At one of the peaks of the Barossa Ranges, Yalumba consider that this area will produce the best white wines they make.

AUSTRALIA AND NEW ZEALAND
COMPLETE BOOK OF
WINE

COMPILED BY LEN EVANS

Acknowledgments

Grateful thanks are extended to the following people for
their assistance and advice in the compilation of this book:
Mrs Jaki Ilbery, Mr Jack Ludbrook, Mr John Parkinson; the
Departments of Agriculture in all States; the State Tourist
Bureaux; and the Mitchell Library (NSW) for the historical
photographs ; Dan Murphy for the use of wine labels.

Appropriate metric sizes for beer, wine and spirits
have been determined and confirmed for bulk sales,
package sales and sale by the glass in hotels, etc.
The end of 1973 is expected to see the completion
of conversion in beer and a significant proportion of
wines and spirits. The original proposals for wine
bottle and container sizes are:

75 ml	—miniature
200 ml	—replacing 6 fl oz
375 ml	—replacing 13 fl oz
500 ml	—new size
750 ml	—replacing 26 fl oz
1 litre	—new size
1.5 litres	—existing magnum
2.25 litres	—replacing ½ gallon
3 litres	—existing jeroboam
4.5 litres	—existing rehoboam
6 litres	—existing methuselah

Published by Paul Hamlyn Pty. Ltd.
176 South Creek Road, Dee Why West, NSW 2099
First published 1973
Reprinted 1974
Copyright Paul Hamlyn Pty. Ltd. 1973

ISBN 0600 07123 5

Printed in Hong Kong by Leefung-Asco Printers Ltd.

Editor: Judith Dine
Photographer: Reg Morrison

AUSTRALIA AND NEW ZEALAND
COMPLETE BOOK OF
WINE

Paul Hamlyn sydney london new york toronto

CONTENTS

FROM VINEYARD TO TABLE *Anders Ousback* 387

THE CHANGING SCENE

WINEMAKING *John Stanford* 443

SOILS AND CLIMATE *Norman Hanckel* 463

WINE OF NEW ZEALAND *Frank Thorpy* 475

INTRODUCTION

The wine industry of Australia and New Zealand had modest beginnings, particularly in Australia where beer was firmly entrenched as the beverage of the people and beer drinking part of the national identity. Few were conscientious wine lovers.

Today, however, wine is enjoying increasingly widespread recognition and appreciation. Wine production has grown into one of the major industries of this country.

Australia finishes its annual grape harvest with a yield of about 250,000 tons. This produces 40-45 million gallons of wine each year. These figures will increase, for the modern equipment of local wineries and distilleries is equal to the finest in any European country; quality wines are being produced in greater amounts each year; more vineyards continue to be planted; and new winemakers and merchants are appearing on the scene. As interest increases, output goes up, and the standard improves.

New Zealand's wine industry is enjoying an unprecedented boom. The grape acreage increased from 1,252 acres in 1965 to 4,500 acres in 1972. This produces more than 5 million gallons of wine.

Both Australia and New Zealand have well defined wine regions. In Australia they range from the immense Barossa Valley and Murray Valley irrigation areas to small areas such as Mudgee, NSW, and Drumborg, Vic. While in New Zealand the major wine producing areas are centred around the Auckland (Henderson and Kumeu areas) and Hawkes Bay-Gisborne-Waikato areas.

Whether large or small, all these regions have their own history, their own characteristics, their own styles of wine and life. This book is written about the wines, the vignerons, the vineyards and the styles of these regions.

Another book on Australian and New Zealand wine? Despite the vast outpourings on the subject in recent years, there were, and are, many gaps to be filled. And we have attempted to do just that. The task was staggering—to produce a comprehensive and up-to-date book on the complete Australian and New Zealand wine scene, including an encyclopaedia of every currently available wine in Australia. The whole industry is changing at a breathtaking rate—takeovers are commonplace, new areas are springing up, long dead vineyards are being revived, more and more people are drinking and becoming interested in wine and the U.S.A. is showing an unprecedented interest. It is an exciting time.

FOREWORD

(by the Rt. Hon. J. D. Anthony)

Environmental and other factors have stamped on the people of
Australia and New Zealand some special characteristics—and on
their industry, their art and their general mode of living.

The wine industry typifies this development. We have taken an
old established art and moulded it into a modern sophisticated
industry—moulded it so as to retain the personal touch of art, but
to superimpose those efficiencies so necessary in the modern world.

Yes, we've come a long way since those first vine cuttings
travelled by sailing ship from Europe surrounded only by cloth
and hope, to be buried in New South Wales soil. The hope was
justified. In Australia we've come from nothing to 6,000 wine
grape growers and a yearly production of 250,000 tons of grapes;
and from nothing to 175 winemakers and 40 to 50 million
gallons of wine.

Since the days of the first grape pressing, Australian wine has
received many international awards for excellence. I have
confidence that such international recognition will continue.

However, many changes have taken place in Australia during
this time. We have seen the establishment of the Australian Wine
Research Institute, now recognized amongst the top such
organisations in the world. We have seen the emergence of the
River Districts of South Australia and the Rutherglen area of
Victoria (to name only two localities) as being producers of some
of the finest sherry and dessert wines in the world. We have seen
the development of an industry with a local character in the
truest sense—a character which has won international acclaim.

On the production side there has been a change in emphasis
away from fortified types of wine to table wines.

There have been new and modern methods, not only introduced,
but developed in Australia.

Some truly Australian concepts have evolved in the industry.
The favourite flagon is a classic example.

With this industry development has come an enthusiastic
response from the peoples of both Australia and New Zealand.
The traditional—and once suspect—tu'penny dark image has been
displaced by an attitude of respect and appreciation creating
almost an aura of a kind never achieved by any other Australian
industry.

This change, while being partly due to some of the development about which I've already spoken, has not evolved without encouragement or assistance. The industry many years ago recognized a need for change and set about to achieve it. It has been successful—so successful, in fact, that many other industries could do well to observe and adopt.

The industry also owes much to a group of intelligent and knowledgeable supporters. These men, devoted to their cause, have become household names within Australia. Men like the author of this publication, Len Evans, the foundation director of the Australian Wine Bureau, by advice, by education and by devotion to an ideal, have lifted and placed the industry on the very top shelf.

It is these men, with their knowledge and enthusiasm, who will continue to support the industry in its newly acquired place in the community. It is to these men that the industry owes so much. To these men, this book is a tribute.

Doug Anthony

HISTORY
OF WINE
IN AUSTRALIA

*Mrs Ilbery is a research worker in history at the
University of New South Wales. She became
seriously interested in wine during an extended
stay in Europe and now dabbles in working with
Len Evans as a research assistant. Jaki Ilbery is
married to an architect and lives in Greenwich,
N.S.W.*

An old grape crusher used by Roly Birks' father early in the 1900s.

The first vines

Although the grape vine is not indigenous to Australia the history of viticulture in this country begins with the birth of the penal colony in New South Wales. Captain Arthur Phillip, R.N., later the first Governor, was in command of the expedition and was in effect Australia's first vigneron.

This First Fleet which Phillip led to New South Wales consisted of eleven small ships with a total tonnage of 3,890 tons, and carrying an extremely disparate group, numbering just over 1,000, of men, women and children, convicts and free men. The hazardous voyage took eight months with stops at Rio de Janeiro and the Cape of Good Hope, where supplies for the new settlement were taken aboard. Included in these supplies were vine cuttings and grape seeds which were the first to be planted on the continent. Phillip was a remarkable leader of great ability, as is evidenced by the extremely low death rate on the long voyage—at most thirty-two people. In view of the mortality rate in England at the time which may have been even higher than this, Phillip's attention to the diet and living conditions of his party showed a humanitarian and enlightened policy.

The motley group of settlers disembarked on 26 January, 1788 to begin the task of establishing a new gaol for convicts from the British Isles. Phillip faced a huge number of problems at this time—the main task being simply to keep the convicts, soldiers and officials alive. Supplies of food from home were irregular, and ignorance of local conditions meant that early agricultural enterprises were often unsuccessful. An adequate supply of food was thus not easy to obtain. Not least of the problems must have been the convicts themselves. Although historians have never been able to agree about the character of the people who committed offences punishable by transportation there were undoubtedly some real criminals among them.

Life for all the settlers was hard, and although Phillip imposed reasonable restrictions on the issue of spirits, from the origins of the colony there is an unfortunate record of widespread drunkenness. Although Captain Phillip encouraged the brewing of beer, then regarded as an essential item of diet, he deplored the excessive use of hard spirits. He was a naval officer, schooled in the wine-drinking traditions of the wardroom and it is reported that in the year of his arrival in Sydney he planted the vine cuttings which he had brought carefully packed in damp soil from the Cape and Rio de Janeiro. Early records mention that grape seeds of 'the claret grape' (probably cabernet sauvignon) were planted as well. The vines were planted at Farm Cove, near the site of the present Botanical Gardens. Those early settlers had no knowledge of soil or climatic conditions, and probably chose the site because of its proximity and ease of clearance of natural vegetation. The humid sub-tropical conditions of Sydney Harbour are not conducive to cultivation of the vine, and although those early vines grew they were attacked by the fungoid disease anthracnose or 'black spot', and no wine was made.

But Governor Phillip did not give up, and by 1791 had established three acres of vineyard in more favourable conditions some twelve miles away on the Parramatta River. A settler named Schaffer had planted one acre by that time, and was thus Australia's first private vigneron. Nothing more is known of Mr Schaffer but it is reasonable to assume that if he had much success some record of this would remain.

Because of ill-health Phillip resigned his position as Governor in 1792 and returned to England. Although local wine was of no significance at that stage he can be credited with the start of the Australian wine industry. From that time things began to move, and some vineyards were planted by private settlers, generally as part of mixed farming operations. There must have been quite some interest in viticulture in the colony as the very first issue of an Australian newspaper, *The Sydney Gazette*, dated 5 March, 1803 published an article of directions on how to plant a vineyard. The development of new vineyards continued and 'appreciable quantities' of wine were made by the opening years of the nineteenth century.

It is interesting to speculate on the reasons why England, not a wine producing country, should right from the start be interested in making wine in Australia. Furthermore, the British people as a whole were not wine drinkers, and certainly not table wine drinkers. The wealthier classes, who were also the governing classes, were, however, used to drinking table wines from France and Spain, and their influence dominated. First of all, the imperialistic British desired to have their own source of wine which could be relied upon to supply their needs at all times without relying on the unpredictable European nations with whom war was an ever-present possibility. The idea of Australia as vineyard for the United Kingdom continued for many years, and is aptly summed up in the title of Hubert de Castella's book *John Bull's Vineyard* published in 1886. In addition, the British government naturally wanted its colonies to be successful in establishing primary industries, which would be able not only to supply produce but to create revenue.

At the local level the authorities encouraged the planting of vineyards and the making of wine, not only for the economic value but in an attempt to convert the populace to moderation in drinking. Among the enlightened men who realized the value of drinking wine as against the debauched and excessive consumption of rum were Dr John Lang, and at a later date Dr Lindeman, and James Busby who wrote in 1830 that light table wine was 'designed to increase the comforts and promote the morality of the lower classes of the colony, and more especially of the native-born youth...where...the unlimited use of ardent spirits and the excitement they produce is more likely to terminate in mischievous results.'

The settlers themselves were farming in a new and untried environment, and thus aimed to experiment with as many varieties of farming and grazing as they could. So, in addition to their sheep and cattle, wheat and other crops, vegetables and orchards, many planted small acreages of grape vines for winemaking. The influence of natural conditions combined with the skills of the producers determined the degree of success of these ventures. Further, Max Lake believes that 'the move to winemaking in the last century was a genuine new and national thing, spurred by revolt against the excesses of the unfortunate rum currency in the new colony.'

The pioneers: Gregory Blaxland, John and William MacArthur, James Busby

We will not debate the claims of Blaxland, MacArthur and Busby to being 'father of Australian viticulture' or argue about who did the most for the industry. Suffice to say that they each contributed a great deal and it is not necessary to rank them in order of importance.

Gregory Blaxland, an explorer who crossed the barrier of the Blue Mountains in 1813, is also remembered for his pioneering viticultural activities. On his arrival in the colony he purchased 450 acres near the present Eastwood in the Parramatta Valley. from D'Arcy Wentworth. He named the property 'Brush Farm' and planted some vines which he had brought from the Cape of Good Hope between 1816 and 1818. His vineyard was largely based on the 'claret' grape which proved most resistant to the troublesome vine blight anthracnose.

In 1822 Blaxland made history by shipping a quarter pipe of red wine fortified with brandy to London, where the Society for the Encouragement of Arts, Manufactures and Commerce awarded him a Silver Medal in 1823. Five years later Blaxland was awarded the gold 'Ceres Medal' for a further two samples, which were considered to be decidedly better than his first effort. It was at this time that the basic assumption that Australian wines could not stand the journey to Britain without fortification was made.

No more was heard about Blaxland and winemaking, but in those few years he had achieved a great deal. Above all he had shown that sound, drinkable wine could be made, which demonstrated the possibility of a colonial wine industry to the English, and to local settlers who were no doubt encouraged by Blaxland's success. He also experimented with varieties of grapes until he found blight resistant vines, and was aware of the influence of the nature of the soil and position of the vines on the character of its wine.

Captain John MacArthur (1767-1834) arrived in Sydney with the New South Wales Corps in 1790, and thus began a turbulent and colourful career in the colony. Posterity chiefly honours MacArthur for first importing merino sheep to Australia but we are more interested in the fact that he was one of the first settlers to plant a vineyard for winemaking on a commercial scale. From 1809 to 1817, as the result of a violent and bitter quarrel with the Governor, Captain Bligh, MacArthur had been an exile in Britain. He took with him his sons James (born 1798) and William (born 1800), and in 1815 and 1816 the three made an eighteen-month tour through France and Switzerland, to quote William MacArthur 'for the express purpose of collecting vines, and of obtaining information respecting their culture'.

On their return to the colony the MacArthurs planted their first vineyard at Camden in 1820. After some trial and error they removed this vineyard to a twenty-acre property on alluvial soil sloping down to the Nepean River near Penrith. This was Australia's first commercial winemaking enterprise, and by 1827 the MacArthurs' vintage totalled 20,000 gallons. In the 1830s they commenced another vineyard on a different site.

James MacArthur died in 1867 after quite an active public career. His brother William, who died at the age of eight-two in 1882, was really the vigneron of the family and also held various public offices—as a member of Parliament and Commissioner for the Paris Exhibition. William had a high opinion of the skills of European vine dressers, and imported some Germans to carry out this skilled operation. He exported some of his wine and secured awards for Camden Park wine and brandy in 1841. More important for the industry as a whole was William MacArthur's belief that knowledge of local conditions, which differed so markedly from those in Europe, was of prime importance. He published this knowledge in book form in 1844 under the title *Letters on the culture of vine, fermentation and the management of wine in the cellar.* William MacArthur's contribution to the infant wine industry was in dissemination of practical information through his book and articles, and by example— the success of his vineyard being proof of what could be done. In the 1850s he was instrumental in founding the New South Wales Vineyard Association. He built up the reputation of being of extraordinary importance to the wine industry.

James Busby, the best known of the pioneers of the early nineteenth century, has long held the reputation of being the father of Australian viticulture and

Delivering grapes at Penfold's 'Kalimna' vineyard, in the Barossa Valley, S.A., at the start of this century.

founder of winemaking in the Hunter Valley. While in no way detracting from Busby's undoubted achievements, recent research by W. P. Driscoll has cast new light on this pioneer. It seems that the best title for Busby is 'prophet' as his main influence was as a teacher and theoretician, and as such his influence was indeed considerable. Eric Ramsden in *James Busby: the Prophet of Australian Viticulture* (1941) was the first to characterize him thus.

Busby was born in Edinburgh on 7 February, 1801 of an old Northumberland family. In 1810 his father took over the management of the Irish estates of the Marquis of Downshire, and it was there that young James first became interested in agriculture. He came to Australia on the *Triton,* arriving on 24 February, 1824 with his father, John Busby who was an engineer and mineral surveyor, and other members of the family. Before leaving Scotland he had become convinced that there was a great future for viticulture in the colony, quite an extraordinary conclusion in itself, and to this end spent some months studying viticulture and winemaking in France.

On 8 May, 1824 Grant 125 of 2,000 acres on the Hunter River was made to Busby. This he named 'Kirkton', and later under the management of his brother-in-law, Kelman, it became well known for its

wines. Shortly after his arrival in 1824 James Busby was engaged to teach viticulture to the boys of the Male Orphan School at Bull's Hill, near Liverpool. His job involved taking charge of the 12,300 acre estate and organizing an agricultural institute there, with the special objects of teaching the boys the cultivation of the vine and other suitable but previously neglected products. In March of the following year Busby planted a vineyard at the orphan school, which yielded, under the management of Richard Sadlier, a 'sound wine of Burgundy character' in 1829.

In 1825, after he had been in New South Wales only a short time, Busby published his first book of 270 pages entitled *Treatise on the Culture of the Vine.* The book consisted largely of translations of the writings of Chaptal and other French authorities. Although quite an achievement in view of his youth, the book had a less than favourable reception if some articles in *The New South Wales Magazine* are any indication. The anonymous reviewer was hostile to the *Treatise,* accusing Busby of lack of practical knowledge, and of giving an abstruse scientific discourse instead of simple directions.

Busby had his troubles in other areas also. When the Corporation of the Clergy and School Lands took control of the-school in 1826 they decided in view of the running costs to close the school down, and Busby was involved in a wrangle about a financial settlement. The corporation kept on the vineyard, but there is no evidence that Busby himself actually made any wine there. His career for the next few years did not go smoothly. He held various government offices, such as Collector of Internal Revenue, but considered that he was badly treated. Busby did find time between his other activities to publish in 1830 his most successful book, *A Manual of plain directions for planting and cultivating vineyards and for making wine in New South Wales* (brief titles must have been most unfashionable). The ninety-six page book was aimed at the small farmers and was well received by the press critics. In his book Busby extolled the virtues of the daily drinking of light wine as against the excessive consumption of spirits with its unfortunate consequences. Busby believed that there should be a vine arbour in every home, and wrote in an oft-quoted passage 'The man who could sit under the shade of his own vine, with his wife and children about him, and the ripe clusters hanging within their reach, in such a climate as this, and not feel the highest enjoyment, is incapable of happiness and does not know what the word means.'

The year after the publication of the *Manual*, 1831, Busby left for Britain to attempt to redress his grievances. However, more than self-interest was involved, for Busby took the opportunity to tour the wine producing areas of Spain and France to examine the influence of climate, soil and viticultural practices on the wine of each area, and to collect samples of different varieties of vines. Busby spent four months travelling, starting from Cadiz and ending in Paris. The bulk of his collection (of which there are various estimates of numbers) of 433 vines came from the Botanic Gardens at Montpellier, but 110 came from the Luxemburg Gardens, forty-four from Sion House near Kew Gardens in England and ninety-one from other parts of France and Spain. Busby generously donated the collection to the government 'for the purpose...of forming an Experimental Garden at Sydney, to prove their different qualities, and propagate, for general distribution, those which may appear most suitable to the climate.'

Early in 1832 the cuttings were packed in cases of moss and shipped to Australia. The collection was planted in the Botanic Gardens, where Busby's enthusiasm was not shared and after initial successes the vines were neglected and subsequently lost. Fortunately distributions from the collection were made to 'Kirkton', Camden and the Adelaide Botanic Gardens, from where thousands of clippings were taken and spread throughout South Australia. The Adelaide collection was also neglected and ultimately destroyed, but some cuttings were taken at the time to Spring Vale and Watervale, and thus Busby's efforts were not wasted although their potential was not fully realized.

In 1833 Busby published a work of great importance to ampelography entitled *Journal of a Recent Visit to the Vineyards of Spain and France*. The book lists a catalogue of all the vines he collected on his tour. That year he left for New Zealand where he took up the post of British Resident. He felt in later years that his efforts on behalf of the wine industry were not appreciated. James Busby died in England in 1871, and posterity at least has recognized his achievements, as W. P. Driscoll writes 'His enthusiasm and ardent propaganda, his publications and collections of vines were of great importance to the infant industry.'

The Hunter Valley

By the time of Busby's departure to New Zealand there were over twenty acres under vine in the Hunter Valley. This area was to become one of the finest wine centres of Australia, but let us begin at the beginning.

In the very early days of the colony—1797— Lieutenant Shortland discovered and named Hunter's River, and also discovered vast coal deposits there. Coal was not considered too important then, but timber was, and lumbering operations were soon established inland from Newcastle. At that time the only way to get to the area was by sea, but in 1820 John Howe discovered a way through the mountains from Windsor to the Singleton district. In April, 1823 Major Morriset made the first overland journey from Newcastle to Sydney, establishing the feasibility of overland passage. In 1826 the area was opened up with the construction of a roadway.

The first significant numbers of settlers arrived in the Valley in the 1820s and turned to grazing and agriculture. We do not have any records of who actually planted the first vines in the Hunter Valley, but vines were planted initially as part of mixed farm holdings. Among the earliest vineyards which were later to achieve considerable reputations were George Wyndham's 'Dalwood' and William Kelman's 'Kirkton'. What Max Lake has called 'the first grape rush' began, and by 1843 the Hunter had 262½ acres of vines which produced 16,472 gallons of wine and 140 gallons of brandy. Seven years later, in 1850, there were over 500 acres owned by thirty-two vine growers. The pattern in the Hunter was for large properties, from 500 to 2,000 acres, with in most cases only small areas being devoted to vines as a hobby.

One of the earliest vignerons was George Wyndham, a settler from Wiltshire, who first attempted to grow vines on his grant 'Dalwood' in 1830. His first vintage was 1835; it was not successful and Wyndham noted in his diary that the wine 'should make good vinegar'. The following year his vintage was 1,650 gallons. More is said of Wyndham in the section on the Dalwood vineyard.

Busby's connection with the Hunter was chiefly through William Kelman, a fellow passenger on the *Triton,* who married Busby's sister Catherine. Kelman planted 'Kirkton' with some of Busby's vines in 1830, and in 1834 boldly decided to extend his vines to ten acres. After some years of trial and experimentation Kelman did quite well, and by 1843 had fifteen acres of vines and was having particular success with the white hermitage grape.

Another successful settler was James King, one of the most prominent vignerons of the nineteenth century. King was born in Hertfordshire in 1800 and arrived in New South Wales in 1827 as a free settler, where he took up a grant of 1,920 acres on the Williams River, a tributary of the Hunter. On this property, which he named 'Irrawang', he grew grain and raised cattle, but for some years his main interest was in establishing himself as a merchant in Sydney. In 1832, however, King planted a vineyard on the property near Raymond Terrace, and made his first wine in 1836. A cautious man, King had only fifteen acres under vine in 1854, of which six were an experimental vineyard, and he only then was expanding with another nine acres. His most successful variety was Shepherd's Riesling, now known as Hunter riesling or semillon, which is the main white wine variety of the area.

King was fully aware of the value of experimentation and scientific study. He carried out an extensive correspondence with Baron J. von Liebig, a great German chemist and philosopher. This had a two-fold effect—King learned a great deal from von Liebig, and his correspondence helped to publicize the industry overseas. Further attention was gained by King during a trip to Europe, where his wine won a medal at the Paris Exhibition of 1855, and was chosen with some wine of MacArthur's to be 'placed on the table in front of the Emperor (Napoleon III) during the ceremony of closing'. Although King did not record what became of the wine he was 'well satisfied' with the compliment. On the same trip King showed his wines to von Liebig and the Duke of Nassau who approved of them.

Back home King spent a great deal of time and money trying to make champagne, with little success. He also developed a pottery at 'Irrawang'. Of greater interest to us here was the slim book King published in Edinburgh in 1857 entitled *Australia may be an extensive wine-producing country,* in which he shared the belief of Busby and others that the consumption of light wines was far more desirable than hard spirits. King was instrumental in founding the Hunter River Vineyard Association (of which more will be said later) and passed on a considerable amount of the knowledge he had gained. James King died overseas in 1857 after a career in which his intelligence and enthusiasm earned him an honoured position in Australian wine history.

Mention here must be made of Dr Henry John Lindeman who planted 'Cawarra' in 1843, and

thereby founded one of Australia's great winemaking enterprises. His life and career are dealt with in the section on Lindemans in the Hunter Valley.

The decade of the 1840s was one of consolidation. Although the colony passed through a severe depression winemaking was not adversely affected and there were about 300 acres of vines in the Hunter Valley in 1846. In January 1843 the Maitland *Mercury* newspaper was established, and this became a most important medium of communication on all facets of winemaking (and incidentally an invaluable primary source for present day historians). Winemaking in the Hunter Valley made such strides that by 1847 an association of those interested in winemaking was formed. This organisation arose largely from the conflict between the pastoralists and vignerons in the Hunter River Agricultural Society. Those credited with the formation of the new Hunter River Vineyard Association were James King, Henry (later Reverend) Carmichael, M.A., Government Surveyor for Gloucester, Durham and Brisbane, of Porphyry vineyard, and Dr Andrew Lang of Dunmore. The inaugural meeting was held on 19 May, 1847 at the Northumberland Hotel with James King in the chair, and the association was formed, 'for the purpose of promoting the culture of the vine and turning its products to the most profitable account.' The society met twice annually, with members submitting samples of their wine for inspection. One of the Association's successful campaigns was in having Australian wines accepted as 'colonial' wines in Britain, so that they could compete under the same conditions as Cape wines on the U.K. market.

In 1847 the British Government allowed non-British immigration to the colony, and thus trained European labourers could be employed. William Kirchner (a German living in Sydney) visited Germany after consultation with the vine growers and arranged for two groups of vine dressers to go to the Hunter district. Although there were problems with the Germans, their long term influence was undoubtedly beneficial to the industry.

By the mid-century mark the fledgling industry was established well enough to survive the labour scarcities and other problems associated with the goldrushes. By 1852 the Hunter River district had 461 acres of vines from which 59,000 gallons of wine and 1,100 gallons of brandy were made. At this time a whole wave of new plantings began. The Land Act of 1861 reorganized the system of land allocation. settlers paying £1 an acre for their selection of between forty and 320 acres. Vineyards sprang up all over the Pokolbin area.

Martin Bouffier from Nassau, Germany, is credited with being the first vigneron in Cessnock. His vineyard, north of the Wollombi road, was planted in 1866. Another of the earliest settlers at Pokolbin was John McDonald who built the house and winery at 'Ben Ean' in 1870. George Campbell, an Irishman,

Old ruins at Pewsey Vale, S.A. In 1847 a vineyard was planted there by Joseph Gilbert. The original vineyards went out of production in 1927, but have now been redeveloped.

At Reynella, S.A., the oldest underground commercial wine cellar still in use in Australia. It was excavated by John Reynell in 1838 ready for the first vintage in 1842.

had a vineyard on his 200 acre property 'Daisy Hill', where he built fine red-brick cellars. Many of the names of these vignerons have faded into obscurity—long forgotten are J. F. Doyle of 'Kaludah', Frederick Wilkinson of 'Cote d'Or', J. D. Brown of 'Colestoun' and Dr John Glennie of 'Orindinna', to name but a few. From around this time though some of the familiar Hunter names began to appear on the scene—Tyrrell, Drayton, Elliot, as well as the already established Lindeman.

It is interesting that such a similar boom should happen almost exactly one hundred years later. Let us hope that the events of the following years do not parallel those of the last century also. There was a major economic depression and bank crash in the early 1890s, but although the effects of this were severe they were not nearly as devastating to the vignerons of the Hunter as the effects of Federation. With the formation of the Commonwealth of Australia in 1901 customs barriers between the states were removed, and the winemakers of South Australia took full advantage of the situation. There was a veritable flood of all types of wine from there, and as these were cheaper, the Hunter wines could not compete. The upshot was that many vineyards were uprooted and lost to winemaking—the boom had bust!

On 20 September, 1901 the Pokolbin District Vinegrowers' Association was formed to replace the Hunter River Vineyard Association, and at its peak had over forty independent growers as members. The new association held local wine exhibitions and was active in protecting the district against phylloxera. It also achieved some legal measures to discourage adulterated wine coming from other states.

Thus the turn of the century saw the Hunter down, but not out. In fact the Valley was to fall further before the revival sixty years later.

Corowa and Albury

Winemaking in New South Wales in the last century was not solely confined to the Hunter Valley. The towns of Corowa and Albury in the far south of the state on the River Murray were the centre of quite an extensive winemaking district in the 1890s.

Winemaking at Corowa began in the mid-nineteenth century, when many small vineyards were established in the area. In the past, as now, the Lindeman name has been most prominent in the Corowa area. Large scale winemaking began there with Dr Lindeman's purchase of a property known as Haffner's Vineyard in 1872. The phylloxera epidemic at the end of the last century devastated the district, and many of the smaller vineyards were lost forever.

An important vigneron of the times was J. T. Fallon who had an extensive vineyard at Ettamogah, a few miles from Albury. In 1873 Mr Fallon read a paper on New South Wales wines before the Royal Society of Arts in London, the same body addressed by Blaxland in 1823. When phylloxera attacked his vines in 1906 Mr Fallon did not replace the vineyards. A Mr L. Frere attempted to make sparkling wine at Albury in the belief that some of the lighter soils of the district would produce light wines of quality. Unfortunately phylloxera interrupted his plans and we have never discovered just how accurate Mr Frere's ideas were.

A well-known identity of the district was John Delappe Lankester, born in Lichfield, Staffordshire on 20 September, 1837. He arrived in Sydney with his father in 1849, and spent the whole of his adult life working in the wine industry. In 1860 he opened and managed a wine business for Dr Lindeman in Sydney. Lankester was manager of J. T. Fallon's vineyards when they were destroyed by phylloxera. He then cultivated his own vineyards at Ettamogah where he had a grant of 160 acres of land. Lankester died in January 1938; perhaps his longevity was at least partly attributable to a life spent working with wine.

The Sydney area

After the early attempts at growing grapes for wine at Parramatta there were no serious plantings in the Sydney area. Among the early pioneers, no mention has been made of James Ruse (the ex-convict who in 1791 became one of the first settlers to support himself through agriculture), who planted at Rosehill on the outskirts of Parramatta, or of Dr Robert Townson who cultivated the muscatel grape at Bunbury Curran near Campbelltown and made a sweet wine. Close to Sydney, at Rooty Hill, a vineyard was planted early last century. This was named 'Minchinbury', and has become renowned for its sparkling wines.

The land was originally acquired as a grant by Captain William Minchin in 1819, and passed to a Dr McKay after the Captain's death in 1821. Dr McKay planted the first vines there, and built the winery. The property was acquired by Penfolds in the early 1900s. 'Minchinbury' is discussed in detail in the section on the vineyards of New South Wales.

Yet another wine doctor, Thomas Henry Fiaschi, established a vineyard on the banks of the Hawkesbury River, near the Sackville Reach in the 1880s. Dr Fiaschi was born in Florence in 1853, the son of a professor of literature who had wine interests. Fiaschi graduated in medicine from Pisa and Florence, and then did post-graduate study in England. After his arrival in Sydney in 1874, the doctor began practice in Macquarie Street and eventually became senior surgeon at Sydney Hospital. After some years in Sydney Dr Fiaschi decided to make wine in a personal effort to improve the standard of the local wine then available, and in 1886 he started planting a vineyard which he called 'Tizzana' after the family property in Italy. He designed and built a two-storey winery like those he had known in his homeland, and the stone shell still stands. Dr Fiaschi imported French and Italian varieties and appointed a French manager, Mr Sarar. Their wines became well known, especially the light whites, and were sold at the family cellars in the heart of Sydney. The doctor also bought a vineyard at Mudgee, near the present 'Craigmoor', which has recently been revived. He died in 1927 and the firm went out of business about twenty-five years later.

Victoria: the early days

As the founding of the two colonies was so different, so the making of wine in Victoria began in quite different circumstances to that in New South Wales. John Batman founded the settlement of Melbourne in 1834, and according to the *Port Phillip Patriot* the new settlement owed its existence 'to the skill and enterprise of the individual colonists', whereas other colonies depended on governmental decisions. Free settlers flocked to the surrounding districts almost immediately. Governor Bourke proclaimed jurisdiction over the settlement in 1836, but there was a strong separatist movement right from the beginning. The growth of vineyards in the new colony was rapid, and in the absence of intense divisions in the community over the abuse of spirits, and with governmental encouragement in the form of subsidies, Victoria soon became prominent as a wine-producing state with many thousands of acres under vine.

Edward Henty has always been credited with the planting of the first vineyard, when he settled at Portland in the western part of Victoria in 1834, the year of the founding of the colony. There is no further mention in any records of Mr Henty or his vines, so the accuracy of his claim to being Victoria's first vigneron is open to question.

Four years later, in 1838, William Ryrie, a pastoralist who came overland from New South Wales, planted the first vines in the Yarra Valley, at Yering. Ryrie planted thirty acres in this fertile area which was only thirty miles from Melbourne, and the first wine was made there in 1845. By this time, however, Ryrie was no longer alone in practising viticulture; the rush to plant grapes in the area was immediate and on a large scale. By 1848 there were 100 acres under vine, and over the following twenty years this area increased to 3,000 acres.

In September, 1839 Charles Joseph La Trobe became superintendent of the new settlement. By a fortunate chance for Victorian winemaking he had lived for some years at Neuchatel in Switzerland, where he acquired some knowledge and a real appreciation of wine. During his Swiss sojourn La Trobe married Sophie, the daughter of Frederick Auguste de Montmillon, Swiss Counsellor of State.

On their arrival in Victoria the La Trobes named their house 'Jolimont', after Sophie's family's country estate, and planted a small vineyard in what was to be the garden of the first Government House in Melbourne. La Trobe encouraged other settlers to follow suit, and directed, for example, the planting of vines at 'Mayfield', the home of the McCrae family. It is also probable that he advised Skene Craig, Commissariat Officer, who had a vineyard in what is now Collins Street West in the centre of Melbourne. Amiet Pelet, the husband of La Trobe's housekeeper Rose, had his own vineyard in what is now the centre of Melbourne. In fact his wine was honoured by being served at the ball given on 28 November, 1850 to celebrate the separation of the colony of Victoria from New South Wales.

Although these activities were significant La Trobe's great contribution to Australian winemaking was to influence some of the people of Neuchatel to come out to the colony and practise their viticultural skills there. Five years after La Trobe's arrival in Melbourne eleven men had started from the Canton of Neuchatel for Australia. They settled near each other in the district of Geelong, and all planted vineyards around their homes. In 1842 vines were planted at Pollock's Ford where David Louis Pettavell and Frederick Breuget established the Neufchatel (sic) vineyard, on high land near the Barwon with cuttings brought from Dijon. In 1845 they made their first wine.

The de Castellas and the fabled wines of Lilydale

Those early Swiss migrants had an influence which far outweighed their numbers, as they were better educated than most and also had a thorough knowledge and understanding of winemaking and viticulture. Among the Swiss settlers were Clement Deschamps, the son of a head vigneron at Neuchatel, Baron de Pury and his cousins, the de Castella brothers, who were to make immense contributions to the wine industry of Australia.

The first of the de Castellas to come to Australia was Paul, son of the chief physician of the Pourtales Hospital at Neuchatel, who arrived in 1848 with Adolphe de Meuron. Paul bought part of Ryrie's cattle station, Yering, at Lilydale and began to plant a vineyard, for which he obtained 20,000 cuttings (principally cabernet sauvignon) from Chateau Lafite. Most of these struck and Yering soon had a reputation for good red wine. He invited his brothers to join him and in 1854 Hubert de Castella arrived in Australia. In turn Hubert established a second vineyard which he called 'St Hubert's'. This vineyard eventually reached 250 acres with a vintage of 70,000 gallons. Legends have developed about the quality of the Lilydale wines, which were apparently of extraordinary finesse and of a quality never before seen in Australia.

At the great Melbourne International Exhibition of 1881, 'St Hubert's' triumphed by being awarded the prize for the most meritorious exhibit in the entire show. This prize, a silver table set of seven pieces worth £800, was awarded by Emperor Wilhelm I of Germany and one can only wonder how the judges could decide between such diverse items as steam engines, felt hats and wine on equal terms. St Hubert's wine was also honoured with the award of *Grand Prix* at the Paris Exposition of 1889. This was one of only fourteen such prizes given to wines from all over the world, so the quality of the wine must have been commendable.

Yet another part of the Yering cattle station was bought and planted to vines by Guillaume, Baron de Pury, who called it 'Yeringberg' and produced, from all accounts, first class white wines.

Hubert de Castella not only made wine, but wrote a book about it. *John Bull's Vineyard* was published in 1886, and records that Yering vineyard then occupied 100 acres, 'Yeringberg' on the same bank of the Yarra (de Pury) seventy acres, and his own 'St Hubert's' 260 acres.

St Hubert's vineyard later came into the possession of David Mitchell, the father of Dame Nellie Melba. Unfortunately a variety of factors put the Lilydale vineyards out of production in the 1920s, one of the last vintages at 'Yeringberg' being made in 1924. The noxious phylloxera bug was not responsible for the finish of winemaking in the Lilydale area—the reasons were wholly economic. The grape harvest was small compared with other Victorian areas, partly because the choice vines were low yielders, partly because spring frosts became an undue hazard through the clearing of timber, and partly because of the decline in fertility through neglect of manuring. Further, in those days the number of wine lovers was too small and most Australians were not prepared to pay the necessary price for quality. Some properties were bought by people more interested in dairying than viticulture and finally rising land values made it uneconomic to continue with the vineyards. In recent years some devotees have begun modest new plantings in an attempt to recreate old glories, so we may yet discover for ourselves just how good the wines of Lilydale are.

Other nineteenth century Victorian vineyards

It is strange in these urbanized days to think that about a hundred years ago vineyards covered thousands of acres of what is now South Yarra, Hawthorn, Brighton and other suburbs of Melbourne, as well as Geelong and Bendigo. The *Illustrated Australian News* proclaimed in 1866, 'The notable increase of private vineyards is one of the most cheering signs of the times, a few years hence and every

country resident will be enabled to entertain his visitors with the produce of his own little vineyard...'.

In the early 1840s John Fawkner put in ten acres near Flemington and eight years later had a vintage of 2,000 gallons. Hawthorn was another suburb noted for its wine. Count Alinant de Dollon cultivated twenty-nine acres, and adjoining him were the vineyards of L. McKinnon and Neil McLean. Edward Khull, the goldbroker, owned the 'Tooronga' vineyard nearby. The now fashionable inner suburb South Yarra was also a winemaking centre in the last century. A contemporary writer recorded that a young Swiss, Mr Wisewould, made 300 gallons of 'exceedingly good' wine including a riesling there at the 1861 vintage.

At Whittlesea the 'Glenlinton' Vineyard was established towards the close of last century by H. E. Dawson, a solicitor turned vigneron, and a Mr Gilchrist who was chief *Hansard* reporter. The Dawson wines were high-quality dry reds, but wine production was terminated at 'Glenlinton' when the vineyard was turned over to grazing in the 1930s.

North of Melbourne, another area devoted to wine growing was in the region of Bendigo, later to be famous for its gold mining. In the early 1840s there were many vineyards established around Geelong, about fifty miles south-west of Melbourne. By the 1870s they were important wine producers. An apochryphal story which may well be true is that the judges of the wine section of the Vienna Exhibition refused to assess the Bendigo entry of hermitage on the ground that it was fraudulent, since no colonial wine could possibly be so good. Corio, about eight miles north of Geelong was a noted wine region in its day, producing, by all accounts, a very fine dry red.

1875 saw the beginnings of one of the great natural disasters of Australian winemaking history. That year *phylloxera vastatrix* or the grape vine louse, a parasitic aphis which lives on and destroys grape vines, was discovered at the village of Fyansford in the Geelong area, soon spreading to Geelong itself. Some years later it appeared at Bendigo. The Victorian Government took all possible measures to contain the disease and prevent it spreading north to Rutherglen, then the principal wine growing area of the state. No expense was spared in uprooting all the Geelong vines and putting an extensive programme of soil sterilization into operation. This drastic policy was, however, unsuccessful—not only were the Geelong and Bendigo vineyards totalty ruined, but the louse got to Rutherglen anyway.

Rutherglen

Rutherglen in the north-east of Victoria originally sprang into prominence as a gold mining centre in the 1850s. Gold trebled the population in ten years, brought enormous and sudden wealth and gave a greater complexity to colonial society. Merchants and food producers, pastoralists and transport operators shared in the prosperity brought about by the rich gold discoveries of the next decade. But it did not take very long for the surface alluvial gold to be worked out, and many of the disenchanted miners turned to a new industry, viticulture.

Vines were first planted in the Rutherglen district by Lindsay Brown at Gooramadda in 1851 with cuttings from Albury (where German growers were already making wine on a small scale). From then the growth of vineyards was rapid and within a decade Rutherglen was in the forefront of wine production in Victoria. Most of the present winemaking concerns were founded in that era—the Sutherland Smiths of All Saints, Morris of Fairfield, Chambers, Campbells and Gehrigs. Mr P. B. Burgoyne then owned the 'Mt Ophir' vineyard near Chiltern, where he built a beautiful winery in 1893. 'Mt Ophir' produced some legendary wines of a 'burgundy' style. Unfortunately, in the middle of this century the property was given over to other agricultural pursuits and Mt Ophir wines were no more.

By the 1880s Rutherglen was surrounded by some thousands of acres of vines, although the actual acreage has been a controversial statistic. Whatever, in those joyous days the future looked bright indeed. North-east Victorian wines were amassing prizes all over the world. In 1883 the Murray District Vinegrowers' Association was formed with George Sutherland Smith as its first president.

At the end of the decade in 1889 the Victorian Government passed a bill designed to encourage the expansion of the rapidly burgeoning industry, and in doing so helped to bring about its downfall. The 'Planting Bonus Bill' gave a bonus of £2 for every acre of vines planted in Victoria after that date. This action brought into existence many thousands of acres of vines, almost entirely planted by farmers who had little or no knowledge of viticulture, and from them a huge quantity of often inferior wine was made with consequent harmful effects, especially on the reputation of Australian wine in London.

In the nineties Australia passed through an acute Depression from which the Victorian wine industry did not escape. After agitation by the Rutherglen Vinegrowers' Association, the State Government subsidized the growers to the tune of a bonus of one shilling a gallon on Victorian brandy. In the same year, 1896, the Viticultural College was established at Chiltern to instruct young men in the science of vine growing. But the zenith had been reached.

In the late 1890s phylloxera was found at Rutherglen, and it did not take long to devastate the vineyards and ruin the growers of the district. Under the advice and direction of Francois de Castella, the Government Viticulturist, the State Government began a policy of assisting the Rutherglen growers to rehabilitate their vineyards. At the time the cure was a new discovery—the replanting of European scions grafted on resistant American root stocks. Such men as de Castella and the Chiltern Viticultural College did valiant work in advising growers and distributing resistant stocks, but the damage had been done. Many growers decided to abandon wine growing—some vineyards were replanted with other crops and others were turned into grazing land for sheep. The upshot was that the Rutherglen district has never regained its former importance for volume of wine. At least the destruction was not complete as at Bendigo and Geelong, and some excellent wines have continued to be made in the area.

Great Western

Australian history is more notable for floods, fires, droughts and strikes than romance. The story of the beginnings of winemaking at Great Western is thus one of the more picturesque episodes in our history.

It all began in France, in 1825, in the province of Lorraine when Anne Marie Blampied was born to a farming family. She must have been an adventurous girl, for at the age of twenty-eight she and her brother Emile (aged fifteen) left for Australia to seek their fortune on the goldfields. They arrived at Beechworth in Victoria in 1853, and went into business transporting supplies to the miners with another Frenchman Jean Pierre Trouette. Anne Marie married Jean Pierre and they moved to the goldfields at Great Western, in about 1858, accompanied by young Emile.

The gold was soon worked out and Jean Trouette bought land near the village of Great Western, according to Les Francis, because the area reminded Trouette of his homeland (the department of Gers). He planted half an acre of vines on the property which was named 'St Peters' in partnership with Emile Blampied in 1863. The following year their plantings were increased to four acres, and by 1867 they had about 50,000 vines and 2,000 fruit trees. That year 500 gallons of wine was made and in the following years awards were gained at home and abroad.

Jean Trouette died in November 1885 at the age of fifty-two. The following year his only son Nicholas was killed in tragic circumstances, while attempting to rescue a workman from an underground wine tank. Bad fortune continued to plague Anne Marie and after a series of poor seasons and crop failures 'St Peters' was sold in 1897 to an English family named Merton. Anne Marie Trouette died in December 1905, succeeded by her daughter Marie who lived until 1927. 'St Peters' lapsed into obscurity, and wine was no longer made there.

Although 'St Peters' has not existed as a vineyard for many years, the Trouettes and Blampied were the

Shiraz vines at 'Chateau Tahbilk', Vic.

founders of winemaking at Great Western. They were also the inspiration which led the brothers Joseph and Henry Best to plant their vineyards, which have survived, in the Great Western area. These days Great Western is especially well known for its champagne, and the history of Hans Irvine and the House of Seppelt who are responsible for this is recounted on the section on the vineyards of Great Western. Briefly, in 1865 Joseph Best planted grapes on his property which he called 'Great Western'. Best sold out to businessman and politician Hans Irvine in 1888, who expended a great deal of effort on the venture and succeeded in making first class sparkling wine. Seppelts took over at Great Western in 1918, and have continued to make wine at Great Western. In 1866 Joseph Best's brother Henry planted a vineyard on the banks of Concongella Creek, which is now operated by the Thomsons.

Great Western is another winemaking area of Victoria which is now but a shadow of its former self. In the early years of this century there were over 2,000 acres of vines in the area from Glenorchy in the north to about ten miles below Ararat in the south. The decline was not caused by phylloxera but by the economic situation. Great Western produces wines of high quality, but the soils are quite poor and the climate with its frequent frosts is such that yeilds are not high, and are often *very* low. Although many vineyards were uprooted and turned over to sheep, Seppelts and Bests have survived.

'Chateau Tahbilk' and Central Victoria

In central Victoria near the town of Nagambie the Tahbilk vineyards were planted in 1860 by a Melbourne syndicate, eventually bought out by John Pinney Bear. In the eighties phylloxera struck· Tahbilk and wiped out all but 135 acres planted on moist sandy soil. The vineyard then went into a decline until it was bought in 1925 by the Purbrick family who still own it today. The chronicle of 'Chateau Tahbilk' is detailed in the section on the vineyards of Victoria.

Near the town of Shepparton Dalmatian born Trojano Darveniza planted the 'Excelsior' vineyard in 1875, and had numerous successes at overseas exhibitions.

Mildura: the north-west

The town of Mildura on the River Murray depends for its very existence on the water of that river. The men who first harnessed the Murray waters were the Canadian born brothers Ben and George Chaffey, who came to Australia at the request of Alfred Deakin in the 1880s. The account of the development of the irrigation settlement at Mildura is firmly linked with the history of Renmark, ninety miles from Mildura, but 200 miles down river, and as Renmark is the senior settlement the full story is recounted in that section.

In 1887 irrigation from the Murray was begun. The young settlements had to overcome multifarious problems in their early years, not least of which was the bankruptcy of the Chaffeys in 1893. They survived, however, and within a decade of their founding tons of citrus and dried vine fruits were being produced each year. However, at that stage, there was no wine. Many acres of gordo blanco were planted for drying into raisins, but when a new variety known as Thompson's seedless came into favour there was a glut of gordos. In desperation they were distilled for fortifying spirit and later a sweet wine was made. Winemaking at Mildura thus began in rather strange circumstances. This, combined with the Victorian Government's planting bonus, did not help the reputation of Australian wine.

W. B. Chaffey, known as 'The Boss', settled in Mildura and was responsible for founding not only the town but what was to become a great winemaking company—Mildara. The charming old Chaffey home 'Rio Vista' is now preserved as an art gallery. Thus the history of winemaking in Victoria to the beginning of this century was one of acute highs and lows. The few people who can remember or have been fortunate enough to experience the wines of the 'dead' Victorian vineyards must especially mourn their passing. The rest of us can be glad that the remaining vineyards have survived to produce some great and unforgettable wines. We can all be pleased that the wine boom of recent years has meant a series of new plantings which reassure our wine drinking future.

South Australia: the founding years

The South Australian wine industry has also had some misfortunes, but by a combination of good luck, the blessings of nature and the enterprise of its settlers it has long assumed the dominating position in Australian winemaking.

Soon after the founding of the colony in 1836 it was realized that the wine industry could be important. In the *Almanac* of 1849 George McEwin, a pioneer horticulturist, forecast that wine 'would become a source of great wealth to the colony, the climate and soil being ideal' and affirmed that wine 'rivalling the most famous growths of the old world will be produced in South Australia as soon as we gain the requisite knowledge and the practical experience necessary to success.'

Vines were planted almost at the beginning— the first at Chichester Gardens, North Adelaide by John Barton Hack in 1837, and George Stevenson in 1838. The first commercial planting was that of A. H. Davis who obtained cuttings from the Busby collection and established them at his farm in the Reedbeds (now Underdale, a western suburb of Adelaide) between 1838 and 1840. No trace remains of any of these historic vineyards, the development of the city long since having devoured them.

There has been a great deal of dispute among wine historians and the companies concerned as to who made the first wine in South Australia. The rival claimants are John Reynell and Richard Hamilton —whose vineyards of course, still thrive today. Reynell planted vines on his property about fourteen miles south of Adelaide round about 1838, while Hamilton established his vineyard south-west of the city, near Glenelg, about the same time. The matter has not been finally settled—both sides having produced evidence in their favour. John Reynell did not arrive in Australia until 1838, almost a year after Richard Hamilton, but records of the South Australian Land Titles office show that Richard Hamilton took up his land in June, 1838 while the land grant at present day Reynella was transferred to John Reynell in July, 1839. The evidence about who actually planted the first vines and made the first wine is lacking and contradictory. Certainly both men made meaningful contributions to Australian winemaking by the early establishment of vineyards in South Australia, and both were thus instrumental in laying the foundations of the wine industry.

The Adelaide environs

The first vines in South Australia were, naturally enough, planted in the vicinity of Adelaide. As the city has grown many of these vineyards have disappeared but some still remain, and among these are the first vineyards of what have become leading winemaking companies. Foremost among these is Penfolds, which in 1844 had its origins at Magill, some four miles east of the city at the foot of the Mount Lofty ranges. Dr Christopher Rawson Penfold originally began to make wine for its tonic properties in aiding the health of his patients, and in so doing shaped the beginnings of one of the largest wine companies of Australia.

In 1854 Patrick Auld began to plant the 'Auldana' vineyard, now owned by Penfolds. In 1862 Mr Auld formed the Australian Wine Company in London, to sell the produce of his vineyards there. A report in the London *Wine and Spirit Gazette* in 1869 noted that although Australia could not then be considered as an exporting country the wines of 'Auldana' were being sold in London and 'deserve the highest praise of connoisseurs'. The article went on to say that Mr Auld was 'dead against any attempt at artificial fortifying, and his ambition is to obtain the pure juice of the grape without the slightest addition of spirit.' Would that more vignerons of those and later days had thought similarly! Incidentally Patrick Auld's London company later became incorporated in the Emu Wine Company.

Other still existing early Adelaide vineyards are those of Osmond Gilles at Glen Osmond (1856), which was later owned by Woodley Wines; H. C. Clark at Stonyfell (1858), now owned by H. M. Martin and Son; Dr W. T. Angove at Tea Tree Gully in 1884, Douglas A. Tolley at Hope Valley (1893) and Hamilton's Ewell vineyard at Glenelg.

The now prominent firm of Thomas Hardy had its beginnings at his 'Bankside' property, on the River Torrens only two miles from Adelaide. Hardy bought the land in 1853 and began clearing and planting almost immediately. Wine was made there until the early 1920s, when 'Bankside' became a casualty of the expansion of the city. In the intervening years of course Hardys had expanded enormously in South Australia and other states.

A number of attempts were made in the early days to grow grapes on a commercial scale in the wetter parts of the Adelaide Hills, but all failed with the exception of the vineyard planted at Clarendon in 1849 by John Edward Peake. Peake is remembered now because it was he who first imported direct from Spain the palomino, pedro ximenez, doradillo, temprana and mollar negro grapes, some of which have been important in South Australia ever since.

Dr R. M. Schomburgk, later well known as director of the Adelaide Botanical Gardens, planted a small vineyard in 1857 at Buchfelde (now called Loos), west of Gawler on the Para River. Dr Schomburgk was responsible for introducing to South Australia the sultana grape, which was to assume major importance in the irrigation areas of the Murray.

The Southern Vales

The area south of Adelaide on the plains between the Mount Lofty Ranges and the sea was established early as a major centre of wine production. The first of the vineyards in the area was John Reynell's, planted near the township which was later to bear his name, in 1838 or so.

He was soon followed by Dr Alexander Charles Kelly who planted a vineyard which he called 'Trinity', near Morphett Vale in the early 1840s. This vineyard was later owned by John B. MacMahon, but the property was sold and is now covered by houses. About twenty years later Dr Kelly was responsible for founding a company which bought a property near McLaren Vale where there was a vineyard which had been planted by Mr W. Manning in 1850. Dr Kelly expanded the plantings and named the property 'Tintara'. Eventually Thomas Hardy bought the holding. Dr Kelly was a firm believer in the value of wine and had great faith in the future of the wine industry. He published a book *The Vine in Australia* in 1861, in which he emphasized the need for a scientific approach to winemaking and the use of suitable grape varieties. More is said of Dr Kelly in the account of Hardys' Tintara vineyard.

The Seaview vineyard at McLaren Vale was originally planted in 1850 by George Manning, who called it 'Hope Farm'. The latter part of the nineteenth century saw the beginnings of many vineyards whose names we know well today. In 1892 a Mrs Horne planted a vineyard at O'Halloran Hill, south of Adelaide, which became 'Glenloth'. In the McLaren Vale area the 'Ryecroft' vineyard was established by Frederick Wilkinson in 1884, the Kay brothers began planting at the 'Amery' vineyards in 1890, while Mr A. C. Johnston of Pirramimma bought his property in 1892.

Nature has been particularly kind to viticulture in the Southern Vales—frosts are not a problem, droughts are few, the climate is generally moderate and vine diseases (notably phylloxera) have not been a serious worry. Little wonder then that the area has gone from strength to strength as a wine-making centre.

The Barossa Valley

The Barossa Valley, long one of Australia's largest and most important wine areas, was totally unexplored by white men when Colonel William Light led the first party of exploration there in December, 1837. It was Light, the first Surveyor-General of South Australia, who named the valley after an area in the south of Spain. One of the far-sighted though eccentric early explorers was Johann Menge, geologist, who reported, 'I am certain that we shall see the place flourish, and vineyards and orchards and immense fields of corn throughout. It will furnish huge quantities of wine; it will yield timber for our towns, and superior stone and marble abounds for buildings.' How right he was!

The man who was responsible more than any other single individual for the early development of the area was George Fife Angas, the Father of the Barossa Valley. Angas who was born in Newcastle, England in 1789, was largely responsible for founding the South Australian Company and was appointed its director. The Company was formed with private capital to develop the colony, and did much to advance its agricultural settlement.

George Angas settled in the valley, and became something of a feudal lord. The village of Angaston (initially Angas Town) was surveyed in 1841 and named after him. Angas needed labour for his orchards, and being both a practical man and humanitarian realized that the ideal solution would be to bring to Australia some Silesian Lutherans who were being persecuted at the time. Since 1822 the religious Lutherans of Silesia had been oppressed for refusing to annex their church to the State Church of King Frederick III of Prussia, and Angas saw them as highly suitable migrants, being hard-working and sufficiently idealistic to resist tyranny. He thus arranged with Pastor August Ludwig

Pressing the grapes
(Engraving in the Illustrated Melbourne Post
of 19 March, 1866).

Christian Kavel to bring out the first three boatloads of German migrants from Silesia in 1838, and provided the finance which made the venture possible. The first German settlement of twenty-eight Lutheran families took place in 1842 at Bethany, sometimes called Neuschlesien: New Silesia.

Many others followed these first migrants to the new land, where they settled in the Barossa Valley, worked hard and prospered. Naturally many of the Silesians turned to viticulture, and among the German settlers were men whose names are household words today. The first man to plant vines in the Barossa was Johann Gramp, who in 1847 established a small vineyard at Jacob's Creek, just a mile from the present giant Orlando winery. The same year Samuel Hoffmann settled at Tanunda. Joseph Seppelt arrived in Australia from Germany in 1849 and settled in the Barossa Valley in 1851 with the intention of growing tobacco. He soon switched his interests to viticulture, and so began the House of Seppelt.

Although the German settlers were of major importance, the English colonists also did their bit. Samuel Smith founded the Yalumba organization in 1849, and William Salter began his vineyard near Angaston ten years later in 1859.

Thus within a mere two decades from the time the first white man set foot in the Barossa Valley the foundations were firmly laid of the industry which was to be so much a part of the story of Australian wine. Things haven't always gone smoothly of course, there have been depressions and labour shortages and other troubles, but overall the Valley has enjoyed good fortune. Above all it escaped the horrors of phylloxera which did such damage in the neighbouring state, Victoria. This was not due only to good luck—rigid quarantine measures were enforced by Act of Parliament. The vintners of the Barossa have worked for their success, but they could not have done it without the natural advantages of the area plus a dash of good luck.

Clare-Watervale

The Clare area is the most northerly of the South Australian wine areas, about eighty miles north of Adelaide. The countryside there is hilly and no doubt would have reminded the early German settlers of those parts of the Rhine Valley where grapes had been grown for centuries. The only survivor of the early Clare vineyards is the Sevenhills College Vineyard, which was originally planted by a group of Austrian Jesuit fathers in 1848. Other vineyards in the same area, such as the one that was planted by John Ward in 1853 and another planted by Valentine Mayr in 1859, no longer exist.

The first vineyard at Springvale was a small one planted by Francis Treloar in 1865. In 1889 the firm of H. Buring and Sobels bought the Quelltaler property and wine is still being made there although Vignerons Distillers & Vintners Ltd. have since taken over the company and the property.

In the 1890s the Stanley Wine Company was founded, as was the family concern of A. P. Birks. Both these companies are still very much in existence.

Langhorne Creek

In 1860, Mr Frank Potts planted the 'Bleasdale' vineyard twenty-five miles east of Adelaide at Langhorne Creek on the Bremer River. The 'Bleasdale' vineyards are still owned by the Potts family.

Coonawarra

The Coonawarra area is not only isolated geographically, but historically also. The history of the area is most interesting, being quite different and not nearly as smooth-running as the other South Australian wine areas. The name of John Riddoch features prominently in the Coonawarra story but another man whom history has largely forgotten was in fact the first to plant fruit trees and vines in the area. In fact, his success was Riddoch's inspiration.

William Wilson, a Scot, who came to Australia as a shepherd, was the man who discovered without really knowing it the unique red bank soil of Coonawarra. After a modest gold strike at Ballarat Wilson bought two acres at Penola, where the climate reminded him of the Mediterranean regions of Spain and France where he had worked in vineyards. Wilson planted fruit trees and vines, and they flourished.

Enter John Riddoch, the Scottish born 'Squire of Penola'. He bought 'Yallum Park' (Yallum being an aboriginal word for grassy) outside Penola in 1861 and gradually extended his holding to 100 square miles. Riddoch was member for the Victoria district in the South Australian Parliament from 1865 to 1873, and was also a close friend of the poet Adam Lindsay Gordon. In 1881 Riddoch built a magnificent sandstone mansion, which was compared to the Palace of Versailles at the time, and this was surrounded by a deer park, splendid gardens and an orchard. In about 1890 Riddoch decided that the land should be thrown open for closer settlement. Acting on the advice of Professor Perkins, agriculturist with the State Government, he resolved to establish a fruit colony in the belief that 'with intense cultivation the land might be made to support a large population, combining the advantages of rural, healthy life with the pleasures of social intercourse.' Acting on William Wilson's advice Riddoch determined that it should be started on the stretch of red soil on which Wilson had done so well.

In June, 1890 Riddoch advertised the intended Penola Fruit Colony, subdivisions of ten acre blocks being available to the public at £10 per acre at 5 percent per annum interest. The original survey involved 1,147 acres, of which 877 were taken up. Later 812 additional acres were added. Originally twenty-six individuals took up Riddoch's offer, holding from ten to eighty acres each. The colonists planted fruit trees—apples, peaches and apricots, and grapes. Riddoch himself planted 348 acres of vines —181 shiraz, 110 cabernet sauvignon and fifty-seven pinot noir and malbec, and encouraged the colonists to plant in the proportion of one-third cabernet to two-thirds shiraz. During the first planting season 95,000 vines were established.

Riddoch built a winery with cellars which held 75,000 gallons, and bought the colonists' grapes. He intended also to build a jam factory but this never eventuated. The growers formed the Coonawarra Fruit and Winegrowers' Association. The early vintages at Coonawarra showed what the area was capable of, the wines of 1895 and 1896 were of 'superior quality'.

Coonawarra grapes were never much good for brandy because of their low spirit content and thus the area suffered greatly from the lack of demand for table wine. By the beginning of this century Riddoch had thousands of gallons of wine on his hands which he could not sell. John Riddoch died in July 1901—a practical visionary whose plans did not succeed as they should have done simply because he lived at the wrong time.

The year John Riddoch died, 1901, was also the year that Bill Redman arrived at Coonawarra. Redman was to have more influence on the wines of Coonawarra this century than any other individual.

The history of Coonawarra this century is one of crisis after crisis. Although the area made dry red wines of outstanding quality only a few people appreciated them, and it was only in the fifties that Coonawarra began to come into its own. Curious that the three areas (the Hunter, Coonawarra and Great Western) which have made many, if not most, of Australia's top table wines, have shared years and years of hard times and crisis before achieving widespread recognition.

The Murray Valley

It is no exaggeration to say that water is the lifeblood of the settlements along the Murray River. When Captain Charles Sturt first explored the area in 1830, he found only red, sandy alluvial flats, sandhills with 'not a blade of grass', stunted box-trees, some blue gums and scattered aboriginal tribes. Now, of course, the river has been put to use, and acres and acres of vines have yielded millions and millions of gallons of wines and spirits.

The story of this transformation began with Alfred Deakin, later Prime Minister of Australia, who was travelling in the United States as a Royal Commissioner on Water Supply for the Victorian Government in the 1880s. There he met the Canadian born Chaffey brothers, George and William Benjamin, who were involved in establishing an irrigation settlement in California. He persuaded them to come to Australia and begin a similar project there. To his eternal credit Deakin realized that the Murray Valley was ideal for such development and that the Chaffeys were the men for the job.

George Chaffey, the older brother, then aged thirty-eight, arrived in Australia first, and saw Renmark, then a part of the 'Bookmark' sheep station which was nothing but a flat, hot, barren slab of land. In February, 1887 the brothers signed an agreement with the South Australian Government, and later a similar one with the Victorian Government. The plan was that the Chaffeys would prepare and irrigate land, sell it in blocks on time payment and use the revenue for further development. Two settlements were started—first at Renmark and then at Mildura in Victoria. Within a year land was on offer at £20 an acre for orchard blocks, £20 each for town allotments and £100 for residential sites, with ten years to pay. In South Australia the Chaffeys were to receive an acre of land freehold for every £4 spent by them or property owners in development.

Settlers were encouraged, and many came from England in response to highly-coloured descriptions of the glorious future of the area. Life in those pioneering days was hard, and became harder when the Chaffeys went bankrupt with the bank crash of 1893. With the crash development stopped dead and many settlers abandoned their properties. George Chaffey borrowed enough for his fare and went back to the U.S.A. where he later completed irrigation works which made Renmark and Mildura seem small. W. B. Chaffey stayed on at his vineyard at Mildura. During this black period the Renmark Irrigation Trust was created by Act of Parliament in 1893. The Trust was set up to administer the area, and is controlled by the growers themselves. The early years of the Irrigation Trust's control were tough going, but they persevered and eventually prospered.

Before prosperity Renmark had to face the drought of 1914 when the Murray dried up to a mere trickle. Without water the settlement was doomed, and it was realized that a system of locks was absolutely essential. An agreement was made by New South Wales, Victoria and South Australia to erect a series of locks which would ensure that the level of the river remained high throughout the year.

The story of how winemaking began in the irrigation settlements in an attempt to make use of the unwanted gordo grapes which had been grown for drying is told in a later chapter.

South Australia from 1870

It has been noted how the many vineyard areas of South Australia were established so rapidly after the founding of the colony. From 1846 to 1852 the colony's area under vines was quadrupled, and by 1856 the vintage exceeded 100,000 gallons from about 750 acres of vines. Expansion continued at a remarkable rate and from 1861 to 1867 the area under vines had grown from 4,000 to 6,000 acres, and the vintage from 472,000 to 863,000 gallons. South Australian wine was by then finding its way to other states, and there was even some export to England.

In its rapid expansion the South Australian wine industry took no heed of economic limits and by 1870 saturation point was reached. The home market was glutted and interstate markets offered little promise, for both Victoria and New South Wales imposed stiff discriminatory tariffs against South Australian wines to protect their own makers. The bottom fell out of the London market—in haste for profits considerable quantities of poor quality, raw young wine had been shipped to England, and the long voyage did not help either. Some of this wine was sold at only 1/4 a gallon, and some was shipped back at the owners' expense. As a result scores of unprofitable vineyards were uprooted, and between 1865 and 1885 the acreage of vines in the

colony fell from 6,630 to 4,340. It took twenty years before the original ground was recovered.

The eighties and nineties were great years for South Australian viticulture. Through the first of the decades the industry gradually overcame its slump, confidence returned and planting was resumed. By 1889 more than 7,300 acres were under vine, the vintage topped one million gallons and there were seventy recognized winemakers in the colony, half of them in a substantial way. Five years later the vintage was climbing rapidly towards two million gallons, which it reached at the turn of the century. The increased volume was accompanied by increased attention to quality. An incentive to improve standards were the colonial and overseas exhibitions which marked the period, at which the best Australian wines competed with those of European vineyards and were far from disgraced.

By the end of the century Victorian vineyards were being ravaged by phylloxera, which fortunately South Australia had escaped. The parliament of the state promptly passed an Act in 1899 which imposed rigid quarantine measures, under the supervision of a newly established Phylloxera Board. The Act put a levy on winemakers for the creation of a fund to assist the industry with replantings should the need arise. The introduction of any vines or plants from infected areas was prohibited, and a nursery of resistant stocks established in case of need, in Victoria. Despite these commendable measures it is doubtful that without a kindly fate South Australia would have been kept free of disease.

Thus at the turn of the century the South Australian industry was riding the crest of a vinous wave. The area under vines had increased to 20,860 acres yielding over two million gallons of wine. And with Federation came the removal of customs barriers between the states—South Australia was poised to expand its interstate markets and establish itself once and for all as the premier wine state of the Commonwealth.

Other States

Although Western Australia, Tasmania and Queensland have not been important in terms of quantity of wine production, wine has been made in the three states for many years. The first vines to be planted in Western Australia were planted in 1840, by Captain John Septimus Roe, one of the original settlers of the colony. The first commercial wine made was at Houghton in the Swan Valley, in 1859 by a Dr Ferguson.

In Queensland the best-known vineyard was planted at Roma in 1863 by S. S. Bassett, and is still owned by the Bassett family. Winemaking has not been important in Tasmania's history, although a Signor Diego Bernacchi attempted unsuccessfully to establish a vineyard on Maria Island in 1887.

An early scene of grapepickers at vintage time at 'Yalumba' in the Barossa Valley, S.A.

Australian wine this century

The opening years of the new century were particularly favourable for the wine industry of South Australia. A sequence of dry years ended and in 1902 the vintage mounted to nearly 2,500,000 gallons.

There was a temporary halt in about 1904-5 when there was a slump for a season or two. The vintage was down by nearly half and many vines were affected with diseases, the causes of which were not understood. Growers sold for as low as 15/- a ton, or fed their grapes to pigs. The crisis passed fairly quickly and by 1906 the vintage figures were rising again.

Many of the South Australian wine families realized that to continue successfully in business they would need to develop their markets in the most populous States—New South Wales and Victoria. With Federation and the subsequent removal of trade barriers, South Australian wine had free access to the other states, and the big firms such as Penfolds and Hardys were quick to take full advantage of this. In four years the volume exported rose to nearly a million gallons, of which the other Australian states took 846,000 gallons, while interstate sales of spirits mounted nearly tenfold.

This was all to the good for the South Australians, but hit the Hunter Valley winemakers hard. They simply could not compete in price with the South Australian wine, which was cheaper principally because of subsidies to growers by the South Australian government. As a result in the next ten years or so more vines were uprooted in the Hunter than at any other time. All this led to rather frosty feelings between the winemen of the Hunter and South Australia.

The outbreak of World War I severely affected the export of wine to Britain. The effects of this were only felt badly from 1916 and there was an immediate rise in exports after the war. On the home front, the war led to a tremendous amount of hostile feeling to the German settlers, and indeed anything Germanic. This was especially evident in the Barossa Valley where there were many settlers of German descent. There was little ill-will at the outset, but animosity grew with the intensity of the struggle and the increasing Australian casualties. Prejudice was shown in employment, many in public life were subjected to attack and the South Australian Parliament passed an Act to wipe out German associations by a wholesale changing of place names. By this Act Kaiser-Stuhl became Mt Kitchener, Siegersdorf became Dorrien and Gnadenfrei became Marananga. Later some of these names were changed back.

In the post-war years the government instituted a policy of settling repatriated soldiers on the land. The initial success of the river settlements beckoned governments searching for land on which to settle the returned soldiers and so there was in the five years after 1919 a record expansion of the irrigation settlements along the Murray and Murrumbidgee rivers in South Australia, Victoria (at Red Cliffs and Merbein) and New South Wales. Thousands of ex-soldiers, not all suitable for the work, were placed on river blocks planted with vines (many of them doradillos) which promised a quick return, principally from spirit making.

The Hunter Valley shared in the repatriation scheme. Fifty acres was considered to be a suitable sub-division, and several such blocks at Fordwich were given to returned men. For a variety of reasons the plan failed and the newly-planted vineyards were later taken over by Tulloch, and by Elliott.

Also in New South Wales the Murrumbidgee Irrigation Area underwent enormous expansion at this time. The development of this area had begun only a few years previously with the construction of the Burrinjuck Dam. The first farms in the Griffith area were taken up in 1912, and irrigation and planting began in 1913. With the arrival in the area of large numbers of inexperienced farmers numerous problems had to be overcome—some unsuitable grape varieties were planted and unsatisfactory methods of cultivation and irrigation adopted.

In a few years the new wine producing areas on the Murray grew to rank near the top in terms of quantity. South Australia, for long the leading wine state producing sixty to seventy percent of the Commonwealth vintage, went still further ahead to provide up to seventy-five or eighty percent of the Australian total. In 1919-1920 the South Australian vintage was five million gallons, by 1923-1924 it passed ten million gallons for the first time. The expansion was too rapid to be digested and it was realized that wine was being made which could not be sold. Before 1924 was over reaction had set in. Its first manifestation was a glut of doradillos. Grapes which two or three years before had been selling at about £12 to £14 a ton fell rapidly to fetch only £4 a ton or less. It was a story of excessive enthusiasm and optimism which led to production far in excess of demand. The industry was to feel the effects of this over-production for years.

The World War and what followed was no help to the Rutherglen area. The early years of the century had seen something of a revival there, although few growers took part in it. After the war costs of production rose and the land was put to other uses—notably wool. The decline was to continue for many years.

After the slump following the over-production of the early twenties expansion followed a somewhat more orderly and judicious programme. The area under vines increased each year by an average of about 500 acres, so that in the next ten years South Australia's area of vineyards rose gradually to 53,000 acres, while in 1927 its vintage exceeded sixteen million gallons.

The decade of the twenties was not the happiest in the Hunter Valley. World War I helped the vineyards recover to some extent from the problems of the previous years. In 1922 there were 2,700 acres in full bearing, but soon downy mildew hit badly. In 1925 this disease destroyed three-quarters of the crop, the following year a similar loss was caused by drought and in 1927 extensive hail virtually wiped out their entire vintage. After a great year in 1928 (there is always a little silver lining) disaster struck from another direction. In 1929 there was enormous industrial unrest in the mines, with a sixteen-month lock out and considerable civil strife. The local wine market collapsed a year ahead of the world depression of the thirties.

From the late twenties there were many portents of the coming economic storm. The rural industries were facing serious difficulties with apparent overproduction, under-consumption and a disastrous decline in export prices. Other industries, notably the New South Wales coal industry, also showed symptoms of worsening economic conditions. With the real onset of the depression the wine industry passed through one of its worst crises ever. Exports to England fell off, and the local market faded away —Australian consumption of wine declined by sixty percent. The price of grapes fell to £2 a ton for cheaper varieties and total disaster faced the industry.

Many vineyards were torn out and given over to sheep and cattle for though a fortune could not be made from them at least they offered a living. During a big glut at Coonawarra the government intervened, and agreed to pay all soldier-settlers with a fruit block a subsidy of £4/10/- an acre to pull up their grapes and start dairy farms. As a result most of these Coonawarra vineyards disappeared. Of the original 900 acres only 300 remained. Victoria lost thousands of acres of vines around Ararat and Stawell. It lost them all in the Yarra Valley and most of them in central Victoria. The Barossa firms survived by concentrating on fortified and sweet wines to fill what demand there was for wine. The demand in this period was largely for sweet fortified wine, simply because this was the cheapest form of alcohol available.

Recovery from the depression was very slow, and although the situation gradually improved from 1932 to 1938 the industry was in a generally unhappy position. The Second World War gave the wine industry a much needed fillip. Exports were naturally severely curtailed—they fell from 3¾ million gallons in 1939 to 1½ million gallons in 1945. Home consumption increased tremendously in the same period, from 3½ million gallons to nearly nine million gallons. The reason for the increased consumption during the war years may have partly been because wine was sold on a quota system, which made most people battle for their allowance. It seems more likely that the presence of the local and visiting armies had a strong influence on consumption of wine. The great bulk of this wine was fortified, but gradually table (i.e. unfortified) wine became more popular, and by 1946 about forty percent wine produced was in this category. This trend has continued since with table wines gradually becoming more and more popular.

After the cessation of hostilities the government again had a policy of settling repatriated soldiers on the land. It was at this time that the Loxton irrigation area near Renmark was established, as was the Robinvale settlement in Victoria. In other places, however, the decline in vine acreage continued—in the Hunter in 1947 only about 1,100 acres of vines remained (compared with the 1866 peak of over five times that amount), and in Victoria the area under vine also continued to fall.

With the ending of the Second World War came a notable change in the marketing of wine. Before, this, wine, along with many other food commodities, had largely been unlabelled and sold in bulk. Hotels and other supply outlets bought in bulk and sold from the cask by the glass, in the customer's containers or bottled under their own labels. With temporary shortages after the war the big wine companies seized the advantage to sell in bottles under their own labels, with the result that their names became more widely known. This marketing change led to an increase in quality but probably was a large part of the cause of the increased cost of wine.

In the post-war period the level of affluence in the community gradually increased. The fifties did not see any startling developments, but the first signs of a revival were there, for example Wynns and Mildara moved into the Coonawarra area. And with the sixties came the boom. Annual consumption of wine increased from 1.1 gallons per head in the early sixties to 1.8 gallons per head in 1969, and this increase was almost entirely due to the greater popularity of table wines. Evidence for this boom is everywhere—the proliferation of books and articles on wine, the shortage of premium wines and previously unbelievable prices they command, and the wave of new plantings all over the country—many in previously untried areas. Why? Why after so many years did wine drinking become the 'in' thing? For one thing, there was the previously mentioned affluence. People had more money to experiment with the good things of life, and discovered that wine was a very good thing indeed.

This affluence brought with it the motor car, enabling many people to take advantage of the proximity of the vineyards to Australia's capital cities. It became a commonly enjoyed week-end pastime to drive out to the vineyards, sample their offerings, and buy the odd bottle or two. A 'cellar', not an inexpensive investment by any means, became a status symbol. One shudders to think of how much wine is sitting under various houses and staircases and goodness-knows-where, waiting for it to miraculously turn into some form of heavenly nectar. Some of it may come up to its owners' expectations, but undoubtedly many people have

been and are going to be disappointed. At least they have enjoyed the status of having put down a cellar!

Let us not ignore another important factor in the increased popularity of table wines—that is promotion. Simply, the Australian Wine Bureau, some associated writers and other 'personalities' made an organized effort to get people to drink wine. The wine companies increased the volume of their advertising and changed the nature of their promotion. They began to stress the 'drink what you like with what you like' no nonsense theme, and aimed to appeal to young people. And it all worked.

'Cellarmaster' of *The Bulletin* began the first regular wine column in 1962. In 1965 the Wine Bureau began to put editors and writers together, and from about that time things really began to move. We must at least mention writers and journalists such as Frank Margan, Frank Doherty, Jack Ludbrook, Neville Baker, Dan Murphy, Keith Dunstan, and of course, Len Evans, who had inestimable influence in popularizing the drinking of table wine, and were responsible for giving the public considerable education and the background to what it is all about. Graham Kerr, of Galloping Gourmet fame, did his bit for the industry through his extremely popular television programme. And Max Lake, with his books and by his example, helped thousands of people appreciate wine.

Industry figures are not nearly as well known to the public, but those who deserve much of the credit for spreading the word about wine include 'Blue' Geaterix, Arthur Moore, Fred McKeever, John Stanford and Arthur Critchley. The efforts of the New South Wales Wine and Brandy Producers Association were largely responsible for the formation of the Wine Bureau, and the Bureau deserves recognition for its efforts in the promotion of Australian wine.

Various wine and food societies have been both a cause and effect of the boom. The senior bodies, such as The Bacchus Club in South Australia and the Wine and Food Societies of New South Wales and Victoria, played an important role in spreading the appreciation of good food and wine in the community. With this increased awareness many new societies sprang up. And so the snowball effect continued.

Finally, we must not neglect the influence of European immigration which began on a large scale after the war. These new Australians had a great influence on the food habits of the nation, as evidenced by the growth of delicatessens and 'continental' restaurants, and also on drinking habits. They were used to the daily consumption of large quantities of *vin ordinaire,* which itself created a demand as well as setting an example.

And so people everywhere, young and not so young, have begun to drink and enjoy wine without fuss—simply to get through flagons of sound, light wine without worrying which side of the hill the grapes came from. James Busby would be delighted!

The bottle washing department at 'Seppeltsfield', Barossa Valley, which was founded in 1852 (Photo: Seppelt & Sons, Views of Seppeltsfield).

3 Australian wine abroad

As we have seen it was intended from the earliest days that Australia would supply at least part of the demand for wine in Britain. A flood of Australian wine has been sold in Britain over the years, but its quality and the prejudices of the British people have been such that the reputation of Australia as a winemaking country has for long been distinctly unfavourable

The first wine shipped to London was made by Gregory Blaxland at Parramatta in 1822. The Royal Society of Arts awarded Blaxland a silver medal for this, and in 1828 again honoured Blaxland with the award of a gold 'Ceres Medal'. Records show that the Committee of the Society found the wine to be 'a light but sound wine with much of the odour and flavour of claret, or rather holding an intermediate place between that wine and the red of Nice.' Thus, right from the very beginning Australian wine was not considered on its own terms, but rather in comparison with the wines of Europe. This is not surprising as Australia was an unknown land and its products were just as unknown.

In the early 1840s John MacArthur received prizes for wine exhibited in London but it was not until the mid-century that any significant quantities of wine were exported. The first year that the Department of Customs and Excise recorded Australian wine in bond in the United Kingdom was 1854. That year the amount noted was 1,389 gallons but from then on there was a steady increase, until 51,000 gallons entered Britain in 1864. The 1860s marked the beginning of a new era in the export of Australian wine.

From the beginning of the nineteenth century Cape wines had enjoyed a preferential tariff in the U.K. This was ended in February, 1860 from when the import of Cape wines declined considerably, to the advantage of wine from Australia.

The Emu Wine Company Limited

In 1862 the Australian Wine Company was registered in London. The proprietors of this company were Patrick Auld, of 'Auldana' vineyards and a Mr Burton, formerly an employee of the Department of Customs and Excise. Their aim was primarily to sell Auldana wine, but also to sell Australian wine generally. The Australian Wine Company was the first to popularize and distribute Australian wines in the United Kingdom. In 1883 the manager of the company, James Cox, registered the trade mark 'Emu'. Two years later the company was bought by Aylwin Whately Pownall. The Emu Wine Company continued to grow and by 1925 was the largest importer of Australian wines in both the United Kingdom and Canada. Five years later, in 1930, the Company acquired its first vineyards with the purchase of R. C. H. Walker's property at Morphett Vale south of Adelaide. They greatly enlarged and improved the property and now have the capacity for storing one and a half million gallons of wine and a quarter of a million gallons of brandy. The company buys a large amount of wine and brandy to supplement the produce of its own vineyards. All wine shipped to the United Kingdom is sent in casks, but some wine in bottles goes to Canada.

In 1945 the Emu Wine Company expanded in Western Australia with the purchase of the Valencia Wine Company, and four years later they bought Houghtons, one of Western Australia's oldest winemakers.

P. B. Burgoyne and Company

The firm of P. B. Burgoyne and Company commenced business as Australian wine merchants in 1872. Burgoynes later acquired the Mt Ophir and Mt Athos vineyards in the Rutherglen area, although these ceased production in the early 1950s. Burgoynes became part of the Emu Wine Co Pty Ltd in 1956.

The United Kingdom market from 1870 to World War I

With two companies promoting the sale of Australian wine in London the volume of such business increased steadily. From the early 1880s importations began to increase rapidly, the six figure mark being reached in 1886 (145,582 gallons).

A feature of the late nineteenth century was numerous 'great exhibitions' which were held all over the world as a grand form of trade fairs. Australian wines were exhibited at many of these and the results were somewhat mixed. At the time there was a notable controversy about the Vienna Exhibition of 1873 at which Australian wine won numerous awards. A Dr Thudicum alleged that some Australian wines were over twenty-six percent proof spirit, and that these must have been fortified as it was impossible for such a degree of alcohol to be produced naturally. A heated debate followed in the press.

Australian wine was also exhibited at the Bordeaux Exhibition of 1882, and was awarded some prizes there. In a critical report on these wines, however, M. Emile Dubois noted that, 'in general the wines have not been properly clarified before bottling and the bottling has not been done properly'. He found that the grapes were harvested when too ripe and that the jurors 'believe that you put brandy in the wine'. They found the wines have 'a curious taste of bitterness' and believed that the grapes were planted in brackish soil. The highest number of points awarded any wine was sixteen out of twenty-five, and several scored no points at all.

In any event these exhibitions did serve a purpose in bringing attention to Australian wine. These wines usually competed in an 'Empire' or 'Colonial' wines division, and not in open competition with the European products. The awards they won, however numerous, did therefore not mean much to the English.

Exports of Australian wine to Britain increased steadily from 1884 until the outbreak of war in 1914. 1902 was the peak year, when nearly 990,000 gallons were exported.

World War I and after

During the war naturally exports fell considerably owing to lack of shipping space. In 1918 only 176,000 gallons were exported, but after the war the figures went up again. Practically all Australian wine imported into the United Kingdom up to this time was of the full-bodied dry red type with an alcoholic strength of about twenty-seven percent proof spirit. Their quality was, at best, uneven.

In 1914 the New South Wales Department of Agriculture held a blind tasting by leading Australian wine merchants of wines which were available at retail shops in London. Of the thirty-seven wines examined, eighteen were considered good (some excellent), six of medium quality, nine indifferent and four bad. Some of their comments are illuminating. Of a 'burgundy' which sold for 19/- a dozen: *Taster 1:* 'A rather rough wine, but otherwise a very good wine for English market.' *Taster 2:* 'Very rough, sound, good; would not appeal to any wine drinker being too rough.' *Taster 3:* 'Rough, sound, full bodied; typical for the English market.'!

By the early 1920s Australia was faced with a glut of fortified wine, mainly resulting from the vast production from the newly planted irrigation areas. With the home market saturated it was natural for the local winemakers to turn to the United Kingdom. Unfortunately for them, however, Britain had signed a treaty with Portugal in 1916 which legally reserved the names Port and Madeira for the wines of Portugal and Madeira.

According to H. E. Laffer, who wrote the authoritative *The Wine Industry of Australia* (1949), 'the vital need for Australia was to get rid of bulk stocks representing good, sound, and palatable wines which ultimately proved to the liking of the people in the mass.' The Federal Government thus passed the *Wine Export Bounty Act* of 1924. This applied only to wines of at least thirty-four percent proof spirit, as the glut consisted mainly of sweet fortified wine. The bounty was 2/9 a gallon, to which was added a refund of 1/3 a gallon paid in excise for the fortifying spirit used.

The following year, 1925, the British Government decided that blood was thicker than water and granted Empire wine a fifty percent preferential margin over foreign wine. This meant, for example, that when foreign wine paid eight shillings a gallon duty, Empire wine only paid four shillings. This was a tremendous help to the Australian industry. Then, when the situation was looking a little brighter, the Commonwealth Government in 1927 reduced the bounty by one shilling per gallon.

Consider for a moment what sort of Australian wine was being sold in Britain. The wine was sold at a lower price than the European product, partly because it was regarded as inferior to the wines of Europe. The cheap fortified sweet red 'port style' wines sold well compared to more expensive port from Portugal. Heavy, fruity Australian reds were sold as 'Australian burgundy', which was advertised as being good for the health. This burgundy was alleged to contain lots of iron and thus be good for anaemia and invalids (Dr Penfold had thought the same thing—eighty years before. Surely medicine had made more progress than that!). Australian 'boarding house burgundy' had a lowly reputation in Britain and obviously the main reason it was bought was because it was a cheap form of alcohol.

In 1929 the *Wine Overseas Marketing Act* was passed, which set up a Wine Overseas Marketing Board (which later became the Australian Wine Board) with Mr J. Wallace Sandford elected as its first chairman. The following year a London office was opened under the management of Mr H. E. Laffer.

In 1930 the Federal Government imposed steep increases (up to eighty-three percent) in the rate of excise duty on fortifying spirit, and the wine industry successfully pressed the government to place the revenue in a special trust fund for payment of the bounty on exports.

The outbreak of the Second World War gravely affected the Australian wine industry. In the preceding period about 3½ million gallons had been exported to Britain annually, but with war more urgent cargo had priority. In addition, of course, shipping became extremely hazardous because of enemy activity. From 1941 the British Government issued an embargo on all imports of wine and spirits, and in the following years very small quotas were imposed—one thousand tons only in 1943.

During the war years when exports were slight a considerable balance was built up in the Wine Export Encouragement Trust Account, and by the end of 1946 it was worth £1,100,000. The Government then decided in 1947 to discontinue the bounty of one shilling a gallon, because they claimed higher prices being paid overseas for wine and the increased local consumption made it unnecessary. £500,000 of the Trust Account was made available for use by the wine industry (which was used in 1955 to set up the Wine Research Institute) and the balance disappeared into Consolidated Revenue.

Exports to Britain continued during the fifties, and in 1960 the Wine Board opened the Australian Wine Centre in Soho. This was financed by the Board and seventeen leading Australian wine firms to act as a central supply point in the United Kingdom. Britain is still Australia's best overseas customer for wine, taking over a million gallons of our wine a year. Next is Canada, and then much further down the scale come many south-east Asian countries.

Wine is not one of Australia's major exports, and Australia is not a big exporter of wine in world terms. The recent succession of new plantings may mean an improvement in this situation.

An old lever press at 'Bleasdale' winery, Langhorne Creek, S.A. The press, built in 1895, was originally powered by a two-man capstan.

VINEYARDS AND VIGNERONS OF AUSTRALIA

Jaki Ilbery

Roly Birks, winemaker since 1917 at Birks' 'Wendouree' Cellars.

4 New South Wales
The Hunter Valley

The Hunter Valley is one of the great wine producing areas of Australia. Its wines may not always have been fully appreciated, but in recent years the reputation of the Valley has been much enhanced, and the vignerons are beginning to reap their just rewards. Money for development has poured into the area and the wines, despite steep increases in price, are greatly sought after.

Perhaps surprisingly, in view of the extent of its reputation, the Hunter Valley produces less than one percent of Australia's total wine output. Actually the figure is rather misleading, for included in the total wine output is all the wine that is made into distillation material as well as the fortified wine. Speaking only of table wine, the Hunter puts out about five percent of Australia's production, which is not much —its many fans would say not nearly enough—but the recent new plantings should help somewhat.

The chequered history of the area has been described at some length in the section on the history of Australian wine. Why the Hunter Valley has been so successful for wine cultivation is probably due to a combination of factors—soils, climate and not least the efforts of the winemakers. Naturally, success begets success, and legends of great wines and great winemakers, notably Maurice O'Shea, have developed. This has had a two-way effect. It has perhaps stimulated old and new winemakers to recreate, and possibly exaggerate, past glories. The 'Hunter mystique' has also encouraged wine lovers to be interested in the area—to visit it to see the renowned vineyards for themselves, but above all to buy, cellar and eventually drink the wines, and in turn to develop new legends of their experiences.

The Hunter Valley can be divided into two main vineyard areas. The older vineyards are centred in the parishes of Pokolbin and Rothbury, a short distance from the coal town of Cessnock. With the wine boom of the sixties many new vineyards were established in the Upper Hunter area, west of Muswellbrook. As these vineyards are still relatively new, the extent of their influence and reputation is unsure. The fame of the Hunter has been built on the old vineyards of the Pokolbin area, and it is mainly to this area that reference will be made.

The Hunter Valley is the largest area of lowland on the east coast of New South Wales. With the exception of the coastal break at Newcastle, it is bounded by uplands from 1,500 to 4,000 feet high. The Hunter Valley region is about 10,000 square miles in area, but grape growing is concentrated in a relatively small part of the central lowlands.

Geologically speaking, shale, tuffs, sandstone and conglomerates are the principal constituents, with some lava beds in the basal portions. They form most of the lowland area of the Valley, giving rise to undulating country. There is sandstone plateau to the south, with hilly country and alluvial river flats to the north.

The soils are mostly podsolic, with an absence of free lime in the subsoil. They are fine textured, and generally very dark brown to grey-brown. This type of soil is friable when moist, and soft to hard when dry. There are also some areas of loams, which have concentrations of limestone, and vary from red to chocolate in colour. The third type of soil is found in the alluvial river flats. (These differences in soil all have their effects on the grapes produced from them, although the nuances in the wines may not be apparent to any but the real experts.) The most important feature of the soils of the Hunter vineyards is the evidence of the remains of volcanic activity. This is found in a long strip east of the Mount View Range, and in small areas which run in a line north of Mount Pleasant. The majority of top quality reds of the Pokolbin area come from this weathered volcanic soil, which is red clay loam.

Climate has an enormous influence on grape cultivation, and thus on the wine made from them. The average annual rainfall in the Hunter Valley is about twenty-seven inches, but this varies considerably from year to year. The rain is heaviest in summer, with a secondary peak in early winter. There is an average of eighty wet days per year, with thunderstorms in summer.

Temperatures are moderate. In summer, of which January is usually the hottest month, the mean daily temperature exceeds 21.1°C. In winter the mean minimum is about 4.4°C, with July having the lowest temperatures.

It has been said in the past, especially abroad, that vintage years mean very little in Australia—that all years are similar. This is not so, especially in the Hunter area where climatic conditions can and do alter considerably from year to year.

Too much rain is often a problem, particularly at vintage time. This may cause the grapes to split open and decreases the sugar content of the berries. It also increases the likelihood of mildew diseases. The end result may well be very light wines. Unfortunately floods and droughts have been frequent. Between 1908 and 1962 thirty-one years were either flood or drought years, and in one-third of those years the area has suffered both floods and drought. Particularly severe floods have occurred in 1893, 1913, and five very wet years in the early fifties, with further bad floods in 1955 and 1963. Fortunately frost is generally not a problem, unlike Coonawarra and some of the Victorian vineyards.

Hail, however, is one of the major worries of the Hunter winemakers. It can completely destroy an entire year's crop in a matter of minutes. Severe hail damages the wine as well as the grapes, and can affect the vintages of the following few years. Not all vineyards are hit by a single hailstorm. In recent

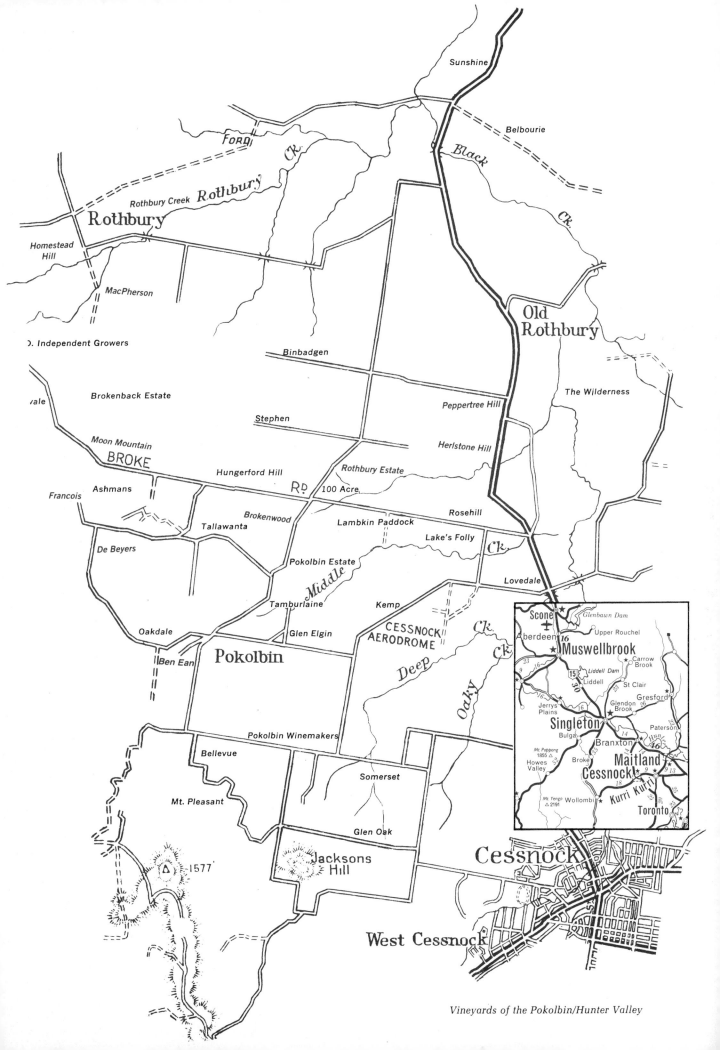

Vineyards of the Pokolbin/Hunter Valley

times 1963 was the worst year for hail. There is usually very little warning of impending hail, although there is little that can be done as a preventative. Murray Tyrrell claims to have had some success in firing imported rockets into the hail clouds, which are meant to disperse them—the other vignerons have generally remained unconvinced.

Bushfires must be added to the catalogue of woes. In 1968 fires badly affected some of the vineyards, such as Tyrrells and Elliotts, destroying many of the vines especially at the perimeters.

Vine diseases present further hazards. The Hunter is one of the few areas to have escaped the dreaded phylloxera, which devastated many Australian vineyards in other states in the latter part of the nineteenth century. The area is (perhaps as some form of divine compensation?) susceptible to downy mildew, a fungus which withers leaves and berries. A wet summer and lack of sunshine favour the disease, which the vignerons attempt to combat by spraying with copper and other chemical compounds. Downy mildew first struck in 1917 and did a great deal of damage over the following years, entirely wiping out some vineyards.

Birds are yet another problem. Packs of starlings do the worst damage to the grapes, while rosellas and currawongs also do their share. Shooting the pests is the only solution.

The fame of the Hunter rests on its unfortified wines—the dry reds and dry whites. Traditionally the reds have been made from hermitage, the local name for shiraz; and the whites from semillon (confusingly known also as Hunter riesling) probably because they have given the best return in quality and quantity. Pinot noir, the great grape of Burgundy, has not done very well in the Hunter in the past, although McWilliams have some which is nearly always used in blends. There is also some blanquette, white hermitage, rhine riesling and verdelho grown. Of recent years some new varieties have been introduced—cabernet sauvignon, traminer, malbec, merlot and Clare riesling.

The justly famous whites are soft, round wines with extraordinary bouquet and flavour. They have a honey character, and some see 'sweaty saddle'. As elsewhere in Australia changes in winemaking techniques have greatly changed the traditional style— the trend now is for delicate, fresh, more acid wines and the techniques of controlled temperature fermentation and refrigeration have made this possible.

The use of imported new oak casks for maturation of the red wine has caused great differences of opinion in the area. McWilliams first introduced this on a fairly large scale in 1961. Max Lake is an enthusiastic promoter of the technique. Many Hunter wines now show the use of some new oak, though it is still used more sparingly than in other areas. Some small makers still cling to the traditional methods—and their reluctance to tamper with methods proven successful is quite understandable.

W. Drayton & Sons Pty Ltd, 'Bellevue'

A relatively small family concern, the Draytons have a long association with the Hunter. Theirs is the only name still actively concerned with the area which is to be found on the original maps of the land grants in the Pokolbin area. The Draytons are one of the three families who have endured through all the bad times, through the Depression of the thirties, to still independently make wine today. In the past some of their wine was sold in bulk and bottled by others, and they relied heavily on the sale of fortified wine to survive. Now, however, they make, bottle and sell their own product.

The founder of this enterprise was Charles Drayton who was born in 1820, at Bellevue in England.

Charles moved to the Pokolbin area in 1850, and bought a 40 acre block with the intention of establishing a small farm. Although grapes were grown in the district even before he settled there, it was not until twenty years later that he decided to make part of his property into a vineyard to produce dry white and red wine.

The Draytons were a prolific family—Charles had four sons and two daughters by his second wife. One of his sons, William, did even better, by producing nine boys and a girl (William, Joseph, Lewis, Walter, Ernest, Wesley, Reginald, Edgar, Ivy and Len). William was a practical man; his son Len describes him as 'a winegrower, cooper, carpenter and blacksmith'. William's youngest son, Len, born at Pokolbin in 1905 and for many years the chief winemaker, is the present Managing Director of the company. As senior wine man of the Hunter, with his life-long association with winemaking there, his knowledge and experience are keenly sought after by younger vignerons. Following family tradition, Len's son Bill is now at 'Bellevue', along with Len's nephews, Ron, Reg and Max.

The boom of the sixties has, at last, brought a measure of prosperity to the Draytons. Life for any primary producer is not plain sailing at any time, and the Draytons lost 50 percent of their crop in a short but severe hail storm in 1963. They were also affected by bushfires at the end of 1968 which nearly destroyed the old family homestead. The 'Bellevue' vineyard is located in the foothills of the Mt View range, just north-west of Mt Pleasant. Much of the soil is light grey loam, which is apparently alluvial, rather than the volcanic soil which is largely found in the area.

Although there was once a wide variety of grapes planted, they now have mostly hermitage (shiraz) for the reds, with the addition of some cabernet sauvignon in recent years. The dominant variety for the whites is semillon, or Hunter riesling, with white hermitage and a small amount of rhine riesling.

Draytons have recently acquired the 'Lambkin' and 'Ivanhoe' properties for development. They now have over 500 acres altogether, with about 130 acres under vine, and plan to expand further. On arrival at Draytons' visitors enter a squat modern building, which is the sales and tasting area. The winery and storage section is of brick and galvanised iron, behind which is the now uninhabited old homestead.

Moving with the times, the Draytons have discarded their famous old 30 ton log press, which could take two days to set up, and they now use a French Vaslin screw press. They have installed other modern equipment—a refrigeration system for controlling the temperature of fermentation, a new bottling plant and a big underground storage area.

The Drayton whites have typical Hunter character, although the style has become more delicate with the new techniques of winemaking. Bottled under cask numbers, both whites and reds can be quite outstanding at their best.

Elliott's Wines Pty Ltd, 'Oakvale'

The history of the Elliott family follows a similar pattern to the Draytons. The Elliotts are another of the family concerns which have survived all the economic and other crises which hit the Hunter vignerons over the years.

The original Elliott was a Scottish coalminer, who bought the property 'Oakvale' in 1893. The winery is located there now. The vines still planted there are very old, and in the style of the time, too closely planted to be easily cultivated today. Oakvale is the name under which the Elliott wines are bottled.

Bob Elliott, his son, was born near Newcastle in the same year as 'Oakvale' was acquired. It was he who, showing great foresight, greatly extended the family holdings, and established the Elliott style of winemaking.

He bought and planted 'Belford' in the thirties and it is from here that the famed and hard-to-get white known as Belford comes. This vineyard is a little away from most of the others in the area, located past Branxton south of the railway line near the New England Highway. At about the same time Bob Elliott also bought 'Fordwich'. This was one of the properties developed by returned servicemen after the First World War, in a government-sponsored repatriation scheme. It is planted with semillon, used in making typical Hunter dry whites.

In 1943 he acquired 'Tallawanta', off the Broke Road, between Tyrrells and the present Hungerford Hill. This vineyard had been established by V. Stevens, who sold it when he returned from fighting in World War II. 'Tallawanta' consists mainly of clay loam and weathered volcanic soils and is exposed to the hot summer westerly winds which can adversely affect the grapes. It is planted with hermitage which is used in the making of Elliott's dry red.

The residue of grape skins and seeds after the juice has been extracted (marc), Lindeman's, Corowa, N.S.W.

Bob Elliott sold his wine from a shop in Cessnock, although through the lean years his wine was also bought in bulk by big makers.

Doug Elliott, born in Cessnock in 1922, took over as winemaker after his father's death in December, 1959. He is progressive in his outlook, and has installed new equipment, giving away the old continuous press. He also extended the winery by adding on a new wing, and then he replaced the old part when it was burnt down. Doug Elliott is a quiet man with a firm belief in the quality of Hunter wines. His son John is now helping with the winemaking.

All the Elliott wines are vineyard bottled. They produce two whites—a standard and a private bin, and one red—Oakvale. These are typical Hunter wines, which itself implies high quality.

Hungerford Hill Vineyards Pty Ltd

This company has achieved one of the largest vineyard areas in the Hunter Valley in a very short space of time. The company was formed to develop vineyards in the Hunter. In 1967 they began operations by buying a holding opposite Elliott's 'Tallawanta'. This property was formerly part of Allan Hungerford's Friesian stud, which he had been reluctant to sell. The soil is rich chocolate basalt, regarded as ideal for red grapes.

Land clearing and contouring was begun in 1968, and shiraz, semillon and cabernet cuttings were planted. Norman Hanckel, who had experience with Yalumba in the development of the Pewsey Vale vineyards in South Australia, was appointed manager of Hungerford Hill Vineyards. As such, he was in charge of the clearing, contouring and planting operations which began the group's activities in the Hunter.

The Hungerford Hill company was responsible for the introduction of several techniques new to the Hunter. The land was deep ripped in addition to the usual contouring, and a unique water injection system was introduced. The latter technique is now widely used in the district.

The first vintage was in 1970, when the vines were about 18 months old. The growth of the vines was remarkably good, and they yielded approximately eleven tons of grapes. The wine from this vintage was not made on the property.

A winery has been built, and a dam of 110 million gallon capacity constructed. The company intends to use this for irrigation only when absolutely necessary, such as during droughts. They wish to maintain the traditional style and quality of the Hunter wines.

By local standards, the scale of Hungerford Hill's activities is enormous. The company has bought nearly 1,000 acres, of which 600 have been planted.

Hungerford Hill Pty Ltd was floated as a public company in 1969. They have established a large winery at Buronga in New South Wales, where they will buy from local growers, and be capable of handling 2½ million gallons of wine. In February, 1970 they took over Reynella Wines in South Australia. The company also has interests in the Woorinen Co-operative Winery near Swan Hill. Hungerford Hill was an entirely Australian owned company with H. C. Sleigh Ltd one of the major shareholders with a twenty percent interest. Recently Rothmans joined forces with the company to form a new wine company called International Cellars.

'Lakes Folly'

'Lakes Folly' is a small vineyard, but its influence and the quality of wine it produces have given it an importance which greatly outweighs its size. Its owner, Dr Max Lake, was born in July 1924, graduated in medicine from Sydney University in 1946 and was a surgeon eight years later. He became a serious student and a lover of wine, and has written some very good books on Australian wine, with a special contribution to research on the Hunter.

Dr Lake decided that he wanted to make his own wine, and establish his own vineyard and this in itself was a remarkable decision. In 1961 he began

searching the Hunter looking for the ideal land. In 1963 he bought sixty-three acres near McWilliams' Rosehill paddock, of which he is aiming to have twenty-five acres under vine. He built an A-frame winery, which is locally referred to by some as the Pokolbin Opera House. This was the first new vineyard to be planted in the Hunter for many years, and probably did much to influence others to follow his example.

The chief variety planted was cabernet sauvignon, the great grape of Bordeaux, with about one-quarter red hermitage. This was a radical departure from the traditions of the Hunter, where hermitage had long been the most popular variety. The vineyards are planted in nine foot rows, with the vines six feet apart. All the vines were planted by Lake's friends, who also picked the grapes at the first vintage in 1966. The quantity of grapes was small, and the wine was made by the ancient method of treading out the juice by bare feet (to the accompaniment of 'Zorba the Greek' played on the piano by Lake himself). This historic grape treading force was Marie Schmid, David & Stephen Lake, Len Evans and David Lynch.

Another departure from Hunter tradition is the use of new oak for maturation. Dr Lake's wines have been highly praised, and are noteworthy as being of a new style for the area. Two wines only are made, a 100 percent cabernet, and a cabernet hermitage blend, although later one wine only may be sold, Lake's Folly Dry Red.

Lindeman's Wines Pty Ltd, 'Ben Ean'

The influence of the Lindeman name now extends far beyond the confines of the Hunter Valley. It stands for one of the major winemakers of Australia, and is closely bound up with the whole history of wine in Australia.

The founder of this viticultural giant was Henry John Lindeman who was born in London in 1811, the son of a doctor. At 23 years he graduated from St Bartholomew's Hospital in 1834 as a surgeon and joined the Royal Navy.

Lindeman married Eliza Bramhall in 1840, left the Navy, and decided to emigrate to Australia. They arrived in Sydney in September 1840, and Dr Lindeman set up as a general practitioner at Gresford on the Paterson River, a tributary of the Hunter River.

In 1843 he was granted some land, which he planted as a vineyard called 'Cawarra', which is aboriginal dialect for 'by running waters'. He was successful for some years, and built up a large stock of maturing wines, reputed to have been of high quality. In 1850 Dr Lindeman joined the Hunter River Valley Association, and later became its president. Disaster struck in 1851, when a fire completely destroyed the doctor's wooden storage shack and winery.

At this stage, Lindeman left for the Victorian goldfields, where he worked as a surgeon and a miner, and incidentally, studied winemaking in the Corowa and Rutherglen areas. He returned to 'Cawarra' with his fortunes restored, rebuilt his winery and expanded his plantings. In 1870 he established the headquarters of his firm and his winery in Pitt Street, Sydney.

In order to supplement the dry wine produced from 'Cawarra' with sweet ones, for which there was a great demand, he extended his holdings to Corowa. In 1872 he bought Haffners' Vineyard at Corowa, on the banks of the Murray River, the border between New South Wales and Victoria. The Felton and Southern Cross vineyards there were also acquired. The Lindeman establishment at Corowa has expanded enormously since then.

Dr Henry John Lindeman died in 1881. He had been a strong exponent of the value of drinking table wine as a deterrent to rum and spirit drinking with its attendant drunkenness and his influence in the Hunter Valley and at Corowa was huge.

In 1879 Dr Lindeman had made his three sons partners in the firm. Charles Frederick Lindeman became manager after his father's death, and built most successfully on the foundations he had laid.

In about 1896 a writer in the *Maitland Mercury*, H. M. McKenzie, was most impressed by the 'immense storage capacity' at 'Cawarra'. He noted that all the casks there, which were made of three inch oak, were imported from Germany and cost £26 each to set up in the 'Cawarra' cellars. There were then about twenty-five acres under vine. Mr McKenzie wrote, 'It is a recognized fact that "Cawarra" is the best vineyard in this district, the wine, especially a light claret which I tasted and found excellent, being bottled at the premises.' The 'Cawarra' clarets were 'light, sound and free from acid, and by no means, as so many colonial clarets are, rough on the tongue.' The Lindemans had an 'invariable rule' that no wine left the vineyard for at least four years, and was then rested for at least one year in the cellars in Sydney before sale. The wines were mostly Madeira and Black Hermitage.

In about 1900 the Lindemans bought 'Porphyry', near Raymond Terrace in the Newcastle district. This vineyard was planted in 1838 by Dr Henry Carmichael. It is no longer cultivated but its name has been given to one of the few sweet wines made from Hunter material.

The next addition was the property named 'Sunshine'. This is located near Branxton on the Cessnock road, and was bought by the Lindemans in 1910. It is now an important vineyard, planted with semillon, verdelho and white hermitage.

One of Charles' brothers, Frederick, bought the 'Ben Ean' vineyard in 1912. This, which was planted in 1870 by John McDonald, is the site of an impressive winery, and is Lindemans chief base in the Hunter River Valley. 'Coolalta,' which is at the back of 'Ben Ean,' was sold by the Wilkinson family to Lindemans at about the same time. 'Coolalta' had been planted in 1866, and is possibly the oldest vineyard in the Pokolbin area.

Dr Lindeman's daughter, Mathilda, married James Kelman, a nephew of James Busby. This marriage added 'Kirkton' to the Lindeman holdings in 1914. 'Kirkton', which is four and a half miles from Branxton, was originally planted by Kelman's father in 1830, with vines which he obtained from Busby. At the turn of the century there were sixty-five acres of vines on the sandy reddish soil, which produced 400 to 500 gallons per acre each year. According to Mr McKenzie, in the *Maitland Mercury*, 'Kirkton' produced 'a delicate wine in the shape of hocks and clarets, amongst which the red hermitage seems to suit the soil better than the majority. The verdelho and riesling are also a very suitable kind for the "Kirkton" soil.' The vineyard was sold after the 1924 vintage, some of which was picked from Busby's original vines, as being uneconomic. It is now used as a farm.

The firm experienced financial problems from the Depression and on through the war years. It recovered, however, in the late 1940s, and a new era of expansion began soon after. In 1953 Lindemans became a public company. In 1960 it established its headquarters in Marrickville, Sydney where it now has a very large modern plant and storage facilities.

Lindemans acquired 'Chateau Leonay', formerly Leo Buring's concern, in 1963, and further increased its influence on the Australian wine scene when it took over Rouge Homme Wines at Coonawarra in 1965. Lindemans buy grapes from other growers for making into wine, and also purchase large quantities of wine for blending purposes.

In 1971 Lindemans was itself taken over by the American tobacco company Phillip Morris.

The 'Ben Ean' vineyard is on rich volcanic loam, and, with the grapes from 'Sunshine', is the source of Lindemans multi-prize winning Hunter wines. The white wines from 'Ben Ean' are particularly famous, and although the reds are very good, too, the output is not very large. Lindemans do blend wines extensively—combining Hunter wine with wine from other areas to put out standard wines of the same style year after year. The areas from which the blends originate are usually noted on the label.

Lindemans were the leaders in changing the style of white wines to the more delicate and fresh style common today. In the Hunter in 1956 they installed pressure fermentation tanks which allow the wine-maker to control the temperature of fermentation. It was in 1965, however, that Lindemans really began to modernize the equipment at 'Ben Ean'. They installed a German Wilmes air bag press, which gets the maximum delicacy and flavour from the grapes, and much other modern machinery which ensures maximum quality in their wines. Lindemans emphasize complete cleanliness as being essential to good winemaking.

In the Hunter Lindemans are constantly expanding. New plantings are being made, and old areas replanted with premium varieties. In looking at the present position of Lindemans wines the contributions made by two of their outstanding winemakers—Hans Mollenhaeur and Karl Stockhausen, should not be overlooked.

Hans Mollenhaeur, a German food technologist who emigrated to Australia shortly after World War II, was winemaker at 'Ben Ean' in the fifties. He was working in the cider industry in Tasmania when he was appointed as manager of 'Ben Ean' after applying to a newspaper advertisement. Some of the wines that he made are now part of the Hunter legend. He also published research papers on winemaking, developing a theory on the rate of maturation of grapes; and on local history. Mollenhaeur returned to Germany in 1959.

He was succeeded by Karl Stockhausen, who was born in Hamburg, Germany in 1930. In 1955 he came to Australia and studied accountancy while staying at the Greta migrant camp. He joined Lindemans as a casual worker, and after a year moved to their headquarters in Sydney, where he worked as a clerk while completing his accountancy studies. Stockhausen passed his degree in 1961. When Mollenhaeur returned to Germany, Karl Stockhausen was offered his job. His experience at that stage was not large, but with much care and meticulous attention to detail, he has succeeded in producing wines of very high quality.

McWilliams Wines Pty Ltd, 'Mt Pleasant'

McWilliams have huge wineries at Yenda, Hanwood and Beelbangera in New South Wales, and at Robinvale in Victoria. The history of the development of the company is discussed under these areas. Many of McWilliams top quality wines, although only a very small percentage of their output, come from their Hunter Valley vineyards, and are sold under the Mount Pleasant label. McWilliams have only been involved in the Hunter since 1932, but the Mount Pleasant label and wines have a much longer history than that.

The small original vineyard of 'Mount Pleasant', in the Pokolbin area near Cessnock, was planted in 1880 by Charles King on a Crown grant. The soil there is weathered volcanic loam, which is very fertile.

Some years later the vineyard was acquired by John Augustus O'Shea, an Irish immigrant, married to a Frenchwoman. After his son Maurice had finished school in Australia, John O'Shea sent him to France,

where he studied viticulture, first at the Agricultural College at Grignon and later at the University of Montpellier. Maurice O'Shea returned to Australia in 1921 with an extensive knowledge and feeling for food and wines. In 1925, when the vineyard was about 120 acres in area, he named it 'Mount Pleasant'. On taking over as winemaker Maurice O'Shea extended the vineyards and began making wine of such quality that he has assumed nothing short of legendary status in Australian wine history.

In 1932 the McWilliam family, interested in dry table wines, and recognizing the potential of the estate, combined with O'Shea in the equal ownership of a company known as Mount Pleasant Wines Pty Ltd. Later the O'Shea family sold their shares to McWilliams Wines. Maurice was retained as vineyard manager and director until he died.

O'Shea was given a free hand by McWilliams, and with their capital behind him, began to extend their holdings. They acquired 'Lovedale' on the Cessnock-Branxton road. Vines were planted, but at the outbreak of World War II the government took over the property and converted it into an emergency landing field for the duration. In 1950 the government released the area and Maurice and McWilliams started again. They planted the area mainly with semillon. 'Lovedale's' soils are mainly alluvial silt with yellow clay, and this vineyard is the source of the dry white wine known as Anne Riesling.

In about 1950, O'Shea planted the vineyard known as 'Rosehill', which is situated along the Broke Road, opposite the present 'Lake's Folly'. 'Rosehill' has volcanic soil, and is the source of the Robert series of reds and much of the Philip series.

Maurice O'Shea died in May 1956. His reputation, however, lives on, and a legendary aura has developed about his name. He had superb judgement of wine, and with McWilliams financial resources backing him, was able to buy the pick of the wine made by other vignerons to be blended as he saw fit. O'Shea certainly made some of the most magnificent wines ever seen from the Hunter, and was largely instrumental in putting the area and the Mount Pleasant name firmly on the viticultural map.

Brian Walsh, the present winemaker at 'Mount Pleasant', took over after O'Shea's death. Walsh was born in Sydney in November, 1931 and graduated from Sydney Technical College as an industrial chemist in 1954. He joined McWilliams as a laboratory assistant in 1952, and three years later was sent by them to Newcastle to learn winemaking from O'Shea. Walsh helped O'Shea with the 1956 vintage, and in June, 1957 he moved to 'Mount Pleasant'. He has a firm belief that the influence of the winemaker is not the major factor, but that the quality of the wine depends on the quality of the basic grapes, and the strict following of such basic rules as cleanliness. To follow the great name of O'Shea was surely an unenviable task, but one in which Brian Walsh has succeeded most admirably.

'Lakes Folly', established by Dr Max Lake in the Hunter Valley in 1963.

Since the time of Walsh's coming to 'Mount Pleasant', the McWilliam enterprise in the Hunter Valley has increased enormously. Over the five years to 1967 their crush rose from 100 to 300 tons, all grown by themselves. Their acreage under vine has also expanded. 'Mount Pleasant' is now about 200 acres, 'Lovedale' over 270 acres and 'Rosehill' over 50 acres. The newest plantings are at the 'Hundred Acre' vineyard next to the Rothbury estate. In 1960 a new winery was started to cope with the increased production of grapes.

The new 'Mount Pleasant' winery is very modern and well equipped. They have a Vaslin screw press and Wilmes bag presses, and a considerable array of stainless steel equipment, underground concrete tanks, etc. It is vastly different to O'Shea's old winery, l'Hermitage, which was pulled down to make room for the expansion of the new winery.

In accordance with the tradition of the Hunter, semillon and hermitage are the main grape varieties.

McWilliams do, however, have a large proportion of varieties which have not been common in the Hunter—pinot noir, traminer, rhine riesling, montils, blanquette, white shiraz and aucerot. These grapes are found at 'Mount Pleasant' and 'Lovedale'.

The wines from 'Mount Pleasant' enjoy the reputation of being of a consistently high standard, and are more readily available than many other Hunter wines.

Penfolds Wines Pty Ltd, 'Dalwood', 'Dalwood Estate'

Since full history of this leader among Australian wine companies and its founders is related in the South Australian chapter, this section is confined to their activities in the Hunter Valley with which they have been associated since 1904. In recent years they have severed their ties with their long-held main vineyard in the lower Hunter, and in an expensive

47

and influential move, have established a large new enterprise in the Wybong area near Muswellbrook.

In 1904, Frank Astor Penfold Hyland, grandson of the founder of the firm, bought the 'Dalwood' vineyards near Branxton. This is the only vineyard in the area which is right on the banks of the Hunter River, and was one of the earliest established vineyards in the district.

It was originally obtained by George Wyndham, an immigrant from Wiltshire, as a Crown grant in 1828. Before he left for Australia in 1827, Wyndham spent many months in the wine-producing countries of Europe, gaining knowledge of the culture and production of wine. He planted a vineyard of five or six acres in about 1831. In the late 1850s Wyndham's son, John, took over the management of the property and with his brother, Alexander, he extended their plantings to thirty-five acres. They continued to increase their scale of wine production, and by 1886 they had 78 acres under vine.

By the 1890s 'Dalwood' was said to be the second largest vineyard in the colony of New South Wales. A contemporary report notes that the varieties planted were hermitage, verdot, burgundy, malbec and lambruscat, and the wines were of a 'rather rich bodied character'. There was a very fine distillery there for brandy making.

Soon after taking over the property, Penfolds built new cellars, and installed a new plant for wine production. The 'Dalwood' wines were stored in thirty gallon casks, and sent for bottling to the company's cellars in Sydney.

In 1920 Penfolds extended their interests in the Hunter Valley with the purchase of the 'Sparkling Vale' property, two miles north of the present Cessnock airstrip. The planting of vines there was commenced under the supervision of Harold J. Davoren in 1921, and the first vintage was harvested in 1924. Planting continued until there was an area of eighty-two acres under vine, the main part of which was semillon. Penfolds eventually abandoned the vineyard after rainy seasons repeatedly bogged the ground.

Frank Penfold Hyland bought the vineyards of the old Hunter Valley Distillery (a mile north of Tyrrells) in 1942. Penfolds considerably increased production from the vines there, which consist mainly of semillon (about forty-five acres), with some chardonnay and blanquette. The soils of this vineyard are mainly sandy loam, and it is from here that most of the whites sold under the 'Dalwood' label have come since the Second World War.

In 1948 the company purchased 'Penfold Vale', and planted it with fifty acres of white grapes. In the same year Penfolds acquired the Matthews' vineyard of fifteen and a half acres of semillon.

Perhaps the most spectacular project of all began in 1960. At the end of the fifties Penfolds was fighting a losing battle in endeavouring to get reasonable yields from the vines at 'Dalwood', which ranged in age from 60 to 120 years. Such old vines bear less and less fruit, and eventually cease to be an economic proposition. Penfolds decided that they could not save 'Dalwood', and that they needed new ground. Eventually they found what they were looking for fifty miles from the nearest 'traditional' Hunter vineyard on land eighteen miles from Muswellbrook, near Wybong Creek in the Upper Hunter Valley. There had been a few vignerons there in the 1920s, but they were wiped out in the Depression of the thirties.

The Department of Agriculture's tests were favourable, and Penfolds bought 723 acres, of which 600 were suitable for growing grapes. The property was named 'Dalwood Estate', Wybong Park. Encouraged by the prospects of the area, Penfolds purchased a further 550 acres of the Simpson property adjoining the 'Dalwood Estate'.

The soil types vary from light sandy loam to heavy, almost black soil, with a few pockets of the famed red Hunter Valley loam. There are traces of seashells to be found, which indicate that the area was once covered by the ocean. The area has a slightly lower rainfall than the Pokolbin area, and should be free of mould and fungus diseases. It is frost free, and outside the hail belt which is such a menace in the Pokolbin district.

The vines are widely spaced in dead straight rows for ease of cultivation. The white varieties grown are Clare riesling, rhine riesling, semillon, blanquette, white shiraz, chardonnay, chasselas and traminer. The reds are hermitage, cabernet, malbec, mataro and pinot noir. In addition, Penfolds imported eleven grape types from overseas. After a period in quarantine, nine varieties were planted at Wybong—among them gewurztraminer, sylvaner, mueller-thurgau and chardonnay. There has been a most successful strike of these new plantings.

Penfolds have built a very modern winery, with the aims of producing better quality and cutting production costs. They have installed stainless steel fermenters for the whites, and new types of concrete vats for the reds. They also have basket type predrainers above each of the two Gradon Whitehill air-bag presses which should provide more free run juice from the white grapes, and an altogether higher yield of clean, high quality juice. Penfolds have retained what they could from the old 'Dalwood', including a 1,000 gallon oak cask from Penfolds first vintage in 1844, which is probably the oldest in Australia.

The Penfold company has made a huge investment in this new project, which will run to about $2 million. Penfolds will enormously increase the output of wine from the Hunter. The style of this wine is obviously not settled yet, and it may well be somewhat different from the traditional Hunter style.

Christopher Hancock, who has a Diploma of Oenology from Roseworthy Agricultural College, is manager of the 'Dalwood Estate' winery. He has been with Penfolds since 1964. After some experience at Magill, Hancock was made senior winemaker at Penfolds winery at Griffith where he supervised the expansion of the plant at a cost of a million dollars.

As pioneers in the Upper Hunter Penfolds have stimulated many to follow them. As wine lovers we can but wish them luck and hope that the fruits of their labours will be worth it all.

Pokolbin Winemakers Ltd (formerly Drayton's 'Happy Valley')

'Happy Valley', the vineyard which until a short time ago, was run by Barrie Drayton, was originally part of Charles Drayton's holdings. To briefly summarize the ramifications of the Drayton family tree, Charles was the pioneer who established Drayton's in the Hunter Valley. Of his ten children, Len now manages 'Bellevue', and one of his other sons Ernst (or Ernest) Roland inherited 'Happy Valley'.

Barrie Drayton, who was born at Cessnock in July 1935 has worked at 'Happy Valley' since he left school at fifteen. He is progressive in outlook and has planted some varieties new to the Hunter, such as mataro and sauvignon blanc, and introduced new equipment and techniques such as the temperature control of fermentation and air bag presses.

'Happy Valley' began selling their wine under their own label only in recent years. Previously much of the best of their wines was sold by Leo Burings as special bottlings. In 1970, Pokolbin Winemakers Limited, a public company, was formed to take over the property. Since then they have extended the winery considerably, added new equipment and increased the storage capacity.

Roberts Rothbury Pty Ltd, 'Belbourie'

'Belbourie' is another of the vineyards established in the Hunter in the new wave of plantings in the sixties. It is run by James Roberts and his wife Janet. Jim Roberts was born in Maitland in 1923, the son of a schoolteacher turned farmer. He has a Bachelor of Science degree from the University of Sydney, and spent some time as an oil geologist. Janet Roberts is a daughter of the previous owner of the property, the late Norman E. Wright of Merriwa. She breeds game birds—pheasants and guinea fowl.

'Belbourie', a property of 1,720 acres between Rothbury and Allandale, runs along the lower slopes of the Molly Morgan Range on the northern side of Black Creek. Until 1964 it was used solely for grazing and still has 1,200 acres of pasture with Galloway beef cattle and Merino sheep.

In 1964 Jim Roberts planted three acres of grape cuttings—they struck well and planting began on a larger scale, with a goal of 200 acres under vine. Many varieties are represented, including semillon, rhine riesling, chardonnay and Clare riesling, with some traminer, sylvaner and sauvignon blanc. The red varieties are black shiraz, cabernet sauvignon, mataro and malbec.

The soils at 'Belbourie' vary from alluvial sandy loams on the creek flats to heavier red podsols on the higher undulating land. The first grapes were processed in 1970. Fermentation was carefully controlled, with great precautions taken to avoid oxidation of the grapes during picking and making. As part of this policy Jim Roberts has invented and had constructed on the property, a mobile crusher which enables the grapes to be crushed and pressed under a head of CO_2 gas immediately they are picked.

The winery at 'Belbourie' is an interesting building, being made from convict-cut sandstone taken from Wyndham's original winery at 'Dalwood'. There is also the remains of one of Molly Morgan's wineshops on the property.

The Roberts have a rather unusual system of merchandising their wines which they sell direct to the public on a subscription system. They are also believers in the value of tourism, and encourage visitors to the winery.

J. Y. Tulloch & Sons Pty Ltd, 'Glen Elgin'

For many years the Tullochs had the largest family vineyard in the Hunter. They are one of the four original families who survived the Depression which wiped out so many of the vignerons of the time. Today, the Tullochs are no longer a family concern.

The story begins with John Younie Tulloch, the Methodist owner of the general store in Branxton. He was quite a prosperous man for he also had grazing interests. In the style of the times he had a large family—nine children, of which five were boys (Hector, Roy, James, Alec, Keith) and four girls (Dorothy, Marjory, Jean and Kath).

In what must be one of the most extraordinary business transactions in the history of the Hunter, Tulloch accepted a fifty acre vineyard at 'Glen Elgin' 'in satisfaction of an overdue debt'. The name of the customer who had no cash is not known, but he had ceased cultivation at 'Glen Elgin', and no wine had been made for a year when Tulloch took over in 1893.

The vineyard was neglected, but, with no experience, John Tulloch made one hogshead of wine from the five acres under vine in 1897. He sought advice from Professor J. Blunno of the New South Wales Department of Agriculture, and planted shiraz vines on the red and yellow clay podsolic soil.

New additions to Tulloch's winery, Hunter Valley (Photo: A. F. D'Ombrain).

John Tulloch had an uncle, J. A. Russell, who was a wine traveller. Russell sold his nephew's wine in Newcastle and the Cessnock district. Thus encouraged, Tulloch began to expand and plant more grapes. He moved his family from Branxton to live at 'Glen Elgin' when wine became his way of life.

With the Federation of the Australian colonies in 1900 Tulloch, with l New South Wales vignerons, faced a flood of cheap Government-subsidized wine from South Australia, which followed the removal of trade barriers. He made fortified wine at 'Glen Elgin' for the first time, but continued to make dry reds.

After the First World War John Tulloch began to buy grapes from the repatriated soldiers the government had settled on fifty acre properties at Fordwich, in the nearby Broke district. He later acquired six of those blocks, and eventually had a second vineyard of 300 acres of sandy soil with basalt subsoil and clay. The grapes from Fordwich have always been processed at the home winery at 'Glen Elgin'.

J. Y. Tulloch held on through the Depression and in 1939 formed his business into a limited liability company.

When J. Y. died in 1940 Hector Tulloch, his eldest son, became manager of the 'Glen Elgin' winery with his brother Keith as his assistant. Another brother,

Jim, took over the management of the Fordwich vineyard, while brother Alec was given control of the company's cattle properties. At the end of World War II it was decided to sell under the Tulloch label, instead of in bulk to big companies. It was a most successful move.

Hector Tulloch and his wife Eileen were well known in the Pokolbin district for their hospitality. He was chief winemaker until his death in 1965. Hector was especially proud of his 1954 Pokolbin Dry Red which won first prize in both the Claret and Burgundy classes of the Sydney Show—which rather made nonsense of the claret and burgundy distinctions, which are not really applicable in Australia.

Keith, one of Hector's brothers, was chief winemaker from Hector's death until his retirement in 1970. He never married, and was assisted by Hector's son Jay. Keith was one of the vignerons of the Hunter district who had a great knowledge of winemaking in the local conditions, and was willing to share that knowledge.

Hector and Keith Tulloch made good wine, and with their efforts Tulloch's Pokolbin Riesling and Tulloch's Pokolbin Dry Red competed successfully in wine shows throughout Australia.

In November, 1969 the company was taken over by Reed Consolidated Industries, a huge Australian public company with strong British connections. The

Tulloch name was not lost entirely—with Jay Tulloch and his cousin John S. Tulloch (also a grandson of the founder J. Y. Tulloch) remaining on.

Reeds built a new winery, replacing the old one which has been described as 'an iron structure resembling a cowshed'. They installed a considerable amount of new equipment—modern presses, stainless steel tanks, etc. Under the supervision of the new manager Dickson Morris (a diplomate from Roseworthy, who has been a winemaker at Berri) more wine is being produced, and great efforts are being made to ensure that it is of the highest possible quality.

The Rothbury Estate

The Rothbury Estate syndicate was formed in 1968, and includes several prominent business and professional men. Len Evans was appointed chairman and marketing director in that year, and Murray Tyrrell, the noted Hunter Valley vigneron, was made vineyard director. They bought a property at Pokolbin, in the parish of Rothbury, with a variety of soils including chocolate volcanic loams, clay podsols and sandy loams. The first plantings were made in 1968; eighty acres of shiraz and semillon. The following year, in addition to substantial plantings of the same varieties, some cabernet sauvignon, chardonnay and blanquette were established. Since then other varieties such as pinot noir, Clare riesling, traminer and pinot blanc have been planted.

The Rothbury Estate now owns nearly seven hundred acres and their associated vineyard properties, Brokenback Estate, Homestead Hill Estate and Herlstone Estate, nearly one thousand. Of this 850 acres are under vine. The anticipated annual crush will vary between 1,600 and 3,000 tons. The impressive new winery, which includes a spectacular Cask Hall which will seat over two hundred people for a meal, won the prestigious Blacket Award for architecture in 1970. The best modern equipment has been installed, including enclosed fermenters, centrifugal filters and the Bucher Guyer presses which are completely enclosed in CO_2 jackets, thus eliminating any possibility of oxidization.

The syndicate aims to make top quality table wines from their own grapes only. They do not purchase grapes or blend their wines with those from local or other areas. Most of their wine is sold from the winery, and they have plans to export overseas, especially in the U.S.A. Rigid standards are applied to the selection of the various wines that are sold under the unique label designed by the famous Australian artist, Fred Williams. Wines not selected for this purpose are disposed of elsewhere. The selection panel includes the celebrated wine judge and art dealer Rudy Komon, Len Evans, Murray Tyrrell and Gerry Sissingh, the winemaker/manager. Gerry Sissingh was production manager at Lindemans for several years, and is also a noted wine judge.

Rothbury's winemaker/manager, Gerry Sissingh sets the controls of the Buchot-Guyer hydraulic presses.

The members of the syndicate are businessmen Ted Gowing and John McDowell; Dr John Burgess, a radiologist; Dr Frank Mills, surgeon; Alan Grainger, dentist; Alan Burgess, orthodontist; Bob Sanders, company director; Rudy Komon, art dealer; Murray Tyrrell, vigneron; Peter Davidson, accountant; and Len Evans, wine merchant and consultant.

Tyrrell's Vineyards Pty Ltd, 'Ashmans'

Tyrrells are the third of the family winemakers that were among the original settlers of the Pokolbin area who are still making wine today. The Tyrrell name is now well known, owing to the enthusiastic promotional efforts of the present proprietor, Murray Tyrrell.

The 'Ashmans' story began with Edward Tyrrell, a nephew of the first Anglican bishop of Newcastle, who bought the land where the vineyards are now in 1858. The original holding, which he called 'Ashmans', was 320 acres in area. First, Edward put up a shack of gum tree slabs, in which he lived. This small hut still stands, adjacent to the present winery. He then cleared some of the land and planted grape vines. The first vintage was in 1864. For nearly twenty years Edward Tyrrell increased and improved his property. A strip of his vines planted in 1879 and still bearing fruit are believed to be the oldest vineyards in production in the Valley.

One of his sons, Dan, whose full name was Edward George, took over in 1883 at the age of fourteen. He was the oldest of Edward's ten children. Dan Tyrrell is one of the winemakers who are part of the Hunter legend. He built up the Tyrrell name and added considerably to the family holdings.

Dan had very strong views on winemaking, and believed simply in good basic equipment and methods. He was convinced that the earth floor of the winery contributed to the quality of his wine and that the fluctuating temperatures in the slab and iron winery helped to make the wines unique. He was a firm traditionalist, who would never use anything but wild yeasts and was quite opposed to the use of sulphur. Dan sold his wine in bulk, to be bottled by others. Maurice O'Shea was one of the buyers, and some of his great wines were in fact Tyrrell's. Dan Tyrrell, who never married, died in April 1959.

Murray Tyrrell, the son of Dan's brother Avery, was·born in February 1922 in Cessnock, and educated at Maitland High. On his return from overseas service with the A.I.F. in 1945, Murray became associated with the vineyard. He took over as winemaker on his Uncle Dan's death in 1959. The early years of his management were not easy. Severe hailstorms almost wiped out the crop in 1958 and 1960, and also hit in 1962 while the 1959 and 1961 vintages were affected by the previous years' hail.

He has clung firmly to some of the traditional methods, and still occasionally uses oak hand presses. In other ways, however, Murray Tyrrell is probably one of the most progressive winemakers of all. His first major departure from the Tyrrell tradition was to bottle and sell his wines under his own label. A firm believer in direct merchandising, he now sells ninety percent of his wine direct to the public. He is well aware of the value of public relations, and encourages visitors to the winery, providing good tasting facilities, barbecue areas, films and other conveniences. Tyrrell is also an enthusiastic promoter of the Pokolbin area; is involved in the Vintage Festival, and encourages tourism generally.

The style of whites made by Tyrrells has been drastically changed in recent years. He picks earlier, and makes fresher, more delicate and acid wines, which have been widely acclaimed. He has also introduced some techniques new to the Hunter, such as fungicide spraying by helicopter to prevent downy mildew.

Although he has been responsible for a great increase in ouput, Murray Tyrrell has remained determinedly independent. He is now vineyard director and a syndicate member of the huge new Rothbury Estate. His two children have both made careers in the wine industry—his son Bruce being associated with the family firm and daughter Ann as cellar manager of Len Evans Wines in Sydney.

The Tyrrell vineyards are on podsolic topsoil, with volcanic subsoil. They are located on the foothills of the Brokenback Range, and some are on the alluvial flats north-east of the Broke Road. Most of Tyrrell's red hermitage is grown on weathered heavy red clay which has natural lime. The whites are made chiefly from semillon, and some blanquette. Tyrrell's wines, both red and whites, are bottled under a system of cask or vat numbers.

Wyndham Estate

Penfolds old 'Dalwood' vineyards have not been allowed to die. When Penfolds moved to Wybong, their Branxton property was bought by Perc McGuigan, who had been winemaker at 'Dalwood' for twenty-eight years. The property was renamed Wyndham Estate, after George Wyndham, the nineteenth century vigneron who originally planted the vineyard. McGuigan later sold out to Tim Allen and Digby Matheson, but retained his connection with the Estate by remaining on as consultant.

The McGuigan family has had a long association with the Hunter Valley and winemaking there. Perc McGuigan and his son Brian were with Penfolds for a long period, and played an important role in Penfolds establishment of their new vineyards at Wybong. Brian McGuigan has left Penfolds to concentrate on the family enterprises, as manager and winemaker at the Wyndham Estate; and brother Ross' venture at 'Chateau Douglas', Scone.

The Wyndham Estate is a 300 acre property right on the banks of the Hunter River. New plantings have been made—the faithful semillon and hermitage, with cabernet, blanquette and rhine riesling as the main plantings plus the addition of some exotic varieties—pinot noir, traminer, malbec and pinot chardonnay.

A unique feature of the Wyndham Estate is the availability of water from the Hunter River. To take full advantage of this a travelling irrigator is used. The machine moves between the vines, shooting water nearly 100 feet into the air and covering a large area with a fine mist, which feeds the vines and protects them from the scorching sun.

The Wyndham Estate group make and bottle their own wine, and sell it ex-vineyard and through an organization in Sydney. In addition, the group plans to process the grapes of smaller independent growers, and bottle and sell this wine under their own particular labels, so that the small growers will retain their identities. The Estate is also interested in encouraging tourism locally as well as in the expansion of the export market.

The Vineyard Areas of New South Wales

The Murrumbidgee Irrigation Area

In terms of volume alone the Murrumbidgee Irrigation Area has been very important in the production of Australian wine, supplying the major part of the wine made in New South Wales, and about one-sixth of Australia's total annual vintage. With the increasing demand for light 'table' (i.e. unfortified) wines, the winemakers in the M.I.A. have made full use of modern technology, and are producing some wines of gold medal winning quality.

Irrigation of vineyards gives rise to enormously increased yields, but in the past this has meant that the quality has tended to suffer somewhat. The berries of irrigated grapes tend to be fuller, and lighter wines result. Traditionally great wines have not come from irrigated areas, with most of the material being used for the sweet fortified styles and making spirits for brandy. Thus although in quantity terms these wines were of great importance, it was widely believed that good wine could not be produced by irrigation methods. The early mistakes of the inexperienced returned soldiers who were the original growers helped to perpetuate this idea.

The winemakers of the M.I.A., led by McWilliams, are doing their best to overcome this image by giving increasing attention to the planting of classic wine grape varieties and using the most modern techniques of winemaking. They do not like the name M.I.A. as they feel it over-stresses irrigation, and prefer the name Riverina.

The M.I.A. or Riverina, is a large area in the south-west of New South Wales, around the towns of Griffith, Leeton and Yenda. Murrumbidgee is an aboriginal term for 'big water' which is really most appropriate. The development of the area only began in the first decade of this century, after the New South Wales Government passed an Act in 1906 authorizing the construction of the Barren Jack (now Burrinjuck) Dam, near Yass, which now has a capacity of 772,000 acre feet. The waters of the Murrumbidgee River are stored and regulated at the dam, whence they flow along the natural channel of the stream for about 240 miles to the Berembed Weir. Here water is diverted into the man-made canal which supplies an area of 451,263 acres.

The New South Wales Conservation and Irrigation Commission has been mainly responsible for land development in the area. Irrigable land is not allowed to be held by companies, but only by individuals, with a maximum permitted holding of seventy-five acres of land for fruit cultivation, or 300 acres for grazing.

After the First World War the government settled repatriated soldiers in the area. There were many problems with totally inexperienced farmers in an untried area. Some unsuitable varieties were planted, and unsatisfactory methods of cultivation and irrigation adopted. Gradually, with experience, things improved and better techniques were implemented.

The population grew with the movement of people to the area as cultivation expanded. With the immigration programme after the Second World War, many new settlers, and especially those from Italy, took up holdings in the M.I.A.

Griffith is situated 396 miles from Sydney by rail, at an altitude of 420 feet. As well as its pastoral industries (rice, wheat and oats, sheep, pigs, cattle, citrus, and, of course, grapes) Griffith has developed secondary industries, such as rice mills and dried fruit processing plants. Temperatures can be very hot in Griffith—an average of over 32°C in February, and cold too—down to 3.8°C in July. The average annual rainfall is only about 15.8 inches, but in view of the irrigation system this is not really important.

The soils of the M.I.A. vary considerably, ranging from heavy clay to light sandy loans, with occasional patches of sandy soils. The subsoil is mostly clay, which holds the irrigation water. There are no rocks in the area. Generally, the soil types are quite heavy, and the grapes there produce more flavour under irrigation than the grapes from lighter irrigated soils in other regions.

The growers of the M.I.A. have always grown grapes suitable for making quality wines. A higher proportion of white grapes than red are planted. White grapes used for sweet and fortified wines are sultana, malaga and muscat. There are also extensive plantings of white shiraz (white hermitage) semillon and riesling, used for table wines. Red grapes are shiraz and grenache used for both sweet fortified wines and dry table wines. There is a constantly increasing acreage of cabernet sauvignon. Lately there have been plantings of some exotics, such as pinot noir, malbec, pinot blanc and traminer.

The irrigation of vineyards increases their yields between three and seven times that of non-irrigated areas. The average yield for all wine varieties in the M.I.A. is about 7½ tons per acre, a very high figure compared to non-irrigated areas where yields are perhaps two tons per acre. The total area in the M.I.A. under wine grapes was 6,589 acres in 1969. In the period from 1960 to 1968 the area under vine expanded by fifty percent. Production doubled in the same period. In the 1969 vintage 43,210 tons of wine grapes were harvested in the M.I.A., out of the total New South Wales crop of 54,313 tons. In 1970, 53,857 tons were harvested.

The M.I.A., as can be seen from the governmental regulations on the size of properties, is an area of small farmers, most of whom sell their grapes to one of the big winemakers for processing. This is a fragmented system, but the big companies are now exercising greater pressure on the growers, on such matters as the time of picking and the desirability of planting certain varieties. Some co-ordination is exercised by the Irrigation Research and Extension Committee. This body was set up in 1947 under the auspices of the various governmental authorities concerned with the area, such as the CSIRO and N.S.W. Department of Agriculture. Mr Vivian Charles Williams, a leading vine and citrus grower was its first chairman. The I.R.E.C. has set up a conference on plantings which makes recommendations to growers on the planting of the most suitable varieties.

The most outstanding feature of, winemaking in the M.I.A. in recent years has been the transformation of its wines: from emphasis on the sweet fortified styles and spirit for brandy to concentration on light table wines, of as high a quality as possible. To achieve this, winemakers have encouraged the planting of premium grape varieties. The introduction of earlier picking of grapes, especially the white wine varieties, has been most important, as a better balance of acid and sugar has resulted in improved quality wines. As excessive heat at vintage time is a great problem, the introduction of refrigeration techniques to control the temperature of fermentation has allowed more delicate wines to be made—the esters and aromatic flavour substances not being destroyed by the heat of fermentation. Other techno-logical advances such as centrifuges have also helped the production of good quality wines.

McWilliams Wines Pty Ltd, Hanwood

In any discussion of the M.I.A. the name McWilliam is the one which immediately springs to mind. They were the first in the area and dominated it

Reg Drayton tests the sugar content of a white wine grape fermentation.

for the years of its early development. McWilliams have also been leaders in producing quality table wines in an irrigation area.

Samuel McWilliam, the founder of the firm, first planted a few acres of vines at Corowa, on the Murray River, in 1877. It was his son John James, however, who began the expansion of the family enterprise which has grown to become one of the major winemaking companies of Australia.

It was in the Murrumbidgee Irrigation Area that the McWilliam empire really flourished. In 1912, almost before the main irrigation canal reached Hanwood, four miles from Griffith, two fifty acre blocks were bought and planted with about 35,000 cuttings. From 1916 their grapes were processed at the Junee winery. In 1917 the McWilliams built themselves a winery at Hanwood.

Three years later, in 1920, another winery was built at Yenda, near Griffith. A distillery was also installed there, and later on cellars for the storage of their sparkling wines.

McWilliams is still a family concern, with many of the McWilliams playing active roles in the organization. Various relatives of the four brothers who were sons of the original founder are doing different jobs for the firm. McWilliams has a huge centre at Pyrmont in Sydney. Their activities in the Hunter have already been discussed.

Back in the M.I.A. McWilliams built a third plant at Beelbangera. Their latest enterprise is a winery at Robinvale, on the Victorian side of the Murray River, south of Euston which is on the Sturt Highway in New South Wales. Construction of this new and still growing winery was commenced in 1961.

The present technical director and supervisor of production is Glen McWilliam. He is based at Hanwood, where he has been since he left school in 1931 (Scots College, Sydney, where many of the family were educated). Since then he has not missed a single vintage at Hanwood.

Glen McWilliam was appointed a director of the company in 1943, and since then has been involved with its expansion programmes. Three of his sons are working in the family company.

It has been under Glen McWilliam's supervision that the standard of McWilliam's irrigation area wines has been raised. It was his cellars which first produced quantities of light commercial table wines from irrigated vines, which had been regarded as suitable for making only fortified and sweet wine.

The sheer size of the McWilliam operation is staggering. They have a 100,000 gallon stainless steel tank at Hanwood, and eight stainless steel rail tankers. McWilliams produce nearly two million gallons of wine per year—a sizeable percentage of Australia's total output for a single maker. The Hanwood winery has an almost unbelievable storage capacity of over five million gallons.

Despite the huge quantities of wine involved, quality has by no means been overlooked. The McWilliams have actively encouraged local growers to plant better varieties, even providing them with the new vines. They have co-operated with the CSIRO and Department of Agriculture in the first significant trials on the scientific control of irrigation to improve wine quality and these efforts have begun to pay off. In the late 1960s McWilliam's Cabernet Sauvignons from Hanwood began winning many gold medals. They followed these successes with other gold medals for local rhine rieslings. These breakthroughs were evidence to prove that irrigation areas *can* make top wines.

Penfolds, Griffith

Penfolds have also been associated with the M.I.A. from its earliest days. Frank Penfold Hyland visited the area, and in the Hanwood Hall addressed soldiers who had just returned from the war, advising them to take up viticulture. He said that Penfolds would establish a modern winery at Griffith to process grapes, and would help in any way to establish culture of the vine in the district. As evidence of the company's good faith, he offered an eight year contract to growers for all grapes produced at a minimum of £8 a ton.

The task of organising growers, many of whom knew nothing at all about growing grapes, fell to Mr H. E. Laffer, who later represented the Australian Wine Marketing Board in London.

Penfolds sent to Griffith cuttings from their vineyards elsewhere in Australia. The plans for their winery were drawn under the supervision of Leslie Penfold Hyland and the winery was built right by the railway very near Griffith in 1913. A distillery and storage facilities were added later. The first vintage at Griffith was made in 1921, and Mr A. Day of Farm 131, Hanwood, claimed to be the first settler to have delivered a load of grapes over the weighbridge.

By 1929 the Griffith area had advanced so rapidly that extensions had to be made to the winery and distillery buildings. Expansion has continued until now, the winery is capable of storing one million gallons of wine and brandy and has an intake capacity of over 250 tons of grapes a day during vintage.

Wynn & Co Pty Ltd, Yenda

Of the big wine companies, Wynns is a latecomer to the M.I.A. where they have established a winery and vineyards at Yenda. David Wynn, son of Samuel, who founded the family firm, advocated in 1959 that Wynns should begin operations in the M.I.A. According to brother Allan Wynn, his father opposed David firmly, as he held a strongly-felt prejudice against irrigation wines, believing good wines could not be made by irrigation area methods.

David Wynn triumphed, however, and acquired a winery previously owned by Caldwell's at Yenda,

Dr Max Lake, a Sydney surgeon, takes a sample from a young red grape ferment to test the sugar, in the winery at 'Lakes Folly', Hunter Valley, N.S.W.

near Griffith. He enlarged and modernized the plant and began making table wines there, especially dry whites. It has grown to such an extent that it is now the largest winemaking unit owned by Wynns.

Wynns do buy in bulk from the local growers, but they have also established their own vineyards, largely from cuttings grown experimentally in their own nursery. Their major varieties are semillon, trebbiano, shiraz and grenache. They also have plantings of cabernet sauvignon and touriga, as well as pedro ximenez and palomino for sherry and white shiraz for vermouth. The company is continuing to experiment with new varieties to examine their suitability for the area.

The Yenda plant is a large modern concern. Wynns have huge refrigeration systems to counteract the effects of summer heat on the wine, as well as the customary stainless steel storage tanks. They also have paraffin-waxed concrete tanks for the whites.

Wynns take advantage of the usually unwelcome heat to mature their port in oak casks more rapidly than would otherwise be possible. They are continuing their expansions in the Riverina, with a new vineyard being established in the Binya Hills, near Griffith.

Other makers, Griffith

There are several growers in the Riverina who do make their own wine. Many of these are immigrants from Italy who brought the tradition of making and drinking their own wines with them.

Among these are Rossetto's wines at Beelbangera, five miles from Griffith. This enterprise was founded by the present Governing Director of the firm, Angelo Rossetto in 1945. Mr Rossetto migrated from Treviso in the north of Italy in 1922, and settled on his present site in 1928. Rossettos market a full range of wines and liqueurs.

Fellow countryman Vittorio de Bortoli arrived in Griffith in 1923 and worked at various jobs until 1927 when he obtained a plot of land to start a winery. The first two vats of 900 gallons each were built in 1928, the year the first wine was made. They battled through the Depression years and by 1936 had a capacity of 25,000 gallons. Since 1963 tremendous strides were made by the company, and in 1970 a million gallons of wine was handled. De Bortoli's winery now has a storage capacity of over one million gallons, including 65,000 gallons of wood storage. The company owns fifty acres of vines at Bilbul, and another 100 acres at Nericon, about twenty miles from the Bilbul Cellars. De Bortolis market about fifty varieties of wines, liqueurs and spirits, through a wide variety of retail outlets including large department stores.

Calamia Wines at Griffith purchased their winery from an Italian grower, Frank Calabria, who was making a dry red from the brown muscat grape.

This line has been continued. Calamia is the only winery using the Italian variety, Uva di Troia, and are specializing in dry reds although a full range of wines is marketed. The winery is now under the supervision of 'Scotty' Ireland, a celebrated winemaker who was formerly with McWilliams.

Rooty Hill
Penfolds Wines Pty Ltd, 'Minchinbury'

Minchinbury is well known throughout Australia as a brand name for champagne. To motorists driving on the Great Western Highway from Sydney to Penrith the site of the winery is notable for the crashed aeroplane which acts as a signpost.

The original owner, Captain William Minchin, received the land as a grant of 1,000 acres on his retirement from the Army in 1819.

After his death in 1821 his daughter inherited the property. Shortly afterwards it was purchased by a Dr McKay, who planted the first grapes at 'Minchinbury' and used convict labour to work the land. Dr McKay built the winery of dressed stone with walls eight foot thick in places—the original cellars are still in use.

Jas. Angus, a railway contractor, bought the vineyards towards the end of the nineteenth century. He set up the firm of J. Angus & Son, extended the vineyards and cellars, and started making wine. In the late 1890s he began making champagne under the direction of Leo Buring. It was during this period that the dreaded phylloxera attacked the vineyard, necessitating complete replanting with grafted, resistant vines. Several new varieties were planted at this time.

Frank Penfold Hyland was sufficiently impressed with the Minchinbury wines so that he bought the vineyards and cellars in 1912. Their first manager was Leo Buring, who was there until 1918. Ivan Combet joined the staff at 'Minchinbury' in 1919 and stayed there as winemaker until his retirement at the end of the sixties. He was succeeded by his son, the late Tod Combet.

The present 'Minchinbury' estate is located thirty miles from Sydney between Parramatta and Penrith. The urban development of the area has made the land so valuable that Penfolds' vine acreage is now much less than it was in its hey-day. In 1949 there were 250 acres under vine at 'Minchinbury', this has been whittled away until today only about thirty-four acres remain, at the Southridge vineyard, three miles from the winery. The grapes grown on the clay loam there are traminer (fifteen acres), riesling, white shiraz, and some chasselas.

The wine of 'Minchinbury' is champagne, but it has also been the source of Penfolds' famed Trameah, first marketed in 1920. This is made from the traminer grape—a variety which yields lightly and, sadly the wine is extremely rare. Various show Traminers of the sixties were outstanding as single varietal wines. Today, most of the material is blended into the private bin wine, Traminer Riesling.

Corowa

Corowa's fame as a wine producing area lies chiefly with its sweet fortified wines, and is especially connected with the Lindeman name. The area is located about 400 miles south of Sydney, on the north-west bank of the River Murray, the border between New South Wales and Victoria. It lies thirty-five miles west of the border town, Albury, and is just across the river from Wahgunyah. Corowa really belongs in the Rutherglen area geographically speaking but as our classification is on a state basis will be considered with the other vineyard areas of New South Wales. The country round Corowa is undulating, with varying types of soil.

Winemaking at Corowa began in the middle of the last century. There were many small vineyards in the area, but Dr Lindeman's purchase of the Haffner's property in 1872 was the start of large-scale winemaking there.

Corowa suffered badly from phylloxera at the end of the last century. As a consequence many of the smaller vineyards were abandoned and the land put to other forms of production. The winemaking area once extended to Albury, which used to have some important vineyards. The largest of them was owned by J. T. Fallon, who abandoned his vineyard as such after it was wiped out by phylloxera in 1906.

In discussion of the history of the district, mention must be made of John Delappe Lankester, who was associated with wine all his life. He was born in Lichfield, Staffordshire in September, 1837, and arrived in Sydney with his father in 1849. In 1860 he opened and managed a wine business in Sydney for Dr Lindeman, and later managed J. T. Fallon's vineyards. His later years were spent on his own vineyards at Ettamogah, a few miles from Albury, where he had a land grant of 160 acres. He died at the ripe old age of 100 in January, 1938.

Lindemans

Lindemans' 'Southern Cross' and 'Felton' vineyards are the largest in the district. 'Felton' is near Balldale, about twelve miles from Corowa, and consists of 120 acres of heavy clay loam which produce brown muscat and frontignac grapes, and three Portuguese varieties—bastardo, alvarelhao and touriga which are grown for port. Recently part of the vineyard has been replanted with shiraz and granouis, the latter being a vintage port variety.

The 300 acre 'Southern Cross' vineyard was planted in 1910 at Hopefield eight miles from Corowa. The clay loam soils at 'Felton' and 'Southern Cross' are heavier than those found on the sandy river banks. Lindemans do not irrigate the vines, despite their proximity to the river, which allows the berries to develop a good acid-sugar balance.

The Corowa winery, based on a two-storey building originally built in 1877, and now covering a large amount of ground, both under roof and in the open, is used by Lindemans chiefly for making fortified wines and brandy. The ports and muscats of the Corowa-Rutherglen area are of outstanding quality. Lindemans also buy grapes for processing on a large scale from local growers.

Mudgee

Mudgee is located on the central western tablelands of New South Wales, 160 miles by road north-west of Sydney. The town was settled in 1836 and is now the centre of a grazing district featuring pigs, poultry and dairying and other pastoral activities.

The climate is moderate although the area is subject to occasional floods and frost. Being on the same latitude as the Hunter Valley, Mudgee enjoys the same benefits of a summer dominant rainfall as does the Hunter, however, its location on the western slopes of the Divide means that the total summer rain is less than the Hunter. The average rainfall is twenty-four to twenty-six inches annually, but falls of double this are not uncommon. The other dominant influence on the Mudgee climate is altitude. 'Craigmoor', for example, is approximately 1,700 feet above sea level. The effect of the altitude is to produce a slower ripening period and a harvest some six weeks later than the Hunter Valley. The Mudgee area now has one of the highest vineyards in Australia at Botolbar which is 2,000 feet above sea level.

The soil in the areas where vineyards have been established is red loam, containing limestone and ironstone. The sub-soil is heavy clay and needs to be ploughed to a depth of at least six to nine inches to enable the young vine roots to strike successfully. Grape vines were planted in the area in about 1855, and winemaking began a few years later.

'Craigmoor'

'Craigmoor' was established in 1858 by Adam Roth, a German immigrant who settled at Mudgee within a few months of his arrival in Australia. His original grant of land was ninety-two acres on the banks of the Pipeclay or Eurunduree Creek. The first vineyards were planted in the same year and the land has been in continuous cultivation to vines ever since. The business became firmly established in 1872 when gold was found at Home Rule and before long the closest diggings were a mere half-mile from the 'Rothview' Vineyard. The family prospered, supplying, wine, fruit and vegetables to the miners.

By the 1880s there were thirteen established wineries in the Mudgee district and over 400 acres under grapes. The Roth family operated six of these wineries with five of Adam's six sons having been established in separate ventures of their own, while the youngest helped his father in managing the principal business. The largest winery in the Mudgee district in this period was 'Fredericksburg' which adjoined 'Rothview' and had nearly 200 acres under grapes.

The Depression of the 1890s was a severe blow to these wine producers and the 'Fredericksburg' Winery collapsed financially. From then on the wine industry in Mudgee went into a gradual decline which was reinforced by the fact that most of the younger members of the wine producing families moved out of the industry, into grazing, share cropping and fruit production. By the thirties there were only two significant wineries left in the district, being 'Craigmoor' and Dr Fiaschi's vineyard at Bumberra, some two miles away. In 1935 'Craigmoor' passed into the hands of Adam Roth's grandson Alan S. (Jack) Roth who ran the business until his death in 1969. The business was then sold to Van Heyst & Co Ltd interests in Sydney. The present winemaker is Pieter van Gent, originally from Holland, who spent over ten years with Penfolds.

The 'Craigmoor' Vineyards now consist of 190 planted acres. Of these forty-six acres are planted to white grapes being principally semillon (eighteen acres), chardonnay (six acres), traminer (seven acres), trebbiano (eight acres) with some gordo and pedro. Of this total area there are thirteen acres yet to come into full bearing. Presently 144 acres are planted to red grapes with 105 acres still to come into full bearing. The dominant grape is shiraz (ninety-six acres) with thirty-six acres of cabernet, and some grenache, frontignac and black muscat.

'Craigmoor' makes dry red and dry whites, as well as ports and muscats. They have won several medals in shows under their new owners.

Dr Fiaschi's Vineyard
—now Augustine Vineyards

A new venture in the Mudgee district is the recent revival of Dr Fiaschi's vineyard which was abandoned in the mid 1940s. In 1969 the only surviving vines were of the aleatico grape, a variety imported from Italy, so a programme of replanting has started, with plans to plant about 200 acres of vines—about half of this has been done. Varieties planted are aleatico, hermitage, cabernet sauvignon and semillon.

Mudgee Wines

Mudgee Wines, under the control of Alf Kurtz, is a long established company in the area. (Recently, Ivan Combet became associated with the venture.) Dry white and red table wines and port and muscats are made.

New vineyards

With the scarcity and high cost of land in the Hunter, many aspiring vignerons have cast their eyes on the Mudgee area and in recent years new vineyards have been planted, notable among them Bob and Wendy Roberts of the Huntingdon Estate. They have established excellent vineyards and built a small, well-planned winery. The infusion of new blood and new money gives rise to hopes for good wines in the future.

Other areas

Forbes

At Forbes, in the central-west of New South Wales, J. Genet of Sandhill Vineyards has thirty acres of vines. Shiraz is his chief variety. The Chislett family also have a property on the outskirts of the town and are developing their wine growing potential.

Hungerford Hill Pty Ltd, Buronga

In addition to their vineyard development project in the Hunter Valley, Hungerford Hill have established a winery at Buronga, which is in New South Wales but quite close to the Victorian town of Mildura. The winery is open air, with the equipment all out in the open, and it will have the capacity for handling 2½ million gallons of wine. They have long term contracts with local growers to supply specified varieties.

B. Seppelt & Sons, Barooga

In the late twenties Seppelts acquired the Barooga property, in New South Wales just down the River Murray from Rutherglen. The main purpose was to establish a nursery for phylloxera-resistant stocks which could be used for South Australian vineyards should the need arise, but there were supplementary objects of vineyard research and general viticultural experiment. Its proximity enabled Barooga to be worked in conjunction with the Rutherglen wine areas.

An old French continuous press and driving belts at Bailey's winery, Taminick, Vic.

Victoria

The North-East

The north-east of Victoria has had an extraordinary number of ups and downs in its winemaking history, and has come through it all with a reputation for making the top fortified and dessert wines in Australia, as well as very big generous dry reds. The area is roughly triangular, with its base along the River Murray, bounded on the east by a very complex series of highlands which form part of the Australian Alps and the west by the open Oxley plains. Winemaking is carried out on the flat Murray plain, with the towns of Corowa (actually in New South Wales) as the northernmost point of the region, Glenrowan and Taminick to the south and Barnawartha to the east. A box thirty miles long and fifteen miles wide would cover it.

The centre of the wine growing district is Rutherglen, which is on the Murray Valley Highway, 170 miles north-east of Melbourne, and 396 miles south-west of Sydney. Rutherglen has a large reputation for a small town of 1,700 people, in a shire of only 3,000 and an area of fifty miles radius. Rutherglen has an almost fairytale history of rises and falls— it boomed during the gold rush, then boomed again during the grape rush with about 14,000 acres under vine at Rutherglen alone. Phylloxera ended that run of success, and then economic conditions caused the area to decline further. Now the wheel is commencing to turn full circle, as the area prospers again. (Refer for detail to the section on the history of Australian wine.)

The renaissance was marked in 1967 by the first Rutherglen Wine Festival, which was enormously successful. Thousands of people poured into the area and enjoyed all kinds of activities—a wine ball, luncheons, barbecues, tours of the wineries, rodeos, seminars, a wine auction, and all the fun of the fair washed down with lots and lots of local wine.

The surrounding highlands have a moderating effect on the climate of the region, which does not vary much from year to year. The summers are long, hot and dry. The rainfall is about twenty-five inches per year and falls largely in winter and spring. The nights in winter are very cold and frosts are frequent, though the days are bright and sunny. The country is only a few hundred feet high—Rutherglen is at an altitude of 555 feet above sea level. The vineyards are mostly centred on the King, Ovens and Murray Rivers, where the soils on the flats are well drained sandy loams.

The climatic conditions of Rutherglen, combined with the nature of its soil, have contributed to the nature of the wines of the district, which have traditionally been big, dark, highly alcoholic 'wines for heroes'. However, some Rutherglen winemakers have been making use of modern technology to successfully lighten the style of their wines. The dessert wines of the district are of supreme excellence, but have not always enjoyed the respect they deserve. Now that the Rutherglen district has regained some measure of its former glory the outlook for increased production of its very special wines looks bright indeed.

Bailey Brothers, 'Bundarra' Vineyards

At Taminick, which is four miles west of Glenrowan and 143 miles north-east of Melbourne, are the 'Bundarra' vineyards of the Bailey brothers.

The Bailey family came to Australia in the 1840s from Manchester, where they had a coaching business. Richard Bailey settled his family in Melbourne, and started another cartage contracting business. One of their jobs was to transport bricks for the old Melbourne mint. In the sixties the Baileys moved to the north-east of the state, where there was gold, and the need for transport. When the gold began to run out in the mid-seventies, the businesses which depended on filling the miners' needs suffered and the Baileys turned to viticulture.

Richard Bailey bought some land at the foot of the Warby Ranges, and between 1875 and 1889 planted vines there. He did not confine his activities to winemaking, but became a pastoralist, involved over the years with cattle, wool and crops. The property has remained in the hands of Richard Bailey's descendants, and his great-grandson Alan Bailey is now making wine there. A versatile man, Alan Bailey is a keen pilot and very interested in geology, in addition to his winemaking activities.

There are over 200 acres under vine in the gently undulating country at 'Bundarra'. Baileys also have 140 acres of shiraz at Huceynia, nine miles west of Glenrowan. Varieties grown at the home vineyards include shiraz, Rutherglen tokay, brown muscat, chasselas, aucerot, cabernet sauvignon and rhine riesling. These are all grown on phylloxera-resistant stock. The 'Bundarra' soil is an extremely rich, friable red granite loam of great depth (about thirty feet). The soil has very good moisture-retaining properties, thus long dry spells are not such a problem as elsewhere, and irrigation is not used. These natural conditions mean that the Baileys enjoy very high yields—about three tons per acre, which is often double the yield of other vineyards in the area.

The winery, with its dirt floor and what Dr Samuel Benwell has called 'functional untidiness' reflects the individuality of its owners. But it is the wine made there which really taxes any writer's supply of adjectives and descriptive powers. Keith Dunstan said they were 'liquid steak and eggs', and a Frenchman noted, 'they are food, wine and a good cigar'. Dr Benwell writes that 'Bundarra' wines are 'nothing less than a tour de force.... They are red wines in another language.' Suffice to say the Bailey reds are unique—big, gutsy, and very long living. Both dry reds and whites, and dessert wines—muscats and ports are made. As well over the years Bailey's wines have been greatly in demand for blending.

Booth Brothers, 'Taminick' Vineyards

Nearer the Warby Ridge than the Bailey Brothers' vineyard, is that owned by Booths. The vineyard was originally planted by a Mr Opie in 1892. His viticultural venture was short-lived, as phylloxera destroyed his vines ten years later. At this stage, school teacher Eska (or Ezra or Escar) Booth, came on the scene. The son of an implement maker from Wallan who eventually became a warden at Pentridge, Eska Booth had been interested in viticulture for a few years, and worked at 'Chateau Tahbilk' to gain experience. He then went to 'Taminick', and replanted Opie's vineyard with phylloxera-resistant stocks of chasselas, shiraz and white hermitage. The vineyard property of approximately fifty acres is now run by the brothers Clifford and Geoffrey Booth, with the help of Cliff's sons.

The attractive old stone winery contains some very fine casks, including one from de Castella's Lilydale vineyard, 'St Hubert's', and another 900 gallon beauty which was shown by E. Bonetti at the Great Exhibition in 1888.

For many years the Booth brothers sold all their wine in bulk for blending but they now have their own bottling facilities and their red wines can be quite formidable.

Vineyards of North-West Victoria

Brown Brothers, Milawa Vineyards

The beautiful Ovens Valley lies between the King and Ovens Rivers which flow down from the dominating Australian Alps. At Milawa, in this valley, six generations of the Brown family have established an enduring winemaking enterprise. Their story really begins with one John Graham, a Scot, who had farmed for a time in Canada before he arrived at Milawa in 1857. He was among the first purchasers of land in the district, and three years later he built a high gabled barn on his property like those he had seen in Canada. Then George Harry Brown came along, and married John Graham's daughter Rebecca.

George Harry planted vines on his father-in-law's property, and his son John Francis Brown made the first wine at Milawa in 1889, and found that the Canadian-style barn was most suitable for maturing his wines. Phylloxera wiped out the vineyard before the First World War, but by 1920 John Brown I had replanted the vineyard with resistant stocks. By the time John Brown's first son, John Charles, was ready to leave school in the early 1930s, the manager who had been helping with the winemaking left. So young John gave up his vague ideas of a career in chemistry and in

1934 made his first vintage, and thus became John Brown II of Milawa. Since his father died in 1943 at the age of seventy-six, John II has been in charge. He now has the help of his four sons, the oldest being John Graham Brown, who is overseer, and whose young son John Andrew Brown is the fourth John Brown at Milawa. All four brothers, (John, Peter, Ross and Roger) have attended Scotch College in Melbourne, where many of the winemaking families of north-east Victoria have been educated. Peter is developing the vineyard, Ross is in charge of the books and young Roger will be involved full-time when he is old enough.

The Browns have 125 acres at Milawa, ten miles south-east of Wangaratta, of shiraz (forty-three acres), cabernet (ten acres), mondeuse, rhine riesling (twenty-three acres), tokay and patches of pinot, malbec and mataro. The vineyard is at an altitude of 600 feet above sea level. The soil is red-brown loam over about fifteen feet of clay, below which there is water-bearing river gravel. There is some irrigation from an underground piping system. Nearby at Everton, on the foothills of the ranges, Browns have about thirty acres mainly of shiraz and cabernet on the gravelly quartz-laden shale and loam. At 'Mystic Park' the Browns have twenty acres of the eighty acre property planted with gordo, with plans for more of carignane, mataro, grenache and oelliade.

The average rainfall is about twenty-five inches, with useful winter rain and some showers at flowering. The most serious climatic problem is the occasional spring frost which did much damage in 1954, and again in November 1967 when a severe frost completely wiped out the crop.

The Browns really work as a family unit, and when in the sixties, they needed increased storage space, they simply built a new bottling hall and cellars themselves. John Brown III designed the buildings, and he and Peter, with help from Ross and Roger (the latter then aged twelve), laid the bricks and poured the concrete, welded the trusses and sheeted the roof. The only thing they did not do was install the electrical wiring. The Browns have some modern equipment to go with their new buildings—the Bucher Guyer hydraulic press, a centrifugal filter and refrigeration system, which has done much for the delicacy and quality of their whites especially. The best of the past has been retained, and they have some magnificent old casks made by the famed Sullivan of Barnawartha.

Milawa is the source of some fine and very individual white wines, and a range of reds which include a straight shiraz, cabernet shiraz blend and shiraz mondeuse blend. Smaller quantities of dessert wines and sherry are also made. Some grapes are bought from the irrigation area for making into sherry.

A self-effacing man, John Brown is highly regarded by those who know him. Len Evans describes him as 'a great enthusiast, dedicated, knowledgeable and with a great "feel" for making wine.'

R. L. Buller & Son Pty Ltd, 'Calliope' Vineyards

The 'Calliope' vineyard at Rutherglen was first taken up by the present proprietor's father in 1921 under a soldier settlement scheme. The property was owned originally by the Callen family who had worked it successfully until the outbreak of phylloxera. Approximately sixty acres of reconstituted vines were bearing when Mr Buller senior purchased the vineyard. R. L. Buller junior started work on the property in 1947 after a course at Roseworthy.

The Bullers now have about ninety-five acres under vine at Rutherglen. Varieties grown include shiraz, pedro, semillon, tokay and muscat. Since 1952 the 'Calliope' winery has been run in conjunction with a second winery and distillery at Beverford in the mid-Murray area. They have thirty-five acres of vines there.

Bullers used to sell all their output in bulk for blending but they have now installed their own bottling plant. They buy grapes for processing, including those of Tod Graham who works part of the 'Netherby' vineyard (which he now irrigates), and which was planted in 1859 by John Graham.

A. D. Campbell, 'Bobbie Burns' Winery and 'Silverburn' Winery

The Campbells' 'Bobbie Burns' winery is situated three miles west of Rutherglen on the Echuca road. John Campbell first planted seventy acres with vines in the 1880s. Along with the other Rutherglen vignerons he was badly hit by phylloxera, but before the First World War John Campbell's son, David, undertook the replanting of fifty acres of vines grafted on resistant American root stock. David continued adding to the property until his death in 1933, when his son, Alan, took over. Alan Campbell still works the establishment, and is now helped by his sons, Malcolm and Colin. Malcolm joined the business in 1962 and is mainly concerned with the farming side, while Colin, the younger brother, started work in 1967 after he graduated from Roseworthy.

They have 110 acres under vine, of which about one-third are flood irrigated. On the red clay loam a wide variety of grapes are grown—shiraz, muscat, Rutherglen pedro, malbec, blue imperial, white hermitage and cabernet sauvignon. In addition to their vineyards, the Campbells own 900 acres of land which are under wheat and sheep.

A new processing plant for table wines has recently been installed, and the Campbells began bottling and labelling their own wines in 1968. Further development is taking place, and some fine wines are being made.

W. H. Chambers & Sons, 'Rosewood'

The Chambers are another small family concern, with their winery only half a mile from the Rutherglen township on the road to Corowa, adjacent to Seppelts. The site was originally established as a vineyard by German-born Antony Ruche, one of the earliest vignerons in the district.

By 1891 the original Mr Chambers had purchased the vineyard and planted additional wines but he was badly affected by phylloxera and had to begin a replanting programme.

The present winemaker is Bill Chambers, grandson of the first of the Chambers of 'Rosewood'. Of their seventy acres under vine there are still some vines, over eighty years old, planted by Bill's grandfather at the end of the last century. Bill is enthusiastic about redeveloping the vineyards, and getting them back into top condition. He has been replanting at the rate of about five acres per year since 1964, including some cabernet vines. Many varieties are grown including brown muscat, tokay, shiraz, Rutherglen pedro, and rhine riesling. Bill Chambers, popular wine judge at shows in Melbourne, Adelaide and Sydney, has plans to modernize and improve the winery once the vineyards are developed to his satisfaction.

The Chambers make big full wines. They are noted for their sherry and dessert wines, especially an excellent fortified tokay, and a superb Brown Muscat.

R. N. & K. B. Gayfer, Chiltern Winery

When goldmining in the Chiltern area began to decline in importance early this century many people drifted away from the district. In an effort to establish a new industry to bring prosperity to the area a group of prominent townspeople formed a company under the leadership of a local physician, Dr C. F. Harkin, and chose winemaking as the new venture. They selected a 150 acre site about a mile south of Chiltern on the Hume Highway. Prior to the purchase there had been no vines on the property which had been a mixed farming business owned by the McLean family.

R. N. Gayfer was appointed to manage the business. He had formerly been manager of a station at Balranald, and although he had grown grapes he had not made wine before. In the first instance sixty-five acres of vines were planted, beginning in 1913. At the first vintage wine was made in the ex-engine house of a gold mine under the open sky, as the roof on the winery was not completed until the following year. The necessary vats and casks were manufactured locally and bought from defunct wineries in the area. The winery building, now over one hundred years old, was originally located at three different pit heads above mines in the Chiltern Valley before being shifted to its present site in 1919.

In time Dr Harkin bought out his business partners and owned the property until 1948 when he sold it to the Gayfer family. The present owner is K. B. Gayfer.

There are now forty-five acres of vines, and economically over-age vines are being replaced gradually. Good dessert and table wines are made.

G. T. Gehrig, Barnawartha Vineyards

Barnawartha is a small settlement between Rutherglen and Wodonga. The Gehrig vineyards located there are now run by Barney Gehrig with the help of his sons Bernard and John, who are all descendants of Philip George, the original Gehrig of Barnawartha.

The vineyard was originally planted by a joint stock company, 'The Barnawatha (sic) Vineyard Company' in the latter part of the last century. Philip Gehrig bought the property, then about fifty acres, a few years later, and a contemporary noted that 'the present owner is working the vineyards profitably and producing some excellent wine'. He built up the property to over 100 acres of vines before phylloxera wiped them out. Son Frederick replanted sixty acres, but this has since been reduced.

Gehrigs now own thirty-six acres of vineyards on clay loam soils, which are irrigated from the Murray. Varieties grown include shiraz, white hermitage, palomino, Rutherglen pedro and Rutherglen pinot. In the mid-sixties B. T. Gehrig decided to develop his table wines and with this in mind plantings are gradually being extended, with pinot noir and cabernet being introduced.

The original homestead built of bricks fired on the property is still used by the family. A feature is a tall tower which once had a bell which used to toll hourly for the information of the vineyard workers. The century-old cellars are still in use, but renovations have recently been made. The majority of their storage is oak, but recently two 500 gallon and one 1,000 gallon steel tanks for making white wines under refrigeration have been installed.

L. Jones, Rutherglen

The smallest vineyard in the district at present lies about a mile from Rutherglen on the road to Chiltern. The present owner, Les Jones, bought the property in 1927 when it had already been long established as a vineyard. Prior to 1927 the winery was owned by the Rhue family, who had originally come from Germany and were thought to have first settled on the site in the 1860s. An interesting remnant of their era still to be found on the property is a barn of hand-made bricks which is now used as a cellar and winery. The original bark roof remains extant beneath the new roof, and is a most effective means of insulation.

It was on this property that phylloxera was first discovered in 1897 and all the vines were destroyed although they were soon replanted.

When Les Jones (who had worked on another vineyard before deciding to go into business for himself) bought the property there were forty acres under vine. He has since reduced this to twenty acres of shiraz, white hermitage, muscat and pedro.

There was no winery when Mr Jones came onto the property, probably before this the grapes were sold to other wineries. There were some oak casks, and the new owner bought more. He now makes dry red, port, sweet whites and muscats, which he sells in bulk or flagon. In addition to his vineyard Les Jones has land under cattle, pigs and wheat.

Morris Wines Pty Ltd

The Morris company is not large but the family has been concerned with making wine in the Rutherglen area for over one hundred years. And the particular wine they have made throughout their long history which is hallowed among the *cognoscenti* is their superb liqueur muscat.

The 'Mia Mia' vineyard, ten miles east of Rutherglen, was originally planted by George Francis Morris, a Bristol born Quaker, in 1859, and has been owned and run by his direct descendants ever since. This is itself rather remarkable, as very few small family concerns have survived the various disasters, notably economic depressions and the phylloxera scourge,

Mr Charles Morris in the wood storage area of his Rutherglen winery, Vic.

which have hit the wine industry over the years. The Morrises stuck at it, however, and after phylloxera had destroyed their vines, entirely wiping out the 600 acre 'Fairfield' vineyard, G.F's son, Charles Hughes, replanted them in 1904.

After Charles H. came his three sons—Charles Tempest, Gerald and Frederick. Gerald retired in 1953 and management of the business passed to Gerald's brothers Charles and Fred, and his two nephews, Charles Henry (Charles' son) and Frederick John (Fred's son). Charles Henry, born 1928, is far better known as Mick. Mick Morris went to school at Scotch College, Melbourne, and then gained a Bachelor of Science degree from Melbourne University, followed by an oenology course at Roseworthy. A strong individualist, Mick Morris is especially devoted to his liqueur muscat, and regrets that the style is not as popular as it deserves to be.

The 'Mia Mia' vineyard at Rutherglen is now 110 acres, the soils consisting of red clay loam with a yellow pebbly clay subsoil. The chief variety grown is brown muscat, with tokay, shiraz, chasselas and pedro for dessert wines and dry reds. In conjunction with 'Mia Mia' the company runs another vineyard fourteen miles away at 'Balldale' across the New South Wales border. The 'Balldale' vineyard was planted in 1908. The grenache, rhine riesling, and Rutherglen pedro grown on the sandy soils there are used for dry wines and sherry; these are ungrafted vines as they escaped phylloxera. Neither vineyard is irrigated, the vines depending on natural rainfall which is about twenty-four inches at 'Mia Mia' and twenty-two at 'Balldale'.

The climate is not always kind to the Morrises—such as during the 1968 vintage when a heavy November frost burnt off a large percentage of buds at 'Mia Mia'. This was followed by a dry spell, which meant that the surviving berries did not fill out, and nearly half the crop was not picked. At other times there is too much rain at the wrong times, which brings the associated problems of oidium and downy mildew.

Fortunately much of the time things go well enough for some top wines to be made. As previously mentioned the Morris' Dessert Muscat is their chief claim to fame. The muscat is not their only such claim, however, for they also make dry whites and reds, other dessert wines, and port. All their wine is made at 'Mia Mia', the grapes from 'Balldale' being transported there for processing. In addition to their own crop the Morris company also buy quite large quantities of grapes from the Murray Irrigation Area for making into wine.

Now in their fourth generation, Morris' have been taken over by Reckitt and Colman. The injection of new capital gives rise to hopes that production of their characteristic wines will be increased.

Rutherglen Viticultural Research Station

The Viticultural Research Station (or Victorian Government Viticultural Station) near Chiltern, ten miles south-east of Rutherglen, was originally opened in 1896, during the pre-phylloxera boom, as a college to train boys for a diploma in viticulture. When the numbers of students decreased as phylloxera hit during the following decade, the project was abandoned. The college then became a research station for the investigation of wine diseases, and for improvements in winemaking. It also was the centre for the anti-phylloxera grafting programme, with the propagation and distribution of grafted phylloxera-resistant nursery stock as its main function.

In 1908 the Victorian Government sent Francois de Castella, Government Viticulturist, to Europe to investigate grafting techniques and new varieties. This collection was planted at the Viticultural College, and in later years was very useful in identifying varieties already grown in the area and known only by their local names. Since then new stocks have been imported, for purposes of comparison, from France and from other parts of the world. The new varieties are held in quarantine for some years. The station now has several hundred varieties of vines, from which various experimental wines are made. As well, the research station studies pasture improvement, cereal development and animal husbandry.

At Wahgunyah the Victorian Government maintains a nursery (part of it is leased by South Australia) which was established under the direction of Francois de Castella subsequent to the phylloxera outbreak, for the propagation of phylloxera-resistant stocks. At the nursery Research Station staff graft thousands of European scions on American vine stocks. These grafted vines are insurance should phylloxera ever strike again in Australia. This worthy work goes largely unpublicized, and deserves greater recognition.

B. Seppelt & Sons Pty Ltd, Rutherglen

Seppelts is the only large wine company with a property in the Rutherglen area, being active there since the early years of the century. The Rutherglen vineyards were then still suffering the devastating effects of the phylloxera plague which had almost wiped them out a few years earlier. By the beginning of the First World War there were signs of revival, and some growers had begun replanting with phylloxera-resistant stocks.

It was about this time that the 'Clydeside' vineyard and cellars at Rutherglen came on to the market. Although the winery had substantial stone buildings and good equipment, it had seemed for a time almost a mockery, for there were no grapes in the district to be made into wine. However, replanting of the vineyard with resistant stocks had begun, and seeking an insurance against phylloxera invading South Australia and ruining local vineyards, B. Seppelt and Sons bought the property.

The vineyard had been owned by D. G. Hamilton who owned the Rutherglen general store and first planted vines in 1886. A clearance sale of winemaking equipment and casks was held on 24 March, 1915 and soon after Seppelts took over. They purchased an additional 185 acres from Mr J. Neilsen and planted several varieties on resistant root stock in about 1918-1919. Up till 1929 wine was not made on the property, but on 26 February of that year the first part of the present winery was opened in the presence of 200 guests including many local dignitaries. The property was expanded further in 1938 when the winery, distillery and vineyards of Masterton and Dobbin were purchased. The distillery was put to use and the winery section used for storage. In 1946 the winery was doubled in size.

At Rutherglen Seppelts own 500 acres, about half of which are planted to vines. A programme of new planting is being carried out and a further sixty acres of vines under irrigation are being established. Varieties grown include Rutherglen brown muscat for liqueur muscats, shiraz, mataro and Portuguese varieties for ports, and frontignac and tokay for white dessert wines. The company is also developing pinot noir. The vineyards on the river flats are irrigated, but those on higher land rely on natural rainfall. A sprinkler irrigation system was introduced to fifty-five acres in 1966. The soils are mostly red-brown, with sandy loam on the river flats.

The wines made at the Seppelts Rutherglen winery are the typical fortified wines of the area; outstanding among them is a full sherry which is aged in Spanish oak casks, and private bin vintage ports. They also make dry red wine which goes into various commercial blends.

G. S. Smith & Sons, 'All Saints'

The impressive turreted winery of 'All Saints' stands at the end of a drive lined with elm trees as a living monument to the founder of one of Victoria's foremost winemaking families, the Sutherland Smiths of Wahgunyah.

In the 1860s George Sutherland Smith bought property on the Murray, planted grapes, and called his vineyard 'All Saints'. In less than a decade his wine won an award at the Vienna International Exhibition—not bad for a builder-ferry operator turned vigneron. The time George spent running ferries may not have been much use in winemaking, but he made full use of his knowledge of building in the construction of the winery at 'All Saints'. He made the bricks himself on the property, and used these to build a winery unique in Australia and one which is strongly reminiscent of the old Castle of Mey in his native Scotland. This beautiful old building with its battlements, large arched doorways and thick cavity walls is well worth visiting. George died soon after the winery was built in 1884.

The first George's son, David Bank, inherited the property, and in turn passed it to his sons, David and George. And now their sons, George Junior, Ian and Peter are the fourth generation of Sutherland Smiths to make wine at 'All Saints'. In recent years George Junior has played a large part in the promotion of the popular Rutherglen Festival.

The vineyard is about three miles north of Wahgunyah on the banks of the Murray River, just across from Lindemans at Corowa in New South Wales. There are about 350 acres of vines at 'All Saints', grown on the alluvial river flats of sandy loam, and some clay loam. About one-third of the acreage is devoted to shiraz, the main single variety grown, and they also have plantings of cabernet sauvignon (about twenty acres), pedro, palomino, marsanne, white hermitage, chasselas, white grenache, rhine riesling and tokay. The average yield is about 2½ tons (or 400 gallons) to the acre. The Sutherland Smiths are reconstituting the whole vineyard area at the rate of five to eight percent per annum with new varieties being introduced, such as Clare riesling and pinot noir.

The rainfall is usually about twenty-two inches per year, although there have been years when considerably more has fallen, resulting in floods. As the summers can be very wet, while the growing periods in late spring are dry, there is a spray-watering system installed making use of the river adjacent to the property, which adds about eight to ten inches of water per year when necessary. In addition to the problems of rainfall, 'All Saints' have suffered attacks of downy mildew, frost and damage by birds. During the 1890s the vines were destroyed by phylloxera and were later replanted with varieties grafted onto phylloxera-resistant stocks.

Despite these problems the wines of 'All Saints' have been of high quality over the years, and as they have made up a large part of the total wines of north-east Victoria, they have greatly contributed to the high reputation of the wines of the area. Traditionally, the dry reds have been very big, full, fruity, long-living wines—'wines for heroes'. In recent years the Sutherland Smiths have been leaders of attempts to lighten the style, and also to make dry whites of a more delicate nature than formerly. It is perhaps ironic that this change of emphasis has been made, as the fame of the area was built up in the past on its big, highly alcoholic and delightfully aromatic fortified wines. The demand for these dessert muscats and ports (both vintage and tawny) has diminished as the demand for light table wines has increased, and thus the change in 'All Saints' wines. In their winery the Sutherland Smiths claim to have the largest oak storage in the southern hemisphere. They have a capacity of about a half a million gallons, and most of this is oak. Many of their enormous old casks were made by Peter Sullivan, an exceptionally talented and well-known cooper who worked at Barnawartha until about 1905. Sullivan won many prizes for his barrels (generally made of American oak) which have been called the Rolls-Royces of casks. In addition to their oak the Sutherland Smiths naturally have much modern equipment, such as the air bag press and centrifugal filter.

The 'All Saints' vineyard has its offices and bottling plant in Melbourne. For eighty-four years the city headquarters were located in Selborne Chambers, but in 1960 they were forced to seek larger premises. A move was made to Queensberry Street, North Melbourne, where there is now a modern bottling plant and modern facilities for distribution.

'Stanton and Killeen'

Mr Jack Stanton of the 'Stanton and Killeen' vineyard has been making wine on the property since before the First World War. His great-grandfather, Timothy Stanton, first came to the district in the mid-nineteenth century about the time Antony Ruche was planting 'Rosewood'.

Timothy Stanton came from Wales and his great-grandson doubts if 'he had ever seen vines' before he came to Australia, where he took up land on the Black Dog Creek in 1862. In the following years his son J. L. Stanton established 110 acres of vines on a property one mile west of Rutherglen. In turn his son J. R. Stanton took over the business, and later purchased the present 'Gracegarry' vineyard from a family called Hughes.

The Hughes had established 100 acres of vines on their property which is situated three miles west of Rutherglen off the Echuca road. After the phylloxera devastation J. R. Stanton replanted European varieties on resistant root stock. At present there are thirty-six acres planted to vines with an additional ten acres which have recently been planted and will come into full bearing soon. Their soils are mostly sandy loams on which muscat and shiraz are grown. They also have 900 acres of wheat, sheep and cattle.

The present proprietor is Jack Stanton who works the property with his son-in-law, Norman Killeen, who was formerly manager of the Rutherglen Research Station. They have recently started bottling their own wines, which include ports and muscats as well as big 'old-style' dry reds.

Goulburn Valley

Tahbilk Pty Ltd, 'Chateau Tahbilk'

'Chateau Tahbilk' is undoubtedly one of the most picturesque wineries and cellars in Australia. It is located in the Goulburn Valley, less than eighty miles north of Melbourne and about five miles from the town of Nagambie. The Chateau is one hundred miles from Rutherglen, and should not be included as part of the north-eastern area as conditions there are quite different, with the result that the wines of 'Chateau Tahbilk' are also quite different to those of the Rutherglen area.

The name of the property is derived from a place on the Goulburn River, which the aboriginals called 'tabilk tabilk', meaning a 'place of many waterholes'. The nearby township is known as Tabilk, and why the Chateau has added the extra 'h' nobody really knows.

The first owners of a huge area which includes the present Chateau property were Hugh Glass and John Purcell who acquired it in 1845. Hugh Glass was one of the largest landowners and richest men in Australia, and eventually split with Purcell, taking for himself the southern part of their holding consisting of one square mile which included 'tabilk tabilk'.

Glass appointed a young Frenchman from Burgundy, Ludovic Marie, as his manager. Marie was a well-known local identity as he owned a general store and ran a ferry service across the Goulburn River. He planted some table grapes in the garden of his homestead, and was so successful with these that he experimented with wine grapes. Marie then convinced Hugh Glass and others that both soil and climate were highly suitable for viticulture, and the Goulburn Vineyard Proprietary Company was formed on 16 March, 1860.

The company intended to purchase the 'Noorilim Estate' to develop as vineyards, but the sale fell through with the drunken death of its owner Andrew Sinclair. On 6 June, 1860 a new company was formed, called the Tabilk Vineyard Proprietary. Richard Horne was secretary and Marie manager. An important addition to the new board was John Pinney Bear, an Englishman of some wealth and with a knowledge of farming, who also had rather grand ideas. He proposed that an advertisement for one million vine cuttings be placed six times in the major newspapers of Victoria, New South Wales, and South Australia.

The newly formed company, with a capital of £25,000, took over on 1 August, 1860 the 640 acres of the Tabilk run purchased from Hugh Glass for £5.10.0 per acre. Legend has it that the poet Horne actually planted the first vine at Tabilk. Under the supervision of J. P. Bear, 150 acres of land was cleared of its gums and honeysuckle and sixty-five acres planted with vines by the end of 1860. At this time

Vineyards of Northern and Central Victoria

also, though there was no wine, large vaulted underground cellars were built, which are still in perfect order. Ludovic Marie left Tabilk in 1862, but clearing and planting went on under the control of Mr Bear, who gradually bought out the other shareholders.

1875 was a significant year in the annals of the enterprise for it was then that the 'new cellars' were built. These were designed by the architect W. A. Zeal of Melbourne; the extensions to the cellar being about 100 feet long and bringing the cellarage capacity to 200,000 gallons of wine. A bulge at one corner appeared to endanger the building, but never has had any ill effects. To mark the opening of the new cellar a bottle each of the 1875 dry red and dry white was sealed in a space in the wall. These wines were removed in 1947 and found to be in good condition.

In 1887 Francois de Coueslant came to 'Chateau Tahbilk', as it was now known, as manager. Copies of the letters he wrote as manger are still preserved and give a good picture of the daily life at the vineyard at the time. He was a far-sighted man, interested in experimentation, and he put several of his more unusual ideas into practice. He planted olive trees, with the idea of establishing an olive oil industry. Earlier he had planted a double avenue of mulberry trees leading to the homestead, with the hope of beginning a silk industry. De Coueslant planned for the wives and daughters of the vineyard workers to look after the silkworms and spin the silk. This rather ingenious idea did not come off, but the trees still stand in memory of an original idea. It is believed that de Coueslant erected the splendid tower which is featured on the label of Tahbilk wines.

John Pinney Bear died in October 1889 in his mid-sixties, after an association with 'Chateau

Tahbilk' of more than a quarter of a century. The credit for really getting the vineyard going belongs to him. An additional blow at about this time was that phylloxera hit and destroyed all but 135 acres which were planted on moist, sandy soil which protected them from the disease. (Seven rows of these original shiraz vines have been left for sentimental reasons.) The final factor which marked the end of the good old days was the departure of Francois de Coueslant soon after Bear's death.

The vineyard then went into a long period of decline. It was owned by Bear's widow who lived in London until her death in 1925 at the age of ninety-two. When the vineyard came onto the market it was bought by his Australian agent for Reginald Purbrick, then Conservative member for Walton in the House of Commons, and father of the present proprietor, Eric Purbrick, M.A., L.L.B.

Eric Purbrick was born in Sydney and educated at Melbourne Grammar. After he graduated as an M.A. from Jesus College, Cambridge in 1925, he studied law and was called to the bar of the Inner Temple four years later. While holidaying in Germany that year he decided to act on his mother's suggestion to go to Australia to manage 'Chateau Tahbilk'. With an academic English background and absolutely no experience of winemaking Eric Purbrick arrived just in time to preside over the 1932 vintage of a rather run-down, neglected winery at a time of acute economic depression. He applied himself energetically to learning his new business and to its rehabilitation. The twenty-eight year old lawyer learned winemaking from books, a winemaker he hired called McDonald, Arthur Pearson, and above all from those eminent personalities of the time—T. C. Seabrook and Francois de Castella. De Castella, Government viticulturist, advised on improvement of the soil by ploughing, manuring and winter irrigation, and further advised that some areas should be replanted with phylloxera-resistant stocks. The quality of the new owner's success was shown by the request of Tom Seabrook to act as agent for Tahbilk wines, a short two years after he had rejected such a request from Eric Purbrick on the grounds of inadequate quality of the wines. Things were not easy in those days, and Eric Purbrick worked hard to sell his wines. Originally it was sold in bulk for one and tuppence a gallon delivered in Melbourne, and he drove an old truck around Victoria selling his wares to wine saloons. In addition to the vineyards the farm activities had to be managed which was no mean task.

In 1936 most of the old homestead was pulled down, and an attractive new one designed by the architect (now Sir) Roy Grounds was built on to what remained. Eric Purbrick also added to the atmosphere of the winery with the installation above the main entrance of the cellars of a large wrought-iron sign, a copy of an eighteenth century one he saw outside a *weinhaus* in the Black Forest in Germany.

In 1955 Eric's son John took over the running of the farming side, leaving his father free to concentrate on winemaking. Four years later in 1959 the cellars were classified by the National Trust as being of historical and architectural interest. The following year, 1960, the centenary of 'Chateau Tahbilk' was celebrated, and the then Prime Minister of Australia, Sir Robert Menzies addressed the gathering, and entombed two bottles for future generations.

The property now covers 2,800 acres of river flats but only 100 acres of these are planted to vines. Cabernet and shiraz plantings are being extended to meet the increased demand for their red wines. Varieties grown are cabernet sauvignon and shiraz for reds, and rhine riesling, white hermitage and marsanne for the whites. The soil varies from sandy loam on the river flats to grey alluvial types. Being close to the lake there is moisture in the subsoil which aids the growth of the vines. The annual rainfall is about twenty-two inches, and it is supplemented with irrigation. The summers are very hot—sometimes over 43.3°C, which can lead to too much sugar in the berries, and consequently to rather fat, low acid wines. Downy mildew is a problem, as are frosts. Despite this, the average yield is about two tons per acre. An unusual feature of the winemaking is that the must is fermented in big oak vats. The old screw press has been replaced by an air bag press. 'Chateau Tahbilk' makes only unfortified wines, reds and whites, which have long been labelled under their varietal names rather than such misleading names as 'claret' or 'chablis'. The style of the Tahbilk wines is individual and very distinctive, and the quality of a high standard.

'Chateau Tahbilk' really is a lovely Australian version of a chateau, with its old buildings set among big trees and gardens. Eric Purbrick, a true gentleman and member of the *Confrèrie des Chevaliers du Tastevin*, has been more than successful in his rehabilitation of the Chateau. He can be well satisfied with what he has achieved—the wines are well known and much in demand, and widely exported.

Cottage Vineyard

A recent enterprise is the 500 acre vineyard development by Ross Shelmerdine at Mitchelton on the bank of the Goulburn River opposite 'Chateau Tahbilk'. As consultant, Colin Preece of Great Western fame has supervised the project.

Darveniza Brothers, 'Excelsior' Vineyard

The forty acre 'Excelsior' vineyard of Trojano Darveniza is situated two miles from Mooroopna near Shepparton in the fertile agricultural area of the Goulburn Valley. This little known family-run firm has been making wine here, and once with con-

Large wood cellar below the winery at 'Chateau Tahbilk', Nagambie, Vic.

siderable overseas success, for nearly one hundred years.

The original Darveniza, also Trojano, was born in Dalmatia of Austrian parents, and came to Victoria during the gold rushes. He was successful enough to afford 320 acres of land in 1871, where he planted wheat. By about 1875 Trojano feared possible over-production of wheat, and planted a few acres of grapes as a standby. Within fifteen years he had over 100 acres under vines, including shiraz, cabernet, mataro, muscat, chasselas, pedro and riesling. Darveniza won an amazing number of awards for his wine in European exhibitions—over 300 altogether!

Although there are still Darvenizas—John and Trojano, grand-nephews of old Trojano, making wine at the 'Excelsior' vineyard, today there are only dim remnants left of the heyday of the 1890s. The vineyard is planted on flat land near the river, and is now irrigated. The major variety grown is shiraz. There are a few acres of vines, including cabernet and malbec, over sixty years old and still bearing well.

The winery is now a rather weather-beaten but somehow charming sprawl of wooden buildings. The oldest part of the cellar dates back almost a century, and holds two rows of 250 gallon casks. The winery has a wood storage capacity of 50,000 gallons. 'Troji' believes that no great training is required for winemaking, 'you just make the wine the way it turns up'. But this is not winemaking from ignorance, for among the maze of vats and butts is a large centrifugal press and other modern equipment.

Most wines from 'Excelsior' are sold locally, and are especially popular with settlers in the area who have come from Mediterranean lands. Darveniza makes light dry whites and reds, and sweet fortified wines from grapes bought from the Murray Irrigation Area. Interestingly, the crest on their labels, registered long before Federation, resembles that of the Commonwealth. The Darveniza version improves on the State's in that the kangaroo and emu support a wine-cask instead of a dreary shield.

L. Gravina

Gravina's also have vineyards in the Shepparton area. They have about fifteen acres of shiraz and grenache and use flood irrigation from the Goulburn River. The firm also buys large amounts of grapes from the Murray Irrigation areas for making into wine.

Other Vineyards

C. Conte, Ardmona.
V. Curcio, Ardmona.
Goulburn Valley Winery, Shepparton.
G. & V. Scrimizzi, Ardmona.

Great Western and Surrounds

In Australia the name Great Western is now almost automatically associated with champagne. The township after which the wine was named is not well known, and is certainly nothing like the picture its name engenders. Great Western is situated 136 miles west of Melbourne, midway between Stawell, which is chiefly famous for its annual Easter running race, and Ararat. The country is hilly, with the Grampian Mountains twenty-five miles to the west. The area is not kind to viticulture —the soil is poor, frosts are severe, rainfall is insufficient and yields are low. And yet it is this small area, where for about the last fifty years only two companies have made wine, that has produced some of Australia's greatest wines.

The height above sea level at Great Western varies roughly between 950 and 1,200 feet. This and the latitude, 37° south, gives the cool temperatures which are desirable for slow ripening of the fruit and the retention of acid. The average mean temperature of the hottest month in this district is 20°C. This, with the pattern of ripening and harvesting, is said by Dan Murphy to be similar to the great wine districts of the world.

Rainfall at Great Western is about twenty to twenty-five inches per year, mainly in the winter. This amount is not sufficient for the development of healthy vines, and drip irrigation systems are desirable. Unfortunately the underground water is too salty for this, but dams, tanks and the Concongella Creek are used. The winter rainfall is adequate to store water for use in late spring and early summer. The major climatic disadvantage of the Great Western area is frost. As often as every three or four years spring frosts destroy the young shoots on the vines on the flats. Sometimes a second budding saves the situation, but all too often whole vineyards are unproductive for the year. Obviously the economic repercussions of this are extremely serious.

Generally speaking the Great Western soils are among the poorest vineyard soils in the country. The soil is volcanic, varying from red-brown gravelly loam to grey granitic sand; the subsoils are clay and granite, with sedimentary soils in the Concongella basin. The flats along the Concongella Creek have a good soil which is heavier and deeper. Most of the other soil in the area is badly leached podsol and quite unsuitable for growing grapes.

Varieties grown for red wines include hermitage, malbec, cabernet sauvignon, cinsaut, esparte (which is the Spanish name for mataro) and miller's burgundy. The latter is the local name for pinot meuniere, and is so named because in the summer the underside of the leaves carry a whitish down which resembles a light dusting with flour. The white varieties are chasselas, folle blanche, tokay, semillon and rhine riesling. According to Peter Weste of Seppelts, cabernet really needs more water than the district has.

Vine diseases had been rare for many years, but downy mildew struck severely in the early sixties. A load of infected irrigation area grapes were brought to a winery in the area, and the wind did the rest. Intensive spraying with copper and other chemicals has since been carried out in an attempt to control the mildew but patches of the disease still flare up.

One of the serious problems of the Great Western area is the low yields there, often only a ton to the acre, with at very best four tons to the acre. Unlike the serious frost problem, this can be overcome to some extent by the use of improved scientific knowledge of viticulture, such as close selection of vines and the planting of more suitable varieties. It does mean, however, that 'straight' Great Western wines are, justifiably, likely to be expensive.

It is one of the ironies of nature that the greatest wines are often made from areas with the poorest natural conditions. And so it is at Great Western. The champagnes of the area are well known, but the rarer unblended dry whites and reds of the area are often superb. The economics of winemaking and the qualities of the wine are such, however, that Great Western wines are often used for blending.

Seppelts, Great Western

Seppelts, for much of the time under the guidance of Colin Preece, have been the dominating force at Great Western for most of this century. They have been there since 1918, though the history of their vineyards goes back a lot further than that.

Flor sherry at Mildara Wines, Merbein, Vic.

The original planter of what is now part of Seppelts Great Western vineyards was Joseph Best, who was born in Richmond, Surrey in 1830. He arrived in Australia as a child with his brother Henry, their father David and his brother George and their wives in 1834. After a stay of four years in Launceston, David Best, who was a builder, moved his family to Port Phillip, where the boys were educated at St James School, Melbourne. By the 1850s the young brothers had succumbed to the call of the goldfields, where they made their gold from a cattle yard and slaughterhouse at Great Western which provided the miners with meat. As the gold rush subsided so did their business, and by 1864, inspired by the pioneers Blampied and Trouette, the brothers decided to turn to viticulture, and each planted his own vineyard.

Joseph purchased a property south of the village of Great Western on gently rising land and in 1865 began fencing and clearing the land. The following year he began planting, with cuttings obtained from the Trouettes and others, including de Castella at Yering. In 1868 he had his first vintage at Great Western—thirty-eight gallons. Planting continued and by 1877 his vintage was 7,000 gallons of wine.

While excavating his cellars, about 1870, Best discovered in the subsoil a stratum of soft granite, ideal for tunnelling. Thus he had local gold miners dig a system of tunnels, seven feet by four feet, in which to store his maturing wine. The miners' name for these tunnels was 'drives' and so they are known today. Joseph prospered, and his wines won prizes all over the world. He never married, and lived with his father and sister Elizabeth in a plain four-roomed cottage. At the height of his success, Joseph Best died suddenly on 8 January, 1887 at the age of fifty-seven, and was buried in the Great Western cemetery.

As Joseph died intestate the Great Western property was disposed of, and the proceeds divided among the members of his family. The purchaser was Hans Irvine, a Ballarat businessman, who paid the not inconsiderable sum of £12,000 for fifty-five acres of vines, 450 acres of grazing land and the stock of wine in the cellars. Although Joseph Best began winemaking at Great Western, Hans Irvine, with enormous energy, took the operation to new heights. He wanted to make champagne, not just sparkling wine but champagne equal to the best from France, and spared no effort to attain this end. He made several trips to France (in itself quite an achievement in those slow-travelling days) and brought back a skilled team of champagne artisans headed by Monsieur Charles Pierlot, an expert of considerable repute who had had experience at the Champagne house, Pommery.

In 1890, the same year as Pierlot joined him, Irvine began planting at Arawatta, two miles south of the cellars, where he had purchased 145 acres. Arawatta is said to be the aboriginal name for a

waterhole in the area. The variety he chose was white pinot (since re-named Irvine's White; it is probably folle blanche); the classic champagne grape is black pinot but it was subject to disease at Great Western. Expansion continued and new red brick cellars were built in 1892 at a cost of £2,000. Special machinery was imported from France, as were champagne bottles, as no bottles of adequate thickness were made in Australia at the time. In an effort to take his wine directly to the British public, Irvine opened a depot at Dowgate Hill near Cannon Street in July 1905. The investment of all this energy (and money) was rewarded with the considerable successes Irvine's wines achieved at exhibitions.

Irvine realised that the drives provided the ideal conditions for the maturation of sparkling wine—the temperature is maintained at an even 14° to 15°C the whole year, freedom from vibrations, dryness—and that these were similar to the great chalk caves of Epernay. Thus he had the drives extended, the dome-shaped tunnels were cut, on average, roughly twelve feet wide by seven feet six inches high and sixteen feet underground. By 1907 one mile of drives had been excavated.

Hans Irvine, born 1856, was a politician in addition to being a vigneron. In the 1890s he was elected a member of the Legislative Assembly, and in 1903 became Member for the Grampians in the Federal Parliament. He was president of the Viticultural Society, and in his 'spare' time he turned his attention to transforming the homestead.

While all this was going on Irvine did not by any means neglect his winemaking. He had begun to buy grapes from other growers mainly for distillation for brandy. His wines were very popular, and made more so by Irvine's belief in the value of advertising. He acquired the St George's winery and vineyards from a Mr Skyrmes. At the age of sixty-two Irvine decided to retire. In 1918 Irvine severed his connection with Great Western, and Seppelts became its third owners. Irvine died four years later while on a visit to London.

A new era began at Great Western with the resources and experience of the new owners, and Reginald Mowat, a Roseworthy graduate, was appointed manager, which post he held until his resignation in December 1932. At that time the Depression was at its height—hardly an auspicious beginning for the new manager, who was, however, to become one of the great Australian winemakers of the century. This man was Colin Preece. Born in Adelaide on 5 May, 1903, he graduated as dux of Roseworthy in 1923, after which he joined Seppelts, and had been attached to the technical staff at Seppeltsfield before his promotion to Great Western.

It was not until the 1940s that any real expansion was made at Great Western, however, over the following twenty years a considerable amount was achieved. In that period about 340 acres of new

'All Saints' winery at Wahgunyah. In 1864, George Sutherland Smith decreed that his vineyard would be called 'All Saints', as several local vineyards were named after a saint.

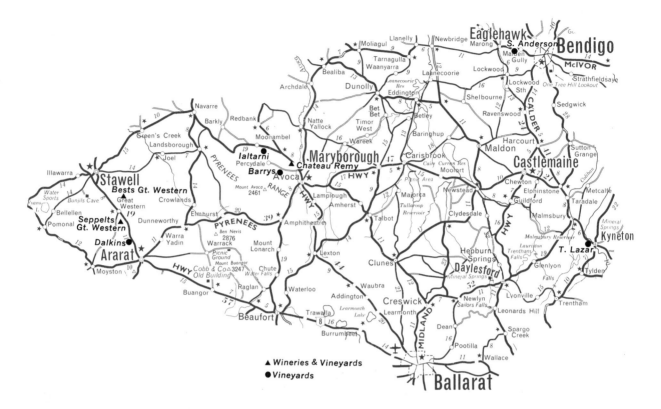

Vineyards of Great Western and Surrounding Areas

vineyards were established, and eighty acres were replanted. The holdings were extended in 1945 with the purchase from Maria Salinger of the properties 'St Ethels' and 'Hockheim', which are about one mile south-east of the cellars. The first stage of an imposing new building was erected in 1946, and a second floor added thirteen years later. By 1964 increasing sales again made it necessary to extend the cellar area, and a modern fermentation cellar was completed in time for the 1965 vintage. During this time the drives were completely given over to the storage of sparkling wine, and when space was still insufficient were extended. An early one was opened by Lady Somers, wife of the Victorian Governor-General in 1928, and others by Governors Lord Huntingfield in 1934 and Sir Dallas Brooks in 1950. The drives now have a total length of three and a half miles and have been given an 'A' rating by the Victorian National Trust.

In 1963 Colin Preece retired due to ill health. Most commentators on the wine scene label him 'master', and rank him with two other greats—Maurice O'Shea and Roger Warren. Under Colin Preece's management Great Western champagne far outstripped all its competitors. He also began making still wines in the forties which led to the successful commercial range from Great Western—Moyston claret (named after a village south of the

vineyards), Chalambar burgundy (from Mt Chalambar east of the vineyards), Rhymney chablis (from a neighbouring locality where there were gold diggings) and Arawatta riesling (after the most well known of the Great Western vineyards). When Colin Preece retired after an outstanding career, his place was taken by Les Francis. He had been with Seppelts since 1925, and at the time of his appointment to Great Western was on the technical staff at Seppeltsfield. In addition to ably carrying out his winemaking activities, Mr Francis has contributed a great deal through original historical research to our knowledge of winemaking at Great Western.

Present winemaker at Great Western is Peter Weste. His father was a pioneer who in 1908 took up a neglected vineyard block on the Murray where he lived in a tent until he got established. He then went on to become director of the Renmark Co-operative. He also wrote a weekly column on viticulture in the *Murray Pioneer* newspaper for thirty years. Peter was born in 1929 and studied oenology at Roseworthy. He joined the Renmark Co-operative in 1947, and then spent the next seven years with the S.A. Grapegrowers. After a time at Quelltaler and then at Stanley he worked a short while with Hamiltons before going to Great Western.

Seppelt's winery at Great Western is not surrounded by vineyards in the usual way. The winery and some vineyards are on a hilly slope near the township, but there are other plantings on scattered sites, some miles apart. These lie to the south on the road to Moyston, with others bordering the Western Highway near the township and running along the flats of the Concongella Creek. Seppelts have fifteen named vineyards at Great Western, with a total of 518 acres under vines of a holding of 1,500 acres. About one-quarter of the vines are black varieties, which are esparte (mataro), miller's burgundy, cinsaut, malbec, shiraz and cabernet sauvignon. White varieties are semillon, rhine and Clare riesling, white hermitage, tokay, chasselas and Irvine's white (formerly thought to be a pinot variety, now thought possibly to be folle blanche, and named in honour of Hans Irvine). Whatever its origin this variety is the basis of the famed Great Western champagne.

Seppelts use their winery at Great Western as the centre for making their 'prestige' table wines, in a similar fashion to Penfolds at 'Auldana'. A considerable amount of modern equipment has been installed, necessary to make delicate base material for champagne. This equipment includes ultra cooling in stainless steel tanks, and big steel centrifuges for clarifying the must. More equipment, larger buildings and more technicians, as well as the use of the transfer method have meant a considerable increase in production of Great Western champagne in the last ten years. In addition the still wines have by no means been neglected—the 'commercial' Great Western wines are very popular, and the small quantity of straight Great Western wines, although rare indeed, are well worth obtaining.

Best's Wines Pty Ltd, 'Concongella'

The history of the only winemaking concern at Great Western apart from Seppelts runs parallel with the history of Seppelts. For when Joseph Best planted vineyards he inspired his younger brother to do likewise. Thus by the end of the 1860s Henry Best (born 1832) had bought a property on the banks of the Concongella Creek, about two miles north of the Great Western township which he fenced with red-gum sawn on the property, and commenced to plant with a wide variety of vines. These included frontignac, 'burgundy', esparte, hermitage, black prince, muscatel, malbec, sweet water and chasselas.

Henry Best aimed at making light-bodied table wines rather than the fortifieds which were so popular. Most of his wine was sold in Britain to fill standing orders for it there. Henry Best died in 1913 at the age of eighty-one.

Henry's son Charles carried on making wine at 'Concongella' until the twenty acre vineyard and cellars were sold to the Stawell Vineyard Company who owned a large number of vineyards in the area at the time. Later Mr F. Thomson bought out the company, and his sons have run the vineyard to this day. The managing director is Eric F. H. Thomson, and his partners are his brother W. H. Thomson and his son E. V. H. Thomson. With the winery the Thomsons bought the right to use the Best name, and have continued to do so.

Bests now have about fifty acres of vines situated on the low-lying flats of the creek where they are unfortunately highly susceptible to frost. The soil there is clay loam over yellow clay subsoil. Their varieties are shiraz, malbec, miller's burgundy, esparte, rhine riesling and chasselas. The Best's winery is largely made of timber, and is situated over an underground storage area. Only dry red and white wines are made from Great Western grapes.

In addition to 'Concongella', Bests have a vineyard at Lake Boga in the Swan Hill area for making fortified wines.

Other Growers

Des McRae, with his sons Greg and Michael have a property of nearly forty acres at Ararat. It is situated on red volcanic loam on a frost free patch of hillside, and in addition has plenty of water.

The Dalkin Family, on a tall hill only a few miles from Great Western have planted twenty acres of vines on dark chocolate loam and gravel.

Nathan and Wyeth, Avoca

Avoca, on the site of a gold rush township of the last century, still with old mine shafts sunk by Chinese diggers, lies forty miles north-east of Great Western, in hills which are part of the complex Great Dividing Range. Avoca is about 790 feet above sea level, and recently has been the site of several new vineyard developments. These have the advantage over Great Western of being frost free.

Nathan and Wyeth of Melbourne in conjunction with Remy Martin of France have developed more than 200 acres of vines, about three-quarters of which are white hermitage with the remainder doradillo. Planting will continue steadily until 600 acres are developed. The grapes from the Chateau Remy vineyard were intended to be made into brandy, which is the reason for the selection of the above named varieties. John Robb (formerly of the Hunter Valley) as manager supervised the development, from virgin bush to budding vines on the gentle slopes of rich soil in only a few years. A distillery has been completed at Avoca for processing the company's grapes.

When it seemed clear that the demand for champagne was soaring it was decided to divert up to half the Avoca production into fine champagne. Colin Preece was retained as consultant, and some French experts bought in for good measure. The

Avoca champagne is being made by the completely classical method, including disgorging by hand. It is marketed under the Quelltaler label, as Nathan and Wyeth also own that company.

Several other large properties have been planted in the area. It appears that most of them will wish to market their grapes instead of going to the capital expense of building and equipping a winery. One of these vineyards is being developed by Wal Henning, a teacher-earthmoving contractor, who is planting 400 acres of land having a quartz and limestone subsoil with cabernet, doradillo, malbec, pinot, rhine riesling and white hermitage.

Seppelts, Drumborg

A few years ago Seppelts wished to expand, but Great Western was overtaxed for grape growing and it was very difficult to find suitable land in the area. Accordingly the company sought land similar to the Great Western area where the same grape varieties could be grown. It was not possible to plant any of the Great Western vines in South Australia owing to the quarantine regulations, and thus the new land had to be in Victoria.

After much searching Seppelts found a 470 acre property of undulating farmland 100 miles away at Drumborg. The property is situated on the Princes Highway, four miles from Heywood, just outside the town of Portland. This is almost one degree of latitude further south than Great Western or Coonawarra.

There were no existing commercial vineyards in the area, however, in the early years of the colony of Victoria wines were produced around Geelong.

Seppelts believe the soil at Drumborg is very similar to that of the Arawatta vineyard at Great Western, which is considered the best vineyard on the estate at Great Western. The Drumborg soil comprises red-brown volcanic earth interspersed with iron stone gravel.

The climate at Drumborg is cooler than Great Western though above century conditions do occur in summer and the rainfall is much higher. Average rainfall is about thirty inches per year and records have shown that no month in the year averages less than an inch. Even with this very high rainfall, drainage is good and aids the vine roots in penetrating the soil to a considerable depth. Sunshine hours are low due to the maritime climate but the company claims that heat absorption by the brown earth gives a long and moderate ripening effect to the grapes.

Seppelts intend to develop their Drumborg vineyards to produce top quality grapes to make top quality table wines, especially champagne. Over 200 acres have already been planted, with varieties including rhine riesling, tokay, miller's burgundy, chasselas, sylvaner, gewurztraminer,

Flor sherry 'houses' at Mildara, near Mildura, Vic.

and pinot chardonnay. There are also substantial plantings of Irvine's white which is the basis of Seppelt's Great Western Champagne. All grapes from Drumborg are processed at Seppelt's Great Western winery.

The North-West

The town of Mildura, the business and commercial centre of the Victorian Murray Irrigation settlements, was (like Renmark in South Australia) founded by the Chaffey brothers in 1887. The surrounding scrubby grazing land was virtually useless for agriculture until the Chaffeys organised irrigation from the Murray River. Water brought life to the desert and after the First World War settlements for ex-servicemen were established at Red Cliffs and

An old hand press in use at Chambers' winery, Rutherglen, Vic.

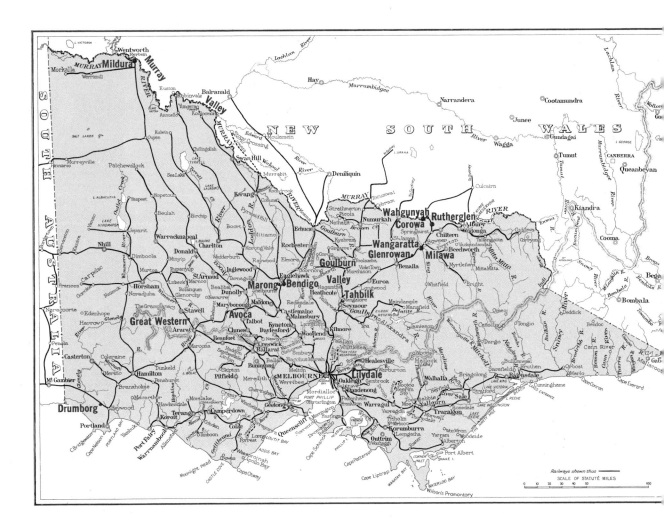

The Vineyard Areas of Victoria

Merbein, with similar expansion at Robinvale after the Second World War.

Mildura is now a big town, with a population of over 12,000. A wide variety of fruit and vegetables pour from the fifteen to twenty acre 'blocks', as the farms of the area are known. The district specializes in dried vine fruit and citrus in addition to grapes for wine. The method by which the water makes this cultivation possible is as follows: from a central pumping station water is led through main channels and smaller concrete-lined distribution channels to each block. Supplementary electrical pumps are widely used to get the water up the steep banks of the river. Within the blocks earth channels or furrows are dug, or sprinkler systems are used. Irrigation water is usually applied from August to the end of March.

The landscape in this part of north-west Victoria is gently undulating and quite monotonous. The altitude is usually under 300 feet above sea level, with long, very hot summers. Occasional severe spring frosts are a problem, and oil burners and other devices are used in an attempt to protect the vines. The area has been phylloxera free, but spraying is necessary to control insect pests and mould. The soils are the typical pinkish-brown Mallee variety and below the red surface sands are limestone and clay, which can lead to drainage problems.

Grapes are grown in settlements—the largest of which is in the Mildura-Merbein-Red Cliffs area. Other grape growers are found at Lake Boga, Swan Hill and Robinvale. The growers are independent, and grow their choice of varieties, for table use, drying or winemaking. Shiraz and semillon, of use only for winemaking, are widely grown, while varieties such as the seedles sultana, waltham cross and gordo which have other uses are also grown on a large scale. In addition to the local wineries, growers sell to many winemakers from other areas, such as Griffith and Rutherglen.

All sorts of wines are made from grapes grown in the Murray Valley. As discussed elsewhere the river wines have not enjoyed a good reputation in the past. With improved winemaking techniques and the use of suitable varieties, such as shiraz and semillon, the wines are now usually of at least moderate quality, and fill a lot of flagons which give many people great pleasure. And the quality is still improving. In addition to wines, brandy and fortifying spirit are made in large quantities.

Mildara Wines Ltd

The only large company at Mildura is Mildara Wines. The winery is situated at Merbein, about five miles west of Mildura, on a high bank of the Murray River. The headquarters of the company were not always at the present site, although Mildara has been connected with Mildura since almost the beginning. The town was founded in 1887, and the following year the Chaffey brothers planted a vineyard and built a winery at Irymple, near Mildura. They made their first wine in 1891, and continued to plant more and more vines. In 1914 the Mildura Winery Pty Ltd, as it had become, moved its headquarters to the present site. Expansion continued, they were renamed Mildara Wines Ltd, and became a public company. They are now prominent among Australian winemakers, making some outstanding wines, brandies and sherries and selling widely throughout Australia.

The company owes its present position to the hard work and progressive outlook of the men associated with it since its inception. W. B. Chaffey was the chairman from the beginning until his death, and his son, W. H. Chaffey, was the company's secretary from 1917 to 1963. H. R. Haselgrove, O.B.E., was for many years chairman and managing director, and is very much part of the Mildara story He was one of the pacemakers and one of the major influences on the contemporary wine scene. Ron Haselgrove is a winemaker of unquestioned skill and judgement, and one of Australia's leading brandy distillation experts.

Mildara has long been famous for its sherries and brandies, and these remain the real raison d'etre of the company. In the late forties they decided to market a quality red, and since the local Mildura area was not suitable for its production they had to look elsewhere. Ron Haselgrove believed in blending—of both different grapes and different regions—to ensure consistency of style and quality. Through the years he has stuck to this, ably abetted by executive Syd Wells, his son Richard Haselgrove and, formerly, Les Ekert. Since 1955 to ensure supplies from Coonawarra and having great faith in that area and its future he master-minded the development there of the Mildara winery and vineyards. The result of this effort has been some very good wines indeed.

The winery at Mildura, high on a bluff, is one of the best kept and smartest in Australia. There are concrete buttresses on the cliff face, as the soil there is very friable and it was quite possible that the winery would otherwise have ended up in the river. Dr Benwell describes the winery as resembling a well-established country golf club. Inside the winery efficiency and organization reign supreme over the impressive array of expensive equipment. The company retains its connection with Irymple, where it has storage cellars and 140 acres of vineyards. Varieties cultivated are cabernet sauvignon, malbec, rhine riesling, Clare riesling and listan, a specially selected Spanish strain of palomino of which sixty acres have been developed. This is the only Australian vineyard of this variety which is used to make high quality sherry.

Naturally these grapes comprise only a small percentage of those processed by Mildara. They purchase the major part of their requirements from about 400 local growers. As the only big company in the area the growers depend on Mildara for their income, and the company can thus exert considerable pressure on the growers as to varieties grown, methods of cultivation and picking times. The grapes used by Mildara for their sherries are palomino, pedro and doradillo. They distil large quantities of grapes, mainly doradillo, for their brandies.

McWilliams, Robinvale

McWilliams, the pioneers of irrigation area wine in the M.I.A. in New South Wales, have established themselves in a big way at Robinvale, on the Victorian side of the Murray River, south of Euston which is on the Sturt Highway in New South Wales. They began construction of their Robinvale winery in 1961 with plans to process 5,000 tons of grapes annually and with provision to double this figure. They buy locally grown grapes both for making wine and for the distillation of brandy and fortifying spirit.

Other Murray Valley Wineries

It should be noted that although Rutherglen is geographically in the Murray Valley it is not included in this area. Apart from its quite different history, the Rutherglen area is not generally irrigated, and irrigation is the raison d'etre of the Murray vineyards.

In the Swan Hill area at Beverford, the Rutherglen firm, Bullers, have a winery. They also have vineyards there planted mostly with shiraz, with some cabernet and semillon. The Thomsons of Best Wines Pty Ltd, Great Western, have a winery and a vineyard called St Andrew at Lake Boga in the same area. They make fortified red and white sweet wines, fortified dry wines, as well as fortifying spirit and brandy.

Tasting last year's vintage in new oak small wood at Lindeman's 'Rouge Homme', Coonawarra, S.A.

6 South Australia

The Vineyards of Adelaide

Adelaide, the capital of Australia's premier wine producing state, is an attractive modern city located on the banks of the River Torrens.

In 1836 at the time of the creation of the colony of South Australia Colonel William Light decided on the location of the main town. The site chosen was at latitude 35°56' south, and longitude 138°36' east, on the eastern side of St Vincent's Gulf where the soil was moderately fertile and there was an attractive vegetative cover of long grass and widely spaced tall gum trees. The new city was named after Queen Adelaide, wife of William IV.

The climate was moderate, with generally equable temperatures ranging from 11.6°C in July to 23°C in February and with seven hours of sunshine daily.

The average annual rainfall was about twenty-one to twenty-two inches.

From the earliest days vineyards have been cultivated in the area, but the building of factories, shops, houses and other 'progress' has meant that few of the old vineyards survive. The first vines were planted at North Adelaide by J. B. Hack in 1837 and George Stevenson in 1838. The first commercial planting was that of A. H. Davis, who obtained vine cuttings from the Busby collection and planted them at his farm in the Reedbeds (now Underdale, a western suburb of Adelaide) between 1838 and 1840. No trace remains of these historic vineyards.

Many of Australia's most prominent wine companies had their beginnings in the Adelaide environs—Penfolds at Magill, Hardys at Bankside, Hamiltons at Glenelg and Martins at Stonyfell. Many other vineyards were established, but have since disappeared under the pressures of urban expansion.

In the city itself there is not much apparent evidence of the wine industry which is so important to the state of South Australia. There are of course the odd patches of vines in the suburbs. Most hotels and restaurants have a good range of South Australian wines, but if the visitor wants to experience more of the well-known wines of the state he must travel to the vineyards and wineries themselves. And that is an enjoyable experience.

Angoves Pty Ltd, Tea Tree Gully

As in so many instances, the winemaking firm of Angoves was founded by an immigrant doctor—he was Dr W. T. Angove, born in Cambourne in Cornwall in May, 1854, the son of Thomas Angove, a captain of mines. He graduated from London Hospital and then practised medicine at Mildern Hall in England. In 1880 he married Emma Carlyon, and soon after migrated to South Australia.

Dr Angove began practice at Tea Tree Gully, near Modbury, some twelve miles north of Adelaide. He made an arrangement with the Reverend Archdeacon Farr to make wine in Farr's Brightlands cellars, which had been established before the 1870s. Angove's first vineyard, which consisted of five acres of shiraz and riesling, grown on the steep hills and kept weed free by canterbury hoes, was planted in 1884. He later built his own winery and transferred operations there. A correspondent of the S.A. *Register* who visited the vineyard at vintage in 1903 noted that Dr Angove produced 2,000 gallons of cabernet, which was a 'medium quantity of first class wine'.

Dr Angove's family believe that he started making wine for his family and friends to enjoy, and also for the medicinal use of his patients. Later Dr Angove distilled wine for brandy, which he called St Agnes. He chose the name after the village of St Agnes in his native Cornwall, and also in honour of the patron saint of purity.

Apart from his medical practice and his interest in winemaking Dr Angove had many hobbies. He held a commission in the Volunteer Mounted Rifles and was a very good shot; built an eighteen-foot yacht which he sailed; and was also interested in horticulture and photography. Dr Angove built up a famous collection of birds' eggs and for many years was President of the Ornithological Society. He died on 25 March, 1912 on a return journey to England.

Dr Angove's eldest daughter Miss H. S. Angove trained as a nurse, and then went to England where she did pioneering work in physiotherapy. His eldest son, Thomas Carlyon Angove, followed his father into the family business, and in 1910 moved the headquarters of the firm to Renmark on the Murray River. The firm's activities there are related in the section on the River areas.

At Tea Tree Gully Angove's have 240 acres of pedro ximenez, rhine riesling, shiraz, cabernet and grenache. The soil there is heavy loam. The average rainfall in the area is between twenty and twenty-five inches. Grapes are still processed there, and Dr Angove's original stone cellars are used. The vineyard is now rather old, however, and is feeling the effects of its years with reduced productivity.

Australian Wine Research Institute

Formal research into wine began in the early 1930s with the establishment of a Wine Research Unit at Adelaide University. In 1935 the unit was transferred to the Waite Research Institute at Glen Osmond on the outskirts of Adelaide. The Oenological Research Committee carried out research there with the support of the Commonwealth Scientific and Industrial Research Organisation for the next twenty years.

In 1955, to extend its functions, the Australian Wine Research Institute was formed. The Federal Government set up a Wine Research Trust Fund of $1,000,000 which had accrued from a special excise duty levied on fortifying spirit, for the purpose of paying an export bounty on fortified wines. The money was available as the bounty payments had ceased in 1947, and the newly created fund was used to establish the Wine Research Institute and to provide for its future income. The Institute is a registered company in South Australia, limited by guarantee and without share capital. Its income is augmented by grants from the Australian Wine Board and the CSIRO. It is controlled by a council, responsible to the Commonwealth Minister for Primary Industry and the Wine Board.

The new laboratories and pilot winery of the Wine Research Institute were opened at Glen Osmond in 1958. The buildings house chemical and microbiological laboratories and a library, and a fully equipped pilot winery. These facilities, with an increased staff, have allowed for an extensive research programme.

The late Mr John C. M. Fornachon, then Director of the Institute, wrote in 1965, 'In broad terms the research programme of the Institute has been concerned with a study of the factors which influence the quality of wine, with the objective of so controlling these factors as to improve quality.' Their research covers both specific problems and basic work on the chemistry of grapes and wines. An important function of the Institute has always been the provision of technical advice on oenological problems to members of the Australian wine industry. The Institute also supplies pure cultures of tested and selected yeasts to vignerons.

John Fornachon had a world-wide reputation for his work, and particularly for his research on flor sherry. Bryce Rankine, senior research officer, has published widely on many aspects of wine research. In

Adelaide Metropolitan

Vineyards of Adelaide Metropolitan

addition to his scientific activities Mr Rankine has been a wine judge for many years, and has written a most informative book on the Barossa Valley. The work of the Wine Research Institute has contributed considerably to the high overall standard of Australian wine.

Hamiltons Ewell Vineyards Pty Ltd, Glenelg

Richard Hamilton is one of the two claimants to the position of first winemaker in South Australia. He was born on 13 February, 1792 in Scotland.

Before he was twenty-one Hamilton had married, and he and his wife Ann produced nine children. On 7 June, 1837 he bought a Land Order, signed by Robert Torrens and Rowland Hill, which gave him the right to take up land south of Adelaide on his arrival there.

When the Hamilton family (except for son Henry who was born in 1826 and had been left in England at the Bluecoat School) landed at Port Adelaide in October, 1837, they took up a block of land and settled in the Marion district. The property, which was called 'Ewell' after his former home in Surrey, was near Glenelg, seven miles south-west of Adelaide, and only two miles from the sea. Hamilton must have begun clearing and planting the land with the vines he had brought from Cape Town almost immediately. His original planting was five acres but the vineyard grew in extent, until there were eventually 156 acres at Glenelg. It has been claimed that 1,200 gallons of wine were made at 'Ewell' by 1840.

The Hamiltons (like many other Australian wine-makers) developed a family tradition of sons following their fathers into the business. Henry Hamilton followed Richard (who died at the age of sixty) and was responsible for quite considerable new plantings in 1860. Henry's son Frank, was eventually followed by his grandson, Eric. Eric's son Robert is now general manager.

84

Today some of Richard Hamilton's original vines are still kept at 'Ewell' vineyards for historical purposes, as well as quite a number of those planted in 1860. The vineyards are now surrounded by suburban houses, and there is a drive-in cinema right in the middle of the vines. Such are the pressures of urban development that only forty-five acres of vines remain on the rich red-brown loam.

Hamiltons have, however, expanded in other areas. They own vineyards in the Barossa ranges, at Eden Valley and Springton, and also at Nildottie on the River Murray. Near Reynella, at Happy Valley Hamiltons own fifty-five acres which are planted with pedro and grenache. They are partners with the Adelaide Steamship Company in a large new enterprise of vineyard development near Sandy Hollow in the Upper Hunter Valley. Hamiltons also own the Old Mill Bond Store at Bridgewater, which was built in 1860 for the grinding of wheat into flour. The mill has an unusual waterwheel, which measures 36 feet in diameter and weights 17½ tons. Hamiltons have added spacious floors and use it for bond storage of maturing whisky and other spirits, and for the storage of wines.

The 'Ewell' vineyards have plantings of pedro and verdelho which are used in Hamiltons' most famous wine, their Ewell Moselle, which has been made since 1929.

A Russian winemaker, Mr Seeck, joined Hamiltons in 1929 bringing with him a strain of flor yeast which had been brought from Spain in 1913 by a Dr Harris of Rutherglen. Fermenting wines with flor yeast was a pioneering procedure at the time. Mr Seeck had studied winemaking at Heidelberg, Germany for seven years before his first visit to Australia in 1880. In 1903 he returned to Russia, but ran into disfavour with the secret police, and fled Russia eventually to return to Australia. He remained with Hamiltons as winemaker until his retirement in 1941. Mr Seeck died in Victoria in 1942 at the age of eighty-three.

In 1944 Hamiltons installed refrigeration to control temperatures in the winemaking process.

Hamiltons now make over one million gallons of wine, brandy and other spirits per year. Their winemaker is Maurice Ou, who has been with them for over twenty years. He is a Frenchman, and spent some years before World War II working in the vineyards of Nimes, Bordeaux and Beaune.

H. M. Martin and Son Pty Ltd, 'Stonyfell'

The 'Stonyfell' vineyards are located in the hills at Burnside, an attractive suburb five miles east of the Adelaide G.P.O. The name means 'mountain of stone' and is appropriate as the origins of the vineyard are associated with the nearby stone quarry.

The Martin family were not involved in the earliest days of viticulture at 'Stonyfell'. Henry Septimus Clark, at only fifteen years of age, planted the first in July, 1858, probably where the Stonyfell Quarry office now stands, about a mile from the Auldana vineyard. He had come to Australia from Birmingham with his father Francis, and mother Caroline, in 1850. Henry Clark's mother was a niece of Sir Rowland Hill, who became famous for the penny post. He was involved in the administration of the colony of South Australia in the 1830s and may have been responsible for the decision of the Clark family to emigrate.

The first year young Henry planted one and a half acres of mataro with the help of a friend, Robert Slape. They later planted 32½ acres, mostly Black Portugal, with some muscat, sercial and doradillo. Henry Clark built two-storeyed cellars of locally quarried stone, which are still in a good state of preservation. The winery was a lean-to adjoining the top floor. During the first years they had no machinery at all, and trod the grapes by foot power in the cool of the evening. The wine was stored in 300 gallon casks, some of imported timber and others of local red-gum, some of which are still in use.

Henry Clark was employed full time as secretary and engineer to the East Torrens District Council, and thus needed help in running the vineyards and cellar. He appointed Joseph Crompton, aged twenty-two, manager at £120 a year. In 1862 Henry Clark, his brother Algernon, and Crompton, formed a firm named Clark and Crompton. Two years later Henry Clark died. In 1866 Crompton married Susan Mary (Algernon's and the late Henry's sister), and in 1873 he bought out Algernon Clark's share, and became sole owner of 'Stonyfell'.

Although Crompton was producing 9,000 gallons of wine per year he was so affected by the economic reverses of the 1880s that he was forced to sell the property. In 1888 the Bank of Adelaide transferred 'Stonyfell' to Henry Dunstan, a quarryman and road contractor, with no interest in wine.

At this stage the Martin name came on the scene. Dunstan employed as secretary Henry Maydwell Martin, who had come from England in 1851 and married one of Henry Clark's sisters (thus making him also Crompton's brother-in-law). In 1892 Henry Dunstan decided to separate the quarries and vineyards of 'Stonyfell', and appointed Henry Martin manager of the new firm of H. Dunstan and Company, winegrowers. Martin planted new and better vines, and sold 'Stonyfell' wines interstate and overseas. Their wine won prizes in Paris and London.

In 1902 Henry Martin's younger son Ronald joined his father as partner at 'Stonyfell'. They bought the stock and plant from Dunstan, and leased the cellar and vineyards. The Martins traded under the name of H. M. & R. H. Martin Stonyfell vineyards until 1926, when they formed a limited liability company known as H. M. Martin and Son Ltd.

Ronald Martin was a friend of Leslie Salter, and in 1920 he purchased a third share in the 'Saltram' vineyard. W. Salter & Son ceased to be a partnership and became a limited liability company with Ronald Martin as chairman of directors and Leslie Salter as managing director. Henry Martin died in 1936 at the age of eighty-nine, and Ronald then became chairman of the Board. During this period improvements continued to be made at 'Stonyfell'.

When Leslie Salter resigned as manager of 'Saltram' vineyard in 1937, H. M. Martin and Son took over its management. The 'Saltram' wines were marketed in conjunction with the wines from 'Stonyfell'. In order to run the two vineyards efficiently as one unit 'Saltram' vineyard became a wholly owned subsidiary of H. M. Martin and Son. Ronald continued as chairman of H. M. Martin until he was killed in a car accident in 1950.

Michael Auld, great-grandson of Patrick Auld of 'Auldana', became general manager and then managing director. In 1962 Ronald Martin's son Henry M. Martin II became chairman and managing director.

The company owns 95 acres of vines at Langhorne Creek, planted with shiraz, cabernet and paulo (palomino). At the home vineyard, 'Stonyfell', there are thirty-six acres of tokay, sweetwater, pedro and grenache, grown on the deep red loam over limestone and slate soil. No new plantings are being made at 'Stonyfell', although replantings are being carried out constantly. H. M. Martin only grow about ten percent of the grapes they crush, the remainder being bought from other growers.

Most winemaking is now carried out at 'Saltram', and 'Stonyfell' is used mainly for maturing and bottling. The winery at 'Stonyfell' is terraced like an Italian vineyard, necessitating climbing from one level to another by ladders and steep companionways. The winery has a storage capacity of about one million gallons.

Winemaking at 'Stonyfell' has been under the control of Bryon Dolan since 1959, when he was transferred from his managership at 'Saltram' to become general manager of H. M. Martin. He can be credited with the high quality of their wines and especially the Stonyfell Metala wines.

In March, 1972 Dalgety Australia Pty Ltd, who had long been wine distributors, took over H. M. Martin and Co.

Penfolds Wines Pty Ltd, Magill

The wine giant, Penfolds, had its origins at Magill at the foot of the Mount Lofty Ranges.

It was at Magill that Dr Christopher Rawson Penfold, the founder of the firm, first planted his vineyard. The son of a Sussex vicar, the Reverend John Penfold, Dr Penfold was trained at St Bartholomew's Hospital and worked in private practice spending some years at Brighton. He married Mary Holt in 1835, and a few years later decided to try his fortune in the colonies. Before his departure, Dr Penfold arranged the purchase of a grant of land at Magill, for which he is reported to have paid £1,200, a large sum in those days.

Towards the end of 1844 Dr Penfold arrived with his wife and baby daughter, Georgina, at the port of Largs Bay in South Australia. They had made the then rather hazardous and uncomfortable voyage on the 350 ton barque Taglioni, under the command of Captain W. Black.

The family settled at Magill, and built a whitewashed stone cottage which they named 'The Grange'. As well as practising medicine and looking after his farm, Dr Penfold planted vine cuttings which he had brought out with their ends dipped in sealing wax to keep the sap in the vines until they were planted. He did not approve of the quality of the imported wine of the time so he made his own for the use of his patients with anaemia. Whether the wine was in fact any help to the anaemic is debatable, but this now discredited cure was 'the start of something big'.

Dr Penfold's acreage under vine increased, and he devoted more and more of his time to winemaking, with which he was assisted by his wife Mary and her servant, Ellen Timbrell. Mary Penfold's diary gives some details of winemaking at Magill, and lists some of their maturing wines, which included a white wine ('mixture Sweet Water and Frontignac') and a red wine 'mixture'.

Dr Penfold died at the age of fifty-nine in 1870 and was buried at St George's churchyard at Magill. He had become well known in the district and had been made first mayor of Burnside. The doctor, as befitting his profession, originally. believed primarily in the use of wine as medicine, but his winemaking ambitions soon outgrew these limited horizons. In his twenty-six years in the young colony Dr Christopher Rawson Penfold laid the basis of a veritable viticultural dynasty.

In 1861 Penfold's daughter, Georgina Ann, at the age of nineteen, married Thomas Francis Hyland, a 30-year-old Irishman and officer in the Victorian Civil Service at Castlemaine. At the time of Penfold's death the business was experiencing some financial problems associated with the shortage of capital necessary for expansion. After the death of his father-in-law Thomas Hyland conducted the management of family affairs with Mary Penfold. Between them they overcame their temporary difficulties. In 1880 he resigned his post to devote himself to the family business.

By 1881 Mary Penfold handed over the management of the vineyards to Joseph Gillard whose vineyards and cellars she had just bought. She continued to oversee affairs at Magill until her death in 1895.

Penfolds was becoming an important wine producer. It is recorded that the stock of wine at the Magill winery in 1881 was 107,000 gallons. At that time the total quantity for South Australia was about 312,000 gallons. Wine production continued to increase and by 1885 trade was flourishing between

Magill is the headquarters of the Penfold organization in South Australia and the centre of their blending operations.

Magill and all the states as well as New Zealand. The total land under grape was 1,000 acres. In their early days port and sherry were the main wines made, but the range was expanded to include table wines.

Thomas Francis and Georgina Hyland had four children. Of the two girls, Inez died at the age of twenty-eight, and Estelle married a Major Knight and lived in England. Frank Astor Hyland (born 1873) and Herbert Leslie Hyland (born 1875) spent some years at Melbourne Grammar School and finished their educations in England. In memory of their grandfather the brothers changed their name to Penfold Hyland. Frank entered the business in 1892, and spent three years in Europe studying winemaking. With Federation of the colonies in 1901 interstate trade was made easier, and Frank Penfold Hyland opened a branch office in Pitt Street, Sydney.

Joseph Gillard retired in 1905 and Leslie Penfold Hyland took over the management of the South Australian branch. He was active in bringing about the amendment of the 6 o'clock closing law to permit the drinking of wine with meals up to 8 p.m. During his years of managership the company established wineries at McLaren Vale, Nuriootpa and Eden Valley.

Frank supervised the expansion in New South Wales, which is discussed in that section. Vineyards and wineries continued to be added to the company's holdings. The McLaren Vale cellars, south of Adelaide, were bought in 1910, and worked in conjunction with the parent organization at Magill. The following year saw Penfold's entry into the Barossa Valley.

In 1913 T. F. Hyland, who had remained as a senior partner, retired and the business was formed into a company under the governing directorship of Frank Penfold Hyland. At about the same time Penfolds ventured into winemaking in the Murrumbidgee Irrigation Area. Over the years the expansion of the company continued; at Griffith, in the Hunter Valley and elsewhere.

Leslie Penfold Hyland died in 1940 after a long illness, and his elder son, Francis William, who succeeded him at Magill, died a few years later in 1946. Jeffrey, Leslie's second son, returned from active service and rejoined the company, becoming a director, in 1945. He later became managing director. Penfolds acquired 'Auldana' in 1943, and 'Modbury' and 'Kalimna' in 1945.

Frank Penfold Hyland died in 1948, at the age of seventy-four. He had controlled the company for almost fifty years, during the period of its growth from a comparatively small family business to one of the major Australian wine companies. Frank had been active for the good of the entire wine industry, and had been elected as first president of the Federal Viticultural Council.

Since the death of Frank Penfold Hyland the company has been administered by a Board of Directors. Penfolds became a public company in 1962. A lot of wine has been produced since Dr Christopher Rawson Penfold started to cure his anaemic patients at Magill.

Magill is the headquarters of the Penfold organization in South Australia. They have enormous storage capacity there—redwood storage tanks, concrete vats and oak casks. There is a vast and impressive array of winemaking machinery and equipment. However, with the expansion of Adelaide the land at Magill has become so valuable that there is little vineyard within the immediate vicinity of the winery.

'The Grange', the family's small old whitewashed stone cottage, is still maintained at Magill in its original condition and is used as a museum. Grange is now famous to wine lovers as the name of one of Australia's greatest and hardest-to-get wines, which is made at Magill. Dry whites, champagne base material, dry sherry and aperitif mixer drinks are also made at Magill.

Magill is the centre of blending operations in South Australia. With the huge diversity of vineyards and wineries owned by Penfolds there is a need to maintain uniform blends and styles, which is carried out at Magill.

Today Penfolds is a household name in Australia. They own many wineries and have thousands of acres under vine. There are Penfolds offices and distribution centres in every Australian state and in New Zealand. In 1968 Penfolds headquarters were moved from South Australia to Tempe in Sydney. Here, with a vast complex of buildings and equipment, is housed the company's head office and main bottling and distribution centre.

These are claimed to be the largest bottling cellars in Australia, and one of the most modern plants of its type in the world. The centre was built in 1957 at a cost in excess of two million dollars. The Tempe cellars have a storage capacity of 5 million gallons of wine—which could fill a row of bottles 1,420 miles long!

Penfolds Wines Pty Ltd, 'Auldana'

The vineyards at 'Auldana' have a history as old as the neighbouring Penfolds vineyards at Magill. Patrick Auld bought two sections of 230 acres in 1842 at the usual Crown price of £1 per acre. He planted some small plots with vines, and on his return from a visit to England in 1852 was impressed with their growth, and decided to devote himself to wine growing.

He laid out the vineyards, and planting was commenced in 1854. In 1861 Auld floated a company known as the South Auldana Vineyard Association, with a capital of £12,000. The Association's first vintage the following year yielded 3,000 gallons of red and white wine. This was the first attempt by an Australian wine producer to establish an independent organization to sell Australian wine, especially his own, in London.

The varieties at 'Auldana' then were primarily verdelho, with some tokay, muscat of Alexandria and a little gouais. At the southern part of the vineyards were grenache, more verdelho and donzelinho. There was also an acre of 'Carignan grafted with Carbonet'. The vines were all planted at ten feet by five, except the verdelho which was seven by seven. Auld did not consider it necessary to trellis or stake his 'luxuriant' grenache vines. The vineyard was hand weeded, as he regarded the horse hoe as 'at the best a slovenly and incomplete process'.

Patrick Auld was aware of the importance of classification of his grape varieties, and the qualities which each variety gave to the wine made from them. He also carried out some experimental grafting such as verdelho on muscat. The newspaper also reported that Auld did not use a press for his wines, but relied solely on a crushing mill and fermentation.

In 1897 new cellars were built at the foot of the hill, and under the management of Edmond Mazure, a Frenchman, 'Auldana' wines began to build up a good reputation. Mazure made some unique innovations. In 1903 he protected the vines from birds by tying kerosene tins filled with marbles to the vanes of windmills—which must have made sufficient din to frighten away the neighbours as well! The cellars are interesting, built with unusual stone columns and Norman arches. The original building still stands but has been modernized.

The 'Auldana' property was sold to Sir Josiah Symon, a notable Senator, barrister and one-time Chief Justice of South Australia, before Penfolds purchased it in 1944. The winery has been used for making champagne, but much of its present fame lies with the St Henri wines which are made at 'Auldana'. John Davoren, winemaker, must take much of the credit for these wines. The Davorens are another family with a long association with winemaking for Penfolds. John's father, Harold Davoren, was winemaker at 'Dalwood' in the Hunter many years ago and was responsible for some of the great wines

Penfolds made at 'Dalwood' earlier this century. John Davoren has more than adequately measured up to his father's stature as a winemaker.

Roseworthy Agricultural and Oenological College

Many readers will have noticed the almost monotonous regularity with which reference has been made to Roseworthy College graduates. This is the only centre in Australia where the science of oenology—winemaking—is taught. And it must be remembered that despite the art involved in making wine (and undoubtedly natural talent and feeling for wine are important) winemaking is a science, and an increasingly complex one. The sophisticated techniques and machinery used for the production of top class wines these days require a thorough technical knowledge and considerable skills. A great many Australian winemakers have studied at Roseworthy College, and it is significant that describing someone as a 'Roseworthy Graduate' means that 'he knows what he's about'.

The college is situated to the west off the road to Clare, about thirty-five miles north of Adelaide. This worthy institution was originally an agricultural college only, and a course in winemaking was established in addition to the agricultural course in 1936. Now students are required to study two years of general agriculture before specializing in wine for one year. They are also expected to do practical work in a winery.

Some vines are grown on the property, and the college has a winery which processes a few hundred tons of grapes annually. Their cellars are well equipped and have 18,000 gallons of oak storage, the casks being very fine specimens. In addition the college has a very good laboratory as a study of chemistry is part of the curriculum. From the 1920s Samuel Wynn bought the entire output of wine from the college.

Roseworthy has been an important force in changing the situation described by Dr Alexander Charles Kelly in *The Vine in Australia* in 1861: 'It is a notorious fact that modern science has not found its way into the cellar of the vigneron, who follows exactly the same routine his fathers have pursued for centuries.' Were the good doctor aware of the qualifications of modern Roseworthy graduates he would certainly approve!

Douglas A. Tolley Pty Ltd, Tea Tree Gully (Hope Valley)

Douglas A. Tolley was one of a family of brothers involved in the firm of Tolley, Scott and Tolley Ltd. In addition to his interest in the family firm Douglas A. Tolley developed his own vineyard and winery.

In 1893 Douglas Tolley established a vineyard and winery at Hope Valley in the foothills of the ranges at Hope Valley several miles eastwards of the St Peters distillery. A contemporary writer noted that it was a beautiful vineyard 'some hundred acres or more in extent . . . considered one of the show wineries of the state, and where he has made some very fine wines especially of the dry variety.'

In later years Douglas' son, Len, looked after the affairs of the vineyards and winery. He developed winemaking there on a substantial scale. The wine was mainly sold in bulk, to be bottled all over Australia.

The company has vineyards at Tea Tree Gully, Modbury and the Murray Valley. They also have a vineyard called 'Medlands Estate' at Dorrien near Tanunda in the Barossa Valley and a small winery there. It is used as a fermenting cellar only. The wine is then sent to the main winery at Hope Valley for maturing and bottling.

Len Tolley died in 1965, and his three sons, Peter, David and Reg, now look after the company's affairs. They have begun to sell their wine under their own label—Pedare, which name is composed of the first two letters of the christian names of the brothers.

Woodley Wines Pty Ltd, Glen Osmond

The Woodley Wines vineyard and cellar are located at Glen Osmond, four miles south-west of the city of Adelaide. Glen Osmond takes its name from Osmond Gilles, the first Treasurer of the colony of South Australia, who planted the original vineyard.

J. W. Bull, author of a book, *Early Experience of Colonial Life in South Australia,* obtained an option to buy the land where the vineyards are now located, in 1838. He decided, however, that the land was too stony for easy clearance and planting, and gave the option to his friend, Osmond Gilles, who planned to build a 'suburban residence' on the site. The next year silver-lead deposits (lead sulphide) were discovered there.

Gilles resigned as Treasurer, and leased the site to the Woodley Company which had been formed to mine the land, from which he received considerable royalties every year. He planted a vineyard at Glen Osmond in 1856, and appointed his friend J. W. Bull manager of the vineyard and winery. The vineyards were planted chiefly with shiraz, malbec and mataro, with some grenache and verdelho.

After a few years the ore was mined out and the miners departed, leaving a system of underground workings, approximately two and half miles long. Gilles found that these tunnels, which had occasional shafts for ventilation, maintained a natural temperature of 15°C and were ideal for the storage of wine.

The vineyard and winery changed hands several times after Osmond Gilles' death. First his nephew, Osmond Horne Gilles, inherited the property, and after his death it passed into the hands of Lewis W. Gilles. In 1892 Benno Weidenbach bought the concern, and extended the vineyard as far as Milne's Road. He also planted olive trees which are still standing on the northern and western boundaries of the vineyard. The President of the Vignerons' Association, Mr H. V. Pridmore, bought the property in 1900.

In 1924 the vineyards were sold for suburban building blocks, but the cellar itself was bought by Lieutenant Colonel David Fulton. He was the former commanding officer of the Third Light Horse during World War I. In 1926 Captain C. E. Hawker joined the firm, and Woodley Wines was floated as a limited liability company. Not much is known about Colonel Fulton, but he must have had considerable knowledge of winemaking. It was he who advised Bill Redman to make a light claret-style of wine, instead of the heavier, riper style that Redman had been making. Bill Redman regards Colonel Fulton as one of the great influences on his winemaking.

Tony Nelson, who was born in Vienna and became an expert winemaker, joined the company at the beginning of July, 1940. When Colonel Fulton retired Nelson became managing director of Woodleys.

Although Woodleys itself is located at Glen Osmond, it was in Coonawarra that Tony Nelson had his greatest influence. He acquired the present Wynn's Coonawarra Estate for Woodleys in 1946, long before Coonawarra rose to its present prominence, and sold it to Wynns in 1952. In that period Nelson did his best to sing the praises of the area to all who would listen.

In 1963 Woodley Wines Ltd was taken over by the Melbourne chain store company, Crooks National Holdings. Tony Nelson was retained as consultant, but he has since retired.

S. Wynn & Co Pty Ltd, 'Modbury Estate'

Wynn's Modbury Estate' vineyards are in the Modbury/Golden Grove area amongst the Adelaide foothills, a distance of thirteen miles north-east of the G.P.O., in latitude 34.9 degrees south, about 550 to 700 feet above sea level, and approximately twelve miles from the sea.

Samuel Wynn was responsible for the purchase of 561 acres which was then the 'Surrey Farm'. It is a gentle undulating property on the western slopes of the Mount Lofty Range. The main soil types are red and chocolate loams over limestone, slate schists and ironstone gravel, with small areas of black soil. Vine plantings were arranged on the basis of suiting the variety to the soil type—the limestone area being planted with sherry grapes and the quartzite with white wine varieties.

The planting and cultivation of a new vineyard on a large scale was a complex and costly task. J. L. (Jock) Williams joined the firm as vineyard manager at 'Modbury', and the success of the operation was primarily due to him. He had previously been in charge of the winemaking section at Roseworthy Agricultural College.

Of the total holding of 561 acres, 500 acres is suitable for viticulture, the remaining area being too steep for economical cultivation. Of the 500 acres 443 are planted to vines, with 57 acres being taken up by headlands, waterways, creek, workshop and domestic areas. Many varieties of vine were planted experimentally, but the most suitable proved to be pedro, semillon, rhine riesling, palomino, trebbiano, shiraz, cinsaut, mataro, grenache and doradillo.

The climate is temperate, with the average rainfall at 'Modbury' being 21½ inches, varying from 17 inches (1954) to 29.9 inches (1947). After many years of experimentation Wynns showed that a single critical irrigation of three acre inches applied in summer has doubled the yield of an average rainfall season and trebled the yield of a season of below average rainfall. When the rainfall of any year is less than 19 inches Wynns have shown that a watering of three inches at the critical time is enough to transform the situation from 'dry' to good moisture conditions. In seasons above 25 inches rainfall, watering is not necessary.

Acting on this information Wynns constructed a dam across a creek conveniently located between the two main vineyards in 1963. The creek flows only in winter after moderate rain. The dam's capacity is 22 million gallons which is sufficient to apply a single watering of three acre inches to 228 acres of vineyard. The dam was designed by the Water Conservation Branch of the Department of Agriculture.

A system of portable aluminium irrigation tubing equipped with sprinklers was installed. The water was secured at a capital cost of £137 ($274) per million gallons, and the increased grape tonnage obtained in the 1964 vintage, as a result of the single season's watering, almost paid for the investment.

Since 1947 all Wynn's plantings have been on the contoured plan, as this saves about 25 percent of the rainfall which is lost, together with some good topsoil, on the old square planted areas.

Vineyard cultural operations are completely mechanized. Vintage begins in early March with rhine riesling, and is continued until late April. The table wines varieties are picked first, when the acid is high, and the sherry and dessert wines later. The grapes are transferred to the winery at Magill, and with the aid of mechanization, not more than one hour elapses between picking and processing. The best wine is sold under the Modbury Estate label with the remainder being used in blends.

Century-old cellars at 'Sevenhill' vineyard, eighty miles north of Adelaide, where most grapes go into making altar wine for sacramental purposes, and a small quantity of dry red table wine.

From mid-February until the end of April is vintage time,
when brightly-clad pickers enliven the vineyards of the
Barossa Valley, S.A.

We have not yet discussed the history of the Wynn family who have contributed so much to Australian winemaking.

Shlomo (or Solomon) Weintraub was born in a village in Russian-occupied Poland in 1892. The period following his birth was not auspicious for Jews, as they were a suppressed and persecuted minority in Poland at that time. Shlomo's family had a long but modest connection with winemaking—they made wine principally from raisins for use in Jewish religious ceremonies, and when Shlomo grew up he took part in the family business. When he was twenty he married Chava, and the young couple decided to leave Poland quickly because Shlomo's call up for military service was imminent. On 12 November, 1913 Shlomo and his bride disembarked at Port Melbourne, with a total worldly wealth of four gold sovereigns.

One of Shlomo's first actions in his new country was to change the name Weintraub (which appropriately enough means wine grape) to Wynn.

By the end of 1918, after various menial jobs, Sammy used his hard-earned capital of £135 to buy a little wine shop in Bourke Street. It was an immediate success. He sold good wine but his fortified wines were far more in demand than table wine, the most fashionable being Madeira.

Samuel Wynn did not stop with this first success, and in 1920 became the proprietor of a restaurant, the 'Cafe Denat', which he had been supplying with wine. He took into partnership the head waiter, George Hildebrandt who knew the business. In 1928 Wynn met Rinaldo Massoni who agreed to take over the 'Denat', but changed the cuisine to Italian and the name to the 'Florentine'. The new restaurant was an immediate success.

Another facet of the wine trade in which Sammy had become involved in 1922 was wholesaling. This soon dwarfed the retail operation, and was based on the same principle of sound wine at low cost. He made regular wine buying trips to South Australia, often chartering a two-seater aeroplane, then a rather dangerous and novel exercise. He became acquainted with the Roseworthy Agricultural College, and to help the College decided to buy its output. He continued to do this and to help the College in other ways.

In about 1925 Wynn discovered how to make vermouth by the infusion of various herbs with a base wine. He adopted the marque 'Boronia' for his new product. In this same year Samuel Wynn became involved in winemaking at Magill.

In 1933 with the Depression at its height Samuel went to London in an attempt to resume the export trade in wine with the United Kingdom. Southard & Co placed a small order, and by 1939 he was exporting 2,000 hogsheads of wine annually to the United Kingdom. But the war put a stop to these exports.

Samuel had three sons—two of them were doctors, and the third, David was the managing director of S. Wynn & Co Pty Ltd; Samuel Wynn being the governing director. David became the motivating force behind the company's progress and he began a marketing policy designed to make the consumption of wine a pleasure to be enjoyed by all. At the beginning of the fifties the Wynn organization began to market wine in half-gallon returnable flagons. Their aim was to produce and sell good quality, economical quaffing wines, which could be enjoyed without any of the traditional mystique and fuss associated with wine drinking. Wynn's advertising stressed the everyday use of wine with food. Although Wynns were certainly not solely responsible for the wine boom of the sixties, they did play a significant part in having wine accepted as an everyday pleasure.

It was to ensure a supply of suitable grapes for their flagons that the 'Modbury Estate' was established. Wynns later expanded by establishing themselves at Coonawarra, and then at Yenda in New South Wales.

The success story of Samuel Wynn is an example of what can be achieved by a combination of natural talent and the opportunities of a developing country. The creation of such a valuable enterprise from virtually nothing in 1913 is certainly an admirable feat.

The headquarters of the firm are in Melbourne. In 1970 Wynns became a public company, and were listed on the Adelaide stock exchange. In February 1972 the company was the subject of a takeover, and is now in the hands of the giant brewing concern, Tooheys Limited.

Australian Wines Pty Ltd, S. Wynn & Co Pty Ltd, Romalo, Magill

Romalo is a trade name known throughout Australia for sparkling wines and champagne. The company, now a subsidiary of Wynns, is located adjacent to 'Auldana' at Magill. The chequered history of the organization began with Leon Edmond Mazure, a French cook and former manager of 'Auldana'.

In 1919 Mazure decided to go into business on his own account, and bought the Longbottom property of about twenty acres where Rosslyn Park is now situated. He called his property the 'La Perouse' cellars, and began to make champagne in two stables in which he installed shaking tables. Mazure later built the winery at Romalo.

Hurtle Walker, who ended up as manager of the company and a renowned champagne maker, was associated with the property from the beginning.

Mazure, who was then at 'Auldana', offered Hurtle a job when he was fourteen. He began as errand boy, buying cigarettes and newspapers for Mazure. When he was eighteen Hurtle was promoted to the sparkling wine cellars, where he spent the next three years working under a Frenchman named Duray. When Duray decided to return to France because of ill health Hurtle Walker was virtually left in charge of the sparkling wine cellars, at the age of twenty-one.

World War I broke out, and Walker joined the artillery in January, 1915.

After his war service he went back to 'Auldana' in 1919, and was invited to go with Mazure when he set up his own winemaking operation.

Bertram Reginald Collins, a New Zealander, became associated with the enterprise in about 1920. Collins was responsible for coining the name Romalo, which was a combination of his daughter Roma's name, with the name Malo, who was the daughter of his friend Charlie Watts. Mazure's destination is obscure, but in 1920 the property was taken over by Collins.

Leo Buring came to the company as advisor for two years and it was he who brought the culture for Romalo's sparkling wines from France in 1919. The same culture has been used ever since.

In 1925 Reginald Collins, a charming *bon vivant*, talked Samuel Wynn into investing heavily in the company. About the same time a large winery was added for making table wine for export to England. Collins was somewhat reckless with his expenditure, and sank the company deeply into debt.

In 1926 Hurtle Walker was appointed manager of the company then known as Australian Wines Export Pty Ltd. At that stage 200 hogsheads, mainly of fortified wine, were being exported to London each month.

By 1927 the beginnings of the great Depression were having their effects. The export market collapsed with the withdrawal of the Government bounty of one shilling a gallon, and badly hit Collins' company. The company came under the control of a Receiver and stocks and equipment were sold at any price. After the liquidation of the company Collins returned to New Zealand.

Samuel Wynn undertook the rehabilitation of the company, and on 20 December, 1929 the first meeting of directors of the new company was held in Melbourne. Samuel Wynn became majority share-holder in 'Australian Wines Ltd'. The export trade was relinquished as Wynns could find sufficient markets for the wine in Melbourne.

In the late twenties Wynns built a winery in the Barossa Valley midway between Nuriootpa and Angaston. It was known as Wynvale, the name being coined by Reginald Collins. Cyril Pollit was in charge there. Wine made there was taken by lorry to Magill where it was blended for export. After the debacle of 1927, Wynns were forced to sell, and in 1930 the winery was bought by S. Smith & Sons Ltd (Yalumba Wines). S. Smith operated it as a subsidiary, the Vinters Co Ltd, a crushing and storage plant.

Wynns continued to increase the still-winemaking at Magill. By 1935 more than 2,000 tons of grapes were being crushed there each vintage, and storage for more than half a million gallons had been installed.

By 1944 the output of Australian Wines Ltd reached 10,000 bottles of sparkling wine per year. Sammy Wynn hired Ken Ward, a Roseworthy graduate, to manage Wynn's South Australian operations, and so free Hurtle Walker to devote himself to the manufacture of sparkling wines. Walker was appointed a director with Lloyd Babidge, David and Samuel Wynn and Frank G. Herman.

Hurtle Walker had married Ellen Eliza Gratton in 1923, and they had two children. Their daughter Joyce worked in the office of the winery before her marriage to Don King, a geologist. Hurtle's son Norman was educated at St Peter's College, and then studied at Roseworthy Agricultural College. On his graduation in 1951 Norman began work in the Romalo cellars. For several years at each vintage Norman went to Coonawarra to assist Wynns.

In 1953 a further underground cellar was built of 10,000 dozen capacity, and yet another of equal size was built in 1959.

Hurtle Walker retired from the managership in September 1963, although he remained actively associated with the firm. Norman followed his father and was appointed manager on the latter's retire-ment. Jack Ludbrook has summed up Hurtle Walker's contribution to Australian winemaking very well: 'With a lifetime of hard work over long hours, and an ever-willing hospitality to callers . . . , Hurtle Walker has contributed much to the tradition of the Australian vigneron. His strength of character and firmness of purpose, his able management and pro-gressive outlook, have always been combined with a willingness to undertake the humdrum task, the common round of duty . . . . At the same time his quiet twinkling good humour has always shone out with something of the sparkle of the champagne which he has spent a lifetime producing.'

The well-known champagne from Romalo is made by the traditional *methode champenoise* (see glossary). The cellars there have the capacity to store over half a million bottles of champagne. Pink champagne, sparkling burgundy and sparkling moselle are also made.

The winery at Romalo makes champagne and other sparkling wines for other companies, which is sold under the other companies' labels. In some cases the other company or merchant provides Wynns with the base wine for making into champagne.

Wynns also continue to make still wines at their Magill winery. Grapes are taken there from the Modbury vineyards (eight miles away) at vintage time. They are crushed and fermented, and the wine is processed and conditioned, and kept before being transported to the firm's main storage cellars in St Kilda Road, Melbourne, for final conditioning and bottling.

The Southern Vales

The area known as the Southern Vales has been established for more than a century as an important centre for vine cultivation and winemaking. The Southern Vales are located south of Adelaide, on the road running to the coastal resort, Victor Harbour, with some of the vineyards as close as thirteen miles from the city. A visit to the area is a thoroughly enjoyable experience, beginning with a drive through the urban sprawl which stretches south from the city of Adelaide in a ribbon development following the road, until just beyond Morphett Vale where the green rolling hills are dotted with massive old blue gums. There are magnificent views over the undulating slopes and flats of pasture land, orchards and vineyards, which stretch between the Willunga escarpment of the Mt Lofty Ranges and the sea at St Vincents Gulf. About twenty-five miles from Adelaide, across the Onkaparinga River, is McLaren Vale, an area which has been singularly blessed for the making of good wine without the problems of frost, drought and pests which beset vignerons elsewhere.

Recently the name 'Southern Vales' has fallen into disfavour, as it can easily be confused with the Southern Vales Co-operative winery. Dan Murphy suggests that a more accurate name would be Reynella-McLaren Vale, as the Reynella district includes most of the Morphett Vale vineyards.

The suitability of the area for viticulture was recognized long ago, when, soon after the colony of South Australia was proclaimed, John Reynell planted the first vines there in 1838. The vales are well suited for fruit growing, and particularly suitable for grape growing. The climate is temperate with a reasonably mild summer, cool vintage and freedom from frost. The rainfall is fairly reliable at twenty-two inches, and droughts are not common. The soils vary considerably, from pure sand through sandy loam, limestone, ironstone, to rich alluvial soil in the valleys and heavy red clay on the eastern flats. In addition, the area is relatively free of pests.

The wines of Reynella and Tintara have been widely known and successful for many years while the wines from the neighbouring McLaren Vale were enjoyed, though quite anonymously, in blends made by the big wine companies. Much of the McLaren Vale wine was also exported in bulk to the United Kingdom. In recent years, since the success of companies such as Ryecroft, Seaview, Osborne and the McLaren Vale Wine Pty Ltd (formed under the leadership of Jim Ingoldby) these wines, to quote Walter James, 'are flying under their own colours'. And most successfully, too.

Thomas Hardy and Sons Limited, Tintara

On 14 August, 1850 the sailing ship *British Empire*, skippered by Captain McEwin, arrived at Port Adelaide with 243 passengers including Thomas Hardy, a twenty-year-old farmer from the village of Gittisham near Honiton, Devon. He was first employed by John Reynell, on whose vineyard he spent about one year, before going to a cattle property at Normanville, south of Adelaide. There he was infected with 'gold fever' and made his way to the Victorian diggings, where he was soon arrested for not having a digger's licence, spent the night in the lock-up and was fined £1. Hardy did fairly well at the Forest Creek field, not from gold, but from a butchering business, for which he drove cattle from the Normanville station to the gold fields.

After eighteen months he returned to Adelaide, where he married his cousin, Joanna Hardy of Somerset, a fellow passenger from the *British Empire*. In 1853 Hardy invested his newly-acquired earnings in a property beside the River Torrens, not far from Adelaide, which he called 'Bankside'. Hardy worked hard, and by 1861 he had planted sixteen and a half acres with vines and stone and orange trees. 1857 was the first vintage at 'Bankside', the wine was matured in a cellar (which held three 100 gallon casks) that Thomas Hardy dug out in the evenings after his day's work. By 1859 he shipped two hogsheads to England—possibly the first export of wine in any quantity from the colony.

From then on Hardy went ahead by leaps and bounds—he extended his holdings under vine in 1863 to thirty-five acres, and produced ever increasing amounts of wine. His output doubled between 1863 and 1864, and quadrupled to 14,000 gallons in 1865. By then he was buying about half the grapes processed from other growers, and blending them to make the sorts of wine he wanted, thus laying the basis for Hardy's winemaking practices for the next century.

A major milestone in the development of the Hardy enterprise was his purchase in 1876 of the 'Tintara' vineyard, about five miles north-east of McLaren Vale, which had been developed by Dr Alexander Charles Kelly. Dr Kelly rates an important place in our wine history. He wrote significant books on wine, *The Vine in Australia* (1861) and *Wine Growing in Australia* (1867), and believed in a scientific approach to winemaking. He was also responsible for the planting of sauvignon blanc vines. Interestingly, these vines were contour planted—evidence of his advanced ideas on the prevention of soil erosion. Dr Kelly, a Scot, had practised as a physician in Adelaide before he planted his first vineyard, 'Trinity', about 1842 to make wine for its medicinal value. He then persuaded some influential Adelaide men — Sir Samuel Davenport, Sir Thomas Elder, Sir Edward Stirling and Mr R. W. Barr-Smith to invest in the Tintara Vineyard Company, and purchased a 700 acre property at

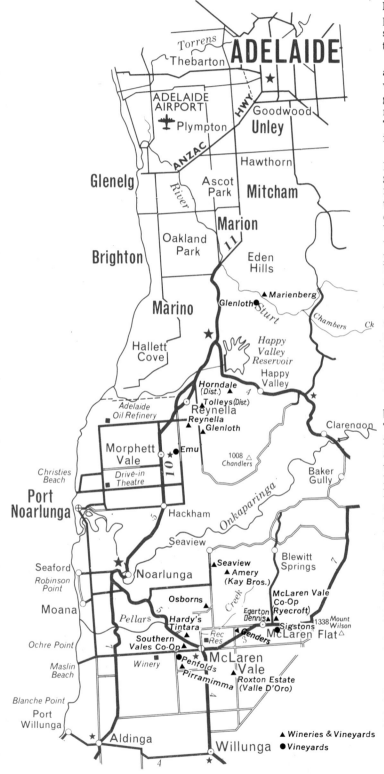

Vineyards of the Southern Vales

McLaren Vale, where a settler named Manning had planted vines in the fifties. The first meeting of shareholders of the new company sought a name for the vineyard, and chose 'Tintara'.

'Tintara' was affected by the Depression of the 1860s, and was bankrupt by 1873 despite its full cellars of wine. Dr Kelly may have been a good doctor, and a good winemaker, but he was not a successful business-man. The only bidder for the bankrupt company was Thomas Hardy—and he recovered the purchase price in the first year from the sale of wine in stock.

'Tintara's' new owner set to work to develop the property—Hardy cleared more land, planted good grape varieties, and conducted far-sighted experiments in contour cultivation to stop soil erosion. He expanded the cellars and built accommodation for his employees. In 1878 he bought the disused McLaren Vale flour mill and converted it into a winery, which became known as the Mill Cellars. Three years later Hardy built a 'substantial' bluestone building in Currie Street, Adelaide, for a head office and bottling cellars.

This building was the headquarters of the company, with the basement used for the production of champagne, until 1961 when it was sold, and later demolished. A further development was the purchase in 1884 of 480 acres adjoining 'Tintara'. He was helped in the establishment of the new vineyard by J. G. Kelly, the doctor's son, and Thomas Hardy Nottage, a Hardy nephew.

The business continued to grow at such a rate that by 1887 Thomas Hardy took his three sons James, Thomas Nathaniel and Robert into partnership, forming the company known as Thomas Hardy and Sons Limited. James specialized in sale and distribu-tion, T.N. in management and Robert in winemaking. In 1893 an impressive new cellar was built at Mile End, about one mile west of Adelaide, to provide additional storage capacity of 80,000 gallons and an up-to-date laboratory. And still the company grew, until by 1895 they were the largest winemakers in the colony, with a vintage of 350,000 gallons.

The Hardy company was now well on the way toward the position of prominence it still holds today. When Federation abolished duties on wine between the states, the family opened up branches in Sydney (where they erected one of the first electric bulb advertising signs in Australia), Melbourne and other centres. A major set-back in their progress was a disastrous fire in October, 1904 which destroyed the 'Bankside' winery.

Thomas Hardy died in January 1912, two days short of his 82nd birthday. Two of his sons, James and Thomas Nathaniel, had predeceased him, leaving only Robert and the next generation to carry on the business. Thomas Hardy was an exceptionally able and energetic man, and by the time he died could look back on a full and happy life during which he personally built up a vast and successful business enterprise. He was active in a wider sphere also—

as president of the Vigneron's Association he threw his support into the fight against phylloxera; he participated in the agitation for Federation, and was elected president of the Chamber of Manufactures. The people of McLaren Vale honoured Thomas Hardy with the erection of a memorial in the centre of the town, which is believed to be the only such monument to a winemaker in Australia. Undoubtedly, however, the most important memorial to Hardy is the company he created and the fine wines it has made and continues to make.

The family carried on, and expanded to Waikerie on the River Murray and Dorrien in the Barossa. As new steps were made, old links were broken. 'Bankside' was sold in the early twenties as the land had become very valuable with the growth of the city. In 1926 'Tintara' had outlived its usefulness as a winery, and activities there were transferred to the old Mill Cellars. By this time Tom (Thomas Mayfield) Hardy had gradually taken over control of the business from his uncle Robert, who died in 1927. Tom built up a fine reputation as a wine man, but was killed prematurely in an air crash in 1938.

Robert's second son Kenneth T. Hardy took over management at the head office, and became a prominent identity in South Australian wine and commercial circles.

Tom M. Hardy's three sons are now all actively associated with the company—Tom is managing director, with Jim (of sailing fame) in charge in Sydney and David playing an important part in the company's viticultural activities. Kenneth's son Robert is another member of the fourth generation in an executive position with the firm.

Now there about 800 Tintara acres at McLaren Vale, of which about 320 acres are under vine. A wide variety of grapes are gown including cabernet sauvignon, sauvignon blanc, rhine riesling, grenache and malbec; and lesser varieties such as doradillo which are given supplementary spray irrigation as necessary. The soil is largely sand or light loam over limestone and clay, with some ironstone.

The old Mill Winery is large and well equipped, processing considerable quantities of grapes bought from local growers in addition to those from the company's own vineyards. The Mill Cellar is a show place; set in immaculate gardens with fascinating reminders of the old days amongst all the modern machinery. The McLaren Vale cellar is noted especially for its dry reds, Hardy's premium whites largely being made at Dorrien in the Barossa.

Hardy & Sons used to sell under the Tintara label, but have since realized the value of the Hardy name and gradually featured it on their labels. The fame of Hardys has developed largely from their exceptional ability in blending wines, rather than from their straight wines (although Bob Hagley, winemaker at McLaren Vale, has made some fine straight dry reds). In any discussion of the Hardy blends pride of place must be given to Roger Warren, whom Max Lake has described as 'that master of blenders', and who ranks with Maurice O'Shea and Colin Preece as the greatest wine blenders of the century. As technical manager for Hardys, Roger Warren was responsible for the high quality and often greatness of their wines, which considerably enhanced the Hardy reputation. Dick Heath, another name to be reckoned with, took over as technical manager after Roger Warren's sudden death in 1959. Heath graduated from Roseworthy College in 1941, at a time when Henry Martin of Stonyfell and Phil Tummel now of Tolley Scott & Tolley were students, and Tom Angove was a year ahead of them. Now a director of the firm, Dick Heath has been with Hardys since the early 1930s, and technical manager since 1960.

Thomas Hardy and Sons Pty Ltd are by no means standing still. They have their headquarters in Adelaide, with branches in every state of Australia and several agencies overseas. They are expanding into new areas such as Keppoch near Coonawarra.

Walter Reynell & Sons Ltd, Reynella

The Reynell name goes back to the very beginnings of the wine industry in South Australia, when John Reynell planted some of the first vines in the infant colony, in the area which was later to bear his name. This pioneer of the grape was born at Ilfracombe in 1809; of a Devonshire farming family.

Reynell arrived in South Australia two years after the founding of the colony. Soon after his arrival he married one of his fellow passengers from the *Surrey*, Mary Lucas, the daughter of an admiral. The newly-weds settled on a property thirteen miles south of Adelaide and three miles east of St Vincent's Gulf which John had bought from the South Australian Company in London. He was primarily interested in farming—sheep, cows, wheat and potatoes, but did plant some vine cuttings which he had brought with him from the Cape of Good Hope.

In 1845 Reynell obtained a supply of vine cuttings from John Macarthur in New South Wales to enlarge his vineyards. A letter from Macarthur's son, William, which is in the Reynell archives, names prices for riesling, cabernet sauvignon, malbec, gouais, dolcetto, constantia, verdelho, tokay and others. The prices were mostly 20/- per 1,000. These cuttings were planted on the banks of the Panalatinga Creek, where they were sheltered with almond trees. It seems that was the time when Reynell decided to concentrate on winemaking, for that year he excavated the Cave Cellar, the oldest of the underground cellars still in use in Australia.

Reynell never had much ready cash, and so in 1854 he sold part of his extensive holdings as the site for a town. Blocks were surveyed and sold by auction to form the township of Reynella. That year also saw

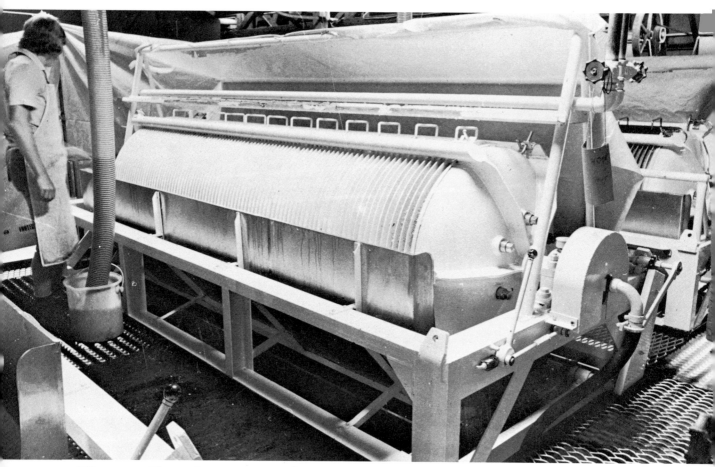

Wilmes press, 'Chateau Leonay', Barossa Valley, S.A.

the birth of John's son Walter, who was to build most successfully on the foundations laid by his father. John Reynell died in June, 1876 at the age of sixty-seven, and must always be given the credit for his pioneering work in the South Australian wine industry, and his tenacity in keeping on going through the many difficult periods he encountered.

The Reynells are one of the oldest of the many families in which the management of the winemaking business was handed on from generation to generation. Walter Reynell was intelligent, energetic and a hard worker, and built up the family fortunes with the creation of the firm now known as Walter Reynell & Sons Ltd. Walter was well known in Adelaide business circles by the time he died in April 1919.

The two world wars were responsible for the deaths of two generations of Reynell heirs.

Thus for some years the only Reynell blood in the firm was its chairman, Ian Thomas, grandson of Walter Reynell's sister, while Colin Haselgrove, well-known winemaker and yachtsman, was managing director. In April, 1970 Reynella joined the contemporary trend and was taken over by Hungerford

Hill Vineyards Pty Ltd, of which the petroleum company H. C. Sleigh is a twenty percent shareholder.

There are 430 acres under vine in the beautiful rolling country at Reynella, with another sixty acres at McLaren Flat. The soils vary considerably, although the subsoil is basically limestone. The main soil groups are fairly shallow red sandy loam over lime-stone, and a heavy gravelly clay loam over marl subsoil. Irrigation is not used, and they rely on the natural rainfall, which is usually about twenty-two inches per year. The climate is most suitable for viticulture, with moderate temperatures, and beneficent sea breezes from the nearby St Vincent's Gulf in summer.

For many years Reynella was proud of having one of the largest South Australian acreages of cabernet sauvignon, which now stands at seventy-two acres, and is being increased with new plantings. Of the other red wine varieties a large proportion of shiraz is grown, with mataro, grenache and malbec also. For sherry and white wines Clare riesling, gouais, pedro and palomino are cultivated, with some white hermitage and doradillo which are being replaced with better varieties as they become economically over-age. The company purchases almost two-thirds of the grapes processed from other growers.

The charming old main cellar building is still the centre of operations, although a separate bottling plant was installed several years ago, and has since been considerably extended. They have in excess of 100,000 gallons storage capacity, which is not large in terms of the Barossa Valley, but Reynella claims that this scale enables them to exercise greater control of quality. John Reynell's Cave Cellar is still used; it holds about 40,000 gallons of selected wines, including a museum of special reds. The winery houses a distillation tower for brandy making, as well as some modern equipment, including a refrigeration system.

Reynella is renowned for its reds, which are called claret and burgundy. They also produce flor and other sherries, brandy, port, good red flagon wines, and recently white table wines.

Edwards & Chaffey Pty Ltd, 'Seaview' Winery

The vineyards now known as 'Seaview' are over 120 years old, a considerable period in terms of Australia's relatively short history. The property is east of Noarlunga in a hollow of the hills which divide Morphett Vale from McLaren Vale, just south of the Onkaparinga River. The 'Seaview' vineyards have passed through the hands of several owners since they were established as part of the Hope Farm by George Pitches Manning many years ago.

In 1948 the property was bought from Mr G. W. Kay by Messrs. Ferguson and Chaffey, the latter owners were Messrs. Ferguson and Chaffey, the latter a Roseworthy oenology graduate and grandson of one of the pioneering brothers who established the Murray irrigation settlements. Three years later F. H. Edwards, who had extensive viticultural experience in the Marion district, replaced Mr Ferguson in partnership with Benjamin Chaffey. Gradually the surrounding area became known as 'Seaview', taking the name of a neighbouring estate which was once the summer residence of Sir Samuel Way, the Chief Justice of South Australia. Now, of course, Seaview is well known as the label under which Edwards and Chaffey's wines are sold. The 'Seaview' vineyards came under new ownership once more when the British company Allied Breweries, in association with Tooheys of N.S.W., took over from Edwards and Chaffey in early 1971, and eventually Tooheys became the sole owners.

The 'Seaview' vineyard is five miles from the coast of St Vincent's Gulf, and 500-550 feet above sea level. The average annual rainfall is twenty-three inches, which falls mostly in winter, with the odd inch or so about the end of January. The summers are fairly mild, with very rare spring frosts. These climatic conditions, with a long cool ripening period and useful sea breezes are kind to the growing grapes.

The gravelly soils are rather poor and low yielding, a similarity with French and other European vineyards. The shallow top soils consist predominantly of ironstone impregnated gravel, over a subsoil of chalky soft marl. With the help of the Conservation Branch of the S.A. Department of Agriculture, Edwards and Chaffey treated by hand the areas worst affected by soil erosion, and also applied modern contouring techniques. A new type of higher trellising was also gradually installed.

There are about 180 acres under vine at 'Seaview', of which about fifty acres are of cabernet sauvignon, yielding about 11,000 gallons per year. There are also substantial areas of rhine riesling and sauvignon blanc, the latter, though famous in Bordeaux is an unusual variety in Australia. Palomino, pedro ximenez and albillo are used for sherry, while the plantings of shiraz, mataro and grenache are used with the cabernet for reds.

A feature of the winery are six wall plaques, sculpted from vat timber, mounted on the heads of 1,000 gallon casks in the front cellar. These jarrah plaques, which each depict one of the stages of wine production are the work of Professor Paul Beadle, Dean of the Faculty of Fine Arts in Auckland, New Zealand, who also created the American War Memorial in Canberra. The winery also features paintings by Kenneth Jack and David Dridan, and a stainless steel fountain by Richard Howard which portrays a trellised vine. It is good to see the natural beauty of the area complemented by the art of man.

Glenloth Wines Pty Ltd, O'Halloran Hill

Nowhere but in Australia could the name of a wine company be taken from a racehorse, and this came about in the following manner. A Mrs Horne planted a small vineyard in 1892, the year a five year old horse called Glenloth won the Melbourne Cup at fifty to one, thus inspiring Mrs Horne to name her vineyard after the horse.

The 'Glenloth' vineyard was in the O'Halloran Hill district, a few miles south of Adelaide. It was behind Reynella, near the Happy Valley Reservoir. At the time it was planted Reynella had already been established for many years, and probably prompted the beginning of Glenloth.

In 1921 Mr and Mrs. J. R. Harper Robertson bought the vineyard; and they built a winery in the centre of the vineyard during the following years. They made their first wine in 1923, and went on to win many awards for their range of table and dessert wines.

In 1942, to cope with the expanding volume of business, a winery and distillery situated at Happy Valley, a few miles from the original 'Glenloth' property, were purchased. The newly acquired premises were modernized, and subsequently most of the winemaking activity was transferred there. 'Glenloth' was made into a private limited company with the Harper Robertsons as Directors. Subsequently their son, J. R. W. (Bob) Robertson looked after the winemaking and development of the company.

In 1966 Seager Evans and Co of London took over Glenloth Wines. Much of the company's wine is sold in bulk in London. At present all the grapes processed are purchased from other growers, but the company has bought 400 acres in the Keppoch area of south-eastern South Australia. These will be planted at the rate of 100 acres per year. Morgan Yeatman, a well-known winemaker who worked at Quelltaler, went to 'Glenloth'. In 1971 Glenloth Wines was taken over once more, the first 'double' in contemporary times. Tooheys Ltd, Sydney-based brewers, are now the sole owners.

Ryecroft Vineyards Pty Ltd

'Ryecroft', now one of the leading vineyards in the McLaren Vale district, was originally a pig farm.

Frederick Wilkinson gave up his job with the bank of South Australia and bought the farm in 1884; two years later he planted vines there. His first vintage, a burgundy-type wine, was 1895, and he followed it with bigger plantings and better wine. Wilkinson's son was to have inherited and carried on the running of the winery, but he was killed in the First World War. Thus in 1919 Frederick sold the property to James C. Ingoldby, lately returned from service in France with the first A.I.F., and his father-in-law, T. C. Walker.

The new owners, with the help of winemaker Aub Chapman, doubled the acreage and increased storage to 200,000 gallons. For about five of their early years of winemaking Leo Buring came to 'Ryecroft' at vintage to give advice. 'Ryecroft' mainly produced sweet wine which was sold in bulk for the export trade.

Jim's elder son Peter studied at Roseworthy College, and it was intended that he would take over the winemaking. World War II intervened, however, and Peter was killed. Peter's brother Jim had been studying fine arts, with the intention of becoming an artist. After service abroad with the RAAF Jim went back to his art studies, and later joined an advertising firm in Adelaide. In 1950 he returned to 'Ryecroft'. For seven years he learned every facet of the art of winemaking from Aub Chapman, a well-known McLaren Vale identity, who has been described as an 'autocratic old man, barely literate but with a magic touch with wine'. When Aub died of a heart attack in 1957, Jim took over as winemaker, and a new era began for 'Ryecroft' wines.

Jim Ingoldby had great faith in the quality of his dry reds, and began bottling under his label from the time he took over. Prior to this, along with most other small concerns in the area, they had sold their wine in bulk to the big companies. For some

years he continued to make sweet wine for export, but he concentrated on his good dry reds, and sought to firmly establish the identity of the area.

There are over 270 acres at 'Ryecroft', the vines consisting of cabernet, shiraz, grenache and pedro. The soil is good red clay, with some sandy patches. 'Ryecroft' shares in the advantages at McLaren Vale of mild temperatures, reliable rainfall, frost-free conditions and proximity to the sea.

By 1965 'Ryecroft' was producing about 100,000 gallons each year. Almost two-thirds of this was sweet wine for sale overseas, mainly through the Emu Wine Company. About 34,000 gallons of shiraz and 8,000 gallons of cabernet were made. It was these wines that interested Jim Ingoldby and it was about 1965 Jim Ingoldby had an unusual idea.

This man decided that the time had come when the wines of McLaren Vale should be known in their own right, it was time for credit to go where credit was due. So he joined with Egerton Dennis and Burr Dodd and formed McLaren Vale Wines Pty Ltd in February, 1965, with the aim of buying wine from local small makers, bottling it separately and, the crux of the matter—each label stating full details on where the wine came from, who made it and so on. The advantages of such a scheme are enormous. The small companies have a ready outlet for their wine, without the necessity for bottling machinery or the problems of storage and marketing, and yet they retain their own identities. The consumers can buy under one label wines that are varied and interesting, with a full knowledge of grape variety, vineyard, soil type, style of wine, as well as the name of the cellar from which the wine originated. The local winemakers Kay, Johnston, Osborn, Southern Vales, Dennis and of course 'Ryecroft' take part in the scheme. And now many people throughout Australia know about McLaren Vale Wines, all because Jim Ingoldby believed in them.

The company was taken over in September, 1970 by Reed Consolidated Industries, the British industrialists who also own Tullochs in the Hunter Valley. Egerton Dennis believes that this move can only be for the good of the wine industry, as it secures the future of the company and the production of fine wine.

F. E. Osborn & Sons Pty Ltd, d'Arenberg

This enterprise can be said to have commenced with the planting of shiraz and some mataro grapes in the 1890s by the Milton family in the hills south of Adelaide, overlooking McLaren Vale. Some of these original vines are still bearing.

In 1912, Mr Francis Ernest Osborn (died 1957) purchased the 195 acre property, sixty of which were planted, naming it 'Bundarra' (believed to be aboriginal for 'on a hill'). The winery was built and first vintage made in 1928. Most of the production was dry red, with the remainder being whites made from palomino grapes, plus a small amount of port. By 1928 the area to vines had been increased to ninety acres.

d'Arenberg, the founder's son, born in 1926, began taking an interest in his early twenties and in 1957 took over completely after the death of his father. He was determined to succeed and worked extremely hard to build up the vineyards, winery and equipment. He has increased the annual crush to over 900 tons, most of it for red wine, with a production of 150,000 gallons. ·

They now have about 155 acres under vine. The varieties cultivated are cabernet sauvignon, shiraz, grenache, mataro, doradillo, palomino, and albillo. The soils at the Osborn company's vineyards are mostly sandy soil over iron stone subsoils, with portions of limestone.

The winery, which has been modernized in recent years to include bulk handling and auto fermenters, still uses a hydraulic press. The increased demand for table wine has encouraged the recent extensions to the premises and the installation of a modern bottling plant, with warehousing and bottle ageing facilities.

D'Arry Osborn has lightened the style of his reds somewhat though they still retain much 'generous' character, and has since been most successful at wine shows. As well as selling under the d'Arenberg label he supplies wine to McLaren Vale Wines Pty Ltd.

Southern Vales Co-operative Winery Ltd

The Southern Vales Co-operative was formed in the early sixties to make wine from the grapes of growers who did not have their own wineries. They own a fairly large winery in the township of McLaren Vale, where they had their first vintage in 1965, under the chairmanship of Wine Board member Ambrose Tonkin. Neil Lindsay was the winemaker responsible for the continuing improvement of their wines.

Horndale Distillery Pty Ltd

The Horndale Distillery company has its headquarters in the Happy Valley district, about fourteen miles south of Adelaide. From 1898 it was under the control of Bernhard Basedow who purchased the property in 1909. Under Basedow's guidance the company soon became well known for its dry reds and brandy, which did very well in shows. In those days 'Horndale' comprised five sections, totalling approximately 209 acres of vineyard; however, the present company has no land under vines.

In 1965 Gilbeys Limited purchased Horndale from the New South Wales company of Swift and Moore,

for the supply of brandy to its Australian subsidiaries, and also to manufacture fortified wines for the United Kingdom market. Since then Horndale have also exported large amounts of brandy to Malaysia and Canada, and fortified sweet red wines to Canada, Jamaica and Trinidad.

Over the last few years Horndale has made the aperitif 'Dubonnet' under licence. This wine consists of a blend of red and white mistelle infused with ingredients imported from France. The company purchases mainly grenache, doradillo, pedro and sultana from the irrigated river areas.

The cellars and buildings cover one-quarter of an acre, and are built into the side of a hill in the form of terraces. Many tons of rock were blasted out for the purpose, and all stone needed to build was quarried on the property. The walls are two feet thick and twenty-five feet high to ensure a cool even temperature all the year round. The storage capacity of the winery is about 160,000 gallons of brandy in wood, and about 155,000 gallons of wine in wood and concrete.

A. C. Johnston Ltd, 'Pirramimma'

The 'Pirramimma' property, which is situated on the Willunga Plains just outside the township of McLaren Vale, was originally bought by Mr A. C. Johnston in 1892. At the time there were only a few grenache vines there. Wine was made for the first time in 1900, and rapid progress was made from that time, both in extension of the vineyards and improvements to the winery and cellars.

Mr Johnston's sons Alex and Digby ran the affairs of the company for many years. Their sons, Alex and Ian, have also joined the family firm. They have 150 acres under vine, and also own thirty acres of almonds and 500 acres of farm land and grazing. The greatest wine acreage consists of shiraz (almost two-thirds of the vineyard). There are also plantings of grenache, pedro ximenez, and palomino, with about three acres of cabernet sauvignon. The 'Pirramimma' soils vary in type from sandy on the rise to rich dark loam on the flat, with a red clay subsoil over limestone marl.

The Johnstons make mainly dry red wine, with some sweet red. From 1916 to 1946 they sold their whole output to W. A. Gilbey Ltd of London. Since 1946 Gilbeys have continued to purchase wine, but the Johnstons also sell under their own label, as well as through McLaren Vale Wines Pty. Ltd.

Kay Brothers Pty Ltd, 'Amery'

The 'Amery' vineyards near 'Seaview' were established in 1890 by two brothers, Herbert and Frederick Walter Kay. They built the magnificent stone cellars on the lines of a model exhibited at the Adelaide Chamber of Manufactures by Dr J. G. Kelly. The cellars were enlarged in 1927, and again in 1938. Their storage capacity is now about a quarter of a million gallons. The brothers enjoyed winemaking in partnership for fifty-seven years, until Frederick died in 1947. This lengthy association between brothers must surely be unique in the wine history of Australia. When Herbert died the following year his son Cuthbert (Cud) took over the management of the winery. The family tradition is being continued —Cud's son Colin was a gold medallist at Roseworthy and has studied winemaking overseas.

The 'Amery' vineyards cover 130 acres, but they plan to almost double this figure in the future. Shiraz and mataro comprise the largest plantings, with about twenty acres each of cabernet sauvignon, and rhine riesling. Other varieties such as grenache, pedro and frontignan are also cultivated. The soil varies from biscay loam to deep sand, with alluvial soil on the valleys and water-washed quartz in the ridges with drifts of shallow sand and a little limestone. The vineyards are not irrigated.

As consideration of their grape varieties shows, the Kays have made mainly red wine over the years. They sold substantial quantities of wine to P. B. Burgoyne in England for many years. Kays continued to sell some dry red to this company after it was taken over by the Emu Wine Company in 1956, but ceased sales there in 1961. Kays also belong to the McLaren Vale Wines' organization.

Roxton Estate

The winery at McLaren Vale, known in recent years as 'Valle d'Oro' was founded in the early 1930s by B. B. Mason, a firm of general merchants from Hull.

Standing on an area of about twelve acres, initial plantings were grenache, shiraz, and mataro grapes for the production of port wines for which there was an increasing demand in the United Kingdom.

Due to the shortage of labour and transport at the beginning of the Second World War, the winery closed down until 1946 when it was re-opened by Mr Con Sparrow. He continued to make fortified and dry red table wines but ill-health forced him to sell his interests which were purchased by two Italian winemakers, John Rosetto and Lorenzo Cosometto.

Their aim was to specialize in making quality dry red table wines. The winery, using its own grapes as well as the production of neighbouring vineyards, expanded and the business flourished. However, it became clear that substantially more capital would be needed to develop the enterprise.

In 1970, Dalgety Australia Limited in search of other avenues of interest purchased control of the winery. Under the new ownership a programme of development with the latest equipment and modern technology has proceeded and new plantings have been made, including eighty acres of cabernet sauvignon and shiraz.

Total production has now risen to a capacity of 400,000 gallons per annum comprising 75 percent red wines to which the greatest emphasis has been given, the balance of 25 percent being white table wines.

Production from the winery will now be marketed by Dalgety under the brand Roxton Estate; a return to its original name. Roxton Estate wines at present on the market are claret and burgundy styles.

Southern Vales Growers

Egerton Dennis: Ege Dennis is probably best known as one of the founders, with Jim Ingoldby, of McLaren Vale Wines Pty Ltd. Dennis had been employed by the Bank of New South Wales before the war, but when he returned from war service in England he decided to branch out into growing grapes, about which he knew little. He bought fifty-five acres at McLaren Flat, about three miles north-east of the township, and set about learning the business of viticulture.

Dennis has now increased his acreage to eighty, planted with shiraz, and cabernet sauvignon. The soil at his property varies—light and heavy, with good subsoil, and is particularly suitable for shiraz and cabernet.

He has never actually made wine, as his grapes have always been sold off the vine and the making handled by others. Until 1964 Dennis sold his berries in bulk to various big companies, but since McLaren Vale Wines was formed he has sold his crop to them. The method by which McLaren Vale Wines operates has given Dennis the satisfaction of seeing wine made from his grapes, labelled as such, and then attain success in wine shows.

Ege Dennis was largely instrumental in the acquisition of McLaren Vale Wines by Reed Consolidated Industries in September, 1970. He felt the time was appropriate to secure their future. Since the takeover he has remained with Jim Ingoldby as joint managing director. Dennis' wife Sue takes a large part on the running of the vineyard. *K. D. & M. Genders:* This vineyard is on the heavy soil of the Daringa Swamp, almost part of the town of McLaren Vale. The vines are so profuse that the pickers have to reach rather than stoop. Recently Keith Genders has had success as a winemaker. *D. G. Sigston:* Sigston's vineyard is just over the road from 'Ryecroft', on heavy red clay that once carried huge stands of old red gums. They sell through McLaren Vale Wines Pty Ltd.

Other Winemakers

In the McLaren Vale area the G. A. Pattritti company at Dover Gardens, founded in 1926, processes a few hundred tons of grapes each year, of which they buy about two-thirds.

Continuous air bag press at Leo Buring's 'Chateau Leonay', Barossa Valley, S.A.

The Barossa Valley

The beautiful Barossa Valley is one of the best known, if not *the* best known, of the winemaking areas of Australia. The appearance of the many rows of green vines, interspersed with orchards and olive groves on the grassy slopes, is as pleasing to the eye as their products are so often to the palate.

The Valley lies about thirty-five miles north-east of Adelaide, at an altitude of about 1,000 feet above sea level. The highest peak is near Pewsey Vale, at 2,064 feet, and the lowest point is at Lyndoch, 595 feet. Tanunda in the centre of the Valley is 864 feet above sea level. The Barossa is about seven miles wide, varying down to two miles at its narrowest, and twenty miles long. The three main towns in the Barossa are Tanunda, Nuriootpa and Angaston, each having a population of about two thousand people. There are also a number of smaller communities throughout the area.

The history of the Barossa Valley and its early settlers is discussed fully in the section on the history of Australian wine.

In the general consideration of the Barossa Valley we include for convenience the Keyneton, Springton and Eden Valley areas, which are actually in the Barossa Ranges. In fact the soils and climate of these areas differ somewhat from those in the Valley itself, and separate mention will be made of these where relevant. As a generalization, better quality table wines come from the hilly areas than from the Valley floor.

With regard to climate, research has established that the Barossa Valley has no direct counterpart in the viticultural areas of France or Germany, but that it comes closest to the climate of Portugal.

The climate in the area does differ from year to year, but the fluctuations are not nearly as marked as in some other Australian areas, notably Coonawarra, or especially, as in the European areas. The climate varies within the Valley. The rainfall, for example, and consequently the yield of grapes, is greater in the southern part than on the western perimeter.

Overall the Barossa is quite an arid region, and is hotter and drier than most European areas. The average rainfall is about twenty inches, but this varies from about eighteen inches on the west to about thirty inches in the hills. The rainfall is low in summer, when the vines need it most, and some irrigation is thus desirable. There is little underground water to be found, but many vineyards do have some irrigation from wells or bores. The problem of lack of water in summer can be quite severe. In addition to the low summer rainfall there is a high rate of evaporation, and it is common for vines to show the effects of the heat and dryness by their dull colour and some leaf drop.

Average temperatures vary considerably—the hills being much cooler than the Valley floor, and thus having the advantage of being able to produce more delicate wines. The average mean January-February temperature at Nuriootpa is 20.5°C, although temperatures in the eighties are not uncommon. In July the average temperature is 8.3°C, although the minimum is around 4.4°C.

The soil types found in the Barossa are very diverse, varying from heavy loams to light sandy soils. The most fertile are the red-brown earths, which consist of loam over clay subsoil, which contains some lime. Also commonly found are grey-brown soils known as solodized solonetz, which have yellow-brown to grey subsoils which contain limestone. There are also patches of terra rossa and rendzinas.

The soils in the Eden Valley-Springton area differ from the Barossa soils. There the soil is podsolic, consisting of grey-brown sandy loams over limestone, ironstone, quartz or yellow to grey-brown clay. There are various mineral deposits in the area, such as asbestos, talc and copper. At Angaston limestone is mined for a cement works, and some marble is also found.

The Valley has escaped phylloxera, for which it can thank strict government quarantine regulations, and good luck. The vines there are thus not grafted onto other roots as in so many areas of the world.

A wide variety of grapes is cultivated in the Barossa Valley. There are many acres of shiraz, grenache, pedro ximenez, mataro and doradillo in descending order of acreage. There is also a considerable area of riesling (rhine and clare, plus semillon which is sometimes given the name madeira, to confuse the matter further).

Traditionally the Barossa has been known for the production of fortified wines, such as sherry, port and frontignac. With the increased demand for light table wines the focus of production has changed, and the new plantings reflect this. The greatest areas of new vines have been planted with shiraz, grenache, riesling, cabernet sauvignon and mataro.

In the 1970 vintage 38,400 tons of grapes were crushed in the Barossa. This was 16 percent of the total for South Australia, and 11 percent of the Australian total of 350,000 tons. In March, 1970 there were 16,700 acres of vines bearing grapes in the Barossa, and nearly 4,000 newly planted acres.

The yield of grapes per acre is determined by such factors as rainfall, soil and grape variety. The average yield per acre in the Barossa is 1.65 tons. In varietal terms the yield can range from 2.70 tons for Clare riesling down to 0.62 tons for the shy bearing cabernet sauvignon.

The minimum prices for grapes are fixed each year by the South Australian Prices Commissioner. Although premium varieties command higher prices, their often low yields do not encourage growers to plant them as the differences in prices are not large enough.

As has already been mentioned the fame of the Barossa has rested in the past on its fortified and dessert wines. The winemakers of the Valley do, however, turn out the complete range of wines, from aperitif wines, such as sherry and vermouth; through dry white and dry red table wines and sparkling wines to dessert wines, port, muscat, tokay, etc. In recent years there has been an increasing emphasis on the production of high quality table wines. The Valley has shown that it is capable of producing some very good table wines indeed. The whites from the hilly areas, especially Eden Valley and Springton, and more recently Pewsey Vale, have been very delicate and quite delightful and may be regarded as among the best in Australia. Some of the big reds made in the Valley are unquestionably top class, notably those made from cabernet.

Why has the Barossa Valley developed as the heartland of South Australian winemaking? Why is the name Barossa synonymous with wine? The reasons lie in the combination of natural factors—such as soils, terrain and climate, with the influence of the Silesian migrants who made up the majority of the early settlers of the area. The German colonists brought their winemaking traditions with them, and by their hard work ensured the beginnings of traditions new to their adopted land.

Signs of this early German settlement are still evident throughout the Valley. Most obvious, of course, are the vineyards everywhere, although these are not Germanic as such. Occasionally the German dialect known as 'Barossa Deutsch' is still heard, although unfortunately this is dying out. Many German family names are still in evidence, although during the First World War many place names were changed by an Act of Parliament. Throughout the Valley there are charming and orderly little settlements, with unique stone houses and scrupulously maintained Lutheran churches.

The Silesian migrants brought their eating habits with them also, and some of their traditional foods are still to be found in the shops. Among these are

Vineyards of the Barossa Valley

cakes such as streuselkuchen; sausages and small-goods of all sorts—mettwurst, leberwurst, blutwurst and many more; and other delicacies such as sauerkraut and pickled cucumbers.

The Germanic love of music is evident in many ways. In Tanunda there is a choral society, the Liedertafel, which has been strong since 1861. There are many brass bands, which happily take part in annual competitions, and also play a prominent part in the Vintage Festival.

The biennial Barossa Vintage Festival is clearly influenced by wine festivals of a similar nature in Germany. The festival has been held since 1948 as a carnival at vintage time, the proceeds going to charity. Numerous functions are held during this period of music, dancing, drinking and feasting. There are grape picking contests, processions and parades, a wine auction, an art exhibition and much else besides. Unquestionably, it is the best organized and attended wine festival in Australia, and is one of the outstanding festive occasions of any kind in the country.

Thus the Barossa Valley is a unique area, and is of major importance in Australian wine production. The Valley is the heartland of the primary wine producing state of Australia, with over 20,000 acres of vines and thirty wineries. A toast to the memory of the men who started it all—George Angas, Samuel Smith, Joseph Seppelt, Johann Gramp and the rest!

Tolley, Scott and Tolley's new fermentation and storage facilities with modern bottling lines in the foreground, Nuriootpa, S.A.

Barossa Co-operative Winery Ltd, Kaiser Stuhl

The Barossa Co-operative is the only co-operative winery in the Valley, and with a progressive team leading the enterprise it has enjoyed enormous expansion and success in recent years.

This present prosperity is a long way from the rather unhappy beginnings of the company. During the Depression the market for wine had virtually collapsed and in May, 1931 a group of growers in the Barossa joined forces for their own security to process their grapes under the name of the South Australian Grape Growers Co-operative Ltd. It was a great struggle to keep going in the early years, but they managed to remain solvent, and built their first modest cellars in 1933. Their main market was in the United Kingdom, but the outbreak of World War II had a disastrous effect on the export trade. The Co-operative survived these trials and continued

to sell its output in bulk, mainly, to other wineries. In 1966 the name of the company was changed to the Barossa Co-operative Winery Ltd.

In 1958 the company developed its own label, Kaiser Stuhl, which means 'the seat of Kings'.

The new label soon became a force to be reckoned with. This was due in no small measure to the enthusiastic, efficient and well-qualified managerial and technical team running the organization. The chairman of the Co-operative and its 450 grower-shareholders was for many years Oscar Semmler, whose family originally settled in the Valley over one hundred years ago. Yugoslav born George Kolarovich has been the technical director and winery manager since 1961. He comes from a family of vignerons well known on the Austrian, Hungarian, German and Yugoslav markets since 1850. After several years' practical experience, Mr Kolarovich gained a Bachelor of Agricultural Science degree from the University of Munich. A. R. (Robert)

Litchfield is secretary of the Co-operative, and as such controls the multitudinous financial details affecting the interests of the members.

The Co-operative has followed a policy of marketing wines from individual vineyards since 1958. The grapes for these wines are from single vineyards, all individually owned, and the growers have the satisfaction of their wines retaining their own identity, with the advantages of national marketing organization and a well-known label. Wine lovers can enjoy these individual wines in full knowledge of their origins.

One of the first of these was a late-picked rhine riesling from Eric Stephens' vineyard, 'Wyncroft' in the Eden Valley. The name of the vineyard is taken from the Scots name for 'house on the hill', as a token of Mr Stephens' Scottish origins. He has been a director of the Co-operative for many years, and also served for a long period as chairman of the Phylloxera Board, the quarantine patrol organization which has succeeded in keeping South Australia free of the disease.

W. C. (Collis) and R. V. Rogers' 'Eden Valley' vineyard is humorously known as 'Sunburnean'. The grapes from this property are used for an individual vineyard dry riesling.

In 1970 the first individual vineyard red was put on the market. This was from A. E. Materne's vineyard at Greenock.

In addition to their individual vineyard wines the Co-operative markets a full range which includes appetizer and dessert wines. They specialize in sparkling wine and their Rosé which was launched in 1962 has also been very successful. They make huge amounts of sparkling wine which is sold under the labels of other major companies.

The Kaiser Stuhl winery is fully equipped with the wide range of expensive and highly developed machinery necessary for the production of large quantities of quality wines, especially sparkling wines. These include thermostatically controlled pressure tanks and self-emptying centrifuges. A new bottling plant has been installed which has an output of 8,000 bottles per hour. There is a place for tradition among all this modern technology, and the cellar area has hundreds of hogsheads of French oak containing maturing reds.

It is encouraging that growers, as primary producers, have been able to co-operate so successfully for their mutual benefit. Naturally the fruits of their co-operative not only benefit the growers, but the wine drinking public as well.

O. Basedow Wines Ltd

The Basedow winery is a small family concern, with headquarters on the Sturt Highway just north of Tanunda, in the midst of a residential district. The Basedow family has been making wine at their 'Illapara' winery since the end of the last century, with John Basedow being the fourth generation involved.

The winery and its output are small, but the wines are of a high quality. They have won many medals in shows. Basedow wines are all made from Barossa-grown grapes, and are good examples of true regional wines.

In 1971 the company was taken over by a group of businessmen.

Leo Buring Pty Ltd, 'Chateau Leonay'

The 'Chateau Leonay' winery is on the east bank of the North Para River about a mile north of Tanunda.

Leo Buring, a cousin of the Burings of Buring and Sobels, graduated in 1896 as Gold Medallist and Dux of Roseworthy Agricultural College. He then studied oenology at Geisenheim on the Rhine, and at Montpellier in France. Two years later he returned to Australia. Leo Buring was associated with many wine companies over the next quarter of a century as manager, technical adviser and director. He was responsible for some magnificent wines, including champagne from Minchinbury, and others from Great Western, Seppelts and Lindemans.

In 1931 Buring went into business for himself. With Reginald Mowat of Great Western he formed a Sydney-based company, whose first wine—from Emu Plains, thirty-nine miles west of Sydney—appeared on the market in 1934. Buring's semi-sweet white, Ringolde, was almost synonymous with wine during the early 1930s. The name came from the German 'reines gold', meaning pure gold; this referred to the colour of the wine, not to the Rhine in Germany. Buring took all of Phillip's Hunter Valley production of 10,000 gallons or more and used this with other Hunter material to make Ringolde. (The main Hunter vineyard is now Brokenback Estate.) The Second World War was a big stimulus to the demand for the wine, the American soldiers especially buying large quantities. Building his popular fame on Ringolde, Buring's firm prospered and expanded, taking over the Melbourne firm of Matthew Lang in 1941.

At about this time Albert Charles Shipton began to work for Leo Buring as cellar manager at the Olde Crusty Cellars in George Street, Sydney. He had a long association with Burings and was with them until his retirement in 1952. A. C. Shipton's youngest son, Ray, started with Burings in 1942 at the age of fifteen. He spent the four years to 1949 at Roseworthy after which he returned to George Street, Sydney to work under his father and Leo Buring. Ray continued there after his father's retirement in 1952.

Leo Buring's connection with the Barossa dates from 1945. In that year, at the age of sixty-eight, he purchased the small Orange Grove winery which had been built by Gottlieb Hoffman in 1897. Buring began to rebuild the winery, adding turrets to the corners of the building. He planned to build Flemish towers, and designed a label with a drawing of his dream winery. He did not neglect the interior of the winery, and gradually improved its equipment. In the beginning he handled vintages of between 300 and 400 tons in small fermenting vats, five feet square and five feet deep. By 1953 he was able to afford a Coq mill crusher. In 1955, John Vickery, a Roseworthy graduate who was to do so much for the wines of 'Chateau Leonay', joined the firm. The following year Leo Buring retired. John Vickery continued his struggle to make fine wines with rather inadequate equipment. In 1959 a second-hand bottling plant was installed.

In 1961 Leo Buring died at the ripe old age of eighty-five, before he was able to complete the rebuilding of 'Chateau Leonay'. He has been called 'truly an ambassador of wine'. Leo Buring made a great contribution to the Australian wine industry—through his influence on the many firms with which he was associated, through introducing thousands of people to drinking wine via his Rinegolde, and through his establishment of 'Chateau Leonay'.

Lindeman's Wines took over the company in 1962, and they, not unreasonably, preferred to spend their money on equipment rather than on ornamentation of the buildings. After improvising a cooling plant in 1962, refrigeration equipment was installed in time for the 1963 vintage. And that was just the start of it.

'Chateau Leonay' has now expanded enormously—handling over 5,000 tons of grapes annually. A spectacular array of sophisticated modern machinery has been installed. There is a continuous pneumatic press, air bag presses, stainless steel tanks, Uncle Tom Cobley and all. There is a storage capacity of over 600,000 gallons, and the bottling plant has been vastly increased in size. And the winery is continuing to grow at a great rate.

The company owns about fifty-five acres of vineyards at Tanunda, and a further sixty-five acres at Watervale, which were purchased by Leo Buring from Malcolm Allan. They have recently planted a further six acres. They grow a wide variety of grapes, including palomino, shiraz, pedro, rhine and clare riesling and trebbiano. 'Chateau Leonay' buys about ninety percent of its crush from outside growers.

Over half of the wines made at 'Chateau Leonay' are white table wines. The company's search for perfection, John Vickery's ability and the above mentioned technology have resulted in some very good whites which have been covered in medals at shows. A wide range of wines are made at Leonay, including dry reds and a dry sherry called Florita after the company's Watervale vineyard.

Chateau Yaldara Pty Ltd

'Chateau Yaldara', one of the most unusual winery complexes in Australia, is situated near Lyndoch, at the junction of the North Para River and Lyndoch Creek. The winery does not have a very long history under its present owners, but has a wide reputation among tourists as a place worth visiting.

The proprietor of 'Chateau Yaldara', Hermann Thumm, comes from a German family which has been involved in winemaking on the Rhine for centuries. Following this tradition Hermann Thumm gained a diploma in oenology after he left school, and then worked with a large winemaking company. In 1930 Thumm went to Persia where he was involved in several business enterprises, including a winemaking firm. The events of the World War interrupted these activities. In 1941 Persia was occupied by the British and Russians, and all German residents were interned. Hermann Thumm was sent to Australia as an internee, and spent the rest of the war in internment centres.

In 1946, the war over, Thumm returned to winemaking. After a year with a winery in the Barossa Valley, he took over the ruins of a mid-nineteenth century winery and flour-mill at Schlenke's Gully. He began to rebuild this shell, which had birds nesting in the ruined walls and waist-high weeds everywhere, along the lines of a formal European chateau.

'Chateau Yaldara' is now a flourishing enterprise. It is best known for its sparkling wine and champagne which is appropriate as Yaldara comes from an aboriginal word meaning 'sparkling'. The vineyards are planted with riesling, pedro, shiraz, grenache and mataro. The company supplements its own grapes considerably with purchases from other growers in the locality.

The actual chateau, built in the sixties, is filled with art treasures, as a result of Hermann Thumm's idea of creating a place of beauty with a European atmosphere. An ornamental lake has been built as part of the beautification programme. New cellars were built when the original ones became too small, and a new champagne cellar was recently built overlooking the lake. Thumm has also been involved in the construction of the new Barossa Motel at Lyndoch.

Hermann Thumm's sons are following the traditional family occupation. His eldest son Robert studied oenology at Geisenheim on the Rhine, and youngest son Dieter studied economics at the University of Adelaide.

Matara Pty Ltd—Augustine Barossa Valley Estates Pty Ltd, 'Glen View'

The 'Glen View' winery is situated to the north-east of Rowland Flat, near the tiny village of Kabminye, with sweeping views overlooking the Valley. P. T. Falkenberg Ltd, which owned the winery, was taken

Woodley Wines vineyard at Glen Osmond, S.A., was once mined for silver-lead deposits. After the ore was mined out there was a system of underground workings left which was ideal for the storage of wine.

over in 1970 by Matara Pty Ltd, and is now operated by Augustine Barossa Valley Estates Pty Ltd.

This newly formed company is managed by Jim Irvine. Irvine has had considerable experience in the industry, having spent many years working with Thomas Hardy & Sons, working at one stage with Roger Warren and Dick Heath. He was also manager of Siegersdorf and state manager of Hardy's in Victoria.

'Glen View' has 112 acres of many varieties, including grenache, mataro, madeira, sercial, carignane and pedro. The new company has installed modern winemaking facilities, and aims to produce high quality table wines.

G. Gramp & Sons Pty Ltd, 'Orlando'

The 'Orlando' label is well known throughout Australia. Their popular appeal rests with their Barossa Pearl, and their later wines—such as Sparkling Star Wine. These are both highly successful, easy to drink sparkling wines, which resulted from major technical innovations introduced by the Gramp family.

It all began with Johann Gramp who was born in 1819 at Eichig, near Kulmbach in Bavaria, the son of a prosperous land owner and farmer. At the age of eighteen Johann left home. He sailed in the 400 ton barque *Solway* with fifty-two other migrants, via Rio de Janeiro and the Cape of Good Hope to Kangaroo Island off the coast of South Australia. Soon afterwards, on the mainland, he worked for the South Australian Company, and then took a job with a baking business before taking up land at Yatala, near Adelaide, where he built a log cottage.

In 1847 Gramp moved to Jacob's Creek, a small tributary of the North Para river, to a site one mile north-east of the present 'Orlando' winery. He planted a small vineyard there, the first vineyard in the Barossa, and had his first vintage in 1850, the same year as his son Gustav was born. The entire vintage filled one octave, and was a hock-style of white wine.

The acreage under vine and scope of operations was gradually increased; and in 1887 Gustav took over the management of the vineyards. The same year he moved the winery to Rowland Flat, where it is today. By 1912 the business had become most successful, and a limited company was formed. In 1920 Gustav's son Hugo became managing director.

In 1938 tragedy struck, which affected not only the Gramp family, when the 'Kyeema' aeroplane crashed at Mount Dandenong near Melbourne. On the 25th October of that year Hugo Gramp, Tom Hardy and Sid Hill-Smith were killed, along with Charles Hawker, a Federal Minister. After Hugo's death his only brother Fred took over as managing director. Management of the firm remained with the family after Fred Gramp retired, his sons Sid and Keith playing active roles, while their cousin, Hugo's son Colin, was in charge for many years.

In December, 1970 the family relinquished control of their company to Reckitt and Colman Australia Ltd. Some of the Gramps have remained on the board of directors.

The headquarters of the firm is still at Rowland Flat. 'Orlando' make millions of gallons of wine every year, and to do this purchase far more grapes from outside growers than they grow themselves. 'Orlando' own over 1,000 acres of vineyards in full bearing. They grow among others, rhine riesling, cabernet sauvignon, shiraz, and trebbiano. The vineyard in the Barossa is planted with between 450 and 600 vines to the acre, usually planted on the twelve feet by seven feet plan. There is only a little irrigating done, the vineyards relying mainly on natural rainfall. The soils at Rowland Flat mainly consist of a gravelly sandy loam over red and yellow clay.

The firm purchased 253 acres for new vineyards in the Eden Valley in 1969. Of these, 180 acres are suitable for viticulture. Rhine riesling, gewurztraminer and frontignan are being planted on the soils there, which are of skeletal group. Gramps also have holdings at Ramco on the Murray River, near Waikerie. Naturally these are irrigated, an overhead permanent sprinkler being used.

With great enthusiasm Colin Gramp supervised a unique experiment in the early sixties. This involved the establishment of a new vineyard appropriately known as the 'Steingarten', or garden of stones, at an altitude of 1,600 feet high on the mountain behind Rowland Flat. The soil there is very rocky and Gramps had great difficulty in preparing the area for planting. The stony schist rock which is a soft shale type of rock had to be broken up with stone hammers before planting of vines could commence. The vineyard, which is only six acres in area, is reminiscent of those on the Mittel Mosel in Germany. There is no trellising—each of the rhine riesling and gewurztraminer vines is supported by a tall stake as is the German practice. The climate at 'Steingarten' is unreliable, but the cool temperatures are conducive to a good retention of acid, which can lead to wines of delicacy and finesse. The venture cost thousands, and such an adventurous investment certainly deserves success.

The winery at Rowland Flat is more functional than beautiful. The oldest part of the winery is a little tasting room. It is an ultra-efficient operation, equipped with a vast array of all the most modern equipment, with the capacity for storing a staggering four million gallons of wine.

These headquarters have been the source of some remarkable technical innovations which have had enormous effects on Australian winemaking. In 1953 Gramps, in what has turned out to be a revolutionary move, adopted the cold and pressure-controlled

'Seaview' vineyard, originally known as 'Hope Farm', was first planted by George P. Manning in 1850, and is now owned by Messrs Edwards and Chaffey.

Commemorative plaque at 'Yalumba' where the first grapes were planted in 1849 by Samuel Smith.

Hamiltons Ewell Vineyards Pty Ltd, Springton and Eden Valley

Hamiltons have their headquarters at Glenelg, but the pressures of urbanization have forced them to expand in other areas, and they have acquired fairly small wineries at Springton and Eden Valley.

The winery at Springton was built by William Rayner in 1890, on land which originally belonged to Oscar Benno Seppelt. Hamiltons acquired the winery in 1938. They renovated it considerably, using the gravity principle, in the next decade. Hamiltons' Springton winery has, unlike most others, always been used for table wines. They have forty acres of rhine riesling, shiraz, white frontignac, grenache and cabernet sauvignon at their Springton vineyards.

Hamiltons came on the scene at Eden Valley much more recently. In 1965 they bought a winery which had been built by Penfolds in 1922, and 110 acres, of which 105 are under vine. The varieties grown include shiraz, cabernet sauvignon, riesling and white frontignac. A subsidiary company known as Eden Valley Wines and Vineyards Pty Ltd controls the running of the winery and vineyards at Eden Valley.

Both the winery at Springton and the recent acquisition at Eden Valley are equipped with refrigeration equipment. Only table wines are made there—both whites and reds.

fermentation system that had been developed in Western Germany and Austria. This resulted in white wines of outstanding flavour and bouquet for which Gramps have become famous. Three years later Gramps introduced Barossa Pearl, a naturally sweet sparkling wine which had a huge impact on the Australian market. This was an expensive wine to produce as a great deal of sophisticated and expensive equipment such as large pressure tanks was necessary.

Good material and good equipment can only lead to good wines if good technical people are around to make them, and Gramps have developed a very good team. Gunter Prass, the associate technical director and production manager, has a background of extensive experience in Germany, and is aided by other able men such as Mark Tummel, Harold Pfeiffer, Jeff Virgo and Tony Kluckzo.

Gramps have been among the leaders in the use of most of the highly complex technological innovations of the sixties. They pioneered with such machinery as centrifuges, gravity separators and the Mac four stage press. Under the new owners they are assured of the necessary capital for future· developments, and also have the advantage of marketing through Reckitt and Colman's large network of outlets, which is all a far cry from a young German immigrant and his infant vineyard a short 120 years ago.

Thomas Hardy and Sons Pty Ltd, 'Siegersdorf'

The well-known Hardy firm is represented in the Barossa by their winery 'Dorrien', between Tanunda and Nuriootpa. Hardy's first involvement with winemaking in the Valley was in 1918, when they began to buy grapes from growers there, transporting the grapes to their 'Mile End' winery for processing.

Two years later they commenced the building of a winery, which they called 'Vine Vale'. The new cellar had its first vintage in 1921. The name of the winery was later changed to 'Dorrien'. Jim Irvine, the manager at 'Dorrien' from 1959 to 1965 (see 'Glen View' for more on him) proposed to call the winery 'Siegersdorf' which was the original name for the area. His suggestion was implemented, and 'Siegersdorf' it is called today.

As is so often the case, the winery concentrated on fortified wines for many years. It was only with the recent demand for table wines that the emphasis was changed to table wine production. Now nearly all the wine made at 'Siegersdorf' is table wine, with only about ten percent being fortified. The grapes for the winery are purchased in the Eden Valley-Springton area. 'Siegersdorf' has been specially successful with their rhine riesling wine.

C. A. Henschke and Co, Keyneton

Keyneton is a small village eight miles south-east of Angaston. Although geographically close, the area is really rather different to the Barossa Valley proper. The land is more open than in the Valley, sparsely wooded with poorer soil. The altitude at Keyneton is higher, and it occasionally has frost in winter. The average rainfall is twenty-one inches, although this varies considerably from year to year.

In the early years of this century there were five wineries, all with large vineyards, in the Keyneton area. The area was known as North Rhine, as it reminded the early German settlers of that part of their homeland. The Barossa wineries who had the advantages of higher yields and better access to Adelaide may have been too much for the Keyneton wineries. For whatever reason only one remains today.

This is the firm of C. A. Henschke, whose winery is two and a half miles north of Keyneton. The origins of the firm lie with Johann Christian Henschke, wheelwright and builder, who was born in Jutschlau, Silesia, in 1803. He arrived in Australia in 1842 after a voyage on the ship *Skjold*, and settled at Bethany near Tanunda. He began farming on a small holding near Keyneton soon after. It was Johann Christian's son, Paul Gotthardt born 1847, who planted the first small vineyard to make wine for his friends and family. He had his first vintage in 1868.

Paul died in 1914 and was succeeded by his son, Paul Alfred who extended the property holding and the cellars. At the turn of the century he began making fortified wines which were then very much in demand locally. During the period from 1920, drought years and the Depression hit hard, and farming again became the major pursuit. Of Paul Alfred's seven daughters and four sons Cyril Alfred, born in 1924, grew up to become interested in winemaking. Together they built a new cellar in 1949, and then turned their attention to making dry table wines. Cyril Henschke assumed sole charge nine years before his father's death in 1964. The family tradition is being continued, with Cyril's younger son, Stephen, who will be the fifth generation of Henschkes at Keyneton.

Henschkes own about 700 acres, but only about 140 of these are under vine. They have recently planted a new seventy acre vineyard about two miles north of Eden Valley, in a frost-free area. Replanting of old vines is being carried out with premium varieties. Two of Henschke's vineyards have given their names to two of his top red wines—'Hill of Grace', named after the nearby Gnadenberg Lutheran Church, and 'Mount Edelstone', the original meaning of which was noble stone. The shiraz vines at the 'Hill of Grace' were planted in 1900 on rich silty soils. The soils generally are clay loams and podsols.

Cyril Henschke does not have a very large output, with an average annual crush of 400 tons, but he makes only table wines from his own and other local grapes. He makes an interesting range of varietal whites as well as the aforementioned reds, and has won many prizes throughout Australia.

The cellars cover over 10,000 square feet and are all built of local field stone. They have a storage capacity of over 100,000 gallons and a cool deep cellar can store almost 200,000 bottles of wine. The small winery is not particularly modern or mechanized and has considerable charm. Cyril Henschke, who is the only Australian vigneron to have won a Churchill Fellowship, is noteworthy as one of the few who make only unfortified wines of the district.

Hoffmann's North Para Wines Pty Ltd

The Hoffmanns are one of the number of Barossa winemaking families who can trace their history back several generations. In their case, the family tree begins with Samuel Hoffmann, who was born in 1795 at Richenau in Silesia. He was a trooper in the Prussian army, and fought at Waterloo in 1815. He then became a farmer, but not very successfully. In the hope of a better life free of religious persecution, Samuel applied for a migrant permit. After many years of waiting this was eventually granted, when he was fifty-three years old.

Thus in 1847 he sailed with his wife, daughter Johanne, and eight sons on the sailing-ship *Gellert* from Hamburg. Shortly after his arrival, in 1848, he took up some land on the west bank of the North Para River near Tanunda. This is the land his descendants own to this day.

Samuel's daughter did not marry, and seven of his sons left home to work and live elsewhere. Samuel Hoffmann died in 1878, thirty years after his arrival in the new land. His youngest son Christian (1844-1915) stayed with his parents, and grew up to plant the first, small Hoffmann vineyard. His son, Christian II (1868-1947) built a winery and greatly enlarged the vineyard. The fourth generation of Hoffmanns was represented by Erwin (1898-1970) who devoted his life to viticulture and winemaking and became one of the best-known personalities in the Valley. With his wife Laurel, Erwin Hoffmann was renowned for his hospitality, and together they made considerable contributions to charity.

Their son Bruce is now in control. Bruce has three sons, Stephen, Gregory, and Roderick. It is really remarkable that in a country as young as Australia the sixth generation in a direct male line should be living on the original property. The Hoffmanns have been a prolific family—there are now over three thousand of their descendants in Australia.

The Hoffmann winery is one of the smaller ones in the area. It has concentrated on making dessert wines and dry red.

B. Liebich & Sons, Rovalley Wines

The 'Rovalley' winery near Rowland Flat is another of the Barossa's family enterprises. The business was begun in 1918 by Benno Paul Liebich, who was then aged twenty-eight. After his death in 1941 his two sons took over management of the winery. C. W. Liebich is now the technical manager and H. K. Liebich in charge of the sales side. Apart from their involvement in winemaking, the family have had a continuing love of and interest in racehorses.

The Liebich company owns 650 acres, of which 400 acres have been established as vineyards. The winery which is close to the North Para River, has been considerably enlarged in recent years, and now has a storage capacity of half a million gallons.

'Rovalley' markets a wide range of wines, and does much of its business with the sale of wines in bulk to hotels.

Penfolds Wines Pty Ltd, Nuriootpa and 'Kalimna'

Among the largest of the many large wineries in the Barossa is the one owned by Penfolds at Nuriootpa. Penfolds began operations there in 1911 when the local growers guaranteed that they would deliver at least 1,000 tons of grapes a year to the new Penfold winery. In return Penfolds guaranteed a minimum price of £4 a ton. A fifteen acre vineyard formerly owned by a Mr J. Large was bought, and building commenced. At the time it was planned that the new winery would be subsidiary to the one at Magill, but the new winery soon overtook the home one at Magill in size.

By 1913 a cellar was completed to handle the grapes, but storage was limited and the company built a large distillation plant to convert part of the vintage into rectified spirit and brandy. This plant included a 5,000 gallon still, the largest pot-still in Australia. In 1920 Penfolds built a cellar and distillery at Eden Valley, sixteen miles east of Nuriootpa. The wine was taken by road to Nuriootpa for blending, but as road transport facilities increased the grapes could be more efficiently processed at the Nuriootpa winery and the Eden Valley cellars became a storehouse for flor sherries. Expansion of business made further building necessary at Nuriootpa, and two acres of land adjacent to the winery were purchased in 1948. Throughout the Valley Penfolds have wineries and stores and vineyards, all contributing to the output at Nuriootpa.

The winery is enormous, the buildings covering over seven acres. They have a storage capacity of five million gallons. The building known as the 'Bird Cage' (because of its open wire mesh sides) has the capacity to store one million gallons of port in 14,000 sixty gallon hogsheads. In addition to the facilities provided by up-to-date machinery, spacious cellars

and a railway that enters the winery enclosure itself, an efficient laboratory has been established at Nuriootpa, where the scientific staff keep a check on the wines at all stages of manufacture and maturation.

Until recently the winery at Nuriootpa concentrated solely on making fortified wines, being specially well known for its ports. All Penfolds' brandy is made there.

For many years the Nuriootpa winery was under the control of Paul A. Scholz, who joined Penfolds as a cellar hand in 1913. Fifty-one years later he retired as manager. He was succeeded by Ray Beckwith, a Roseworthy graduate, who joined Penfolds in 1935 after two years with Hardys. He became chief chemist in 1951.

Penfolds are believed to have at least 1,000 acres of vineyards in the Barossa. Of these 700 acres are at the 'Kalimna' vineyard, at Moppa, only a few miles north of Nuriootpa. Penfolds acquired the estate in May, 1945 from D. & J. Fowler Ltd., a grocery firm who had been making wine for export to Britain. Previously, at the beginning of the century, Mr William Salter ran 'Kalimna'.

Penfolds' purchase included vineyards, winery and distillery. The winery contained oak storage of the best quality for 100,000 gallons of wine. The vats, built at the beginning of the twentieth century by a well-known cooper, J. Keuper of Nuriootpa, were transferred to the Nuriootpa winery. The Kalimna cellars are now used for storage and maturation of wines, including a large quantity of sherry on flor.

The vineyard is one of the largest in Australia, and is planted with many varieties including cabernet, doradillo, mataro and shiraz. Most of the wine from 'Kalimna' goes into various private bin dry reds. It is also the source of cabernet sauvignon used by John Davoren in the making of the famous St Henri at Magill. Jeffrey Penfold Hyland must be credited with much of the success of the 'Kalimna' material, for it was he who developed it after it was bought and who planted many of the varieties which have resulted in such classic wines.

St Hallett's Wines Pty Ltd

'St Hallett's' winery between Rowland Flat and Tanunda is named after Hallett's Valley where the first vines for the winery were planted. The winery is of comparatively recent origin—it was founded in 1918 by the Lindner family.

In the traditional manner of the Valley, the Lindners can trace their family back to their arrival in Australia. The original Lindners were Silesians who arrived in Australia in 1860 and settled at Bethany. A son of one of the original immigrants, Carl Lindner, spent many years as a butcher in the Barossa Valley. In 1912 he bought land at Hallett's Valley and planted his vines— a small winery was built in 1918, only dry red and dry white wines being made. He then bought the vineyard opposite the cellar from Mr John Jacob, the first surveyor in the area.

Mr Lindner's son, Carl Wilhelm (better known as Bill) worked for Gramps where he learned the art of winemaking. In an enthusiastic effort to learn all he could about making top quality wine he also took correspondence lessons from California. In 1944 Bill started winemaking and in 1948 left his employment and expanded the family business.

The cellar expanded in four stages—from a storage of 21,000 gallons to the present 200,000 gallons. The last addition was a major project, mainly for the purpose of producing dry wine. The underground cellar has a storage capacity of 1,000,000 bottles of dry wine; the top cellar being used as a bottling section.

The company is a family concern—Bill and his wife (Norma) and three sons, Merv, Carl, and Elmore. Carl is responsible for managing the vineyard area which has increased to 140 acres—fifty of these acres can be irrigated from two bores in dry years. Elmore is the cellar manager.

The company has a policy of quality before quantity and with this in mind use maximum quality grapes. They have also purchased hundreds of oak hogsheads, quarter casks and octaves for maturing wines. 'St Hallett's' market a wide range of wines including some distinctive dry reds.

W. Salter and Son Pty Ltd, 'Saltram'

The story of the old winemaking firm of W. Salter and Son began with William Salter, who was born in Exeter, England in 1804. He arrived in South Australia in the very early days of the colony—in December 1839 on the *Caroline*, a 495 ton sailing ship.

When the Barossa Surveys were thrown open for selection William Salter purchased a section in the new district. In 1844 he moved his family to the property—the fifty mile trip by bullock wagon took four days. William Salter was a deeply religious man and called his property 'Mamre Brook', after a verse in Genesis describing some of Abraham's land. He built, with no previous experience, a plain-fronted six-room house which is still in good condition.

His first interest was in cattle, but prices were low, and Salter turned to sheep. His young son Edward, then aged ten, helped as shepherd and night watchman. Salter began to prosper, and became a man of standing in the community. He was elected Treasurer of the first District Council of Angaston, and was for many years Deacon of the Congregational Church at Angaston which he had been instrumental in founding.

When copper was discovered on his property, the ever versatile Salter opened the Crinnis Copper Mine. There was an influx of miners, and an extensive plant was erected. When prices for copper fell in the late sixties, the mine was closed and the Cornish miners departed.

In the meantime, William Salter formed a partnership with his son Edward, then aged twenty-two. In 1859 they founded the firm of W. Salter & Son, and began operations with the clearing and planting of ten acres at the eastern end of the property. A shed for making wine and a cellar, which was simply a cave cut into a hill, were built. Details of father and son's winemaking activities were faithfully recorded by Edward in his Vigneron's Journal—an admirable exercise by one who had relatively little formal education. Their first vintage was in 1862 from shiraz grapes, and 1,800 gallons were made.

In 1863 a screw press was used for the first time, but it was unsuccessful. Another mill was tried later, but foot power proved to be most satisfactory, and the grapes were crushed in treading boxes until steam power was introduced in 1891. The treaders wore special knee boots, made by a local bootmaker named Schulz who charged twenty-five shillings a pair.

From 1863 onwards the Salters fortified their wine with an average of seventeen percent of absolute alcohol. Grapes from other growers were first bought in 1868 when sixteen tons of shiraz was purchased.

The selling of their wine presented the Salters with many difficulties. William Salter began to travel throughout South Australia and to Melbourne from 1865 to find a market for his wine. In 1871 William Salter died, and Edward continued managing the property, which he had already been doing for many years.

More vines were planted, and by 1873 grapes were picked from thirty acres of shiraz and ten acres of 'sherry'. The previous year Edward had engaged Alfred Birks who introduced 'Saltram' wines to New Zealand, and a few years later they employed two more travellers, Anderson and Fleming, for the South Australian trade. In 1882 Salters made an arrangement with Thomas Hardy & Son, wine merchants, who undertook to buy and then find a market for all the Saltram wine. This arrangement lasted for ten years and a firm market was established in London in that time.

Expansion continued and by 1891 the vintage was about 40,000 gallons—three-quarters of which was dry red for export. These quantities meant that the days of treading boxes were over, and a hydraulic press and pump driven by a five horse-power steam engine was purchased. That year also Edward overcame the heat problem of fermentation which had bedevilled him from the beginning, by running cold water through copper pipes in the vats.

In 1898 Edward's sons, Charles and Leslie, entered the partnership each holding a quarter share. Charles was appointed manager. It was intended that winemaking would be conducted as a separate business from grape growing. In 1902 Charles went into his own business, and Leslie was appointed manager, a position he retained until he resigned in 1937. The firm continued to concentrate on making red wine for export; the quality of which must have been good as many awards were won. In 1913 Edward Salter died at the age of seventy-six years.

The first cellar, 1851, at Seppeltsfield, Barossa Valley, S.A. (Photo: Seppelt & Sons, Views of Seppeltsfield, *1921).*

Leslie Salter, who had been educated at Roseworthy College, became well known in the industry and held various important offices on such bodies as the Federal Viticultural Council. During this period he became a good friend of Ronald Martin of 'Stonyfell', who purchased a third share in W. Salter & Son in 1920, when it became a limited liability company with Ronald Martin as chairman of directors. When Leslie Salter resigned as managing director in 1937, 'Saltram' vineyard was managed by H. M. Martin of 'Stonyfell', and in 1941 it became a wholly owned subsidiary of Martin's. The 'Saltram' winery works closely with 'Stonyfell', winemaking being carried out at 'Saltram' with 'Stonyfell' being used for maturing and bottling.

For sixty-three years Fred Ludlow worked at the 'Saltram' vineyard and winery—an outstanding record of service. Byron Dolan, of Metala fame, was manager of 'Saltram' for some years before he was transferred to 'Burnside' in 1959, when he became general manager of H. M. Martin & Son. Winemaking at

'Saltram' has been in the hands of Peter ('Mudflat') Lehmann since 1960. He was born at Angaston in 1930, the son of a Lutheran pastor, and worked for thirteen years under the guidance of Rudi Kronberger at Yalumba. Lehmann has lightened the traditional style and made some fine red wines and port.

'Saltram' has about 200 acres under vine. Varieties grown include semillon, clare and rhine riesling, grenache, shiraz, cabernet sauvignon, pedro, palomino, dolcetto and tokay. The soils at 'Saltram' vineyard are limestone and quartz. The vineyards get about five inches of supplementary water from their own bore, by spraying in winter and flooding in summer. Only about ten percent of all grapes processed are gown on their own properties.

Since winemaking has been concentrated at 'Saltram', the winery has been expanded and modernized, and now has a million gallon capacity. The winery is well equipped, and their wines have developed a fine reputation.

B. Seppelt and Sons Pty Ltd, 'Seppeltsfield', and 'Chateau Tanunda'

'Seppeltsfield', near Greenoch on the western edge of the Barossa Valley, is the imposing headquarters of the huge firm of B. Seppelt and Sons. The winery is a tourist magnet, attracting many thousands of visitors.

The story began in Silesia in the early years of the nineteenth century. Joseph Ernest Seppelt, born 1813, grew up to head the family business which dealt in tobacco and snuff and the production and sale of various liqueurs, in the town of Wustewaltersdorf.

In 1849 with his wife and children—two sons, Oscar Benno Pedro and Hugo, and a daughter, a group of young men from his factory and thirteen neighbouring families from Wustewaltersdorf, Seppelt sailed for Australia. Joseph had bought an eighty acre block of land at Golden Grove near Adelaide before his departure, but when he found tobacco would not do well there, the party moved to Klemzig, a settlement of Lutheran escapees from Prussia, near Adelaide.

Seppelt spent a year looking around before he bought two sections in the Hundred of Nuriootpa, and two lots in the township of Tanunda from Hermann Kook, farmer. The deal was registered in February, 1852. The families settled in Tanunda while the men set to work to clear the land and establish 'Seppeltsfield'. When gold fever struck, however, most of the young men headed for Victoria.

'Seppeltsfield' also turned out to be unsuitable for tobacco cultivation and Joseph Ernest began again with corn and wheat, and also planted a small vineyard. He encouraged his neighbours to plant grapes, planning to buy their crops to make into good wine. The first wine was made in Frau Seppelt's dairy which Joseph then converted to a storage cellar, twenty-four by thirty-six feet in extent.

Joseph built up the business, selling his wine at Gawler and along the Murray before he died in 1868 at the age of fifty-five from a sudden attack of pneumonia.

Joseph's son Benno was twenty-one at the time of his father's death. He devoted his hard-working life to winemaking and left an enviable record of achievement. Benno built up the business from its humble origins to a huge interstate concern, well known for the quality of its products, and made the Seppelt label a household word. A very energetic man, it has been said that his abstemiousness at table and regular habits kept him youthful. He supervised the building of the famous winery, the first part of which was built in 1867.

In 1875 the stone cellar was extended, and doubled in size. The holdings and vineyards were gradually extended. A grand new distillery was built, and opened with some pomp in 1877. Extensions continued and by 1878 the capacity of the 1875 building was quadrupled. Benno Seppelt's era of almost continuous expansion was rounded off in 1882 with the completion of a new vinegar section. In 1885 a new winery was begun. At the turn of the century 'Seppeltsfield' was producing 400,000 gallons per year. As a result of the continued growth of the business, in 1902 it was registered as a company.

Seppelts expanded its winemaking activities and interstate markets. At about the time of the outbreak of the First World War the 'Clydeside' vineyard and cellars at Rutherglen came onto the market and were bought by the company. These facts are only a bare outline of Benno Seppelt's achievements. By the time he retired in 1916 he had created a vast enterprise which his father would hardly have recognized. That year the concern was made a limited liability company.

Ever active Benno Seppelt had nine sons and four daughters. On his retirement his eldest son Oscar, who had spent several years studying winemaking in Europe in the 1890s took over as chairman of the board. 1916 was also the year in which Oscar bought 'Chateau Tanunda', five miles away after it had suffered prolonged financial difficulties and the effects of a drought. 'Chateau Tanunda' was already well known as a large scale brandy producer. It had once been owned by the Adelaide Wine Company, whose winemaker until 1910 was R. George Mann, father of Jack Mann, of Houghtons fame.

Two years after the purchase of 'Chateau Tanunda' Oscar Seppelt bought the Great Western champagne cellars in Victoria. Under Oscar's control in 1927, a new winery was set up at Nuriootpa to cope with Seppelts' greatly increased production. At the end of the war a winery was established at 'Dorrien', beside the railway to Nuriootpa.

In 1930 Benno Seppelt died at eighty-five years of age, at a time when the Depression was just making itself felt. Oscar naturally could not continue with any expansion, but did manage to consolidate the Seppelts' position. It was at this time that he began the planting of the date palms at 'Seppeltsfield' which are now a sign of Seppelts' wineries everywhere. Before its centenary year Seppelts achieved a vintage of three million gallons.

After twenty-three years as chairman, Oscar retired in 1939 and was followed by Leo R. for three years, who was in turn succeeded by Waldemar. The fourth generation of the family becoming prominent, Ian, Waldemar's son, was made chairman. He is also chairman of the Australian Wine Board and holder of other important posts in the Australian wine industry. Robert is general manager and has also made a considerable contribution to the industry in general. He and brother John, the sales director, are Leo's sons. Cousin Bill is production manager and cousin Karl vineyard manager.

The fifth generation has now appeared on the scene. Robert's son, Nicholas, a graduate of the University of California, is now manager at 'Seppeltsfield'. Ian's sons Malcolm and Graham and Bill's son Bill are also taking their places in the company.

In 1970 Seppelts was floated as a public company, although many members of the family retained important positions.

'Seppeltsfield' itself is actually a complex, almost a village, of winery, cellars, distillery, administrative buildings and vinegar plant. The winery and storage buildings are built of local bluestone. At the time it was built ingenious use was made of gravity, obviating the need for pumping, the fermenting vats being set in stepped down rows on the side of a hill. Grapes go in at the top, and the must is then moved down by stages until it reaches storage vessels lower down.

There is enormous storage capacity at 'Seppeltsfield', whole cellars being devoted to making sherry and port alone. 20,000 hogsheads of brandy are stored—and to give some idea of what this means, 20,000 gallons of it is written off to evaporation!

The modern and well equipped laboratory at 'Seppeltsfield' is the quality control centre for all Seppelts' production, and wine is brought there from all the other wineries for analysis. Only fortified wines are made at 'Seppeltsfield', but the scale of production is staggering. 3,000 tons of grapes are processed each year, twenty percent of them being brought in from outside growers.

'Chateau Tanunda' at Tanunda, another Seppelts winery in the Barossa, is an unusually beautiful old bluestone winery which was built in 1889 with a holding capacity of over one million gallons. It has recently been considerably extended for making table wines. Seppelts also have a winery at 'Dorrien'.

The Barossa wineries are used for processing the grapes of the company's River Murray (Qualco) vineyards.

Overall Seppelts own over 5,500 acres in three states. They have 500 acres under vine at 'Seppeltsfield', where they grow grenache, mataro and palomino varieties on the red-brown earth.

Seppelts do not plan to extend their vineyards in the Barossa Valley. They do have a policy of systematic replanting; replacing vines that have outlived their economic life, or are of a variety no longer required, with varieties that will yield grapes of the highest quality. Seppelts have been expanding in new areas—at Keppoch, Drumborg and Qualco, planting at a rate of over 100 acres per year. They still have about 1,000 acres suitable for development as vineyards.

As well as their enormous output of wine, Seppelts make three-quarters of a million gallons of vinegar each year. Doradillo grapes are used for the vinegar, the vinegar bacillus transforming the wine into acetic acid.

S. Smith & Son Pty Ltd, 'Yalumba'

The 'Yalumba' winery, just out of Angaston, is a good example of a gracious Australian version of a European winehouse. The solid winery, built of local blue marble, is set among green lawns and tall trees, and the whole scene is somewhat reminiscent of an English country estate.

As well it might be, reflecting the origins of the founder of the organization, Samuel Smith, a brewer from Wareham in Dorsetshire. In 1847, at the age of thirty-five he left England with his wife, son and four daughters on the sailing ship *China*, for South Australia. They settled initially at Klemzig, on the banks of the Torrens, near Adelaide. After a short time he moved his family by bullock waggon fifty miles to the north-east, where the township of Angaston was forming.

He was employed by George Fife Angas, who was at the time virtually a feudal lord, to work in his garden and orchard. Samuel Smith was quick to realize the potential of the area for viticulture, and bought thirty acres to establish his own vineyard. He called it 'Yalumba', an aboriginal term meaning 'all the country around'. In 1849 he began the planting of his vineyard by night, as he was still working for Angas during the day.

In the early 1850s Samuel succumbed to the lure of the goldfields, hoping to be lucky enough to be able to acquire capital for the expansion of his vineyards.

After four months he returned to Adelaide with £300 worth of gold, which, although not a fortune, enabled him to expand. For £80 he bought a further eighty acres, and spent a further £100 on a plough, two horses and a harness. Samuel Smith then devoted himself to winemaking and began to really develop the enterprise. His son, Sydney, became a partner, and in 1863 they made sixty hogsheads of wine. Within ten years 'Yalumba' had established a reputation for quality, and by 1866 won a bronze plaque at an Intercolonial Exhibition in London.

When Samuel died in 1888, Sydney took over management of the Estate. They continued to prosper and expand, and built the well-known two-storey blue marble winery with its clocktower which replaced the old thatched cellar.

Sydney Smith's two sons, Percy and Walter Grandy, joined the business, eventually taking it over. Percy managed the cellars and Walter travelled the world looking for markets for their wines. He was successful in building up an export market in England and India.

In 1923 Percy Smith retired, and a private company was formed with two of Walter Smith's sons as directors—Sidney Hill Smith and Wyndam Hill Smith. As mentioned, Sidney was one of the victims of the 'Kyeema' air crash in 1938. After this, his brother, Wyndam, then aged twenty-eight, who was looking after the company's affairs in Perth, returned to headquarters to become managing director and chairman. 'Windy', as he is affectionately known, and still managing director, is a colourful character. He loves wine, as well as horse racing and cricket. He has bred many winning racehorses, and is part of the syndicate that bought the estate once owned by George Angas and which is now used as a racing stud, Lindsay Park.

'Yalumba' made it through the Depression, and just before the Second World War began producing brandy on a large scale. At the same time they commenced business as general wine and spirit merchants with agencies as distributors of various spirits, such as White Horse Whisky and Gilbeys Gin. This period also saw the beginning of production of Flor sherry.

Mark Hill Smith, Sidney's eldest son, who is the present managing director, returned from war service in the navy to join the company, the first of the fifth generation of Smiths at Yalumba. His younger brother, John, has since joined him, as has Wyndam's son. Mark Hill Smith's two sons, Michael and Matthew, are the sixth generation of the family at Yalumba.

The Smith family has also been fortunate with the company's personnel. Rudi Kronberger has been making wine at 'Yalumba' for over forty years, which must be something of a record. Viennese born, he graduated from the Institute of Oenology in Vienna, where Tony Nelson of Woodley Wines, and much earlier, Oscar Seppelt, also studied. Rudi came to Australia in 1929 after an apprenticeship in the Rhineland. He has been influential in the technique of the early bottling of riesling, and has done much in the cultivation of the Flor Fino type of sherry. Now, over sixty years of age, he is in charge of the technical and scientific aspects of the business and is still 'Yalumba's' chief authority on blending. Alfred Wark, a chartered accountant, has been with the company since the retirement of Harold Yates, who had been with 'Yalumba' for fifty years. Wark became company secretary on his discharge from the RAAF. He is also widely known for his culinary ability and has published a book, *Wine Cookery*.

Since the end of World War II 'Yalumba' has grown tremendously. The company's vineyards cover many hundreds of acres and their cellars now house over four million gallons of maturing wines. In the Barossa Valley 'Yalumba' owns over 400 acres of vineyards, and they have developed about 400 acres of their 600 acre holding at Oxford Landing on the River Murray. A wide variety of grapes are grown in the Barossa, where the soils are mostly sand or sandy loam over clay.

A huge building project to provide additional storage and modern bottling facilities was recently completed. The latest types of bottling; filling and labelling and filtering machinery have been installed and the new insulated bottle storage holds over 150,000 dozen of maturing white and red table wines. Many hundreds of French Nevers and Limousin oak casks have been purchased in recent years, their influence being reflected in the quality of the dry reds.

The scale of winemaking at 'Yalumba' is reflected in the size of their annual crush, which is over 16,000 tons of grapes in a normal season. Seventy-five percent of the crush is purchased from outside growers in both the Barossa and Murray Valleys. An indication of the value of this buying to the economy of the State is that over one million dollars was distributed to the growers for their grapes in 1970.

'Yalumba' is especially well known for their range of ports, but they also produce renowned sherries and white and red table wines. In recent years 'Yalumba' has had considerable impact with their Pewsey Vale Riesling.

In 1961 'Yalumba' began a new and exciting venture—the establishment of vineyards at 'Pewsey Vale', in partnership with Geoffrey Angas Parsons, the present proprietor of 'Pewsey Vale Station', 1,800 feet up in the Barossa Hills. This area had been a vineyard once before, the original vineyard there having been planted by pioneer Joseph Gilbert in 1847.

'Yalumba' believed that 'Pewsey Vale' had enormous potential for the production of top quality table wines. Under the supervision of Norman Hanckel over 160 acres were contour banked and planted with rhine riesling and cabernet sauvignon, and some semillon. The climate at that altitude is relatively cool, with about twenty-five inches of rain annually. There are huge outcrops of rock at 'Pewsey Vale' and the soil is podsolic—mostly gravelly sandy loam over a very pebbly subsoil.

The young rhine rieslings of 'Pewsey Vale' have been multi-medal winners, justifying the faith and investment of 'Yalumba'. Let us hope that wine companies like 'Yalumba' continue to progress and that the results of new projects are always as successful as 'Pewsey Vale'.

Tolley, Scott and Tolley Ltd

Tolley, Scott and Tolley is widely known for their brandy, but in recent years they have moved into the table wine field. Their present large winery, adjacent to the Penfolds mammoth at Nuriootpa, is worlds apart from the East Torrens Winemaking and Distillation Company Limited.

The company with the long name was formed on 23 August, 1858 with a capital of £2,000 in 400 shares of £5 each. With Thomas Mildred as chairman the company was formed to purchase grapes for the manufacture of brandy and spirit for fortifying wine and methylating. After a few years of trading the distillery at Nelson Street in the inner Adelaide suburb of Stepney was closed down. It was later purchased by a Mr H. Linde, who appropriately called the business The Phoenix Distilling Company.

In 1888 Mr Thomas Scott with Messrs Ernest and Douglas Tolley purchased the distillery, and began trading as Tolley, Scott and Tolley. Scott had experience in distillation in the United Kingdom and Peru, and organized the new business on a sound basis, fitting new equipment, to specialize in the manufacture of brandy, gin and rectified spirit for fortifying wine. He eventually sold his distillery in London and settled in South Australia.

Ernest A. Tolley was born in Adelaide in 1862, and educated at St Peter's College Adelaide before going to England in 1879. He studied at Kings College London for three years, and then spent a further three years at Epernay and Narbonne in France, learning a great deal about winemaking, especially sparkling wines. Ernest returned to London, where he joined the Abbey Street Distillery in Bermondsey, South London, which was owned by Thomas Scott, his future partner. There he learned the art of distilling. Ernest's brother, Douglas, is described in the section on his own firm, Douglas A. Tolley Pty Ltd.

The Tolley brothers returned to Australia in 1887 and went into business with Mr Scott. Another T.S.T. personality of those early days was John Linnett, a partner of Thomas Scott's in London. London born, he emigrated to Melbourne in 1875 where he became a baker. Some years later he went back to England and spent seven years with Scott before coming back to Australia to join Tolley, Scott and Tolley.

In 1904 a new and up-to-date distillery was erected at Angas Park, Nuriootpa. Four years later Tolley, Scott and Tolley purchased a winery which had belonged to S. & W. Sage at Nuriootpa, with forty acres of vines. They gradually bought and extended their holdings until they had 600 acres under vine.

In January, 1921 the firm was formed into a limited liability company, with Mr Linnett as secretary. The capital of the company was then £150,000. The reason for the re-forming of the company was to allow the members of the respective families to participate in the business. Albion James Tolley, father of Ernest and Douglas, put some capital into the venture, as did two of their brothers, Albion Everard and Frederic Osborne.

Ernest's son, Sam, and Douglas' son, Len, followed their fathers into the business, and later the next generation also joined the board. In 1961 Tolley, Scott and Tolley was the subject of a takeover by the Distillers Company Ltd of England.

The whole of the grape processing operation is now conducted at Nuriootpa. Part of the output goes by tanker to Stepney for further storage, blending and bottling. The modern bottling plant at Stepney can turn out over 24,000 bottles a day.

The winery at Nuriootpa has been expanded and modernized at a cost of one and a half million dollars, to cope with making table wines. In 1965 the most modern crushing, fermentation and skin disposal facilities were installed. In the early seventies a new red wine fermentation cellar was completed, and the bottling and storage cellars were greatly increased. The employment in distillation of wooden Coffey stills, which combine the advantages of continuous and pot still, is unique in brandy production.

The grapes come from the Barossa and new plantings at Eden Valley. The company has established 1,000 acres of vineyards at Waikerie in the irrigation area of the Murray. They also buy grapes from McLaren Vale and Langhorne Creek.

Wolfgang Blass took over as winemaker from Gordon Nilsson, in 1968. Blass has a diploma from the Wuerzburg Oenology College in Germany, from whence he came to Australia in 1960. He worked for several years for the Barossa Co-operative Winery before launching himself as a free-lance winemaking consultant and technical adviser. He also began making wine under his own Bilyara label, establishing a small winery on the Sturt Highway about two and a half miles north of Nuriootpa. Wolfgang Blass has been called 'enthusiastic, irrepressible, ebullient, efficient' and has made some very good wines indeed. There is little doubt that we shall be tasting many more good, and even great, dry wines from this company in the future.

Wilsford Wines

This relatively small concern, near Lyndoch, has been owned for many years by the Burge family. The founder of Wilsford Wines was John Burge, who settled in South Australia, from England, in 1859. His son, Percy, now runs the winery with the help of his sons, Noel and Colin. Noel Burge was one of the first graduates in oenology from the Roseworthy Agricultural College. The fourth generation of Burges is now at Wilsford, represented by Noel's son, Richard and Colin's son, Grant.

Wilsford Wines own ninety acres of vineyards which are planted with rhine and clare riesling, cabernet sauvignon and shiraz. They get yields of two to four tons per acre and crush about 500 tons annually. About half the grapes processed are purchased from other growers in the area.

The Burges have in the past concentrated on making dessert wines, but in recent years they have given increasing emphasis to the production of table wines. Some new French oak has been bought for their reds.

'Chateau Rosevale' Winery

The 'Chateau Rosevale' winery is in the western part of the Barossa near the little hamlet of Gomersal. There are no vineyards in the immediate vicinity and the company has its small vineyard in the Valley proper.

The winery is fairly old, and was owned by the Fromms until 1964 when it was taken over by Waldemar Lehmann, and his son-in-law, Ron Burton. They are modernizing the whole set-up. 'Chateau Rosevale' markets over one hundred wines and liqueurs, which are all made on the premises. They specialize in sparkling wines.

Bernkastel Wines Pty Ltd

This company now operates the 'Paradale' and 'Arrawarra' wineries just west of Tanunda. The 'Arrawarra' winery was founded in 1879 by the Petras

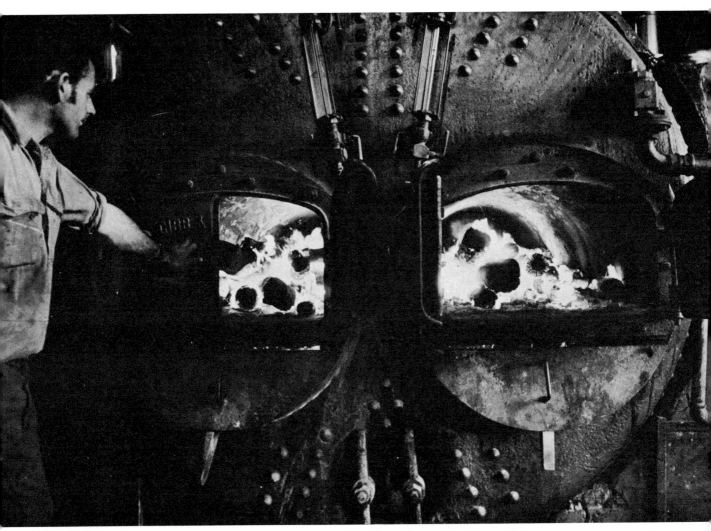

This 50-year-old wood-fired boiler is still in constant use at the Waikerie Co-operative Winery, S.A.

family. The founder's son, J. W. F. Petras, inherited it, and later sold it to a Mr and Mrs Dyer. 'Paradale' was previously owned by Arthur Hanisch.

K. I. Kies, 'Karrawirra'

Ken Kies is the owner of the 'Karrawirra' winery, a few miles south of Lyndoch. 'Karrawirra' is aboriginal, meaning 'forest of red gums'. The winery was built in 1969 to process the grapes of Ken Kies' seventy acre vineyard. He was one of the largest grape growers in the district.

Tarac Industries Pty Ltd

This organization does not make any wine but is worthy of mention as it is closely connected with winemaking in the Valley. The firm, which has its headquarters at Nuriootpa, was founded in 1930 by Mr A. J. Allen.

Tarac recovers winery wastes, processing the marc for tartaric acid, grapeseed oil and fortifying spirit. They have branches at Berri and Griffith.

Viticultural Research Station, Nuriootpa

In 1938 the South Australian Department of Agriculture established a viticultural research station two miles east of Nuriootpa. The property covers fifty acres, of which forty-five are under vine. They carry out research into grape varieties and viticulture generally. A considerable amount of research has been done on vine-bud mite and vine disorders. Field days are held at which the results of their labours are communicated to growers.

121

Clare—Watervale

Clare, about ninety miles north of Adelaide, is the most northerly of the South Australian vineyard areas. It lies on the main road north from Adelaide through the centre of Australia, which ends eventually in Darwin.

The little town of Watervale is at the southern part of the area, while Clare itself is about ten miles on. Clare is at an altitude of 1,305 feet above sea level— Watervale is slightly lower at 1,200 feet.

The area has long been a centre of the wine industry. The 'Quelltaler' winery has the most historic connections at Watervale, their vineyards being originally planted in 1865. Details of the company's early history are included in the section on 'Quelltaler'. The 'Sevenhill' College vineyard, originally planted in 1848, is the sole survivor of the early Clare vineyards. Some of the other early vineyards no longer exist, such as those planted in 1853 by John Ward and Valentine Mayr in 1859.

By 1903 there were 1,200 acres under vine in a radius of six miles from Clare. It was then very difficult to buy land in the district, anything arable fetching £10 per acre, while premium plots brought up to three times that sum.

The Clare district has a hot climate, and quite a low rainfall, about 24 to 26 inches. The country is hilly and wooded. The soils are similar to those in the Barossa. There is widespread limestone with a considerable amount of sandstone. The vineyards are generally not irrigated. These factors mean that a very distinctive style of wine is made—a rather big and long living style.

The ubiquitous shiraz has been the mainstay of most Clare wines, although there are also substantial plantings of mataro and grenache, with some cabernet. Lately, more of the latter variety has been planted.

A. P. Birks, 'Wendouree' Cellars

Winemaking at 'Wendouree', two and a half miles south-east of Clare, began as a hobby for the founder of the firm, Alfred Percy Birks, who established his vineyard in the bush in 1892. His hobby grew and by 1895 his vintage was 140 gallons. By 1913 this had grown to 4,000 gallons.

Those early wines were stored in semi-underground thatched roofed cellars. New cellars were built in 1914, and extended in 1921 and again in 1924. These cellars are still in use, with a total storage capacity of 60,000 gallons.

A. P. Birks died in 1948 at the age of eighty. His third son, Roland Napier Birks, has been winemaker since 1917, with his wife Olive Wakefield Birks.

'Wendouree' has a vineyard of over seventy acres, with planting gradually increasing. The main grape varieties grown are shiraz, mataro, riesling and pedro, although there is also some quantity of grenache, albillo, malbec and cabernet sauvignon. Roly Birks' output is now 40,000 gallons per year, but over half the grapes processed are purchased from other growers.

Winemaking at 'Wendouree' is still carried out in the old manner, producing very much the old style of wines—big reds noted for their longevity. Recently the firm was taken over by a Victorian company.

H. Buring & Sobels Ltd, Quelltaler

In German 'Quell' denotes a bubbling spring of pure water, and in the idiom of a few generations ago 'Thal' meant a vale. The combination of these words into 'Quelltaler' is the equivalent English 'Springvale', and it is this area which has a history of over a century in the making of Australian table wine.

Mount Horrocks, named after the original settler, overlooks the 'Springvale' vineyards, and it was at the base of this mount that Francis Treloar planted the original fifty acre vineyard in 1865. It is recorded that the Treloar vineyard was located 'where the calcareous soil was kindly suitable, the site well-chosen (1,300 feet above sea level) and the vines the finest procurable'.

Treloar sold his property, the vineyard and the grazing land to Captain Walter Watson Hughes (later

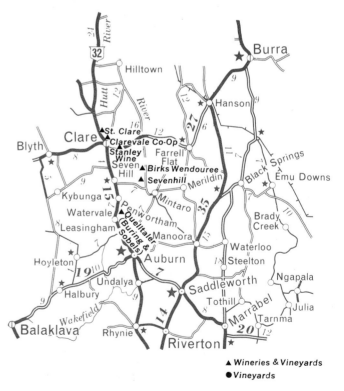

Vineyards of Clare-Watervale

Sir Walter Hughes), but stayed on as the manager. He established the wine cellars in 1868, engaging Carl A. Sobels as the winemaker. Sir Walter Hughes later became the original founder of Adelaide University.

Carl Sobels was born at Quedlinberg, Germany and arrived in South Australia with his parents in 1847. He married Meta Dohrnwendt at Lobethal in 1867. He had been living in Tanunda where his parents had made their names as winemakers. Carl came to 'Springvale' in 1869 with his wife and two young children, the beginning of a family which eventually grew to thirteen. He completely handled the vintages at 'Springvale', and made many extensions to the cellars.

In 1889 a partnership was formed between Carl Sobels and T. G. Hermann Buring to purchase the vineyards and cellars from James McKinnon Richman.

It is quoted by one of their descendants: 'Enterprising, they acquired neighbouring lands; far-sighted they uprooted acres of unsuitable vines and planted other varieties better suited to produce table wines of the quality for which "Quelltaler" was becoming noted; prudent they adapted their cellars, their implements and methods to keep pace with the industry's progress.'

The ripping out of the unsuitable vines must have taken considerable courage. While they waited for the earth to be rested the two partners gathered cuttings of shiraz, rhine riesling and semillon and others such as dolcetto, malbec, cabernet and grenache from the experimental vines planted in the Adelaide Botanic Gardens. Their aim was to make only quality table wine. Things did not always go smoothly, and in 1900 a severe frost wiped out the complete vintage. But Buring and Sobels persevered, and prospered.

In 1935 the company's head office, bottling and distribution plant moved from Currie Street to a building now known as 'Quelltaler House', one of the oldest sites in the heart of Adelaide, Gilbert Place. The design of the building has a strong Spanish influence. The bottling plant has now been transferred, and the despatch has been moved to larger premises at Flinders Street. There is now a steak restaurant in the old cellar.

The family influence was strong for many years. At the centenary luncheon in 1965 there were present thirty direct descendants of Carl Sobels. The firm has now been taken over, and is entirely owned by Vignerons Distillers and Vintners Ltd, a holding company for several liquor companies. Nathan and Wyeth Pty Ltd of Melbourne and Remy Martin of France are the two major shareholders.

The 'Quelltaler' winery, with its central stone cellar, has a unique and delightful atmosphere. A feature of the winery are the 1,200 gallon slate fermenting vats, the oldest of which have seen more than seventy-five vintages. These are made of sheets of solid grey Mintaro slate, three inches thick, quarried from the Watervale hills. They are ingeniously bolted together, externally, so that the metal does not come into contact with the wine. The complete vessels are massive, as they weigh more than five tons. The material is uniquely suitable for its function, the thickness of the walls efficiently dissipating the heat of fermentation. The tanks are almost maintenance free. Unfortunately no more of these vats will be made, as the cost of the Mintaro slate is now prohibitive compared to the cost of concrete.

In the early fifties the 'Quelltaler' winery underwent a major renovation and reconstruction, but the efficient and unique slate tanks were retained.

The vineyards at 'Springvale' are situated over an artesian basin, and bore water is used for winery operations, but not for irrigation. The soils are red-brown loam over soft limestone, shale and clay. The average annual rainfall is about twenty-five inches.

There are 480 acres under vine, of which sixty are non-bearing. 'Quelltaler' still has about 200 acres for future planting, and are expanding at the rate of twenty to thirty acres per year. They have a wide variety of white grapes, among which are semillon, rhine and clare riesling, and pedro. The red varieties include shiraz, grenache, cabernet sauvignon and malbec. About one-third of the grapes processed are bought from local growers.

'Quelltaler' has been especially noted for its dry white wine known as hock. The company claims proudly to having produced the first Australian wine served at the Lord Mayor's Banquet in London. Their 'Granfiesta' sherry also enjoys a very good reputation.

Clarevale Co-operative Winery

The Clarevale Co-operative operates from its winery right in the centre of Clare. It has been established since 1928. The managing director was for many years the then Minister of Lands in the South Australian Government, Mr P. H. Quirke.

Clarevale markets a large amount of fortified wine and brandy. It also produces some table wine, made from grenache, mataro, and shiraz. Recently a cabernet blend did very well in national wine shows. All wine made by the Co-operative is from grapes bought from its grower/shareholders.

Manresa Society Inc, 'Sevenhill' Cellars

The 'Sevenhill' winery is known especially for its production of sacramental wines. The winery is run by the Brothers of the Jesuit College of St Aloysius. It is believed that 'Sevenhill' was named by one of the early priests in relation to the fact that Rome is built on seven hills.

The College is set in a great circle of hills, and has been there since the community settled on the site in the mid-nineteenth century. The history of the Order in Clare began with two Jesuit fathers who accompanied a party of Silesian settlers to the district in 1845. One of the priests, Aloysius Kranewitter, stayed on to acquire the land for the Order. According to Bagenal, an early writer on the area, it is from this immigration that the cuttings of the varieties now known as 'Clare Riesling' and 'Tokay' are believed to have come to Australia.

The pioneer Austrian priests and brothers of the Society of Jesus had come from a traditional vine growing country. They must have been concerned about their supplies of altar wine, separated as they were from European sources. It was thus natural that they should decide to make their own wine. In 1852 the first vines were planted, the cuttings having been obtained from the Hawker estate at Bangaree, twelve miles from 'Sevenhill'.

In 1863 the order had its first winepress, until then the ageless method of foot power having been used to press the grapes. The press was entirely made on the property (except for the screw) by the brothers, the blacksmith and the carpenter. This press enabled the winemakers, Brother John Schreiner and his assistant Brother John Schneider to press about four buckets at a time.

Since then the cellars have been extended and plantings have continued, until now about one hundred and ten acres are under cultivation. Winemaking has also progressed with the times. In 1963 an air-bag press was installed. Brother Downey was in charge of the cellars and its activities for thirty years before his retirement in 1951. Then Brother John Hanlon took over, and was winemaker, with the assistance of Brother John May, until his death in February, 1972. Brother Hanlon was born in 1918, and joined the Order at the age of twenty, having previously been a furrier in Melbourne. Over the next decade he spent much of his time in the college's kitchen, before being instructed to help with the winemaking, which he did for three years before Brother Downey's retirement. Len Evans has written of Brother John: 'He had a wonderful sense of humour and unique twist of imagination. There was none of the unctuous do-gooding bit for him—he loved man, loved his fellow, understood his foibles and weaknesses, yet could, and did, prick holes in the pompous and eschew the pretentious. He was a great man, a good man, and a maker of fine wine.'

The country at 'Sevenhill' is undulating, the soils ranging from white sandy to heavy black types. The low (about 24 inches) rainfall and high amount of sun mean that the vineyards have a low acre yield, but produce a big style of wine. A great variety of grapes are grown, including albillo, frontignan, tokay, grenache and shiraz.

At all times winemaking takes second place to the religious activities of the Order. The chief winemaking concern of the brothers is the manufacture of altar wine, approved by their Archbishop as pure sacramental wine to be used by priests at Mass. This wine, which is used in Anglican as well as Roman Catholic churches, is sent all over Australia, and is exported to the Pacific, Japan, India and Indonesia. When the requirements for altar wine are met, the remaining grapes are made into table wine—a big dry red, dry whites, and vintage port. Table wines have only been sold since 1954. The proceeds from all wine sales go to supporting the College, and its Indian mission.

'St Clare' Vineyards

J. B. Barry, winemaker at 'St Clare', is a graduate of Roseworthy College. After finishing his course in 1947 he joined Clarevale Wines, and eventually held the dual position of general manager and winemaker for a number of years. Later he joined Tolleys, where he worked on the planning of their vineyards.

In 1960 Jim Barry purchased a property in Armagh (an Irish name) very close to the town of Clare.

Barry started off with the original vines that were on the Burton Cottage Estate, and later he bought another seventy acres north of this property. A burn runs across the flat bisecting the holding, with vineyards on both sides. This district is known as Ben Burnie, and is where vines of cabernet, clare riesling and shiraz varieties are grown. At Watervale there are fifteen acres of rhine riesling with a few acres of pedro.

Dry red and white table wines are made, and marketed, under the 'St Clare' label.

Stanley Wine Co Pty Ltd

The Stanley Wine Co Pty Ltd was founded in 1894 in the Clare area. The name was derived from the old State electoral district of Stanley. The founders were J. H. Knappstein, merchant; Dr O. Wein Smith, a Scottish born doctor who was practising in Clare, Magnus Badger, a solicitor; and John Christison, a brewer, and the managing director; Alfred Basedow, who was general manager. Basedow had continental training and was reported to be recognized as one of the best winemakers in the country.

J. H. Knappstein known as 'one of the most enterprising wine men in South Australia' bought out the interests of Dr Wein Smith and Mr Badger, and on the death of John Christison in 1912 Mr Knappstein acquired his share. From that time onwards the company was under his control. In 1903 he made a trip to the United Kingdom to try to find markets for Clare wine.

The Stanley Company had its first vintage, of 3,000 gallons, in 1895. In 1896 the cellars were built and improvements were made steadily after that. By 1903 the vintage had grown to 100,000 gallons, and a contemporary reporter noted that 'practically speaking the Stanley Wine Company buys all the grapes in the district'.

Following J. H. Knappstein's death in 1919 the business was controlled by a trustee company, with the consequence that very little progress was made during those years. In 1938 the company reverted to the control of the Knappstein family with Fred W. Knappstein as winery manager, and Otto as Chairman of Directors.

On Fred's death in 193! Bernard was appointed manager. He carried on until his death in 1954, when Alex succeeded him and was later appointed Chairman of Directors on the death of Otto in 1959.

In 1948 the company established vineyards in the Watervale area, south of Clare. From 1954 onwards old unproductive and uneconomic vineyards in Clare were sold, to concentrate on the development of the virgin land at Watervale. Development went on steadily. In the Leasingham/Watervale area they have over 500 acres of red clay over limestone. At Clare itself they have 100 acres of acidy sandy loam and at East Clare about 50 acres of clay with limestone subsoil.

Alex died in 1962, and K. H. (Mick) Knappstein was appointed manager and Chairman, with John as vineyard manager. Hugh and Bob are two other Knappsteins who were on the board.

The Stanley Wine Co Pty Ltd was taken over by the food giant, H. J. Heinz, in 1971. Tim Knappstein, a Roseworthy graduate and grandson of the founder of the company has been retained as winemaker.

The grape varieties grown are rhine and clare riesling, cabernet sauvignon, shiraz, tokay, grenache and pedro. In the planting programme, commenced in 1957, the chief varieties planted were rhine and Clare riesling, cabernet sauvignon and shiraz.

The average yield is approximately 2½ tons per acre at Watervale, on established vineyards in average years with a rise and fall according to extreme seasons. The vineyards are not irrigated.

Over half the grapes processed are purchased from other growers. The varieties purchased are mainly pedro and grenache in quantity for bulk wines, with most other varieties supplied in lesser amounts.

Both red and white wines are made with about 95 percent of these being dry table wines. For many years the Stanley Company sold mainly for export, and then later sold its products in bulk to big wine companies. In recent years the company has been increasingly selling under its own label, and has won many medals for these wines. Lately the Leasingham dry whites have achieved a particularly good reputation.

In the 1960s the Stanley Company invested heavily in a vast array of new equipment. This includes two 12,000 gallon glass lined steel tanks, six 10,000 gallon concrete and six 1,000 gallon oaks. Fermenting facilities were also increased and modernized with the purchase of two German Wilmes presses, and a new crusher. Since then more large fermenting tanks have been added, as well as a centrifuge for clarification of the juice.

Unloading the grapes at Birks' Wendouree Cellars, S.A.

Part of the two-level wood storage area at Potts' 'Bleasdale' winery. The timber for the building and all the big vats was hand hewn on the property.

125

Coonawarra

Coonawarra, the aboriginal meaning of which is 'wild honeysuckle' is one of the magic names of Australian winemaking. This tiny area in the southeast of South Australia, miles from anywhere, now enjoys the reputation of being one of those at the very top of the winemaking ladder.

Coonawarra is a tiny isolated area near the South Australian-Victorian border, on the road between Naracoorte and Mount Gambier, about forty miles from either of them. The nearest township is Penola. Coonawarra is 264 miles from Adelaide. The countryside is absolutely flat for miles around, with tall pines growing in profusion. It is the centre of a dairy cattle and wool producing district.

This little area is one of the most southerly of Australia's vineyards, situated as it is between the 37th and 38th parallels of latitude. It is only 200 feet above sea level, and but fifty miles from the cold southern seas.

Geographical location, and thus climate, combined with the influence of its famous soils, are natural factors which have enormous potential for the production of quality wines from Coonawarra. The influence of the climate, however, is a two-edged sword.

The number of hours of sunshine is one of the single most significant factors influencing quality in table wines. Ideally there should be no more than an adequate amount of sun to ripen the grapes slowly over a relatively long period. This allows full flavour to develop, while the acid is retained. Scientifically speaking the product of temperature and days of sunshine is called heat summation. At Wynn's Coonawarra Estate it is 2175 degree days, the lowest of any Australian vineyard, and even less than Epernay (Champagne): 2200, or Beaune (Burgundy): 2300. The advantage of this is that grapes ripen slowly and late. This can also be the growers' biggest headache. In many years the summers are cloudy or cool and rain falls. The grapes may thus ripen insufficiently, and the sugar content will not build up enough before the autumn rains set in. The grapes will be too acid. It may be difficult to pick the grapes at 10 degrees Baumé.

Vintage at Coonawarra is later than in most other Australian areas. The grapes are usually not mature enough for picking until the end of April, sometimes vintage can even extend into June. By this time, however, the autumn rains are due, and if these are early considerable damage can be done to the grapes, making picking very difficult and increasing the danger of fungus diseases. Vintage in cool weather does have its advantages though. It means that cool fermentation is natural, and the wine made is thus more delicate.

Frosts at Coonawarra are always a hazard, the vineyards being particularly susceptible to late spring frost. Heaters, 'smudge pots' and sprinkler systems are used to protect the vines. In some years, however, many growers have lost their entire crop.

These climatic variations mean that the differences in the quality of Coonawarra wines are considerable from year to year. The vintage label on a bottle of Coonawarra wine is an important indication of quality, a characteristic shared with the Hunter Valley. The other major natural influence on Coonawarra wines is the unusual soil of the area, which is particularly suitable for the production of wines of the highest quality. In geological terms the area is of podsolic soil, associated with old sand dunes and sand sheets. There are some swamps dotted throughout the area.

There are actually two main types of soil at Coonawarra, a black and a red. They both had their origins in the same limestone, and although the weathering process was the same throughout the years of the soils' formation, the harder sections of limestone developed into soil differently from the softer parts.

The famed red soil of Coonawarra is known as 'terra rossa'. This rare strip of soil is an island, nine miles long and less than one mile wide. In some parts it is only 200 yards in width. The surface soil is a rich red loam, which is friable and porous, and from a few inches up to two feet in depth. The subsoil is calcareous and chalky consisting of nodular travatine limestone and clay to a depth of six to ten feet. The heavy black soil which adjoins the terra rossa is a rendzina. It is almost clay-like in texture and much more difficult to work than the red soil. There are tiny sea shells found here, a remnant of the time when the seas covered the area. The subsoil is similar to the subsoil of the terra rossa.

Under the layer of limestone subsoil is an unusually high water table. No one is sure where this water comes from. The importance of this subterranean water cannot be overstressed. The roots of the vines can quickly and easily penetrate to the water, resulting in vigorous and healthy vines giving very good yields. This is natural irrigation at its best. These factors, combined with the excellent drainage, which is also necessary for good grapes, are ideal for the cultivation of top quality grapes, which go to make top quality wine.

And there is no doubt at all that Coonawarra wines are, at their best, among the finest produced in Australia, and justly take their place among the quality wines of the world. Cabernet and shiraz have been the main grape varieties for the reds. The cabernet sauvignon grape was originally planted by John Riddoch. He also attempted to cultivate pinot noir, the great grape of Burgundy, but with little success. Riddoch also established areas of malbec and shiraz.

Coonawarra reds are very refined in flavour, akin, if we must make comparisons, to the wines of Bordeaux. When young, Coonawarras are a dark purple colour. This gradually changes to a dark red. The bouquet of a mature Coonawarra is most complex

*Hermann Thumm began 'Chateau Yaldara', at Lyndoch,
in the 1940s. Since 1960 he has been carefully remodelling
and extending the buildings at Yaldara aiming to
reproduce something of the atmosphere of European
vineyard chateaux.*

Stainless steel DuCellier-Isman red wine grape fermenter tank where maximum colour extract is obtained by constant rousing of the must, which is automatically triggered by the pressure of carbon dioxide formed during fermentation, at Thomas Hardy's winery, McLaren Vale, S.A.

—Max Lake considers they 'defy description'. The wines have a high acid and austere but strong and rich flavour, with a strong tannin grip. They age well.

In recent years rhine riesling has been cultivated at Coonawarra. Wynns and Mildara have both marketed straight Coonawarra rhine rieslings. The first Wynns offered for sale was the 1968. The conditions which make for great reds—the slow ripening which enables full flavour to develop while retaining acid—also are beneficent to whites. As the rieslings of Coonawarra are a comparatively recent innovation we look forward to the consolidation of the style in the future.

The big wine companies dominate Coonawarra today—Wynns are the largest with over 1,000 acres, but Lindemans, Mildara, Penfolds, and the newest-comers, Hungerford Hill, all have substantial holdings. There are several growers who do not make their own wine but sell to the big companies. The two independent winemakers there are Redman and Brand. A total of over 3,200 acres are owned by wine interests in Coonawarra. The terra rossa strip is almost entirely planted with vines—and what land is left commands previously undreamt of prices.

Hungerford Hill Ltd

In addition to the quality Hunter River (N.S.W.) and Reynella (S.A.) vineyard areas controlled by Hungerford Hill Ltd, the company has moved into the Coonawarra area. It purchased 405 acres in 1971 from Mr D. I. Balnaves who has been retained as Development Manager and who has spent his lifetime in this area. The first vine was planted on 24th July, 1971, by Bill Redman.

At present 250 acres have been planted with cabernet sauvignon, shiraz and rhine riesling. The first vintage is anticipated to be ready for harvesting in March/April, 1973, and will assuredly add to the already excellent reputation of wines from this region.

Mildara Wines Ltd, Coonawarra

Mildara entered the Coonawarra scene in 1954, with the purchase of thirty acres of red soil, selected by the Redmans, for £3,500. The price was very high in those days, and many sceptics thought it was wasted money. The Redmans ran the property until 1962. Mildara bought more land, and built their own winery and cellars, across the Penola Highway from Wynns.

The winery is a large solid building, containing a multiplicity of expensive equipment. Two banks of concrete tanks carry an arch of overhead fermenters under which a log press waits with gaping mouth. Amongst the cleanliness and efficiency sits an Amos crusher, nickel lined pumps and stainless steel lines. The cellars have a storage capacity for 40,000 gallons of wine.

Situated on the eastern fringe of the terra rossa strip of soil, Mildara now has over 300 acres under vine, and plan to extend their plantings gradually until their entire holding of over 850 acres is in production.

The majority of their vines are red grapes—chiefly cabernet sauvignon and shiraz. They also have experimental plantings of other varieties such as malbec, clare riesling, sauvignon blanc, semillon and palomino. Mildara also has plantings of rhine riesling which has been marketed as a straight Coonawarra rhine riesling since 1960.

The vines are generally not irrigated, except for some watering during the first two years after planting to help in the establishment of the young vines.

Mildara's Coonawarra wines are of a very high quality. Their high reputation has been achieved under the influence of Mr H. R. (Ron) Haselgrove, formerly the company's managing director, who had great faith in the future of the area in the 1950s, and his chief winemaker Mr Syd Wells. Dan Murphy, who has written with great knowledge and understanding of Coonawarra wines, believes that there are basically two styles of Coonawarra wines—the Mildara style on the one hand, and the Wynns-Redman style on the other. In his opinion the Wynns-Redman style is similar to the Medoc wines of Bordeaux, while the fuller-flavoured Mildaras do depart from this style.

S. Wynn & Co Pty Ltd, 'Coonawarra Estate'

Undoubtedly it was the leadership of the Wynn family which has helped to bring Coonawarra back into prominence in recent years. Before they became involved in the area in the early fifties the grapes off what is now the Wynn's Coonawarra Estate were used for distillation into brandy. An unthinkable waste in terms of today's demand for table wines from Coonawarra!

The present Coonawarra Estate vineyard was developed in the first instance by the Barossa firm Chateau Tanunda, who bought the Riddoch winery in 1919, and planted more vines to make brandy. Their enterprise was unsuccessful, and by 1921 they had sold out to Milnes of Adelaide. Milnes believed that Coonawarra grapes were only suitable for making brandy.

In 1946 Woodley Wines, under the direction of Tony Nelson, acquired the property and renamed it 'Chateau Comaum'. Woodley's restored the cellars to production by coming to an arrangement with the Redmans, that Bill and his sons would make their wine and manage the vineyards. The new enterprise had an inauspicious beginning with an attack of downy mildew which had not struck before. Despite the quality of the wines made there, and the efforts of Tony Nelson, the going was tough and by 1951

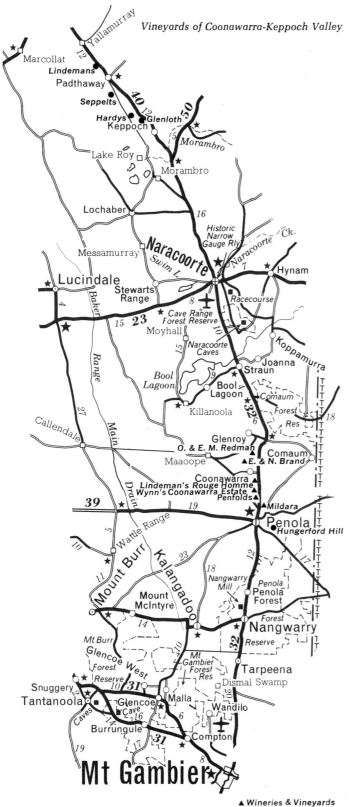

Vineyards of Coonawarra-Keppoch Valley

they had decided to sell the place to grazing interests —at the time wool was booming. This would have meant that the vines would be uprooted and the cellars used as a woolshed.

It was at this stage that Wynns stepped in. Samuel Wynn, migrant from Poland and founder of the firm, had been buying wine from Coonawarra for a number of years. He was particularly impressed with some of Bill Redman's old wines—those of the early thirties—and with how well they had aged. Samuel Wynn was grieved and appalled at the idea of allowing a vineyard of such quality to become defunct. He determined to try to prevent this. Initially he tried to interest a number of large wine firms in forming a consortium to run the vineyard as a non-profit making venture. This idea was not warmly received, and so he determined that his firm would buy the property and attempt to rehabilitate it as a vineyard. At this stage he could not have expected to make any profit from his investment.

Fortunately for Australia's growing number of wine lovers, and for Wynns, the venture finally turned out to be highly successful. Wynns have been followed into the area by other big firms such as Mildara and Lindemans.

At Wynn's Coonawarra Estate the soils are both of the terra rossa and black rendzina types. They now have about 350 acres under vine at Coonawarra, with claret ash trees planted round the perimeter, as a wind break. The pride of the Coonawarra Estate is the plantings of cabernet sauvignon, of which there is over 120 acres. They have also established about fifty acres of rhine riesling. Although Wynns also have over 120 acres of shiraz, and some plantings of other varieties such as pedro, palomino, doradillo and clare riesling, they feel that it is from the 'exotics'—the cabernet and rhine riesling—that their best will come.

David Wynn believes that Coonawarra is a unique area and it should not be concerned with the commonplace, which is why Wynns have given prominence to the exotics in their planting programme. They have planted these varieties despite the fact that they are not easy to grow. They take much longer to get established than shiraz, for example, and their cropping is less reliable. In addition, they are shy bearers. David Wynn says that the consumer must decide whether the results achieved are worth the extra cost and effort, because ultimately he has to pay for it. Wynns have also tried to plant pinot noir. This variety was planted in the early days of the colony but was unsuccessful.

The unique winery, which is featured on the labels of Wynn's Coonawarra wines, was originally built by John Riddoch in 1891. It has all the conventional old winery details of beam, cellars, oak and smell; and all the pleasantness associated with them. The reds are stored in oak casks ranging in capacity from 300 to 1,400 gallons. Some are new

French casks and some are eighty to 100 years old. The wine is kept in oak for two years.

Wynns usually market only three wines from Coonawarra—a cabernet, hermitage and a riesling. If the vintage was a poor one a blend may appear instead of the cabernet and hermitage. The first Coonawarra Claret was 1950, but this was not made by Wynns as they only bought the vineyard after the vintage. Rhine riesling was first vintaged in 1962.

O. D. & E. M. Redman, Coonawarra

The Redman name is synonymous with the Coonawarra area—the pioneer Redman, William Leonard, having an enormous influence on the wines of the area. Indeed Bill Redman is to Coonawarra what O'Shea was to the Hunter and Colin Preece to Great Western.

Bill Redman arrived at Coonawarra in 1901, the year of John Riddoch's death. He was fourteen at the time, the sixth in a family of seven boys and three girls. His father John Redman, born in Manchester, England, was a railway ganger at Stewart's Range, near Naracoorte, where the family ran the local post office.

William had left school in the fourth grade, and gone to work for a skin buyer at Naracoorte for 5/- a week. In the vintage of 1901 William and his older brother, Albert (Dick) aged sixteen, went looking for work at Coonawarra. They were employed at Riddoch's winery—Dick picking grapes and Bill working in the cellars. Bill was then paid £1 salary for a six-day week. At the end of the grape-picking season he was given a permanent job.

He learned to make wine there under the guidance of Ewen Ferguson McBain, a Roseworthy graduate, and a good teacher. Bill stayed at Coonawarra until he was nineteen and head cellarman, through a bad period for Coonawarra. After a short spell doing farm work at Pinnaroo, Bill returned, never to work outside Coonawarra again.

By then Bill's father was working a dairy at Coonawarra with two of his other sons. Bill joined them for two years, until forty acres of Riddoch's vineyards came up for sale. The family bought the property on very generous terms—£150 deposit and the balance of £750 over ten years at four percent interest. Bill went into partnership with his father and brother Robert in 1908.

The Redmans did very well out of their first vintage, which went to make Riddoch brandy—the only time their grapes were not used for wine. Bill Redman got the backing of Douglas Tolley in 1909 for the making of wine for export to Britain—he sent hogsheads to Coonawarra and agreed to pay 1/- per gallon. The Redmans had no winemaking equipment and began with a crusher bought from a teetotal family named Alexander—on the curious grounds that none of the wine made from it could be sold in the area. They had little other equipment, and simply improvised —using hogsheads with the tops removed for fermentation!

Tolley eventually refused to buy any more of Redman's wine. Bill Redman then arranged with Lieutenant-Colonel David Fulton of Woodley Wines to take his wine, provided it was matured in casks at Coonawarra for two years. Colonel Fulton advised Redman to make a light claret-style of wine, with earlier picking, and thus the forerunners of today's famous Coonawarra clarets were made.

Grape growing at Coonawarra was never a proposition that ran smoothly—until the Second World War Bill Redman's was almost the only wine produced there. The Redmans survived all the crises which affected the area, and kept on making wine— although they were a strictly teetotal household for Bill's wife, Lilian Neilson, whom he married in December, 1913, was a strict Presbyterian.

In 1942 an arrangement was made by which the Redmans took the grapes from the local growers and made the wine which would be marketed by Woodleys. At the end of the war when Bill's sons Owen and Leonard returned from service it was agreed that Bill and his sons would make wine for Woodleys, who had bought Milne's cellars and vineyards.

Bill and Robert Redman dissolved their partnership in 1946 and Bill joined the Board of a new company formed by Woodleys, known as 'Chateau Comaum'. Bill and Owen took the forty acres of vineyards and 250 acres of open country and formed their own company: W. L. & O. D. Redman.

In 1947 the Redmans entered their claret in the Adelaide wine show, and won first prize, the first recognition of wine under their own name. In 1950 the company was re-named W. O. & D. Redman, when Len left the company and Don, just out of the RAAF, joined.

Redmans continued to sell their wine to Woodleys, even after the Wynn's takeover in 1951, and for several years they competed in wine shows against themselves—the Redman label against the Woodley label (although the Redmans had made both wines).

It was in 1954 that the first Redman wine was put on the market under their own label—Rouge Homme, the literal French translation of their name. That historic year also saw Bill Redman's retirement, after a career which certainly did not receive the recognition it deserved at the time. It is good that at last Bill Redman's contribution to Australia's wine history is being recognized.

In the fifties the fame of Coonawarra was beginning to spread. The Redmans were still selling their wine in bulk, as well as managing Mildara's vineyards and bottling under their own label, which did very well in shows. By 1965 the fame of the area was established and the big companies had moved in. At this stage the Redmans sold out to Lindemans. Rouge Homme then owned 400 acres of the red bank, and seventy-five acres of vineyards in full bearing.

Vintage in Australia takes place between February and April and in the northern hemisphere between September and November.

Within days of the sale to Lindemans, Owen Redman bought forty acres from Arthur Hoffman, a descendant of one of the original colonists. Bill himself stayed on in Coonawarra, living with his daughter Nancy and son-in-law, Eric Brand. From 1966 to 1968 Owen made his wine in Brand's cellars, although his output was small—only 2,000 gallons a year. Owen returned from a round-the-world tasting trip, and opened his attractive new Redbank Winery on 15 March, 1969. He has installed small fermenting tanks (each holding four to five tons of grapes) and 13,000 gallons of oak storage. Since 1965 he has bought a further ten acres of red soil and has increased his plantings of cabernet sauvignon.

Owen Redman has a home in Adelaide, and his vineyards are managed by Arthur Hoffman, the previous owner. He owns seventy acres in partnership with his wife, Edna.

Bill Redman must be amazed at all the development at Coonawarra. It is said that 'he dreamt of Coona-warra becoming a kind of Medoc of the Southern Hemisphere—but he never really expected it to happen.' And all wine lovers of Australia can be devoutly thankful, not only for what the Redmans have given us in the past, but that the Redman family are continuing to make their wines for our future pleasure.

Eric Brand

In 1965 Eric Brand started making wine. His property of sixty-six acres includes the original vineyard of Captain Stentiford, who retired there from the sea towards the end of the last century. Brand bottles some of his own wine under the 'Laira' label—Laira being the name of a ship of Captain Stentiford's time. He also sells wine to Thomas Hardy. In 1971 he made a superb Cabernet Sauvignon that will be talked of for years to come.

Keppoch

The Keppoch name is new to the Australian wine scene and not much has been heard of it—yet. With the demand for land at Coonawarra sending prices there skyrocketing, some of the big companies began searching for additional suitable land, as yet undeveloped viticulturally.

The Keppoch area which is located about forty miles north of Coonawarra had been regarded as being virtually a desert—the vegetation there was very sparse, in places almost non-existent. After World War II soil reclamation was begun, and sheep grazing became the major land use in the area.

Some interested wine companies, following Seppelts' lead, were attracted to the area, which they thought had great potential for making high quality table wines. Although Keppoch is quite near to Coonawarra there are many geographical differences between the two. The soil at Keppoch is of the red-brown earth variety, with clay and limestone underneath, as against Coonawarra's terra rossa and rendzina. The wind and frost patterns of the two areas may prove to be quite different, also.

Seppelts

About ten years ago Karl Seppelt, the company's vineyard manager, decided that part of the Padthaway Estate (a name registered by the family which originally owned the property, and therefore unavailable to winemakers) some twenty-six miles from Naracoorte, was suitable for development as a quality table wine area.

All told, Seppelts purchased 880 acres. A trial vineyard was planted in 1963 with quarter-acre plots of premium wine grapes. The initial fifty acres of vines were planted the following year. Plantings have continued until now about 500 acres are under vine.

The soil at Seppelts' Keppoch holding consists of rich brown sandy clay loam overlaying limestone. The varieties planted include cabernet sauvignon, shiraz, malbec and rhine riesling, with various experimental plantings of recently introduced varieties. The grapes from Keppoch are processed at Seppelts' Great Western winery.

Thomas Hardy, Lindemans, Glenloth

Hardys are one of the companies who followed Seppelts into Keppoch. They bought 532 acres in 1968, and are planting between fifty and one hundred acres each year. Varieties planted include cabernet sauvignon and shiraz. Wines from their vines will not be available until 1974.

Lindemans bought 1,060 acres in 1968 also, and began planting in 1969.

Glenloth Wines have also purchased 400 acres in the area.

Langhorne Creek

The area known as Langhorne Creek is twenty-five miles east of Adelaide on the Bremer River. Langhorne Creek was named after Alfred Langhorne who had brought a mob of cattle overland from New South Wales in 1841 and settled there. It lies between Strathalbyn and the northern shore of Lake Alexandrina, the outlet of the Murray River.

A unique feature of the area is the very rich and fertile alluvial loam on the riverflats. This soil is enriched with silt by the annual flood of the Bremer. The rainfall is low—only about fourteen inches—which makes irrigation a necessity. These features add up to wines which have a distinctive and individual character. There are several vineyards in the area which sell their grapes to the 'Bleasdale' winery, or to other wineries outside the area. A prominent grower (with a seventy acre vineyard) is Angus Borrett, who married one of Frank Potts junior's daughters. The chief grape varieties grown are palomino (known locally as paulo), muscat, grenache, doradillo, verdelho, cabernet and frontignan.

A feature of the irrigation system is that it is of the flood control. When the River Bremer is high a system of flood gates are operated which forces the waters over the banks of the river onto the vineyards.

Bleasdale Vineyards Pty Ltd

Frank Potts, of 'Bleasdale', was the pioneer vigneron of this area. He was born in 1815, and came to Australia from England at the age of twenty-two.

Frank Potts was impressed by the fertile soils and huge red gums at Langhorne Creek, and settled there. In 1850 he acquired a total of 312 acres on a Crown grant at the cost of £1 per acre. He named his property 'Bleasdale', after his friend the Rev. J. I. Bleasdale who was an influential figure in the wine world of the time. The resourceful, inventive and hard-working Potts built a hut for his large family of six sons and four daughters. His wife died in childbirth, and he later married Anne Flood and had two more sons.

In the early 1860s he planted thirty acres on either bank of the Bremer with shiraz and verdelho. He dug a water channel along either bank of the creek, and constructed a water pumping mill of his own design. By using a weir he constructed, which blocks off the creek, the entire vineyard can be flooded to a depth of several feet.

Ever resourceful he made his own bricks for the cellars from clay on the property and made twin presses, wine pumps and casks—all of red gum sawn on the place. Potts also built a still.

Frank Potts appointed his third son, Frank, to take over the responsibility of the operation as soon as he was old enough. Sons Fred, Henry and Edward planted their own vineyards. Edward established his own winery, 'Kookaburra Cellars', which was absorbed by the 'Bleasdale' cellars on Edward's death in 1919.

Later in life Frank senior confined his activities to boatbuilding and constructed everything from paddle-steamers to racing yachts. He died in 1890, after a very active life, and surely one of the most amazing men who have a place in the history of Australian wine.

In 1904 his son, Frank, purchased the Bridge Hotel at Langhorne Creek and ninety adjoining acres were cleared and planted. He died in 1917 leaving a widow, six sons and four daughters. Frank junior's wife, Alice, carried on with the enterprise, and made progress even through the Depression. On her death in 1935 the estate was divided among her children, Arthur B. Potts inheriting the winery and original 100 acres.

In 1948 the business was converted into a company. The fourth generation of Potts are now working at 'Bleasdale', still making the distinctive wines for which the family is known.

'Metala'

In 1890 Arthur Formby planted thirty acres of cabernet and shiraz at the vineyard he named 'Metala'. In the early twentieth century, Ronald H. Martin of 'Stonyfell' at Burnside took over the vineyard and cellars at 'Metala' and considerably extended them. At that stage the winemaking operations and storage were moved to 'Stonyfell', near Adelaide.

The 'Metala' vineyard is now owned by Denys Butler, but the grapes are still processed by H. M. Martin & Son at 'Stonyfell'.

There are about seven acres of cabernet sauvignon and twenty acres of shiraz at 'Metala'. Despite the low rainfall of the area the flooding of the Bremer River results in very good yields—about 300 gallons per acre. The winemaking process makes extensive use of modern technology to produce wines of the optimum delicacy. The Metala Cabernet Shiraz, which is sold in individually numbered bottles, is justly renowned throughout Australia.

The Murray Valley: Renmark, Berri, Loxton, Waikerie

This area has been the source of vast quantities and varieties of wines and spirits since irrigation settlements were begun there towards the end of the last century. There is little apparent romance or excitement in concrete pipes or pumping stations, but these have been the means of bringing water to the arid and otherwise agriculturally useless regions of the Murray Valley.

The Murray River flows for 3,500 miles from the source of its longest tributary to its mouth on the South Australian coast. It drains 265 million acres, one-seventh of the continent. This great river, fed by the melting snows of the Great Dividing Range, used to flood each year, and with nothing to stop it the water dispersed and was wasted. Under an agreement early this century by New South Wales, Victoria and South Australia, a plan was evolved to erect a series of locks which would retain the flood waters and maintain the river at a high level throughout the year. In the first instance ten locks were constructed, ranging from Blanchetown to Mildura, 1,000 miles from the mouth of the river. Today the irrigation system is extensive and highly developed, with a complex system of dams, locks, pumping stations and irrigation channels.

The irrigation system affects viticulture in New South Wales, Victoria and South Australia, with particular emphasis in the latter wine-State. As the Murray meanders through such a vast area of country there are naturally some variations in climate and topography between the different grape growing districts. Nevertheless, these conditions are basically similar. The vineyards have generally been established on level or gently sloping land which is easily irrigated. The soils are basically alluvial sandy loams of low humus content, overlying limestone subsoils. Although the soils along the Murray vary from fairly heavy clay to limestone and red sand, the area round Renmark consists of pure sand, and this is characteristic of the areas where grapes are grown. Climatically speaking, the area is hot and dry, with summer temperatures in the nineties and a rainfall of usually under ten inches. These conditions are suitable for growing many crops under irrigation.

The vineyards vary considerably in size. Typically they consisted of individually owned areas of about twenty-five acres, although some were as small as five acres. The big proprietary companies, however, have enormous areas under vine, some with hundreds of acres at a time. On the plains, shelter belts of eucalypts and almond trees are common as wind protection round the vineyards.

The site for the town of Renmark, which is located on the west bank of the Murray 225 miles by rail from Adelaide, was chosen by George Chaffey in 1887. It was he who named the town Renmark, the name which the aborigines had given the area, the meaning of which is 'red mud'. Renmark is a well-designed town with broad avenues and parklands along the river frontage, and but one hotel which is owned by the community. The town is the centre of Australia's first irrigation area, which is administered by the primary producers themselves through the Renmark Irrigation Trust.

The area administered by the Trust includes more than 12,000 acres of orchards and vineyards. The Trust has been responsible for repairing and concreting the water channels which were near a stage of uselessness when it took them over in 1893. In 1937 the Trust began a massive drainage project to combat the problems caused by overwatering.

Other towns around which irrigation areas have been developed in South Australia are Berri, Loxton and Waikerie. Of these the Berri irrigation area was proclaimed in 1910, and the Loxton area is the newest, being established by the Commonwealth and State governments after World War II in a scheme to settle returned soldiers on the land.

In the early days the most popular grape variety planted was gordo blanco, of which large areas were planted for drying as raisins, commonly called lexias. The purple Zante currant was also widely grown. In later years a new variety, the seedless sultana, was introduced, and soon outstripped the gordo in favour with the buying public. This resulted in a huge glut of unsaleable gordos, an unhappy situation which threatened the livelihood of many growers. In order to get some return from their crops the growers at Renmark decided to form a co-operative distillery, each putting up a proportion of the capital required. This eventually turned out to be a most successful move and these co-operatives are now an important feature of winemaking in the Murray Valley. However, they first had to overcome many problems.

Initially, only fortifying spirit for sale to established wine companies was made. There was a limit to the demand for this commodity, however, and the distilleries began to use the spirit in making their own sweet white wines. Finding a market for this wine was not easy as the public did not take readily to its unusual flavour. This was overcome with the development of a market in the United Kingdom, and the use of the wine in wine cocktails. Sales increased and the whole output of the co-operative wineries was readily absorbed. Since those days the co-operatives have considerably expanded their operations and now make all types of wine.

The co-operatives are run by the grower-shareholders themselves. In order to operate efficiently the management instructs the growers when to deliver their grapes, after the growers have given estimates of their crops. Thus the wineries are kept running smoothly and at full capacity. The growers are paid for the proceeds of the sales of wines and spirits. This sytem of co-operation has worked well on the whole, resulting in fair returns to the growers and general prosperity for the formerly barren irrigation settlements.

The whole range of grape varieties is now grown under irrigation—many thousands of tons of gordos, doradillo, grenache, shiraz, riesling, palomino, mataro, frontignan and others are crushed each year. Millions of gallons of wine and brandy are made, in the past brandy and sweet fortified wines almost exclusively. The brandy is light and clean, and has been very popular. The table wines have not had a good reputation, until recent advances have resulted in greatly improved quality.

Serious wine lovers have tended to ignore or deride irrigation area wines in the past. The vast amount of wine made from river areas does keep flagon wine drinkers content, and with the improvement in quality in recent years these and other river wines can no longer be ignored.

Angoves Pty Ltd, Renmark

Thomas Carlyon Angove is generally regarded as the pioneer of winemaking from grapes grown by River Murray irrigation. He was the son of Dr W. T. Angove, who began making wine at Teatree Gully outside Adelaide in the 1880s, and thus founded the firm which bears his name.

It was in 1910 that Thomas Carlyon established a distillery and processing house at Renmark. This was not the first use of the settlement's products for winemaking. A year earlier there had been a glut of lexias, and about 400 tons of these went to Angove's Teatree Gully distillery, where they were made into wine spirit. Angoves grew and grew over the years, becoming a vast business, which passed the million gallon a year mark long ago.

In 1947 Thomas William Angove became the third generation to lead the company. Thomas Carlyon Angove died in 1952, after seeing all that he had believed possible about winemaking on the Murray eventuate.

Angoves market a wide range of wines and brandy under their own label. They also sell a considerable amount of their material in bulk in England. Angoves is possibly best known for their St Agnes brandy. Since the Second World War their field of activity has expanded to include table wines; and vermouth which enjoys an export market in Canada.

Their acreage under vine is enormous, with about 2,000 acres at Murtho (near Lyrup) and sixty acres at Renmark. Varieties grown at Renmark include rhine riesling, cabernet sauvignon and shiraz, with a wider range grown at Murtho. The scale of Angoves' production is made obvious by the fact that despite the size of their own enormous vineyards, these supply only ten percent of the grapes processed, the balance being bought from other growers.

Over: At Hardy's, McLaren Vale, S.A., these 2,500-gallon maturation vats, containing ports and sherries, are made from Australian red gum and unlined.

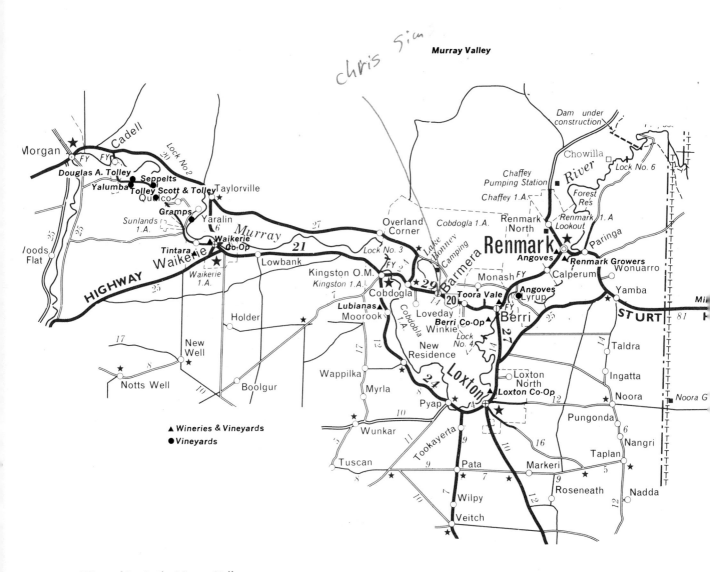

Winemaking in the Murray Valley

Renmark Growers' Distillery Ltd

The Renmark Growers' Distillery was the first co-operative winery in Australia. It was established in August 1916, when 130 Renmark grape growers registered the co-operative. They bought the 'Chateau Tanunda' distillery which had operated at Renmark in 1915, before its owners suffered a financial collapse.

The winery was originally built to handle 500 tons of fruit each vintage. For the co-operative's first vintage in 1917 they processed about 1,000 tons of grapes. The plant has now grown to cope with an annual crush of between 10,000 and 15,000 tons of grapes. It can put through 200,000 gallons of distillation wine in a week.

At first the function of the Growers' Distillery was to make use of grapes not suitable for the dried fruits market, but by 1922 beverage wines were being made, and by 1925 the Distillery's products were being exported. Now the company uses the wide variety of grapes its growers send in to make a big range of wines. These include table wines, as well as fortified and sparkling styles and brandy, which are sold under the Renmano label.

The Distillery itself is well-equipped with modern machinery, but it still preserves within its walls, as part of the spirit store, the original freestone front of 'Chateau Tanunda'. Since World War II the Growers' have concentrated on streamlining operations and have been in the forefront with winemaking innova-

138

tions and techniques. The co-operative has a small vineyard which is used chiefly for experimental purposes.

Now with over 500 grower-shareholders, a sound technical staff and a well-developed marketing organization, the Renmark Growers' Distillery has come a long way since it was first established to save losses from fruit not good enough for drying.

Berri Co-operative Winery & Distillery Ltd

This Co-operative had its beginnings in 1918 at Berri, which is midway between Renmark and Loxton. That year a distillation plant was established for producing fortifying spirit from the waste dried fruit left after packing operations were complete. Four years later a new company was formed to take over the distillery and increase its capacity to deal with the large tonnage of grapes produced by the repatriated soldiers. Mr H. R. Curren of Berri was active in gaining support for the formation of the Co-operative. Mr W. Gillard was chosen as the first chairman.

From a very small beginning—one continuous still, three 2,000 gallon spirit storing tanks and a grape crusher which crushed less than one hundred tons in the first year, the company has grown enormously. They now handle an annual crush of over 20,000 tons, and have a storage capacity in excess of five million gallons. The Co-operative proudly claims to have the largest single winemaking and distilling plants in Australia.

In 1958 a decision of major importance was made, resulting in the establishment of a separate winery plant costing £100,000. This winery was designed to make table wines, for which there was an increasing demand. To meet this demand varieties such as shiraz and riesling, varieties suitable for table wines, had been planted on an increasingly large scale.

The Distillery is now a modern plant in every respect. It handles an average intake of 400 tons each day at vintage time, while 8,000 gallons of wine pass through the pot still and pot rectifiers each day for the manufacture of brandy and spirit. In addition to the pot stills, continuous stills which handle 30,000 gallons of wine per day are operated. An extensive refrigeration system has been installed. Other modern equipment includes such items as a Westphalian centrifuge and stainless steel ethanol stills.

As a Co-operative, all grapes processed are supplied by the 500 grower-members. The company makes red and white dry wines, fortified wines, brandy and grape fortification spirit. Their wines are marketed under the 'Mine Host', 'Karooma', 'Berri' and 'Berrivale' labels, and are also exported to the United Kingdom and South-East Asia.

Thomas Hardy & Sons Pty Ltd, Waikerie

The Hardy firm was one of the first to appreciate the possibilities of growing grapes in the irrigation area of the Murray. The first venture of the company in the Waikerie district was the erection of a small winery on the banks of the river for use at the 1915 vintage. The first year's intake was eighty tons of grapes. Four years later the winery was sold to a group of returned soldier-growers, and is still in operation as the Waikerie Co-operative Distillery Ltd.

Also in 1915 Robert Hardy, in conjunction with Samuel Sage, purchased irrigable but virgin land at Waikerie. It was cleared and planted under Mr Sage's supervision, and became known as the 'Cyrilton' vineyards. Mr Sage's interests have since been acquired by the Hardy company.

A further step in 1916 was a contract made with Mr Fred Matters for the purchase of grapes from his property at 'Murray View', some ten miles down river from Waikerie, with the condition that the company erect a winery there. John Stoward, a great-nephew of the founder of the Hardy firm and a skilled engineer and winemaker, who had previously supervised the erection of the Waikerie winery, was commissioned to erect the Murray River plant. The 1,300 to 1,400 hogsheads of wine of the first vintage were shipped downstream to Morgan in a steamer towing barges, for railing to 'Mile End'.

When the Waikerie winery was sold, a winery was erected at 'Cyrilton', again under the supervision of Mr Stoward. The winery was ready for the 1921 vintage and has since expanded to a point where it now plays an important part in the company's production. A large continuous still for the production of fortifying spirit was erected, and has resulted in the intake of a very great tonnage of grapes, not only from the Waikerie area, but from Barmera and Loxton, also.

Hardys have over one hundred acres under vine at Waikerie, where they grow doradillo, gordo, grenache, palomino, pedro, rhine riesling, shiraz and sultana.

Jack Nielsen, a great host, has been the central figure in this operation for many years. Much loved in the district, he has welcomed thousands of visitors in his unique entertainment cellar, and has done much to spread the word of wine.

Loxton Co-operative Winery and Distillery Ltd

The Loxton Co-operative is a comparative newcomer. It was formed in 1949 and began production four years later. The Co-operative is now operated by 250 growers in the Loxton Irrigation Area. This settlement was government-established with the aim of re-settling ex-servicemen as primary producers. An area of about 6,000 acres was developed.

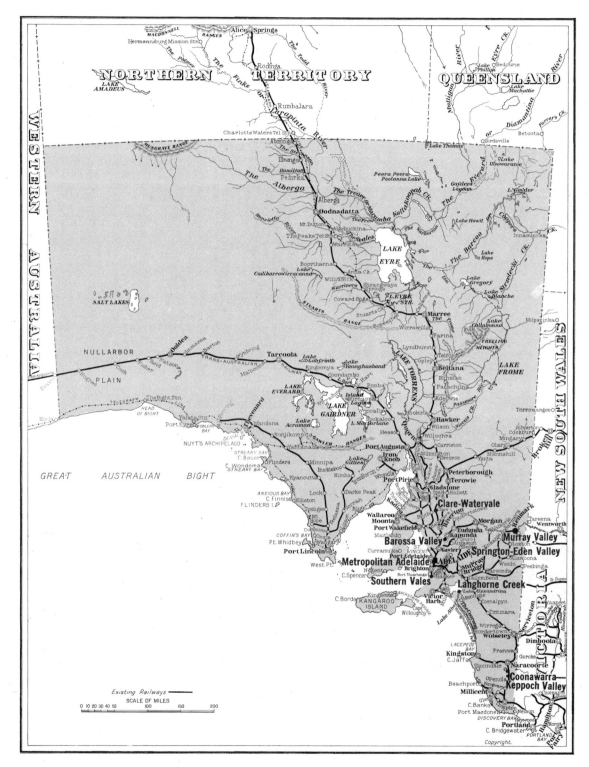

The Vineyard Areas of South Australia

The Co-operative has grown remarkably in its short history and is now a major producer of wine and brandy, most of which is supplied directly to the trade for blending or re-labelling.

B. Seppelt and Sons Pty Ltd, Qualco

Seppelts began their venture in the Murray Valley with the purchase of land at Qualco, in the Waikerie area in the early sixties. They now own 1100 acres, of which about 500 acres have been planted to vines.

The soil at their vineyards is coarse red sandy loam, over limestone and marl subsoil. The varieties grown include palomino and hermitage for use in sherry production, shiraz, doradillo, cabernet sauvignon and tokay. Seppelts have also planted malbec, which they feel is extremely suitable to the soil and climate of the area from both the quality and yield aspects. The vines are irrigated with permanent and portable overhead sprinklers.

The company does not have a winery at Qualco. They transport all their grapes, from their own vineyards and those bought from other growers, to their main Barossa winery for making into wine.

Seppelts believe that with the planting of premium varieties, and the use of sophisticated equipment, high quality wines will be made in the Murray district.

S. Smith & Son Ltd, 'Yalumba River Estates'

In 1958, Yalumba purchased 600 acres of land adjoining the River Murray at Oxford Landing, between Waikerie and Cadell, and established 'Yalumba River Estates' for the purpose of growing grapes under irrigation.

This venture is one of the largest areas in Australia under overhead spray irrigation. The Murray water is lifted 130 feet by a powerful pump and circulated through pipelines ranging from fifteen inch steel lines to two inch plastic pipes. Permanent overhead sprinklers are installed throughout the vineyard, and thirty acres may be watered at any one time.

The first year fifty-six acres were planted, and the first vintage from these grapes was 1961. All the planted areas have been trellised. 'Yalumba' now have over 370 acres under vine. A wide variety of grapes is grown, including doradillo, gordo, palomino, grenache, cabernet sauvignon, shiraz, dolcetto, semillon and sauvignon blanc. Several of their wines made from the cabernet sauvignon of these vineyards have won Gold Medals in various shows.

Tolley Scott and Tolley

Tolley Scott and Tolley own about 1,000 acres at Waikerie on the Murray, of which about 800 acres have already been established as vineyards. The soil there is sandy loam and limestone marl. Spray irrigation is used in the cultivation of grenache, doradillo, cabernet sauvignon and some other varieties. The grapes are processed at the Tolley Scott and Tolley winery at Nuriootpa.

Waikerie Co-operative Distillery Limited

The Waikerie Co-operative Distillery was formed and registered in 1919. One of the main objects in forming the company was to endeavour to secure better prices for the grapes produced by local growers. The share capital necessary to promote the company was subscribed by the grape growers and general public of the district of Waikerie.

On the death of the first chairman, Mr T. H. Dunstan, in 1922, Elliot Miller was appointed to the position which was to be his for fifty years.

The company purchased the winery built by Hardys in 1919. For the first few years about 400 to 500 tons were processed annually. This intake has increased gradually with a dramatic leap after the Second World War, until now over 5,000 tons are handled each year.

In 1921 a pot still was installed. The two rectifiers at the winery have been replaced by continuous stills. The increased output of the Co-operative has led to several extensions to the buildings housing fermenting and storage tanks, and bond store capacity. As well the working plant has been kept up-to-date.

The Co-operative built up a substantial export trade with the United Kingdom, following a trial shipment of five hogsheads of sweet white wine in 1927. At its peak 4,000 hogsheads were exported annually, but during the 1950s the demand in the United Kingdom decreased considerably and the market there has largely fallen away.

The chief lines produced by the company are fortified sweet wines, fortifying spirit and brandy spirit, which are disposed of mainly in bulk.

Other Growers

Gramps own about 150 acres in the Qualco area which include experimental plantings of sauvignon blanc, pinot blanc, pinot chardonnay and malbec.

Douglas A. Tolley has over 100 acres at Qualco, plantings including cabernet, shiraz, semillon and rhine riesling.

Nildottie, near Swan Reach, is the location of the Greenways irrigation settlement. They started planting in 1961, and in 1968, 120 acres of vines completed the 550-acre settlement. Hamiltons have a big connection in this area.

7 Western Australia

The Swan Valley area around Perth has long been a centre of winemaking. Today it is probably best known for Houghtons' famous White Burgundy. Houghtons are, however, by no means the only winemakers in the Swan Valley for there are about sixty wineries in the district, although most of these are small concerns run by migrants from Europe.

The vineyards of the Swan Valley are not far north-east of Perth, and are centred on the banks of the Swan and Canning Rivers, at a latitude of thirty-two degrees south and an altitude of less than a hundred feet above sea level. Summer temperatures are very high, often maintained at 105°F during the ripening period. The rainfall is about thirty-four to thirty-five inches per annum, and falls almost entirely in winter—there is usually no rain at all after December. The Swan River is not suitable for irrigation as it is tidal and brackish. The soil is a deep alluvial sandy loam, the best of which is known as Marri land, which has ease of soil penetration and moisture at a depth of twenty feet.

The hot sunshine and fertile soil conditions combine to produce grapes with a very high sugar content, and the resultant wines are very full, flavourful and low in acid.

'Sandalford' Vineyards

This is the oldest vineyard in Western Australia, situated twelve miles from Perth on the West Swan Road. The original vigneron was Captain John

Vineyards Near Perth and in the Swan Valley

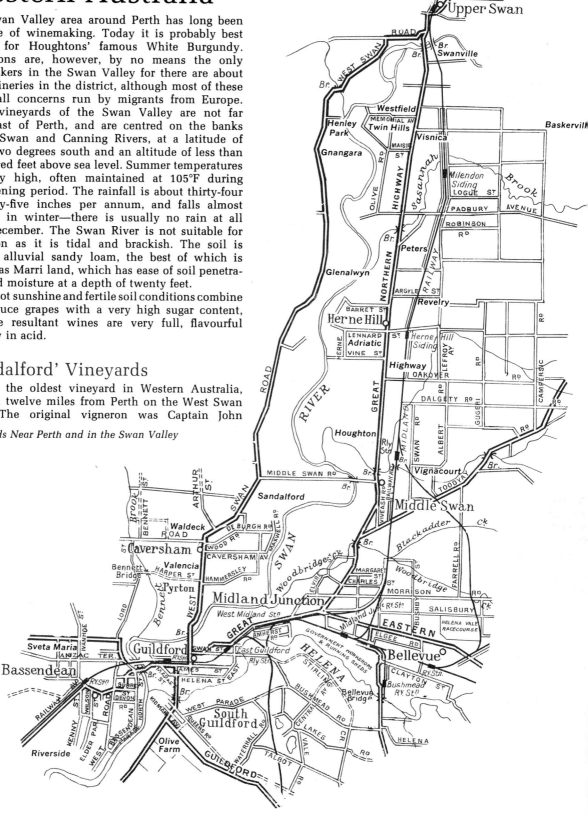

142

Septimus Roe, one of the original settlers of the colony of Western Australia who arrived on board the *Parmelia* in 1829. He became the State's first surveyor-general, and in 1840 planted a vineyard, which he called 'Sandalford' after an historic estate owned by his family in the mother country.

For over a hundred years 'Sandalford' was mainly concerned with grapes for the export trade, winemaking being a hobby and a sideline. The first wine was made by Captain Roe's son, John Frederick, in 1910. In 1945, after the Second World War, Captain Roe's descendants began to seriously make wine on a commercial scale. His great-grandsons John and David Frederick now run the business.

There are about 300 acres of vines at 'Sandalford', some of which are devoted to table grapes for export. Varieties for wine are semillon, shiraz and cabernet with some verdelho and pedro. The soils are deep river channel loam and shallow clay. The yield is about two tons to the acre.

In addition to being the oldest vineyard in Western Australia 'Sandalford' is the only one in the hands of the family of the original owner.

Houghton Wines

'Houghton' is very near to 'Sandalford' in the Middle Swan Valley, and is the first vineyard in Western Australia where wine was made commercially. The vineyard was originally planted by a retired army officer, Colonel Houghton of the Indian Army, in 1833 with cuttings from South Africa. The vineyard was purchased by Dr John Ferguson in 1859, the year wine was made there commercially for the first time. The doctor had arrived from England in 1842 to become Colonial Surgeon for the colony of West Australia, and what prompted him to buy a vineyard seventeen years later is a mystery.

Dr Ferguson's son, Charles Walter established a more formal vineyard and built the imposing cellars. Legend has it that it was here that Western Australia's lone bushranger, Moondyne Joe, was captured in 1869 while helping himself to the best cask. In addition to C. W. Ferguson's activities as a vigneron he began the Middle Swan Cricket Club in the 1870s. In 1910 R. George Mann left the original 'Chateau Tanunda', then owned by the Adelaide Wine Company, and joined 'Houghton' as winemaker—and there have been Manns making wine there ever since. Jack Mann, R. G.'s son is the present incumbent, and is quite a character. He joined his father in 1922, and took over completely as winemaker in 1930—which means that he has seen over fifty vintages with the one firm. Jack Mann has strong convictions, and is dedicated to Western Australia, its white wines and cricket—although not necessarily in that order. In July, 1950 the Ferguson family surrendered their long control of 'Houghton' to the Emu Wine Company of South Australia, but Jack Mann remained as winemaker.

There are 245 acres under vine—semillon, tokay, shiraz, pedro, malbec (fifteen acres), cabernet sauvignon (fourteen acres), grenache, verdelho and madeleine. The latter variety makes a delicate wine most suitable as a base for Flor sherry. Although the Swan River forms the western boundary of the 353 acre property it is too salty to be used for irrigation, for which bores are used. The yield is about 300 gallons to the acre. The Emu Wine Company has bought 2012 acres at Gingin, about fifty miles north of Perth, for future development.

The 'Houghton' winery is immaculate and charming, with 1,800 vessels of European oak, the casks ranging in size from ten to 10,000 gallons. These are in excellent condition, some with highly-polished ornamental brass screws in the cask doors, others beautifully carved 120 gallon cognac ovals.

Undoubtedly Houghton's most famous wine is the White Burgundy, but also made are other table wines including a Verdelho, Rosé, and dry reds, as well as fortified wines. Of the latter, there are formidable wood-matured ports and muscats.

'Valencia' Vineyards, Caversham

The 'Valencia' vineyards are at Caversham, less than one mile from the town of Guildford in the Swan Valley. The vineyard was originally planted in 1890 by J. L. Nanson, editor of the Perth *Daily News*, Lindley Cowan, head of the Government Bureau of Agriculture, and Adrian Despeissis, Government Viticulturist at the time. Its original name was 'Santa Rosa'. In 1945 the vineyard was acquired by the Emu Wine Company.

There are now about 100 acres of semillon, tokay, malbec, shiraz, pedro, grenache and doradillo vines there. 'Valencia' do all the bottling of Houghton's wines, which are transported there in stainless steel tanks protected by blankets of CO_2 gas.

New Norcia

The Benedictine Monastery eighty-four miles north of Perth, had their own vineyards from which they made wine until 1972 when the Wyening Cellars, as they were known, went into liquidation.

N. K. Waldeck, Caversham, Bindoon

The Waldecks have a property of twelve acres in the Swan Valley and over forty acres at Bindoon, planted with cabernet, grenache, semillon, tokay and shiraz. In the past few years, with the graduation of son Phillip from Roseworthy, a programme of expansion and modernization has begun. The Waldecks have about one hundred acres at Bindoon of deep loam soil which are suitable for planting vines. Spray irrigation is used, but sufficient water for the new development may be a problem.

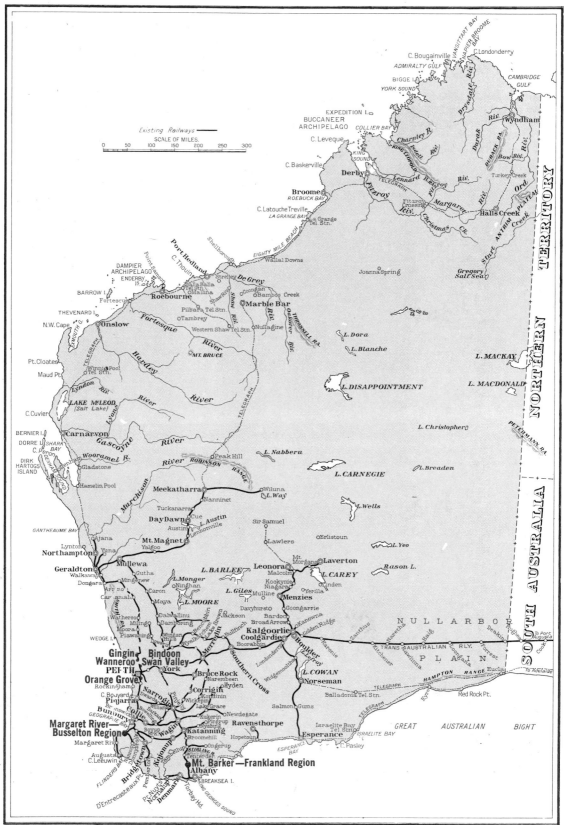

The Vineyard Areas of Western Australia

Miss Vera L. Shuster from Freeling, S.A., has been picking grapes for fifteen years in the Barossa Valley.

Noack and Sons

This company has fifty-four acres at Upper Swan and about 100 acres at Bullsbrook, planted with shiraz, grenache, rhine riesling, pedro, gordo, frontignan and hermitage. The soils here are deep red loam, unlike most of the other Swan Valley vineyards, and are not irrigated. An astonishing but mysterious sweet wine of delicious flavour was once found in the earth at the foot of a tree, several bottles being in perfect condition.

Other Growers

There are numerous growers who sell their grapes to the above-mentioned winemakers, and many who make wine for their personal consumption, and some who make small quantities for commercial purposes.

OLIVE FARM: On the Great Eastern Highway at South Guildford, it is owned and run by Vince Yurisich and family. The old underground cellar which dates back to 1830, is delightful and cool. Wines from here have been consistent Gold Medal winners.

RIVERSIDE VINEYARD: On the West Road, Bassendean. Laurie Nicolotto's wines have distinguished themselves in the last three year's wine shows. He won gold awards in Local and Open Classes in the 1970 Royal Perth Show and his Red Burgundy was judged the best West Australian wine in any class.

SVETA MARIA: On Ivanhoe Street, Bassendean. Ted Grassi has consistently won prizes for the last six years in wine shows. His Claret won a gold award in 1969 and the White Burgundy a silver. His silver 1970 Claret has just been released together with the Red Burgundy.

LUISINI WINES: Wanneroo Road, Wanneroo. Situated on the 11 mile peg from Perth, Luisini Wines feature a fine range of vintage wines including some twelve year old vintage port. The main cellar is underground and this keeps the wines at a consistently cool temperature.

CONTEVILLE: At the 12 mile peg, Wanneroo Road, Wanneroo. Proprietor, Paul Conti, has been very successful in recent wine shows for rosés, reds and a white frontignac. Paul has an ideal underground cellar for maturing his quality table wines and he has just built a new crushing and storage cellar.

PARRI WINES LTD: On Wanneroo Road, Yanchep. The only major producer of champagne and sparkling wines in the State. One of the largest producers of all varieties and the biggest exporter to the Eastern States. The log cabin is a welcome place for visitors to sample Parri Wines.

JADRAN: On Reservoir Road, Orange Grove. This place specializes in high quality fortified wines. Its winery and sales rooms are most attractive.

WESTFIELD WINES: On Great Northern Highway at Baskerville, this attractive clean underground cellar stocks a complete range of wines. John Kosovich is concentrating on making top quality table wines and has won two gold awards in the 1970 Royal Perth Show.

TWIN HILLS: On Great Northern Highway at Baskerville, this vineyard is run by Steve Kraljevic who specializes in red and white table wines. In the 1969 Royal Perth Show Twin Hills won a gold in the Local Class for rosé and a silver for red wine. They also won other medals for their ports and sherries.

VISNICA WINES: On Great Northern Highway at Baskerville. Visnica make their wine from grapes grown in their own vineyards. All types of wine are available from quality sherries to clarets and burgundies and they have won numerous prizes for their wines in the Royal Perth Show.

REVELRY WINES: In Argyle Street, Herne Hill. Produces quality bulk wines and is an ideal place to buy clarets in oak casks for bottling parties.

ADRIATIC WINES: On Great Northern Highway at Herne Hill. Phillip Jurjevich, the proprietor, makes both fortified and table wines from grapes grown on the property, but is now concentrating on good quality clarets.

BASKERVILLE WINES: Haddrill Road, Baskerville. This company specialize in table wines and make a true Champagne and Sparkling Burgundy by the Methode Champenoise. There is a most attractive old style cellar.

GLENALWYN WINES: On West Swan Road at West Swan. G. Pasalich and Son specialize in all wines. In the 1969 Royal Perth Show, Glenalwyn were the most successful W.A. Exhibitor, Local Class, winning a gold award for claret and muscat.

HENLEY PARK: In Swan Street at West Swan. Henley Park is owned and run by Mark Yujnovich who has a stock of vintage ports, sherry and claret. He has just produced a vintage port fortified with old brandy. Mark has available a full range of quality table and fortified wines with his vintage selections.

New Areas

In about 1964 trial plantings were made at Mt Barker, about 200 miles south of Perth. The soil is gravelly loam and the climate slightly cooler than the Swan Valley, and is claimed to resemble that of Bordeaux. Six acres of cabernet and riesling were planted on a site about twelve miles west of Mt Barker township with the advice of the State Government Viticulturist, Bill Jamieson. Other trial plantings have been made at Frankland River and in the Busselton-Vasse region, where eight acres of cabernet, riesling, malbec and shiraz were planted. It remains to be seen as to how successful these areas could become.

One of Australia's most famous winegrowing areas, the Barossa Valley of South Australia, begins at Lyndoch.

৪৪ Queensland

The Queensland climate is not especially suitable for the cultivation of grapes for wine so it is not surprising that little wine has been made there. However, it is remarkable that one family-owned vineyard has kept going for over a century. The story of winemaking in Queensland is completely dominated by the Bassett family, but there are at least twenty other winemakers, mainly in the Stanthorpe area (south-west of Brisbane, very near the New South Wales border), who each crush at least five tons of grapes annually. This group including names like Zanzatta & Co., A. & S. Pugilisi and Musumeci & Deluca, are mostly settlers from Europe who have brought their traditions with them, and who make wine without fuss primarily for their own and their friends' and neighbours' consumption.

Romavilla Vineyards Pty Ltd, Roma

The town of Roma, now famous for its oil and natural gas, is the centre of the small Queensland wine industry. It is located about 320 miles west of Brisbane, one thousand feet above sea level, and in the dry belt west of the Great Dividing Range. The long summers in Roma are hot indeed, and often dry, though the average annual rainfall is twenty-two inches. It was in this unlikely environment that Samuel S. Bassett, a Cornishman who had spent some time in the Hunter Valley, established a vineyard in 1863.

He began by clearing the scrub in an area along the banks of the Bungil Creek—which only runs after heavy rain—and had vine cuttings sent by bullock wagon from Toowoomba. Most of the cuttings withered and died on the journey, but Bassett planted the few survivors on the sandy loam creek banks, and eventually built up his vineyard until he had 440 acres planted to vines. Varieties grown were (and are) riesling, solverino, syrian, portugal, red muscat, white muscat, black muscat, black cluster, red hermitage and mataro. Samuel Bassett travelled throughout Queensland selling his wine, and won numerous prizes for them at the Brisbane Exhibition.

Samuel Bassett's son William, now over eighty years old, has continued to make wine with a family company, Romavilla Vineyards Pty Ltd, controlling the vineyard and winery. The area under vine has declined to 210 acres although the company has over 370 acres for development.

The galvanised iron winery has underground cellars with a storage capacity of 120,000 gallons. The crushing machinery can process forty tons of grapes per day and a hydraulic press is also used. The majority of their wines are fortified, with a dry and a sweet white table wine also being made. Only their own grapes are processed.

In addition to the often unfavourable climatic conditions, the area is subject to hailstorms—in 1966 half the vintage was destroyed by hail. Frost is a further problem, with old tyres being burned as smudge pots. Birds too can do their share of damage, and carbide guns are used in an attempt to combat them.

William Bassett has three sons and a daughter, all married and on the land, who do not intend to become vignerons. Incidentally, one interesting claim to fame of the Romavilla winery (which has nothing to do with wine) is that Billy Hughes, one time Prime Minister of Australia, worked in the vineyards there before the Boer War. Is this the only time an Australian leader has laboured in a vineyard?

৭ Tasmania

Little wine has been made in Tasmania in the past, probably mainly because the climate is unsuitable for the production of fortified wine because of low heat summations. It is also probable that early attempts to grow grapes were frustrated by the inability to control powdery and downy mildew and some of the vine pests.

A few valiant aspiring vignerons did attempt to establish vineyards in Tasmania in the early nineteenth century. In 1827 Bartholomew Broughton produced wine from grapes grown on 'Prospect Farm' situated between the New Town road and what is now the Brooker Highway, somewhere near Maypole Inn. The farm was later bought by Captain Swanston, and one report indicates that in 1848 he received an award for wine shown at the Paris Exhibition. In 1844 he had five acres of vines in bearing. In the 1840s Dr Gaunt of Windemere, East Tamar, was making his own wine from grapes growing on his property. In about the 1830s William Effingham Lawrence had approximately four acres of vines planted near the junction of the South Esk and Tamar Rivers within the city of Launceston.

There are a number of other indications that grape vines were grown for wine at this time, none of these areas being extensive. All trace of the plantings has now disappeared except for two or three varieties suspected as being progeny of the original vines and now located generally as single specimens throughout the State.

In 1887 a Signor Diego Bernacchi formed the Maria Island Company and planted vines and mulberry trees. His chosen site, Maria Island, is an isolated rocky outpost off the east coast of Tasmania which had been used as a whaling station and later as a convict settlement. Bernacchi succeeded in making some wine there, and even exhibited in Paris, but the venture eventually failed. Legend has it that the wily Signor, in an attempt to convince his backers of the security of their investments, actually bought grapes and wired them to the vines to impress the visitors!

John F. Miguet, 'La Provence'

For many years after the Bernacchi debacle the wine industry in Tasmania was non-existent. It took the arrival of a Frenchman in the early 1950s to revive winemaking there. The Frenchman in question, John F. Miguet, scion of a family of vignerons, arrived in Tasmania with a French construction company. He determined to plant vines on his land, a mile from Lilydale, where the soil was rich and brown and there were trees to protect the valley from strong winds. In his spare time Miguet cleared the site of brambles and blackberries and began collecting vines. All vines introduced into Tasmania must go through the Department of Agriculture, who were not especially interested in viticulture at that stage, but they eventually imported a few cuttings. Miguet slowly continued planting and developing his infant vineyard in the face of massive indifference. He now has three acres under vine at his 'La Provence' vineyard including rhine riesling, cabernet sauvignon, white hermitage, grenache, pinot noir and pinot blanc, from which he makes small quantities of table wines.

Claude Alcorso, 'Moorilla Estate'

John Miguet has been rewarded in some way for his remarkable tenacity, as others have now followed him. Claude Alcorso, of music fame, began planting his 'Moorilla Estate' at Berriedale near Hobart in 1964, with the main planting in 1966. He now has one acre which includes rhine riesling, cabernet sauvignon and shiraz.

Windemere Vineyards

In 1965 'Windemere Vineyards' (located not at the original site but on the West Tamar at Robigana) was planted by a syndicate of six Launceston professional men, some of whom have now left the area. Messrs G. S. M. Green and R. P. Wyly now carry out most of the maintenance work from their homes in Launceston. Their vineyard is one acre in extent and grows rhine riesling, white hermitage, semillon and cabernet sauvignon.

'Chateau Legana'

'Chateau Legana' some eight miles up the Tamar Valley from Launceston was started in 1969 by two Tasmanians, Mike Curtis, a townplanner, and Geoffrey Wiltshire, proprietor of a squash court. With help from the Department of Agriculture they imported some rootlings from the mainland, and now have four acres planted with several varieties, including cabernet sauvignon, rhine riesling, shiraz and grenache. The vineyard is mainly trellised, but part of it is trained on stakes in a similar method to the German Kaiserstuhl system.

Other Growers

There are a number of other plantings from which wine is made in small quantities, generally for home consumption. In Hobart and Launceston there are several families from Italy, whose home gardens contain a number of vines, the yield being sufficient to provide some wine for their own consumption. Most home garden vines are trained on overhead trellis systems, whereas commercial plantings are on normal trellises, with a vine density of 600 to 1,000 vines per acre.

The Tasmanian Department of Agriculture believes that selected sites, particularly in the north-east, east and south-east, of the island have climatic conditions suitable for the production of wine, provided that care is taken in varietal selection, site selection and training and pruning systems. In fact, research has established that Launceston has 1964 degree days per year, compared to 1674 at Geisenheim Germany and 1827 at Auxerre in France.

The vines in Tasmania do not, however, achieve a very high Baumé in a normal season, which makes them unsuitable for the production of sweet fortified wines.

The Tasmanian Department of Agriculture holds stocks of most of the vine varieties which are suited to cool climatic conditions, and an observation plot is being planted with these varieties. They are also investigating techniques of rapid propagation, with the aim of planting out larger acreages of selected varieties from the small supply of parent material available.

At this stage in time the winemaking industry is Tasmania is poised for expansion—Mr Miguet may feel that his long years of pioneering work have at last been recognized.

Wine Producing Areas of Australia

1. Hunter Valley
2. Muswellbrook
3. Mudgee
4. Rooty Hill
5. Murrumbidgee Valley—Riverina
6. Swan Hill
7. Robinvale
8. Mildura
9. Murray Valley
10. Tahbilk
11. Shepparton
12. Rutherglen—Wahgunyah—Corowa
13. Glenrowan Milawa
14. Great Western
15. Coonawarra
16. Langhorne Creek
17. Southern Vales
18. Adelaide Metropolitan
19. Barossa Valley
20. Clare—Watervale
21. Swan Valley
22. Roma

GRAPE VARIETIES

Graham Gregory, B.Sc.Agr., R.D.Oen., graduated from Sydney University in 1953 and subsequently obtained the Diploma in Oenology at Roseworthy Agricultural College, South Australia, in 1956. He occupied the position of Viticultural Specialist for the N.S.W. Department of Agriculture from 1957 to 1968. In 1970 he was appointed Chief of the Department's Division of Horticulture. As well he holds the position of Chief Quarantine Officer (Plants) for N.S.W. and is Chairman of the N.S.W. Dried Fruits Board. In 1966 he undertook an extensive official study tour of wine grape production in Europe, America and South Africa. For many years he has acted as a wine judge at various major wine shows throughout the country.

A new red grape ferment in open concrete vats, McWilliam's Wines, Hanwood, N.S.W.

The characteristics of the grape, more than any other factor, predetermine the style and quality of a wine.

All commercial wine grapes in Australia are varieties of the species *Vitis vinifera,* commonly referred to as the European or Old World grape. It is generally accepted that this species, which is responsible for over 90 percent of the world's grape production, originated in Asia Minor where viticulture began.

There are many other species of *Vitis,* the majority of which are native to the American continent, particularly North America. The most important of these is *V. labrusca* which, together with hybrids of *vinifera* and *labrusca* and other American species, is extensively grown in the eastern States of North America. Here, *vinifera* will not thrive due to its susceptibility to winter freezing and certain pests and diseases endemic in the region.

Other American species and hybrids are widely used as rootstocks throughout the world because of their resistance to root pests. The most important of these is the 'vine louse', phylloxera, which devastated large areas of European vineyards in the mid 1800s and changed the course of viticultural development in Australia when it spread from southern Victoria to the Rutherglen area in 1899. Fortunately the incidence of phylloxera in Australia is confined to north-eastern Victoria, the Corowa district of New South Wales and areas close to Sydney and Brisbane. Consequently, the use of phylloxera-resistant rootstocks is unnecessary in the majority of the grape producing areas of Australia which lie outside these infested districts.

There are innumerable varieties of *V. vinifera.* In France alone the official statistics list over 270 separate wine varieties, although less than half of these assume any real commercial significance.

The number of commercial grape varieties grown in Australia is comparatively small. This is partly a reflection of the strict quarantine prohibition which was applied on the importation of grapes up until the early 1960s, because of the dangers of bringing in exotic pests and disease. By that time, methods of identifying the presence of disease, particularly virus diseases, had been developed to a stage which allowed introductions to be made safely, but only subject to strict post-entry quarantine procedures.

As a result, many varieties which are new to Australian viticulture have been imported over the last ten years. Some of these are important overseas and are likely to prove worthwhile additions to the varietal composition of the vineyards here. Notable examples amongst the reds are merlot of the Bordeaux region, gamay of Beaujolais and zinfandel of California, whilst amongst the whites there are chenin blanc of the Loire Valley, pinot gris of Alsace and the German varieties silvaner and muller thurgau. Also worthy of appraisal are several of the recently introduced Italian varieties such as sangiovese of Chianti and nebbiolo of Piemonte.

Apart from new varieties, big benefits are likely to result from the introduction of high performance clones (or strains) of varieties that are already here. These clones have been selected for their freedom from virus diseases and high productivity and should do much to improve the acceptability of the higher quality wine varieties, some of which have tended to be shunned because of their poor cropping capacity.

In this chapter, descriptions are provided of the commercial wine varieties which are currently grown in Australia. Reference is also made to the significance of each variety in other countries as this assists in their appreciation. The relative performance of wine grapes, both in agronomic characteristics and wine-making quality, is remarkably consistent from region to region.

Except where otherwise stated, the Australian acreage statistics quoted throughout the text were compiled by the Commonwealth Bureau of Census and Statistics and apply to the position as at 30 June, 1971. Overseas statistical data has been derived from the official publications of the countries concerned.

Red Wine Varieties

Shiraz

Synonyms: syrah (France), petite sirah (California), red hermitage.

Shiraz is Australia's principal variety for the production of fortified and non-fortified red wines. This is in contrast to the situation in other wine growing countries where the variety is comparatively unimportant.

In France, only 4,000 of the 3.2 million acres of wine grapes grown there are planted to the variety.

Nonetheless, the red wines of the small but famous region of Hermitage in the Rhone Valley are made totally from shiraz. It is also grown elsewhere in the Rhone Valley, notably at Chateauneuf-du-Pape, near Avignon, where it is one of the several specified red varieties, and although grenache predominates, shiraz is regarded as a better quality type.

Several thousand acres of shiraz are grown in the two quality districts of California, the Napa and Sonoma Valleys. The principal red wine variety of South

Africa is called 'hermitage', but is in fact cinsaut; the true shiraz accounts for less than one percent of the plantings there

In Australia, there are 17,951 acres of shiraz, more than any other true wine variety, red or white. It is grown in virtually all districts and there are few quality red table wines or ports produced here of which shiraz is not the major varietal component.

Although it is often blended with other varieties, notably cabernet sauvignon, a big range of straight shiraz wines are made and many of these equal or surpass the best of the blends in quality and popularity.

Shiraz wines are of good colour, contain moderate amounts of acid and tannin and possess a positive though mild fruit flavour. As with all varieties, the intensity of its colour, acid and tannin increases as the temperature of the region in which it is grown decreases. This accounts for the marked difference between the Hunter Valley and South Australian shiraz dry reds, the former being lighter and softer in style, due to less tannin and acid, than the more assertive and full bodied wines of the cooler Barossa Valley, Clare and Coonawarra districts.

With the exception of a few acres of pinot noir, shiraz was the only red grape grown in the Hunter Valley until the last few years. In this district its wines, while being soft on the palate, develop a big, 'earthy' flavour which is unique, not only amongst the wines of Australia, but those of the world. Because of the softness to their finish, similarities are sometimes drawn between the Hunter shiraz reds and the red burgundies of France, but the flavour of the two is totally different.

The shiraz wines of Rutherglen and other parts of north-eastern Victoria are usually more full bodied and fruitier than those from both South Australia and the Hunter. At least a part of this can be attributed to the tendency in these districts to pick the grapes at a rather more advanced stage of maturity than elsewhere.

Shiraz is a good growers' grape. It is vigorous and produces good crops of medium sized bunches which are midseason in maturity. It is easily distinguished in the vineyard by the whitish tips to the young shoots and its trailing growth habit.

Grenache

Although the area of grenache in Australia, namely 15,565 acres, is less than shiraz, in 1971 over 40,000 tons of the former were processed for wine as against 29,500 tons of the latter. This is due to the variety's greater productivity and the fact that the non-bearing acreage of shiraz is three times greater than that for grenache. The latter demonstrates that of the two, vignerons are preferring shiraz for new plantings.

In New South Wales and Victoria, there is very little grenache grown outside the irrigation areas, but in South Australia the majority of plantings are in the non-irrigated districts near Adelaide, the southern vales, and in the Barossa Valley.

Grenache is grown extensively in other parts of the world. It is an important grape in France where there are about 62,000 acres, located almost entirely in the southern parts of the Rhone Valley and in the Midi (Languedoc) region bordering the Mediterranean. Although it is mostly used here for Vins Ordinaires de Consommation Courante, grenache is also an important component of the higher quality Appellation d'Origine Controlee (A.O.C.) wines of Chateauneuf-du-Pape and Tavel where it constitutes 80 percent of the red grape plantings. The distinctive roses of Tavel originated from the natural tendency of the grenache wines grown there to oxidize and become light in style. In addition, the sweet, fortified, aperitif wine of Banyuls, which lies on the Mediterranean coast bordering Spain, is made from grenache.

In California it ranks third to carignane and zinfandel in order of importance as a red wine grape. It is also a significant variety in parts of Spain.

Grenache wines mature at an early age and because of this it is favoured by Australian winemakers for 'commercial' grade dry reds and ports. It is also commonly used for roses for which it is well suited. Grenache dry reds are pleasant when young, having a light, fresh style and a grapey palate. However, when compared with the better quality varieties, its wines are lacking in colour, tannin and character, particularly when grown in the hot, irrigation districts, where deficiencies of this kind tend to be accentuated.

The variety is readily identified by its erect growth habit and shiny, entire leaves which are hairless on both the upper and lower surfaces. It is a heavy producer of medium sized, tight bunches which are predisposed to breakdown when wet weather is experienced near vintage.

Cabernet Sauvignon

Cabernet sauvignon is Australia's premium quality grape for dry red table wines, the use to which its production is entirely applied. Total plantings of cabernet amount to 4,247 acres, of which more than 25 percent are young non-bearing vines, demonstrating its increasing importance in the local oenological scene.

In France, over 19,000 acres of cabernet sauvignon are grown, the plantings being concentrated mostly in the Department of Gironde (Bordeaux). It is regarded here as the best quality grape of the five red varieties whose wines are permitted, by law, to carry the Bordeaux appellation. The others are merlot, malbec, cabernet franc and petite verdot, the first being the most extensively grown with an acreage more than double that of cabernet sauvignon. The Bordeaux reds are invariably made from blends of several of these five varieties. There are also limited plantings in the Anjou region of the Loire Valley where it is blended with cabernet franc to produce the best of the two types of rosé made there, namely Rosé de Cabernet, the other being Rosé d'Anjou.

Cabernet is grown extensively in Chile and in California where it produces the finest of the red table wines.

Cabernet wines possess a strong fruit flavour and bouquet which has been likened by some to the smell of freshly crushed young gum leaves. Being high in acid and tannin, they mature slowly but retain their quality and freshness for many years. As in France, few straight cabernets are made in Australia, where it is usually blended with shiraz. The fact that blending is normal practice with the variety supports the claim made by many that cabernet on its own does not make a complete wine, but rather one which is 'lacking on the middle palate'. This may be so, but there have been too few straight cabernets made here to reach any firm conclusion. So far the main reason for blending has been its limited availability.

Nearly three-quarters of Australia's cabernet is grown in South Australia where it is fairly evenly represented in all major districts. The Coonawarra cabernet blends are, rightly, the most highly regarded. They are of outstanding quality, possessing a rich purple colour and strong fruit flavour which, for want of a better analogy, is often described as 'minty'. Another feature of these wines is their clean, crisp finish to the palate which is derived from a combination of relatively high levels of acid and tannin. Some of the Coonawarra cabernets bear a remarkable resemblance to the reds of Bordeaux which is not surprising in view of the similarity in climate of the two regions and the common component of this fine wine grape.

The cabernets of Clare, the Barossa, Adelaide and the southern vales areas tend to be more full bodied and slightly softer on the finish. Although their fruit flavour is usually less intense than the Coonawarras, many cabernet blends of top quality originate in these districts.

Cabernet has become a significant variety in the Hunter Valley where at December, 1971, there were 670 acres, all planted since 1963. The young Hunter cabernet wines show considerable promise and there is no mistaking their varietal composition. Only time will tell whether these varietal characteristics will be subordinated by regional flavours of the kind which develop in the Hunter shiraz wines.

Cabernet has been grown in the irrigation districts for only a short time, but already it has proved to be the best quality red variety presently available for these areas. Its inherent capacity to produce flavoursome wines of high colour, tannin and acid content balances the combined influence of high temperatures and ample soil moisture which normally results in red wines that are lacking in these components.

It is a vigorous yet poor cropping variety of loose and rather small bunches. In the irrigation districts yields average between four and five tons per acre as against eight tons for shiraz. However, the price which winemakers are now prepared to pay for it compensates for this deficiency.

In appearance cabernet can be identified by its strongly lobed, shiny leaves and straggly growth habit. Because of its loose bunches, cabernet is resistant to rain damage, a factor much in its favour in the Hunter Valley where precipitation during the harvest period is higher than in any other Australian district.

High performance clones of cabernet which have been either selected here or imported from overseas are now becoming available and this will further encourage its wider acceptance amongst Australian grape growers.

Mataro

Synonyms: morrastel, burgundy

On an area basis, mataro ranks fourth as a red wine variety in Australia. Of the 3,960 acres grown, all but a few hundred acres are located in South Australia where it is represented in most districts. However, it assumes greatest importance in the Barossa Valley where there are 2,012 acres.

On the world scene, mataro is not an important grape. There are only about 1,500 acres in France and 2,500 acres in California where it is regarded as a grape without merit and is not recommended for further planting.

Some winemakers have used it to good effect in blends with shiraz, but the overall performance of mataro in Australia only rates it as average in quality. The wines are of neutral flavour and usually possess a rather hard finish. Nevertheless the area of young vines is more than sufficient to maintain the existing acreage and it must continue, therefore, to hold appeal to some vignerons. It is used for both table wines and ports.

Malbec

Synonym: cot (France).

The present area of malbec grown in Australia is only 648 acres, of which two-thirds (485 acres) are located in South Australia, mostly in the irrigation districts.

Malbec is notorious for its irregular cropping characteristics due to the frequent failure of its berries to set normally. However, improved clones have been recently imported into Australia and the variety could become more popular when these are available to growers.

Despite its agronomic faults, malbec is one of the specified Bordeaux varieties where, of the reds, it ranks third in importance to merlot and cabernet sauvignon. Here, its productivity has been improved

The vintage comes in at the Drayton brothers' 'Bellevue' winery at Pokolbin in the Hunter Valley, N.S.W.

by the use of less vigorous rootstocks and, more importantly, the planting of selected virus-free clones.

It is also grown extensively in Argentina where, in contrast to other regions, it apparently crops well. In California, it is of little importance and is not highly regarded as a quality grape. These differences in performance could well be due to genetic variations between clones of the variety, coupled with differing levels of virus infection.

The limited quantities of malbec wines made in Australia are of a good standard quality, rich in colour and in tannin, a description which could be applied equally as well to the French wines of this variety.

It is a moderately vigorous grape with a spreading growth habit and its fruit matures early in the season.

Carignane

Synonym: carignan (France).

Plantings of carignane in Australia amount to 492 acres, of which 359 acres are located in the Barossa Valley. There is some doubt as to the authenticity of the Australian carignane as it does not exactly match the European description.

Carignane is the most extensively grown red variety in France where over 400,000 acres are devoted to its culture. The plantings are concentrated in the southern departments bordering the Mediterranean, which consititute the regions of Roussillon in the west, Midi (Languedoc) in the centre and Provence in the east. Here it is used for Vins Ordinaires de Consommation Courante (V.C.C.) and the somewhat better quality Vins Délimités de Qualité Supérieure (V.D.Q.S.) red table wines. Although carignane is

157

recommended for planting in these regions, the proportion of the variety in relation to others is regarded as being too high as its wines require long ageing.

In California, also, the area of carignane exceeds that of all other red wine varieties. Here it produces wine of only standard quality but continues to be recommended for planting in the warmer regions.

Wines made solely from carignane are rare in Australia. Little interest is being shown in the variety and it seems unlikely to enjoy any great importance in the future of Australian winemaking.

It is a vigorous and productive grape of midseason to late in maturity.

Cinsaut

Synonyms: oeillade, blue imperial.

There are 377 acres of cinsaut in Australia, with most plantings located in the Barossa Valley (118 acres). It is also grown to a limited extent at Rutherglen, Corowa and in the Murrumbidgee Irrigation Area, but it is not being favoured for new plantings.

Cinsaut is an important variety of the Midi and Provence regions in the south of France where it is grown in association with grenache and carignane. Of no importance in California, it is nonetheless the principal red wine variety of South Africa where it is called 'hermitage' and constitutes about 27 percent of the total wine grape plantings there.

Cinsaut is productive, midseason in maturity, and of average vigour. The berries, though not large, are fleshy and more agreeable to eat then most other wine grapes.

It is used for both red table wines and port which are of standard quality with no obvious varietal character. Some winemakers in Australia produce good dry red blends of cinsaut with shiraz and even cabernet.

Pinot Noir

The 1971 statistics show a mere sixty acres of pinot noir planted in Australian vineyards. Of these, twenty-five acres are in New South Wales, mainly in the Hunter Valley and thirty-five acres in Victoria, mostly in the north-eastern districts. Nevertheless, winemakers are beginning to display considerable interest in this famous variety and plantings made after 1971 are expected to be significant, particularly in the Hunter Valley.

The exploitation of pinot noir in Australia has been thwarted by the lack of reliable clones. There is considerable genetic variation within the variety and it is often infected with virus diseases of varying severity. However, a locally selected pinot noir clone is now being distributed to growers and a wide range of high performance clones have been imported from France, Switzerland, Germany and California and these should become available soon.

Pinot noir is the earliest maturing of all red wine varieties and for this reason it can be grown successfully in the cold grape growing regions of Switzerland, Germany and northern France. Plantings in France amount to about 21,000 acres. All the red wines of the Cote-d'Or portion of Burgundy that are entitled to the appellation of 'Bourgogne' or higher Burgundy classifications must be made solely from pinot noir.

It is one of the three principal varieties in Champagne where it ranks second in importance to pinot meunier, another black grape. Normally blends of pinot noir and chardonnay base wines make by far the best champagne, pinot providing the strength and fullness while the chardonnay provides the delicate bouquet and elegance to the wines. The former on its own produces wines that are too big and apart from exceptionally good years, those of the latter are too delicate.

It is an important grape of Beaujolais where it is planted on the calcareous soils, while gamay, to which pinot noir is closely related, is grown on the granite soils.

Pinot noir and gamay are also the two red grapes of Switzerland, where in the Valais they are usually blended to produce the wines labelled 'Goron' and, the lesser quality, 'Dole'. The very best wines of the Valais, however, are made solely from pinot noir and are labelled 'Dole-Pinot Noir'.

In the Napa and Sonoma Valleys of California, pinot noir and a variety called 'gamay beaujolais' are also widely grown. It is now accepted that the latter is not the true gamay but rather one of the numerous clones of pinot noir.

The most famous Australian pinot noir wines have been made in the Hunter Valley. This is somewhat surprising because the variety usually develops insufficient colour and produces thin wines when grown in such warm regions. For this reason it is mostly blended with shiraz, although amongst the few straight pinots made in the Hunter are some magnificent wines. Whether blended or not, there is no mistaking the distinctive floral bouquet and flavour that the variety imparts to its wines.

From its performance overseas, it would seem that pinot is more suited to cooler districts than the Hunter and an indication will be given in this regard when the new Mudgee plantings come into bearing. There are no commercial plantings in South Australia but this situation should change soon, following recent relaxation of restrictions governing entry of vines to that State. It is surely worthy of trial in districts such as Coonawarra and Clare.

Pinot noir is a moderately vigorous variety with a spreading growth habit. It is a poor yielder but this is more than compensated by its high wine making quality.

The dry red table wine of the future streams from Dr Max Lake's new Howard Rotapress at his Hunter Valley winery.

Frontignan

Synonyms: Muscat de Frontignan, frontignac

There are several clones of frontignan which possess different berry colours, ranging from white to black. The red (or brown) clone is most widely grown in Australia, but the others are also present and often intermixed in the one vineyard. The total Australian acreage of frontignan is 887, of which 528 are in South Australia, mostly in the Barossa Valley. It is also an important grape in north-eastern Victoria, Corowa and the Murrumbidgee Irrigation Area.

Frontignan is responsible for the best of the muscat dessert wines made in Australia. The rich, luscious character of these wines is unique and probably unmatched by any from elsewhere in the world. The frontignan muscats of Rutherglen and adjoining districts have acquired the greatest fame but wines of equal quality are made in the Barossa and the M.I.A.

The variety is also becoming popular for dry white table wines. These possess the distinct fruity flavour of the muscat grape but are often rather austere, particularly on the finish to the palate.

In the A.O.C. region of Muscat de Frontignan in the south of France, only the white clone of frontignan is grown commercially. It is used for one of the few sweet fortified wines, vins doux naturels, made in that country. The red and white clones are grown to a limited extent for table wines in Alsace under the name of Muscat d'Alsace.

The vine has moderate vigour and produces reasonably good crops of compact, cylindrical bunches, the berries of which are inclined to shrivel before harvest.

159

White Wine Varieties

Sultana

Synonym: Thompson seedless (California).

In recent years there has been more sultana processed for wine in Australia than any other grape variety.

This is partly a reflection of the current wine boom in that the production of true wine varieties has been inadequate to meet the demand. However, the variety has distinct advantages to the winemaker, particularly for distillation wine. It is productive and, in contrast to other distillation varieties, is early maturing. This enables fortifying spirit to be distilled from wine made early in the vintage, thereby avoiding the need to hold large stocks from one year until the next.

Despite its neutral flavour, the usage of sultana is by no means confined to distillation wine. Commercial from it, including dry and sweet table wines, sparkling wines and sherry. Thus there is justification for its nickname of 'Murray Valley pinot'. The quantity of sultana crushed in Australia reached a peak of 81,809 tons in 1970 but declined to 42,817 tons in 1971 due mainly to unfavourable weather conditions. With the increasing availability of other white varieties, it is reasonable to assume that its importance as a wine grape will decline. But winemakers have learnt to use it to advantage and because of the large area planted, big quantities of sultana are bound to be vintaged for a long time.

It is significant that in California, more Thompson seedless, as it is known there, is crushed for wine than the combined total of all other varieties.

Nearly all of Australia's 51,757 acres of sultana are grown in the dry Murray Valley irrigation districts of Victoria, New South Wales and South Australia. It is principally used for drying and being a seedless variety, is popular as a fresh table grape. Successful cultivation of sultana is only possible in dry climates due to its susceptibility to downy mildew, berry splitting and bunch rots.

Muscat Gordo Blanco

Synonyms: muscatel, Muscat of Alexandria, hanepoot (South Africa).

Muscat gordo blanco is another dual purpose grape which has assumed considerable importance as a wine variety. It is the principal component of Australian cream sherry to which it imparts its mild muscat flavour. Also it is often fermented to dryness to produce a fruity, slightly aromatic, white table wine.

As with sultana, it is also sold as fresh fruit—the common white muscatel—and is the main variety used in Australia for dried raisins.

Plantings of gordo blanco in Australia amount to 9,906 acres which are concentrated in the Murray and Murrumbidgee irrigation districts as well as the Swan Valley of Western Australia.

The vine lacks vigour but when planted comparatively close together, the yields per acre are quite high. Its bunches are medium sized, loose and of midseason maturity.

In California it is an important drying grape and is also used for dry and sweet wines. A similar situation applies in South Africa where it is called hanepoot.

It is grown in several regions of Spain, being an important component of the sweet Malaga wines. A little is grown in Jerez where after partial drying it is used to make sweetening material for Spanish sherries.

Doradillo

Doradillo is probably Australia's most prolific wine grape and, as such, is traditionally the nation's principal distillation variety. It produces wines of neutral flavour which are, therefore, well suited for the distillation of fortifying and brandy spirit. Some winemakers also regard it highly as a base wine for premium quality dry sherry and the results achieved justify its use for this purpose.

Of the 5,815 acres devoted to the variety, most are located in the irrigation districts where it commonly yields crops of 15 tons or more per acre. It is also well represented in the Barossa Valley and other non-irrigated districts of South Australia.

The noted, early viticulturalist, de Castella, considered Doradillo to be synonymous with the Spanish variety Jaen. However, it is not clear whether this is the case. Certainly, apart from the possibility of Spain, the variety does not appear to be grown to any extent in other parts of the world.

The vine is only moderately vigorous and rather more sensitive than most to poor drainage. Doradillo may be distinguished in the vineyard by its dark green, lobed leaves which carry a heavy white felt on the under-surface. Its extremely heavy crops of large, conical bunches are late in maturing.

Palomino

Synonyms: paulo (at Langhorne Creek, S.A.), listan, white French (South Africa).

Because of past confusion in distinguishing between palomino, pedro ximenez and common palomino (false pedro), the latest available statistics of Australian grape plantings do not separate these three varieties in all States. However, their combined area is 8,300 acres.

Of the three, palomino is the most important, having become very popular since the early 1960s as a premium quality dry sherry grape. It is represented in most districts of South Australia, particularly the Barossa, Murray irrigation areas and Langhorne Creek. There are also significant plantings (475 acres) in the M.I.A., and in the Sunraysia district of Victoria and New South Wales (197 acres).

Palomino constitutes almost 90 percent of all of the 30,000 acres of grapes grown in the Jerez region of Spain which, under the appellation laws, is responsible for all that country's sherry production. The other varieties of Jerez are mainly pedro ximenez (about 10 percent of plantings) and a little muscatel (gordo blanco), both of which are only used for sweetening material being partially dried in the sun on esparto grass mats before crushing.

Palomino is one of the most widely distributed wine varieties in California and is wrongly called 'golden chasselas' in the Napa Valley. It also comprises over 20 percent of the plantings in South Africa where it is grown under the name of white French. Surprisingly, in neither of these countries is palomino regarded as the best dry sherry grape, being too low in total acidity. The best sherries in South Africa are made from stein (chenin blanc).

It is a vigorous, highly productive variety carrying large, loose bunches. The distinguishing features of palomino are its dark green, deeply lobed leaves which are heavily felted on the undersurface. It may be mistaken for doradillo, but matures much earlier and has more red colouration on the leaf stalks and shoot tips. Common palomino, on the other hand, has leaves which are only slightly lobed and carry strong bristles as distinct from felty hairs on the undersurface. Pedro ximenez is quite different, possessing shiny leaves which are hairless, like grenache, on both the upper and lower surfaces.

Palomino is not a suitable grape for table wines.

Pedro Ximenez

Pedro ximenez is a vigorous growing variety and in good seasons produces extremely heavy crops of large, easily harvested bunches. Yields of 20 tons per acre have been recorded in irrigation districts. However, its berries are highly susceptible to splitting following the incidence of rain when the fruit is approaching maturity. Because of this serious disadvantage, it has been replaced by palomino as the top dry sherry grape in Australia. Although the acreage is declining, the variety is represented in most districts.

Despite its agronomic faults, the clean, neutral flavoured wines of pedro ximenez continue to be highly regarded for flor sherry, particularly the more delicate fino styles.

Additional information is given under palomino.

Common Palomino

Synonym: false pedro.

Common palomino is also a heavy yielding variety of large bunches but is less vigorous than pedro ximenez. Most plantings are in South Australia, especially the Barossa and Murray region, where there is an estimated 500 acres. There are also 145 acres of common palomino in the M.I.A.

Its wines are of neutral flavour and possess no particular attributes. There are practically no new plantings of the variety.

Additional information is given under palomino.

Semillon

Synonym: Hunter River riesling, greengrape (South Africa).

Semillon must be regarded as Australia's most important dry white table wine variety. There is a strong similarity between semillon and Clare riesling, both in the morphological characteristics of the vine and in the winemaking qualities of the grape. Because of this, there is considerable confusion, particularly in South Australia, as to the true varietal identity of the two. The situation is compounded further in that semillon in the Barossa Valley is often known under the name of white madeira.

Official statistics give the area of semillon in Australia as 4,983 acres. The majority of these are in New South Wales, 3,281 acres, followed by South Australia, 1,602 acres. In New South Wales, 1,800 acres of semillon are located in the M.I.A. and 1,400 acres in the Hunter Valley. The South Australian plantings are mostly in the Barossa but it is gaining in popularity in the Murray irrigation districts.

There are over 60,000 acres of semillon in the Bordeaux region (Department of Gironde) of France, more than any other wine variety planted there. The white, Appellation d'Origine Controlee wines of Graves, Sauternes and Barsac must be made from semillon, sauvignon blanc and muscadelle, but the proportion of each is not specified. In practice, however, semillon predominates and all contain 10-15 percent of muscadelle. Traditionally, infection of the fruit with *Botrytis cinerea* ('noble rot') is necessary to produce the best of the luscious wines of Barsac and Sauternes. Semillon is also grown fairly extensively in two of the adjoining departments to Gironde, namely Dordogne and Lot-et-Garonne.

Semillon constitutes about 9 percent of the wine grape plantings in South Africa where it is called greengrape. There are also moderate plantings in the Napa, Sonoma and Alameda counties of California.

The reputation of Hunter Valley white table wines has been established primarily on the semillon variety which represents 75 percent of the white grapes grown there. The Hunter semillons are undoubtedly the most distinctive and readily distinguished regional wine style in Australia. The unique flavour of these wines is such that persons unaccustomed to them often need time to acquire a true appreciation of their worth. They contain only moderate amounts of acid, except when the grapes are picked immature, and are consequently soft on the palate. The mild fruit flavour of the grape is supplemented by characters which develop after bottling, providing a rich complex wine. Because of their softness, Hunter semillons are ready to drink at an early age, but this belies their capacity for comparatively long storage and for best value, should not be consumed before three years, preferably longer.

Semillon, either by itself or in blends with trebbiano and verdelho, produces wines in Australia which are more akin to white burgundies or chablis than those made from the more aromatic and fruity flavoured grapes like rhine riesling.

The variety has also proved extremely valuable for white table wine in the hot inland irrigation districts, which accounts for the growth of its popularity in the M.I.A.

The most distinguishing features of semillon are the bronze tips and reddish brown streaks on the actively growing shoot tips, contrasting with those of clare riesling which are grass green. The leaves are mostly 5-lobed, sometimes 3-lobed, and their upper surface has a distinctive rough texture.

It possesses moderate vigour, is midseason in maturity and highly productive of medium sized, compact bunches which have a tendency to break down following wet weather near vintage. The berries of semillon are slightly larger than those of clare riesling and do not develop the typical pronounced copper colour of the latter when exposed to the sun.

Clare Riesling

Not only has clare riesling been confused with semillon, but also with rhine riesling, the name by which it is called in the Murray River districts. Accordingly, the exact area of the variety is not known, but, unlike the situation in other States, clare riesling assumes far greater importance in South Australia than semillon.

It was thought to have been brought to the Clare district by the Jesuits who founded the Sevenhill Monastery about 1850. However, its close similarity to semillon suggests that it is no more than a clone of that variety.

The winemaking qualities of clare riesling are virtually identical to those of semillon and both are used almost exclusively for table wines.

Additional comments are given under semillon.

Rhine Riesling

Synonyms: riesling (Germany and France), white riesling (California).

Whereas Australian winemakers look mostly to semillon for white burgundy style table wines, rhine riesling is rightly regarded as the premium grape for the fruitier and more acid German hock styles. The majority of plantings are located in South Australia where it is becoming increasingly popular in all districts. Also, there has been considerable recent interest in the variety in the irrigation areas and in the Hunter Valley.

Rhine riesling, as the name implies, is the premium variety of Germany where it accounts for 26 percent of the total area of wine grapes of around 200,000 acres. In a quantitative sense, however, it ranks second to silvaner which makes up 35 percent of the plantings there. Rhine riesling, nonetheless, assumes pride of place in the quality Rheingau and Mosel regions where its acreage represents over 72 percent and 95 percent of the totals, respectively.

Although traminer is the variety which comes first to mind when thinking of Alsace, the Alsatians regard riesling as their premium wine type and are jealous of its high quality and dryness in relation to the German rieslings which now are usually slightly sweet.

Riesling is also grown in Italy, Switzerland, Austria, Chile, California and South Africa where, in all cases, it is rated amongst the best of the white table wine varieties.

The cool South Australian districts are responsible for the best local riesling wines. Here the prominent, fruity aroma and flavour of its wines are well balanced by a fresh crispness to their finish, brought about by comparatively high levels of acidity. They are fine, elegant wines when young but develop an 'oily' consistency and complexity with bottle age, that many favour.

In the Hunter, as with other aromatic grapes, the varietal flavours of riesling tend to be subordinated by regional characteristics. However, this could well be changed by the greater care now being exercised during vinification to avoid oxidation.

A distinguishing feature of rhine riesling is its red shoots in the spring. It has round, 3-lobed leaves which are rough and often puckered on the upper surface. Other distinctive features of the variety are its small, tight cylindrical bunches, short bunch stalks and spotted berries. It is comparatively early in maturity.

Riesling has moderate vigour but it is a relatively poor yielder. It is hoped that the release of a big range of selected clones that have been imported from Europe will correct this situation.

Traminer has the most pronounced varietal characteristic of any white grape, producing a wine with a very aromatic, pungent aroma and flavour.

1

Grenache is widely grown in South Australia and to a lesser extent in New South Wales and Victoria, where it is used for both table wines and ports.

2

Cabernet sauvignon is used for the production of premium-quality red table wines, particularly of the claret type. It is the famous grape of the Bordeaux district of France.

3

Chardonnay produces wines of clean, delicate character, particularly favoured as a base for high-quality Champagne. This grape is one of the earliest to mature and is moderately productive.

4

*Rhine riesling is the famous grape of the Rhine Valley in
Germany. In Australia it is used for the production of
quality white table wines. It produces wines of strong,
distinctive fruitiness which are fresh and grapy when
young and which become luscious when aged.*

5

*Clare riesling, grown mostly in the Clare Valley and
Watervale districts of South Australia, is a variety producing
high-quality, delicate wines of the hock type. It is a good
cropper of moderate vigour.*

6

*Semillon is the major white table wine variety of Australia
and is in abundance in most of the winegrowing districts
of New South Wales and South Australia.*

7

Sauvignon blanc, one of the grape varieties used in the composition of French Sauternes, is grown to a limited extent for light, dry wines in Australia.

8

The sultana grape, the basis of the Australian dried fruits industry, is also used for making wine. Because it matures early it can be used as a distillation wine for the manufacture of fortifying spirit, thus avoiding the need to hold large spirit stocks from year to year.

9

Pinot noir is a highly regarded grape of the Burgundy district of France and the premium grape for the production of French Champagne. Winemakers in Australia are interested in this famous variety and plantings made after 1971 are expected to be significant.

Trebbiano

Synonyms: white shiraz (N.S.W. districts), white hermitage (South Australian districts), ugni blanc (south of France), St Emilion (Cognac).

There are 2,773 acres of trebbiano in Australia, of which 1,410 acres are in New South Wales and 1,065 acres in South Australia. With the exception of about 120 acres in the Hunter Valley, the majority of the New South Wales plantings are in the M.I.A. and most of those in South Australia are equally distributed between the Barossa and Murray districts.

The name trebbiano comes from Italy where the variety assumes considerable importance. It is not commonly known that trebbiano, in combination with malvasia bianca, traditionally makes up 35 percent of the varieties used for the production of the red wines of Chianti. The other varieties are all red grapes, namely sangiovese, canaiolo nero and colorino. The two white varieties are no doubt responsible for lightness in character of this classic regional wine style. Trebbiano is grown elsewhere in Italy and contributes to many of the better quality dry whites of that country.

Under the name of St Emilion, it is best known throughout the world as the grape of Cognac. In this region, which extends over the Departments of Charente and Charente-Maritime, to the north of Bordeaux, over 90,000 acres of the variety are grown. Emphasising its value as a distillation grape, there are also significant plantings in the Armagnac region in the Department of Gers. It is known as ugni blanc in the Midi and Provence regions of the south of France, where it is frequently blended with clairette for dry white table wines.

The versatility of trebbiano overseas is reflected in its use for all classes of white beverage and distillation wine in Australia. It produces rather austere table wines of neutral flavour but blends well with more fruity types.

Trebbiano is a vigorous, highly productive variety of midseason maturity, though significantly later than semillon. It is distinguished in the vineyard by its large, thick leaves and long, cylindrical bunches which are often forked at their tip.

Tokay

Although a famous grape of the Rutherglen district in north-eastern Victoria, 762 acres of Australia's total of 1,076 acres of tokay are grown in South Australia, mostly in the Barossa Valley where it is still being planted to a limited extent. There are 169 acres in Victoria and 122 in the Swan Valley of Western Australia.

It is commonly accepted that the variety came from Hungary and is thought to be Harslevelii which is one of the two varieties of the Tokaj-Hegyalja district where the original tokay wines are made. These are natural sweet wines of comparatively high alcoholic strength, which are said to match the best of the French sauternes and German trockenbeerenausles in quality. The other variety of Tokaj-Hegyalja is furmint.

In Australia, tokay is the traditional grape for the production of fortified, sweet white dessert wines for which it is unsurpassed by other varieties. These wines are not often seen commercially, but are equally as luscious and distinctive as the frontignan muscat dessert wines, without, of course, the muscat flavour. Tokay is also used for sherry and occasionally dry white table wines that possess a rich, full flavour.

Tokay matures early in the season and produces moderate crops of medium sized, well filled bunches. However, many of the plantings in Australia are obviously heavily infected with debilitating virus diseases.

Albillo

Synonym: sherry.

Of the 428 acres of albillo grown in Australia, all but 10 acres are located in South Australia, mostly in the Barossa Valley. It has been used mainly for the production of sherry and for this purpose it is reputed to have considerable merit.

Albillo is a comparatively weak growing variety which yields moderate crops of early maturing fruit. The vine in appearance resembles riesling except that the bunches are somewhat larger and the berries oval in shape. The origin of the grape is not known.

There have been no new plantings of albillo in recent years and the variety seems destined to decline further in significance.

'Irvine's White'

'Irvine's white' is grown exclusively in Victoria, particularly in the Great Western district between Stawell and Ararat where there are 211 acres of the total 297 acres of the variety.

Elsewhere in the world, no variety is grown under this name and it is now thought that 'Irvine's white' is in fact folle blanche which was formerly the principal variety of Cognac. In good years, folle blanche is a heavy cropping grape, but, due to its extreme susceptibility to bunch rots, it has been replaced in Cognac by trebbiano (St Emilion).

No doubt the variety acquired its name in Australia from a Hans Irvine who acquired a property at Great Western in 1888 and brought a team of French experts there to develop champagne production in the district.

Much of the credit for the supreme finesse and elegance of the best Great Western champagnes is attributed to 'Irvine's white', from which they are made.

Sercial

The only Australian plantings of sercial are located in South Australia where there are 237 acres, of which 220 acres are in the Barossa Valley.

Sercial is one of the four main grape varieties grown in the island of Madeira, a Portuguese territory in the Atlantic Ocean, 530 miles from Lisbon. The fortified, aperitif/dessert wines of this region carry the name of the variety from which they are made. Sercial produces the best of the dry madeiras, the others in ascending order of sweetness and richness are verdelho, bual (boal) and malmsey, the last being made from the malvoisie grape.

In Australia it is regarded as an average quality variety used for dessert wines and in blends for white table wines. Although it is unlikely to increase in relative importance, there have been a few new plantings of the variety.

It is moderately vigorous and produces big crops of early maturing, small to medium sized bunches.

Chasselas

Synonyms: sweetwater, gutedel (Germany and Alsace), chasselas dore (California), fendant (Switzerland). The total area of chasselas is 213 acres, of which ninety-seven acres are in Victoria, mostly in the north-eastern districts, seventy-six acres in Western Australia and forty acres in New South Wales. As well as being used for wine, it is sometimes sold as an early maturing table grape, under the name of sweetwater.

Chasselas is grown in Switzerland, Alsace and Germany as a wine variety but even more widely throughout Europe as a table grape. It is the principal wine grape of Switzerland where it is also known under the name of fendant.

In Alsace it represents about 20 percent of the total plantings and is used there for wines of only standard quality.

In Europe chasselas is one of the heaviest producing white varieties, having rather large, loose bunches of medium sized berries. This contrasts with the situation in Australia and California where it is far less productive and has smaller bunches and berries. However, the foliage characteristics of the vine in Europe and Australia are very similar which suggests that there is only a clonal difference between the two. In addition, many of the Australian plantings are known to be heavily infected with virus disease.

The best Swiss and Alsatian clones of chasselas have been recently imported and it will be interesting to compare their performance with vines in the older plantings.

The European chasselas wines are by no means in the premium quality class but they are pleasant, well balanced and have a mild, fruity flavour. Some Australian winemakers regard it as an ideal grape for champagne.

Traminer

Synonym: gewurztraminer.
All but one of Australia's 123 acres of traminer are grown in New South Wales. The oldest and best known plantings are at Rooty Hill (Minchinbury) and at Pokolbin (Mt Pleasant). The remainder are young plantings located mainly in the Hunter Valley and in the M.I.A. There is one acre in Victoria.

On world standards, the best known traminer wines are made in Alsace where the variety accounts for about 17 percent of the total plantings. Because of the wide range of different flavoured grapes grown there, Alsace is one of the few regions in France where the wines are given a varietal nomenclature.

Gewurztraminer and traminer are one and the same variety. Normally in Alsace the two names are used simply to denote the strength of character in the particular wine, gewurztraminer being applied to those with the the strongest flavour. However, some makers label all wines gewurztraminer except when the merchant specifically requests traminer.

There is marked clonal variation within the variety in respect to berry colour and strength of flavour. The berries range from a deep pink (almost red) to white in colour. With the exception of one small village where a white, strongly flavoured clone is grown, only the pink clones are grown in Alsace as these are regarded as producing the best flavoured wines.

On the other hand, in Germany where traminer is a comparatively minor variety, it is maintained that both pink and white clones may be strongly aromatic and, if anything, the white tends to be superior in this respect.

Under the name of savignin, traminer is grown in other parts of France to Alsace, notably in the Cotes-du-Jura to the east of Burgundy where it is responsible for the curious vins jaunes or yellow wines. These are subject to a flor yeast treatment during the course of their preparation.

Of all the white varieties, traminer produces table wines with the most obvious varietal bouquet and flavour which may be described as aromatic, spicy or honeyed. In Australia the Rooty Hill traminers are the most famous and closely approach the best of Alsace in quality. Because of the similarity in the climate and soils, the variety should perform equally in the Hunter but so far the varietal character of traminers made there is little less pungent.

Good clones of traminer are moderately vigorous and yield comparatively good crops of small, early maturing bunches. The variation in berry colour that exists in Europe also applies in Australian plantings.

Brian Falkenberg and John Vickery, winemakers for Leo Buring, checking a load of freshly picked grapes.

Clairette

Synonym: blanquette.

Clairette, which is known in Australia as blanquette, accounts for 121 acres of Australia's grape plantings. There are seventy-five acres in New South Wales where it is grown exclusively in the Hunter Valley. The remainder are located in Victoria, mostly in the northern and north-eastern districts.

Clairette is grown extensively in the Midi and Provence regions of southern France. Here, practically all the white table wines are blends of this variety and ugni blanc (trebbiano). It is also grown commercially to a small extent in South Africa.

In France, as in South Africa, clairette makes wines with a distinctive though rather aggressive fruity aroma and bouquet. They have a reputation for their tendency to oxidise. Its winemaking performance in Australia is similar although occasionally some fine elegant wines are seen which carry the blanquette label. It is often used to advantage for blending, in small quantities with varieties like semillon.

The foliage of clairette is very similar in appearance to that of doradillo with which it is sometimes confused. However, its berries are oval in shape whereas those of doradillo are round. It is a vigorous variety producing good crops of moderately large, loose and late maturing bunches. Some vines have a marked tendency towards poor berry setting which is caused by virus infection.

Verdelho

There are 105 acres of verdelho in Australia, forty-six of which are in Western Australia and the balance are equally distributed between the Hunter Valley and the non-irrigated districts of South Australia. It is incorrectly called madeira in the Hunter.

Classically verdelho is a top, white port variety of the Douro Valley of Portugal. It is also responsible for one of the four types of fortified aperitif/dessert wines of the Madeira Island.

In Australia, verdelho has proven attributes for blending with semillon and trebbiano, adding richness and fullness in flavour to produce wines of a white burgundy style.

Sauvignon Blanc

Synonym: Surin (in parts of the Loire).

Despite the importance of sauvignon blanc in France, there are a mere sixty-three acres in Australia, the majority of which is grown in South Australia where it is represented in most districts.

In France there are close to 14,000 acres of the variety, half of which is planted in the Gironde. Here it is blended with semillon and muscadelle to produce the famous wines of Sauternes, Barsac and Graves. It is also grown extensively in the Loire Valley where it is responsible for the A.O.C. wines of Pouilly Fumé, Sancerre, Quincy and Reuilly.

In California it is grown in both the cool and warm areas and is highly regarded for its distinctive wines. It is considered to be one of the best quality varieties for the hot San Joaquin Valley and this is in keeping with its limited though favourable performance so far in Australian irrigation districts.

Sauvignon blanc produces soft wines of pronounced varietal flavour. The vine is vigorous but a comparatively poor yielder of small, early maturing bunches. Because of its small bunches, it is costly to harvest but despite this, it is likely to become far more important in Australian viticulture.

Chardonnay

The area of chardonnay in Australia is insufficient to be recorded separately in the official planting statistics. Recently, however, there has been renewed interest in the variety and it is bound to be grown far more extensively in the future.

Chardonnay is often referred to as white pinot, but in fact the two are quite distinct, the former being readily identified by its naked petiolar sinus on mature leaves, a characteristic unique to the variety. Although there are a few vines of pinot blanc in both the Champagne and Burgundy regions, in France this variety only assumes commercial significance in Alsace. It now appears that virtually all the so-called white pinot plantings in Australia are truly chardonnay.

Chardonnay is grown extensively in northern France, where it is responsible for all the grand A.O.C. white wines of the Cote-d'Or and of Chablis. It is also the white variety of Champagne where it is normally blended with pinot noir to produce the finest wines, except in very good years when the blanc-de-blancs made solely from chardonnay may be superior. In all there are about 18,000 acres of chardonnay in France.

It is also regarded as the premium white table wine variety in California.

Chardonnay wines possess a distinctive vinosity and are impressive either as straight varietals or in blends. The quality of some of the more recent Hunter and Mudgee chardonnay/semillon blends indicates that the variety holds considerable promise for Australian conditions.

It is a rather vigorous vine and a reasonably good yielder of smallish, early maturing bunches.

Marsanne

All of Australia's plantings of marsanne which only amount to fifty-seven acres, are grown in the northern Victorian districts where it is used for white table wines that possess a definite varietal vinosity. Nearly half of this area are young vines coming into bearing.

Marsanne is grown in the south of France for white table wines, but is of only minor importance there.

Aucerot

Despite the frequent references which are made to it, at December, 1971, there were only thirty acres of the so-called aucerot variety grown in Australia and they are all confined to the Hunter Valley. In the past the variety assumed minor significance in this district but it is at least ten years since an aucerot wine has been bottled and marketed as such. Most of the present plantings are young vines and perhaps more will be seen of the variety in the future.

The similarity in the names suggests that it is the same variety as auxerrois which accounts for about 3 percent of the grape plantings in Alsace. Here the practice is to blend auxerrois with pinot blanc and the resultant wines are sold under the label of Pinot Blanc. The latter variety, by itself, produces wines which are too acid and neutral in flavour.

The distinct fruitiness and softness of the Alsatian auxerrois blends is consistent with the reputation of the Hunter aucerots.

The inside of a press gets a scrub down at Morris' winery, Rutherglen, Vic.

WINE
OF AUSTRALIA

*Len Evans was born of Welsh parents in England.
He became interested in wine, women and golf
when he was fourteen. While writing for television
and radio, he worked in a hotel on a casual basis
and, typically, he became immersed in the industry
within months. By 1960 he was Beverage Manager
of an international hotel and built the largest retail
cellar in Australia at that time. In 1962 he began
the popular Cellarmaster column in* **The Bulletin.**
*On the first day of 1965 he joined the wine industry
and suggested the formation of The Australian
Wine Bureau, of which he was the founding director.
In 1966 and 1967 his* **Cellarmaster's Guide to
Australian Wines** *became a bestseller.*

*Len Evans is now a professional wine consultant,
chairman of a syndicate of vignerons, restaurateur,
a lecturer and broadcaster on wine and food, and
Australia's most widely-read wine writer. His
interests have remained the same since he was
fourteen, only he now has little time for golf.*

Stainless steel storage tanks at McWilliams, Hanwood, N.S.W.

The modern Australian winemaker is well informed and well equipped. The great Australian wine firms have the latest and most scientifically devised equipment and highly qualified trained staff. Consequently there is a lot of good wine made in Australia. Not that all wine made in Australia is fine wine, for like all other wine-producing countries Australia produces much wine that is *ordinaire* or plain wine.

The following encyclopaedic survey is a comprehensive description of wine in Australia. Many are entitled to rank among the world's really fine wines. The entries are alphabetically listed by the name of the producing company.

All Saints

All Saints' Beverleys Blend Riesling
From new semillon vines planted at Wahgunyah in north-east Victoria. Made under controlled fermentation conditions and containing some residual sugar. A pleasant clean wine of medium acidity. It is named after Beverley Sutherland Smith and was first marketed in 1970.

All Saints' Cabernet Shiraz
Made from ten percent cabernet and ninety percent shiraz grown in Wahgunyah in north-east Victoria. Most of the material is aged in 500 and 1,000 gallon oak casks for eighteen months before bottling; but some is matured in small Nevers oak and blended back.

From 1972 this wine was made under enclosed fermentation principles. Prior to this it was made in open fermenters, under heading boards. The wine has a medium acidity with a firm, clean finish. It is normally sold after about one year in the bottle.

All Saints' Champagne
A soft, sparkling white of medium sweetness; made from chasselas grapes grown locally.

All Saints' Claret (30 percent Cabernet)
That rather unusual heading speaks for itself. The balance is shiraz; all the grapes are grown locally and blended together in a fermenting vat. From 1972 the wines were fermented in enclosed tanks; prior to this, in open vats with heading boards. Approximately one-third of the wine is matured in Nevers oak hogsheads, the balance in 1,000 gallon casks. The two wines are blended prior to bottling after approximately eighteen months of wood age. They are normally released after one year in the bottle.

The wine has a good fruity nose; a fairly full palate, rather soft and pleasant; and usually the acidity is fairly low—although in 1960 it was quite high. The wine has a firm finish due to the oak and cabernet tannins. It usually needs further bottle maturation after release.

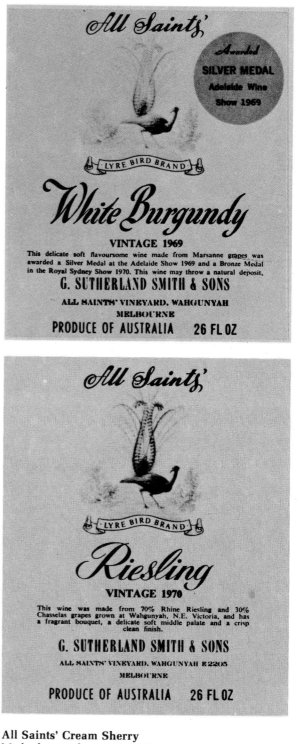

All Saints' Cream Sherry
Made from tokay and pedro ximenez grapes grown locally at Wahgunyah, with some muscat gordo blanco from Robinvale. The wine is matured in small oak for three years.

All Saints' Estate Claret
Made from shiraz grown at Wahgunyah. A soft wine which spends two years in big wood before being released.

All Saints' Estate Riesling
Made from semillon and white hermitage grown at Wahgunyah. Made under enclosed and controlled fermentation process and bottled at six months.

All Saints' Estate White Burgundy
Made from marsanne and chasselas, grown at Wahgunyah. Again the enclosed fermentation methods are applied and the temperatures are controlled. The wine is bottled at six to seven months. It is rather a broad, soft, pleasant wine.

All Saints' Hermitage
A light red made from shiraz grown at Wahgunyah. It has soft fruit, low acidity on the finish and is an early, pleasant drinking style.

All Saints' Light Amontillado Sherry
A very pleasant, nutty sherry made on the Flor principle from palomino grapes. The wine spends one year on Flor in oak hogsheads and then is further matured in 1,000 gallon casks for three years. A quantity of ten to fifteen year-old amontillado, matured in Spanish 25 gallon casks, is then blended in with the base wine. The result is a soft, oaky wine without excessive sweetness; and of considerable sherry flavour.

All Saints' Lyre Bird Burgundy
Made from the marsanne grape picked at medium ripeness; the usual controlled fermentation methods are applied. The wine is quite soft, full-flavoured, very clean finish—there is some grip on the back of the palate; the acidity is well balanced: all in all a pleasant flavoured, round, soft white style.

All Saints' Lyre Bird Claret
A specially selected cask (1,000 gallon) of a red wine with high cabernet content (approximately thirty to forty percent). The balance is shiraz and this is blended with a similar wine which has been matured in new Nevers oak hogsheads. The wine is usually matured for at least two years in the bottle, after eighteen months in oak. All the material is locally grown.

This is a good fruity wine of considerable flavour and body, with a quite firm, strong finish.

All Saints' Lyre Bird Riesling
Made from seventy percent rhine riesling and thirty percent chasselas under the normal enclosed fermentation methods which are temperature controlled. The wine is fairly full flavoured showing marked varietal fruit and has a reasonably crisp acidity.

Not much of this wine is made and it can be reasonably assumed that it is the most delicate of the white wines made by the company. It has won a number of Bronze Medals and one Silver Medal in recent years in young White Wine Classes.

All Saints' Marsanne
A sweet white dessert wine made from the marsanne grape; picked when quite ripe; fermented on skins for three days before pressing and fortification; matured in big oak for three to five years. The wine has a very pleasant, quite unique, flavour—which some people liken to the honeysuckle.

All Saints' Medium Dry Sherry
This is a blend of two wines—a Flor sherry made from palomino grapes, which has been matured in big oak; and a sweet white dessert wine made from chasselas grapes, matured in hogsheads. The wine after blending is matured in 500 gallon oak casks for a further twelve months.

All Saints' Old Liqueur Muscat
From Rutherglen brown muscat (frontignac), which is allowed to shrivel on the vine until 17 to 19 degrees Baumé is reached. This can go as high as 20 degrees in a good year. The grapes, after crushing, ferment on the skins for about two days and are then pressed in the continuous press to gain maximum extraction of colour and flavour. The wine, after clarification is matured in small oak for some years.

This is an extremely sweet, very flavoursome dessert wine of considerable power and body.

All Saints' Old Madeira
A very old blend of marsanne, matured in 500s and 1,000 gallon oak casks together with tokay matured in hogsheads. The wines are up to twenty years old when finally sold. The blend is allowed to marry in oak 500s for two years prior to release.

It is a very mellow soft wine, but not as sweet as might be expected. The oak tends to dry off the finish. In fact it is a quite elegant wine of good flavour, with this rather dry finish.

All Saints' Old Muscat
From Rutherglen brown muscat (frontignac) grown at Wahgunyah and muscat gordo blanco from Robinvale in north Victoria. The wine is matured in big oak for three years.

All Saints' Old Port
From shiraz grown at Wahgunyah, matured in big oak for three years.

All Saints' Old Reserve Sherry
A Flor sherry made from palomino and pedro ximenez grapes (which are locally called Spanish pedro). The wine spends one year on Flor in oak

175

hogsheads and then a further two years in oak 1,000 gallon casks.

It is full flavoured and fairly dry.

All Saints' Old Sherry

From pedro ximenez and palomino grapes grown at Wahgunyah and made on the Flor process, using bulk methods, the wine spending a further two years in big oak.

All Saints' Old Tawny Port

A high quality dessert wine made mainly from shiraz, together with some Portuguese port varieties, which are quite common in the district, from Wahgunyah in north-east Victoria. The wine is wood matured and has a general age of about twelve to fourteen years. Some of it is matured in oak hogsheads; a portion of the wine has been matured in old brandy casks and this has added to the dry finish of the wine.

All Saints' Pale Dry Flor Sherry

Made from palomino grapes grown locally. The first drainings are separated and used exclusively for this wine, which spends one year on Flor in underground sherry storage. It is then matured for three years in oak 1,000 gallon casks. Only the most delicate material is selected for this blend. The wine is normally almost bone dry with a very low acidity, soft middle palate and pleasant oak finish.

All Saints' Pearl

A sparkling wine of medium sweetness made from the chasselas grape.

All Saints' Pinot Shiraz

Made from approximately one-third pinot noir and pinot meuniere; the balance being shiraz grown locally. The wine is mostly matured in big oak, but with a small proportion matured in new oak hogsheads and blended back. The wine is medium bodied with a very soft middle palate and a soft, pleasant finish.

This wine provides most interesting flavour and the first ones produced by the company had marked promise, although they suffered from some acetic acid volatility. Recent vintages show much promise for the variety and it will be extremely interesting to see the pinot noir as a straight varietal wine without any other fruit being mixed with it.

All Saints' Rosé

An interesting style, made from white grenache grapes. The wine has pleasant fruity nose, a soft middle palate without any sweetness, and a reasonably clean, acid finish. There is also a slight tannin grip at the back of the palate.

The wine is fermented on skins for one day under a CO_2 blanket and then pressed lightly; fermentation taking place under controlled conditions. The colour comes from the pink skins of the white grenache grape. The wine has been an award winner.

All Saints' Show Muscat ('58/'64 Blend)

Made from the Rutherglen brown muscat (frontignac). When the summer is extremely hot and dry the muscat grapes really shrivel and Baumés of 19-20 degrees are attained. When this occurs, wines of extremely high sugar content can be made. The grapes, after crushing ferment on the skins for a couple of days. They are then pressed in the old-fashioned continuous presses, to gain maximum extraction of colour and flavour.

The 1958 wine won a great number of medals over the years and has now been freshened up with the '64, which also has a most creditable record. The wines are matured in oak 500 gallon casks, rather than hogsheads as otherwise the company believes the wines would become too flat and too woody. It is a magnificent dessert wine of the greatest character.

All Saints' Special Bin Cabernets

Normally high quality red wines which have won medals at various shows. Some are straight bottlings of one special 1,000 or 1,200 gallon cask. Others are a cask of this size, blended with a portion of the wine which has been matured in new Nevers oak hogsheads. The wines are mostly sold under the claret label, although the one 1967 red wine which was made from late picked grapes won a Silver and a number of Bronze Medals in open Burgundy classes. A 1969 blend won a Gold Medal in Sydney in 1970.

Normally these wines are given at least three years' bottle maturation prior to release. They have a high colour, full rich flavour on the middle palate and some oak is also evident. The wines have a clean, firm finish, on which again the cabernet fruit and oak are evident.

All Saints' Special Tawny Port

Made from shiraz grapes grown in the company's River Vineyard: fermented on skins in open vats under a false head for two to three days before fortification; and then matured in oak hogsheads for three to five years.

This is a soft round wine of good colour, with a clean finish.

All Saints' Sweet Sherry

Made from tokay and pedro ximenez grapes grown at Wahgunyah in north-east Victoria; blended with some muscat gordo blanco from Robinvale. Matured in big oak for two years.

All Saints' Vermouths

The Dry Vermouth is made from doradillo grown at Wahgunyah and the Sweet Vermouth from

Rutherglen pedro (pedro ximenez). Both wines are infused with herbs and matured in small oak.

All Saints' Very Old Sweet Sherry
A very rich, old, rancio style wine made from pedro ximenez and marsanne grapes; matured in oak 1,000 gallon casks and blended with an extremely old Rutherglen tokay, which has been matured in hogsheads for many, many years.

The wine is soft, round, luscious, with a very strong oak finish.

All Saints' Vintage Port
Made entirely from shiraz, grown on the Top Ten Block. Only a small quantity is made each year. The grapes are allowed to become very ripe—usually about 16 degrees Baumé—and the fermentation is made on skins for as long as possible, consistent with the finished sugar content.

The result is an extremely full-flavoured wine of considerable tannin, which is quite smooth on the middle palate; but with a very firm, dry finish. The wine is matured in fully topped up oak 1,000 gallon casks for two years before bottling.

Normally this style wins at least one Gold Medal as a young wine. The '65 was probably the most famous edition of the line—a wine of considerable 'blackberry' fruit, with a very strong, smooth, rich palate and a firm finish. The wine definitely needs considerable years in the bottle before it shows its best.

All Saints' White Muscat
Made from muscat gordo blanco grown at Robinvale in northern Victoria and matured in big oak.

All Saints' White Port
A blend of tokay and pedro ximenez with some muscat gordo blanco and matured in big oak.

Angove's Ltd

Angove's Amontillado Sherry
Made from a blend of palomino and pedro ximenez grapes and matured in oak casks for at least five years. A fairly dark coloured full-flavoured wine, with some trace of sweetness on the middle palate.

Angove's Bin Ref. Claret
This is a blend of cabernet sauvignon grown at Renmark in the River Murray districts of South Australia, together with shiraz from Tea Tree Gully, near Adelaide. The wine was stored in small wood for eighteen months and then bottle aged at Renmark for another two years.

A full-flavoured wine, showing considerable varietal fruit and some oak.

Angove's Bookmark Riesling
'Bookmark' is an aboriginal word given to the original station property in the Renmark area.

The grapes are picked early in the season, approximately during the second week of February and crushed in the early morning. The fermentation is temperature controlled and the crisp young wine is racked one week after fermentation, fined and filtered and then is bottled as soon as possible.

Angove's Brightlands Burgundy
The original Brightlands Cellars still stand at Tea Tree Gully near Adelaide, where the first burgundy was vintaged in the 1880s. Cabernet sauvignon, shiraz and mataro are the grapes used to achieve this full-bodied, characteristic dry red. It is aged in small wood for a period before being blended, bottled and laid down to gain more bottle age.

It is a wine of considerable fruit and body.

Angove's Fino Dry Sherry
Made from pedro ximenez grapes, this delicate and pale dry sherry shows considerable Flor character and distinctive wood flavours. It is a high quality wine which has gained a string of successes at overseas wine shows, including some in France. The wine is made on the Flor process, the Flor film growing on the wine in part-filled hogsheads for a period of four years or more. At this stage the wine is racked, fortified to the appropriate strength, fined and filtered and returned to the hogsheads for a period for further blending and maturation. Finally, it is blended with older Flor sherries, bottled and laid down for a further six months before sale.

It is a wine of considerable sherry character, good balance; one which is always good value.

Angove's Golden Murray Sauternes
A blended medium-sweet, white table wine, aged for two to three years before being released.

Angove's Ingleberg Hock
A clean white wine made from the semillon variety.

Angove's Liqueur Frontignac
Made from straight frontignac. A rich fruity dessert wine showing considerable 'raisin' character and some oak. A full-flavoured wine of considerable power.

Angove's Liqueur Muscat
Made from muscat gordo blanco grapes grown in the Renmark district near the River Murray. A fruity wine with a soft middle palate, and clean finish showing some oak on the back of the palate.

Angove's Marko Vermouths

These are high quality wines which are considerably better than the trade vermouths generally available on the Australian market. Fresh free-run juice is used and aromatic herbs from France and Italy are steeped in spirit and infused to give the delicate character of these very good wines.

The Bianco Vermouth is pale, sweet and light in character. The Sweet Vermouth is quite dark in colour, sweet to the taste and robust in character. The Dry Vermouth is my particular favourite, being very pale, dry to the taste and delicate in character —with very subtle use of herbs.

These wines have been known for some considerable time and have long been exported. In fact, one won a Gold Medal as early as 1935 at the London Brewers' Wine Exhibition. Since that time the wines have done considerably well at local and overseas exhibitions and wine shows.

Angove's Nanya Moselle

A light wine with a slightly sweet middle palate, made from young palomino grapes grown in the River Murray area. Fermentation is temperature controlled and the resulting wine is light, fairly delicate and is bottled early to retain characteristic fruity bouquet. It is best enjoyed when quite young.

Angove's Nanya Rosé

The name Nanya comes from that of an aboriginal warrior and his tribe who roamed the Renmark area some considerable time ago. This particular wine is made from grenache grown in the district.

The wine does not carry a vintage date, though it is always from a recent vintage. The skins which impart the colour, of course, are separated from the fermenting juice at an early stage so there is no complete colour extraction. The rosé is a light, clean wine showing the bouquet of the parent red grape.

Angove's Old Brown Sherry

One of the oldest wines produced by the company. It is eight to ten years old in its youngest constituents. Both oak and considerable advanced fruit character are evident in this rather full, rich wine.

Angove's Old Choice Port

Made from a blend of shiraz and mataro grapes and matured in oak for some years.

Angove's Oloroso Cream Sherry

A full-bodied dessert wine made from pedro ximenez grapes grown in the River Murray district. The wine has considerable residual sugar on the middle palate. A solera system of blending succeeding vintages is used to achieve a balanced wine, matured in wood. The wine is developed without the Flor process and consequently retains the original fruit characters of the variety used.

Angove's Premium Vintage Port

Made from shiraz grapes grown in the River Murray district—always of a particular year. The wine is matured in the bottle for a number of years. Only a sticker label is used with this particular style, giving full information of vintage year, bottling date, grape variety and so on. The wine is only made in a good year. It is not blended and the period spent in wood, of course, is comparatively short.

The wine has considerable 'blackberry' flavour and a fairly full, strong tannin on the finish. It needs many years in the bottle before being mature.

Angove's Reserve Sweet Sherry

A blend of pedro ximenez and grenache grapes grown in the River Murray district of South Australia.

Angove's Rich Tawny Port

Made from a blend of grenache and mataro grapes grown in the River Murray district. When the fermenting must reaches the desired degree of sweetness, brandy spirit is added to arrest the fermentation. A long period of wood maturation follows.

This is a wine of full flavour and clean spirit finish.

Angove's Sauvignon Blanc

A white wine vintaged from that famous variety grown in Renmark in the River Murray district of South Australia. It is control fermented in small oak vats, racked under a blanket of CO_2 and bottled early to retain the crispness and characteristic aroma of the variety.

Angove's Sevogna Egg Marsala

An aromatic sweet wine which contains whole eggs and is infused with a wide variety of spices and herbs.

Angove's Special Bin Claret

An honest dry red wine blended from shiraz and mataro and grenache grapes. Some of this wine may come from the company's Tea Tree Gully's vineyards; but they are predominantly River Murray reds. These are not vintage wines and the sameness in quality through the years is one of their engaging features. The wines are very well priced and take some bottle age.

Angove's Special Bin Hock

Made from semillon grapes grown in the River Murray district, the Riverland. Fermentation is temperature controlled and the finished wine is bottled early to retain freshness and crisp acidity.

Angove's Special Bin Riesling

Made from riesling grapes grown in the River Murray district. Fermentation is temperature controlled and the finished wine is again bottled early; a wine of pleasant, refreshing character, with some crisp acidity on the back of the palate.

Angove's Special Bin Sauternes

A blended wine of some sweetness which is aged for up to five years before being bottled.

Angove's Special Vintage Port

This wine is made from River Murray shiraz and is matured in the bottle for a number of years. It sees little wood in its lifetime and heavy encrusting occurs in the bottle.

Angove's Tregrehan Claret

The name Tregrehan originates from the small town in Cornwall, the birthplace of an ancestor of the Angove family. This dry red is made from cabernet sauvignon and shiraz. The company claims that the shiraz lends the typical delicate bouquet and full round softness to the middle palate and the cabernet balances this with the crisp tannin finish and firm body. The grapes which go into making Tregrehan Claret are all grown on the company's own vineyards —the Anchorage, the Chowilla Block, Tea Tree Gully and others. The soil is generally clay loam, ironstone or alluvial. Some of these vineyards are in the Adelaide foothills, others along the Murray at Renmark and each yields a characteristic wine —which is kept separate until the winemaker blends them before bottling for further ageing.

Aspen

Aspen Cream Sherry

This was the name originally given to the wines being marketed by Harvey's, the famous Bristol sherry firm when it launched this brand in Australia. Now they have dropped the Harvey's because of problems of identification in other countries, with the result that the name Aspen is used both for the company and the product in Australia.

Of the various sherries marketed under the Aspen label in Australia I prefer the Cream Sherry as being the truer to type. This is more like the true cream style made famous in England and not quite the same thing as the rather fruity, muscaty style which is more common throughout Australia. For many years Harvey's had an arrangement with Seppelts and had access to some of the tremendous and quite remarkable sherries that are stored in wood at Seppeltsfield. The oldest wine of the cream goes back to the 1936 vintage and the rest of the material is round about the eight years old mark. There are several different wines and grape varieties in the blend and these are matured in small oak until blended. They are made mainly from palomino and pedro ximenez and there are also bits of madeira, sercial and white shiraz to add variety and complexity. All the material comes from the Barossa Valley. Incidentally there is no such grape variety as madeira. The madeira of the Hunter Valley is verdelho and that of the Barossa is indistinguishable from the semillon.

The Cream Sherry is of the Oloroso style which in Spain is usually quite dry, though there can be some sweetness or an impression of sweetness. The sweetness becomes pronounced when the wine is sold abroad and the English, Dutch and American markets are said to have different levels of sweetness requirements. This sweetness is, of course, added to the mature Oloroso—the sweetening agent *vina dulce* being made from ripe pedro ximenez grapes which have been dried in the sun for a couple of weeks.

Cream is an English term for a type of rich Oloroso Sherry which has been sweetened and particularly belongs to the famous Bristol shippers. The colour of this wine is a deep amber, the nose is complex, nutty and pungent with good wood showing through. The flavour is rich and subtle and the finish clean and dry. The sweetness is not cloying. The Baumé reading for the sweetness is about 5 degrees proof and the proof spirit content, 22.5 degrees.

Aspen Extra Dry Sherry

Made mainly from pedro ximenez grown in the Barossa Valley and developed under Flor culture, then matured in small oak casks for some years prior to bottling. This is a youngish wine as sherries go and has a certain freshness on the back of the palate, with just a touch of sugar on the middle palate, which makes it acceptable as a good quality commercial sherry.

Aspen Medium Dry Sherry

This sherry averages an age of six years and is made predominantly from pedro ximenez grapes grown in the Barossa Valley. Although an 'each-way' wine it has good flavour, good oak character and is probably one of the better grade medium dry sherries on the market.

Aspen Pale Dry Flor Sherry

The finest selected palomino grapes are used exclusively for this very good quality dry sherry. This is matured under the Flor culture and then matured in small oak casks for several years. I would imagine that very little liquering is added to the wine, which has excellent colour, very clean nuttiness, a delightful balance of oak character, very good flavour and oak astringency. The Flor character also shows very well in the complex flavours of the wine.

Aspen Tawny Port

A pleasant, light, soft dessert wine made from grenache grapes grown in the Barossa Valley and matured in oak for an average of seven years during which time a very light, clean style of dessert wine emerges.

This wine is probably less sweet than many of the tawny port styles available in Australia and has that slight licorice quality and rather firm finish which is said to be the hallmark of Portuguese wood-matured ports.

A pleasant wine of good character, soft, clean, light and cf interesting flavour.

Augustine Vineyards

Augustine Vineyards Aleatico Rosé
This rare variety was planted by the famous Dr T. Fiaschi in Mudgee and is the only survivor of the vineyards which were abandoned in the 1940s. The planting of the vineyard area was started again in 1969 when the Aleatico was reconstituted.

A rosé was made in 1971 and 1972, having a most unusual flavour and character; quite unlike any other rosé being made in Australia. I suppose one could call it Italian in character.

Augustine Vineyards Cabernet Sauvignon
From new plantings of cabernet sauvignon made in 1969. This variety in the Mudgee district makes reds of great depth of colour and a distinctive varietal character. The wine has a firm finish and will unquestionably keep for many years in the bottle.

Augustine Vineyards Hermitage
Small quantities only are being made of a full-blooded dry red from the Mudgee district, which after being matured in wood will keep for many years in the bottle.

Augustine Vineyards Semillon
Produced from semillon grapes grown in the district. A full-flavoured wine which develops roundness and softness in the bottle with a hint of coarseness on the back of the palate.

Augustine (Barossa Valley)

Augustine Barossa Valley Baccarat Rosé
Made from the carignane variety of the Barossa Valley. Picked when fully ripe and vintaged in the traditional way for a short time on skins to gain colour. This wine has a pleasant colour and is made in the Portuguese style—that is, it has some sweetness on the middle palate and there is some considerable spritzig apparent.

Augustine Barossa Valley Red Wines
The 1971 vintage provided a high degree of success for this company at the Brisbane, Melbourne, Perth and Adelaide Wine Shows. One fine dry red wine was awarded one Gold, two Silvers and two Bronzes at these shows, which is a commendable effort for a new company.

James Irvine, the winemaker, was with Thomas Hardy for many years and ran the Siegersdorf Winery in the Barossa Valley at one time. We look forward to top quality dry reds coming from this company.

Augustine Dry Tokay
An unusual dry white wine made entirely from the tokay grape grown at H. H. Zander's 'Wroxton' vineyard in the Eden Valley and picked when fully ripe at 12.5 degrees Baumé. This unusual style has considerable full fruit, crisp acidity on the finish and some sweetness on the palate.

Augustine Rhine Riesling
Made entirely from rhine riesling grown in the Barossa and Eden Valleys. The wine has a slight nose, full flavour on the middle palate with some sweetness apparent and a crisp, clean finish.

Bailey's Bundarra Vineyards

Bailey's Bundarra Claret
Another labelling of their celebrated dry red. *See* Hermitage.

Bailey's Bundarra Hermitage
Made from shiraz grapes with a small percentage of cabernet added. Possibly one of the most celebrated dry reds in Australia since it has a most individual character, coming from the ferruginous soils of the district. In the early sixties, with Max Lake, I visited this vineyard for the first time and was struck by the incredibly rich character of these dry reds. We were drinking a wine which was at least ten years old and which appeared to be only about two. Dr Sam Benwell tells of an amusing story in which the wines were described by an Australian as being 'steak and eggs'. A Frenchman added 'no, a three course meal *and* a good cigar'. Since then the wines have become slightly lighter, though they do have a most unique flavour and character.

Bailey's Bundarra Madeira
Made from palomino, chasselas and riesling grapes and matured in wood.

A full flavoured dessert wine.

Bailey's Bundarra Muscat
Made from the brown muscat (frontignac) grape which is grown in the local district.

A full flavoured dessert wine that perhaps lacks full wood development.

Bailey's Bundarra Muscat Liqueur
An extremely interesting wine made from the brown muscat (frontignac) grape. The grapes reach incredible Baumés which can reach up to the thirty plus mark. The resultant wine, after many years' maturation in wood, is bottled at up to 14 Baumé, which is

Alan Bailey of 'Bundarra' Vineyards, Taminick, Vic., evaluates last year's red.

outstanding in a finished wine. This is a most interesting and individual wine, first grown in the vineyards in 1934. Alan Bailey states that they are the originators of the style, though of course there have been other muscat liqueurs going back into the early part of the century, and, indeed, the latter part of the last century. Whatever, the wines have an extremely rich, luscious flavour and are superbly well balanced. They are quite unique to Australia. Elsewhere, in the south of France and in Spain where wines are made from much the same variety, they are not able to obtain the richness and depth of flavour that can be obtained in this area.

Bailey's Bundarra Port
Made from shiraz grapes picked at very high Baumés.
A full-bodied, rich dessert wine.

Bailey's Bundarra Riesling (also labelled Hock)
Made from rhine and aucerot riesling (sometimes called accroit) in the district.
A full-flavoured, big, white wine, verging on the coarse side.

Bailey's Bundarra Sauterne
A sweet, white table wine, made from chasselas blended with angelica.

Bailey's Bundarra Sherry, Dry
A wine made from palomino and chasselas and matured in wood for eight years; having a rich oxidized character and being fairly dry at the back of the palate.

Bailey's Bundarra White Port
Made from tokay grapes picked at up to 18 degrees Baumé.
A rich dessert wine of clean flavour.

Basedow Wines Ltd

Basedow's Claret
A light, soft dry red made from shiraz and mataro grapes grown in the Barossa Valley.

Basedow's Cream Sherry
A fortified sweet wine made from muscatel (muscat gordo blanco) and pedro ximenez, grown in the Barossa Valley.

Basedow's Family Port
A soft, light style of wood-matured port, made from mataro and grenache and kept in wood for two to three years.

Basedow's Illapara Claret
A medium to full style dry red, made from shiraz grown in the Barossa Valley. A low-priced wine which has good fruity flavour and can stand some age in the bottle.

Basedow's Illapara Riesling
Made entirely from clare riesling grapes grown in the Barossa Valley. A light, clean fruity, dry white wine.

Basedow's Illapara Sparkling
A slightly sweet pearl type of low alcoholic strength.

Basedow's Medium Dry Sherry
A soft, slightly fruity sherry, made from palomino grapes and matured for two to three years in wood.

Basedow's Moselle
A fairly full, fruity style, with a quite soft middle palate and clean finish, made entirely from clare riesling grapes.

Basedow's Muscatel
A full fruity muscat wine made from muscat gordo blanco and kept in wood for only one to two years.

Basedow's O.B. Port
Made from shiraz, grenache and mataro grapes, grown in the Tanunda district of the Barossa Valley, and a blend of various wood-matured ports aged from three to ten years.

Basedow's Rhine Riesling
Made entirely from rhine riesling, half of which is grown in the Basedow vineyards at Vine Vale and half of which is grown in the Eden Valley; control fermented in stainless steel and bottled young to retain a rather fresh, delicate, fruity character.

Basedow's Special Bin Dry Red

These are occasional wines produced by the company, some of which have been of very high quality. There was in particular a cabernet shiraz blend made in 1968 which won the Jimmy Watson Trophy at the Melbourne Show. This was made up of 10-20 percent cabernet sauvignon which came from the Basedow's vineyard at Vine Vale, plus some shiraz from the same vineyard and the total was made up of shiraz from Eden Valley and Barossa Valley areas. The grapes were picked at between 13 and 14 Baumé, fermented in open concrete tanks and then kept in big oak and also French puncheons until the wine was ready for bottling. At bottling it did seem to suffer a knock and there was sulphur evident when the wine was opened for examination; but I am sure this wine was typical of the style that can be made in the Barossa of high quality, good body and good fruit with plenty to it.

Basedow's Special Claret

A blend of shiraz and cabernet grown in the Barossa and Eden Valleys. They have tended to make an effort with these wines and are rather proud of their quality; being full-flavoured, medium to full-bodied wines, with a good clean finish.

Basedow's V.O. Dry Sherry

An old woody style of dry, fortified wine with no Flor character. Aged in wood for several years.

Basedow's V.O. Frontignac

A rich wine made from muscat and frontignac grapes, matured in old oak casks. A blend of wines from between three and sixteen years old.

Basedow's V.O. Madeira

Made from the madeira (semillon) variety, grown locally and matured in oak casks for between three and ten years.

Basedow's Very Old Port 1952 Blend

Blended from various wood-matured tawny ports made from shiraz and ranging in age from 1952 to 1965. This is a tawny style of good quality, having plenty of vinosity with a full flavour and a good, clean spirit finish.

Basedow's Very Old Tawny Port 1928 Blend

A blend of various wood-matured tawny ports of the years 1928, 1945, 1947 and 1952—all made from shiraz grapes grown in the Barossa Valley. This wine has an excellent, full-flavoured, tawny style and shows plenty of wood, plenty of developed, intense, concentrated flavour, and very good spirit.

Bassett's Wines

Bassett's Wines from the Romavilla vineyards of the company, is situated at Roma in Queensland. This company is by far the most important of the Queensland vignerons. The vineyards comprise about 220 acres of vines and are owned by Mr W. A. Bassett's family. Mr Bassett helped with the 1972 vintage when he was eighty-five years of age.

The grapes are grown on various types of soil which range from alluvial flats to sandy loam. There is no irrigation. The average rainfall is between 22 and 24 inches. Vintage time extends from January to March, but is mainly in January and February.

All the grapes are grown in their own vineyards and no other purchases are made. The wines are aged in wood—English oak—for three years or more and the average age of the wines sold is about six years. A variety of wine is made which is sold to people who call at the cellar door, or who send their orders to the company. Various wines are made which are listed together with their grape varieties:

BLENDED SHERRY (solvorine)
BROWN MUSCAT (muscat)
DRY SHERRY (solvorine)
FRONTIGNAC (muscat)
FRUITY BURGUNDY (mataro)
FRUITY SHERRY (solvorine)
HOCK (riesling)
MADEIRA (made from Portugal)
MUSCATEL (red and white muscat)
OLD INVALID PORT (black cluster)
OLD MUSCAT PORT (muscat)
RICH PORT (mataro)
ROYAL RESERVE PORT (black cluster)
RUBY PORT (black cluster and mataro blend)
SAUTERNES (riesling)
SWEET SHERRY (solvorine)
TAWNY PORT (shiraz)
TOKAY (tokay)
WHITE PORT (solvorine)

Berenyi

Berenyi McLaren Gold-White

A most unusual white wine with rich colour and its own quite marked individual taste. The charming owners of the vineyards, Garbor and Gisda Berenyi, claim that it is made in the traditional Hungarian manner from the juice of selected, fully ripened, red grenache grapes which are grown on their own vineyards.

They age the wine in wood for eighteen months. Sufficient to say that it has a most distinctive flavour and character and is sought out by a considerable clientele.

Berenyi McLaren Ruby-Red

A mellow red table wine, made again in the traditional Hungarian manner from fully ripened grenache grapes, to which is added a blend of shiraz and cabernet sauvignon; all the grapes being grown on their own vineyards.

The cask room at Tyrrell's Vineyards, Hunter Valley, with an earthen floor and slab and iron walls.

The wine is aged in wood for two years and proudly, the owners claim, 'without the use of chemicals during the whole production'.

Bernkastel Langmeil

Bernkastel Langmeil Burgundy
A full-flavoured, round, soft wine made from shiraz and mataro grapes, grown in the Light Pass and Tanunda districts of the Barossa Valley.

Bernkastel Langmeil Claret
A blend of shiraz and mataro grown in the company's Tanunda vineyards in the Barossa Valley. This is a very big, fruity wine containing some older dry red material that was blended into it before bottling. It will keep for a considerable time.

Bernkastel Langmeil Medium Dry Sherry
An each-way wine containing some pleasant old sweet material.

Bernkastel Langmeil Muscat
A rich dessert wine of considerable age.

Bernkastel Langmeil Port
A pleasant, light, soft, smooth, tawny style which is a blend of various wines—average age, about eight years.

Bernkastel Langmeil Riesling
A blend of rhine riesling and Clare riesling grown in the Tanunda and Marananga districts of the Barossa Valley. Fermented under controlled temperature and matured in wood for some months.

Bernkastel Langmeil Sweet Sherry
A typical dessert wine of the Barossa Valley.

Berri Co-operative Winery and Distillery

Berri Burgundy
A full, soft, round dry red made entirely from shiraz grown in the Berri/Barmera district and matured in small oak.

Berri Cabernet Sauvignon
This is a soft, quite well flavoured, balanced dry red made completely from cabernet sauvignon grown in the Berri/Bermera area. The wine was first made in 1963 and with the improved vinicultural and winemaking techniques has developed rapidly. It is a wine which can be drunk quite early because of the good fruit, but it also has quite a good bottle life. It is matured in French Limousin oak. The 1969 and 1971 vintages have been awarded Silver Medals in major shows. The 1972 vintage promises to be the best produced, possessing more colour, consider-ably more tannin and more flavour than earlier vintages.

The wine does mature quite well as a cellar test has shown. I have kept two or three vintages of the wine over the years and though the wine does not achieve distinction and complexity of flavour, after being in the bottle it *does* develop as an extremely pleasant, round, fruity wine of good character and one that takes bottle age quite well and does develop with this kind of maturation. One of the assets about the wine is of course that it can be bought at very reasonable prices.

Berri Cabernet Sauvignon-Shiraz
This is a fairly clean, quite firm dry red of good colour and body, made from equal parts of cabernet sauvignon and shiraz grown in the local district and also matured in small French oak casks.

The wine has quite pleasant body, good fruit and a clean, firm finish which is pleasant and is quite good drinking early.

Berri Claret
This is a lighter style of dry red made entirely from shiraz grapes grown in the district, cold fermented on skins and matured in small oak. The oak in question of course is not the new oak, which is reserved for the cabernet sauvignon, but those casks which have been used a few times.

Berri Dry White Vermouth
A fairly typical Australian dry white vermouth style, made from doradillo grapes, grown in the district and infused with imported herbs.

Berri Fruity Gordo Moselle
Brian Barry, winemaker of considerable renown, who is in charge of winemaking at Berri, describes this as a flamboyant moselle. I am grateful to him for his new wine word. This is, for the variety used, quite a delicate wine—made entirely from muscat gordo blanco grown in the Berri-Barmera-Cobdogla Loveday areas. The grapes are picked at quite an early stage of maturity to retain the sugar/acid balance. After cold fermentation which is carried out at 50 degrees Fahrenheit the must is centrifuged and filtered to retain a slight natural sweetness and is bottled almost immediately.

For a river wine and for a river gordo this is a considerable triumph. The wine has been a consistent medal winner as a young, fruity wine in the Moselle classes of major Australian shows. The 1971 vintage won a Gold Medal and the 1972 vintage has the same kind of pronounced fruity flavour. I think the winemaker is to be congratulated on the style.

Berri Hock
A blended dry white made from clare riesling and pedro ximenez and palomino grapes from the district; bottled young to retain full grape flavour. A rather

Champagne storage in the underground 'drives' at Seppelt's winery, Great Western, Vic. Each 'drive' is named after a famous Australian.

full-flavoured wine, slightly coarse on the back of the palate.

Berri Rhine Riesling

The winemakers take trouble here since they asked the grape growers to take extreme care in the selection of locally grown rhine riesling grapes, which are picked very early in their maturation stage when the sugar/acid level is right. The grapes are gently crushed and the separated juice is control fermented over quite a long time—about three to four weeks. This retains the full varietal fruit character and the wine is bottled only one week after fermentation ceases. They really move to get the wine filled and cleaned and stabilized and then it is put into bottle only one week after fermentation to ensure that all flavour is retained and that the maximum delicacy for the area is achieved.

The wine is quite clean, delicate, refreshingly acid and fills out with age in the bottle. The '71 vintage won a Gold Medal and the '72 vintage was a wine of considerable vinosity, varietal character, and full fruit. A very clean, well made wine.

Berri Riesling

Made entirely from clare riesling grapes; well balanced, and quite fruity, a clean wine with a soft acid finish.

Berri Rosé

This is another good example of the winemaker's art. It is made entirely from grenache grapes grown in the district. The grapes are allowed to reach full maturity so they get the maximum fruity flavour and ripeness. The juice is separated from the skins shortly after fermentation begins to get that delicious, delicate, rosé pink colour. It is then fermented under controlled temperatures, 10 degrees Celsius, until it is completely dried out. They bottle again extremely early to gain this flavour retention and there is plenty of gas in the wine. I find this particular rosé a trifle coarse on the back of the palate, though the wine is very popular indeed and has featured well at shows.

Berri Sauternes

Made from pedro ximenez, doradillo and muscat gordo blanco grapes grown at Berri. A medium sweet table wine, which is quite pleasant and has no particular distinction. It is matured for two years in the bottle before it is sold.

Berri Sparkling White

A straightforward commercial pearl, made from clare riesling, pedro ximenez and doradillo grapes.

Berri Sweet Red Vermouth Amaro

A bitter-sweet red vermouth made from local grenache and gordo grapes and infused with imported herbs, then finally wood-matured before blending.

Berri Sweet Red Vermouth Italian Style

A sweet red vermouth made from local grenache and muscat gordo blanco grapes infused with imported herbs and matured for three years before blending.

Berri Sweet White Vermouth Bianco

A luscious sweet white muscat gordo blanco wine, used as a base, of at least three years' maturity, and blended with specially selected imported herbs.

Berri White Burgundy

Made from white hermitage (trebbiano) grapes, locally grown and selected at the right degree of sugar/acid balance. Fermentation is controlled and after a period of maturation in carefully chosen oak casks the wine is immediately bottled.

This wine has a good soft, full palate. It requires at least one year in the bottle before it begins to develop its full flavour and style and then I would suggest that the style is rather rich, almost chewy, with considerable mouth filling qualities. Perhaps it lacks finesse, but it is a good, round, soft drink.

Berri Karooma Cream Sherry

Made from pedro ximenez and muscat gordo blanco grapes grown in the Berri area and matured in oak for two years.

A fairly full-flavoured, rich, dessert wine of the cream sherry style.

Berri Karooma Dry Sherry

Made entirely from pedro ximenez grapes and matured in small oak for two years. It has quite considerable flavour and oak character.

Berri Karooma Medium Dry Sherry

A pleasant each-way bet; neither too sweet, nor too dry, made from pedro ximenez and matured in small oak for at least two years.

Berri Karooma Muscat

This is a fairly fruity, full-flavoured muscat made from frontignac grapes, grown in the Berri/Barmera area and matured for four years in small oak to develop the rancio character.

Berri Karooma Sweet Sherry

Fruity wine made from pedro ximenez grapes and wood matured for four years.

Berri Karooma Tawny Port

Made entirely from grenache grapes grown in the local districts of Berri and Barmera. It is then wood-matured in small oak for from four to five years, during which time it picks up a tawny colour and this rancio character that they are looking for.

This is a pleasant, sweet dessert wine.

Berri Mine Host Amontillado Sherry

Made exclusively from local pedro ximinez grapes. Made on the Flor process and matured in small oak for three years to produce a fairly full-flavoured amontillado style.

Berri Mine Host Champagne

A clean, crisp, sparkling wine made from clare riesling, pedro ximenez and white hermitage grapes from the local district.

Berri Mine Host Dry Sherry

Made from pedro ximenez grapes, not on the Flor process, and matured in small oak casks for three years, developing a full, fruity, but dry style.

Berri Mine Host Flor Sherry

Each year the best of the pedro ximenez is put to one side and selected for delicacy and style and then sown with a special Flor yeast strain to develop a true Flor character. When they have sufficient character in the wine they fortify it and mature it in small oak for a further three or four more years to produce a rather mature, mellow, but dry flor sherry, which has a slightly fuller palate than most sherries made under this style.

Berri Mine Host Frontignac

An old, sweet dessert wine made exclusively from locally grown frontignac grapes and matured in small oak casks for five years. This concentrated development in small oak hastens and concentrates the flavour process and develops a lusciousness and rancio character because of extreme evaporation in the district.

Berri Mine Host Marsala All'uovo

An old luscious marsala style made from overripe muscat gordo blanco and doradillo grapes and to which is blended specially imported herbs, plus eggs. Matured in large oak.

Berri Mine Host Muscat

An old sweet muscat style wine made from local frontignac grapes and matured in small oak for five years or more.

Berri Mine Host Muscat Liqueur

This is a very old liqueur wine made from local frontignac grapes and matured in very small oak quarter casks for over ten years to produce the full lusciousness required. Only very small lots are bottled at any one time so that the wine keeps its traditional rancio development.

Berri Mine Host Nutty Brown Sherry

Made from specially selected white hermitage grapes and matured in oak quarter casks under an iron roof for at least ten years to produce a tremendous rancio character and a very full nutty flavour.

Berri Mine Host Pink Champagne

A light sparkling wine of considerable sweetness.

Berri Mine Host Ruby Port

A wine of good ruby colour, as the name suggests, made entirely from shiraz grapes grown locally and matured in large oak for a minimum period of three years before bottling. A good light dessert wine.

Berri Mine Host Sparkling Burgundy

Made from local shiraz grapes. A sparkling wine having considerable sweetness.

Berri Mine Host Sparkling Moselle

Made from locally grown clare riesling grapes. Again of quite marked sweetness on the middle palate.

Berri Mine Host Sweet Sherry

Made from pedro ximenez, palomino, white hermitage and malaga grapes and matured in small oak for at least five years. During this time it picks up a very concentrated good, sweet sherry style.

Berri Mine Host Tawny Port

A blend of shiraz and grenache grapes grown in the Berri/Barmera areas and matured in French oak hogsheads under an iron roof for more rapid maturation; the warmer and smaller the cask, the greater the evaporation of water and therefore the more concentrated the wine becomes. This wood development therefore hastens a very rich, quite marked rancio and tawny character. It's a blend of wine ranging from five to fifteen years old and is a very full-flavoured, rich dessert wine.

Berrivale Moselle

Carefully selected clare riesling grapes grown in the local district are used. The grapes are picked early to ensure good natural acidity and flavour. The fermentation is controlled and goes on for some weeks. Immediately on completion they centrifuge filter and clean up the wine so that they can get it into a bottle immediately.

The wine has quite good, full flavour, an aromatic nose and a good crisp, clean finish on the palate. It does contain some natural sweetness and considerable gas.

Best's Wines Pty Ltd

Best's Bubbly-Crimson, Golden, Pink

Light, pleasant, carbonated sparkling wines made from grapes grown at Lake Boga and at Great Western in the 'Concongella' vineyards (Victoria).

Best's Claret No. 0—'Concongella' and 'St Andrews'
A light to medium-bodied dry red made from shiraz grown at 'Concongella' vineyards at Great Western and the 'St Andrews' vineyards at Lake Boga.

Best's Claret No. 0—Special Vintages
The Thomson's of Best's Wines feature a number of Claret Number 0's including the previous entry. Under this label they also sell varietal wines from the malbec, pinot meuniere (Miller's burgundy) variety and the shiraz grapes. They have maintained the Number 0 since they believe that identification was used in that district some years ago as a wine classification, i.e., No. 0, No. 1, No. 2, etc. They have maintained this old label which has changed very little since its original inception before the turn of the century.

All the special vintage varieties are made entirely from Great Western material which is grown at 'Concongella' in Victoria. They have distinctive characters, distinctive flavours and are good examples of quality, varietal wines.

The malbec is a fine-flavoured wine, which has considerable style and a quite assertive flavour. Wolfgang Blass, the celebrated South Australian winemaker, often uses this material in his own particular prize-winning blends. The pinot meuniere has a much rounder, softer style, and a most distinctive middle palate flavour. The shiraz is fairly robust wine, with a good firm finish.

Best's Fine Old Muscat
A full-flavoured, fruity style of fortified wine made from muscat gordo blanco grown at Lake Boga.

Best's Gold Vintage
A light, relatively dry style of sparkling wine which is made from grapes grown at Lake Boga and at Great Western. The base wine is stored in old oak 500 gallon casks until after the second winter, and then carbonated and bottled.

Best's Hock No. 0
There are two wines which appear under this label made from rhine riesling and golden chasselas respectively. Thomson's have made some very fine white wines in the past, and interesting wines because they always left them in wood: in some cases I believe for from three to four years in wood, although they have since restricted this practice. I have tasted wines that were a couple of years in wood before being bottled, and found them excellent.

The rhine riesling is of the older style with a very full-flavoured palate, and extremely interesting style of white wine. The golden chasselas has not got the fruity, aromatic character of the other variety, but it is a very full-flavoured, round, rich, soft wine of considerable charm and distinction. After their wood maturation these wines live in the bottle for many, many years and I have drunk wines, in Melbourne particularly, of this company which are ten to fifteen years old and which really have a tremendous character and flavour: an almost honeyed style, without any sweetness.

Best's Liqueur Muscat
A heavy, full-flavoured, sweet wine made from muscat gordo blanco grapes grown at Lake Boga.

Best's Moselle
A light dry moselle style, blended from sultana grapes grown at Lake Boga and golden chasselas from Great Western.

Best's Muscanti
A fruity, carbonated, sparkling wine made from the muscat gordo blanco variety.

Best's Pink Cham
A carbonated sparkling wine, blended from white grapes grown at Lake Boga and red grapes grown at Great Western.

Best's Royal Reserve Port
A full-bodied, sweet port style made predominantly from hermitage grapes grown at the 'St Andrews' vineyards at Lake Boga.

Best's Sparkling Burgundy
A carbonated, sparkling wine blended from grapes grown at Lake Boga and Great Western in Victoria.

Best's

GREAT WESTERN

Hock No. O

CONCONGELLA VINEYARDS
GREAT WESTERN, VIC., AUSTRALIA

NET 26 OZS.

The variety frequently dominating this blend is malbeck (malbec), grown at Great Western.

Best's Special Reserve Cream Sherry
A light, fruity, sweet wine, made from muscat gordo grapes grown at Lake Boga.

Best's Special Reserve Medium Dry Sherry
A full-bodied sherry of some sweetness and plenty of wood character, heading towards the amontillado style.

Best's Special Reserve Sweet Sherry
A fairly rich-flavoured wine with a clean, dry woody finish.

Best's Special Reserve White Port
Another of the muscat gordo blanco styles from material grown at Lake Boga.

Bilyara, Wolf Blass

Bilyara Wolf Blass Dry Red Gold Medal
These are increasingly significant dry red wines of the highest quality, made by an ebullient German winemaker called Wolfgang Blass 'Kellermeister Diploma' who arrived in Australia in 1960. He was brought out here to help with the technical staff of the rapidly expanding Barossa Co-operative Winery of the Barossa Valley, under George Kolarovich. Blass stayed with that company for four years and then began a hectic and rather interesting period of freelancing, in which he sold his talents to a number of smaller South Australian winemakers. There is no doubt that he did a great deal in lifting the quality of their wines with his aggressive attitudes and tremendous integrity in relation to winemaking quality. He won all sorts of awards for these various people and really helped a number of them, influencing their ideas and their techniques, so that they have continued to do well with their wines.

In 1966 he began making wine under his own rather decorative label which I have often described as an 'O come all ye faithful' example. The majority of the material which he used was cabernet sauvignon and shiraz from Langhorne Creek.

In 1969 he started work as the Technical Director of Tolley, Scott and Tolley in the Barossa Valley at Nuriootpa, though he retained the right to make his own individual wines. His winery, 'Bilyara'—an aboriginal word meaning Eagle Hawk, is situated two and a half miles north of Nuriootpa. Wolf has done well with his dry red Gold Medal series. The Gold Medal is no euphemism.

The wines represent between seventy-five and eighty percent cabernet and the rest shiraz. One feature of them is their tremendous fruit, which is coupled with plenty of oak. This oak he blends in magnificently with fruit to make outstanding claret-style wines.

The 1967 was the first of them and did extremely well. It won several medals and also had the distinction of getting the highest price for young dry red at the Vintage Festival Wine Auction. He followed this up with the 1968 vintage, which won three Gold Medals and a Trophy in the Adelaide Wine Show. This was a very good wine, showing extremely good balance of oak and fruit and a great deal of intensity of flavour. There is no question this wine will go forward for a long time.

The 1969 again won Gold Medals, but it was a lighter style of wine, probably reflecting the year. The oak penetration wasn't quite as deep. I think Wolf probably intentionally lightened the oak so that there would be a better oak-fruit balance. Still, for that year it was a good wine.

The 1970 Gold Medal had tremendous deep, rich, almost royal purple colour: extremely strong cabernet sauvignon fruit flavour, that deep berry character which is so evident. Though oak was strong in this wine I think it found it hard to compete with the tremendous fruit of the wine and there is no question that when these flavours come together it will make an outstanding dry red.

The 1971 has been acclaimed throughout Australia: a wine of incredible fruit and flavour, tremendously well-balanced and supple on the middle palate with a firm, strong finish. It has won several Gold Medals already as a young wine and will unquestionably develop into one of Australia's outstanding wines.

There is no doubt that Wolfgang Blass has made an enormous impact upon Australian winemaking techniques, especially red wine techniques, in the last few years, with his ability to extract from the material tremendous fruit and then to couple this with his extremely good handling of small oak. There is no doubt in my mind that he will make a much greater future contribution to Australian dry red styles, both through his own Bilyara Wines and those from Tolley, Scott and Tolley.

Bilyara Wolf Blass Dry Red Show Wine

This high quality dry red style, whilst not having perhaps the complete significance of the Gold Medal line, still is an important one for the wines are extremely well made, full of fruit and wood flavours and provide very good drinking. They are basically Langhorne Creek cabernet shiraz material, which consists of about eighty percent shiraz and twenty percent cabernet sauvignon. These wines are matured for a minimum of twelve months in small French Nevers oak. The combination of the blends over the years have been with malbec from the Great Western vineyards of Thomsons, 'Concongella'.

The 1966 in fact was a combination of Langhorne Creek cabernet shiraz and Great Western Concongella malbec.

The 1967 was eighty percent Langhorne Creek cabernet shiraz material in the same proportion (twenty percent cabernet and eighty percent shiraz), together with twenty percent shiraz from the Clare Districts. This wine was a very firm wine which will undoubtedly age well for many, many years.

The 1968 reverted to the Great Western blend and had again eighty percent Langhorne Creek cabernet shiraz material, together with twenty percent malbec from Great Western. Again this wine was full of flavour and showed extremely well. The malbec was detectable once you read it on the label. Altogether, a wine of good fruit and oak.

The 1969 was of the same blend structure. The twenty percent malbec from Great Western was again quite assertive. This wine spent twelve months in French Nevers oak and won awards as a young show entry. The flavour was quite strong. It had good colour, but when young it had all sorts of flavours clamouring for attention—cabernet, malbec and also oak, fighting each other for supremacy. Wolf once, in an amusing letter to me, said that he thought that the malbec was going to win.

The 1970 Show Wine indicates the quality of the wine, for although this unquestionably is his lesser wine of the two dry red styles (the '70 Gold Medal as I mention is an extremely good wine), still the '70 Show Wine won three Silver Medals and two Bronze Medals. This was a combination of cabernet

shiraz again from Langhorne Creek, making up eighty percent proportion, and twenty percent shiraz from Wilton in the Eden Valley. The wine had a good flavour, a full middle palate and delicious light oak—a very well-balanced wine indeed.

These unquestionably are very good styles of red wine and again are a compliment to Wolfgang Blass as a winemaker.

Bilyara Wolf Blass Frontignac Rhine Riesling

An aromatic, yet very full-flavoured, rather big white wine made from thirty percent Barossa Valley frontignac and seventy percent rhine riesling from Clare. The wine was matured in big wood for twelve months and shows a rather developed character, 1969 particularly.

Bilyara Wolf Blass Rhine Riesling

These are aromatic, very well-made white wines that can contain a measure of some sugar on the middle palate, because Wolf tries to fill out the middle palate a bit; and the material is obtained from wherever he can get quality rhine riesling.

The 1969 Rhine Riesling which did well at shows, came from the Clare district—a wine full of flavour with a very clean, rather high acid finish.

The 1970 Rhine Riesling was from the Eden Valley and Barossa Valley. There was a slight residual sugar left on the middle palate, about 8 grammes per litre, and some considerable spritzig in the wine. A good style, very refreshing, quality drinking—again, if you don't object to this trace of sugar, a very fine wine.

Wolf has also made some extremely good dry white wines for Tolley, Scott and Tolley. Many of these are sold as B.O.B.—BUYERS' OWN BRAND—for the trade. There is no doubt that they will shortly be marketing these wines and they will have a national significance in a very short space of time.

Birks' Wendouree Cellars

Birks' Wendouree Burgundy

Made variously each year from these red wine varieties: shiraz, mataro, malbec, cabernet sauvignon and grenache. The Birks' burgundy wines are noted for their robustness and rich character. Douglas Seabrook, the noted Melbourne · wine merchant, has bottled some of these over the years and some most distinctive wines of great colour and rich flavour have emerged. Mr Roly Birks sells a great deal of his red wine to the trade and there would be various labellings of them; but amongst the most notable are the Seabrook bottlings. Roly Birks bottles a number himself and these wines are most interesting whenever you should come across them. They live for years, retain their colour, and many people tasting them on the blind come unstuck when trying to pick the age and location.

Birks' Wendouree Claret
Much the same sort of wine as the Burgundy, though the wines would be firmer and probably slightly harder and could contain a bigger quantity of cabernet sauvignon, the shiraz being used in a greater proportion in the Burgundy.

Birks' Wendouree Rhine Riesling
A well-made wine made from straight rhine riesling, having very big varietal flavour and considerable crisp acidity on the finish.

Birks' Wendouree Sweet Sherry
A sweet, luscious wine made from albillo grapes grown in the district.

Birks' Wendouree Muscat
Made from frontignac grapes grown in the district; a luscious, rich wine of considerable longevity.

Bleasdale Vineyards Pty Ltd

Bleasdale Belvidere Claret
A young dry red made from shiraz and oeillade. Good for immediate drinking.

Bleasdale Bremer Claret
Made from shiraz and oeillade. This dry red carries the earthy character associated with the Langhorne Creek styles. The shiraz is allowed to ripen more than normal for dry red winemaking and is then blended with the oeillade, which matures with a much lower sugar content.

1970 and 1971 are quite good vintages and the 1972 is showing excellent promise at this stage.

Bleasdale Brut and Demi-Sec
Selected grapes from the company's own vineyards are harvested before becoming too ripe. The juice is taken from the crushed fruit as soon as possible and fermented under controlled temperatures. The wine is then blended with suitable material from previous vintages to produce the style they are looking for; to which is added the Tirage Liqueur for process under the Charmat method in 500 gallon pressure vessels. It is then allowed to age before being marketed as Brut, or Demi-Sec, depending on the sugar content—the Brut being the driest.

Bleasdale Claret
A minimum priced wine produced from the shiraz and grenache varieties. This wine is a medium-bodied dry red of good fruity drinking and of an average age of one to two years.

Bleasdale Hock
A full-flavoured, relatively undistinguished dry white wine made from palomino and doradillo grapes.

Bleasdale Bremer Gold
A light, sparkling white wine of considerable sweetness.

Bleasdale Cabernet Sauvignon
Cuttings were obtained from the McLaren Vale area in 1963, planted in 1964 and the first cabernet grape from Bleasdale was produced in 1967. For the first few years this was blended in the fermenting tank with shiraz, until 1971 when further plantings enabled the company to produce a straight cabernet sauvignon. The wine spent one month in new French Limousin puncheons and then twelve months in 300 gallon ovals before being bottled in June 1972. It has been shown three times and awarded one Silver Medal and two Bronze Medals.

It has a very dark colour, quite good fruity variety and showing a touch of very pleasant oak. It is a big wine that will need considerable time to mature.

Bleasdale Cabernet Shiraz
A blend of one-third cabernet sauvignon with two-thirds shiraz. This is a very robust red produced from the young plantings of cabernet sauvignon and the much older shiraz vines, which are twenty-five to forty years old. The grapes are blended together in the fermentation so that they start marrying straight away. The pressings are added back into the free run and then the wine is allowed to undergo

its malo-lactic conversion before being cleaned up and matured in puncheons for the early stages of its maturation. A further twelve to fifteen months' maturation takes place in 300 gallon ovals before the wine is bottled as a typically sturdy Langhorne Creek red, which should develop for many years.

The label on this wine is of particular interest as it features H.M.S. *Buffalo* on which South Australia's first Governor arrived at Holdfast Bay in 1836. Among the passengers was Frank Potts, who founded 'Bleasdale' in 1850. This incredible man—engineer, carpenter and workman—made all sorts of things including ferry boats, steam boats, a huge gum press and even a piano out of red gum.

Bleasdale Cream Sherry
Made from palomino, doradillo and muscat gordo blanco varieties—a fruity, sweet, soft, fortified wine.

Bleasdale Dry Sherry
The palomino variety at Langhorne Creek is well-suited for sherry making and this variety is blended with doradillo, and aged in small wood. After maturation it develops into a pleasant, straight-forward dry sherry.

Bleasdale Dry White Frontignac
The frontignac grapes are harvested early and the temperature is controlled to produce a very fruity and dry white which is fairly high in acid.

Bleasdale Liqueur Port
Made from grenache and shiraz and showing some wood age: a pleasant medium-bodied dessert wine.

Bleasdale Madeira
A pleasant dessert wine made from verdelho and palomino varieties (called in the district, paulo) and sold after about two and a half years in wood.

Bleasdale Malbec
Production of this variety in Langhorne Creek is limited to a very few tons, but the wine is interesting in that it has a most unique flavour and style and is quite individual. It does show the true varietal character of this variety which is used so much in Bordeaux. Since 1970 a blend of malbec and shiraz in equal proportions is being produced and the '70 and '71 vintages are shaping up very well. I use the wine quite often to show the varietal character of malbec and it is interesting to compare it against other malbecs that are becoming available throughout Australia.

Mr Ron Haselgrove of Mildara fame used some of the Bleasdale Malbec in the mid-fifties in his famous cabernet shiraz blend in an attempt to use this Bordeaux variety to fll out the style of the wine. He did not find it successful and he finally settled upon his famous Hunter, Coonawarra, Southern Vales blend.

Bleasdale Medium Dry Sherry
A wood aged sherry made from palomino.

Bleasdale Muscat
A dessert wine made from the muscat gordo blanco.

Bleasdale Pink and Sweet Sekt
Both of these wines are light sparkling wines. They are fermented in pressure tanks and bottled under high pressure in heavy bottles.

Bleasdale Pioneer Port
A good style of tawny port blended from fine old shiraz and grenache wines which have been matured in small wood for several years—the average age being approximately eight years.

The label of this wine is quite interesting because it does portray the old red gum wine press which is a great relic of the earlier winemaking days of Langhorne Creek. This was another of the great inventions of that unique pioneer, Frank Potts.

Bleasdale Reserve Port
Made from shiraz and grenache grapes and showing some wood age.

Bleasdale Semillon
This wine is produced from vines of unknown origin but having some riesling characteristics. It is very difficult to identify apparently and should be future work for ampelographers. It is a pleasant, fruity, dry wine.

Bleasdale Shiraz
A very robust, rich red wine made entirely from the shiraz variety. This variety thrives in the rich alluvial soil of Langhorne Creek and the wine produced is often noticed to have a distinct district, earthy character. Crops of six to eight tons per acre are common and generally speaking the wine should reach full maturity between the ages of five to ten years.

Bleasdale Sparkling Burgundy
Selected red wines are blended to form a suitable base to be refermented and bottled under pressure—matured in bottles for twelve months before marketing.

Bleasdale Spumante Mòscato
This wine is produced from very ripe muscat gordo blanco and frontignac grapes. It's a full-bodied, very fruity, sweet, sparkling wine.

Bleasdale Sweet Sherry
Made from palomino grapes, aged two to three years in wood. A good style having a developed lusciousness and showing nice wood character.

Bleasdale Tawny Port
Made from grenache, aged from two to three years in wood and then blended with some older material to produce a fairly full-flavoured wine.

Bleasdale Verdelho
This variety has been grown at Langhorne Creek for many years and has been used exclusively in the past for fortified wines. The vines produce comparatively small bunches and crops of four to six tons to the acre are generally picked.

The dessert wine produced from this variety is matured in small casks (twenty to sixty gallons), close to the roof, where it benefits from the extremes of temperatures and, although the maturation is more beneficial under these conditions, evaporation losses are as high as 20 to 25 percent over a period of six to seven years. What of course is being lost is water and alcohol, but the water rate of loss is by far the highest. Therefore the wine becomes more and more concentrated. By blending the resulting wine with younger verdelho and palomino also, a fine madeira style of wine is produced.

Bleasdale Vin d'Amour
The mind boggles. This most interesting name applies to nothing more than a sparkling, sweet wine, made under the Charmat process. It's certainly not the wine for my 'idee d'amour'.

Bleasdale White Burgundy
This is a relatively new style which is being made from the verdelho grape. The grapes are picked at approximately 12 Baumé and then fermented under temperature controlled conditions. The wine has quite marked varietal character, very rich middle palate, and is very popular as a full-flavoured white burgundy style.

Booth Bros

Booth's Taminick Dry Red
Made entirely from shiraz grown in the Taminick district near Glenrowan in north-east Victoria. This wine was formerly sold in bulk and bought by Wynns, who used it either straight or in blends to produce the famous Ovens Valley Burgundy. The wine has extremely high colour and rich full flavour. The grapes are left on the vine until quite late in the harvest and the Baumés therefore build up to as high as 16 and 17 Baumé. Generally the grapes are picked at round about 14 Baumé. Consequently, there is a great deal of colour and flavour. Bottled as a straight Booth's Taminick Red, unquestionably the wines will live for many, many years.

Brand, Eric

Brand's Laira Cabernet Sauvignon
A very well-balanced wine of excellent fruit and character and tremendous vinosity and power of volume of flavour, with a good, clean, firm tannin finish. The bouquet is of the typical big berry variety and owes a lot to the fruit and also to the region. The oak has been judiciously handled; the finish is firm and clean; but this wine is possibly a little more astrigent than the blend.

Brand's Laira Cabernet Shiraz
Produced from cabernet and shiraz grapes grown on the Terra Rossa soils of the famous district of Coonawarra in South Australia.

These vines are some of the original plantings in Coonawarra and are still bearing crops of up to 5 tons per acre, although over seventy years of age. A lot to do with this of course is the extremely beneficial water table that exists at Coonawarra.

The wine is matured in French oak, has good balance of body and acid and shows good grape flavour with a very fruity bouquet, which is combining well with the oak. The oak and fruit carry on through the palate and the finish is firm, clean and astringent.

I am very fond of Mr Brand's efforts in this area since he started in 1965 and 1966 and he is now making some very fine wines. Incidentally, the wine has the distinction of being the only Estate Bottled wines of the district.

The 1971 wine made by Mr Eric Brand did extremely well at Brisbane; I think it was the champion young red of the show. This is an excellent Australian wine which will live and live for many years. I'm looking forward to tasting it over the years.

Eric Brand, of course, worked for many years for his father-in-law, Bill Redman at Rouge Homme. When Rouge Homme was sold he set up his own place and decided to make his own wines from the vineyards that he had owned for some considerable time. Eric Brand is dedicated to the principle of making fine wine and I was absolutely delighted with the success of the 1971 Cabernet, which was truly one of the best wines I saw of that vintage in the whole of the country. I am looking forward to seeing many more of his wines in the future and I do hope he continues with his success. Incidentally, his wife Nancy, makes the best pickled walnuts I have ever tasted in Australia. She also grows extremely fine fruit.

Brand's Laira Rosé
Made from the grenache grapes grown in the district, this wine has the soft flavour of the grape, combined with the acidity that is associated with the Coonawarra area. The wine has a delightful pink colour, and a clean acid finish, with a very pleasant

middle palate of quite unusual fruit. The vines are also quite old and it is most interesting to see a grenache from the district. It drinks very well.

Brown Bros

Brown's Milawa Cabernet Sauvignon
A rich, full-flavoured wine from the cabernet sauvignon grape grown at both the local vineyards at Milawa in north-east Victoria and also at Everton, some miles away. There is not a straight bottling of this wine year after year, but the bottlings which are shown contain very rich flavour, high colour and a certain austerity in the finish which is very pleasing to those who have developed a liking for this style.

Brown's Milawa Cabernet Shiraz
This is a much more common blend of cabernet sauvignon and shiraz grapes, common in that it is repeated generally year after year. Of recent bottlings I like the '67, '66, '65 and '62. The wines of north-east Victoria have a distinctive character and within this district the wines of John Brown at Milawa have an added dimension. They are more elegant, generally speaking, and less round, soft and earthy than the other north-east Victorian red wines.

Brown's Milawa Cabernet Shiraz Mondeuse
A most interesting and consistent bottling which John Brown has been showing for some years. The cabernet shiraz, the more usual blend, is combined with the mondeuse because the latter grape contributes a good deal of soft, persistent tannin to the wine. This variety has a distinctive flavour. John Brown uses it very well and brings out a most distinctive, good-flavoured red of usually very high quality. The 1962, for example, which I saw some years ago at their Centenary Celebrations, is a wine of considerable character, having quite a nose which had built up over the years into the most pleasant bouquet, having plenty of good, clean flavour, light-bodied yet intense, with none of the marked earthy style and no hint of the coarseness that can characterize other wines from these districts. The '61 had something of the same flavours, though it was bigger, riper and fruitier.

Brown's Milawa Chablis
From trebbiano, palomino and riesling grapes grown on the Everton Hills vineyards some distance from the Milawa vineyards of the same company. The soil there is a shaly, gravelly kind of soil and this may have some bearing on the distinctive flintiness of this white wine.

Brown's Milawa Gewurtztraminer
From experimental plantings of the variety in the district made first in 1972.

Brown's Milawa Graciano
Probably the only planting in Australia which exist of this variety and the cause for much consternation at blind tastings. The material yields a rich, robust, individual kind of earthy flavoured wine which has some similarities to certain Italian wines. A good interesting drink at a barbecue.

Brown's Milawa Muscat
Made from the so-called brown muscat of the district which is almost certainly a frontignac. Not of the usual Rutherglen liqueur muscat type, but a much lighter style of wine.

Brown's Milawa Port
Made entirely from shiraz grown in the local district and matured in wood to make a rich, tawny port of considerable flavour and pleasant aftertaste.

Brown's Milawa Rhine Riesling
John Brown, a pioneer in the making of white wines in the north-east Victorian district, is to be congratulated for leading other winemakers into producing some of the excellent commercial wines which are now available. The rhine riesling grape, however, has been grown at Milawa since the last century and five acres of this variety are over fifty years old and still bearing well.

The grapes are picked when the sugar acid balance is considered favourable to produce a wine which John Brown considers delicate in style, but which does not lack fruit in the middle. All things are relative. Many winemakers in South Australia who use the delicate Eden Valley and Watervale rhine riesling fruit would consider John Brown's wines rather big and full-flavoured. But they are the most delicate wines produced in the whole of the north-east Victorian district.

They have plenty of flavour, are well-balanced, have a most distinct aromatic nose, and the fruit continues onto the palate. The acidity is always quite crisp. The 1972 wine was remarkably fine.

Brown's Milawa Rosé
An interesting wine made from the mondeuse grape grown on the Everton Hills vineyard. The wine is crisp and refreshing with a rather unique flavour and a most brilliant colour which continues for some time.

Brown's Milawa Sherry
John Brown makes a variety of sherries from material obtained from the Tresco and Mystic Park areas and mostly grown under irrigation systems. These grapes produce a softer and blander wine than the Milawa grapes from the local vineyards.

Dick Buller about to sample a 1971 red at his 'Calliope' winery, Rutherglen, Vic.

A dry, a medium and a sweet sherry are made—all are rather clean, pleasant, fortified wines, but of no great distinctive character.

A better wine is the extra dry light amontillado style—a completely dry sherry which is matured in oak hogsheads and made on the Flor principle.

Brown's Milawa Shiraz
Made from shiraz grown on the local vineyards. These wines are generally much bigger and fuller than the usual run of Brown's dry reds. They have a distinctive full flavour which is delightful with big, robust dishes.

Brown's Milawa Tokay
From tokay grapes grown on the Milawa vineyards. The grapes are picked when very ripe and a very rich, full-flavoured dessert wine is made.

Brown's Milawa White Frontignac
Since 1965, white frontignac has been made into a dry white wine which is extremely aromatic with a great deal of full, rich flavour. Before that the variety had been used to make a rich dessert wine of quite distinctive character.

Brown's Milawa White Grenache Tokay White Hermitage
The Milawa vineyard has one of the few remaining plantings of white grenache which is used in a blend with tokay and white hermitage to produce the soft and rather full-flavoured, somewhat coarse, flowery style, liked by so many people.

Buller, R. L., & Son

Buller's Amontillado Sherry
A rich, full flavoured aperitif wine, matured in oak for twenty years.

Buller's Beverford Cabernet Sauvignon
The 1971 Beverford Cabernet was the first made. Only 700 gallons of this wine were made from cabernet sauvignon grapes grown in the Lake Boga district. In spite of the fact that the grapes were irrigated the material has a very good high colour and will pick up more interesting flavour from being matured in new French oak hogsheads.

Buller's Beverford Shiraz
Made entirely from shiraz grown at Beverford in the Lake Boga district and matured in big wood.

Buller's Cream Sherry
A blend of tokay and chasselas, both of the 1943 vintage. These are wines of great richness of flavour and advanced wood character.

Buller's Fino Sherry
Originally a Fino, but now developing an extremely rich, full, dry character; produced in the Rutherglen district and matured in wood for up to twenty years.

Buller's Liqueur Frontignac
A rich dessert wine made from brown frontignac and matured in wood for over twenty years.

Buller's Oloroso Sherry
A rich, sweet, dessert wine showing advanced rancio character, having been matured in wood for over twenty years.

Buller's Retsina
This wine is made for a specific section of the trade and it sells extremely well.

Buller's Rosé
A light, clean wine of full flavour, made from local Rutherglen material.

Buller's Rutherglen Shiraz
A rich full-flavoured wine of high colour and full finish which lives for many years.

Buring, Leo, Pty Ltd

Buring's Altar Wine
A sacramental wine which is a light, tawny port made from grenache grapes grown in the Barossa Valley.

Buring's Barossa Cream Sherry

A pleasant, fruity sweet sherry, made from pedro ximenez grown in the Barossa Valley and muscat gordo blanco from the Upper Murray in South Australia.

Buring's Black Label Bin 13 Burgundy

Five wines are marketed under the Black Label; all are essentially vintage wines, and each has its own distinctive style. The Bin number is repetitive and on each change of vintage the label is changed, outlining a short description of the wine and its history. This range of wines is next in grading to the top Reserve Bin line and has an impressive show record since its introduction in 1969. The red burgundy was introduced to the range at a later stage.

The Bin 13 wines are made from shiraz, oeillade and grenache grapes grown in the Barossa and Eden Valleys and at Watervale in South Australia. The wines are medium in body, round, soft and fruity. The 1968 vintage won a Gold Medal and a Bronze Medal in Burgundy Classes in 1970 wine shows.

Buring's Black Label Bin 7 Claret

The 1966 vintage was the first Bin 7 marketed and the subsequent vintages are increasing in popularity. The wines made for this blend come primarily from shiraz grapes grown in the Barossa and Eden Valleys. Occasionally lesser quantities of other varieties are used in the blend—the label for each vintage telling the story for the particular wine concerned.

The wines are made at 'Chateau Leonay' in the Barossa Valley near Tanunda in the traditional manner; fermenting on skins, but in enclosed stainless steel tanks under controlled conditions. After cleaning up, they are matured in French and American oak casks and then bottled at two to three years of age. The wines are bright in colour and the palate is medium-bodied to soft with oak and varietal, a rather pleasant flavour. They are good clean wines that can be enjoyed when young but also take a certain amount of age, though not more than ten years. They are sold for reasonable prices and the four vintages '66 to '69 inclusive have won three Gold Medals, three Silver Medals and three Bronze Medals at various shows; a good record for a straightforward trade wine. I particularly liked the 1968 vintage, which I thought was a very flavour-some, pleasant wine with a nice, clean, firm finish.

Buring's Black Label Bin 21 Moselle

The grapes for this wine have been primarily white tokay, with semillon and clare riesling grown in the company's own vineyards in the Barossa Valley and at Watervale. The wines are fruity, clean and aromatic, with the varietal character evident. The palate is round and soft, slightly

sweet, but well-balanced with acid and body—a good style of wine for those who do not like their wines dry all the time.

A great feature is the colour and freshness of these wines, which is consistent throughout the whole range of Buring's whites—surely one of the most celebrated of Australian white wine styles. Show awards have been four Silver Medals and four Bronze Medals for the vintages '69 to '71.

Buring's Black Label Bin 33 Riesling

The '68 vintage was the first wine marketed and subsequent vintages have been excellent. I think these wines are among the best for their price in Australia. They are very good when young, but, with age, they pick up a delicious depth of character on the middle palate, whilst retaining considerable freshness.

The consistency of these whites—particularly the rieslings—is shown by their green-gold colour, which tends to deepen more towards gold with bottle age. The delicacy, freshness and frequently 'spritzig', the intense fruit flavour and flowery varietal character, all combine to make these wines great. They are probably at best with from one to three years' bottle age, but they will continue to develop the pungent riesling character and flavour with additional bottle age without any fear of oxidation.

The Bin 33 is labelled merely 'Riesling'. In most vintages it is wholly rhine riesling and in others it is predominantly so, with a small quantity of other rieslings and sometimes a rare variety known as rouschette. It depends on the particular year. In the 1968 to 1971 wine shows Bin 33 gained two Gold Medals, four Silver Medals and five Bronze Medals. I don't think they were really trying, however, since they were probably putting their Reserve Bin Rhine Rieslings in the same shows. Whatever, this style is a tremendous value for money. Of the range I particularly like the 1969, Bin 33, a Gold Medal winner and a wine which picked up great character after about eighteen months in the bottle. It is a wine of quite remarkable quality.

Buring's Black Label Bin 86 White Burgundy
The 1971 introduced in early 1972 was the first Bin 86. The wine was well accepted and collected favourable show awards during its first year—results being, I believe, one Gold Medal, one Silver Medal and two Bronze Medals.

It is made from clare riesling and trebbiano (white shiraz, white hermitage) grapes grown at the company's own vineyards in the Barossa Valley and at Watervale. The colour is the typical light green-gold, which greatly signifies the style of the company. It is soft and smooth with a round fullness on the middle palate and sufficient acid balance to keep and build up the flavour with bottle age. I still prefer my Hunter whites in the white burgundy category, though I continue to be impressed with the advances being made by South Australian winemakers in this softer, rounder style.

Buring's Celeste Champagne
A low to medium-priced good quality sparkling wine, the base wine for which comes from the vineyards of the Barossa Valley; made primarily from clare riesling and liqueured to a medium degree to suit the popular palate.

Buring's Champagne Rosalie (Pink)
The production details are outlined under Leonay Champagne. Leo Buring was the first to introduce pink champagne commercially in Australia. The only real difference between pink and white champagne is the colour. This actually stems from a different base wine. The material used in this wine comes from lightly pressed shiraz grapes, which retain their fresh pinkness better than most varieties.

Buring's Chateau Leonay Vintage Wines
This range of wines, commonly tagged C.L.V., is in the price bracket below those of the Private Bin Black Label line. The quality is high and these wines represent extremely good value for money. Over the years they have gained a considerable number of show awards. The styles may be slightly different, but they are all well made. It is often a matter of personal preference anyway.

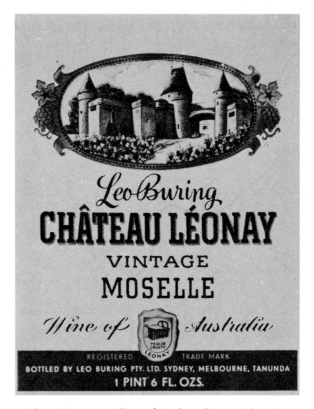

The wines are all marketed under a rather jazzy label depicting a picture of the Chateau as it might have been had Leo Buring finally had his way. The origin of the label is of German design. These wines are strictly vintage wines and this is the only change in the label from year to year.

Buring's Chateau Leonay Vintage Burgundy
A good, medium-priced dry red made from shiraz and grenache grapes grown in the Angaston Hills of the Barossa Valley and at Watervale in South Australia. Made in the traditional manner by fermenting on skins, but under controlled conditions in stainless steel tanks for a limited time. After cleaning up, the wines are stored in large oak storage casks for a number of years, bottled, and then aged in the bottle. The aim is to achieve a light to medium bodied wine, well-rounded and soft, with a flavour of the fruit showing.

Buring's Chateau Leonay Vintage Chablis
This wine, made from semillon and clare riesling grown in the Barossa Valley and the Clare districts, has good light colour, is clean, dry and crisp. It is a pleasant drinking wine, fairly neutral in character and without a predominance of fruit or aromatic quality.

Buring's Chateau Leonay Vintage Hock
Hock is an English term for a German wine from

the Rheingau. It has been adapted for Australian use as a 'dry white table wine', without prejudice to variety or district. This dry white wine has attractive colour, the first indication of a good wine, and is fresh and delicate but without any particular varietal character. This is not usually the type of wine entered in Shows, for it is not singularly outstanding against other wines which have more varietal and aromatic character.

Buring's Chateau Leonay Vintage Moselle
The clare riesling grapes from which this wine is made come from the deeper sandy soil in the heart of the Barossa Valley. The wine is pleasant, fresh and fruity with a slight degree of sweetness which will please many palates. Show awards in recent years have been two Silver Medals and two Bronze Medals.

Buring's Chateau Leonay Vintage Riesling
Another outstanding white wine from the company and good value for money. This wine has been featured for many years in the different vintages commencing in 1963. It has won an extraordinary number of show awards and continues to do so. The 1963, for example, one of the forerunners of all the great rhine rieslings from the company, has been smothered in Gold Medals.

The wine is made from the rhine and clare riesling varieties, with a greater proportion of rhine riesling in the Bin, sufficient to give the flowery lift and fragrant character of the variety. The clare gives more fullness to the palate. The mid-1960s were outstanding wines made up of a high proportion of rhine riesling. Towards the end of the 1960s ('68 and '69) some semillon was used and this seemed to flatten the middle palate just a trifle, though the wines remained very good value for money. In 1970 the wine was a blend of rhine riesling and clare and the company now seems to be maintaining this blend in the rough proportion of about sixty percent rhine riesling to forty percent clare.

Buring's Chateau Leonay Vintage Red Hermitage Claret
Not altogether different in style from the Bin 7. The same varieties of grapes, grown in the nearby areas, are used in the blends and the difference in grading is in the hands of the blender. The making follows a similar pattern as with all the other reds and it is interesting to observe the influence of new grape crushing techniques introduced in 1972 and the effect that this will have on future wines.

The controlled fermentation in stainless steel tanks and pressing in the more gentle Wilmes-type presses has undoubtedly lifted the quality of these wines. Awards gained in wine shows in recent years have been a couple of Gold Medals, a

Silver Medal and nine Bronze Medals. This is a pretty fair indication of the quality of what is after all a fairly reasonably priced wine.

Buring's Chateau Leonay Vintage Sauternes
A sweet white table wine, full in body, with fruity grape flavour; made from well-pressed clare riesling grapes grown in the heart of the Barossa Valley. The grapes are allowed to ripen fully, making a very pleasant rich wine for those people who like to taste some sugar and some of the natural grape remaining in the wine.

Buring's Chateau Leonay Vintage White Burgundy
This wine came to the forefront with the 1968 vintage when it was first exhibited and gained recognition. Since then it has gone from success to success and the 1971 vintage has gained a number of awards.

Semillon, tokay, white hermitage and rouschette are used but the proportions may vary from year to year, depending on the seasons. Rouschette is an unusual grape variety. There is not much of it about, but it is most useful, being negative in flavour, but very clean, very well balanced with good acid. It helps balance the bigger flavour of the clare riesling.

I liked the 1970 edition of this wine. It had delightful green-gold colour and a perfumed, fresh, very clean fruity nose. There is a ton of flavour on the palate and the finish was soft and lingering: a well-balanced, complete wine of good quality. Wine show awards in the '69, '70 and '71 years were six Gold Medals, seven Silver Medals and twelve Bronze Medals, which is remarkable for a trade wine in such a price range.

Buring's Clairette
This is a light red slightly fruity table wine, made from grenache and shiraz grapes, grown in the Barossa Valley, and retaining a little of the natural sugar of the grape. It is most suitable for drinking with curry dishes. I believe it was originally invented to be enjoyed with the curry featured at the Buring's Olde Crusty Cellar in George Street, Sydney.

Buring's Delicado Port
An aged, rather light tawny port, specially made by drawing the fermenting juice from the red skins of the shiraz grapes before too much of the colour has been extracted. The wine is then aged in small wood for an average of ten years prior to selecting blends to maintain uniformity of style. The wine is not bottle aged to any extent for the object is to carry out the maturation in wood and then to put it on the market as a light dessert wine.

Buring's Extra Special Table Wines
The three wines in this range, claret, moselle and riesling, are the most economically priced of all

the bottled table wines of the company; though they still retain the stamp of quality of this company that does produce so many fine table wines. They are up to show standard and Silver Medals were awarded in 1971. The wines have a fairly plain white label and were first introduced in late 1969 to provide reasonable quality wines in the lower price bracket.

Buring's Extra Special Claret
A wine of good value, being quite light in style, pleasant, and suited for everyday economical drinking. It is made from shiraz, mataro and grenache grapes grown in the Barossa Valley.

Buring's Extra Special Moselle
Made primarily from pedro ximenez grapes grown in the Barossa Valley and clare riesling from the Murray River Valley. This wine has a light, good colour, pleasant fruitiness on the nose and palate, is fresh and clean, slightly sweet and well balanced with acid. Although the cheapest of all the company's table wines, this wine has gained two Silver Medals in 1970 and 1971 shows—the only times the wine was exhibited.

Buring's Extra Special Riesling
This is the dry twin of the Extra Special Moselle. It is a good, clean, fresh wine showing a little fruitiness and is quite crisp. Not a wine for laying down, but very popular for everyday drinking.

Buring's Fino Solero Fruity Sherry
A somewhat ambiguous name, but nevertheless a wine blended basically on the solera system to produce an even standard. The wine is for those who prefer a sherry that is half sweet, half dry.

Buring's Florita Flor Sherry
A high quality Flor sherry; made by the age-old Spanish method of growing a cultivated Flor yeast on a suitably selected base wine in an ullaged sherry butt of approximately 100 gallons capacity. Initially, the alcoholic strength of the wine is kept at a level to allow the growth of the Flor yeast over the surface of the wine; and at the same time at a sufficient level to inhibit the growth of the micro-organism acetobacter, which would otherwise convert the alcohol of the wine to vinegar. The control of the situation is critical and great care is needed from the winemaker. The wine is allowed to stay in this state for a number of years, during which time many chemical changes take place, converting what was originally a hock type of wine into a Flor sherry. When the right time has come the wine is raised in alcoholic strength to something over 31° proof spirit and is then allowed to

mature further in larger vessels, finally being bottled and sold without further bottle ageing.

The base wines for this style come from pedro ximenez and palomino grapes grown in the company's 'Florita' vineyard at Watervale. The soil is rich loam over a limestone subsoil and is considered most suitable for this type of wine. Show awards for 1969, 1970 and 1971 have been phenomenal; this wine, which is after all a trade Flor, has gained eight Gold Medals, five Silver Medals and three Bronze Medals as well as a Trophy for the best sherry in classes at Perth.

Buring's French Vermouth
A popular style, light in colour; fairly dry, with a good blend of herbs to give a clean, dry style vermouth.

Buring's Granada Dry Sherry
A standard-type dry sherry, made from pedro ximenez grapes grown in the Barossa Valley, matured in wood prior to bottling.

Buring's Granada Sweet Sherry
A smooth, sweet, fruity sherry made from pedro ximenez, palomino and muscat gordo blanco, grown in the Upper Murray district of South Australia.

Buring's Italian Vermouth
A good quality sweet wine, darker in colour and sweeter of course than the French style and infused with imported herbs.

Buring's Leonardi Aperitif
A light vermouth-flavoured white wine, lower in alcoholic strength than the vermouths with milder flavour and slightly sweet. Nothing personal, but I wish they had reserved the name for something with a little more character!

Buring's Leonay Champagne
Made by the traditional French process of carrying out the secondary fermentation in the bottle, disgorging, liqueuring, and then marketing in the same bottle in which it is fermented (the famous Methode Champenoise).

The base wine comes from the Clare district and the resultant wine is light and delicate with a shade of sweetness, making it a most agreeable sparkling wine.

Buring's Leonay Champagne Brut
A similar wine to the Leonay Champagne, except that the wine is unliqueured and consequently quite dry. It has considerable character and takes some bottle age.

Buring's Liebfrauwein
This wine with its colourful German-style label has been produced to meet the demands of popular

taste and is a widely accepted white table wine. It is made from various white varieties from the Barossa Valley. The colour is an excellent light-green-gold, the nose fresh and delicate, with fruit character, and the palate is soft, clean, fresh and well balanced. The degree of sugar retained in the wine makes it very agreeable to a lot of palates.

Buring's Maywine
A sweet white wine which originated in Holland, it has been blended with herbs to give an interesting and pleasant character. The alcoholic strength is equivalent to a sweet sherry.

Buring's Reserve Bin Wines
The Reserve Bins are the premium grade wines of the company. These wines are marketed under a plain white label which shows the wine type, Bin identification number, vintage, a short description of the wine and its origin. The best wines available from any district are selected. Particular care is taken in their making and handling. They are individually bottled, binned and then released once or twice a year—but only when they have attained sufficient bottle age.

There is no need to go back over lots of Bin numbers. I've reviewed these wines throughout the years in magazines and in my consultancy sheet. However, I will make special reference to some of the whites.

The red wines are mostly grape or material purchases from other growers and companies. The Buring's winemakers are extraordinarily skilful and the reds still have the stamp of the company, yet they can be other people's wines. The whites are always made by Burings and I think these are the most famous wines of the company.

Buring's Reserve Bin Reds—Burgundy and Claret
In this entry I have put these two types together under the heading of 'Reserve Bin Reds'. The bulk of these wines come from the Eden Valley, Watervale, the Barossa Valley, Coonawarra and the Southern Districts of South Australia. The grapes from which the wines are made are predominantly shiraz and cabernet sauvignon although occasionally there are other varieties on the labels. The varieties of grapes and the districts in which they are grown generally tend to produce wines more towards the claret style, or something like a round, soft-flavoured burgundy middle palate with a claret finish. That is why I prefer to call them 'Dry Reds'.

Although not as prolific award winners as the outstanding rhine riesling range, the red wines have done fairly well in gaining fourteen Gold, thirty-five Silver and fifty-six Bronzes in recent years.

The wines are made in the same manner as other reds, now being crushed in a new imported grape mill, which separates the berries from the stalks as if picked by hand and thus keeping the stalk juice

out of the fermentation tanks. Following vintage, the wines are cleaned up and stored in either French or American oak casks between 65 and 500 gallon capacity. Bottling takes place at two to three years and the wines are then binned to bottle age for a number of years, the length of time varying with individual wines. Burings also purchase wines from other people and these they then control and handle their own way; finally blending them with other varieties and districts to produce their very good quality Bin Dry Reds.

Buring's Reserve Bin Rhine Riesling—Spatlese—Moselle
Once again the wines are grouped under one heading because a general description does suffice for them all. These unquestionably are the pick of the wines from the Leo Buring Cellars. They have long since established a very high reputation and this is evidenced by the great public acceptance of the wines and the tremendous number of show awards.

The quality control for these wines begins at the vineyard, where chosen vineyards are kept under very strict surveillance. The grapes are picked at the exact degree of maturity and taken to the winery with the minimum of handling to avoid broken berries. They are crushed as gently as practicable in the absence of air and the juice is immediately separated from the skins. Very careful control of fermentation and fermentation pressures follows. The wines are cleaned up immediately after vintage and bottling takes place soon afterwards under the most sterile conditions with very up-to-date equipment. Bottle ageing follows until the wines are ready for release.

The Reserve Bin whites are made entirely from rhine riesling grapes grown in individual vineyards in three separate districts: the hills around Eden Valley, parts of the Barossa Valley and the 'Florita' vineyard at Watervale. The higher and cooler districts of the Eden Valley and Watervale, with their particular soils, are generally a little better, though certain picked areas of the Barossa are selected for high class wines. As a result of the grape selection and careful winemaking techniques and skill, the wines have a delightful green-gold colour which turns more towards golden with bottle age. The wines have intense varietal fruit character, a delicate flavour, are fresh and frequently have residual gas or 'spritzig'.

The best wines made in the range are not easy to pick, but I must mention a few which were my particular favourites. The 1966 Eden Valley—DWV 12 —which I reviewed in 1969 must have been one of the best rhine rieslings every made in Australia. At that time it had never won a Gold Medal, which was quite amazing, although it had won numerous other awards. 1966 was an acid year in the Eden Valley and the DWV 12 probably needed plenty of time to fill out and soften. The colour was a beautiful full green-yellow, there was a trace of gas, but the

Red grape skins after pressing at Osborns 'd'Arenberg' vineyard in the hills overlooking McLaren Flat, S.A.

Lunchtime for grape pickers in the Barossa Valley.

wine had an extremely full flavour; intense and complex, yet still delicate and of considerable finesse. It finally started winning Gold Medals and received no less than twenty show awards and eventually the W. W. Senior Memorial Trophy for the best dry white in the Melbourne Show. The 1967 DW 83 was another wine I particularly liked. It was an extremely good wine that won many medals. The 1963 won five Gold Medals and the Bert Bear Trophy for the best young white in Sydney. The 1964 won several Silver Medals; the 1965 won Gold Medals all the way. The DW 73 of 1966 was a very good wine indeed and then we had the excellent DWY 13 of 1969—all very good wines that rank among the best in Australia. Perhaps they don't have the extremely volatile, estery nose of some other rhine rieslings, but they have a magnificent rich middle palate flavour.

Another feature which I like about the wines is that they don't pick up the so-called 'kerosene' character—'flytox'—a development in rhine riesling which, when aged, starts to pick up this rather pungent character. They remain fresh and delicate for years.

The Reserve Spatlese and Moselle wines are mainly from the 'Florita' vineyard at Watervale, where the vines are grown with a northerly aspect in a rich clay-loam soil over the limestone subsoils. The grapes are allowed to ripen more than for the lighter and more delicate dry wines and the district ensures the retention of acid while the grapes are fully ripened; the result being a more luscious wine with the rich flavour of the rhine riesling fully ripened fruit. Again this is a case of the altitude allowing acid retention, whilst the sugar slowly builds and the grape is allowed to become fully ripened and develop all its flavour characters.

The pattern of winemaking is similar to the dry rieslings, but fermentation is arrested to retain a degree of natural grape sugar in the wine. Some of the better wines have been the 1967 DW 93, which secured fourteen medals, including six Golds and the 1968 DWX 39, which gained eleven medals, including four Golds. Future wines are expected to achieve the same standard.

The Reserve Bin whites are unquestionably top wines of this company and have made an enormous contribution to wine standards in Australia. Burings are to be congratulated for their efforts and Reg Shipster and John Vickery should be honoured for their enormous skills in establishing the fame of these white wines.

In recent years, the Reserve Bin white wines have gained sixty-five Gold Medals, fifty-seven Silver Medals and sixty-one Bronze Medals. In addition, seven Trophies have been awarded since 1967.

Buring's Rinegolde Moselle
The name Rinegolde is adapted from the German 'Reines Gold', meaning 'pure gold' and is a reference to the wine's colour; there being no claim for any association with Rhine wine. The wine was first introduced by the late Leo Buring in the 1930s. In those days and in the 1940s it was largely a Hunter Valley wine coming from Jack Phillips' 'Glandore' vineyard, which is now the Brokenback Estate—one of the associated vineyard companies of The Rothbury Estate Group.

Modern techniques have changed the wine from the early days; but it is quite similar to the original in concept. It is not a vintage wine but is continually blended to give a uniform product from year to year. The wine is made at 'Chateau Leonay' from chosen vineyards in the Barossa Valley and some pedro ximenez and clare riesling from the Murray Valley. The wine has stood the test of time and for many years, in its familar squat bottles and vine leaf label, it became known as Australia's national table wine—before the huge upsurge in table wine consumption in the 1960s. Now it is sold in tall, green hock bottles and is still very popular throughout the country.

Buring's Royal Reserve Muscat
A rich, fruity, full-flavoured, sweet, fortified wine made from muscat gordo blanco grapes, grown in the Barossa Valley and the Upper Murray districts of South Australia.

Buring's Royal Reserve Tokay
A sweet, fortified, well-flavoured wine with a pleasant aroma and palate. Made from tokay grapes grown in the Barossa Valley and the Murray Valley districts.

Buring's Sparkling Burgundy
A red, sparkling wine made by the French Charmat process in which the secondary fermentation is carried out in large high pressure bulk tanks under controlled refrigeration conditions. On completion of fermentation, the wine is liqueured and then bottled under pressure. The grapes used in the base wine are shiraz and grenache from the Clare and Barossa Valleys.

Buring's Sparkling Hock
Made by the same process as Sparkling Burgundy. The base wine comes from various districts in South Australia and is blended to bring about a uniformity of product. It is liqueured to a degree between champagne and sparkling moselle.

Buring's Sparkling Liebfrauwein
Made by the same process as the previous sparkling wines and liqueured more highly. The grapes come from several varieties grown in the Barossa Valley, giving a full, fruity wine of some sweetness.

Buring's Sparkling Moselle
Again the methods of making are the same as the previous sparkling wines and the liqueuring of the moselle is higher, making it the sweetest in the

range. It is a full-flavoured wine, with a fruity and pleasant aroma.

Buring's Sparkling Rinegolde
An economical sparkling wine designed to meet the popular market. It is a light, white, fairly sweet fruity wine which has natural effervescence. Large quantities are sold and the blends are made up primarily from clare riesling, pedro ximenez and white hermitage grapes grown in the Barossa Valley and in the River Murray districts.

It is a natural sparkling wine of medium pressure, marketed in a hock shaped bottle and stoppered with a polythene plug and plastic screw cap. The gas, or effervescence, is the product of natural fermentation, made under the French Charmat method. This is a very popular sparkling, clean wine, with some sugar on the middle palate.

Buring's Sparkling Rinegolde Pink
The method of production and packaging is the same as for the standard Sparkling Rinegolde, the difference being in the making of the base wine, which is produced from grenache grapes grown in the Barossa Valley. The juice is run off the skins early, when sufficient colour is extracted to give the degree of pinkness required.

Buring's Special Burgundy Flagon
Made from grenache grapes grown in the heart of the Barossa Valley: light in style, soft and fruity. One of the best of the flagon reds available.

Buring's Special Claret Flagon
Made from grenache, mataro and carignane grapes grown in the Barossa Valley. Light to medium in style, it has fruit flavour with good balance. It is a good quaffing red of high standard and very good value for money.

Buring's Special Moselle Flagon
Made from mixed varieties of grapes grown in the Barossa Valley and from the Murray Valley. Good light colour, clean and fruity; the wine is light, delicate, with some fruit flavour and a touch of sweetness.

Buring's Special Riesling Hock Flagon
Made from clare riesling, palomino, pedro ximenez and white hermitage grapes grown in the Barossa Valley and the Murray Valley. A good bright colour wine with clean, fresh fruit flavour.

Buring's Special Rosé Flagon
Made from grenache grapes grown in the Barossa Valley. It has a nice, light rosé colour, a good, clean, fresh palate and light fruit flavour.

Buring's Suprena Oloroso Sherry
In the blending of Flor fino sherries some Flor wines are put to one side because they may be too full in body for the delicate Florita Fino style. These wines are aged for a longer period in wood and ultimately liqueured with a very old sweet white wine and thence marketed as Oloroso Sherry. The wine has a pungent aroma. The colour is that of old gold. The sweetness is well-balanced with wood and the high volume of extract which has now built up in the wine. Its average age is from ten to twelve years.

Buring's Vintage Port
The vintage ports marketed have been wines of individual years and of the unique 'blackberry', full, rich, style with a firm tannin finish. They have come mainly from the southern districts of South Australia, Clare and the Barossa Valley. The wines have a deep rich colour, plenty of esters, character, are full-bodied with a dry and crisp finish. They are bottled at about two years of age and then allowed to bottle age indefinitely, depending on the individual wine and its character and substance.

Buring's Vintage Tawny Port
An old tawny port is generally available, but because of its age distribution must be controlled, otherwise ageing stocks are quickly depleted, especially if there is a run of popularity in a particular marketing area. The average age of the wine is about twelve to fifteen years, the greater proportion of this time being spent in oak casks.

Basic wines of the blend are shiraz, with a lesser proportion of mataro and grenache, all grown in the Barossa Valley.

Buring's Vin Rosé
The Rosé wine is made from grenache grapes grown at the 'Florita' vineyard at Watervale and the 'Chateau Leonay' vineyards at Tanunda. The crushing and commencement of fermentation are carried out in the same manner as for the red wines, but the juice is run off fairly early when the colour is right.

The wines are of a high standard. They are a light rosé colour, delicate and dry, with a very fresh, pleasant grape aroma. The wines were first exhibited at wine shows in 1968 and since that date have secured two Gold Medals, nine Silver Medals and six Bronze Medals.

Calamia

Calamia Bin 29 Shiraz
A full-flavoured dry red made from black shiraz grapes grown in the Griffith area in the Riverina district of New South Wales. The wine is matured in French oak and is always given a vintage year.

A full-flavoured wine of both good fruit and good oak with a nice clean, fairly astringent finish.

Calamia Bin 17 Troia
The only wine of its kind in Australia containing the uva de troia. A blend of black shiraz and uva de troia, this dry red is matured in French oak and is a repetitive Bin, produced under a vintage label.

The general manager of the company, Mr D. W. 'Scottie' Ireland, a fine winemaker who was for many years with McWilliams, considers this a most complex wine. It certainly *has* got a different varietal character, plenty of fruit and flavour and once again the oak shows through very well. A most interesting and individual wine.

Calamia Brown Muscat
A fortified sweet red from the black muscat grape with plenty of fruit and some wood maturation to soften it.

Calamia Burgundy
A blend of shiraz and grenache material—a quite light dry red, typical of the district, and with no pressings added to it.

Calamia Chablis
From semillon and white shiraz (trebbiano), with pleasant fruitiness and some clean, fresh tannin and acid on the finish.

Calamia Claret
Made from shiraz with a soft undertone of fruit from the troia grape.

Calamia Cream Sherry
Cold fermentation retains the muscat flavour from the gordo blanco grapes used for this young fortified wine.

Calamia Dry Sherry
From the palomino grape, aged in wood for some time. A fairly dry wine with adequate rancio character.

Calamia Frontignac
A heavier fortified style from the frontignac grape, with considerable wood maturation. This is a wine of deep flavour and plenty of style.

Calamia Hock
Cold fermentation and early marketing has enabled the company to present a full fruity style of white from the semillon grape.

Calamia Italian Vermouth
This heavy, rather gutsy vermouth of Italian style is extremely popular with the Italian people in the local Griffith community.

Calamia Private Bins
Calamia is one of the few companies that now really sticks to the Private Bin system with some of their wines and doesn't repeat the bins with all wines year after year as most companies do. Just as their names indicate, these are small amounts put out under a unique handwritten label. They are wines with a difference, and are evidence of the winemaker's love for the area and for the wines he produces.

The A.25 was a dry red from the mataro grape, light in style, easy to drink with plenty of mataro character. This wine has won many friends and it is anticipated that there will be a regular binning of straight mataro.

Other Private Bins which will be made in the future are dry frontignac, which has plenty of fruit character, and a straight cabernet sauvignon.

Calamia Riesling
A wine with plenty of flavour, blended from semillon and rhine riesling grapes and made with extra care to ensure retention of the fresh character. This wine is always marketed early because of the quick maturing qualities of Griffith wines.

Calamia Rosso Secco
This Italian style dry red with a muscat fruit flavour is unique in Australian winemaking. It is completely dry and extremely popular with the Italian community.

Calamia Ruby Port
A light port from the shiraz, grenache and mataro grapes, with very little age.

Calamia Sauternes
From semillon, this semi-dry white is well-balanced with not too much sweetness.

Calamia Semi Sweet Sherry
A blend of the sweet and dry sherries to satisfy the 'in-between' drinker.

Calamia Sparkling Wines
All sparkling wines are from South Australia using a semillon base supplied by the company, which is then made into a delicate neutral style.

Calamia Sweet Sherry
From the trebbiano (white shiraz) grape matured in hogsheads. This sweet sherry has a good balance of rancio character and sugar. It is a very good product of the local Griffith district.

Calamia Tawny Port
A blend of the same grapes as the Calamia Ruby Port (mainly mataro, grenache and shiraz), but with hogshead wood maturation, giving it a desirable depth of flavour and tawny colour.

Calamia Vin Rosé
A completely dry style from the grenache grape; young, fresh and pink.

Calamia White Burgundy
A round, full-flavoured style derived from the trebbiano or white shiraz grape. Once again marketed early before the wine gets too big in the bottle.

Calamia White Muscat
Made from muscat gordo blanco grapes, a heavy, full style selected from the heavier soils of the Griffith district. With a small amount of wood maturation this wine becomes the company's White Muscat.

Calamia White Port
Again the trebbiano or white shiraz grape is used to yield a very full-flavoured sweet dessert wine, heavier than a sweet sherry, and matured in hogsheads.

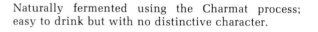

Campbell, A.D.

Campbell's Aged Muscat
A pleasant muscat style without great depth of character, made from brown muscat (frontignac) and matured in wood for some time.

Campbell's Bobbie Burns Shiraz
Made from straight shiraz and aged in big French oak for eighteen months. Not typical of Rutherglen district, since this wine, although it has plenty of big rich fruit and a broad soft character, lacks the portiness which the red wines often get and has a much firmer tannin finish than usual.

Campbell's Cabaret
A sparkling light white wine with some sweetness, made on the Charmat process.

Campbell's Cabernet Shiraz
A blend of eighty percent cabernet with twenty percent shiraz pressings. A dry red wine of high colour and pleasant flavour with a good acid tannin finish.

Campbell's Chablis
Made from the pedro ximenez variety; a big, rather coarse, full, soft wine, the style of which belies the name.

Campbell's Champagnes
Made in various styles—Brut, Demi-Sec and Spumante —and therefore ranging from dry to semi-sweet.

Naturally fermented using the Charmat process; easy to drink but with no distinctive character.

Campbell's Claret
A smooth, soft, pleasant-drinking red, made from shiraz.

Campbell's Hock
Made from white hermitage and bottled fairly young, this light, crisp wine is easy drinking.

Campbell's Madeira
An interesting wine, rather sweet with a heavy almost caramelized flavour.

Campbell's Marsala
A fortified wine made for local sale.

Campbell's Moselle
Made from white hermitage and containing some sweetness and gas.

Campbell's Muscat—Aged
Made from brown muscat (frontignac), this wine has a pleasant muscat character with rich grapiness and reasonable sweetness. It lacks full wood age.

Campbell's Muscat—Brown
Again the frontignac grape (called brown muscat in the district) produces a soft, flavoursome wine of moderate sweetness and pronounced raisin character.

Campbell's Muscat—Liqueur
Made from brown muscat this liqueur muscat has a fuller character than the brown muscat, a bigger, more 'essency' nose and richer flavour. It is quite sweet and can be used as a liqueur. However, I still prefer to see more wood age on the wine.

Campbell's Muscat—Old
Again made from the brown muscat variety, this is a special wine which is aged in quarter casks close to the roof. The high evaporation rate concentrates the liqueur character and produces a wine of quite distinctive flavour. It is very sweet, with tremendous raisin fruit, balanced by a full oak flavour on the back of the palate.

Campbell's Port—Empire 1964
Made from shiraz grapes and kept in quarter casks stored near the roof. A ruby port developing tawny character; bottled only when required.

Campbell's Port—Old Reserve
Made from shiraz and aged in wood for many years. A developed, tawny port of full colour and flavour, containing considerable character and bhdy.

Campbell's Port—Red
A light-coloured trade fortified wine for the local market, made from shiraz.

Campbell's Port—Reserve
Made from shiraz; fuller in flavour and depth of colour than the Red Port. A pleasant drinking wine.

Campbell's Port—Tawny
Made from shiraz; it has light colour and body; a smooth sweetness, and is easy to drink though not of definitive tawny style.

Campbell's Port—Vintage 1965
Made from fifty percent shiraz and fifty percent cabernet; it has a deep purple, rich colour, full body and plenty of character. Fortified with brandy spirit, bottled after two years in oak and now improving. This wine was tasted on a couple of occasions and impressed because of its full, rich character; it will mature and develop for many years.

Campbell's Rosé
Made from the blue imperial variety (cinsaut). Fuller coloured than usual with a slight sweetness and some gas. A pleasant drinking wine.

Campbell's Rutherglen Blue Imperial
Made from cinsaut, it has light colour and body; a wine for easy drinking in quantity.

Campbell's Sauterne
Made from pedro ximenez. A full-flavoured, sweet wine for local trade.

Campbell's Scotsburn Malbec
Made for the first time from the variety in 1970. A full-bodied red wine, having the somewhat stalky flavour of the malbec grape with a high acid and firm tannin finish.

Campbell's Sherry—Cream
Made from the muscat gordo blanco grape. A rich, creamy, rather full, smooth, sweet wine.

Campbell's Sherry—Dry
A blend with a deep rich colour, not made on the Flor process and being rather rancio in wood character. Aged in quarter casks before bottling.

Campbell's Sherry—Fruity
Made from pedro ximenez; it is a medium dry trade wine for the local market.

Campbell's Sherry—Old Dry
Made from pedro ximenez and matured in wood for many years. Old wood character, deep colour, slightly sweetened; more of the amontillado style.

Campbell's Sherry—Sweet
Made .from pedro ximenez; it is quite sweet, but again of very old rancio wood character.

Campbell's Shiraz—Cinsaut
A blend of fifty percent shiraz and fifty percent cinsaut. Aged for twelve months in 500 gallon casks and then for six months in new American oak. Light in colour, a medium bodied wine, which is pleasant drinking.

Campbell's Silverburn Shiraz
Made entirely from shiraz. Aged for twelve months in big wood and then given six months in new American oak. A big soft fruity wine with the fruit matched by the oak flavour, with a firm tannin finish. A wine which lives for many years· in the bottle.

Campbell's Sparkling Burgundy
A blend of red wines; tank fermented, pleasant to drink.

Campbell's Tokay
Made from the Rutherglen tokay variety. A rich dessert wine with considerable finesse in flavour. These wines can be quite outstanding. Aged in wood for some years and having quite typical district and variety flavour.

Campbell's Trebbiano
Made from the trebbiano (white hermitage) and picked at a very low Baumé (under 10 degrees). The acid is fairly high at this stage and this does retain a fruitiness and natural crispness which is not basic to the area. Bottled young to retain

fruitiness. This was made in 1970 for the first time under pressure and temperature control. The wine was fermented at 10°C throughout fermentation.

Colin Campbell has done well with the early vintages of the trebbiano and it is unusual to see this variety making such a clean, crisp wine. The fruitiness of the wine is considerable and would fool many people at a masked tasting.

Campbell's Vermouth—French—Italian
Flavoured fortified wines made for the local market.

Campbell's White Burgundy
Made from the trebbiano (white hermitage) under temperature and pressure control and then aged for twelve months in 500 gallon oak casks. A pleasant full-flavoured wine having a quite nutty middle palate.

Chambers, W. H. & Sons

Chambers' Amontillado (Old Dry Sherry)
Made from pedro ximenez and matured in old wood for many years. A rich, old, dry wine of considerable flavour.

Chambers' Blue Imperial, Alicante Bouchet and Grenache
A blend as stated. Soft, pleasant, good quality drinking with typical north-east Victorian rich character; a wine I have enjoyed many times in Victoria and which always appeals for its rugged simplicity.

Chambers' Bulk Red
A mixture of all the red varieties of the Chambers' vineyard. Bill Chambers was at his delightful best when a customer tasted the wine and wanted to know what variety was in it. 'Hell', he said, 'take your pick.'

Chambers' Cabernet 60 percent Shiraz 40 percent
A dry red of the varieties and proportions as stated in the name. It has a full, rich colour and a lot of fruit. The wine will live many years in the bottle. It combines the big character of the regional district with the added richness of fruit from the cabernet variety. A firm, clean finish.

Chambers' Muscat Brown
Made from brown muscat (frontignac). A light, clean dessert wine, with pleasant raisiny fruit, but without great depth of character.

Chambers' Muscat—Liqueur
From the brown muscat variety again, but containing more wood development and having therefore more lusciousness and richer character.

Chambers' Muscat—Old Liqueur
An outstanding dessert wine that is a blend of wines going back many years. Bill Chambers still has some of the 1890 Muscat made by his grandfather which he uses in the blend. The blend needs to have different years in it. The older years give the wine depth of flavour, character and advanced wood style, the younger years give the wine life and freshness. These wines, unquestionably among the finest of Australian wines, are outstanding value and tremendous drinking at all times. Often disregarded, they are probably the most indigenous wines made in Australia.

Chambers' Port—Ruby
Made from shiraz, a light, pleasant port of distinctive character and style.

Chambers' Port—Tawny
From shiraz again, but a more developed wine, having had a considerable time in wood and therefore being more concentrated in flavour and more complete in character.

Chambers' Port—Vintage
Made from shiraz and sometimes shiraz and cabernet. A very high-coloured and full-flavoured wine of considerable character with rich, firm finish. This wine matures very well in the bottle and remains outstanding drinking for years.

Chambers' Sherry—Cream
A rich, full-flavoured dessert wine made from tokay. It is probably better than the name suggests.

Chambers' Sherry—Dry Flor
A full-flavoured wine with typical Flor astringency and oak character.

Chambers' Sherry—Medium
A pleasant, soft wine of medium sweetness, made from pedro ximenez.

Chambers' Sherry—Sweet
A sweet dessert wine of medium quality.

Chambers' Tokay
A magnificent dessert wine made from the tokay variety. This wine has been matured in big wood for many years and has a most distinctive flavour and character. The rich earthiness of the bouquet is typical of these old wines and this is carried through onto the palate. A magnificent dessert wine by any standards.

Chateau Rosevale

Chateau Rosevale Bianco Vermouth
A full-flavoured, delicate white vermouth made from palomino and pedro ximinez grapes grown in the Barossa Valley.

Chateau Rosevale Burgundy
A blend of cabernet sauvignon and shiraz grapes grown in the Barossa Valley. A full-bodied wine with a smooth tannin finish, aged in French oak for two years.

Chateau Rosevale Champagne
A blend of Barossa Valley semillon and tokay grapes and produced by the traditional method. Three styles are made—Brut, Demi-Sec and Sec.

Chateau Rosevale Cream Sherry
A fruity, but fairly delicate and light, sweet sherry which is a blend of pedro ximinez and muscatel (muscat gordo blanco) grapes of Barossa Valley origin.

Chateau Rosevale Dry Red
A blend of Barossa Valley cabernet sauvignon, shiraz and malbec. This wine has very good colour, a strong varietal fruit, combined with small oak. The finish is very firm and quite persistent with just a touch of that furriness that one associates with the Barossa Valley. The wine spends up to two years in small French oak and then is bottle aged by the company for a further twelve to eighteen months before release. The wines need considerably more time than that to reach their full character, with the marriage of oak and the various varieties developing into a rich flavour with pronounced bouquet.

Chateau Rosevale Dry Sherry
Made from doradillo grapes grown locally. Aged in oak for three years prior to bottling.

Chateau Rosevale Frontignac
Produced from locally grown frontignac grapes. A rich, full-bodied wine which is aged in wood for two years.

Chateau Rosevale Hock
Made from semillon and tokay grapes grown in the Barossa Valley. It has a nice fruity, full-bodied palate and a crisp, acid finish.

Chateau Rosevale Italian Vermouth
A full-flavoured vermouth with plenty of fruit and sweetness, made from local pedro ximenez and doradillo grapes.

Chateau Rosevale Light Port
A blend of locally grown shiraz, grenache and mataro grapes. Aged in oak for two years prior to bottling.

Chateau Rosevale Mecklenburg Port—1959 Vintage
A premium grade, rich dessert wine produced from local shiraz and mataro grapes and aged in wood for many years prior to bottling.

Chateau Rosevale Muscat
Produced from the local muscatel variety (muscat gordo blanco). A full-bodied and highly flavoured wine which is aged for three years in wood prior to bottling.

Chateau Rosevale Perle
Produced from semillon and white hermitage grapes and made by the Charmat process.

Chateau Rosevale Pink Champagne
A blend of semillon and mataro grapes and produced by the traditional method; a wine having some sweetness and fruitiness on the palate.

Chateau Rosevale Pink Schaumwein
A blend of white hermitage and mataro grapes. A sparkling wine made by the Charmat process.

Chateau Rosevale Pink Vinspa
A sparkling wine with a muscatel/grenache base.

Chateau Rosevale Rhineland
A sparkling wine made from the semillon and white hermitage dry white base. Produced in Brut, Demi-Sec and Sec styles.

Chateau Rosevale Riesling
A fruity, but delicate, table wine, produced from rhine riesling grapes grown at the Barossa Valley. It has good varietal style and a crisp, acid finish.

Chateau Rosevale Rosé
Made from grenache grown locally. The wine has a pleasant palate and a soft, acid and very clean tannin finish.

Chateau Rosevale Schaumwein
A sparkling wine made from local semillon and tokay varieties and produced by the Charmat process. Also made in Brut, Demi-Sec and Sec styles.

Chateau Rosevale Sparkling Riesling
A blend of rhine riesling grapes grown in the Vinevale area of the Barossa Valley. Slightly sweet in character.

Chateau Rosevale Sparkling Burgundy
A blend of locally grown shiraz and grenache grapes produced by the traditional champagne method.

Chateau Rosevale Spumante
A honey-based, sparkling wine. Pedro ximenez and doradillo of Barossa Valley origin are the base grape varieties.

Chateau Rosevale Sweet Sherry

A full-flavoured, agreeable sweet wine, produced from pedro ximenez and aged in wood for three years.

Chateau Rosevale Tawny Port

A full-bodied wine of good flavour produced from locally grown shiraz and grenache grapes. The wine is aged in French oak for three years prior to bottling.

Chateau Rosevale Vinspa

This sparkling wine, based on the local muscatel (muscat gordo blanco) variety, is a clean, fresh, fruity wine with a soft acid finish.

Chateau Rosevale Vintage Claret

A well-balanced dry red showing an agreeable tannin and acid finish. It is a blend of locally grown shiraz and grenache. The wine is aged in small oak for two years prior to bottling, has good colour and pleasant flavour.

Chateau Tahbilk

Chateau Tahbilk Cabernet

A dry red wine produced each year, mainly from cabernet sauvignon grapes, which used to be called burgundy and now, fortunately, is not. The blend is now eighty percent cabernet and twenty percent shiraz, the grapes being grown on heavy loam soil at the 'Chateau Tahbilk' vineyards. They are usually picked between 12 and 13½ Baumé and are kept in big wood for eighteen months to two years. After bottling they are usually kept for at least a year before selling. Of the recent cabernets for sale (and this doesn't include the classic Special Bin Cabernets which generally sell for quite high prices), the 1969, 1968 and 1965 were very good wines, having considerable colour, very marked cabernet fruit flavour and a clean, firm, soft finish. Of previous vintages of this variety, the 1964 had pleasant flavour and a firm palate; the 1963 suffered from excess tannin on the finish and will do so for some considerable time yet; the 1962 wine was a good, straightforward, full-flavoured wine; the 1961 and the 1960 were both wines that seemed to lack complexity. They were pleasant, straightforward wines showing considerable character, but not having that final depth of character which one wishes to see with a classic wine of the country. The 1959, too, was slightly hard, and seemed to lack flavour on the middle palate. I preferred the 1958 which was an extremely well-balanced wine, having a delicious, delicate, developed bouquet showing strong oak and cabernet, and a very clean, full-flavoured palate with a soft, persistent finish.

Reverting to the younger vintages, the 1965 has always shown very well. It always had plenty of

flavour with almost a touch of Coonawarra mint on the nose; the flavour was extremely delicate, complex, with plenty of finesse. In fact, the wine gets better the longer one sees it in the bottle. This was a wine which sold very cheaply, which shows that Australian wine can still be an enormous bargain.

Chateau Tahbilk Marsanne

Made from the marsanne grape which originated from the lower parts of the Cote du Rhone. This is grown at 'Chateau Tahbilk' on soil which varies from sandy to heavy loam. It is usually picked at between 10½ and 11 degrees Baumé with a fair amount of acid showing. It has most distinctive flavour and a rather aggressive skin tannin, almost flinty, finish. This wine is very popular and has been served at many important occasions. It holds pride of place with the winemaker who considers it an outstanding white wine. It does have a unique honeysuckle character which makes it quite definitely a regional wine of particular distinction. To me the variety lacks the depth and finesse of flavour that can be achieved with the chardonnay and semillon in the Hunter Valley, or the aromatic qualities of the Rhine Rieslings of South Australia.

It improves with age in the bottle and we have on many occasions enjoyed some of the old wines that have been stored for over ten years in the cellar. These drink extremely well with an almost honey flavour, although not sweet, a character which I find most appealing.

Chateau Tahbilk Moselle

Sometimes made from the chenin blanc grape, but usually from the marsanne. They are grown on medium loamed soil and picked between 9½ and 10 degrees Baumé. A little natural sugar is left in this wine which still has a crisp, pleasant, acid finish.

Chateau Tahbilk Riesling

Made from the rhine riesling grape grown at 'Chateau Tahbilk' in Victoria on medium loam soil and picked at about 11 to 11½ degrees Baumé. Some very good wines have been made from this grape variety at 'Chateau Tahbilk', although they have lost out in recent years to the more fragrant Rhine Rieslings from South Australia. In days gone past (at least ten years ago) the Rhine Rieslings from 'Chateau Tahbilk' were among the best in the country since they had very good fruit, were very well balanced and had good, crisp, acid finish. However, developments in South Australia, with various new techniques being used in both viniculture and winemaking, have resulted in wines of great aromatic quality and flavour, whereas Tahbilk wines have stayed and maintained their own particular independent character.

The splendid tower which is featured on the label of Tahbilk wines is believed to have been built by Francois de Coueslant manager of 'Chateau Tahbilk' in 1887.

The wines are good, pleasant, and well made; perhaps now they lack the intense fruit character and aromatic qualities of those wines being made elsewhere.

Chateau Tahbilk Shiraz

This wine is also known as Red Hermitage. The grapes are grown at 'Chateau Tahbilk' on light to heavy loam country; are usually picked from 11½ to 12½ degrees Baumé and kept in big wood for eighteen months to two years. The wine is then further stored in the bottle until it is released on to the market. This is a softer wine than the Cabernet, showing a little less tannin, lighter colour, and less depth of flavour; is usually drinkable earlier than the Cabernet.

Notes of tastings of various vintages of this wine reveal a discrepancy of character, which unquestionably is due to the type of year and how the wine-maker felt at the time. In recent years the Shiraz, or Hermitage wine, has been a very pleasant drinking wine of medium colour, medium flavour, good balance, a soft finish; and I think has contained less acidity and tannin than wines of previous years and almost certainly, too, less colour and depth of flavour—but these wines have remained very good value for the money.

Of previous vintages I liked the 1964 and 1965, which were both good wines; light, pleasant, agreeable, showing good fruit and character. The 1962 was a big wine which must have contained some pressings. A very pleasant soft fruity wine, which matured quite well, was the well-balanced and light 1961 vintage. The 1960 seemed to me a bit dirty and the 1957 was rather dumb and hard. Incidentally, the famous 1954 which drank so well for such a long time, a very big rather porty wine, has now richened to an extent when one feels it is quite separate to many of the styles that 'Chateau Tahbilk' can show us. Whatever, the style of the Shiraz now seems to have settled into a slightly less full-bodied, better balanced and quicker maturing wine which I find very pleasant to drink.

Chateau Tahbilk Special Bin Reds

Over the years Eric Purbrick has made many outstanding red wines which he has sold for rather more than the straight commercial Cabernet and Shiraz wines and which at auction command very high prices. Each year he puts aside a cask or so of young red, usually Cabernet Sauvignon, to watch it develop. I can remember in 1965 selecting a wine which later had a very distinguished show career. It now drinks extremely well and will, I believe, drink even better in the future. These special blendings are put away and forgotten for at least five or six years and then they are released for a much higher price than the usual wine.

Of the special binnings which I have seen over the years, I have liked several of the Cabernet wines and also one or two of the shiraz pressings. In these shiraz pressings styles, Eric Purbrick has squeezed, it seems, something extra from the fruit which has resulted in wines of great distinction and style. I particularly remember the 1960 shiraz pressings, Bin 28. This was, and is, a very big wine. The tannin finish is extremely firm and will be there for years, but the wine has the fruit to balance this tannin and the bouquet is building up tremendously. This wine was tasted recently and unquestionably it will live for another twenty years—a wine of enormous power and body and a quite authentic Australian red of great character. I also like the old Bin 11 of 1948. This was one of Mr Purbrick's favourite wines and indeed he has shown it to me on a number of occasions; one or two of the bottles have gone over the hill, but the wine, at best, remains an outstanding wine which will live on in memory for years.

There are more of the Cabernets in the special binnings and these again provide an extremely interesting range. The 1967 wine in cask had outstanding character, a ton of flavour and volume and a superb balance and depth of flavour which I enjoyed enormously. This wine has now been in bottle for some time. The 1966 I thought was not quite up to the standard. This wine seemed to lack that final fullness and richness of style which one looks for (although, of course, we are not looking for port richness, but for true intensity of character with finesse). The 1965 had considerable finesse with delicious flavour, tremendous cabernet fruit and colour and quite a firm finish. After it was bottled one felt it would go forward for many, many years. The 1964 was much the same, with plenty of style and a distinguished show record. The Bin 26 of 1962 was another excellent wine. It contained pressings and therefore a load of all the wine goodies that one finds in the top wines of Tahbilk: tannin, body, fruit, oak, everything. I said in an article in *The Bulletin* some years ago, this was 'a Falstaff of a wine' and I stick to my words today. We had a bottle quite recently and it opened extremely well.

Another very good special Bin was the Bin 22 of 1961, which had very good balance and style altogether. I wrote in tasting notes that there was just a hint of ripe, sun-scorched grapes in the flavour and Eric Purbrick confirms this. This wine has a lot of fruit style and is quite unique.

I remember the Tyrrell's tastings, the Tulloch's tasting and the Tahbilk tasting. Each of these tastings showed that at best, there were some tremendous wines made by these sturdy, independent winemaking people. But all confirmed a feeling I had that with Australian wines there is little continuity of style.

The 'Chateau Tahbilk' binnings, at their best, are amongst the most unique wines in this country; wines that will live and be enjoyed for years.

Chateau Tahbilk—White Hermitage
Made from the White Hermitage grape (Trebbiano, Ugni Blanc, etc.), grown at Chateau Tahbilk in medium loam soil; a higher bearer, rather acid variety, picked at somewhere between 9½ to 10 Baumé. Incidentally, this wine makes excellent Champagne material and has often been purchased by other companies for blending for this purpose.

In order to overcome the rather pronounced acid, approximately 20 per cent of Marsanne is blended with the White Hermitage, which appears then under the Tahbilk label as White Hermitage. It has a light character, without any tremendously pronounced flavour but with more of an aromatic nose than one would expect. It is interesting to note that this rather uninteresting variety can at times produce quite interesting and well-constructed wines. (See also Campbell's Trebbiano entry.)

Chateau Yaldara

This is a very picturesque spot in the southern part of the Barossa Valley near Lyndoch. The cellars, which have been established over the years, comprise a collection of buildings resembling a German schlöss, a French chateau, a Spanish bodega and so on. Thousands of people visit 'Chateau Yaldara' each year and buy wines at a most reasonable price at the cellar door. There is a flourishing interstate mail order business.

The majority of their wines are sold at most economical prices and they have a very large range of sparkling wines, since the owner, Mr Hermann Thumm is a specialist in this type of wine.

Chateau Yaldara Dessert Wines
Like most wineries in the Barossa Valley, the company has a full range of dessert wines, some of which are of extremely high quality.

Chateau Yaldara Red Table Wines
These are pleasant, fruity wines, with one or two of them containing some residual sugar. The owner believes this fills out the middle palate a little better and that the majority of people like wines with a trace of sugar. The shiraz grape from locally grown vineyards is the most common variety used.

Chateau Yaldara Sherries
A full range of sherries is made of which the Flor sherry is probably the most distinguished. The material from the valley is most suitable for making these sherries. After years in wood the flavour has become concentrated and wines of great depth of flavour are produced.

Chateau Yaldara Sparkling Wines
An extremely broad range of sparkling wines is produced by the company, mostly by the Charmat process. They come in many colours and in

different degrees of sweetness. Among them are Extra-Dry Sekt, Dry Sekt, Sweet Sekt, Pink Sekt, Yaldara Pearl White, Yaldara Pearl Pink, Sparkling Burgundy, Sparkling Moselle, Fiesta Spumante, Extra Dry Champagne, Dry Champagne, Prince's Pink Champagne and finally—the best of them all—the great Barossa Champagne range.

Of the latter the Brut is a very pleasant drink, being almost dry and having a pleasant delicate flavour and very good balance.

Chateau Yaldara White Table Wines
A full range of wines are made which sell at most economical prices. The majority of them contain either a trace of sugar or in some cases quite substantial residual sugar. The most interesting of them is the Riesling Spaetlese, which is of the sweeter variety.

Chatterton

Chatterton's Cabernet Shiraz
Made from twenty percent cabernet sauvignon and eighty percent shiraz grown in the lower end of the Barossa Valley. A firm, clean wine of good colour and flavour and a firm tannin finish.

Chatterton's Grenache
A straight grenache wine with, typically, the light ruby colour of the variety and a slight stalky palate with a clean, acid finish. Good easy drinking.

Chatterton's Shiraz Mataro
Made from forty percent shiraz and sixty percent mataro grown in the local Lyndoch vineyards. This wine is a pleasant red of no great distinction, but which provides easy drinking.

Conteville

Conteville Claret
A light dry table wine made from grenache grapes for the local market.

Conteville Dessert Wines
Conteville make a number of dessert wines which are sold in the bottle and flagon under such headings as Cream Sherry, Dry Sherry, Medium Dry Sherry, Muscat, Port, Sweet Sherry and so on. These are standard commercial wines made for the local trade.

Conteville Hermitage
A light dry red made from shiraz grapes, grown on sandy soil at the 'Marginiup' vineyards of the company, seventeen miles from Perth in Western Australia. This wine has done very well as a style at the Perth Royal Show. This Show features classes for Western Australian winemakers and is to be very much commended because of what it has done to lift their standards and raise the quality of their wines. Judges from the eastern States work with local judges and in this way there is much interchange of information and ideas.

The Conteville Hermitage has always featured very well in these local classes and it's probably the wine in which the proprietors themselves have most pride.

Conteville Vintage Port
A very deep coloured, fruity wine made from hermitage grapes. It is bottled very young and left to mature in the bottle.

Conteville White Frontignac
This is a light, dry table wine made from muscat gordo blanco and, as one would expect, has an extremely distinctive muscat flavour.

Coriole

Coriole Cabernet Shiraz
From a small vineyard of sixty acres of vines of only the cabernet and shiraz varieties. This vineyard is opposite the Seaview Winery at McLaren Vale in South Australia. Most of the wine has been sold in bulk, some of it to other wine companies, but the company did bottle a 1970 Shiraz. They intend to do more bottlings in the future.

The 1971 Shiraz won a prize in the 1971 Adelaide Show.

Craigmoor

Craigmoor Cabernet Shiraz
A blend of approximately fifty percent cabernet and fifty percent shiraz, grown in the Mudgee district. The wine has a very deep bright purple colour—a characteristic of most of the cabernet wines of this area, plus a very strong fruit character. The finish is perhaps less astringent than those of many of the young cabernet wines from other areas and with this good fruit and balance the wines round out after many years in the bottle into wines of tremendous vinosity. Perhaps they lack at times the elegance of wines from other districts, but they certainly have a great deal of flavour and character. Jack Roth, who owned the 'Craigmoor' vineyards before his death, had great show success with some of his wines in the early sixties and these wines now drink extraordinarily well.

Craigmoor Chardonnay
A small quantity of the 1971 Chardonnay was kept to one side, the rest of it going into the Semillon/Chardonnay blend. I liked this wine very much shortly after it was made. It had great delicacy with

a pronounced acid finish, and it filled out fairly quickly, producing more flavour than one would expect for a young wine. Certainly I believe that this variety has a great future in the Mudgee district. It will be interesting to see what this company will do with its new oak maturation. Chardonnay is the classic white variety of the famous Burgundy district of France, and they also use a measure of new oak maturation in that district. I see no reason why the two factors, the chardonnay fruit and the new oak flavours, should not combine well together to make smooth, soft wines of great character and style.

Craigmoor Liqueur Muscat

This is a rich wine from the frontignac variety and shows what the Mudgee district can do with fortified wines, since the grapes are grown in good conditions and can be picked off the vines with such high Baumé. It has an extremely fruity, raisiny quality. The colour is a deep apricot and there is a most distinctive full flavour, which will mature in cask and become more concentrated as the years go by. At this stage the wine is probably too light for the Liqueur Muscat style, and needs further time.

Craigmoor Mudgee Shiraz

This fairly full flavoured, soft wine, with a very nice smooth finish, is made from shiraz grapes grown on the local vineyards. It is a well balanced wine, and coupled with the fruit and big oak flavour drinks very well. The 1971 wine won a Gold Medal and a couple of Silvers, and has a big future. Some of the wine appeared to me to be rather woody in style, but there was a cask variation. These wines mature very well in the bottle. Some of Jack Roth's Shiraz wines still drink well today and indicate the capabilities of this district.

Craigmoor Muscatel

This experimental wine made from muscat gordo blanco and semillon has met with considerable local interest. It is a table wine, containing considerable sweetness and has no great delicacy of flavour, but has a sort of rich voluptuousness which appeals to many people.

Craigmoor Rummy Port

This unique 'Craigmoor' wine which was developed by the late Jack Roth was said to have been made by accident in the first place. The unusual name arose from the practice of putting down young port material into freshly used rum casks. It is then stored in these casks for three to six years and draws the mature spirit from the wood. The wine follows the Mudgee tradition of big colour and flavour, yet accompanying this is a very pleasant dry finish which is derived from the effect of the mature rum. The dry finish makes it an easy drinking port and it certainly has captured the interest of a lot of people who like its unique blend of flavours.

Craigmoor Semillon Chardonnay

This wine was first produced in 1971 and the chardonnay variety has done a great deal to give more elegance to the rather coarser semillon of the district. The style is broad, soft, full and fruity, with a pleasant, clean finish which grows in the bottle. The 1971 achieved considerable show success getting several Bronze Medals in different White Burgundy classes. The flavour is developing in the bottle and for those people who like a rich, full-flavoured, soft style, it provides excellent drinking.

Craigmoor Traminer

An experimental wine from young plantings of traminer; it is aromatic and full-flavoured, and may provide a great deal of interest in the future.

A rhine riesling is being produced on a neighbouring vineyard at an altitude of 2,000 feet above sea level. It will be interesting to note the combined effects of hot days, cool nights, summer rainfall, altitude and rich soils.

Craigmoor White Burgundy

A broad, full-flavoured white wine of considerable fruit, made from the semillon grape grown in the local vineyards. It is an ideal wine for early drinking.

d'Arenberg

d'Arenberg Amontillado Dry Sherry

The base wine for this was made in 1948 and matured in hogsheads until blended with palomino in 1968. Some sweeter material has since been added to give the softer finish. A rich, dry sherry, showing good oak and fruit character.

d'Arenberg Burgundy

Made from shiraz and grenache grapes grown in the McLaren Vale hills and fermented together on the skin. These wines are matured in large oak casks for two years before bottling and pick up a character which I describe as 'cowshed'. This 'cowshed' character is of the farmyard, a unique flavour, with strength of flavour, which makes them quite distinct and easy to pick at tastings. The 1967 wine I liked for it has this character, although the character wasn't as assertive as in the 1968 wine. At their best these Burgundies are full, generous wines, for pleasant drinking. I saw the 1964 Burgundy after it had been some years in the bottle and it drank extremely well. Provided this 'cowshed' character doesn't assert itself, in these days of more delicate delights, I will always like these wines for their generosity, flavour and richness of character.

d'Arenberg Cabernet Sauvignon

Made entirely from cabernet sauvignon grapes grown on the hills vineyards in the McLaren Vale district. The wine has been matured in oak prior to bottling. The 1969 Cabernet Sauvignon, which was a big

wine, is described by the makers as light, but I could never understand this. It has a large volume of cabernet fruit, strong and intense, and a big, spicy, wood character which typifies the d'Arenberg style. The wine is slightly hard on the back of the palate, but the oak and fruit flavour will come together and probably in years to come this will be a big, soft wine providing robust drinking. These Cabernet Sauvignon wines from the district always have plenty of colour and style, good flavour and fruit, and they go on for years.

d'Arenberg Cabernet Shiraz

These two varieties are picked and fermented together on skins. The wines are fairly generous, having good fruit flavour, plenty of oak showing plus quite strong cabernet character. The spicy nose is there and the finish is fairly soft. These are not wines of great elegance, but they provide generous and pleasant drinking.

The 1964 Cabernet Shiraz created a furore some years ago. I wrote about it in *The Bulletin* describing it as a big, generous red from South Australia, in an article indicating that a lot of people were getting tired of the thinner wines. They wanted something of substance, something on their tongues—hence the success of the north-east Victorian reds, and those from McLaren Vale, although the styles are really quite dissimilar. The response was immensely gratifying to d'Arry Osborne, and certainly to me, in that d'Arry sold out of the wine almost instantly: not only sold out of that wine, but sold all the red wine in his cellar. I like to feel that this enabled him to carry on to develop the style and provide wines which are basically very good, generous and full-flavoured.

d'Arenberg Claret

Made from shiraz grown in the McLaren Vale, fermented on skins, and matured in oak for two

years. The wine has a very good, fruity shiraz nose, and lacks the extreme oak aggressiveness of some of the other wines. As a straight McLaren Vale dry red of generous flavour, it is a good drinking wine. These wines mature; they do very well with three or four years in the bottle, and they continue to drink well after that.

d'Arenberg Gold Medal Burgundy 1969

This Burgundy is made from shiraz and grenache grapes grown at McLaren Vale, fermented together on the skins, and matured in large oak casks for two years. It has now developed into a soft, full, round style of wine which contains a hint of the spicy, woody character that I often talk about. The wine has won several awards, including Gold Medals in Queensland in 1970 and in Sydney in 1972, and several Silver and Bronzes.

This wine has more intensity of character and fruit than the ordinary burgundy. It has a stronger character altogether, including more aggressive oak flavours. Is it oak spiciness? I have had several talks about it with the makers and it is not entirely from oak but, from the grenache variety, from the fruit of the shiraz and from the oak combined with them. Certainly it is a big, generous character that a lot of people seem to enjoy, though I feel that the predominant flavour is now slightly overdone. Whatever, this wine is an interesting and unique style from the McLaren Vale and has impressed the judges on several occasions.

d'Arenberg Riesling

This Riesling, made from straight rhine riesling, is a fairly full-flavoured, fruity wine, which lacks the delicacy associated with altitude vineyards and other makers of white wine. A small percentage of white frontignac is blended in with the wine to enhance the fruitiness.

d'Arenberg Special Award Burgundy 1967

This famous wine has greatly enhanced d'Arry Osborne's reputation throughout Australia. It was made from seventy-five percent grenache and twenty-five percent shiraz fermented on the skins together, plus some shiraz pressings matured in oak for two years before bottling. It has won Gold Medals in shows in Melbourne, Adelaide, Sydney and Brisbane.

I reviewed this wine some years ago and said: 'The wine has a highly aromatic nose and this was the first remarkable thing about it. It's heavily spiced, extremely voluminous, quite distinctive. This goes through onto the palate and those lovers of full-flavoured wines, dense and intense, will find everything they want in its richness and full fruit. The finish is quite soft and smooth and shows clean acid and tannin. Again, it is good drinking, althqugh it will go on unquestionably for a number of years yet.'

I think the 1967 wine had more fruit to it perhaps than the subsequent wines, which still seem to me to have more oak character. This fruit was certainly in very fine balance. The 1967 wine is quite unique and has greatly impressed many people. Some people even regard the style as one of the most important in Australia.

d'Arenberg Vintage Port 1969
This Port is made from shiraz grown locally and bottled very young. It has an incredibly intense black, purple colour; an extraordinarily rich, full flavour and a very strong, firm, tannin finish. Possibly the wine is a little too sweet for some people, although there is the compensating fruit and tannin. Unquestionably, it will throw an extremely heavy crust and it should be binned away for at least fifteen to twenty years before it will reach its full maturity. This is wine which will live for at least thirty or forty years.

d'Arenberg White d'Arenberg 1970
This is made from palomino grapes grown in the McLaren Vale and fermented on the skins for twenty-four hours for flavour extraction under controlled temperature conditions. It is an extremely rich, full-flavoured wine that appeals to a lot of people. To me it lack delicacy. The wine has won several Bronze medals in Queensland, Adelaide, Melbourne and Sydney (but has never won the top awards). It is considered a good straightforward, full-flavoured wine without great fault.

De Bortoli

De Bortoli's Burgundy
A medium to full-bodied dry red made from the shiraz grape.

De Bortoli's Chablis
A sweet wine made for the local market.

De Bortoli's Champagnes—Pink and White
Medium sweet, sparkling wines, made on the Italian style for the local market.

De Bortoli's Claret
A rather agreeable, crisp, young dry red, made for quick, enjoyable drinking.

De Bortoli's Crema Marsala
A rich red dessert wine infused with herbs.

De Bortoli's Cream Sherry
A full-flavoured, sweet dessert wine made from the muscat gordo blanco grape and other varieties.

De Bortoli's Dry Sherry
A pale, quite dry, crisp sherry.

De Bortoli's Flor Fino Sherry
Quite an astringent sherry made on the Flor process.

De Bortoli's Frontignac
A rich dessert wine of some wood age.

De Bortoli's King Sherry
A sweet, luscious dessert sherry, matured in wood for some considerable time.

De Bortoli's Marsala All'uovo
A rich red dessert wine infused with herbs and further enriched with egg extract.

De Bortoli's Mavrodaphne
A rich, heavy red dessert wine, made for the Greek market.

De Bortoli's Moselle
A light, semi-sweet wine made from the semillon grape.

De Bortoli's Muscat—Brown
A popular dessert wine with plenty of grape flavour.

De Bortoli's Muscat—White
Another popular dessert wine made from the muscat gordo blanco grape.

De Bortoli's Nericon Estate Cabernet Sauvignon
Made entirely from cabernet sauvignon, grown twenty miles from the de Bortoli's cellar at Bilbul (NSW). The vineyards are on the hillside in red, sandy loam, over lime and stony subsoil. This wine has plenty of colour and fruit flavour and a good firm finish.

De Bortoli's Nerocon Estate Shiraz
A medium to full-bodied dry red, of good shiraz fruit which has been matured in new French oak prior to bottling.

De Bortoli's Passito
A sweet dessert wine made from the muscat gordo blanco variety.

De Bortoli's Private Bin Claret
A clean, dry red wine made from shiraz grapes and aged in French oak.

De Bortoli's Private Bin Golden Cream Sherry
A popular dessert wine.

De Bortoli's Private Bin Medium Sweet Sherry
A popular wine matured in wood for four years.

De Bortoli's Private Bin Muscat
Made from frontignac and matured in large wood for some considerable time.

De Bortoli's Private Bin Port
An interesting ruby, fortified with brandy spirit and matured in French oak for seven years.

De Bortoli's Private Bin Reserve Brown Muscat
Made from the frontignac variety and matured in oak for six years.

De Bortoli's Private Bin Sweet Sherry
A medium bodied dessert wine matured in oak for nearly ten years.

De Bortoli's Retzina
A dry dinner wine with induced pine resin flavour, made for the Greek market.

De Bortoli's Riesling Hock
A light dry white table wine.

De Bortoli's River Gold
A full-bodied, luscious, sweet dinner wine.

De Bortoli's Royal Port
A light, clean ruby port.

De Bortoli's Sauterne
A sweet and light, popular dinner wine.

De Bortoli's Semi-Sweet Sherry
A medium flavoured, medium bodied sherry, which has considerable local popularity.

De Bortoli's Sparkling Burgundy
A tangy, sparkling wine made from the shiraz variety.

De Bortoli's Sparkling Moselle
A semi-sweet sparkling wine.

De Bortoli's Strawberry Marsala
A red dessert wine, infused with herbs, enriched with egg extract and strawberry flavoured.

De Bortoli's Sweet Sherry
A pale, sweet dessert wine.

De Bortoli's Vermouth
A range of vermouths is made—white, sweet and dry, French and Italian style.

De Bortoli's Vin Rosé
Virtually a light, semi-dry red wine.

De Bortoli's Vittorio Lambrusco
A sweet, sparkling red wine.

De Bortoli's Vittorio Spumante
A sweet sparkling wine made of the muscat gordo blanco for the Italian market.

The Dover Wine Company

A range of wines is made from grapes grown on their own vineyards at Aldinga or the 'Blewitt Springs' vineyards. Mr G. A. Patritti is the winemaker. The family has been making wine for over fifty years—the biggest market being the Italians of Melbourne suburbs (in spite of the fact that the company is in South Australia).

Up until the late 1950s the company made entirely dry red wine but then started making fortified wines which are sold mainly in barrels, straight to the families who bottle it off for themselves. However, recently the company bought a semi-automatic bottling line and will be bottling more and more wines in the future.

The wines that Mr Patritti is particularly pleased with are the Claret, Riesling, Vintage Ports and Burgundy.

Drayton, W., & Sons Pty Ltd
Drayton's
Bellevue Dry Red—Cabernet Sauvignon
This wine is not likely to be produced as a straight wine year after year. The cabernet sauvignon was planted in the Hunter Valley in the 1960s by the Drayton family. It seems that they still prefer the shiraz or hermitage variety, but they planted the cabernet to see what could be done with it as blending material and also for its known sturdiness under bad conditions. It seems that in a poor year the cabernet sauvignon will flourish, whereas the hermitage will not. Such a year was 1971. Most of the hermitage wines made in the Hunter Valley suffered badly from grape rot, and this is reflected in the wines. The cabernet sauvignon, however, was picked later and the skins were unbroken so there was very little rot in the bunches. Consequently the wines are full-flavoured. They have magnificent colour and they are sturdy and quite sound.

The 1971 Drayton's Cabernet Sauvignon has been stored in small wood and has the most excellent wood/fruit combination of flavours. This is one of the best red wines I have seen in the Hunter Valley in the 1971 vintage. It appears that it will be bottled separately. This is not always a practice that Drayton's will follow, I am told, but in a poor year, when the cabernet is quite exceptional and the hermitage is poor, they see no point in blending it.

Drayton's
Bellevue Dry Red—Cabernet Shiraz Blend
This style started in 1967, though the Draytons had evolved a Cabernet/Shiraz blend previously. On that occasion in 1965 the cabernet came from another vineyard in north-east Victoria. In 1967, however, the first cropping of their plantings of cabernet came into fruit and this wine was blended in with some

Bill Chambers of Rutherglen, Vic., popular wine judge at shows in Melbourne, Adelaide and Sydney.

The long established 'Bellevue' vineyard located in the foothills of the Mt View range just north-west of Mt Pleasant, Hunter Valley, N.S.W., and owned by W. Drayton and Sons.

Bottle cellars at Henschke's winery at Keyneton, S.A.
C. A. Henschke has built up a fine reputation with his
steely, highly acid rieslings which he makes from grapes
grown in the Barossa Ranges.

shiraz to make the Bin 780. The Bin 780 was a light to medium-bodied wine.

The percentage in the following year, Bin 880 of 1968, was much higher. There was much more cabernet in this wine, being a forty percent cabernet and sixty percent shiraz. It is a very pleasant wine with a lot of flavour, just a touch of oak and the two varieties in the oak have come together to make an extremely well-balanced wine of good flavour and style. The acid finish was clean and pleasant and the wine unquestionably a new addition to the style of Drayton's wines.

Since then they have been putting this style out in approximately the same proportions, forty percent cabernet to sixty percent shiraz and the wine is of uniformly high quality, with good colour, very good flavour and just a touch of oak which makes it so appealing. The style, however, is different from the normal Drayton's dry red style. It's an addition to the range and a new dimension and it also adds a new dimension to the Hunter Valley.

Drayton's
Bellevue Dry Red Hermitage

The Draytons at 'Bellevue' have now been bottling their dry red wines since the late fifties, although, into the early sixties, they still sold a large quantity of their wine in bulk.

The red wines over the years have provided a most interesting spectrum, from the light 1963 and 1967 vintages to the medium-bodied 1964s and the very heavy, full-flavoured 1965s and 1966s. Since the Hunter Valley is very susceptible to vintage variation, these wines in themselves vary from year to year. At their best they are extremely big, full-flavoured wines with all the Hunter earthiness and character. They round out very quickly, fill out the middle palate and have soft, lingering finishes.

The Bins 625 and 650 of 1966 are wines which have enormous flavour and which will live on for years.

In the early 1960s Draytons suffered from some dirty wood problems which affected their wines quite badly. Now, happily, all these problems are overcome and the family is making splendid wines year after year, which are eagerly sought by wine collectors.

Drayton's
Bellevue Dry White—Semillon

This is the standard white production line of the vineyard and is made from straight Hunter riesling (semillon).

These wines are some of the biggest in the Hunter district with a strong, mouth-rich quality, which sometimes verges on the coarse side. This coarseness, however, does not worry winelovers who have learned to enjoy the particular style. In many years the Draytons have produced classic white wines that live for many years and have a tremendously rich, deep flavour after some years of bottle maturation.

They started bottling their own white wines early in the 1960s but, unhappily, these did not meet with immediate success. Indeed some wines that I particularly recall, the C.22 of 1963 is one example, were hardly bought at all. It is now a great pleasure to taste that particular wine, which after many years in the bottle has an enormous flavour and rich robe of great quality and balance. There have been many celebrated wines made by Draytons since then. They drink well as young wines, with a freshness and appealing round palate, which is softer when young than the majority of the Hunter Valley wines. But with years the richness and fullness deepen and develop. These wines are some of the most effective white styles in the district.

Drayton's
Bellevue Rhine Riesling

This is a most interesting wine made from straight rhine riesling grapes grown in the 'Bellevue' vineyards in the Hunter Valley—interesting because the wine itself does not have the aromatic qualities nor the fruit style of the South Australian Rhine Rieslings. In fact, it is difficult to pick it out as a rhine riesling variety at all. On at least half the occasions it is tasted blind, it is picked as a straight semillon. It is usually identified, however, as a straight Hunter, because the area has the ability to give its wines its own character, before the varietal character asserts itself. Indeed, it is an experienced taster who can then start to sort out the various varietal characters within the district itself.

The Rhine Rieslings have an extremely interesting, almost nutty style to them. They mature fairly quickly, in spite of their clean, fresh acid, and they have a delightful balance and full flavour. This flavour is of the white burgundy character, although of course the variety itself has nothing to do with white burgundy in pure terms at all. The wines mature quickly and have a marvellously rich, big middle palate style with a soft lingering finish. They are very mouth filling like most of the quality Hunter whites, and are at their best after some years in the bottle.

Drayton's
Bellevue Sweet Wines

Draytons make a quantity of sweet whites, sweet reds and sauternes within the district. These are sold at the winery as single wines or blended in with other material from other districts.

Drayton's
Bellevue White Burgundy

This is an interesting binning of wine, usually coming out under the 38 sequence of numbers—838, 938 and so on. The style was evolved in 1967 by Reg Drayton and the author. We decided that we were looking for the old style of Hunter white, that is, one with a full, rich, round, quite full-bodied palate and a fairly high acid style of finish. 1967 was the ideal vintage

to evolve the style. The wine was finally collected from a number of casks and put together. It contained a small percentage of pressings wine and also some fresh acid wine to give the necessary flint finish. The success of the wine was considerable, because after some time in the bottle it started to win awards and, finally, won many prizes in various shows.

This is a style of wine which will live for years and may justly be regarded as an authentic Hunter of the particular style.

The 1968 edition 838 was a much rounder, softer wine with a great depth of middle-palate flavour, but a much less acid finish.

The 938 of 1969 was something in between these two wines, having some of the acidity of the 1967 and the early flavour of the 1968. It is to be hoped that Draytons persevere with this style which is rooted in so much of the tradition of the Hunter Valley.

Elliott's Wines Pty Ltd

Elliott's
Hunter Valley Dry Red

This wine is made from straight hermitage (shiraz) in the Hunter Valley. Elliott's main vineyard, 'Tallawanta', situated opposite Hungerford Hill on the Broke Road, has been there probably for forty to fifty years. It has a very low yield, but, the very lowness of the yield does aid quality. The quality is generally high and at their best the wines produced are extraordinarily rich, and intensely full-flavoured wines, which develop a tremendously interesting and complex bouquet over the years in bottle.

Sometimes you may detect in the young wines a quantity of free sulphur (SO2) which Doug Elliott uses to virtually insulate his wines against the

rigours of bottling. Some people have been disappointed with the amount of sulphur; of course, they should realize that they were drinking the wine too young. After a time in bottle this disappears and the wine is the better for it.

Max Lake points out that the Elliott Dry Red reflects more than any other single house in the Hunter the quality of the years in the Hunter. The Elliott differences in vintages *do* reflect the general standard in the Hunter, and therefore it would be most interesting to trace back over the last few years to see what the differences were.

In 1972 extremely rich, heavy wines were made full of tremendous colour, wonderful flavour and great fruit. These wines will live twenty, thirty, forty years.

1971 was a light year with a great deal of rain and most wines suffering from some rot. This rot has cleared up a great deal in some of the wines, but they are still light and ordinary at the best.

1970 was a medium year and generally good wines were made; wines that will mature in four or five years from the vintage date and will hold up for some time after that.

1969 was an extremely big year; very good wines were made with a great deal of colour, power and richness of flavour. The bouquet is building on these wines now.

1968 was a light style. The wines were clean, quite fruity, well-balanced and fairly good drinking two or three years after bottling.

1967 was a medium year. It was a fairly light summer, not very hot, and the wines had good character. They are nice supple wines that will drink very well within five, six, seven years of their being made.

1966 and 1965 were both extremely big years. Elliott's 1965 dry red is a very good wine indeed, something like the 1972, with a great deal of flavour, and heavy fruit. A wine which will mature over the years, but which is already starting to show the depth of quality which it contains. I feel that the 1966 wine is a trifle bigger, but somehow rounder than the 1965; but it has less finesse. However, it is a most enjoyable wine and, although big, is maturing quicker than the 1965.

1964 was a light to medium style. The wines were clean and were attractive quite quickly; they are still drinking very well today.

The 1963 was a more full-bodied style; a wine which had a great deal of depth on the middle palate and which did reflect the change in year of 1963 after the poor years before it.

One of the best Hunter wines I ever saw was the 1945 made by Doug Elliott's father, Bob. 1945 was a big year, and this wine had, over the 20-odd years of maturation, developed into something quite rare in wine in Australia. I am quite sure that this wine, if shown overseas, would startle people into a realization of how good Australian red from certain areas can be.

Elliott's
Hunter Valley Riesling
Made from semillon grown at Oakvale on the Broke
Road and also at the Fordwich vineyard and the
Belford vineyards to the north of Pokolbin in the
Hunter Valley. Doug Elliott has vineyards in these
three separate locations.

The Belford vineyards produce perhaps one of the
most interesting whites in the Hunter Valley. This is
a rich, full-flavoured wine; the description of the
flavour is often called honey style, by this they
don't mean they are sweet, but rather that they have
that peculiar, deep estery quality of honey, and on the
middle palate have a flavour which is quite like that
of a honeycomb. These wines mature marvellously
in the bottle. On some occasions I've called them
'vanillan'.

The Oakvale vineyards are now very small and do
not have a great deal of bearing upon the success of
wines of the company.

The Fordwich vineyards are the main sustenance
of the white wines. The vines are healthy, they bear well
and they provide most of the tonnage available. The
wines are either made separately or are made together
with the Belford wines, or blended with the Belford
wines. There are label distinctions from year to year.

The charm of the Elliott white wines is that though
they vary in style from year to year they do all develop
very well in the bottle and they always have tremendous balance. I cannot recall really acid wines coming
from Elliott's at any time. They all seem to have a
little extra dimension on the middle palate; and yet,
unlike some other small makers in the valley, they
do not suffer from any coarseness and are always very
well-balanced.

1972 was a good quality year. The wines are
medium-bodied; they are not as heavy as the reds
and are much lighter, rounder and softer wines.

1971 again was a poor year. A lot of the semillon
grapes suffered from bunch rot and this is reflected
in the wines. The 1971 Belford, however, was an
outstanding wine, but the Belford area did not suffer
as much as the Pokolbin and Rothbury parishes.

1970 was an interesting year. The wines are medium-
bodied and contain fair alcohol, but they seem to
lack the body and flavour of a good Elliott.

The 1969 whites were really very big, rich, full-
flavoured wines; almost on the verge of coarseness,
if one could say that of an Elliott wine; very much the
old Hunter style, with enormous depth of character.
The nose will build up in the bottle to a very rich,
voluminous style.

The 1968 wines were light to start with, but they
built up very well in character. These wines had more
fresh acidity than is usual with the style of Elliott
white wines, but I like it very much. At a recent
tasting I saw some 1968s which had delightfully
delicate, middle palate intensity of flavour, yet still
with this crisp finish.

The 1967 wines were bigger; more of a medium-
bodied, fuller-flavoured style altogether and more
towards the white burgundy style with quite a rich
complexity of flavour.

The 1967s were very round, quick developing
wines. They had a lot of richness and roundness to
them, being softer wines of a very big white burgundy
style. They developed rather quickly and could be
enjoyed quite soon after vintage.

In the 1966 and 1965 years very good, high quality
wines were made, although they didn't have a great
deal of fullness of body. These wines had depth of
flavour and they matured very well in the bottle,
retaining fresh acid.

The 1964 was rather a light, pleasant, crisp wine,
but one which you didn't feel was going to last and
develop for many years.

The 1963 was a bit bigger, fuller, and rounder.
The 1963s in my cellar certainly still drink very well
today.

The Elliott white wines are outstanding in the
Hunter. From a small vineyard and a small maker,
they represent a very interesting and complex line of
full-flavoured wines which are quite unique and quite
distinct and which contribute a great deal to the
quality reputation of the district.

Faranda

Faranda Claret
A dry red wine made by a small West Australian
company from shiraz and grenache grapes grown
on their own vineyards. They also make a very
small quantity of white wine from the muscat gordo
blanco variety.

Gehrig Brothers

Gehrig Brothers Red Wines
Barney Gehrig, the owner and winemaker, produces
a Shiraz and Cabernet blend and also a straight
Cabernet Sauvignon from grapes grown locally on
the 'Barnawartha' vineyards of the company. The
wines have plenty of colour; a typical north-east
Victorian rich volume of flavour; and a clean, firm,
persistent tannin finish. They soften with bottle age
into very pleasant drinking wines.

Gehrig Brothers White Wines
Various white wines are produced from a variety
which Barney Gehrig calls pinot riesling, also from
rhine riesling and from white hermitage. The latter
variety produces a most distinctive and agreeable
white wine which has quite a delicate flavour (certainly when you take the area and the variety into
mind). This very clean, dry White Hermitage with a

soft acid finish, is well made and is much coveted by other companies. Because of this delicacy of flavour and the very clean, fresh, acid finish, much of it has been used in the past by other companies as champagne material.

Glenloth Wines Ltd

Glenloth Bin 108 Cabernet Shiraz
Made from 25 percent cabernet sauvignon from McLaren Vale; and 75 percent shiraz, most of which comes from the east of the Happy Valley Reservoir, south of Adelaide.

Bin 108 is made from the selected wines of one particular vintage blended together and regarded as the best bottling from the company as far as the dry reds are concerned. This is a wine of considerable fruit and soft, firm tannin that will mature for some years.

Glenloth Bin 105 Rhine Riesling
A selection of the best rhine riesling wines of the vintages made each year and bottled in July. The grapes grown at Langhorne Creek and McLaren Vale show the full fruitiness of the variety and this bin was originally introduced to show that fine whites, as well as reds, can be produced from areas south of Adelaide.

Glenloth Bin 107 Shiraz
Shiraz grapes, grown in the O'Halloran Hill, Happy Valley and Clarendon districts, south of Adelaide, go into this wine. These vineyards are of varying soil types and elevation, the latter having an effect on the temperature during ripening.

The selection of these wines to produce Bin 107 is made soon after vintage when the wines are blended and matured in oak. It produces a fruity wine with a soft finish.

Glenloth Claret
This general drinking claret is accompaniment for light meals and comes from shiraz and grenache grapes grown south of Adelaide.

Glenloth Coromandel Claret
This sound claret style of wine is made from shiraz grapes, 80 percent grown in the O'Halloran Hill area and 20 percent in the Kingston and Moorook areas of the River Murray. The wine is named after the Coromandel Valley, which is local to the 'Glenloth' winery and recalls the ship of that name which brought settlers to the area in 1837.

Glenloth Coromandel Riesling
A blend made from semillon and rhine riesling grapes grown in the Murray River area and also from the

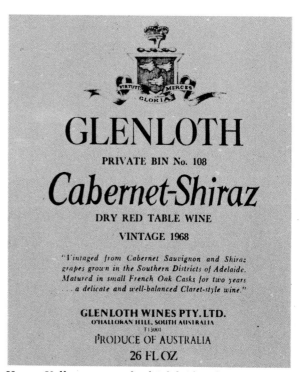

Happy Valley area south of Adelaide. This is an inexpensive, but pleasant, white wine of reasonable balance with quite nice fresh acid.

Glenloth Cream Sherry
A sweet, rather luscious wine, made from pedro ximenez and muscat gordo blanco grapes from the Murray River area.

Glenloth Fino Palido Sherry
The base wine is made from pedro ximenez grapes grown at O'Halloran Hill. The Flor character is obtained after two years on Flor culture, after which the wine is fortified and blended.

Glenloth Glen Pearl
This is a pleasant, bubbly party wine of some sweetness made from sultana and palomino grapes grown in the Murray Valley district.

Glenloth Golden Muscat
Made from muscat gordo blanco grapes grown near Waikerie. It has a distinctive muscat character.

Glenloth Hock
A quaffable drinking dry white, made from pedro ximenez and clare riesling grapes grown around Happy Valley and O'Halloran Hill, south of Adelaide.

Glenloth Lorraine Champagne Brut
Made by the traditional Methode Champenoise. A dry, sparkling wine, showing delicate clean fruit and nice acid crispness on the finish.

Glenloth Lorraine Champagne Private Cuvee
This is basically the same wine as the unsweetened Brut, but is treated with the usual dosage to make it less than bone dry.

Glenloth Lorraine Rhine Riesling
Eighty percent of this wine is rhine riesling from grapes grown in the Southern Vales. Most of the vineyards are on fairly sandy soil, containing a high quantity of limestone. The extra bouquet may be attributed to a combination of factors, including the cooler, favourable ripening period found in these areas.

Glenloth Moselle
This is a slightly sweet wine with a crisp acid finish, and made from semillon and pedro ximenez grapes grown around the 'Glenloth' winery.

Glenloth Old Blended Port
Shiraz and grenache from McLaren Vale have gone into this blend of wine since the early fifties. The wine is matured in casks, kept in a warm spot in the cellars and blended on a Solera type system from year to year.

Glenloth Riesling
A refreshing, crisp, dry white made mainly from semillon grapes grown in the O'Halloran Hill area.

Glenloth Rosé
A clean, fruity wine made from free-run grenache juice. The grenache comes from the local district.

Glenloth Sauternes
A popular sweet wine made from local pedro ximenez grapes grown in the O'Halloran Hill district; bottled when less than one year old.

Glenloth Shiraz
A light, claret style dry red made from shiraz grapes grown in the area south of Adelaide.

Glenloth Solera Medium Dry Sherry
This is a semi-sweet sherry made from local pedro ximenez grapes and matured for eighteen months in small wood before bottling.

Glenloth Sparkling Wines
The company sells both a Sparkling Burgundy and Sparkling Moselle. The burgundy has a fair amount of clean tannin to balance its considerable fruitiness. The moselle is not as sweet as some of the wines sold of this type.

Glenloth Sweet Sherry
Pedro ximenez and muscat gordo blanco grapes grown near Waikerie along the River Murray are constituents of this attractive, round, fairly sweet wine.

COROMANDEL RIESLING

VINTAGE 1970
Here is a crisp, clean white wine made from Riesling grapes grown at Langhorne Creek, and on properties overlooking Happy Valley reservoir in the historic Coromandel district south of Adelaide.

GLENLOTH WINES PTY. LTD. PRODUCE OF AUSTRALIA
NET CONTENTS: 26 FLUID OUNCES

Glenloth Tawny Port
A pleasant, sweet dessert wine, made from shiraz and grenache grapes and matured in big wood.

Glenloth White Hermitage
Made only from white hermitage grapes grown in a vineyard across the road from the 'Glenloth' winery. The original vines were planted in fairly sandy soil about sixty years ago. Each year the grapes are the last to ripen. The wine is soft, full and fruity with considerable forward flavour and just a trace of coarseness on the back of the palate. It is probably best when quite young.

Glenview

Glenview Alouette
A low-priced, bulk-processed, demi-sec sparkling wine made from Barossa-grown pedro ximenez, clare riesling and trebbiano (white hermitage) grapes.

Glenview All'uovo
Typical sweet marsala with added richness from non-irrigated, very ripe grenache grapes.

Glenview Barossa Muscat
A muscat made from muscat gordo blanco grapes from the Barossa Valley and Waikerie District of the River Murray, well aged in oak casks.

GLEN VIEW *Riesling*

Produced and Bottled by
P. T. FALKENBERG Pty. Ltd.
Glen View Vineyards, Tanunda

SOUTH AUSTRALIAN WINE

Glenview Burgundy
Carignane, grenache and mataro grapes grown in the Barossa Valley go into this burgundy which then has a short time in large casks for maturation.

Glenview Cream Sherry
Pedro ximenez and palomino grown in the Barossa Valley, together with Waikerie muscat gordo blanco free-run juice keep the lighter style and freshness of grape flavour in this sherry.

Glenview Dry Red
Made from carignane and mataro grapes from the Barossa Valley, together with Loxton shiraz, this dry red is then matured in large oak for twelve to eighteen months.

Glenview Dry Sherry
Palomino and pedro ximenez grapes grown in the Barossa Valley go into this sherry which is not made on the Flor process. It is aged in wood for three years in old small oak.

Glenview Export Vinade
This wine, bulk fermented on the Charmat principle, is a unique, low-alcohol sparkling wine with a 'head'. It is an excellent summer drink for those who do not like bitterness.

Glenview Fiesta Pearl
There are white and pink varieties of these wines which are made on the Charmat principle from pedro ximenez, palomino and semillon grapes.

Glenview Madeira
An old, sweet, wood-matured white wine, made completely from the madeira (semillon) variety grown in the Barossa Valley.

Glenview Medium Dry Sherry
Made from palomino and pedro ximenez grapes; not made on the Flor process, and blended with an old, sweet, white wine for softness and sweetening.

Glenview Moccambo Coffee Marsala
'Glenview' have produced the first Australian-made Mocha Marsala. They use imported coffee extract of high standard and their own variation of marsala base.

Glenview Montana Spumante
A Charmat produced spumante, using non-irrigated grapes and, therefore, probably more fragrant and perhaps less 'mawkish' than some other Australian styles. It is quite sweet in the traditional manner.

Glenview Moselle
From pedro ximenez and clare riesling grapes, grown in the local vineyards. Temperature controlled fermentation and early bottling have given a rather fresh style, with a little residual sugar on the middle palate.

Glenview Reserve Port
This port is made from shiraz, grenache and mataro grapes from the company's own vineyards in the Barossa Valley and matured in big wood for six years.

Glenview Rich Port
Again, this is a port made from shiraz, grenache and mataro; but it is matured for two to three years only, depending on the size of the vintage. Added character is showing from new fermentation techniques under controlled conditions.

Glenview Riesling Hock
A light, fresh style fermented under controlled conditions from clare riesling, pedro ximenez and palomino grapes from the Barossa Valley.

Glenview Rosé
This rosé, made from grenache grapes, together with pedro ximenez to lighten the colour, is almost an orange-pink colour. The wine shows quite marked development rather than the usual fresh and fruity rosé character.

Glenview Sweet Sherry
Well-ripened pedro ximenez grapes, which are fermented on skins for extra flavour and character, make this sherry which is then aged for three years in old oak 500 and 1,000 gallon casks.

Glenview Vermouth
An Italian-style vermouth made from well-ripened grenache grapes; herbs of a special blend are steeped and infused into the wine. It is a rather bland, sweet

style, and carries a slightly less bitter taste than some other sweet vermouths.

Glenview White Port
A rather rare traditional white port style. Very ripe madeira and pedro ximenez grapes are fermented on the skins and then matured for up to six years in very small casks.

Glenview Krondorf Clare Riesling
One of the new varietal wines now being offered; made by Jim Irvine of the Augustine Barossa Valley Estates. With their new plant and equipment on the site of the old winery at 'Glenview', they are now able to make more delicate styles. The grapes for the Clare Riesling are grown on medium sand over red clay on the foothills of of the eastern Barossa Range at an altitude of about 1,000 feet. These grapes are picked when they have good sugar/acid balance and are made into a delicate, fruity wine of appealing style and character.

Glenview Krondorf Claret
This claret is made from mataro, carignane and shiraz. The mataro and carignane are old vines, grown in Adelaide alluvial clay soils—thick black clay which throws excellent flavour and colour.

Glenview Krondorf Fine Old Liqueur Frontignac
A rich old dessert wine; a vintage from the true frontignac grapes grown at the 'Krondorf' vineyards. The vineyard is sandy loam, with ironstone pebbles. The age of the wine is unknown because they have no records available—but it is extremely old. It has a magnificent, honeyish middle palate, with really concentrated intense flavour. The wine has been stored up high, near the roof and the extremes of

temperature have again mellowed it over the years. There has been a high evaporation rate, but they have been using a modified Solero system in which only a portion is taken from the cask which is then topped up with slightly younger wines. I tasted this wine some years ago when on a visit to 'Glenview' and was delighted with the rich old style of wine.

Glenview Krondorf Fine Old Tawny Port—Vintage 1957
Made from Barossa shiraz, together with grenache and carignane from the 'Krondorf' vineyards; matured, firstly in oak 500s and then in hogsheads until bottling.

The wine has a distinctive fruity flavour, quite developed, with plenty of complexity and intensity of character. Cognac casks which they have used in the final maturation have dried off the finish of this particular wine.

Glenview Krondorf Semillon
A delicate white wine first made in 1972. The grapes were picked when the sugar/acid balance was most suitable for making delicate well-balanced dry whites of well-rounded, soft flavour and smooth finish.

Gracerray

Gracerray Dessert Wines
Made by the company of Stanton and Killeen at the 'Gracerray' winery at Rutherglen in north-east Victoria.

Gracerray Dessert Wines are rich fruity wines made from the distinctive Rutherglen brown muscat (frontignac) and shiraz grapes. They are grown on red loams without irrigation in the vineyards planted by Mr J. C. Stanton in the 1920's. Grapes are picked at Baumé's ranging between 14 degrees and 17 degrees and fortified to finish at 4-5 degrees Baumé for ports and 7-10 degrees Baumé for muscats. These wines retain the full flavour of the grape varieties used and yet have sufficient tannin to offset any cloying sweetness.

Special vintages of them include:

Gracerray Frontignac
Made in the years when Baumé's do not exceed 15 degrees. Lighter in colour and body, but still rich in muscat flavour and bouquet; a wine which will develop enormously over the years.

Gracerray Golden Medal Muscat
This big, full-bodied Rutherglen muscat is the best muscat produced at 'Gracerray' for many years. This wine won a Gold Medal award at Melbourne in 1961. Made from grapes picked at 17½ degrees Baumé. It is a big, full-bodied wine with a deep red colour; rich in flavour and bouquet; yet with a dry,

tannin finish to dispel all trace of cloying on the palate, that shows a maturity far beyond its age.

Gracerray Liqueur Muscat
A blend of muscats from the 1960-70 vintages. It is a full-bodied Rutherglen Muscat with deep colour and a nice balance of fresh muscat character and wood age: a very good dessert wine at a most reasonable price.

Gracerray Old Port
A ruby-tawny blend from vintages 1962-70. A pleasant wine of moderate fullness and sweetness, but with ample flavour and dry finish.

Gracerray 1968 Port
Full-bodied with deep colour and rich, fruity bouquet: a wine full of flavour. There is evidence of the small oak in which the wine was matured. This wine won a first prize in Rutherglen in 1969.

Gracerray 1971 Vintage Port
The best red sweet wine made at Gracerray since 1937. Made entirely from shiraz, which was picked at 16½ degrees Baumé. It is rich in colour, bouquet and flavour; with a good balance of sugar, acid and tannin, and a softness and maturity which belies its youth. This wine is bottled to mature as a vintage port.

Gracerray Dry Reds
In 1969 new plantings of shiraz were begun and the table wines from this vineyard have been given the name 'Moodemere Red' from nearby Lake Moodemere. A proportion of this vineyard was planted to cabernet in 1972. The 1971 vintage represents the first picking of the shiraz. It is light in style and high in acid, but with characteristic Rutherglen bouquet and flavour.

Gravina

Gravina Claret
A full flavoured dry red made from grenache and shiraz grapes grown on vineyards at Shepparton in Central Victoria, which were established in 1945.

Gravina Fortified Wines
The 'Gravina' vineyards produce a number of muscats, ports and sherries, which are made at the winery from material grown on their own vineyards. The majority of this wine is sold in bulk to consumers around the Goulburn Valley area.

Hamilton's Wines

Hamilton's Adelaide Riesling
Made from rhine riesling grapes grown at the southern end of the Adelaide Plains. Bottled young to retain its delicate style.

Hamilton's Amaro Vermouth
Made from pedro ximenez and palomino grapes, infused with selected herbs and spices imported from Italy. The wine has a clean aromatic taste with a pleasant bitter finish.

Hamilton's Barossa Vale Bianco Vermouth
Made from muscat gordo blanco this sweet wine is given an aromatic finish by the infusion of selected herbs imported from France and Italy.

Hamilton's Barossa Vale Burgundy
A light red wine made from a blend of shiraz and grenache grapes fermented in wood to retain a clean, dry finish.

Hamilton's Barossa Vale Claret
A wine of much the same character as the Burgundy being again a blend of shiraz and grenache grapes.

Hamilton's Barossa Vale Cream Sherry
A light golden cream sherry made from palomino and pedro ximenez grapes. Fermentation is arrested and the wine bottled early to retain natural colour and sweetness.

Hamilton's Barossa Vale Dry Sherry
A dry wine from pedro ximenez and palomino grapes, having a clean, dry finish.

Hamilton's Barossa Vale Dry Vermouth
Made from a blend of pedro ximenez and palomino grapes, infused with selected herbs imported from France and Italy, giving the wine an aromatic finish.

Hamilton's Barossa Vale Hock
Made from pedro ximenez and palomino. This white wine has a clean, crisp taste with a dry finish.

Hamilton's Barossa Vale Marsala All'uovo
A thick, rich dessert wine made from muscat gordo blanco to which is added eggs and selected spices.

Hamilton's Barossa Vale Moselle
A slightly sweet white wine made from pedro ximenez and palomino grapes.

Hamilton's Barossa Vale Muscat
A luscious grapy wine made from muscatel (muscat gordo blanco), having the taste of juicy raisins.

Hamilton's Barossa Vale Riesling
Made from pedro ximenez and palomino grapes, this white wine has a clean, crisp taste and a dry finish.

Hamilton's Barossa Vale Rosé
Made entirely from grenache grapes, is clean and light in colour and has a delicate dry finish.

An old press at Drayton's, Hunter Valley, N.S.W.

Hamilton's Barossa Vale Sauternes
Made from a blend of palomino and pedro ximenez grapes. This wine is a light golden colour and has a rich sweetness.

Hamilton's Barossa Vale Sweet Sherry
Made from muscat gordo blanco grown in the River districts. This wine has a pleasant sweet, fruity flavour.

Hamilton's Barossa Vale Sweet Vermouth
Made from a sweetened blend of pedro ximenez and palomino grapes, infused with selected herbs imported from France and Italy.

Hamilton's Barossa Vale V.O. Invalid Port
Produced from a blend of shiraz and grenache; full in colour, with a natural, clean, dry finish.

Hamilton's Barossa Vale White Port
Made from palomino grapes. This port is golden in colour, and lighter than most ports, but it has a smooth, rounded flavour.

Hamilton's Bianco Vermouth
Made from muscat gordo blanco. A sweet white wine of some aromatic character, infused with selected herbs.

Hamilton's Blackberry Wine
A rather unusual blackberry flavoured wine. Fresh blackberries are crushed and the juice concentrated and then added to a fortified wine base.

Hamilton's Burgundy
A blend of shiraz and grenache grapes fermented at Ewell Cellars. Matured in wood this wine is made for the person who prefers a lighter red wine.

Hamilton's Chablis
Made from pedro ximenez and palomino grapes. This wine has a clean, crisp taste, with a pleasant dry finish.

Hamilton's Claret
A blend of shiraz and grenache grapes fermented at Ewell Cellars. Matured in wood this wine is made for the person who prefers lighter red wine.

Hamilton's Dry Red Hermitage (Flagon)
A blend of shiraz and grenache grapes grown at Ewell Vineyards, Glenelg.

Hamilton's Dry Vermouth
Made from a blend of pedro ximenez and palomino infused with selected herbs.

Hamilton's Dry White Riesling (Flagon)
Made from riesling grapes grown in districts south of Adelaide. A clean, crisp wine with a good dry finish.

Hamilton's Eden Valley Cabernet Sauvignon
Vintaged from cabernet sauvignon grapes grown at Nildottie and matured in old wood in the Eden Valley Cellars of the company for two years. This is a true varietal wine with a distinctive cabernet nose and soft tannin finish.

The Nildottie vineyard is equipped with overhead sprinklers to ensure cold, yet adequate water distribution.

Hamilton's Eden Valley Cabernet Shiraz
Made from a blend of cabernet sauvignon and shiraz grapes grown at Nildottie. Fermented in closed wooden vats and matured in small wood until bottled. This wine has been made to improve in the bottle.

Hamilton's Eden Valley Fino Sherry
Made from palomino grapes and then aged in French oak hogsheads, spending two years under Flor. This sherry is pale, clear and completely dry.

Hamilton's Eden Valley Hermitage Dry Red
Vintaged from shiraz grapes grown in the Eden Valley/Springton districts. This wine is matured in oak casks for over two years prior to bottling. It is a full-flavoured soft wine of considerable middle palate varietal character, and a smooth, soft finish.

Hamilton's Eden Valley Liebfraumilch
Made from Springton and Eden Valley rhine riesling grapes which are picked a little later than usual and are consequently riper. The wine has a very flowery bouquet and a late-picked sweetness, with a clean, crisp, acid finish.

Hamilton's Eden Valley Moselle
Produced from rhine riesling grapes grown in the Eden Valley and Springton districts; a wine which possesses a strong varietal bouquet with a noticeably fruity, slightly sweet finish.

Hamilton's Eden Valley Rhine Riesling
Made from straight rhine riesling grapes grown in the Eden Valley and Springton districts, fermented under strict temperature control at Eden Valley and bottled young to retain the natural freshness. The wine has a fresh fruity bouquet, typical varietal flavour on the palate, and a crisp, dry finish.

Hamilton's Eden Valley Rosé
Made from grenache grapes. This wine is drier than most rosés and has a light and clear, clean pink colour.

Hamilton's Eden Valley Vintage Port
Laid down as a Ruby Port of a particular year, this wine is aged in French oak casks for ten years or more. It is made entirely from shiraz grapes, grown at Eden Valley. The wine changes over the years into full, rich, tawny style.

Hamilton's Eden Valley White Frontignac
A delicate, fruity table wine vintaged at the Eden Valley Cellars of the company from frontignac grapes grown at Nildottie. An interesting characteristic of this wine is that because some of the white grapes are dark in colour, the wine develops a slight pink tinge as it ages.

Hamilton's Eden Valley White Burgundy
A full-bodied dry white wine vintaged at the Eden Valley Cellars of the company from white hermitage grapes grown at Nildottie. Matured in small wood, this wine fills out and deepens in flavour with bottle age.

Hamilton's Ewell Moselle
A quite famous and very popular white wine produced from verdelho and pedro ximenez grapes grown at the Ewell vineyards of the company in Glenelg. Following certain French and German practices the grapes are fermented and picked into baskets and wooden boxes to avoid metal contamination. The wine is fermented under strict temperature control and is matured in the air-conditioned cellars of the company at Glenelg until bottling.

Ewell Moselle was the first Moselle to be produced under this method in Australia and has the lowest alcoholic content of any white wine produced in this country.

Hamilton's Ewell Rosé
Made from grenache grapes this wine is drier than most rosés and has a light and clear, clean, pink colour.

Hamilton's Ginger Wine
This wine is made from muscat gordo blanco and is infused with the ginger root. A smooth sweet wine with the spicy tang of ginger.

Hamilton's Golden Cream Sherry
A light golden cream sherry, made from palomino and pedro ximenez. Fermentation is arrested in the wine bottles early to retain natural colour and sweetness.

Hamilton's Graves
A slightly sweet white wine made from pedro

ximenez and palomino grapes. A light wine with a delicate balance of acid and sweetness.

Hamilton's Hock
Made from pedro ximenez and palomino grapes; a wine which has a clear, crisp taste, with a pleasant dry finish.

Hamilton's Invalid Port
Produced from a blend of shiraz and grenache. This wine has fullness and colour, while retaining its clean, dry finish.

Hamilton's Italian Vermouth
Made from a sweetened blend of pedro xinenez and palomino grapes, infused with selected herbs imported from France and Italy.

Hamilton's Langhorne Creek Hermitage
This wine was produced at Ewell Cellars from shiraz (hermitage) grapes grown at Langhorne Creek, South Australia. After fermentation in wood the wine matured in small wooden casks for two years prior to bottling. After bottling the wine is binned for a further year prior to release. A well-balanced wine which should age for some years to come.

Hamilton's Late Bottled Vintage Port
Made from shiraz grapes grown south of Adelaide. Laid down as a Ruby Port of a particular year in oak casks for eight years; after which it is bottled and aged for a further two years prior to release. During its ageing the wine changes to a full tawny style, with a clean dry finish.

Hamilton's McLaren Vale Cabernet Sauvignon
Made from cabernet sauvignon grapes harvested from the vineyards of Mr B. W. Hamilton of McLaren Vale and vintaged at Glenelg. After fermentation the wine was matured for two years in oak casks after which it was bottled and binned for a further year. This wine has a good balance of acid and tannin. It will improve with age.

Hamilton's Marsala All'uovo
This wine, made from the muscat gordo blanco grapes, with eggs and spice added to make a thick, rich dessert wine of tremendous popularity.

Hamilton's Medium Dry Sherry
Made from pedro ximenez and palomino grapes; fermentation is arrested early to retain a small amount of natural sweetness.

Hamilton's Moselle (Flagon)
A slightly sweet white wine made from pedro ximenez and palomino grapes. A light wine with a delicate balance of acid and sweetness.

Hamilton's Nildottie Cabernet/Shiraz
Made from a blend of cabernet sauvignon and shiraz grapes grown at Nildottie. Fermented in closed wooden vats then matured in small wood until bottled. This wine has been made to improve in the bottle.

Hamilton's Nildottie Hermitage
Vintaged from shiraz (hermitage) grapes grown in the Eden Valley/Springton districts. This wine was matured in oak casks for over two years prior to bottling. It will improve in the bottle for a number of years.

Hamilton's Nildottie White Hermitage
A full-bodied dry white wine vintaged at Eden Valley Cellars from white hermitage grapes grown at Nildottie. Matured in small wood this wine will continue to improve with bottle age.

Hamilton's Oloroso Sherry
A genuine Flor sherry with additional 'Jeropiga' added to create a delicately balanced, semi-sweet taste and bouquet. Made from palomino and pedro ximenez grapes, grown at the Ewell vineyards at Glenelg.

Hamilton's Pale Fino Sherry
Made from a blend of palomino and pedro ximenez grapes, grown at Ewell vineyards at Glenelg; aged in oak casks and bottled after two years under Flor. A delicate, pale, completely dry sherry.

Hamilton's Private Bin Muscat
Made from the muscatel (muscat gordo blanco). A luscious, grapey style of wine which is matured for five years in wood.

Hamilton's Private Bin Port
Produced predominantly from the shiraz variety, grown in the southern districts around Langhorne Creek and McLaren Vale. This wine is classed as an 'eight years old wood matured ruby port with full flavour and a clean dry finish'.

Hamilton's Rhine Riesling/White Frontignac
Made from rhine riesling and white frontignac grapes. This is a dry, crisp white wine with a strong varietal bouquet. The two varieties of grapes are blended prior to fermentation, which is carried out in temperature controlled, closed wooden vats. The wine is matured in small wood and bottled young to retain the freshness and flowery bouquet.

Hamilton's Riesling
Made from pedro ximenez and palomino grapes. A wine which has a clear, crisp taste and is quite straightforward.

Hamilton's Royal Reserve Muscat
Made from the muscatel (muscat gordo blanco) grapes. This muscat, matured in wood, is quite fruity and grapey.

Hamilton's Royal Reserve Sauternes
Made from a blend of palomino and pedro ximenez grapes, this wine has a rich sweetness with a light golden colour.

Hamilton's Royal Reserve Port
Produced from a selected blend of shiraz and grenache grapes, the wine has plenty of colour; some wood showing, and a clean dry finish.

Hamilton's Royal Reserve Sherry Dry
Made from pedro ximenez and palomino grapes grown at the Ewell vineyard at Glenelg. This is a light clear sherry with a pleasant dry finish.

Hamilton's Royal Reserve Sherry Sweet
A pleasant sweet wine made from muscat gordo blanco grapes, grown in the river districts.

Hamilton's Sparkling Burgundy
A sparkling red wine fermented in the bottle.

Hamilton's Special Reserve Champagne
A genuine Champagne fermented in the bottle to retain its natural sparkle.

Hamilton's Special Reserve Sauternes
Made from a blend of palomino, pedro ximenez and semillon grapes. The wine is fermented in large wooden vats and then matured in wooden casks at Glenelg. It has the colour of sun bleached straw and is rich and smooth in taste.

Hamilton's Springton Burgundy
A delicate red wine made from shiraz grapes grown at Springton. Fermentation is carried out in closed wooden vats. After fermentation the wine is matured in small wood for two years prior to bottling.

Hamilton's Springton Claret
A delicate red wine made from shiraz grapes grown at Springton. Fermentation is carried out in closed wooden vats. After fermentation the wine is matured in small wood for two years prior to bottling.

Hamilton's Springton Hermitage
Made from shiraz grapes grown at Springton. Fermentation is carried out in closed wooden vats similar to French methods. After fermentation the wine is racked into oak casks and matured for two years. This wine is similar in style to a good Bordeaux and will age in the bottle for many years.

Hamilton's Springton Riesling
Produced from the rhine riesling grape grown in the Springton district. Has a flowery bouquet with a dry finish.

Hamilton's Springton White Burgundy
A full-bodied dry white wine vintaged at Springton Cellars from white hermitage grapes grown at Nildottie. Matured in small wood this wine will continue to improve with bottle age.

Hamilton's Springton White Frontignac
A delicate fruity table wine vintaged at the Springton Cellars of the Company from frontignac grapes grown at Nildottie. Again, an interesting characteristic of this wine is that because some of the white grapes are dark in colour, the wine develops a slight pink tinge as it ages.

Hamilton's Vat 50 Port
Produced mainly from the shiraz variety, grown in the southern districts round Langhorne Creek and McLaren Vale. It is a fairly good quality, wood matured ruby port of some age, with good flavour and a clean dry finish.

Hamilton's Verdelho

Made from verdelho grapes grown in the old and famous vineyard of the company at Glenelg. It is a full-bodied, full-flavoured wine. Fermentation takes place in temperature controlled closed wooden vats and the wine is then matured in small wood.

The verdelho variety originated from Madeira and Ewell is one of the few vineyards in South Australia growing this variety. The vines at Glenelg were planted in the early 1930s. Verdelho is renowned for its keeping qualities.

Happy Valley

Happy Valley Cabernet Sauvignon

A strong-coloured, full-bodied dry red from the Southern Vales district of South Australia which was fermented in stainless steel tanks at controlled temperatures and then aged in small wood prior to bottling. The wine has a full, rich flavour and style with plenty of grip at the back of the palate.

Happy Valley Flagon Wines

A range of flagon wines are produced for sale. These include an Amaro Vermouth, a Bianco Vermouth, Cream Sherry, Creme Marsala, Dry Red Grenache, Dry Sherry, Marsala All'Uovo, Moselle (pedro muscatel), Muscatel, Pedro Hock, Port, Sweet Sherry and Sweet Vermouth.

Happy Valley Hermitage

A full-flavoured wine from grapes grown south of Adelaide. It is made in stainless steel tanks at controlled temperatures and aged in small wood. A straightforward varietal style, with a soft, clean finish.

Happy Valley Moselle

A quite fruity, full-flavoured wine, produced from the pedro ximenez grapes grown on the local vineyards. Cold fermented in wood at 10°C in an attempt to retain big flavours. The wine has a full nose and quite a strong, full palate.

Happy Valley Rhine Riesling

Produced entirely from rhine riesling grapes grown on the local vineyards south of Adelaide; cold fermented in wood at 10°C; and containing considerable varietal character. This style has received awards at the Royal Adelaide Show in the medium dry white class and has also taken out the J. G. Kelly Memorial Trophy for the most outstanding dry white wine at the Southern Districts Wine Exhibition.

Hardy, Thomas & Son

Hardy's Cabernet Sauvignon

This is one of the most famous dry red lines in Australia. Over the years some outstanding dry reds have come from it. The blend has varied. At one time it was a straight cabernet sauvignon from McLaren Vale from vineyards of the company at 'Tintara', from Coonawarra, where the wine was usually purchased from the Redmans and from 'Chateau Tahbilk'. The 'Chateau Tahbilk' part of the blend contained some shiraz since there are shiraz vines amongst the cabernet vineyards, about one in every five. Many of the bin numbers of this famous wine can still be found today and do represent some of the most outstanding interesting Australian dry reds. They date from the 1954 (Bin 766) and include Bin C.9 of 1955, the Bin C.24 of 1957 and so on. These wines are all distinguished by their considerable berry bouquet, by marked elegant fruit on the middle palate, by a slight hole at the back of the palate and then a firm, gripping finish.

The C.24 of 1957 was a wine which has lived for years, it has an elegant style of finish and flavoured fruit. The C.110 of 1958 and the C.111 of 1959 were both outstanding wines, appearing in an era in which many people were very interested in this more austere, delicate kind of wine, yet one which had intense flavour. There was no Cabernet Sauvignon at all in 1960. The 1961 C.340 had enormous flavour and it is still improving.

There were two fine wines in 1962, the 404 and the 407, both were Gold Medal winners. 1963 and 1964 also produced fine wines.

The 1965 wine did not have quite the same style. It appeared to be aggressively out of balance and I wondered if this might have been caused by there being more McLaren Vale fruit in the wine than before. However, the 1966 wine, Bin 626, was magnificent. By this time, of course, the blend had lost the 'Chateau Tahbilk' cabernet sauvignon part, since Eric Purbrick was bottling most of his own red wines. The 626 has considerable flavour and character. It is a blend of McLaren Vale material from the company's own 'Tintara' vineyards in that region, plus cabernet from Eric Brand at Coonawarra. The Hardy's had helped Brand get going in that district with technical assistance and advice and Brand reciprocated by selling some of his wine to them in bulk form. They find it very useful for their top blends.

I think the Cabernet Sauvignon line at all times has shown a most definite cellar style. It has the Hardy's imprint upon it. The wines always have enormous colour, tremendous *depth* of colour, a lot of fruit flavour and are rather austere, elegant wines with this very firm, gripping finish. Unquestionably this Cabernet Sauvignon is one of the classic wines of Australia.

Hardy's Cabinet Claret

Produced from cabernet sauvignon and shiraz grapes grown in several districts. In South Australia the material comes from the McLaren Vale area, the Barossa Valley and the Coonawarra district. The material from New South Wales comes from the Hunter River, where it is called hermitage. Hardy's have always made a practice of buying a certain amount of wine from the Hunter Valley area and this buying tradition has been maintained even during the years of shortage of wine in that district.

The wine is now a light to medium-bodied, dry red, with a fairly fresh acid and firm tannin finish. It shows good fruit and has some oak character coming from maturation in small oak hogsheads. However, I don't think the wine has quite the style and depth of character that some of the older Cabinet Clarets have. Inevitably wine companies have to make their own decisions about their famous lines of wine. In the 1950s the Cabinet Clarets were outstanding and I can remember buying, towards the end of the 1950s, a 1945 Cabinet Claret which was one of the best Australian dry reds I have ever seen.

However, as public consumption grows and demand for the wine increases the wine companies are faced with one of two options. They can either continue the name and the actual blending style of the wine, and then charge a great deal more for it as the material becomes much more expensive; or they can use the name and broaden the scale so that it can be accepted by a lot more people. I think this is what has happened to Lindeman's Cawarra Claret and Seppelt's Moyston Claret, for example, and it also happened to Thomas Hardy's Cabinet Claret.

Of the Cabinet Clarets of the 1950s, I remember with great affection the Bin 265 of 1959, a wine which contained much the same blending material, cabernet sauvignon and shiraz from South Australia and hermitage or shiraz from the Hunter Valley. This was a wine of tremendous fruit and character which was extremely drinkable four or five years after the making; but which held up and stayed deliciously sound, deepening and enriching the flavour, and building the bouquet for many years after.

The Cabinet Claret is a well established commercial dry red, available in most leading stores and restaurants and which is always good value for money.

Hardy's Coronet Port
A well-matured, tawny port produced at the 'Tintara' winery in McLaren Vale from shiraz and selected from grapes available in the district which have always, over the years, produced the necessary flavour and sweetness to produce the best material for high class port.

The wine, which spends at least twelve years in oak casks before being marketed, is a well-balanced, fruity, tawny port of considerable character. It is fortified with mature brandy spirit during making and this does enhance both the flavour and the finish. In spite of considerable sweetness on the palate, the wine finishes quite clean and dry.

Hardy's Courier Champagne
Made by the Charmat process from a base white wine which was made from semillon grapes. This is a pleasant, sparkling, fruity wine with some sweetness on the middle palate and a rather negative flavour. Though in this instance the wine is categorised alphabetically under the Hardy name—in fact, the Hardy name does not appear on the label, so that the wine cannot be confused with the Thomas Hardy Grand Reserve Champagne.

Hardy's Cyrilton Cream
This is a fine rich dessert wine made from the pedro ximenez grape, grown in the McLaren Vale districts and also from the 'Cyrilton' vineyards near Waikerie on the River Murray. This is a very old, rich brown sherry, quite sweet on the palate on first impression, but one which finishes very clean and dry owing to the fine balance of tannin and acid.

The wine is matured in wood for eight to ten years. Cyrilton Cream is almost solely a Flor based sherry, with a considerable addition of concentrated pedro ximenez juice which gives it its rich lusciousness on the middle palate.

Hardy's Eden Moselle
A light, white wine containing some sweetness on the middle palate, made from rhine riesling grapes grown in the Springton, Eden Valley district to the east of the Barossa Valley. It is vintaged at the 'Siegersdorf' winery in the heart of the Barossa Valley, between Tanunda and Nuriootpa.

Basically this wine is a pleasant, well-made rhine riesling, with just a touch of sweetness on the middle palate.

Hardy's Flagon Burgundy
A soft, dry flagon red made at the 'Tintara' winery, McLaren Vale, from shiraz grapes grown in the upper 'Tintara' vineyards on sandy loam sprinkled throughout with ironstone. The wine has a pleasant, fruity, rather distinctive character and a nice fruity nose. It is a line which is sold only in flagons and provides very good drinking at a most acceptable price. Hardy's dry red flagons are among the most consistent and best in this range in Australia.

Hardy's Flagon Claret
A medium-bodied dry red, made at McLaren Vale from shiraz and mataro grapes. It has a pleasant, acid and tannin finish, with reasonable fruit on the middle palate. Both the name and the fairly crisp style of the wine make it one of the most popular flagon wines in this country.

Hardy's Flagon Moselle
This is a slightly fruity wine made from semillon grapes at McLaren Vale. It has a pleasant enough palate and flavour with no special distinction and is an acceptable flagon wine.

Hardy's Florfino Sherry

This fine, dry aperitif wine is produced at the 'Tintara' winery in McLaren Vale from palomino and pedro ximenez grapes, blended with wine made at the 'Siegersdorf' winery from pedro ximenez. The Flor process is carried out exclusively in hogsheads which allows the sherry to mature and pick up the small amount of desirable oakiness during the Flor growth.

This sherry is very dry (amongst the commercial sherries) and has very little, if any, liqueuring at all on the middle palate. It has a very good combination of oak and Flor character and a very good acid, slightly firm finish which makes it an excellent sherry of the Fino style. This is one of the most consistent Australian sherries and is always extremely good buying for those people who want a very dry, delicate and flavoursome sherry.

Hardy's Golden Nectar Sauternes

Made at McLaren Vale from semillon and sauvignon blanc grapes. Both of these varieties are used to produce the classic Sauternes and Barsacs of France. The sauvignon blanc variety helps lift this wine and puts it into a more distinctive class. Golden Nectar Sauternes are among the best of the so-called Sauternes type of sweet wines in Australia and develop remarkably well in the bottle. A chance purchase of one of the trade wines at least ten years old recently showed the depth of character to which the wine can develop. It seems a pity to me that the company has to use the name Sauternes. I am quite sure the wine could be sold excellently well simply as a Sàuvignon Blanc brand, or under the name 'Golden Nectar'. However, the wine does remain good value, having good vinosity and flavour and a clean finish. It is a very good quality sweet, commercial wine. .

Hardy's Grand Reserve Champagne

This is an excellent sparkling wine, one of the best of its kind in Australia, produced at the Mile End Bottling Cellars in Adelaide from the original dry white base wine made from clare riesling and semillon grapes. From time to time there has also been an addition of marsanne, purchased from Eric Purbrick's 'Chateau Tahbilk' vineyards. The semillon in the wine comes from the Springton, Eden Valley areas in the west of the Barossa Valley and here the wine is of a very fine, delicate character with a rather negative flavour, ideal for champagne making.

The wine is put together by Dick Heath. Even when Dick Heath was assistant to Roger Warren (the famous winemaker of Thomas Hardy), it was still his responsibility to make this wine. There are two styles, the Brut and the Extra Dry. The Brut is almost entirely dry and has an extremely good character; a full bouquet develops after the wine is matured, with a very clean, fruity palate and firm, almost hard finish (flinty would probably be a better word). One feature of the Champagne is the time that the wine spends on its yeast lees after the second fermentation process. It gives some of the fine flavour, which is inherent in the style, to the wine. The Brut matures very well, building up considerable volume of flavour with age. The extra dry, which is sometimes affectionately known as 'Gold Top' is a very good drinking, sparkling wine which contains a measure of liqueuring. This liqueuring on the middle palate probably provides more continuous enjoyment than the Brut Champagne with its more acid finish.

Hardy's McLaren Vale Estate Hermitage

Made from the shiraz (hermitage) variety, grown on the rich, sandy loam of the upper 'Tintara' vineyards and vintaged at the 'Tintara' winery, McLaren Vale.

This light, dry red is then matured in French oak hogsheads before bottling. There have been several distinguished wines in this range, particularly the 1962 which had more fruit than is common nowadays and developed magnificently after some years in the cellar. The current wines are probably lighter, being rather firm wines of pleasant character and good fruit, which drink well at all times. Though lighter in style these days, the wine does need a couple of years in the bottle to develop its character.

Hardy's Mill Rosé

Now bottled in the familiar 'Bock' bottle, in which a lot of Australian rosés are sold. At one time this wine was sold in a normal long bottle with a most distinctive artist's label and was probably ahead of its time.

The Mill Rosé is made from grenache grapes grown on the east side of the lower 'Tintara' vineyard and vintaged at the 'Tintara' wineries, McLaren Vale. The wine has a nice crisp, dry acidity on the finish and there is a slight touch of fruitiness on the middle palate which makes it quite refreshing and most palatable to a great number of people.

Hardy's Nottage Hill Claret

This is a good, sturdy red wine made in McLaren Vale from shiraz grapes grown in the 'Nottage Hill' vineyard, which is to the south-east of the original 'Tintara' cellars—the upper 'Tintara' vineyards in that district.

The wine is matured in French oak puncheons for two years and during that time picks up a very good oak complement to the rather strong and fruity varietal material. The soil at 'Nottage Hill' vineyard is sandy loam rich in ironstone and the aspect is westerly. Over the years this area has produced the finest shiraz grapes which have gone into some of the better wines of the district.

In 1967 the company decided to launch this line. The wine was very successful and after some years in the bottle, started to drink extremely well. The 1968 wine was a lighter wine which didn't have quite the same depth of character, though it was still very good. There was no wine bottled under this label in 1969 because the material for that year was not considered good enough.

The 'Nottage Hill' vineyard is named after Thomas H. Nottage, who joined his uncle, Thomas Hardy (the founder of the company), in 1884. He managed the vineyards and cellars at McLaren Vale for over sixty years and the vineyard is on the site of his original home. I think it is a pleasant tribute to one of the stalwarts of the company during its period of rapid expansion and the wine certainly is consistent with this tribute.

Hardy's Old Castle Riesling

A most distinctive dry wine that has been one of the most celebrated of all white wines of Australia. It has been made for over thirty years and during that time it has been well to the forefront in sales of dry whites throughout Australia.

Old Castle is made from rhine riesling grapes grown in the Springton Eden Valley areas of South Australia, to the east of the Barossa Valley, and vintaged at 'Siegersdorf' winery in the heart of the valley itself. The wine is blended with semillon material which is purchased from the Hunter River district of New South Wales. The component from South Australia is dry, fruity, crisp and very delicate. The Hunter Valley material shows more character, both on the nose and palate, but lacks crispness. A small quantity of the Hunter wine in the Old Castle Riesling does build the wine out with age, so that you have basically, well-balanced, quite crisp dry white being filled out with extra flavour which adds to the dimension of the rhine riesling. Many of these wines mature remarkably well in the bottle and keep going for years. Recently I drank a 1942 Old Castle Riesling which was still in magnificent order; wine of superb balance and style, delicious flavour and enormously enriched bouquet. Such is the individual nature of this wine that I don't like it particularly much when it is young, though of course vast quantities of it are consumed at early bottle age.

Hardy's Reserve Bin Burgundy

Over the last twenty years some outstanding full-flavoured dry reds have been produced from this company and sold under the name Reserve Burgundy. In previous years there were selected binnings of the wine such as the 811 of 1954 and the Bin 894 of 1955. These were enormously rich, full-flavoured wines, very pungent and full of character, which drank tremendously well. They won many Gold Medals throughout Australia.

1956 was a disastrous year and I don't think there was a 1956 St Thomas.

In 1957 there was quite a significant change. The C.35 was the wine of that year, but it was a very hard wine as so many of the 1957s were. It was also lighter and without the full richness of the previous wine. The year after was the 184 of 1958, which was again lighter but which matured into very pleasant, soft, round, fruity wine of considerable character.

Hardy's made a practice of bringing out a wine as their St Thomas Burgundy and then retaining some, which would be sold later when it had picked up more age; perhaps under a different Bin number. In some cases they actually left the wine in wood longer. For example, in 1960 there were two bins released, the C.315 and the Bin 405. The Bin 405 was bottled early and picked up fairly pronounced bottle age fairly quickly. On the other hand, its sister wine, the C.315 was kept in casks for much longer, picked up a great deal more character and therefore needed more time to develop in the bottle. The same thing happened in 1961 with the 414 (early bottled) and the C.354 (late bottled); and in 1962 with the 426 (early bottled) and the C.396 (late bottled). All these were very good wines that drank well. I see no point in keeping them for many years since my experience has shown that they drink very well after about four or five years in the bottle.

As consumption grew, Hardy's found it increasingly difficult to maintain stocks of these wines while they developed further; so in the mid-sixties a decision was made by which St Thomas Burgundy became the lighter, more readily acceptable public style. The older, bigger wines were put to one side to mature as reserve bin wines. Thus from the 1963 vintage we had a Bin 421. This wine was extremely good with a very good fruit character; a wine which had a tremendously rich after-flavour and a very soft finish. I didn't like the 1965 Reserve Bin; but the 1966 (Bin 633) had a great deal of character. This was a straight blend of shiraz from McLaren Vale, together with shiraz or hermitage from the Hunter Valley. The Hunter proportion was greater than usual. Generally it is about five to ten percent, but in this case it was nearly twenty percent. This wine had a great deal of fruit and was very soft and round; it was a notable Thomas Hardy blend. The 1967 was also a good wine, although the wines of later vintages do seem to suffer from the rather poor years that occurred in the McLaren Vale.

In all, the Reserve Bin Burgundy line of Thomas Hardy has provided wine lovers with some extraordinarily interesting wines of great character. The style has changed over the years, but it is good to see that they have finally settled upon a line—a blend—which provides extremely good drinking. Again I repeat that I don't think it is necessary to hold these wines too long. The very softness and fruitiness of their character means that they can be consumed after only a relatively short time, so that after say five or six years they make excellent drinking and continue to hold this quality for years.

Demonstration Flor sherry cask at Thomas Hardy's 'Tintara' vineyard, near McLaren Vale, S.A.

Hardy's Reserve Bin Claret

Hardy's did the same with their claret line as with the burgundy styles. They would bring out a claret which was sold as a trade line and then, with further bottle age, renumber it to be sold at a different price under a Reserve Bin Label.

There have been one or two most interesting binnings available during the last ten years, particularly the 1965 Bin 533, which I thought a magnificent red wine. There were also some interesting blends from McLaren Vale, from the Barossa Valley, from Coonawarra and from blended Hunter Valley material.

Unfortunately some of the wines have been somewhat volatile and although the volume of fruit and oak in these wines did tend to compensate, the volatility was too marked in some cases. The company used to buy a lot of material from the Redmans but such material has not been available since the 1965 takeover of Rouge Homme by Lindemans. However, among these bins, many of which are extremely limited in supply and some which don't even appear in more than one state, there are some remarkably fine wines. One should always be on the lookout for the Hardy's Reserve Bin Clarets.

Hardy's Reserve Sauternes

The Golden Nectar Sauternes line of this company has always been good value as a trade line. That is, the commercial line which is always available and which comes out without any great fanfare. But occasionally they make a wine in the line which shows so much character that they tuck it away and make a Reserve Bin. Such a wine was the C.496 of 1965 which, although it sold quite cheaply, had outstanding flavours and characters. It was made from semillon and sauvignon blanc and was probably stored in wood for a little longer than usual. The wood is evident in the flavour and the sauvignon blanc fruit stands out and combines well with it. The sugar is very well balanced and there was no cloying quality to the wine, its finish being quite clean.

In a line-up of Sauternes (sweet wines, I dislike people using this word Sauternes for Australian wines) in Melbourne some time ago this wine was voted the best of all, and it was against some notable show wines from other companies. It had a balance and finesse which was very complex and interesting. There are very few good sweet wines in Australia and it is worth noting that Thomas Hardy occasionally evolve the odd example like the 1965 which has a considerable amount of character and is very good drinking at the price.

Hardy's Riesling-Hock

A fresh, young white wine; also made at McLaren Vale from material grown in the upper 'Tintara' vineyards. It is a crisp, light, clean wine with a nice fragrance, and is good flagon drinking of a fairly high quality.

Hardy's St Thomas Burgundy

This wine is now produced entirely from shiraz grown in South Australia and in the Hunter Valley; the Hunter Valley proportion is less than ten percent. The South Australian shiraz is grown at the 'Tintara' vineyard at McLaren Vale. Earlier vintages of this quite celebrated line have been discussed under 'Reserve Bin Burgundies'.

Today, St Thomas Burgundy is a medium-bodied, very smooth wine, showing much less tannin and acid than the Cabinet Claret. It is not as big as previously, and is now clean and light. The fruit is pleasant, it makes good drinking and the wine gains some depth with a little bottle age, which may come from the small proportion of Hunter Valley. It seems to fill out and soften the other shiraz. This burgundy is a pleasant wine to the palate; it drinks well, after about two or three years in the bottle, and I think it is a most consistent line. Don't get confused over the change of style. The previous style was much bigger, heavier, fuller and the wines could go on for many years. Now, the intention with this line is to produce a most acceptable bottled wine that is available generally to provide good everyday drinking.

Hardy's St Vincent Chablis

This is a dry white wine made at McLaren Vale from semillon grapes grown in the St Vincent vineyard, which is on the top of the hill on the southeast side of the lower 'Tintara' vineyards, overlooking St Vincents Gulf. Here the soil is a light sandy loam over limestone, which gives this wine a rather flinty, dry and somewhat acerbic character on the back of the palate. There is no great distinguishing flavour or nose to the wine, no great aromatic quality, and the bouquet does not build up particularly. It remains a clean, delicate dry white. Incidentally, St Vincent is the patron saint of winemakers, and apparently sailors and bricklayers are also under his auspices. So, if you want an ocean-going, brick winery...

Hardy's Sauvignon Blanc

This is a unique dessert wine made from material which has been quite a long time in the McLaren Vale district. This is the famous sauvignon blanc, a variety which is one of the premier varieties of Bordeaux in France. Here it is made into a sweet white wine, with a very pronounced flavour and an outstanding fruity bouquet. Some of the original vines of this variety planted in 1863 at the old 'Tintara' vineyard are still producing, supplemented by another twenty acres planted about forty years ago. The company uses some of the material for adding sweet material to their Sauternes and Moselle styles, but they also make a dessert wine. Hardy's found that

In 1870 Joseph Best, while excavating his cellars at Great Western, had local gold miners dig a system of tunnels in which to store his maturing wine. They are now given over to the storage of sparkling wine for B. Seppelt and Sons.

the environment in which it grows, which is a ferruginous sandy loam, makes it well suited for producing this fortified dessert wine. It is aged for an average of twelve to fifteen years in oak casks and it has a very rich, mellow character which is quite difficult to describe.

Hardy's Show Port

This is a very old tawny port made from shiraz grapes and matured in oak hogsheads at McLaren Vale for some years. The grapes grown in the upper 'Tintara' vineyards are picked when they are very ripe. Quite old brandy is used in the fortification of this wine. Over the years this wine has picked up considerable rancio style, and has very good flavour, fruit, acid and tannin.

The 1943 wine, Bin 255, was an outstanding tawny port that drank very well and is still drinking very well if you ever see any of it around. It won numerous Gold Medals in several shows and we had this interesting anomaly that even though the wine was of one particular vintage it was still a tawny port. Tawny ports are usually blends of different wines of different years. It was followed by the 1947 Show Port. Again, a very good wine, although something of a lighter style; less rancio character, perhaps less pronounced fruit and less depth of character on the middle palate—but still a fine wine. The Show Port has long been one of Australia's most consistent tawny ports.

Hardy's Siegersdorf Rhine Riesling

This is a straight rhine riesling, made from grapes which have been grown in the Springton, Eden Valley areas and which are then brought down into the 'Siegersdorf' winery in the Barossa Valley to be made. It is made under closed fermentation and the temperature is controlled.

The 1968 and 1969 Siegersdorf Rhine Rieslings are both fine wines with a tremendous essence character —a sort of intense rhine riesling fruit which was extremely appealing, both on the nose and at the front of the palate.

The 1970 wine did not have quite the same character. It was a fresh, pleasant wine, rather acid in style, and with a rather hard finish. The wine didn't perhaps have quite the complex fruit of the previous wines—but it was still a reasonable wine at a reasonable price.

It is now obvious that the company is concentrating on producing a quality Rhine Riesling, which will compete against the other very good wines being put on the market. It must be established that this wine is not a rival to the Old Castle Riesling, which is a unique Australian wine style.

Hardy's Sparkling Perlwein

Made from palomino grapes grown on the sandy loam in the McLaren Vale district and matured for twelve months before undergoing the Charmat process which makes it into a sparkling wine. This is a light, fruity, agreeable sparkling white wine with some considerable sweetness on the middle palate, but which finishes dry. It is a wine made for the pearl-loving public and is an agreeable, light, fruity drink.

Hardy's Special Amontillado Sherry

This is made from one variety, the pedro ximenez, although from two areas. The majority of the pedro comes from McLaren Vale, plus a little from the Barossa Valley. It starts off as a fino under the Flor process, but is always a more fruity, full-bodied style than their famous Florfino. After it has acquired its Flor character it is then matured in oak casks for some considerable time before being slightly sweetened with concentrated pedro ximenez juice. This wine is made under a modified Solera system, whereby the old vintages are from time to time freshened up with younger wine. There have been one or two special binnings which are exceptionally fine old wines of great character.

Hardy's Special Medium Sherry

Another 'each-way bet', but of a more distinctive character. It is made from pedro ximenez and palomino varieties and sweetened with concentrated pedro ximenez juice. After maturation of about five or six years in wood, it is bottled and sold. The flavour is quite pronounced and it is an interesting wine for those people who like these rather bland, medium sherries.

Hardy's Tintara Cellar Seven Sweet Sherry

This rich, brown, sweet sherry is a blend of pedro ximenez with the softer, richer palomino. There is also an addition of concentrated pedro ximenez juice. The wine is matured in oak casks—actually in No. 7 Cellar—and sold as a high quality trade wine.

Hardy's Tintara French Style Dry Vermouth

One of the better dry vermouths available in Australia, being made from a fairly delicate, dry white base which has been fortified by adding proof spirit. After infusing for five to six weeks with some imported herbs, the wine is racked off the herbs and is filtered ready for bottling.

This wine has been a consistent prize winner in Australian Wine Shows.

Hardy's Tintara Full Cream Sherry

Made primarily from the muscat gordo blanco, the juice being taken off the skins fairly quickly. This juice is rounded off with palomino and then kept in big wood for some time before bottling.

Hardy's Tintara Gold Crown Port

Made from shiraz and grenache grapes and matured in oak hogsheads for five years. This dessert wine is of the lighter style—almost a light ruby, and has been made to cater for growing public demand for this style.

Hardy's Tintara Gold Label Liqueur Muscat
This is a luscious dessert wine which is a blend of wines made at the 'Cyrilton' winery in the Waikerie district, together with material from the 'Siegersdorf' winery in the Barossa Valley. The wines from 'Cyrilton' are made from muscat gordo blanco and from the Barossa Valley from frontignac. The wine is blended together and then matured for seven to eight years in oak casks. It has a good balance of muscat, quite rich sweetness and lusciousness and a clean, rather nice brandy finish.

Hardy's Tintara Gold Label Port
Made from shiraz grapes grown in the McLaren Vale and matured in oak casks for eight to nine years. Again this is a fairly light style of port, something between the ruby and tawny styles which has a pleasant fruit and a quite acceptable light style.

Hardy's Tintara Gold Label Sweet Sherry
Made from pedro ximenez grapes and fortified during fermentation to arrest grape sugar. Matured in oak casks for three to four years. This wine, although quite sweet, does not show the fruity flavour of some sherries and is regarded as being of fairly neutral flavour.

Hardy's Tintara Italian Style Sweet Vermouth
Herbs, especially imported from Torino in Italy, are infused into a base wine of muscat of the gordo blanco variety. This wine is therefore fairly sweet, quite aromatic, and has a good clean finish. It has won many awards in shows throughout the country.

Hardy's Tintara Medium Dry Sherry
Made from pedro ximenez grapes and blended as a 'half-way bet' for those people who like neither a completely dry nor a completely sweet sherry.

Hardy's Tintara Old Fruity Sweet Sherry
This is one of the most popular lines in the Hardy range, having great appeal because of its rich, full fruity flavour, which comes from the blend of the muscat gordo blanco material, to which is added some concentrated pedro ximenez juice. This wine is made at the 'Cyrilton' winery at Waikerie and has always been popular as a reasonably priced fortified wine.

Hardy's Tintara Old Vintage White Port
This is a blend of pedro ximenez grapes grown in McLaren Vale, together with muscat gordo grapes grown at 'Cyrilton'. Being made from white varieties it picks up no colour and thus remains a traditional white port. The juice is fermented in contact with the skins, from which it gets the necessary tannin. It is fortified with brandy spirit and then matured in oak for from three to four years.

Hardy's Tintara Sparkling Burgundy
Made from the base wine of the lighter style of burgundy and produced in McLaren Vale from shiraz grapes. Perhaps, surprisingly, it is made by the traditional Methode Champenoise, which is how the company makes all the more celebrated of its sparkling wines. It is liqueured fairly richly, giving it a pleasant fruitiness and a quite marked touch of sweetness on the middle palate.

Hardy's Tintara Sparkling Moselle
This is an extremely popular sweet sparkling wine, made by the Methode Champenoise, the second fermentation taking place in bottles. By the addition of a greater quantity of Expedition Liqueur, the sweetness and flavour have become more pronounced than for the other dry sparkling wines under the Champagne label. The wine is always well made and is most consistent in its style.

Hardy's Tintara V.O. Invalid Port
This port is another big seller for the company throughout Australia. It is a reasonably priced wine and is produced from wines made in McLaren Vale, at 'Siegersdorf' in the Barossa, and at 'Cyrilton' at Waikerie. The grape varieties used are mainly grenache and shiraz with a little gordo blanco added to give the wine a lift on the palate. Brandy spirit is also used for fortification during making and this adds an agreeable after-taste to the wine.

Henley Park

Henley Park Burgundy
A full-bodied wine made from shiraz grapes grown on sloping, rich alluvial red loam soils in the heart of the Swan Valley in Western Australia. Grapes are picked at full ripeness, which results in wine of considerable flavour, with a soft but firm tannin finish. The wine is made by a charming man, Mark Yujnovich, who insists he is only in a small way, though he makes quite a large range of dry and sweet wines. He tends to specialise in robust, Swan Valley vintage ports.

Henschke, C. A., & Co.

Henschke Hermitage
From shiraz grapes from the Springton districts in the Barossa Ranges in South Australia. A rather delicate red wine which is building up something of a show record. This is the lightest coloured of the Henschke reds and the acid is somewhat higher than usual. The wine has plenty of flavour on the middle palate and takes bottle age well.

Henschke Hill of Grace

A rich, full flavoured red wine from the 'Hill of Grace' vineyard near the village of Keyneton in the northern end of the Barossa Ranges lying alongside the Barossa Valley.

Bryce Rankine says, 'In an area where rich and euphonious names abound, "Hill of Grace" could well be unique as a name for a vineyard and its wine. In the Lutheran tradition of the Valley it is singularly appropriate.'

The soils are mostly clay loams and podsols. Rainfall of the district is slightly lower than other areas, being about 22 inches per year. It is a delightful area, rather away from the rest of the Barossa Valley and with a feeling of timelessness. The winery is a very pleasant stone building of great charm. I have enjoyed many 'Hill of Grace' wines there; robust wines, full of flavour, and some with a quite marked 'licorice' character. They have plenty of style and fruit, and a smooth, soft finish.

'Hill of Grace' wine is never shown.

Henschke Mount Edelstone

Mount Edelstone is an anglicized version of Mount Edelstein—'Noble stone'. Cyril Henschke regards this as a most interesting wine. He first entered the 1952 wine in a show in 1956 and won a prize with it. Since then the succeeding vintages have never failed to win a prize each year. The wines have a considerable flavour. The nose builds up with bottle age and the finish is quite firm and pleasantly persistent.

Henschke Rhine Riesling

Cyril Henschke startled the wine world when, with the 1954 vintage wine of this variety, he won many awards from wine shows, including a First Prize in Sydney. This helped establish him in that city and his wines have been extremely popular there ever since.

These wines have tremendous rhine riesling character, moderate to high acid and great longevity. I have tasted the wines going back to the mid-fifties—they have powerful flavour, a quite exquisite nose can build up in this very strong, full flavour, and a very clean, refreshing finish. I prefer the wines after some years in the bottle.

In some years Cyril Henschke makes a wine from grapes which are late picked and consequently have a degree of sugar—though not a concentrated sweetness—on the middle palate which is very refreshing. Like all the other Rhine Rieslings the wine has plenty of varietal character.

Henschke Semillon

A softer, more delicate wine than the Rhine Riesling, and which is generally fuller, very well-balanced and with a clean, soft finish. The wines mature very well and pick up a most concentrated flavour on the middle palate with bottle age.

Again I can remember drinking one of the early 50s—nearly twenty years later—and being enormously

impressed with its flavour, balance, condition and general distinction.

Henschke Sercial

Another wine that develops considerably in the bottle. The grapes are grown on high rocky hills, or on porous soils. Consequently the vine which is usually a heavy bearer produces a very low yield in this district. The result is a fine, delicate wine, with lower acidity—the grapes being picked quite late in the season. This wine has very good flavour; again the palate is soft and round; the finish is smooth, but in spite of its low acidity the wine does pick up considerable character in the bottle with further maturation.

Henschke Ugni Blanc

A rather bland wine, appealing to some palates, which only develops after two or three years in the bottle. The wine has not got the aromatic intensity of the riesling varieties, but is soft and pleasant. Again with age, and somewhat surprisingly, the wine does develop considerable character in the bottle.

Henschke White Frontignac

A powerful, aromatic wine, pioneered by Cyril Henschke, and which has now become one of the company's best-known wines. Superb wines were made in the years 1964, 1967, 1969 and 1972. The wine shows considerable flavour and is aromatic, fruity and fragrant, with a definite muscat flavour throughout. But the flavour is not coarse—none of the heavy 'raisin' style of other wines. The finish is crisp and clean. It is an outstanding wine and shows some improvement in the bottle after twelve months or so.

Hoffman's North Para Wines Pty Ltd

Hoffman's Milpara Claret
The 1969 Claret was made from local Barossa Valley cabernet sauvignon, shiraz and grenache. There was approximately 15 percent cabernet sauvignon in the wine, which is apparent as far as the fruit is concerned. The colour is also very much of the variety, with a very good purple deep rich hue to it. The palate, though medium to full-bodied, is unquestionably lightened by the use of the grenache and the wine is quite soft on the after-palate and the finish.

Hoffman's Milpara Constantia (Light Port)
This light, soft sweet red is made from grenache grown in the Barossa Valley.

Hoffman's Milpara Dry Sherry
Made from pedro ximenez and palomino grapes. This is a bone dry sherry which is aged in small oak for twelve years and then blended with a younger, sweeter wine to yield an acceptable dry sherry, smooth and soft, yet with good wood character.

Hoffman's Milpara Frontignac
Made from frontignac grown in their own vineyard in the Barossa Valley. Its average age is six years. Half of this wine is wood-aged and it is then blended with a small quantity of muscatel, which is the Barossa Valley name for muscat gordo blanco. The wine has a pleasant dessert wine character, with reasonable wood, and obviously, with the varieties used, a raisiny type of flavour.

Hoffman's Milpara Golden Muscat
Made from muscatel (muscat gordo blanco) grown in their own vineyards in the north of Tanunda. It is blended each year to a standard and has approximately three years of wood age. This muscat is a very golden colour and has the distinctively raisiny character of the variety.

Hoffman's North Para Hock
Made from pedro ximenez. A pleasant dry white, rather nondescript style in wine. It is low in acidity and drinks very well when young.

Hoffman's North Para Light Muscat
A light dessert wine of pleasant muscat flavour made from muscat gordo blanco.

Hoffman's North Para Special Reserve Port
Made from mataro, shiraz and grenache. A light dessert wine with some wood age; it has more of the ruby port character than tawny which is then blended with some very old port to give it a good full-bodied character.

Hoffman's North Para Special Ruby Port
Made from mataro, shiraz and grenache, with grenache predominating. This wine has a rich ruby colour and is made as a light, drinkable, sweet red.

Hoffman's North Para Sweet Sherry
Made from pedro ximenez and palomino, together with some sultana, and blended to an acceptable medium fruity standard with a Baumé of about 4.5 degrees.

Hoffman's North Para Very Old Liqueur Tawny Port
Made from shiraz, mataro and grenache. This was a collection of very old port which had been left in small oak for over forty years. I bought some many years ago at a Barossa Valley auction and it gave me a great deal of pleasure because it had tremendous flavour and wood balance. Some of the wine was as high as 12 degrees Baumé. When one considers that it was laid down at 3½ degrees Baumé it illustrates something about rates of evaporation and the acquired density of flavour and concentration of character of these wines.

Hordern
Hordern's Hunter Valley Wines
Made at the Wybong vineyard of Dr Bob Smith. This ebullient character has yet to achieve his winemaking destiny or to arrive at a definitive style. His vineyards look extremely good and his winery is constructed from an old jail which he bought, pulled down and re-erected on the present site.

In 1971 he produced a white which has a most definite character. The 1972 wines were of course much better and he made two white wines; one a free-run semillon which was cold fermented, and the second a combined free-run and pressing wine. The free-run was a very good, clean, flavoursome wine. The red wine of 1972 is predominantly shiraz with a small amount of cabernet and mataro. This wine was subjected to various oak treatments.

Houghton Wines
Houghton's Blue Stripe Burgundy
A very soft, full flavoured, round style of dry red wine; made from straight shiraz grapes grown in the Swan Valley; bottled after twelve months in wood.

Houghton's Blue Stripe Chablis
There seems to be some contention over the grape variety used here. Ampelography—the study of grape

A specially selected white table wine elegant and complete, produced from Verdelho grapes grown on our vineyard in the Swan Valley. being young and delicate, this wine may form a harmless deposit of tartar crystals. Serve chilled.

Verdell

1 PINT 6 FL OZS

PRODUCED AND BOTTLED BY HOUGHTON WINES, W.A.

varieties—will assist in finally determining whether the wines are true to a variety or a clonal variation of a particular type. Anyway, they have the feeling that the Chablis is produced from semillon, but at the same time, they feel that the semillon could be the chenin blanc. Whatever, it is made from one of those varieties in the Swan Valley districts of Western Australia.

This wine has very pleasant middle palate flavour and a clean, soft finish. It is best drunk fairly young.

Houghton's Blue Stripe Claret
From straight shiraz, a very full, rich style, with a fairly firm finish. It is bottled after twelve months in wood.

Houghton's Blue Stripe Cream Sherry
A smooth, soft, sweet wine; muscat gordo blanco and pedro ximenez being the varieties used in the blend.

Houghton's Blue Stripe Medium Sherry
A medium dry wine produced from palomino and pedro ximenez grapes.

Houghton's Blue Stripe Muscat
A rather rich, highly flavoured wine, made from non-irrigated muscat gordo blanco, grown on deep loam.

Houghton's Blue Stripe Port
A wood-matured tawny port produced from shiraz and grenache grapes.

Houghton's Blue Stripe Sauternes
This blend of semillon, muscat gordo blanco and white grenache produces a wine with plenty of fruit and considerable sweetness.

Houghton's Blue Stripe Sweet Sherry
A blend of pedro ximenez and muscat gordo blanco

produces this smooth, sweet sherry. It is aged in wood for about two years.

Houghtons Cabernet
One of the wine styles that is popular in the Eastern States. A fairly well-balanced wine of considerable softness on the middle palate and pronounced cabernet flavour. The finish has a clean, persistent tannin and is most agreeable. This wine is matured in oak for twelve months prior to bottling. It is produced entirely from cabernet sauvignon grown on red loam over clay in the Swan Valley, W.A.

Houghton's Centenary Port
This is a true wood port of great character. It is full of flavour; has a great, rich grapeyness on the middle palate, yet a very clean, desirable tendency towards a dry finish on the back of the palate. This is a top liqueur wine, is produced from shiraz and cabernet sauvignon grapes, grown on Houghton's vineyards in the Middle Swan, W.A.

Houghton's Hermitage
From shiraz grown in Houghton's vineyards in the Swan Valley. A smooth, mellow, rich, full-bodied, full-flavoured, round and generous dry red wine.

Houghton's Hock
A flavoursome white wine, made from verdelho and rhine riesling grapes grown in the Swan Valley. It has considerable aromatic flavour, a rather full, rich palate, and a nice crisp, dry finish.

Houghton's Liqueur Frontignac
This old wine was matured in small casks for a period of not less than ten years. The frontignac grapes used in its manufacture were picked from the vines at not less than 25 Baumé. The resultant fully-flavoured, luscious wine is tremendously powerful; a full, 'raisiny' type of wine with considerable wood. I remember having some on ice cream once with Jack Mann, the famous winemaker of the company who has produced so many vintages. I thought it was quite splendid. With the coldness of the ice cream I couldn't quite understand what the sauce was, and asked Jack if it had taken him long to make. 'Oh yes,' he said, 'about twenty years.'

Houghton's Liqueur Hermitage
There is little doubt that this country is most suitable for making liqueur dessert wines of unique concentration. The combination of sunshine in the climate, which produces almost raisins on the vine, with some years' development in small oak casks, give these wines tremendous flavour and lusciousness. This is an old wood matured wine of the port style.

Houghton's Liqueur Muscat
A luscious deep amber wine; generous, mellow and rich in flavour—as a result of late picking when the

grapes were almost raisins—matured in small oak casks.

Houghton's Liqueur Port
This old wine was matured in small casks for a period of not less than ten years. The hermitage (shiraz), grenache and pedro ximenez grapes used in its manufacture were picked from the vines at not less than 25 degrees Baumé. The resultant liqueur wine is concentrated, rich, luscious and highly flavoured.

Houghton's Liqueur Tokay
A rich, smooth, liqueur dessert wine; a blend of special vintages matured in small oak casks and having the unique flavour of the tokay variety.

Houghton's Madeleine
A dry Flor fino sherry, which is quite delicate and has a certain fruity flavour all of its own. The wine has pleasant acidity with good Flor character. The Angelique Madeleine grape is a perfect base for the wine style and is a favourite of the winemaker, Jack Mann.

Houghton's Malbec
A soft, rich, dry red table wine; possessing considerable generous flavour and rich bouquet of the variety, which is grown in the Houghton's vineyards in the Swan Valley. It is stored in oak vessels for twelve months before bottling.

Houghton's Marsala
This rich, full-flavoured dessert wine is aged in wood, infused with the extracts of egg, coffee, cinnamon, cocoa and vanilla. It is very popular as an after dinner liqueur. (One could probably have it *as* dinner.)

Houghton's Moselle
A pleasant dry style moselle, blended from selected rhine riesling and verdelho grapes grown in Houghton's vineyards in the Swan Valley.

Houghton's Premier Reserve Dry Sherry
A pale, straw-coloured, dry Flor sherry produced from palomino and semillon grapes. It is stored in oak for some time and has soft pleasant acidity and some oak showing.

Houghton's Riesling
A full-flavoured dry table wine vintaged from the refined rhine riesling grapes grown in the vineyards of the Swan Valley. This is unlike a lot of the rhine rieslings of Australia in that it has a much deeper, fuller, middle palate flavour—perhaps lacking the extreme finesse of those other wines.

Houghton's Strelley
A dry red table wine combining the attractive qualities of the cabernet sauvignon, malbec and hermitage (shiraz) grapes, which are all produced in Houghton's vineyard in the Swan Valley. It is matured in large oak casks before bottling.

These wines have a rather lighter middle palate style and a clean, firm finish.

Houghton's Verdell
This is a special varietal wine vintaged from specially selected verdelho grapes grown on deep loam over clay subsoil. It is dry and full of flavour. When young the wines have quite a spicy, aromatic quality—not unlike some of the wines of the Alsace. With bottle age they fill out on the palate quite considerably and get an almost White Burgundy structure; although of course the flavour is quite different. Altogether a most interesting style.

Houghton's White Burgundy
Perhaps the most famous of all the Houghton's wines, this wine is greatly in demand in the Eastern States and there is never enough of it for the customers.

It is a full-bodied, dry white wine, with a unique flavour and character which is very easy to pick at blind tastings. Houghton's have developed this style over the years from chenin blanc (or semillon) and tokay grapes. They claim that the Indian Ocean plays an important part in the production of the wine since the long dry summer, which would be too hot if it was maintained all the time, and the cool ocean breezes that come off the Indian Ocean at night, help prolong the ripening period to the right extent so that they get very good sugar/acid ratios. They like to have their acid on the low side, but they still want the flavour build-up.

The wine has a most distinctive nutty character all of its own and it is, as I have said, greatly admired.

Houghton's Woodbridge Claret
A flagon dry red produced from hermitage (shiraz) grapes, grown in the Swan Valley. It is young and fresh and produced for everyday drinking.

Hungerford Hill Vineyards Pty Ltd

Hungerford Hill Collection—Pokolbin Dry Reds
The plantings of hermitage and cabernet sauvignon in the Hunter Valley district by this company will undoubtedly have great significance in the wine world in future years. Quantities of red wine have been produced which will be matured for some years before being released. Extremely full-flavoured, high coloured wines were produced in 1972.

Hungerford Hill Collection—Pokolbin Semillon
The first wine made from the new large plantings of this company in the Hunter Valley was in 1971. But 1971 was a poor, wet vintage, which resulted in the wines being somewhat light and lacking the usual full flavours of white wines from that district. The wine from this company was no exception. This wine

had quite a pleasant, estery nose on the light side, a light palate, and a crisp clean finish.

In 1972 the vintage produced a much better wine of fuller character and richer flavour. The extended vineyards of Hungerford Hill in the Hunter Valley do not contain much planting of traditional white grape varieties, for they are concentrating mainly on the red varieties, cabernet sauvignon and shiraz.

Johnston, A. C., Ltd

Johnston's Pirramimma Flor Sherry
A full-flavoured, rather robust sherry which is still bone dry. It is made from pedro ximenez and palomino grapes and matured in 65 gallon hogsheads under Flor film to pick up distinctive flavour and character.

Johnston's Pirramimma Liqueur Port
This is a blend of old export sweet reds made from grenache and shiraz and fortified with non-brandy spirit. The principal vintage was 1957 and the wine has been matured since in 40 gallon American oak casks. A rich dessert wine with considerable concentration of flavour.

Johnston's Pirramimma Palomino (White Burgundy)
A rather full-flavoured, robust, dry white wine which has a tendency to coarseness. The palomino grapes ripen fully on the vines and then are crushed in a roller crusher. The must is allowed to rest in contact with skins for a short time before separation, and fermentation is temperature controlled.

Johnston's Pirramimma Shiraz Dry Red
This wine is made from shiraz grapes from the McLaren Vale vineyards of the company. The grapes come from vineyards which vary as far as their soil types are concerned, from sand to sandy loams to heavy black clay. These vineyards have always produced fairly full-bodied types of wines with a great deal of straightforward flavour, and quite a measure of astringency and firmness on the finish. They are matured in big wood for two years and take some considerable bottle age.

Johnston's Pirramimma Sweet Sherry
A pleasant, rich, old, soft, sweet dessert wine made from pedro ximenez and grenache grapes. This is an old export sweet white which has been allowed to mature in 500 gallon oak casks. The wine is from the 1961 vintage and has darkened and mellowed over the years.

Johnston's Pirramimma Vat 12 Shiraz Grenache
Made from forty percent shiraz and sixty percent grenache; matured in large oak for eighteen months. This is a quite light, pleasant, rather stalky dry red, which is quicker maturing than many of the other reds in the district.

Johnston's Pirramimma Vintage Cabernet Shiraz
The proportions of cabernet sauvignon and shiraz in this wine vary from year to year. The grapes are picked and fermented together. The wine is aged for two to two and a half years in big wood and has a very full colour and flavour, a hint of spice on the middle palate and a rather agreeable firm, strong finish.

Johnston's Pirramimma Vintage Mataro
A typical varietal red of the variety, made from mataro grapes grown in sandy loam soil, overlying clay subsoil in the district. The wine has reasonably good colour, a rather vinousy, fruity nose and the characteristic astringent finish.

Kaiser Stuhl (Barossa Co-operative Winery)

Kaiser Stuhl Bin 33 Claret
Made from a blend of shiraz and morastel grapes grown in the Barossa Valley. The morastel is similar to the well-known mataro variety and is probably a clonal selection of it. After blending the Bin 33 is placed in small wood for 12 to 18 months before bottling. The result is a soft, pleasant drinking wine with a rather firm finish and containing more fruit than is usual with commercial blends of this nature.

Kaiser Stuhl Bin 55 Moselle
A pleasant wine made from semillon and clare riesling grapes grown in the Barossa Valley. It can also be produced by the addition of a partly fermented grape juice to a dry wine base. The result is a quite fruity wine which has a pleasant nose, a smooth grapy middle palate with some sweetness showing, but with a dry, clean finish.

Kaiser Stuhl Bin 44 Riesling
Made from clare riesling grapes grown in the Barossa Valley. A pleasant dry wine without the fruity fragrance of a Rhine Riesling, but with plenty of character, a clean middle palate, and a crisp acid finish.

Kaiser Stuhl Champagne
Made from white hermitage and semillon grapes grown in the Barossa Valley. This wine is produced by the traditional bottle fermentation method. Fermentation and maturation on the yeast in the bottle takes approximately one year and then the wine is disgorged and refilled, using the Star Transfer Method. Again it is matured after being cleaned up in the bottle for nearly one year prior to marketing.

This is a Demi-Sec style which contains a small amount of residual sweetness. It has a very pleasant fruit, a trace of coarseness on the back of the palate and a clean, acid finish.

Kaiser Stuhl Champagne—Brut

This wine is produced by the true Methode Champenoise and is made from selected tokay and white hermitage grapes grown in the Barossa Valley. Again the bottle fermentation method means that the wine is on its yeast lees for at least twelve months and then after being transferred and cleaned up is corked and laid down for further maturation for at least another twelve months. The final Expedition Liqueur contains only 7 grammes per litre of residual sweetness. This makes it a fairly dry wine with quite a clean, fresh palate and rather a clean acid finish. It is a very pleasant drinking Brut Champagne suitable for entertainment and pre-dinner drinks.

Kaiser Stuhl Champagne—Gold Seal Brut

This is the top sparkling wine in the Kaiser Stuhl range and is made under the personal supervision of George Kolarovich, the Technical Director of the Company. The wine is bottled in a long-necked, French-type blanc-de-blanc bottle. It is produced by the bottle fermentation method only—Methode Champenoise—and only high quality tokay and white hermitage grapes, grown from specially selected vineyards in the Barossa Valley, are used for this particular wine. It is left for no less than two years on the yeast and yeast lees in the standard champagne bottles. It is then transferred, using the Star Transfer Method, into this rather special champagne bottle after being cleaned up. The Expedition Liqueuring is extremely slight. It is one of the driest of the Brut Champagnes on the Australian market, since it contains only 4 grammes per litre residual sweetness, which is extremely slight. The bead is very fine. The wine is very clean, well-balanced, contains very good fruit and has evidence of this cracked yeast character on the palate, which is the hallmark of a quality sparkling wine.

Kaiser Stuhl Cold Duck

Cold Duck is a 'fun' wine and that is a generous description. This type of sparkling wine has become the largest selling single wine in the United States of America. Noting the success in America, Kaiser Stuhl launched their Australian Cold Duck in September 1970. It is a sparkling red wine that appears to be a blend between Champagne and Sparkling Burgundy. It has considerable sweetness on the middle palate and a fairly clean finish. There is no private bin Cold Duck.

Kaiser Stuhl Cream Sherry

A rather unusual wine in that for a trade wine this is a fairly frequent Gold Medal winner in shows. It is a blend of muscat gordo blanco grapes grown at Waikerie and muscatel from the Barossa Valley. (Almost certainly a variant of muscat gordo blanco.) The wine is fairly sweet, luscious and full-flavoured,

showing a distinctly fruity-muscaty flavour; the finish is quite soft and smooth. This is a well made pleasant wine for those people who like the style.

Kaiser Stuhl Dry Sherry

A fairly light, dry appetiser wine made from pedro ximenez and palomino grapes, grown in the Barossa Valley. The wine spends nine months under Flor culture and is then matured in American oak casks for two years before being bottled. It has a trace of sugar on the middle palate, about 5 or 6 grammes per litre, a pleasant, flowery bouquet that shows Flor and oak characters and a rather astringent, clean finish.

Kaiser Stuhl Flagons—Burgundy

Produced from shiraz grapes grown in the Barossa Valley. A soft, round, easy-to-drink, clean wine of no great pretension or distinction.

Kaiser Stuhl Flagons—Claret

Produced from a blend of mataro, carignane and grenache grapes grown in the Barossa Valley. A rather pleasant, fruity style of wine which has good colour but which is inclined to vary from month to month. At best the Kaiser Stuhl Flagon Claret can be amongst the best value in the country. Sometimes some of the flagons seem to suffer from a trace of volatile acid.

Kaiser Stuhl Flagons—Cream Sherry

Produced from a blend of muscat gordo blanco grapes from the Murray River area and muscatel (muscat gordo blanco) grapes grown in the Barossa Valley. A luscious, creamy, very fruity style of flagon wine.

Kaiser Stuhl Flagons—Dry Sherry

Made from a blend of pedro ximenez and palomino matured in large American oak casks under Flor culture prior to bottling. A clean, slightly astringent dry wine with a trace of sugar on the middle palate.

Kaiser Stuhl Flagons—Dry Vermouth

Produced from white hermitage grapes grown in the Barossa Valley. Imported Italian herbs are added prior to bottling. A light, clean, pleasant aperitif of no great depth of flavour.

Kaiser Stuhl Flagons—Family Port

A rather young, clean, fruity port style—immature, reaching the market two to three years after vintage. This is produced from a blend of shiraz and mataro grapes grown in the Barossa Valley and coming from the Murray River area.

Kaiser Stuhl Flagons—Frontignac

Made from red (or pink) frontignac grapes grown in the Barossa Valley. This is a liqueur type dessert wine which is quite luscious for a flagon wine, quite full-bodied, and very fruity with lots of generous flavour.

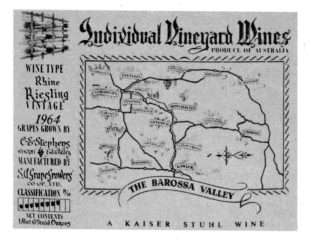

Kaiser Stuhl Flagons—Hock
Made from a blend of semillon, sercial and doradillo grapes grown in the Barossa Valley. This hock is a pleasant, soft, clean blend of no great fruit or distinction. It has very nice freshness and is well made—a good fruity quaffing wine.

Kaiser Stuhl Flagons—Light Dry Red
Produced from grenache grapes grown in the Barossa Valley, this wine is more like a deep rosé than a red wine. It has no distinction at all but is very good, pleasant quaffing wine for everyday purposes.

Kaiser Stuhl Flagons—Light Port
Produced from grenache grapes grown in the River Murray and Barossa Valley areas—a clean, fortified light red wine.

Kaiser Stuhl Flagons—Marsala
A very popular dessert type of wine made with a sweet wine base and Marsala herbs added.

Kaiser Stuhl Flagons—Medium Dry Sherry
Made mainly from ripe pedro ximenez grapes. The sherry is made under Flor culture for six months and then put into the flagon after a small addition of a mature, older sweet sherry, which gives a touch of sweetness and depth of character to the middle palate.

Kaiser Stuhl Flagons—Moselle
Made from clare riesling grapes grown in the Barossa Valley. A pleasant, clean, light wine—quite fruity, with a touch of sweetness on the middle palate and a dry finish.

Kaiser Stuhl Flagons—Muscat
Produced from muscat gordo blanco grapes grown in the River Murray area. It is a light, soft muscaty sweet wine.

Kaiser Stuhl Flagons—Regal Cream Sherry
Produced from muscat gordo blanco grapes grown around Waikerie on the River Murray. A soft, clean, fruity wine.

Kaiser Stuhl Flagons—Regal Sweet Sherry
A blend of pedro ximenez and palomino grapes grown in the Barossa Valley. A soft, clean, sweet wine.

Kaiser Stuhl Flagons—Riesling
Made entirely from clare riesling grapes grown in the Barossa Valley. A rather pleasant, fresh, fruity style of riesling, which has proved extremely popular with the public; having quite nice fruit and being quite clean and well made.

Kaiser Stuhl Flagons—Rosé
Produced from grenache grapes grown in the Barossa Valley. A true rosé style; light with a touch of sweetness on the palate and a clean finish.

Kaiser Stuhl Flagons—Sauterne
Made from sercial and semillon base wines, to which grape juice is added prior to bottling to make a soft, fruity, sweet table wine, having no particular character at all.

Kaiser Stuhl Flagons—Sweet Sherry
Made from a blend of pedro ximenez, palomino and albilio grapes grown in the Barossa Valley. After fortification it matures for two years in large American oak casks and then reaches the market as a pleasant, soft and fruity wine of considerable sweetness.

Kaiser Stuhl Flagons—Sweet Vermouth
This wine is quite dark in appearance, very sweet and suitable for a base for long drinks or 'on the rocks'. It is produced from trebbiano grapes grown in the Barossa Valley with specially selected herb extracts added.

Kaiser Stuhl Flagons—Tawny Port
Produced from grenache grapes grown at Waikerie and the Barossa Valley. Matured in oak casks for between two to four years and then sold as a light red dessert wine.

Kaiser Stuhl Flagons—Vermouth Bianco
Very sweet, white, aperitif type of wine; made from white hermitage and palomino grapes grown in the Barossa Valley, to which special Italian herbs have been added.

Kaiser Stuhl Individual Vineyard Gold Ribbon Riesling
Another wine from a particular vineyard—'Wyncroft'—in the Eden Valley. Certain rhine riesling grapes of this vineyard are left on the vines far beyond normal ripeness; they are then taken down to the cellars and

are temperature controlled and slow fermentated—before all the sugar is converted the new wine is chilled to arrest this fermentation. The wine is then cleaned very quickly and bottled at an early age to retain a maximum flowery bouquet. This wine has a great deal of flavour—a true essence character of the variety, quite concentrated and quite complex: a very flowery, estery sort of nose. Its full, rich flavour contains a fair amount of sugar and a very soft, clean acid finish. The wine actually contains 2.3 percent residual sugar.

There have been many Gold Medal winners in this line; 1971, 1968, 1967, 1965, 1961 all received Gold Medals. Of the late-picked rhine rieslings which are now in vogue this is probably one of the most consistent of the lines, and under this label and ribbon you can always find wines of quite concentrated character and flavour; wines which are always a pleasure to have with chilled fruit at the end of a meal.

Kaiser Stuhl Individual Vineyard Green Ribbon Riesling

This is a special dry wine. These individual vineyard wines of Kaiser Stuhl are an attempt to promote among their grape grower shareholders a true regard for fine quality grapes, the kind of grapes which, with great care and attention, can be selected and then made into really highest quality wine. The grower's name is shown on the bottle, which surely must give the grower some pride in the wines that the Barossa Co-operative is selling. (Kaiser Stuhl is the trade name for their wines.)

The Individual Vineyard Riesling generally comes from the vineyards of Mr C. F. Rogers, who grows his grapes in the Eden Valley area. The grapes are picked fairly late when they are very ripe, but they still retain good fresh acid. At the Kaiser Stuhl Cellars the winemakers carefully control the temperature of the fermentation and the wine is rapidly cleaned and, to retain the flowery bouquet of the variety, is bottled very early. The result is a dry wine with a very full rhine riesling character and just a trace of sugar on the middle palate; it has good clean finish and very well-balanced acid. The outstanding vintages of this particular line were 1968 and 1969.

Kaiser Stuhl Individual Vineyard Late Picked White Frontignan

A selection of white frontignan grapes is made again from selected individual vineyards in the Barossa Valley. The grapes are left on the vine beyond normal ripeness. The wine is temperature controlled and the fermentation is arrested before all the sugar is converted. The resulting wine is a rather sweet, full-flavoured, 'raisiny' type of wine with a heavy muscat overtone, which is surprisingly delicate for the variety of the grape. There is a hint of fullness, perhaps bordering on coarseness, on the back of the palate. I don't particularly like this variety in dry white styles, but the flavour is extremely rich and it appeals to many

people. The bouquet is good, the wine still contains 2.8 percent residual sugar.

The first of these wines was a 1967 vintage. Although both Kaiser Stuhl and Gramp's make outstanding late-picked Frontignans, I still prefer the rhine riesling style of late-picked wine.

Kaiser Stuhl Individual Vineyard Purple Ribbon Riesling

This is an outstanding wine. They call it a sweet white, but I think that you have to go beyond that. Again it comes from the 'Wyncroft' vineyard in the Eden Valley. In this case the grapes were left on in ideal conditions and many, many weeks after the end of harvest; and by this time they were very golden, concentrated bunches of rhine riesling grapes. The fermentation is temperature controlled and a great deal of care is taken in the making, the fermentation being arrested by chilling before all the sugar is converted. They leave 3 percent residual sugar in the wine, which is high and of course this gives quite a rich, complex sweetness to the middle palate.

I feel that this is one of the finest sweet wines that I have seen in Australia with a magnificent nose and full rich flavour, concentrated and complex —but which still has a clean, dry, rather acid finish. This is the kind of wine which will mature for many years, will concentrate even more in flavour and of which the nose and bouquet esters will build. Indeed I believe this will become one of the outstanding sweet wine lines of Australia. It is likened to the German *Auslese*, which means that the grapes are individually selected by hand when they have attained maximum ripeness. We don't have the same *Edelfaule* character (noble rot) because the bacteria doesn't work so well with our varieties; but other than this complex flavour additive being attained, this wine is an outstanding achievement which would be difficult to better.

Kaiser Stuhl Individual Vineyard Red Ribbon Shiraz—Claret

This is made from old shiraz vines from the large 'Dolce Domum' vineyard property of Mr A. E. Materne from Greenock. A small portion of this vineyard consists of old vines which have always consistently yielded extremely good material which has made very good wine.

These old vines, which have very low yield, result in grapes which have great vinosity and character and the resulting wines are extremely full in colour and dense in flavour. There is quite a marked intense flavour. The wine is matured in French Nevers new oak which adds to the complex fruit, so that you get very strong complementary flavours of oak and shiraz. The wines when mature unquestionably will have a great flavour and character. As yet we have not seen the span of life of one of these wines and there is no doubt that in the future, when they have

251

reached full maturity, there will be another added dimension to Barossa Valley red wines.

Kaiser Stuhl—Kaiser Pearl
A slightly sweet, sparkling, clean, fresh white wine made by the Charmat method.

Kaiser Stuhl Light Port
Made from grenache grapes grown in the Barossa Valley. The juice is left for about 24 hours on the skins and this extracts a small amount of pigment and tannin, which accounts for the rather extreme lightness in composition and colour of this fortified wine.

Kaiser Stuhl Medium Dry Sherry
Made from a blend of pedro ximenez and palomino grapes grown in the Barossa Valley. A smooth, rather full-bodied, full-flavoured, 'each-way bet'—appealing to some as an appetiser, or to others as a general all-round fortified wine.

Kaiser Stuhl Regal Cream Sherry
Made from muscat gordo blanco grapes grown in the River Murray area. It has quite a high Baumé of of about 6.5 degrees and has full, rich, creamy, muscaty characteristics.

Kaiser Stuhl Regal Sweet Sherry
Produced from a blend of pedro ximenez and palomino grapes grown in the Barossa Valley, the wine being matured in oak casks. A fairly full-bodied, rich, smooth white wine of no particular distinction.

Kaiser Stuhl Rosé—Gold Medal
This is one of the better of the slightly sweet rosés being made in Australia, if not the most consistent of all. It is made entirely from grenache grapes grown in the Barossa Valley and is produced by leaving the skins on the juice for a short period of time, from 10 to 24 hours, depending on the temperature of the must and pigment quantity in the skins. Only free run juice is used and the sugar content is a natural product of their arrested fermentation methods.

This is a pleasant, refreshing wine with good colour, good flavour and an all-round acceptable balance. It follows the Portuguese style of rosé by also having slight gas in its make-up so that you have a slightly spritzy, sweetish wine with a clean acid finish. I prefer it to the Portuguese style and think it has better character, better flavour, and better composition. It is well packaged in a rather tall, outstanding bottle.

Kaiser Stuhl have always done well with this wine in shows and have received at least one Gold Medal and in some cases several Gold Medals for every one of the vintage rosés for each year since the 1965 vintage.

Kaiser Stuhl Sangria
This unusual drink is a light red made for the young 'pop' market. It is made from Barossa grenache and mataro grapes and has some essence of orange and lemon added. The idea originated in Spain where Sangria is a blend of claret, orange and lemon juice, soda water and often other bits and pieces. This style has been very successful in America as a sort of 'fun' wine and Kaiser Stuhl have copied the product to make a wine which may provide a lot of people with a lot of fun.

Kaiser Stuhl Selected Hock
From semillon, clare riesling and white hermitage grapes grown in the Barossa Valley. A pleasant, dry wine with some fruit on the middle palate; a rather full-bodied style, with a crisp, dry finish.

Kaiser Stuhl Sparkling Burgundy
A very fruity, sparkling red wine with some sugar, made from selected shiraz grapes produced by the Charmat process.

Kaiser Stuhl Sparkling Moselle
Again the Charmat process is used to produce a very fruity sparkling white wine made from semillon, clare riesling and white hermitage grapes grown in the Barossa Valley. This wine has considerable natural sweetness.

Kaiser Stuhl Special Reserve Bin Claret
This is a quality dry red in which George Kolarovich, the winemaker, takes special pride. From each vintage, commencing in 1962, he has selected the best of the shiraz and this has been set aside for making into this Special Reserve line. The selected wine is made and then matured in small French oak casks for two years before being bottled. He started the idea in 1962 and that wine was an outstanding wine which has received seven Gold Medals in Australian shows. It had plenty of fruit, good oak-fruit complementary flavours; it was a

well-balanced wine — marred perhaps only by a slightly furry tannin on the back of the palate. To me this has always been characteristic of the line because this is a tannin that I find so typical of the Barossa Valley. However fine the flavour achieved in these wines, there is generally this slight blemish.

The 1963 and 1964 vintages also produced a number of Gold Medal winners.

The 1965 Special Reserve Bin Claret was an outstanding wine which has won several medals and which also at Montpellier in France was awarded the Diplome d'Honeur. There is no doubt that the winemaker has a special affection for this line and I believe the wines are outstanding reds from the Barossa area.

Kaiser Stuhl Special Reserve Bin Rhine Riesling
Made from the best rhine riesling grapes grown from certain selected vineyards in the Eden Valley. There are several very good Rhine Rieslings from this line. The wine is generally quite dry, has extremely good rhine riesling nose and fruit and is a typical high quality Eden Valley wine. I particularly remember one wine (which I think was the 1965 Special Reserve Bin Rhine Riesling) which was quite outstanding and developed beautifully. This was awarded the 'Bert Bear' Memorial Trophy for the best young dry white table wine at the 1966 Sydney Show.

Kaiser Stuhl Special Reserve Bin White Burgundy
Made from a blend of clare riesling and white hermitage grapes grown in the Tanunda area of the Barossa Valley. The company first produced white burgundy from the 1966 vintage. I remember seeing this wine quite early in shows and I looked at my Show Notes to recall my original impression. The wine did not score very well but it had a fairly heavily complimentary statement about its nose. I had recorded the simple statement 'Montrachet' which meant that I saw on the nose a marked development of fruit which had been matured in small oak casks. Indeed this is the practice of the company with their white burgundy styles. The rest of my notes were not quite so complimentary; in fact they went on to show disappointment, after the initial impact of the oak nose, to state that the wine was rather coarse, flat and lacked distinction. Since then I believe the wine has become slightly lighter, but it has always had this characteristic oak flavour which is very pleasant. It is an easy drinking white table wine.

Kaiser Stuhl Sweet Sherry
Made from a blend of pedro ximenez, palomino and albillo grapes from the Barossa area. Matured in oak for a few years, the wine is a full-bodied, full-flavoured, sweet style, with soft fruit and oak showing.

Kaiser Stuhl Tawny Port
Made from a blend of mataro, shiraz and carignane grapes grown in the Barossa Valley, matured in oak for some time and bottled just prior to sales. A smooth and round, light tawny style with a dry finish.

Kaiser Stuhl Vermouth—Bianco
Produced from a blend of palomino and white hermitage grapes and then infused with herbs obtained from Torino in Italy. It is a fairly delicate, fruity vermouth.

Kaiser Stuhl Vermouth—Dry
Produced from trebbiano (white hermitage) grapes grown in the Barossa Valley. The wine is heavily fined to obtain a light colour and style and then there is an infusion of specially selected herbs.

Kaiser Stuhl Vermouth—Sweet Italian
Again from trebbiano (white hermitage) and infused with herbs. A sweet, full-flavoured style.

Kaiser Stuhl Vintage Burgundy
A full-bodied, dry red produced from shiraz grapes grown in the Barossa Valley. Aged in small oak the wine is bottle matured for some considerable time in the cellars at Nuriootpa. Outstanding vintages have been the 1964 and 1966. The wine is always a fairly pleasant, easy drinking red of considerable shiraz fruit with this touch of oak. Again a rather furry, slightly firm finish dominates the end of the wine. I would like it softer and smoother.

Kaiser Stuhl Vintage Cabernet Sauvignon
The 1968 Cabernet Sauvignon, Bin L.18, was the company's first straight wine of this variety to come on the market. It was a Gold Medal winner in the 1970 Brisbane Show. It has lots of fruit, very rich intense colour, a rather pronounced Cabernet nose ('berry' nose), pronounced oak flavour and plenty of character. It was matured in French Nevers oak and bottled in October, 1971; therefore the period of oak maturation was quite prolonged.

This wine is of the very rich, full-flavoured, complex style that will live for many, many years. It will need at least ten years to show its quality. I believe that the company is developing more of these great varietals; initially for Show purposes and then to be sold to the public after some considerable maturation time.

Kaiser Stuhl Vintage Cabernet Shiraz—Claret
This is a blend of seventy percent cabernet sauvignon and thirty percent shiraz grapes grown in the Barossa Valley. It is matured in French hogsheads for a considerable time and again the oak used is Nevers. This maturation period is not entirely in small oak, since they tend to keep some in concrete and some in oak and then swap the various blends

around. Finally, in this way, correct oak balance is achieved. This is generally the practice adopted by most winemakers throughout Australia, otherwise the wines could become 'over-oaked'.

This is a pleasant well-balanced wine, again showing quite strong cabernet, and some oak. Perhaps it has less of the robustness of the straight Cabernet Sauvignon, but it is a good wine which matures very well.

Kaiser Stuhl Vintage Claret
Made entirely from shiraz grapes grown in the Barossa Valley and again matured in small French casks for a period of up to two years. It is then bottle matured in the cellars for another eighteen months to two years. This means generally that the wine is at least four years old before it is put on the market. The wines will take further bottle maturation. They are nice, typical Barossa dry reds, soft, smooth on the middle palate with the slightly 'matty' or furry finish, which is so typical of the area.

Kaiser Stuhl Vintage Moselle
Made from semillon grapes grown mainly in the Lyndoch area of the Barossa Valley. This is a wine which contains 15 to 18 grammes per litre residual sweetness, which is obtained by the addition of grape juice to a selected dry white wine base. It is a pleasant, fruity wine with a quite marked touch of sweetness on the middle palate, and a dry, clean finish.

Kaiser Stuhl Vintage Rhine Riesling
Made entirely from rhine riesling grapes grown in the Barossa Valley and from the Eden Valley. A pleasant, dry, delicate, white style; quite fragrant and flowery, with a pleasant fruity varietal palate and a crisp, dry finish.

Kay Bros

Kay's Amery Cabernet Shiraz
Made from cabernet sauvignon and shiraz grapes grown in the 'Amery' vineyards at McLaren Vale. The blend percentages vary from 35/65 to 50/50, depending on the crop and grape quality of the year. Made in oak and fermenters, with cooling, and left on the skins for four to five days; matured for from two to two and a half years before bottling, part of this time being in oak casks. It is a long-lived wine and has been a consistent medal winner.

The 1967 wine did particularly well in open Claret classes. The wine always has good fruit, plenty of colour, plenty of character and is quite firm on the middle palate, with a clean, persistent tannin finish. There is always a slight hint of delicate spice to the wine which makes it quite discernable once you can learn to identify it.

Kay's Amery Dry Red
From grenache, shiraz and mataro grapes grown in the 'Amery' vineyards and also from nearby. Sold as a flagon and carafe wine, but a considerable quantity is bottled in favourable years. Always a pleasant medium-bodied red at a very reasonable price.

Kay's Amery Hock
A soft, pleasant wine made from pedro ximenez, palomino and albillo grapes. It is best drunk as a young fresh wine.

Kay's Amery Late-picked Riesling
Made from rhine riesling grapes grown in 'Amery' vineyards and picked at the very end of vintage. Fermented in closed vats under refrigeration and bottled within six months. It improves with several years. The wine has considerable rhine riesling varietal character, a very rich, soft palate in which the varietal fruit shows well, and the residual sugar is well in harmony with the flavour. The finish is clean and crisp.

The 1971 vintage won the top Gold Medal in the Moselle class in the 1971 Adelaide Wine Show and the 1972 vintage shows great promise.

Kay's Amery Muscat
Made from muscatel (muscat gordo blanco) grapes grown south of Adelaide. Mainly used as a flagon wine, it is soft and fruity.

Kay's Amery Port
Made from shiraz and grenache grapes grown in the McLaren Vale district. It is a typical, good quality, fruity dessert wine; develops well in wood and lives to a great age.

Kay's Amery Rhine Riesling
A delicate, dry, crisp wine with a fragrant nose, made entirely from rhine riesling grapes grown in the company's vineyards. It is fermented in closed vats under controlled temperature and bottled within six months. Probably at its best at two to four years of age. Cud Kay, the owner of the company, was the pioneer in bringing rhine riesling to this district.

Kay's Amery Rosé
From grenache grapes grown in the district, with a small addition of shiraz. Crisp, clean wine, with a hint of fruitiness. Best drunk within three years. This wine, generally speaking, has a little bit more to it than some of the delicate rosés and is a very pleasant, refreshing drink.

Kay's Amery Sauvignon Blanc
The first wine from this recent planting in the 'Amery' vineyard was made in 1971 under refrigeration and resulted in a dry, full-flavoured white

Dr Max Lake checks the juice of the first run off his new Howard Rotapress.

with a pleasant spicy nose. Quantity will be limited until further plantings come into bearing. I was most intrigued with this wine when I saw it during 1971; the comparison to a dry Graves must be made and this wine is excellent in that it has very interesting varietal character, plenty to it, a delicious flavour and a lovely dry, rather pleasant clean tannin finish.

Kay's Amery Shiraz
This is a well-tried and proven soft dry red, so typical of McLaren Vale. In recent years the plantings of shiraz have been increased in the district. Amery Shiraz is bottled when two to two and a half years old and improves for many years. The wine is always well-balanced, always has pleasant fruit and there is a hint of spiciness with these reds which is so familiar. A good quality Australian wine.

Kay's Amery Sweet Sherry
Sold mainly in the flagon. Made from pedro ximenez, palomino and albillo grapes, with a little muscatel (muscat gordo blanco), for fruitiness, and kept in oak.

Kay Brothers' Amery Sweet Vermouth
Made from a blend of sweet sherry and port type wines and flavoured with Italian herbs. Stored in oak. Mostly sold for local trade.

Lachlan Valley Wines
Assorted Wines
The Chisletts have run a unique little family establishment at Forbes in New South Wales for some time and Mr F. L. Chislett is the present

manager and winemaker. I visited the winery some years ago and several of the wines were most interesting and had considerable flavour and character. One or two of the reds suffered from volatile acid and Mr Chislett was concerned about this and doing his utmost to correct it. He was also experimenting with some small new wood and was achieving very good blends of flavour between cabernet sauvignon and small oak.

He makes a number of fortified wines which mostly sell to the local trade and among them are a Cream Sherry made from muscat gordo blanco; a Dry Sherry, made from trebbiano (white hermitage) and palomino; a Muscat Brown Frontignac, which is entirely of that variety; and a lighter Muscat, called Muscat White Gordo—again made from the muscat gordo blanco. There is a Port Black Shiraz, which is entirely made from shiraz and a Port Cabernet Sauvignon and Pinot Noir. (Incredibly, there is a small amount of pinot noir in the local vineyards.) It is rather interesting to note that these two great dry red varieties of France come together in a relatively obscure vineyard in New South Wales to make a Port. There is also a Sweet Sherry, made from straight semillon.

The dry reds are variously made from shiraz and cabernet sauvignon, or are blends of both and, free from volatile acid, have a very good flavour character and are fairly full-bodied. There are also some dry whites made for the local trade from semillon and from trebbiano. The latter is a rather full-flavoured, robust dry white.

Lake, Dr Max ('Lake's Folly')

Lake's Fancy Dry Red
Precisely that. This is a unique bottling of a highly individual wine and is the selection of the family's of the wine of the year, being the particular cask that they would like to put aside and keep for themselves. Often there are so many arguments they have to keep two. So for exactly that reason they printed a special label **and** they drink it themselves, which, after all, is their prerogative.

Lake's Folly Cabernet Sauvignon
Made entirely from cabernet sauvignon grown in this now celebrated vineyard in the Hunter Valley. The vineyard has a southerly aspect and is in fact the south face of one of the basalt crowns of the district which are renowned for their red wine quality. Over the road is the summit of the crown and on it lies the famous 'Rosehill' vineyard of McWilliam's. Plantings commenced in 1963 with cabernet sauvignon and were virtually completed by 1965. In this time approximately 13 acres of

cabernet and 4 acres of hermitage were planted, since followed by an acre of merlot and malbec.

Of the wines made so far, Max Lake has produced an extraordinarily interesting range of complex flavoured wines. The wines have been matured in new wood, either hogsheads or 300 gallon casks and Max Lake has handled this wood treatment extremely well. All Folly wines labelled Cabernet Sauvignon are 100 percent.

The 1966 was an experimental wine which was foot-stamped. The wine is now garnet coloured, has a light to medium body, has built up an interesting bouquet and, of course, has tremendous sentimental and romantic overtones.

The 1967 wine has a rich ruby colour; again this distinctive oak cabernet bouquet build-up with a very rich flavour. A wine which will mature for some considerable time yet.

The 1968 was lighter and I think the colour started to fade a little more quickly than the 1967, but 1968 was a fairly light year, a rather wet year, and one would expect the wines to be light from the district. However, the fruit is good, and the 1968 is now showing some 'cigar box' bouquet. Perhaps the fruit of the wine is not sufficiently big to match the oak. One might assume that this wine would be ready for drinking quicker than the 1967.

The 1969 Cabernet Sauvignon is a wonderfully good, rich, 'new-dimension' Hunter: new dimensional in that it has all sorts of new characters. It has regional character to be sure; in addition, it has a much brighter, fuller colour than usual—a very deep vivid colour which still contains purple overtones. There is a huge volume of flavour—extremely rich fruit, plus very good oak indeed. And yet the finish, though firm, is still showing perfect balance. The whole wine I believe will turn out to be a masterpiece. I have always thought it had a quite extraordinary flavour and character and I look forward to seeing it in the future; though in many years time when it reaches its peak of maturation.

The 1970 also had a very good colour. It was a lighter wine. This wine, perhaps, has a style Max Lake was trying to achieve which combines lightness with intensity of flavour. His whole aim apparently, is to make extremely interesting, complex wines ('complex' is a word he uses himself a great deal)—wines of great intensity of flavour, very good balance and finesse and with a concentration of exquisite flavour which comes from cabernet sauvignon fruit and small oak handling. Certainly the 1970 is a wine of great potential and one should be looking forward to seeing **this** in the future as well.

1971 was an extremely wet vintage. Max Lake made a good wine in that year because the cabernet sauvignon stays up better than the hermitage (shiraz). In fact, in 1971 the hermitage went mouldy on the vine and the cabernet didn't. The wine has a very good fruit bouquet; it is a light, very well-

Shovelling lees out of a vat at Hamiltons Ewell vineyards, S.A.

Lindeman's one-year-old plantings in the Keppoch Valley, S.A., are irrigated by water winch from underground sources.

balanced wine and I think this will be very good in years to come. Certainly at this stage again, it is showing the typical combination of fruit and oak that Max is trying to achieve.

The 1972 vintage, although wet to start with, turned out very well and Max has made a surprisingly big wine; a big flavoured, big fruit wine of considerable strength of body. The wine has great depth of flavour and is probably more like the 1969 than any other of the wines in the series: these would be the two comparable wines from the various vintages. I expect this wine to mature as one of the best wines he has made. An interesting conjecture remains. Will the wine finally finish as the rather lighter, more ethereal wine of great finesse that Max is looking for or will good years prevent this? The cabernet sauvignon responds to sunshine, there's no doubt about it. So, will the **years** produce wines which have greater, richer character than perhaps Max wishes to find? Or is the definite style still to emerge with the added benison of malbec and merlot?

Lake's Folly Cabernet Sauvignon Hermitage

These are most interesting wines produced from the two varieties. The hermitage is grown on particularly good soil and produces most interesting wines in its own right. There was no wine which appeared under this label from the 1966 vintage. The 1967 vintage produced a most interesting wine which I liked very much indeed, for it had extraordinarily good varietal flavour and the hermitage was coming through **over** the cabernet. Combined with the oak and the definite regional character the wine had a most interesting combination of flavours; it was extremely well-balanced and had a pleasant soft finish.

The 1968 wine which followed did not have the same complexity of character. It was a lighter wine which reflected the year and again I thought the oak rather assertive. Still, a good wine and one that will drink well for some time.

The 1969 was a bigger wine. The colour was most interesting for it seemed to quickly achieve a rather pleasant, almost brickish colour, which I quite liked and which is rather typical of the area. The bouquet built up very quickly; it was medium-bodied with a rather firmer finish than one would expect from the hermitage variety in the district. A wine which certainly is going to drink very well in the future.

The 1970 wine again was slightly lighter. Again, good oak, cabernet and hermitage flavours. A nice wine with a good nose developing and a wine which one could drink fairly quickly. None of this wine was produced in 1971. The hermitage suffered and did not develop sufficient colour. From 1973 the Cabernet Sauvignon Hermitage will contain merlot and malbec and will be called Lake's Folly Dry Red.

Lake's Hunter Valley Estate Dry Red

Made by Max Lake and sold under the Hunter Valley Estate label from either material which he produces himself or buys from local vineyards.

The 1966 wine was a combination of his own material and some which he obtained from a wine-maker friend nearby. It is a pleasant, full-flavoured wine of a good colour and generous flavour. None of this wine was produced in 1967 or 1968.

In 1969 he produced a most interesting wine (a straight Lake's Folly) which was called The Hunter Valley Estate Dry Red-O'Shea Memorial. This wine was in much demand. Of all the wines that Max Lake has produced it had perhaps the most authentic Hunter character in the traditional sense. It had a very good brick colour and a flavour which was reminiscent of some of the older wines of the district. It is also one of the wines that will mature for many years to come, made, Max believes, by O'Shea's own methods.

None of this Hunter Valley Estate Wine was produced in 1970 and then, in 1971, the hermitage which had not been considered good enough to be bottled by itself was combined with the cabernet to produce a light wine of agreeable flavour and character. It is a wine which developed quite surprisingly from its rather inauspicious start, to show a pleasant light red that will mature fairly quickly.

In 1972 a wine was made from material bought from another vineyard into a fairly robust dry red, which is not really of the Lake's Folly style, but improved by Folly cabernet pressings.

One looks forward with great interest to sampling many of Max Lake's wines in the future. He is a most dedicated winemaker and a man of staggering range of interest; a man who will leave his mark on the wine world of Australia. Many people said that he would not do what he set out to do. I believe that he has now shown them he can produce a unique style of wine. The wines **do** have a complexity of character, considerable finesse, a tremendous combination of fruit and oak and I believe that we shall be seeing many great wines from the vineyard in the future. I am proud to have Max Lake as a great friend and I am continually stimulated by his presence and activities. I believe he wrote his own epitaph one day when in a letter to me he said,

'Yours and the rest
Max Lake
A legend in his time'.

Light Wines

Assorted Wines

In the Happy Valley District, south of Adelaide, there are some fine vineyards and small concerns producing some very good wines.

Lloyd Light was a foundation director of the Southern Vales Co-Operative, but realising the fruit from his own vineyards in these hills was very good, he commenced winemaking in 1969. In 1970 a very good-looking cellar was established and up to 1,000 tons per year are crushed in the winery at Chandlers Hill.

A range of fortified wines, appetiser and dessert, are available for sale on location, but the main purpose of the winery is to produce very good quality table wines which are sold in bulk to other wine-makers and wine companies. There are some table wines available to the public, but as yet the company has not featured its own very good quality table wines for sale, other than in bulk to other companies.

This company has vineyards at Coromandel Valley, Happy Valley, Clarendon, Bakers Gully and Hill Crest, Chandlers Hill.

Lindeman's Wines Pty Ltd

Lindeman's Alpine Mist
Produced at Lindeman's Sydney cellars by the Charmat process of natural secondary fermentation. This wine is a light, pale, straw-coloured sparkling wine with a fruity flavour, some sweetness on the palate and a clean finish.

Lindeman's Aperlwein
Produced at Lindeman's Sydney cellars by the Charmat process. This is a light, pink-coloured, sparkling wine with a fruity flavour, some sugar on the palate and a clean, soft finish.

Lindeman's Auburn Burgundy
A vintage wine, produced from red hermitage grapes (shiraz), grown in the Hunter River area, Clare Valley and at Coonawarra. It is matured in small oak casks prior to bottling, which is done approximately twenty months after vintage, for eventual sale at five years' age.

This is a special and distinctive 'cellar style' created by the Lindeman's people to give a wine with complex bouquet and character, a big fruit flavour with a sound, round, well-balanced palate.

The 1966 wine was an excellent one which provided very good value for money at something just over $2.00 a bottle. It was a Silver Medal winner in various shows, had very pleasant full fruit and style; a very well-balanced wine and plenty of it available.

Lindeman's Ben Ean Moselle
A non-vintage table wine of tremendous popularity; produced from various grape varieties grown in the Barossa and Clare Valleys, including semillon, clare riesling and muscat gordo blanco.

This wine has, therefore, a very soft fruity palate, with a definite grapeyness to it and some residual sugar. This is a consistent wine in its light and pale colour, fruitiness, plus a crisp palate and finish. Among reasons for the great popularity of this wine is its very economical price and its 'maid-of-all-work' quality.

Ben Ean Moselle derives its name from the vineyard of the company and the winery in the heart of the Hunter River Valley, though there is no suggestion that Ben Ean Moselle is a Hunter Wine. The vineyard and winery was purchased by the Lindeman family in 1912.

Lindeman's Bin 50 Burgundy
A vintage dry red wine produced from the red hermitage (shiraz) grapes grown in the Hunter River Valley and Corowa districts of New South Wales, in the Clare Valley, at Coonawarra and McLaren Vale in South Australia. It is a constant Bin number, i.e., it is repeated year after year.

Matured in small oak casks prior to bottling, Bin 50 is a distinctive 'cellar style' wine with a round, soft, generous palate, an attractive flavour and considerable delicacy. Wines used for this style are carefully selected to maintain a consistent character and quality each year and the wine has been awarded two Silver Medals and four Bronze Medals at various Australian Wine Shows. It can be enjoyed immediately upon purchase, although it does take a few years' bottle age with no trouble at all.

The 1966 was a very good wine of this particular class, the 1967 also a good wine. The 1968 seemed a trifle lighter and the 1969 a rather light wine, showing some more advancement than was usual at the time of release which was probably due to the rather poor year in 1969.

Lindeman's Bin 64 Chablis
A vintage dry white produced from white hermitage, semillon and riesling grapes grown in the Hunter, Barossa and Clare Valleys and sold under the year of vintage and with a constant Bin number. Bottling shortly after vintage produces a crisp, delicate wine with typical Chablis flintiness on the back of the palate. This wine is an award winner at many shows and the vintages from 1966 to 1970 won two Gold, one Silver and one Bronze Medal. The wine always has good style and good fruit. It is well-balanced with the marvellous freshness on the middle palate that the company manages to get with nearly all their white wines, and a very pleasant, crisp finish.

Lindeman's Bin 45 Claret
A vintage dry red produced from red hermitage (shiraz) grapes grown in some of the premium areas of Australia, including Watervale, Barossa Valley, McLaren Vale and Coonawarra in South Australia. In fact at one time, Keith Dunstan, the Melbourne writer, said of the Lindeman's wines that the Murumbidgee Irrigation Area must be awfully upset

at being left out! Whatever, their 'cellar style' is most important in Australia, because some of our better wines have been produced by their very skilled oenologists who put together, with tremendous skill, wines from all over the place and still achieve their unique company style and character.

This wine is matured in small oak casks prior to bottling. It is a distinctive dry red with an attractive bouquet and flavour and though it is easy to drink and can be drunk straightaway it has plenty to it. These wines can be put aside for some time and they do improve with age. In recent years, the Bin 45 of various years have been awarded two Gold, four Silver and two Bronze Medals at various shows. This indicates that the wine is extremely good value for money as it can do so well when it is, after all, just a straightforward commercial wine.

Lindeman's Bin 11 Moselle
A vintage white produced from selected riesling grapes grown in the Hunter River Valley, Clare and Barossa Valleys and sold as a constant Bin number, which repeats year after year; the vintage is always shown. A 'Riesling' means semillon, clare riesling and rhine riesling. The wine is bottled shortly after vintage each year and sold at a relatively early age to retain the original fresh flavour and perfumed bouquet—aromatic quality—of the grapes. The Bin 11 is always a prizewinner at shows and in fact from 1965 to 1971 won six Gold, seven Silver and eight Bronze Medals, which shows how well-regarded the wine is. It usually has a trace of sugar on the middle palate, though the 1971 vintage example appeared almost bone dry, certainly much drier than usual. In all, a wine of good balance and fruit, extremely well put together and very good value for money.

Lindeman's Bin 36 Porphyry
A very consistent and well-made sweet wine produced from semillon and other selected white grape varieties at the company's Hunter River Valley and Corowa wineries. It is sold under the year of the vintage and with a repetitive Bin number.

The wine is matured in oak casks until bottling for approximately two and a half years after vintage. Bin 36 Porphyry is a rich, luscious Sauternes style of sweet wine, with a strong grapy bouquet and a clean, dry finish on the palate. Wines used for the Bin 36 are selected each year to maintain a constant style and quality; confirmed by the fact that though Bin 36 was not produced in the years 1961, 1963 and 1965, the remaining vintages from 1960-69 inclusive were awarded eight Gold, twenty-four Silver and thirteen Bronze Medals in Australian wine shows.

The 1968 is a full, luscious wine with a slightly dumb nose, but with very full grapyness and complexity of flavour on the middle palate, yet the wine is not cloying in spite of its considerable sweetness. It has a concentrated, almost muscaty flavour on the middle palate but I find this most appealing, some-what reminiscent of the great Sauternes of France, which have a percentage (about ten percent or so) of the muscat (Frontignac family) variety used in their make-up.

This is extremely good value as a sweet wine. It is a very well balanced, quite elegant style of sweet wine, that finishes very clean and is ideal with chilled fruit at the end of the meal.

Lindeman's Bin 23 Riesling
A vintage dry white produced from riesling grapes grown in the Hunter River, Barossa and Clare Valleys. Again this is a repetitive Bin number which appears each year under the year of its particular vintage. It is bottled shortly after vintage and sold quite early to retain full freshness and flavour.

This is a most consistent line, confirmed when you look at the show record. In 1965 to 1971 this particular wine gained seven Gold, fourteen Silver and ten Bronze Medals in various shows, which is a very good performance indeed for a wine which sells for such a reasonable price.

The 1970 Bin 23 was an extremely good wine which won a Gold in Brisbane and Silvers in Sydney, Melbourne and Brisbane. A wine of terrific fruit and freshness when young with a lot of flavour and character. In addition the compensation is that if you don't happen to drink the wine when young it builds up a delightful full flavour on the middle palate with some age. I can remember drinking Bin 23s of about six years of age which had delightful richness of character.

The 1968 edition of this wine was typical of how good the wine can be. It won a Gold Medal in the Open Hock Class in Sydney in 1968 which is quite an accomplishment for a trade wine, selling for something just over a dollar and the blend did reflect the usual kind of wine that goes into the style. It was composed of 30 percent rhine riesling from Clare Valley, 30 percent clare riesling coming from the Clare and Barossa Valleys and 40 percent Hunter riesling (semillon) from the Hunter Valley. It had a very soft, full, fruity nose; and a very flavoursome palate which is always part of the Lindeman's style; with a soft, acid finish.

This distinctive Lindeman's flavour is very hard to define. Over the years I have called it 'vanillin', and it has just a hint of aromatic spice; very difficult to describe, quite easy to pick once you get used to it. Again, it is a good 'each-way' proposition. This wine was very good when young and then developed well—I am still drinking the 1968 Bin 23. It has delightful full flavour.

The same could be said for the 1966 and also the 1964. All these wines built up considerable character. The fresh acid kept them together and their flavour characteristic was always extremely good.

The 1971 vintage, reflecting the poor year in the Hunter, is not of the usual standard; though it does remain a good stand-by.

Lindeman's Bin 77 White Burgundy

My favourite wine with Chinese food. Again it is a Bin number which is repeated year after year and it is always sold under the label of its particular vintage. It is bottled young to retain fresh fruity flavour and is made from semillon, white hermitage and again the ubiquitous riesling grown in the Hunter, Barossa and Clare Valleys.

It is a round, soft, flavoursome wine which is still crisp, delicate and always very well-balanced and clean. Again this wine has won all sorts of medals and in the six-year period reviewed, it has won four Gold, eight Silver and eight Bronze Medals in various White Burgundy-Chablis classes.

Again the 1971 edition is not quite up to the power of previous wines, probably due to the poor Hunter vintage. There is always a considerable amount of Hunter material in this wine. The wines at the end of the 1960s were very good indeed; the 1970 wine was acceptable, of good style and flavour. The 1968 Bin 77, which won several Silver Medals, was from the usual varieties, white hermitage, semillon and clare riesling. It had plenty of fruit and was a very full style, compensated by a rather austere finish showing quite fair acid and just a trace of the famous flint character which is so much part of the chablis style. Again the wine was very acceptable as young wine and again it built up considerable flavour in the bottle.

The 1967 Bin 77 was an outstanding wine that contained fifty percent of material from the Hunter, the rest was made up from South Australian material. The wine had a delightful gold-green colour, beautiful flavour and tremendous full bouquet which built up in the years after the wine was released. This so-called 'honey' character often comes from Hunter pressings material. They use first pressings in the style and balance them with very fresh, clean material from other areas.

The style was first introduced in 1962. The 1965 was an outstanding wine; the 1966 was very good and won several Silver Medals, and the 1967 wine won Gold Medals as well as Silvers. As I have said previously it is a wine which is very drinkable young because of its soft, smooth freshness—but then matures with extra depth of flavour after some years in the bottle. I think this is a characteristic of all these wines and is a characteristic which I certainly like very much.

Lindeman's Cawarra Claret

This is a non-vintage dry red of great popularity. It derives its name from Doctor Henry Lindeman's first vineyard in the Hunter River Valley, which was established in 1843, though there is no pretence that this wine now comes from the Valley. It is produced from shiraz and grenache grapes grown at Watervale and in the Barossa Valley. Therefore, it is entirely a South Australian wine.

PRIVATE BIN

BIN 23 RIESLING
VINTAGE 1970
HUNTER RIVER BLEND

This wine was vintaged from Riesling grapes grown in the Hunter River, Barossa and Clare Valleys. It was fermented at low temperatures, and bottled shortly after vintage to retain the original, fresh flavour of the grapes. Bin 23 is a light, clean, delicate Hock with a soft, fresh flavour and fruity character, suitable for accompanying all salads and light meat dishes. It may be enjoyed now or kept for many years for further bottle ageing.

LINDEMANS WINES PTY. LTD., SYDNEY
PRODUCE OF **1 PT 6 FL OZ** AUSTRALIA

The wine represents extremely good value for money. It has always been sold at a reasonable price and is a very good drinking red which can be enjoyed straightaway. But, it **was** named after Dr Lindeman's first vineyard and in fact the wines of the 1950s **were** from the Hunter Valley. Lindeman's had the choice of either keeping the price down and using wines from other areas or continuing with just the small produce of the Hunter and raising the price considerably. They made it a very famous wine name because it now sells throughout the length and breadth of the land as a dry red of reasonable price. But I've been fooled by older examples.

Lindeman's Cawarra Riesling Hock

A very popular non-vintage wine produced from a blend of various white grapes from all over the country and bottled at an early age under controlled conditions. It is a soft, clean white showing delicate riesling character with a crisp, fruity palate. And, of course, it is a very low-priced wine. Again, years ago the wines were almost straight Hunters. I can remember the famous 1945 Hock, the so-called 'London Hock', using the same labels as used today. This wine, which was sent to London after the war, was never sold and many years later in the 1960s it was returned to Sydney. It had therefore travelled some 26,000 miles (plus) and was still in superb condition, showing tremendously well-developed Hunter character, great style and great flavour. A complete and devastating argument against those people who say that Australian wines—and Australian white wines in particular—don't travel.

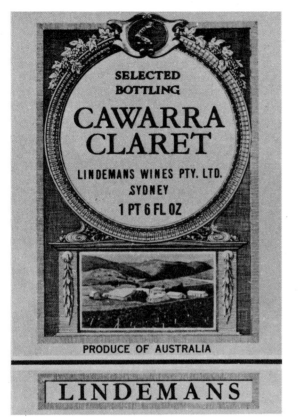

Lindeman's Cold Duck

Introduced to the Australian market in the late 1969 by the company. Cold Duck is best classified as a 'fun' sparkling wine. It is a soft, fruity blend of Sparkling Burgundy and Champagne, with an attractive rosé colour and it is unquestionably a useful wine for those people who don't know quite what they want and indeed, in some cases, may not quite know what they are going to get.

Lindeman's Coolalta Red Hermitage

A vintage dry red sold under the same label every year with the particular vintage registered. It is produced from selected red hermitage (shiraz) grapes grown in some of the premium areas of the country, including Watervale, the Barossa Valley, McLaren Vale and Coonawarra.

This is matured in small oak casks prior to bottling and is a distinctive 'cellar style' red of good flavour, attractive bouquet and nice easy-to-drink character and one which keeps for some years in the bottle and improves during that time.

Coolalta Red Hermitage derives its name from Lindeman's 'Coolalta' vineyard, purchased in 1912 at Pokolbin in the Hunter Valley.

Lindeman's Coolalta White Burgundy

A vintage dry white, produced from white hermitage, semillon and riesling grapes grown in the Hunter,

Clare and Barossa Valleys. It is bottled young under the system that Lindeman's use to retain flavour and freshness. It is a crisp, good medium-bodied White Burgundy which always improves in the bottle with further ageing. It is very much like the style of the Bin 77.

The original wines of this line came out at the end of the 1950s. The 1957 Bin A was a wine which will always live in my memory as a wine of tremendous vinosity and power which developed enormously in the bottle. Over the years I have enjoyed the wine many, many times and have always been most impressed by it.

Lindeman's Corowa Table Wines

This is a range of non-vintage table wines of consistent quality and style, sold at most economical prices which therefore represent excellent value for money for just ordinary, everyday bottled drinking. There are many people who prefer to buy a reasonably priced bottle instead of flagons because of the deterioration of flagons and I applaud this thinking. I think that low-priced bottled wines should become more popular in the future.

These wines are produced from selected grape varieties from the cellars of the company at Corowa on the River Murray. Various wines are sold which include Corowa Burgundy, Claret, Moselle, Riesling Hock, Rosé and White Burgundy. They are all light, delicate wines; soft, clean, with some varietal character showing through them; well put together; well-made wines, which represent very good value for money.

Lindeman's Dry Imperator Brut Champagne

This is a vintage Champagne of fine quality and pronounced flavour, produced in Sydney at the company's cellars by the traditional French Methode Champenoise. The base cuvee is made from specially selected wines from various districts and varieties and brought to Sydney for blending. After addition of yeast and sugar it is bottled to allow secondary fermentation in the bottle and then after some years in its tirage state it picks up tremendous character by resting on its yeast lees during this time. The wine is a blend of different areas and different grape varieties. These are not available for publication because apparently, after a lot of trial and error, they have hit upon their blend and it is a great secret. Certainly, I would imagine, there is both semillon and white hermitage material in the wine and I would imagine further there is some Hunter material as well—just enough to give its great broad flavour. The wines have plenty of character and I think that is their chief virtue. They are not just dry, fizzy wines.

The 1965 wine did well at Shows, had very good character, built up a lot of power and volume of flavour in the bottle and was very good drinking. The 1966 is a good drinkable wine with plenty of

VINTAGE 1968

EST. 1843

Coolalta

Red Hermitage

LINDEMANS WINES PTY. LTD., SYDNEY
1 PT. 6 FL. OZ.

PRODUCE OF AUSTRALIA

style. I believe that these wines are at their best at about six years old, after which time they tend to become too full-flavoured.

In the vintages from 1965 to 1968 the wines won five Gold Medals and eleven Silver Medals. And when you consider the competition given by the famous Seppelt's Great Western Wines, it shows that Lindeman's definitely were producing some Champagnes of outstanding quality.

Lindeman's Dry Imperator Champagne

A premium quality Champagne, again produced by the traditional method, and made predominantly from semillon and pedro ximenez grapes grown in the Barossa and Clare Valleys of South Australia. This wine is also available in Magnums (two bottles), Jeroboams (four bottles) and Methuselahs (eight bottles). Again, this is a good, full-flavoured wine which is less dry than the Brut.

Lindeman's Dry Imperator Champagne—Pink

A premium quality sparkling wine produced under a vintage label and made in the Sydney cellars of the company by the traditional French Methode Champenoise. It is slightly sweeter than the White Dry Imperator Champagne; and is an Australian Pink Champagne style.

Lindeman's El Rey Port

A fine old wood-matured tawny port produced from shiraz and grenache grapes grown on the company's vineyards at Corowa in New South Wales. This wine is matured in a modified Solera System to give a wine of consistent value and style.

Lindeman's Extra Special Dessert Wines

These are made at Corowa and are a range of dessert wines which represents excellent value for money for everyday drinking. The range is comprised of: Extra Special Frontignac which is a sweet, luscious dessert wine of pronounced grapy flavour and taste; Extra Special Madeira, a pale-coloured medium-dry Madeira, with a nutty character on the finish; Extra Special Tokay, a pale-coloured, luscious dessert wine; and Extra Special White Port, a golden-coloured white port, sweet and luscious, yet with a slightly dry finish to the palate.

Lindeman's Flagon Table Wine

Wines from one or more districts and varieties are put together in Lindeman's Sydney cellars to produce this range of quality flagon table wines. They are bottled and matured under strictly controlled conditions to ensure a high degree of consistency throughout the range and represent very good value for money. There is no question that the flagon wines of this company are of good style, well-made, well-balanced wines which provide very easy everyday drinking.

The wines include: Flagon Burgundy, which has a round, soft palate and pleasant flavour; Flagon Claret, a medium ruby-coloured red, with a soft bouquet and flavour, yet firm dry finish on the palate; Flagon Moselle, a light-coloured dry white, with a distinctive slightly muscaty bouquet and rather fruity palate, a clean, fresh, delicate wine with just a hint of sugar; Flagon Riesling Hock, a delicate dry wine with a fresh, clean bouquet and soft, pleasing taste; Flagon Rosé, a light pink rosé with a fruity bouquet and clean, delicate astringency on the palate; Flagon Sauternes, a light golden-coloured Sauternes with a rather fruity grape, almost muscaty bouquet and flavour; and Flagon White Burgundy, a very good-quality, well-flavoured, soft, round dry white, with a smooth finish.

Lindeman's Flor Amontillado Sherry

A light, soft, aged sherry, made from palomino and mont baden grapes grown at Lindeman's Corowa vineyards. It is produced by the Spanish Flor method, in which a special Flor yeast is allowed to grow on the surface of the wine in oak maturing casks, imparting a typical Flor sherry bouquet and flavour which marries extremely well with the oak quality gained from the maturation.

Lindeman's Flor Fino Sherry

A pale, dry, delicate sherry made from palomino and mont baden grapes grown at Lindeman's Corowa vineyards. It is produced by the Spanish Flor method and is a drier wine of some considerable astringency and Flor, with a very nice, clean, flavoursome middle palate.

Lindeman's Golden Velvet Champagne

A light, sparkling wine made by the Charmat method which combines a trace of sugar with pleasant freshness to present good value for money.

Lindeman's Hunter River Burgundy

These are vintage dry red wines made from the red hermitage or shiraz grapes grown at Lindeman's 'Ben Ean' and 'Sunshine' vineyards at Pokolbin in the Hunter Valley. Each year at vintage, only wines which attain a certain pre-determined standard of quality are selected for maturing in oak casks, bottling and ultimate sale at approximately five years' age. Lindeman's generally use a four bin number system for these wines or at least has done so in the last decade.

Of the past ten vintages, no wines were bottled from the 1965 and 1971 vintages, due to drought and heavy rainfall respectively. The balance of the decade of vintages have been consistent prizewinners in various shows throughout Australia, winning eleven Gold, nine Silver and five Bronze Medals to date and I have no doubt that this total will be enlarged in the future.

Bin 3603 of 1967, one of the best wines of that vintage from the Hunter, is very round and soft, and has full flavour. Yet when one considers that this is a fairly light wine and of a fairly light vintage it is surprising how much flavour it does have. It has a clean, soft finish and will drink very well for some time yet.

The 1966 vintage wine was Bin 3303. This was a wine of considerable depth of flavour and had more to it than the 3603: balanced flavour, richness, bouquet—all showing typical Hunter Valley character and yet that added dimension of character that Lindeman's seem to be able to provide with their Hunter wines. It is certainly a wine which drank extremely well and had a lot of style. It appears that this line is 'one-off' their top. They reserve their greatest wines for further ageing and these slightly lighter wines are sold first. They remain among the best of Hunter red wines.

Lindeman's Hunter River Chablis

This wine is now produced from semillon grapes grown at the 'Sunshine' vineyard in the Hunter Valley. The 'Sunshine' vineyard is on the Branxton Road between Cessnock and Branxton, and comprises sandy soils, sand and sandy loam, over clayey subsoil. It is therefore quite quick draining and the yields are lighter and perhaps produce grapes with a higher concentration of delicate flavour. At one time the wine contained some white hermitage material, also from the Hunter, but the blend varies from year to year. Now it is usually straight semillon.

The Chablis is usually a light, well-balanced and quite delicate wine with an appealing clean rather firm acid finish—the so-called 'flinty' finish of the chablis style. Since 1965 the style has been very successful in Australian wine shows, having won a Championship, fifteen Gold, ten Silver and ten Bronze Medals which is a good record for a single line of wine in about six or seven years.

The Championship was in 1968. This was awarded to the famous Bin 3475 of 1968, which I wrote about in 1969—before it received all its gongs I hasten to say—and said it was the best young Chablis I had ever seen from Lindeman's. Although I deplore the name, I still understand the style and what they are trying to convey by the name. That wine had enormous flavour and character, and was beautifully made. A delicious wine of very fine nose and flavour—beautifully balanced and very fruity. In all a very good wine that was delicious when young; but that I said would improve with further bottle ageing, and it has improved mightily and will go on doing so for many, many years.

There have been some extremely good wines of this line. You can go back to wines of the 1950s, the Bin 1340 of 1959 for example, and there was a wine of 1958 which had a lot of flavour and character. There was also the Bin 224 of 1954. All of these wines drank very well for ten years or more after they were made. Unlike a lot of the white wines of Australia these wines pick up a considerable depth of flavour and considerable character with their slow madeirization. Generally speaking, therefore, the wines are very good delicate, fresh, crisp whites when young and they build up considerable character with age in bottle.

I wasn't so impressed with the 1970 edition, the Bin 3875, which I don't think was quite as delicate as they usually are when they are young. Whatever, this is one of the outstanding dry white styles of Australia.

Lindeman's Hunter River Porphyry

This is an occasional sweet wine which is always of great character. It does not appear year after year. When conditions are right the company will make a wine which they generally keep for Show purposes. The wines are always of extremely good character and style with tremendous vinosity. I particularly remember a 1949 wine which had enormous power; the 1956, which had considerable character, a tremendous lusciousness and distinct flavour; and the 1967, which was the Bin 4180. My tasting notes on the latter wine read: 'Estery, essencey, pungent nose. Very good Sauternes colour—deep golden; good sugar, quite sweet, fairly luscious—must contain some concentrated grape juice; flavour acceptable— one of the better sweet wines available. Essence overtones puzzle. May come from traminer pressings or muscat concentrate of some kind.' That particular wine was not of the usual standard of the Hunter River wines because of this overlay of different flavour character. But it was a very good wine, extremely well made with great power, plenty of flavour, a lot of lusciousness and a very good, clean acid finish.

The Porphyry top line is a very good sweet wine with great charm and character. Indeed, it can be the classic sweet wine of Australia when it appears. The Bin 1270 of 1956 was perhaps typical: in various shows the wine has done quite marvellous things. It has won altogether four Championship Awards; 28 Gold and 9 Silver Medals, and I don't think they bothered counting anything else. It was one of the best sweet wines ever seen in Australia.

Lindeman's Hunter River Riesling

Produced from the Hunter River riesling (semillon) grown in the Pokolbin district of the Hunter Valley on Lindeman's 'Ben Ean' and 'Sunshine' vineyards. One of the most celebrated dry white styles in Australia and a wine for which I have a particular affection. Since the 1960 vintage the line has achieved remarkable success in wine shows throughout the country and in major shows has been awarded three Special Trophies, three Championships, 33 Gold, 40 Silver and 13 Bronze Medals.

The wines are 'each-way' wines. They do not have the fullness of the white burgundy style, nor the dry, flinty delicacy of the chablis. In fact they are high quality dry whites from the Hunter Valley made from the dominant white grape available and made by a company that really knows what it is doing with its material. There was a slight—a marginal—falling off in quality at the beginning of the seventies. Why this has happened is hard to understand. Perhaps it is just the 'off' years. 1971 wasn't a good year and the 1970 wine seems to have just a trace of coarseness; in 1969 the vintage was not a big one and the better wines were of the white burgundy style. Certainly I am being rather hypercritical, but I am being hypercritical with wines that I admire greatly.

I have always had an enormous affection for this line because of its 'each-way' propensities. By 'each-way' I mean that as a young wine, the wine has tremendous flavour and character, real delicacy, fruitiness and freshness about it—so much so that even the Semillon, which is not an aromatic variety, has won many prizes in the Hock Classes in shows. For a Semillon to do this is quite rare indeed; but Lindeman's have done this time and time again with their Hunter Semillon. Then, after about two or three years' bottle age the wine is neither fresh and aromatic, nor is it soft, round and fullsome. It goes through a half-way stage and I believe this is almost the worst time to drink it. Leave it to pick up more character, to deepen and enrichen; for then the true value of the wine is attained. It is a value which, in my terms (and I'm a great lover of the highest quality French White Burgundies, of Graves, and of great German wines, especially the great Auslese styles) is one of the classic white wine styles of the world. It is not White Burgundy, it is

not a Graves, it is not a German wine style; it is a unique style all of its own and it comes from the Hunter Valley area of Australia. It is a style which has good fruit, superb balance and tremendous development in the bottle; and I think the style is best exemplified year in and year out by the Lindeman's Hunter Riesling. The wines: Bin 4055 of 1971 is a good wine, but one which reflects the very poor vintage. The 3855 of 1970 does not have the final quality. It is a wine of good flavour and style with a clean fresh acid, but it does not have this great depth of quality or the latent qualities that are going to produce a marvellous rich style after some years' bottle maturation.

The 1969 edition was Bin 3655 and as stated that was produced in a year in which the wine favoured the broader, rounder, softer White Burgundy style. It was a good wine nonetheless. The Bin 3455 of 1968 was a wine of considerable flavour and character—an extremely good wine that is going to live for a long while. Perhaps it is initially overshadowed by its famous sister, the Bin 3475 Chablis, but it is a wine of great charm and distinction. The 3255 of 1967 was a lighter wine which pleased me very much as a young wine and is now drinking magnificently, having five years or more bottle age on it.

Going back through the years, the Bin numbers sound to me like a roll-call in Australian wine fame. The Bin 2955 of 1966 was a wine of delicious flavour. I drank this quite recently and it was outstanding in its depth of flavour on the middle palate. (And don't forget this is a flavour which is unaided by massive small new oak.) The 1965 wine was the Bin 2760—a lovely, round, soft style. The 1964 wine, Bin 2464, contained a trace of traminer and this was from the celebrated 'fruit salad' vineyard at 'Ben Ean' which contains one or two assorted varieties. It was a wine which had a faint strawy character to it when it was young and I didn't like it as much as some of the others. I am now told that I would eat my words. The Bin 2222 of 1963 was a wine which I sold in some considerable quantity, for it was a wine of lovely style— a very fresh, clean acid style.

The 1962 was the famous Bin 1930—the celebrated wine with an enormous show history which was sold when quite young and then was retained for show purposes and then released again in 1972. Then it was sold for a premium price and it showed that by this time it was getting slightly too full. It still remained a magnificent rich wine, but one showing age. The 1961 wine was Bin 1760; the 1960 the famous Bin 1616—one of the greatest white wines ever made in this country, a wine of enormous vinosity, flavour and power. The word 'enormous' is not used lightly, because this wine had tremendous character—and is still doing extremely well in shows.

The 1959 was the Bin 1575, which was called 'Sunshine Riesling' for a while. It was quite delicious when young. It is a lighter wine with very clean acid, which is still drinking well.

The point of all this is that these wines have always been top drinking; good wines when young and with age upon them, and available at reasonable prices in relation to their quality. I hope that the ensuing decade sees the release of wines of comparable quality which we may continue to enjoy so much.

Lindeman's Hunter River Trebbiano

This wine is vintaged from very late picked trebbiano (white hermitage) grapes, grown in the company's 'Windmill Paddock' vineyard near Pokolbin in the Hunter Valley. The wine is strongly flavoured with a crisp, slightly fruity taste, some residual sugar and a spritzig character.

The Bin 3650 from the 1969 vintage was a very fulsome, unusual style. The slight sugar content and rather unusual flavour was most interesting and complex.

Lindeman's Hunter River White Burgundy

If the Hunter River Rieslings have provided the classics, then certainly the White Burgundies of the same company have provided some wonderful drinking as well. Generally the wines are softer, broader, rounder with lovely nutty clean aftertaste. They develop quicker, and are possibly enjoyed better a little earlier than the Rieslings. They certainly have a lot going for them and develop magnificently with four or five years in the bottle. Again the wine is made entirely from semillon grapes grown in the Pokolbin area of the Hunter Valley, both from the 'Ben Ean' and the 'Sunshine' vineyards, probably with a predominance of material from the latter vineyard.

Again, the wine has done extraordinarily well in shows, except in 1964 the wine has been bottled each vintage for the last ten years and during this time it has been awarded one Special Trophy, one Championship, twenty-one Gold, fourteen Silver and seven Bronze Medals. So again, you have this enormous depth of quality, and quite shattering success in show after show.

The Bin 3870 of 1970 was the outstanding Lindeman's wine of that particular vintage; a wine which had a lot of flavour, a ton of style, extremely good balance and all the qualities of the traditional line—roundness, softness, delicacy, soft acid. A most acceptable drink when young, but one which again improves in the bottle.

In 1969 the Bin number was 3670. This was a good Hunter year for white burgundy styles, as against the flinty, drier perhaps more acerbic kind of wine; very soft and rounded and lacking the slightly hard flint finish of the more traditional style. Yet the wines that were made were not big, full wines that can get so fat in the bottle after a year or so, but of the more delicate style. The acid is clean, the balance sound and one felt the wine would live for many years. Certainly this is being borne out at this time.

The 3470 was a fuller style. That wine was made in 1968, and it was compared with two remarkable wines that were made alongside it, the 3455 Riesling and the 3475 Chablis that did so well in shows. It was a very good wine, big, round and soft, and it mostly came off the 'Ben Ean' vineyards. The grapes were picked at about 11½ degrees Baumé during the advanced part of the vintage, though the acid level remained fairly high at 6.8 grammes per litre. So the latter factor certainly holds the wines together for some time after they have been in the bottle. An extra flavour dimension of these wines may also come from the pressings material which is often used in them. White pressings in the Hunter are quite valuable and fill out the white burgundy style. Certainly some of the pressings could come from the 'fruit salad' vineyard and therefore could contain traminer, verdelho and chardonnay, although this is pure conjecture.

The 3270 of 1967 was the gorgeous wine that was covered in show medal honour and one which has been drinking remarkably well for a number of years and will still, one feels, go for a few years yet. The line goes back and back: 1966 the 2970 and 1965 the 2790, in 1963 the 2240, to the great vintage, Bin 1333 of 1959. This was a magnificent wine that rounded out fairly quickly and by 1963 was drinking at its top. I think this is a characteristic of the White

Burgundy line, that they may be enjoyed earlier than the Rieslings in this more developed context.

I swore at a masked tasting that this wine was a French White Burgundy of fairly high quality. I said I would eat my hat if this were not so. Well, I was wrong and half an hour later I was offered a large pastry hat, Tyrolean style. Having had a three-course luncheon, I faced the thing with some alarm. Fortunately a son of a member of the party was going to a fancy dress ball and had no costume, so we baked him some pastry shoes and he went as a meat pie.

Lindeman's Kirkton Chablis
A non-vintage wine displaying a crisp, clean flavour and a quite pleasant dryness and crispness on the back of the palate. It is produced predominantly from pedro ximenez and semillon grapes bought from various areas and bottled under controlled conditions in Sydney.

The vineyard from which the wine derives its name was planted by James Busby (or by Kelman, his brother-in-law) in 1830 and is no longer in existence. There is no suggestion today that the wine is a Hunter wine of that area or of that vineyard, although many years ago it was made almost entirely, even totally, from Hunter Valley material.

Lindeman's Langhorne Creek Oeillade Shiraz
The original French grape variety known as cinsaut is believed to be synonymous with the distinctly flavoured oeillade variety which is grown to advantage in the Langhorne Creek district of South Australia.

This wine is made by the Potts family of 'Bleasdale' fame. Lindeman's buy the wine in bulk from them, both the Oeillade and the Shiraz, and do the blending and maturation in their own cellars. Some interesting wines of unusual flavour have been produced—not wines that I feel are of the top quality, but interesting wines at reasonable prices.

The 1967 was a wine of a very clean, lighter and less porty style than usual (Langhorne Creek is a very fertile area and produces material that can make rather big wines). It was not a big wine but was clean and delicate, austere with a firm, clean finish and had good balance and nice flavour. The oeillade seemed to have a lightening effect. The 1966 was very full and fruity, almost a porty style, and had too much residual sugar apparent. It is the sort of wine that I believe is now out of style, although some people do like it. The 1965 was also a big wine, full of fruit, rather hard and not perfectly balanced. The 1964 was a lighter wine again—still quite tart and acid, but of considerable finesse and developed flavour.

It will be interesting to see what Lindeman's do with the wine because the style does tend to differ from year to year and, after all, they are not making the wines. However, it is an interesting line with unusual varietal character. A departure from the usual style of cellar reds that the company produces.

Lindeman's Liebestein
This is a light, fruity, slighty effervescent, sweet white table wine, similar to a moselle style. It is fresh, delicate, with pronounced sparkle and life—suitable for any party or occasion.

Lindeman's Limestone Ridge Vineyard Claret
In 1966 Lindeman's planted a 60-acre block of land at Coonawarra, South Australia, following their acquisition of Rouge Homme Wines Pty Ltd in 1965. The block included some of the highest land in the Coonawarra area, being the crest of a well-defined ridge of limestone. Plantings comprised 55 acres of red hermitage (shiraz) and 5 acres of cabernet sauvignon; the first full crop from the new vineyard was harvested in 1971. After ageing in Nevers oak hogsheads for 15 months the wine was bottled and given further maturation in bottles before sale. As expected, the wine from the 'Limestone Ridge' vineyard is a full-bodied, delicately astringent, strongly-flavoured style reflecting the hard soil conditions in which the vines are growing. It is anticipated that the maximum annual production of this vineyard will be approximately 25,000 gallons and labels will bear the bottle number plus details of the particular year's vintage.

Lindeman's had a wine which appeared under this name some years ago and this was the 1959 Limestone Ridge Claret, which was a part of the acquisition of the Rouge Homme. It was made by Owen Redman and was an austere, slightly hard wine with great complexity of flavour that will undoubtedly live for many, many years.

Lindeman's Liqueur Muscat
A commercial line of quality wine sold at a reasonable price for everyday customers. It is carefully blended by the company's winemakers to give a luscious flavour and pronounced fruit character. Made from various muscat varieties.

Lindeman's Litre Table Wines
Recognizing the impact of the change from Imperial weights and measures to Metric standards, Lindeman's designed an attractive easy to handle 1 litre capacity bottle for a special range of everyday beverage table wines. The wines are: Litre Burgundy; Litre Claret; Litre Moselle; Litre Riesling Hock; Litre Rosé; and Litre White Burgundy.

All are pleasant well-balanced fruity wines which provide good drinking for very reasonable prices.

Lindeman's Macquarie Port
A very old wood-matured tawny port, produced predominantly from shiraz grapes grown at the Corowa vineyards in New South Wales. It is blended from prizewinning and other wines in a modified Solera

system to give uniformity of style and consistency of quality. Each vintage at Corowa for the past ten years has produced first prize or Gold Medal winning wines which are subsequently blended for this style. The wine has excellent flavour, very good wood development and pleasant oak astringency and considerable sweetness on the middle palate. It is a soft, medium-bodied port, with some sweetness and a dry finish.

Lindeman's Mature Tawny Port
A good standard trade port available at a reasonable price. Produced at Corowa from wood-matured, fortified wine.

Lindeman's Montillo Sherries
These wines comprise one of the largest selling ranges in Australia. They are offered for sale in five varieties in both flagons and bottles. The wines are produced at the Corowa cellars of the company from purchased grapes and wines and are distinguished by their strong fresh, clean grapy bouquet and character. The combination of consistently high quality and excellent value for money has unquestionably contributed to the success of the range over the years.

The range includes: Montillo Cream Sherry, a wine with a noticeable richness of flavour, with an appealing full and luscious character on the palate and a clean, dry finish; Montillo Dry Sherry, a wine showing some oak, plenty of fruit and a soft, round palate with some sweetness, but which is still predominantly dry, with a dry finish on the back of the palate; Montillo Medium Dry Sherry, a light, reasonably dry tasting wine with a pleasant nutty character derived from the oak casks in which it is matured; Montillo Semi-Sweet Sherry, an 'in-between' wine, sweet, but less sweet than the sweet sherry; Montillo Sweet Sherry, probably one of Australia's most popular sweet sherries, it is a well-matured, very grapy wine containing many varieties.

Lindeman's Nyrang Claret
Made from red hermitage (shiraz) grapes grown in the Hunter and Clare Valleys and at Coonawarra. The wine is matured in small oak casks before bottling and can be enjoyed when young because of its round, full fruitiness; but it takes age very well. The wine was first produced in 1962. In the next five years the wines took two Gold, eight Silver and six Bronze Medals in wine shows, which for a standard, if high quality, line was quite a good result. It is distinctly Lindeman's cellar style, having good balance, good fruit, and agreeable softness on the middle palate, although the finish is quite firm. This wine does not differ greatly from the Auburn Burgundy in actual flavour, though the Claret has a firmer palate and finish. It has a little more body, some oak showing and therefore would appear to be the better keeping proposition.

The 1966 vintage was a wine of good flavour, reflecting the year. A wine which had plenty to it.

Lindeman's Porphyry Sauternes
A light golden-coloured, sweet table wine with a fruity nose and soft palate. It is a wine which has matured in the bottle for some time before release and is always consistent value for money. It derives its name from the old Lindeman vineyard, planted at Raymond Terrace in the Hunter Valley by Henry Carmichael in 1833. The vineyard name, in turn, was based on the presence of porphyry type rocks in the vicinity. The vineyard no longer exists, nor is it suggested that Porphyry Sauternes is now made entirely from Hunter material.

Lindeman's Raisin Liqueur Muscat
An old, luscious and grapy dessert wine—a blend of show-winning and other wines, produced from frontignac (Rutherglen brown muscat) grapes, grown at the Corowa vineyards. It is blended in a modified Solera system to give uniformity of style and is always good value for money.

Lindeman's Reserve Amontillado Sherry Z.898A
This wine won first prize (when there was only one first) in the 1961 R.A.S. Sydney in the Open Amontillado Class. It is made from palomino and montbaden grapes grown in the Corowa vineyards. It was made by the Flor process in small oak casks and finally matured in a Solera numbered Z.898A. The wine is of considerable age, showing quite flavoursome wood and Flor character, very well-balanced and integrated, though it is still quite delicate and light. The wine has plenty of character and body, yet it has finesse, and finishes with that delightful clean astringency so typical of a good dry sherry. Another character I liked is the nutty flavour on the palate. This comes from the ageing of the Flor wine in small wood and has a mouth-filling, distinctive quality. There is also a trace of sweetness on the middle palate, though this blends in favourably with all the other qualities of the wine.

The wine is of a considerable average age and a prizewinner at shows, having been awarded one Gold, two Silver and one Bronze Medal since 1971.

Lindeman's Reserve Amorosa Cream Sherry Z.96
Another famous prize-winning wine from the renowned fortified wine cellars at Corowa, run by the celebrated winemaker, Ron Prince. This wine comes from a Solera numbered Z.96. It is a magnificent old, luscious, dessert sherry produced entirely from pedro ximenez grapes grown on the 'Southern Cross' and 'Felton' vineyards. 'Southern Cross' soil is sandy loam over clay, in sharp contrast with that of 'Felton' which is much heavier and richer dark red-brown soil.

This wine is very soft, round and smooth, having almost a velvet quality. It seems to me to be remark-

269

ably like the true nutty brown styles that one gets in England. This wine is quite sweet as one would expect, but sweet in the best sense, having no cloying quality on the tongue and finishing very clean—again the age wood acid is apparent on the finish. A lovely sweet, dessert wine.

Lindeman's Reserve Fino Sherry RP.10

(I wonder if the RP stands for Ron Prince.) These sherries are produced at the Corowa cellars by the Flor process, from palomino and montbaden grapes grown on the 'Southern Cross' and 'Felton' vineyards. Each year wines which have developed pronounced Flor characteristics are selected for even greater development under the Flor yeast and eventually these selected wines are transferred to a modified Solera system, where they are blended with older wines at a higher alcoholic content. The wine is ultimately sold under the number of the final Solera—RP.10—and is of constant quality and style, due to the method of ageing. It is a very fine, clean wine with a distinct Flor astringency, and pleasant oak.

It was exhibited in shows in Australia during 1971 and 1972, and was awarded three Gold Medals and one Bronze Medal in the Open Classes for Fino Sherries.

Lindeman's Reserve Hunter River Burgundy

Produced from red hermitage (shiraz) and pinot noir grapes grown at the 'Ben Ean' vineyard in the Hunter Valley. Following vintage each year the new red wines are tasted and graded. The best, provided they reach a predetermined quality standard, are matured in small oak casks, mainly of Nevers oak, for some eighteen months and then bottled and matured in bottle, preferably for ten years, before sale. Generally two different styles are produced annually, reflecting the characteristics of different soil types and aspects of various portions of the 'Ben Ean' vineyards. Some parts of this are comprised of 60 to 70 year old vines which are now bearing very slight crops, but which yield material of the highest quality suitable for making top reds.

Exceptional years of top quality wines have been 1953, 1956, 1957, 1959, 1965, 1966, 1968 and 1970. No wines were bottled of this quality standard from the 1954, 1955, 1960, 1962, 1964 and 1971 vintages. The wines include many Championship prizewinners.

The 1959 Bin 1590 was an extraordinarily interesting wine that was first called a Claret and then became a Burgundy in subsequent labellings. It had not done very well at all at shows until 1963 when it was entered in the Burgundy classes. It then won a Gold Medal, the top Gold Medal, the Best Red of Show and finally, I think, the prize as the Best Wine of Show.

The Bin 1111 of 1957 was another wine of tremendous character, although it was firmer than many of the Hunter reds. 1957 was a rather strong sunshine year and the wines picked up a fair amount of tannin. This wine has lived for many years, a wonderful wine of extraordinary complexity and flavour.

In 1961 the company produced a couple of very good wines which they kept for some considerable time for show purposes and then released about ten years later. These are the 1961 Bin 2015 and the 1961 Bin 2011. They charge a lot of money for the wines, but after all they had kept them for ten years. The 2015 was a very big wine of rich, powerful flavour. The must contained some considerable amount of pressings, which contributed to the very big earthy style, with very rich flavour and a really firm, big, solid finish. There was quite an amount of hardness there, which unquestionably will be there for many years to come—quite unusual for a Hunter wine to have this firm finish. The 2011 of the same year was very soft, pleasant wine. I've shown this wine to many visitors from overseas and they have liked it very much indeed and have said it is a most complete soft red wine. It is a very balanced wine; with a beautiful, gorgeous round, soft palate and a clean, smooth, lingering finish. There is no doubt that it is a wine that will keep for many, many years.

I showed this wine to a most distinguished wine man from overseas (I think his company crushes over 70,000 tons of grapes per year). He was tasting some Bordeaux wines with me and I sneaked this one in. He was amazed at its quality and praised the flavour, bouquet and style and just went on and on. When I told him the price he caught his breath, and then said, 'but you are a rich young country, so I suppose it doesn't matter.' Sometimes, I feel it does!

The 1963 was a later release and the Bin number was 2511. This was a Gold Medal winner, though it was slightly less 'giving', less generous than some of the other Hunters; a slightly dumber wine of less impact, but a very good Hunter wine nonetheless.

If the three major red wine areas of Australia, from a natural quality point of view, are Coonawarra, the Great Western and the Hunter, then top wines from those areas must be paid particular homage; undoubtedly the top Lindeman's dry red releases of any particular year must be among the top wines of the Hunter Valley district. I consider they are among the top red wines of Australia.

Lindeman's Reserve Hunter White Wines

These wines may be either generic (Hock, Chablis, White Burgundy or Sauternes), or varietal (Traminer, Verdelho, Trebbiano, Chardonnay or Riesling). The Hunter River white wines of the company are sold at one or two years of age as, for example, the Lindeman's Hunter Riesling four-number bin wines described previously. Some stocks are held back for further bottle ageing and ultimate sale at about ten years of age. As described, the Bin 1930 was

Storage cellars at Mildara, near Mildura, Vic.

available for sale as a young wine, then some was kept for further show purposes and finally released about ten years after it was made.

Plantings of varietal grapes have been substantially increased over the years; particularly traminer, verdelho and chardonnay. Consequently, from time to time a special release of a special bin of a certain year is made. Sometimes the amount of wine available for sale is extremely small. Lindeman's sold a Chardonnay which had great character, delicacy and flavour but it was only seen by a few lucky people. Another wine which had a quite assertive and different charm was the Hunter Traminer Riesling of 1965. The traminer variety in the Hunter is not the aromatic wonder that it is elsewhere. It has a much broader, softer style and it does not have the flowery, varietal character that we see in Alsace or in Australia at Rooty Hill. It has a very full, quite intense flavour, which adds something to the Hunter dimension, but it is still a Hunter

wine first. The 1965 wine had tremendous flavour, structure and power, and a strong, nutty, soft finish. This was a wine which was immensely enjoyed shortly after its release in 1969, four and a half years after it was made. And proved the interest that one may find in a 'special'.

These wines are always well worth inspection; they are different and, being up to ten years old, show just what the area can do.

Lindeman's Reserve Liqueur Muscat No. 1625

This is a magnificent, luscious, developed, concentrated, flavoursome Muscat, made from brown and red frontignac (Rutherglen brown muscat) grapes grown at the 'Southern Cross' and 'Felton' vineyards.

This is an aristocrat of the Muscat family and the various wines in it average over twenty years of age. It is made on a modified Solera system and maturation takes place in small oak casks. The blend tree resembles a giant inverted pyramid—endless back-tracking in blend books fails to reveal any source. It is quite possible to believe that some of the wine in this final blend is over fifty years old. A cask of the best Muscat of the year is kept back for it and is eventually added to the main blend. The young wine gives the blend its strong muscat, raisin flavour, adding freshness to the extremely aromatic, rich, oaky quality of the old wine. The aged wood acid again shows on the finish of the wine. The grapes are picked when they are extremely ripe and the whole wine gives an impression of concentrated, luscious, grapy, raisiny flavour. Add to this the oak and maturation, and you have a wine of great complexity and style.

Lindeman's Reserve Madeira 1940 Solera
This is a very dry wine, made from the verdelho variety grown in the 'Sunshine' vineyard in the Hunter Valley and blended together with some white hermitage material grown at Corowa.

The verdelho variety, used today for making table wines, is bottled separately, or blended with a light semillon to help fill it out. However, in the past in the Hunter Valley, it was used for making some magnificent dry dessert wines of great character. (Of the four Madeira varieties in the island of Madeira itself verdelho makes the second driest after sercial, the others being boal and malmsey (malvasia.) The variety called madeira in South Australia is not any of these at all, but probably a semillon.

However, this particular wine was matured in small oak casks and the Solera begun in 1940. Basically the wine is still an old Hunter. The 1940 Madeira has a most distinguished nose, a sort of bone smelling austereness. The palate is clean, with a delightful combination of fruit and oak, and the finish is almost tart with a lovely aged wood, acid character. Altogether a most distinctive and distinguished wine.

Lindeman's Reserve Tawny Port RF.1
Another very old dessert wine blend, the various wines in it having an average age of over twenty years. This is a very rich, wood-matured port—a wine of pronounced and quite distinctive character. It comes from the Corowa vineyards of the company. There are so many grapes in it that the list almost seems an ampelographer's manual of grape varieties: grenache, black shiraz, blue imperial, alicante bouschet, aramon, touriga, bastardo, alvarelhao, grand noir and belzac—what a list! This wine has true Portuguese character, having great elegance and finesse. The palate is actually quite light, with concentrated intense flavour on the middle palate. There is no cloying and the finish has a marked aged wood character—astringent, but not too sharp. This wine has won endless prizes. The most recent blend—and the blend changes of course from year to year as the Solera goes on—since 1970 has been

awarded one Championship, four Gold and four Silver Medals; proof indeed that this is one of the top wood matured ports in Australia.

Lindeman's Reserve Tokay WH.2
A full-bodied, luscious, dessert wine produced from tokay grapes grown at the 'Southern Cross' and 'Felton' vineyards at Corowa. The grapes hang on the vines until very late in the season when they become sweet and raisiny, producing a very full-flavoured wine with a dry finish on the palate. The young wines are placed in small oak casks and later are blended with older vintage wines in a modified Solera system. The final aged blended wine is drawn for sale from Solera No. WH.2, which is then in turn topped up with a younger Solera.

Lindeman's Rouge Homme Claret
A vintage dry red of great quality, produced from shiraz grapes grown at Lindeman's Rouge Homme vineyards in Coonawarra. It is matured in small oak casks prior to bottling, approximately eighteen months after vintage for ultimate sale at about five years of age.

These vineyards were planted in 1908 and have consistently produced wine which is full of flavour, light and delicate with a fine clean tannin astringency on the palate. These wines of course have assumed the mantles of the famous Rouge Homme wines produced by Bill and Owen Redman over the years and, since Lindeman's took over the wines have continued to do well at shows. The vintages 1963 to 1971 have been awarded four Gold, eight Silver and six Bronze Medals.

There have been some fine wines in this particular collection. The 1963 was a rather light wine, but one of considerable fruit. The 1966 was a most interesting wine. The fruit was good, all round balance was excellent, but there was a slightly dirty character to the wine which I found offensive. The 1967 had just a touch of this character, but the rest of the wine was very good indeed with a complete fruit flavour and reasonable balance of tannin. Since that year Lindeman's have made some very fine wines which are now waiting to be released.

Lindeman's Royal Reserve Fortified Wines
This range of wines has been successfully satisfying heavy consumer demands in the lower-priced market for many years. It is specially produced to cover the main sections of the fortified wine market and the range consists of: Cream Sherry, Sweet Sherry, Dry Sherry, Muscat and Port.

Lindeman's Royal Reserve Sauternes
A light golden, sweet table wine aimed for the lower-priced Sauternes market.

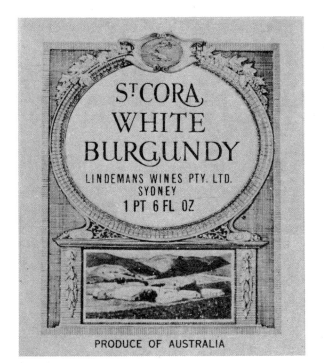

PRODUCE OF AUSTRALIA

Lindeman's St Cora Burgundy

A non-vintage companion to Corowa Claret. Grapes used in this production are red hermitage and grenache, grown in the main at Watervale and in the Barossa Valley. The result is a soft, rounded Burgundy with a smooth, velvety flavour and taste, and economically priced. The name St Cora is derived from the original Burgundies produced at the historical 'Kirkton' vineyard in the Hunter Valley. There is no inference that the wine now contains a bulk of Hunter material.

Lindeman's St Cora White Burgundy

A pleasant, soft, mouth-filling white of quite reasonable character, produced from pedro ximenez and semillon grapes from the Barossa and Clare Valleys and bottled at an early age to retain freshness. This is a soft, round wine with a fresh bouquet and dry finish on the palate, which is very good value for money.

Lindeman's Sparkling Porphyry Pearl

Produced in the company's Sydney cellars by the Charmat process. It is a distinctive, fruity wine with pronounced raisiny, grapy flavour and lots of bubbles. It has been well advertised and has been very popular.

Lindeman's Sparkling Wines

Lindeman's sparkling wines, produced by natural secondary fermentation, have an extremely long history of quality and appeal. They have always had a great acceptance by the public, though since the

inception of the Pearl style, this appeal has probably diminished somewhat. The range comprises: Lindeman's Sparkling Burgundy, which is a soft, full-flavoured, light red sparkling wine; Lindeman's Sparkling Hock, a straw-coloured sparkling wine with a fresh delicate flavour and rather dry finish; and Lindeman's Sparkling Moselle, a pale, golden-coloured sparkling wine, with a pronounced grapy flavour, some sweetness, and a clean, acid finish.

Lindeman's Special Cream Sherry

An old, luscious, wood-matured sherry made from very ripe grapes grown at the Corowa vineyards. It is blended from wines which have won many prizes in shows and other wines in a modified Solera system to give uniformity of style. Each vintage at Corowa for the past ten years has produced a first prize or Gold Medal winning wines, which are subsequently blended for this particular style.

Lindeman's Sunshine Riesling

A vintage dry white produced from semillon and clare riesling grapes grown in the Hunter Valley, Clare and Barossa Valleys and bottled shortly after vintage to retain original freshness and flavour. The wine has a soft, fresh flavour and fruity character. It derives its name from the historical 'Sunshine' vineyard in the Hunter Valley, originally planted by Lindeman's in 1910. At one time the wine was a straight Hunter from this particular vineyard only and indeed the 1959 was such a good wine that it won the outstanding Gold Medal in the 1960 Sydney Show. It was released shortly afterwards as Bin 1575.

Lindeman's Vin De Champeaux

Produced in the Sydney cellars by the Charmat process. This is a Demi-Sec sparkling white wine available at a very modest price. It was first introduced to the market in early 1972 and met with considerable success.

Lindeman's Vintage Port

These are true vintage wines made from material grown at the 'Southern Cross' and 'Felton' vineyards at Corowa. These vineyards have extensive plantings of various Portuguese port grape varieties, chief of these are the alvarelhao, touriga, belzac and grand noir. Only in years of exceptional quality are vintage ports made from these varieties, plus some shiraz. The young wine is matured in oak casks for approximately two years, bottled and then matured in the bottle for many years before sale. During the bottle maturation some of the tannin and colouring matter in the wine precipitates out of solution and forms a deposit or crust on the inside of the bottle and therefore the wines are best decanted before serving.

LINDEMANS

Watervale

RHINE RIESLING

BIN 3295
VINTAGE 1967

A crisp delicate Riesling with fine flavour and character
produced from selected Rhine Riesling grapes grown on the
hillside vineyards, Watervale, Clare Valley, South Autsralia.

LINDEMANS WINES PTY. LTD. SYDNEY

PRODUCE OF AUSTRALIA 1PT 6FL OZ

The 1957, 1962 and 1965 Vintage Ports were awarded prizes at various Australian wine shows. They all had a marked depth of flavour and considerable sugar on the middle palate, balanced by a dry, austere finish—which, of course, is the hallmark of a vintage port.

Lindeman's Watervale Grenache Rosé

A vintage wine made solely from grenache grapes grown in the Watervale district of South Australia.

This is a well-matured, delicate, dry rosé, with a soft fruity flavour and character. The wine has won three special trophies, one Championship, seven Gold Medals and numerous other awards at various shows. This wine, which shows considerable developed character, some people call it oxidized, others bottle matured, is a more advanced rosé style than the rather fresher, younger type, with which we are more familiar. But it has great character and a most definite style of its own.

Lindeman's Watervale Rhine Riesling

These vintage dry whites are produced from selected rhine riesling grapes grown at Watervale, South Australia, and bottled shortly after vintage to retain the original fresh, fruity flavour of the grape. A crisp, delicate riesling with a marked varietal character.

These wines tend to be more mature than many of the fresh Rhine Rieslings on sale and they have quite a marked flavour, very deep middle palate and a smooth, soft finish. Again the show record is impressive: for the 1966 to 1971 vintages inclusive, they won one Special Trophy, eleven Gold, fifteen Silver and twenty Bronze Medals.

There are some very good young, fresh Rhine Rieslings on the market, and of the older ones I am enjoying some from Gramp's and Buring's. Watervale wines can be at their best in the first year of bottling. They do fill out after this time, losing some of that tremendous fresh fruitiness that characterizes them. On the other hand, a lot of people like the developed flavour; if so, then this is the wine for them.

Lindeman's Watervale Shiraz Cabernet

A vintage dry red, produced from the usual combination of shiraz and cabernet sauvignon grapes, grown at Watervale in South Australia, and matured for about two years in small oak casks before bottling; for ultimate sale at about five years of age.

These, at their best, are good straightforward regional wines with plenty to them. The approximate percentages are 75 percent shiraz and 25 percent cabernet sauvignon and both the fruit characters of these varieties, and also the oak character, come through on the palate. The wine needs considerable time to come together. As usual with the area the wine has tremendous colour which does not fade for many years. These wines are quite firm and astringent on the finish, sometimes even rather hard, and they need plenty of time. All in all, very sound, flavoursome wines, with a long way to go.

The 1965 Bin 3155 was a particularly good, straightforward wine. However, I liked some of the later vintages less. The 1967 was a wine which was unbalanced and needed a long, long time before it would show anything; even then I doubted whether it would ever reach the final character of the 1965.

Lindeman's Watervale Spatlese Rhine Riesling

Produced solely from rhine riesling grapes grown at Watervale in South Australia. The grapes are picked late in the season after ripening fully in the sun. The wine is bottled soon after vintage to retain the rich, grapy character of the grapes. It is matured in bottle until sale at about three years (after vintage). Quantities of the best vintages are held back for greater maturation and ultimate sale at up to about 10 years of age. These wines have a tremendous concentration of flavour on the middle palate and quite marked character. The wine has an impressive record at various shows and from 1965 to 1971 has been awarded two Championships, sixteen Gold, twenty-one Silver and eighteen Bronze Medals. No wonder Philip Morris paid so much for the company. They just wanted all that loot!

Heat therapy cabinet at the CSIRO laboratories, Merbein, for heat processing of imported vines to rid them of virus infection. The vines are kept at 37.8°C for at least 400 days.

Loxton Co-operative Winery and Distillery Ltd

Loxton Cabernet Sauvignon
This is a pleasant flavoured dry red wine, made entirely from cabernet sauvignon grapes supplied by the shareholders of this co-operative at Loxton. Of medium colour and fairly light body, the wine drinks very well when young.

Loxton Claret
A light, dry red made from seventy-five percent shiraz and twenty-five percent mataro grapes.

Loxton Cream Sherry
A soft, fruity blend of muscat, gordo blanco and pedro ximenez grapes.

Loxton Dry Sherry
Made from pedro ximenez grapes and matured in 40 gallon oak casks, being fairly full flavoured, soft and round on the middle palate.

Loxton Frontignac
A blend of various years of wines made from the frontignac variety; fruity, with a soft, smooth finish.

Loxton Medium Dry Sherry
A commercial blend made from pedro ximenez grapes.

Loxton Oloroso Sherry
This is a blend of selected wines matured and stored in oak vats. Made entirely from white hermitage grapes, it is a very good trade wine, highly considered by merchants who sell it under their own labels.

Loxton Reserve Port
A light ruby style dessert wine made from shiraz and mataro grapes.

Loxton Retzina
Made from white hermitage and imported resins blended into a Greek-style wine and supplied to wine merchants throughout Australia.

Loxton Rich Port
A tawny port, made from shiraz and mataro grapes, which has been aged in small wood for at least five years.

Loxton Riesling
A fairly full-flavoured dry white, made from clare riesling grapes. The wine is well made, has a pleasant nose, full flavour and clean. finish. The company regards this as one of their better wines and one year it took a Gold Medal in Adelaide.

Loxton Sauterne
A semi-sweet table wine made from a blend of clare riesling and pedro ximenez grapes.

Loxton Sweet Sherry
Made from pedro ximenez grapes and matured in 500 gallon oak vats.

Lubiana

Lubiana Brown Muscat
Made from frontignac, blended with muscat gordo blanco and aged in wood for approximately one year.

Lubiana Burgundy
A blend of selected mataro and shiraz wines aged in wood for six months.

Lubiana Cabernet Sauvignon
From cabernet sauvignon grapes grown on Gardellini's and Lubiana's vineyards at Moorook on the River Murray near Berri, S.A.
Fermented in stainless steel, and after fining and filtration placed in new oak casks for three months, then transferred into old French oak and matured for a further nine months before bottling.

Lubiana Cabernet Shiraz
A blend of forty percent shiraz and sixty percent cabernet material, processed and aged similarly to the Cabernet Sauvignon.

Lubiana Claret
A blend of twenty percent shiraz, twenty percent grenache and sixty percent mataro from the local district.

Lubiana Cream Marsala
A base of light grenache sweet red is infused with selected herbs.

Lubiana Cream Sherry
A soft sweet fortified wine made from local muscat gordo blanco.

Lubiana Dry Sherry
A soft, round, dry, fortified wine made from white hermitage.

Lubiana Dry Vermouth
Made from a base of fortified pedro ximenez material, infused with herbs imported from Italy.

Lubiana Marsala All'uovo
This is a speciality of the company, being a wood-matured, rich, sweet, dessert wine, made from shiraz, infused with herbs imported from Italy.

Lubiana Medium Dry Sherry
A blend of dry and sweet sherries, aged in oak casks.

Mr Allan Antcliff, Research Scientist in charge of vine improvement programmes at CSIRO, Merbein. The CSIRO breeding programme has raised 1,500 hybrids and of these, 300 have been tested.

Lubiana Moselle
A broad-flavoured white wine made from clare riesling, with some residual sugar on the palate.

Lubiana Port Shiraz
A dessert wine made from shiraz, aged in wood for at least three years.

Lubiana Red Vermouth
A pedro ximenez base is used—this time of some sweetness—and this is infused with imported herbs from Italy.

Lubiana Riesling
A Rhine Riesling from selected vineyards in the district, it has full flavour and a good, clean finish.

Lubiana River Gold
A sweet table wine made from riesling material together with muscat gordo blanco.

Lubiana Rosé
A light, clean wine made from grenache.

Lubiana Sauternes
A light, sweet wine made from pedro ximenez.

Lubiana Shiraz
Made entirely from shiraz from local vineyards and matured in new oak for some months before transfer to old oak.

Lubiana Special Claret
From selected local shiraz aged in wood for six months before bottling.

Lubiana Sparkling River Gold
A blend of riesling material with muscat gordo blanco, carbonated to make a sparkling, fruity, rather sweet wine.

Lubiana Strawberry Marsala
A very popular local marsala of strawberry flavour. It is a grenache base infused with specially selected herbs and different flavourings.

Lubiana Sweet Sherry
A well-rounded, soft sherry, made from pedro ximenez.

McLaren Vale Wines Pty Ltd

McLaren Vale Dennis Hermitage
Made at the 'Ryecroft' winery at McLaren Flat from shiraz grapes grown on Mr E. S. Dennis' vineyard, some three miles from 'Ryecroft'.

This wine usually has a very rich, fruity palate with heavy colour and tannin. Most vintages benefit greatly with age. In New South Wales this wine is sold by H. G. Brown and Sons as Bin 60.

McLaren Vale Flagon Dry Red
A blend of shiraz and grenache grown in McLaren Vale. This wine is a soft and pleasant drink. It shows the advantage of the smooth, early ageing character of the grenache, plus the colour and tannin of the shiraz.

McLaren Vale Hermitage
Made at 'Ryecroft' from shiraz (Hermitage) grapes grown in the McLaren Vale district. Selected tanks are blended and aged in wood after vintage to gain wood character and after bottling stored for further ageing. A soft, round, lighter style than usual, of pleasant fruit.

McLaren Vale Ingoldby Hermitage
This wine is selected from the best of the shiraz dry reds made at 'Ryecroft' each year, aged in wood for six months to one year and then bottled and aged further in the bottle.

An outstanding vintage was the 1967 which won a Gold Medal in Adelaide. The wine is fairly typical of the 'Ryecroft' shiraz style having fairly big fruit, rich colour and a full tannin finish.

McLaren Vale Kay Hermitage
Grown and made at Kay's 'Amery' vineyards, these wines are selected after ageing by Mr Cud Kay and bottled by McLaren Vale Wines Pty Ltd to be further aged in the bottle before release. This distinctive wine shows the character of the hilly slopes of the Seaview district, having a lighter, more elegant style than the rather fuller-flavoured darker wines from the valley and flat area.

McLaren Vale Sigston Bin 33 Hermitage
The grapes which are grown on the 'Sigston' vineyards adjacent to 'Ryecroft' have been processed at 'Ryecroft' for forty years. Kept separate and aged in wood, this is a typical example of the big reds of the area with plenty of fruit, plenty of flavour, plenty of 'generosity' and a firm, clean acid and tannin finish.

McLaren Vale Southern Vales Claret
As the name implies the grapes are processed from the whole area. Each year the winemaker makes a selection which gives a good example of the distinctive character of shiraz grapes grown in and around McLaren Vale. Bottled by McLaren Vale Wines Pty Ltd it is aged to further enhance the soft character, the full fruit and the all-round balance of the wine.

McLaren Vale Osborne Hermitage
The Osborne Winery and vineyards, situated two miles north of McLaren Vale, produce the well-known D'Arenberg wines. This wine is made and selected by the Osbornes and bottled and aged in bottle by

McLaren Vale Wines. Full-bodied, with very rich bouquet, it is a typical example of the wines of D'Arry Osborne, having very rich fruit with the typical added spicy character which is so much part of his wines. It is very round, soft and generous with a smooth finish.

McWilliam's Wines

McWilliam's Brut Champagne
Made from a specially selected blend of grape varieties grown in the Riverina District of New South Wales; almost certainly semillon is used and probably white hermitage. It is vintaged at Yenda, near Griffith. Made by the traditional method of fermentation in the bottle (Methode Champenoise) and aged for two and a half to three years on its yeast lees. the wine is not entirely dry, containing about 1 percent liqueuring. Total acid is about 6½ grammes per litre.

This wine has been a consistent Silver Medal winner in shows and represents good value for money. The Brut Champagne always has a pleasant, full nose containing considerable yeast and varietal character; a delightful, full-flavoured, assertive nose which is unusual amongst Australian sparkling wines. Generally this does not continue onto the palate, which is marked by lightness, cleanness and considerable delicacy with almost a negative flavour. The wine finishes very clean. It is a good sparkling wine at a reasonable price.

In an article I wrote some years ago I stated it was a most interesting wine—it was like a middle-weight boxer, all shoulders and thin tapering legs. Well, at least that was new—it certainly hasn't been repeated since!

McWilliam's Champagne
Of much the same style and also made by the Methode Champenoise. This wine spends perhaps a year less on its yeast lees. It is light, medium-dry and has very pleasant gas. This is a slightly less austere, less dry, more commercial version of the Brut.

McWilliam's Cream Sherry
Made in the Robinvale winery in North Victoria from muscat gordo blanco. It has a mellow, fruity flavour and is probably one of the most popular of the sweet sherry styles in Australia.

McWilliam's Dry Friar Sherry
A dry fino sherry produced from palomino grapes, grown in the Riverina district of New South Wales and matured under Flor yeast for at least two years. This is a pleasant, round, fino style with good combination of Flor, oak and fruit characters.

McWilliam's Dry Vermouth
This French style of vermouth is a subtle blend of herbs and good base wine.

McWilliam's Flor Fino Sherry
This wine owes its very distinctive characteristics to the palomino grape from which it is made and to the traditional Spanish Flor process used in its making. It is very dry, with typical pungent bouquet and the delicate flavour expected of a good Flor fino. It is matured under the Flor process for at least three years and then aged further in small wood.

McWilliam's Golden Extra Dry Sherry
A pale, dry, wood-matured sherry, produced from selected varieties grown in the Riverina district of New South Wales.

McWilliam's Golden Medium Dry Sherry
A rich sherry of medium sweetness with an appetizing nutty flavour and smoothness.

McWilliam's Golden Sweet Sherry
A mellow, sweet, full-bodied sherry made from various varieties grown in McWilliam's Hanwood vineyards in the Riverina district of New South Wales.

McWilliam's Hanwood Port
Made from the shiraz variety grown in the Hanwood vineyards. In favourable years a proportion of the crop is often left on the vines for several weeks after the main body of the crush. This gives grapes an extreme richness and body.

This wine is a blend of special vintages over a period of ten years, having been matured in small wood until blending and bottling. It is a wine of considerable wood and fruit character, with good concentration of flavour on the middle palate and a nice clean spirit finish.

McWilliam's Hanwood Riesling
Made from riesling grapes (semillon) grown on the Hanwood vineyards of the company. This wine is bottled early, which helps to retain not only the wine's delicate aroma and flavour, but also plenty of natural effervescence and character.

McWilliam's Mount Pleasant Anne Riesling
A very good quality Hunter dry white made from grapes of the semillon variety grown in the 'Mount Pleasant' and 'Lovedale' vineyards of the company in the Pokolbin area of the Hunter Valley. The 'Lovedale' property is on the Cessnock/Bankston road by the airfield. The Government took over the property during World War II and converted it into an emergency landing field for the duration. In 1950 the area was released and Maurice O'Shea and McWilliam's planted it again, mainly with semillon (Hunter River riesling). These vines have produced

some really first-class white wines from soil which is mostly of a sandy loam nature.

The pick of the white wine is put to one side, bottled in the first year and called Anne Riesling. The young wine is light, well-balanced and with a crisp finish. As it acquires bottle age it develops tremendous character and for this reason I think it is of especial interest.

The 1967 Anne is a top class wine. This year was extremely good for white wines in the Hunter Valley and produced wines of outstanding delicacy with a great depth of flavour. The 1959 Anne was another which I liked enormously and which still drinks very well with tremendous flavour; yet is still fresh and has a clean acid finish. The depth of flavour on the middle palate is its outstanding characteristic.

From these two years my order of the various Anne's is the 1966, which is a full-flavoured wine with very clean acid finish that is still living and still showing a lot of flavour; the 1962, which is a very full wine; the 1965 wine, which is pleasant but lacks some of the depth of flavour of the wines previously mentioned; the 1961 was rather thin and acid early, but is developing well—one of those wines which starts off slowly and then develops character; and the 1964, I didn't like very much for it was rather full-flavoured and slightly coarse.

The point about all the Anne Rieslings is that they acquire considerable character in the bottle, which is not always usual for white wines; but, as stated before, the wines of the Hunter have the ability to do this as long as they are well made and have good fresh acid. Certainly, the Anne Rieslings have these qualities and are very good drinking for many, many years. I suppose you could liken the style eventually to the round, soft, white burgundy style, or just high quality Hunter whites of their own character.

McWilliam's Mount Pleasant Elizabeth Riesling
Again made from the semillon variety (Hunter River riesling), grown in sandy loam, a light soil which helps them develop full flavour and aroma. This is the standard Mount Pleasant and is generally a round, soft wine of considerable flavour and character. Of recent vintages I particularly liked the 1969. The grapes in this year were picked at something over 21 Hunter sugar (Brix)—therefore about 12 degrees Baumé. The wine was bottled not long after vintage in July 1969. It did well in shows, winning Silver Medals in many different locations.

The wine was extremely well-balanced, had a most pleasant fruit flavour, a clean estery sort of nose, and a crisp gentle acid finish. It was a wine that will mature well in the bottle and be good deep drinking in the years to come.

Of previous Elizabeth Rieslings, the 1968 was fat and rather coarse, though it had plenty of generous flavour; the 1967 was light and slightly thin—a marked contrast to the Anne Riesling of the same

year; the 1966 was a rather big wine, and one which developed very quickly in the bottle. Both the 1965 and the 1964 were more delicate wines; well-balanced, with good fruit and clean acid finishes which seemed to have held them together better.

Whatever, Elizabeth Riesling is a good reliable wine at all times; a wine which can be enjoyed when young and which always develops with some bottle age.

McWilliam's Mount Pleasant Philip Hermitage
Made from hermitage (shiraz) grapes grown on the volcanic slopes in the Pokolbin district of the lower Hunter Valley from various vineyards—'Mount Pleasant', the 'One Hundred Acre', 'Rosehill'. All these vineyards are mixtures of basalt crowns with some red clay.

This wine is made entirely from material grown in the district and is celebrated for its flavour and balance, its development of bouquet and soft tannin finish. The wines mature at varying times, depending on the actual vintage year. There is a vintage variation—belying the thought that Australian wines are the same from year to year. In fact the Philip Hermitage varies quite markedly.

The 1969 wine is an extremely good wine that contains a great deal of quality, fruit and general character. The November 1968 bush fires limited the crop in 1969. Consequently there were no special bottlings of that year and the whole of the material went into the 1969 Philip Hermitage which was an outstanding wine. The 1968 wine reflected the year: a light, soft, flavoursome wine that developed rather early and would be pleasant drinking during

McWILLIAM'S MOUNT PLEASANT

PHILIP HERMITAGE
1967

This wine is made from Hermitage grapes grown on volcanic basalt in the Pokolbin district of the lower Hunter Valley. It has the distinctive varietal characteristics associated with this grape, with an abundance of flavour and a firm tannin finish. After ageing in 600 gallon oak casks for two years it was bottled in February, 1969, and it should continue to improve for many years.

From the House of McWilliam, made at our Pokolbin Cellars, a fine vintage wine from the Hunter Valley district of Australia.

A PRODUCT OF AUSTRALIA   26 FL OZ
McWILLIAM'S WINES PTY. LTD., N.S.W.

the 1970s. The 1967 wine was a slightly bigger wine, with more character and which developed after about three years in the bottle. It was then good drinking but one could see that there would be further development and it would take bottle ageing for five to ten years. The 1966 was a very big, generous drinking wine that developed very early. It had tons of body, flavour, and all-round generous character. It showed some of the famous so-called Hunter 'oxidization' within two or three years in the bottle; but there was so much fruit and flavour there that this only tended to help the wine show greater character and flavour. The 1965, also the product of a dry year, was a more austere wine; perhaps the flavour was more elegant for there was more finesse to the wine. It had considerable Hunter flavour with a firmer finish; an all-round, well-made wine. Again it is one that will live for many, many years.

The wines of the early sixties from the 'Mount Pleasant' vineyards varied. The 1963 was a medium-bodied wine of good flavour and it was a welcome change from the rather thin wines of previous years. The 1964 was a medium-bodied wine which drank very well towards the end of the sixties and would continue drinking well for some time.

At this time the wines were simply called Mount Pleasant Hermitage. The 'Philip' name was first introduced in 1965, though some later releases of the 1964 had the name incorporated into their label.

The 1959 Hermitage was a very good wine of considerable keeping qualities that developed flavour all the time it was in bottle. Previous to that the 1957 was a pleasant wine which was rather firm, and wines of the early fifties, 1954, 1953, 1952, were wines that developed considerably in

the bottle and showed a traditional Hunter depth of character. These, of course, were made by the famous Maurice O'Shea.

Mount Pleasant Philip Hermitage is a good quality Hunter wine that shows much generosity of flavour and considerable style. It also has the compensation of being available more than any other Hunter red. Though on quota, being strictly allocated to retailers, merchants and publicans throughout the country—there is usually more of it than other rare reds of the Hunter Valley district.

Incidentally, both the 1965 and the 1966 Hermitage wines contained about 4 to 5 percent of pinot noir.

McWilliam's Mount Pleasant Pinot Hermitage

Made from pinot noir and hermitage (shiraz) grown in the various vineyards of 'Mount Pleasant' and the hermitage from 'Rosehill'. The pinot noir comes from the 'Eight Acre vineyard' which is above the winery at 'Mount Pleasant'. Undoubtedly, the pinot helps lift the flavour of the wine. Usually the wine made from the straight pinot noir is far too light in colour and body to bottle a straight wine by itself. I think the last one the company bottled was in 1957. However, used in blending, it does have a considerable influence on the final flavour. The 1965 Pinot Hermitage, for example, was extremely good, for this was a good year in the Hunter and I can remember seeing the pinot noir not long after it was made. It certainly had a great deal more colour to it than usual. Wisely they decided to blend it with the hermitage variety and there was little doubt that it does take over as far as the nose and flavour are concerned. The 1965 wine contained a quite high proportion of pinot noir—nearly half—and this made the wine one of the strongest pinot flavoured (berry flavoured, flower flavoured—whatever the words are) reds I've ever seen from Australia. It was a wine of great character which will live and live and will certainly show tremendous development in the years to come. The 1966 was another, quite elegant, wine of remarkable pinot noir fruit.

The 1964 Pinot was also a good wine, which developed, and is developing, very well. The 1963 was a lighter wine which was a little more advanced younger. The colour had picked up that typical Hunter brick tinge quite quickly, with the familiar 'onion colour' edges. It has strong nose—aromatic in varietal character and showing much bouquet. It was very drinkable only after three or four years in the bottle and it appeared that it would continue to drink well for some time. Interestingly, 1963 was a split vintage. There wasn't a great deal of rain for most part of the ripening period and then it poured. But the pinot noir ripens early and in this case was picked before the rains. (The same thing happened in Bordeaux in 1964, when the merlot was picked before the rain that split the vintage. Consequently the St Emilions and Pomerols were very good wines, since they are predominantly merlot.)

Back to the 1963 Pinot Hermitage. The pinot noir had good colour and considerable body while the hermitage picked after the rain was soft and rather light. Consequently the wine, overall, was rather light, with the pinot noir dominant. Again it was of early development and very pleasant character.

The 1962 Pinot Hermitage was quite a light wine. The 1961 was a very good wine in that it contained quite strong oak. McWilliam's played with a lot of new oak that year at 'Mount Pleasant' and in some cases it wasn't a great success, but the 1961 Pinot Hermitage was a delightful wine of very good pinot noir fruit and oak flavours.

1960 was rather light, but the 1959 was tops— a wine of considerable power, marked depth of varietal character, strong pinot noir fruit, delightful balance and a firm, clean finish; a wine which will keep for many years.

I have drunk much of the 1957 Pinot Hermitage which I found to be quite hard; a rather big, slightly more common wine, with a very firm finish. Certainly it was a wine that would live twenty, thirty years, but one wondered if the fruit would stay the course. Finally, back to the famous 1952 Pinot Hermitage— a quite gorgeous wine for many, many years and it only started to fade when it was about twenty years old at the end of a long distinguished show career. I enjoyed many bottles of it time and time again. A wine of tremendous flavour, complexity of character and development.

Certainly, the Pinot Hermitage, when found, is one of the top wines of the Hunter Valley district.

McWilliam's Mount Pleasant Sauternes
Made from a blend of semillon and white hermitage grapes grown at 'Mount Pleasant' and matured in 1,000 gallon oak casks until bottled. It generally has a generous, big bouquet. I suspect that they use some of the so-called 'bottoms' and pressings of the white varieties, which is ideal material for this kind of wine. After wood development, the bouquet builds up the development of the aromatic qualities of the varieties used and the wine picks up a luscious, fruity, soft flavour of quite considerable depth of character, with a very soft, smooth finish. The Hunter Valley district can produce outstanding sweet wines and certainly the Mount Pleasant Sauternes is one of the consistent lines which always shows well and has appeal.

There was one particular wine made in the early to mid 1950s which was often shown. Although this wine wasn't as fully luscious as it could have been, it had one of the most remarkable flavours I have ever experienced in an Australian sweet wine; a delicious wine of great depth of flavour. I can remember George Fairbrother on many occasions discussing this wine at shows. He would pick up another famous wine which came from Lindeman's —a 1949 wine of considerably more lusciousness— and he would then put a half glass of each together, mix them up and say 'there's the greatest Australian sweet wine ever made'.

McWilliam's Mount Pleasant (Special Bottlings)
Over the years the company has made a practice of having all sorts of different names and initials used for wines that they consider have special merit. Thence, we see the names Richard, Frederick, Robert, Henry, Stephen, O.P. and O.H. (which means Old Paddock and Old Hermitage, being two vineyards in the 'Mount Pleasant' complex) and so on. I think it would be pointless to run through the various years and names, because the names do appear year after year. Some names haven't been seen for years and then they pop up. A year which is a bounteous one, such as 1959, may give several different bottlings. Some of the most outstanding wines ever produced in this country bear these proud names.

The R.H. Hermitage of 1959, for example, was an outstanding wine of great complexity of flavour and character. There are so many others—P. and O.P. of 1959; O.P. and O.H., 1959; P. and O.P., 1958; and back to the older wines like R.F. 2 of 1947 and 1952 Stephen; the Mountain Range 'Henry' of 1952 and 1947. All great wines and some of the best wines I have ever consumed of the particular style —the soft, round, intense-flavoured style—ones that now command tremendous prices at auctions, because of their rarity, and because of the fame of Maurice O'Shea.

These wines have provided much interest and argument over the years, though it does seem now that the company is concentrating more on the main Philip Hermitage blend, thus eliminating some of these special names. I would hate to think, however, that the company won't put aside a couple of special casks, if such casks were truly outstanding. It would be a shame to see them lost in a more straight-forward wine of the district.

McWilliam's also have some interesting white varietals which appear on labels from time to time; names such as Aucerot, Montils, Rhine Riesling and Traminer. The aucerot and montils are rather interesting varieties that have great austerity, considerable flavour and rather high acid characters. The rhine riesling can make a rather big, full-flavoured wine, which has a lot of roundness on the middle palate. It doesn't have the aromatic qualities at all of South Australian Rhine Rieslings. The traminer can produce a most interesting wine and McWilliam's have a fairly large patch of this variety, above the winery on the hill at 'Mount Pleasant', where they have been making separate wines for some years. It appears that they don't show to much advantage when bottled and need a couple of years or so to settle down and harmonise. They have pro-vided many of the top show wines from the district. After a time they acquire a splendid sort of honey character. This does not mean sweetness but a sort of nutty, mellowed, faintly nectar smelling quality. I like the style considerably.

Outstanding vintages of this variety were the 1967, the 1959, the 1957, the 1953, and, surprisingly, a 1943—a wine, bottled by O'Shea in an old champagne bottle, which picked up great character and flavour. It had this delicious flavour right on the tongue in he middle of the palate. That particular wine was enjoyed well into the late sixties and just shows what the white wines of the Hunter can do—a wine twenty-five years old and still tasting fresh and full in the mouth.

Again I must emphasize that although traminer and riesling, both notable aromatics (in fact the aristocrats of the aromatic family), produce wines of a different character in the Hunter Valley, the area or region predominates. It is always the area which shows first. The wines are definitely of Hunter character first and with varietal variations second. I believe this is one of the most interesting things about the Hunter Valley district and the various varietal wines that are available.

McWilliam's Pink Champagne
A light, medium-sweet, sparkling wine, full of effervescence, made by the traditional Champagne method of bottle fermentation.

McWilliam's Private Bin 14 Burgundy
Made from a blend of hermitage and grenache grapes grown in the Riverina district of New South Wales. A repetitive Bin number which comes out year after year with the year of the vintage on the label.

This wine has the delicate aroma of the fruit, is medium bodied and has a round, soft palate.

McWilliam's Private Bin Cabernet Sauvignon
A triumph for the company and made entirely from cabernet sauvignon grapes grown in the Riverina district of New South Wales. A tremendous amount of care and attention is given to the growth of the grapes, which come mostly from vineyards controlled by individuals who co-operate very well with McWilliam's. Very good fruit is picked from these vineyards to make wines of great interest. The wines have excellent full colour, with that purple tinge about them when young which is characteristic of the variety, an extremely strong, aromatic fruit, the so-called 'berry' flavour which is so distinctive. This combines very well with the oak flavour derived from the maturation of the wine in small new oak barrels. These barrels are generally of the hogshead size and McWilliam's have experimented with certain of the different oaks over the years—Troncaise, Nevers, Limousin and American oak. I've always felt that they derive a most individual quality from their oak maturation—a sort of 'smokey' or 'tarry' quality which is different from the sweeter flavour of the Penfold's style, for example. Whatever, both oak and

fruit marry extremely well to produce an outstanding wine.

The 1964 Cabernet won numerous Gold Medals. It is a magnificent wine of great individuality. In past years the 1967 also won many prizes. Again there is a tremendous depth of flavour of the variety on the middle palate, the so-called 'smokey' quality of the oak and a very firm oak tannin finish. The 1968 wine was somewhat lighter and in a journal of the time I wrote tasting notes about this wine: 'very good wood treatment, lighter style than usual, good Cabernet, light middle palate, firm clean finish: good quality, but lightness on middle palate emphasises oak. Quite delicate.'

This wine has done well at shows, winning different awards including Gold Medals in Brisbane in 1968 and 1971 and in Adelaide in 1971. I understand that the company have produced large volumes of top Cabernet from the Riverina district in subsequent years and we shall be seeing a lot more of these wines in the future.

McWilliam's Private Bin Cabernet Shiraz
This wine is a blend of cabernet sauvignon and shiraz grown in the Riverina districts of New South Wales. It is matured in 600 gallon and 65 gallon oak casks until bottled.

It has pronounced varietal character, good colour, excellent balance and takes bottle maturation very well. The 1966 was an extremely interesting wine that had all the flavours of the straight cabernet sauvignon; oak, fruit and so forth, in just a slighter quality. But since there was so much in the cabernet sauvignon variety the cabernet shiraz blend still had plenty going for it. 1965 saw the first release—a good wine of pleasant initial drinking which also took some bottle maturation. The 1966 was a blend of forty-seven percent cabernet sauvignon and 53 percent shiraz. Again the cabernet showed through quite strongly and the oak flavour augmented the fruit without overcoming it. (The grapes were picked at 12½ degrees Baumé and the wine has finished up with 21.5° proof spirit and 5.5 grammes per litre total acid.)

Later vintages were a trifle lighter, but still had good flavour, good balance and continued to provide excellent drinking.

McWilliam's Private Bin 25 Chablis
This wine is made from semillon grapes grown in the Riverina district of New South Wales, where the soil is mostly heavy loam. The wine is dry, light and fresh; with generous bouquet and flavour and an intensely clean finish on the palate. To retain these qualities it does not receive any wood ageing and is bottled very young.

McWilliam's Private Bin 35 Claret
The hermitage (shiraz) grapes used to produce this vintage wine are picked exclusively from the com-

pany's 'Hanwood' vineyards. Controlled irrigation, accompanied by special pruning techniques, helps produce grapes which give a firmer style than one usually expects. This wine has delicacy, is very clean on the middle palate, and at the same time has full flavour of fruit with a firm tannin finish.

McWilliam's Private Bin 46 Hock

Another repetitive Bin number used year after year, the vintage changing on the label. To produce this wine great care is taken to ensure that the riesling (semillon) grapes, grown in the Riverina district of New South Wales, are picked at their optimum maturity. This, coupled with the quite cold temperature of fermentation which takes a considerable time, helps to make an excellent light style. It is crisp, delicate, has a lovely fruity bouquet, a very clean palate and a crisp finish. The wine is to be enjoyed when young and is often picked by experts as a straight Hunter.

McWilliam's Private Bin 56 Lexia

This is a light, dry white table wine made from the grape variety sometimes called lexia but which is actually muscat gordo blanco. It is produced in McWilliam's Robinvale winery in northern Victoria. During fermentation the temperature is maintained below 13 degrees C and this helps to retain the very powerful aroma of the grape in the wine as well as a tremendous volume of fruity flavour. This is a very aromatic wine showing strong muscat character; but the wine is very well-balanced and, as far as I'm concerned, is an outstanding triumph of winemaking skills.

McWilliam's Private Bin 66 Moselle

Made from semillon and other varieties grown in the Riverina district of New South Wales, this wine has some residual sugar on the middle palate, has a pleasant fragrant aroma, a rather delicate fruity flavour, and a crisp acid finish. It contains some effervesence or spritzig.

McWilliam's Private Bin Pinot Blanc

It seems that there are several variations of pinot blanc which are grown extensively throughout France; but all produce wines of a very distinctive aroma and flavour. This varietal wine, made from pinot blanc grown in the Riverina in New South Wales, has the typical characteristics of the variety: a rather unusual, but pleasant, bouquet; a distinctive flavour with good balance; and a very crisp, firm finish. The balance of the wine, the harmony of all the characteristics, is good. To me this would have been wonderful material for a top quality Champagne. After some time in the bottle, the flavour deepens and develops and the bouquet builds up quite remarkably. The wine does seem to be rather dumb in the first year or so after it is bottled. As the wine grows in the bottles the outstanding delicacy of the

McWILLIAM'S

ESTD 1877

PRIVATE BIN 56
LEXIA

This is a light dry white table wine made in 1970 from the grape variety known as Lexia and was produced at our Robinvale Winery in Victoria. During fermentation the temperature was maintained below 55° F and this has helped to retain in the wine a very powerful aroma of the grape as well as a tremendous volume of flavour.

It is an ideal accompaniment to most foods, particularly seasoned fish dishes and white meats.

It was awarded a Silver Medal in the International Wine Fair at Ljubljana, Yugoslavia, in 1970.

McWILLIAM'S WINES PTY. LTD. N.S.W.

A PRODUCT OF AUSTRALIA   26 FL OZ

variety and the cleanness and crispness of the finish restricts any threat of coarseness or bigness. In fact, this particular white indicated to me that certain of the wines from the Riverina will be able to take plenty of age, though others—of the more aromatic varieties—do tend to fill out rather quickly.

McWilliam's released one of these wines in 1966, and it is still drinking very well and showing a lot of developed character. The 1968 wine was of the same style, although it was probably even more delicate. It is a line of considerable finesse and most interesting character.

McWilliam's Private Bin Rhine Riesling

The company pioneered the cultivation of rhine riesling in the Riverina district of New South Wales and their efforts with the variety resulted in numerous Gold Medals. The 1966 McWilliam's Rhine Riesling won many Gold Medals; I think in one year alone it won no less than six Gold Medals. It was an extremely big aromatic wine of great flavour, great varietal character, with considerable spiciness on the middle palate. Interestingly the 1966 variety contained a small proportion of sauvignon blanc, which helped fill out the middle palate and may have contributed to the spicy quality.

In a couple of years the 1967 wine also won all sorts of prizes. To do that it has to be good. The one thing that worries me, however, is that the wines, having this enormous power and volume of power when young, become, with two or three years of age, very big in the bottle. The flavour seems to develop very quickly and the finish softens off.

So, unlike the Pinot Blanc wine made by the same company, the wine doesn't appear to me to improve with development of bottle character. Certainly, some of the McWilliam's winemaking team disagree with this; they like the wines when they develop; but I like them so much when they are young I can see no point in keeping them. In this they remind me very much of some of the intense Alsatian aromatics, which I believe are best enjoyed within a year or two of their bottling. In that first year or so the Rhine Riesling has this great depth of flavour, a very big aromatic varietal nose and is a wine for those people who want to see more intensity of flavour on the middle palate. The finish is always crisp and clean at this stage. The Rhine Riesling is good value. So what more do you want?

McWilliam's Private Bin 76 Riesling
Again a repetitive Bin number, although the vintage changes from year to year: made from specially selected riesling (semillon) grapes, grown in the Hanwood vineyards in the Riverina. This is a wine of pleasant character, quite considerable delicacy, agreeable fruit and a clean, crisp finish.

McWilliam's Private Bin Tokay (Dry)
Normally the tokay variety is used for making luscious, sweet white wines, but these grapes grown in the Riverina are ideal for producing a most interesting table wine. With the aid of refrigeration, fermentation is carried out at a very cool temperature and this retains the scented aroma of the tokay grape in the wine and its richness of flavour. After bottling it develops a firm, fruity flavour and delicate bouquet with very good balance and soft, round finish.

It is an interesting wine style. Perhaps it does not have the delicacy of the Pinot Blanc, nor the aromatic quality of the Rhine Riesling; but it still has its own character and flavour, and the varietal characteristics are most marked.

McWilliam's Private Bin 91 White Burgundy
Another repetitive Bin number, the vintage label changing year after year. It is made from the grape variety known as white hermitage (trebbiano, ugni blanc) again grown in the Riverina district of New South Wales. This wine is dry, but at the same time full of flavour, with the decided varietal character of the fruit and the aroma of the very ripe grapes used. A broad, soft, pleasant style.

McWilliam's Royal Reserve Brown Muscat
Produced from frontignac grown in the Riverina district of New South Wales. It has a lush muscat aroma and flavour.

McWilliam's Royal Reserve Dry Sherry
Palomino grapes grown in the Riverina are used to produce this dry sherry, which is allowed to mature in oak hogsheads before bottling.

McWilliam's Royal Reserve Port
Made entirely from shiraz grapes, it has a smooth, mellow character and is quite rich in flavour.

McWilliam's Royal Reserve Sweet Sherry
This wine is mellow, sweet and full-bodied. It is produced from various grape varieties grown in the Riverina.

McWilliam's Semi-Sweet Sherry
A medium sherry which is an each-way palate bet—made from several varieties of grapes grown in the Riverina.

McWilliam's Sparkling Burgundy
A rich red, slightly sweet, sparkling wine with a full fruity flavour made from shiraz grapes grown in the Riverina district and produced by the Charmat method.

McWilliam's Sparkling Chateau Gay
A natural sparkling wine made by the Cuvee Close process from a specially selected blend of grape varieties.

McWilliam's Sparkling Moselle
A crisp, white, slightly sweet, sparkling wine with a full fruity flavour, made from riesling (semillon) grapes grown in the Riverina district. Production is by the Charmat method at McWilliam's Yenda winery.

McWilliam's Sparkling Rosé
This is a natural sparkling rosé. It is made on the Charmat process and is slightly sweet and fruity, light with an attractive rosé colour.

McWilliam's Sweet Vermouth
An Italian type sweet vermouth with a deep, rich colour and smooth taste; made from a sound base wine with a generous infusion of imported herbs.

McWilliam's Vintage 99 Port
Made from a blend of shiraz and grenache grapes grown in the Riverina district. It is carefully matured in oak to give a very pleasant, soft blend of wood and fruit.

McWilliam's Wine Cocktails
These cocktails are made from specially selected wines produced in the Riverina wineries of the company. After blending with fruit flavours they are allowed to mature before bottling. At present they are obtainable in the following flavours: apricot, banana, cherry, manhattan, martini, tropical fruit.

Marienberg

Marienberg Claret

Made by a delightful lady winemaker, Ursula Pridham. In 1966 Ursula and Geoffrey Pridham purchased the property in the hills, south of Adelaide, going towards the Happy Valley district. It is a small vineyard now of some 15 acres or so but the significant fact is that Mrs Pridham has made some excellent wines which she matures in new small oak. Her early dry reds won a Gold Medal in the Adelaide Show which is no mean feat against the highly organized and technically advanced larger companies.

The Clarets are very sound indeed, extremely well made, with good fruit, plus an extremely sensitive handling of new oak. Fermentation is closed and temperature controlled. There is no doubt that the extreme care taken in making the wines is reflected in their quality. The Clarets tend to be of the lighter style; very flavoursome and ready to drink not long after bottling.

Marienberg Rhine Riesling

A most interesting and complex wine, being straight Rhine Riesling matured in small oak. To me this is a contradiction, since I believe small oak flavour can augment white burgundy styles, but is not particularly helpful to the aromatic style of rhine riesling. However, these are Mrs Pridham's wines and that's her business.

The 1969 Rhine Riesling was a very full-flavoured wine which had quite strong oak overtones. The 1970 wine, which won a Silver Medal in a couple of shows, was a more aromatic Rhine Riesling showing considerably more varietal flavour and less oak. Whatever the argument, this is an authentic new development and is extremely interesting because of the combination of flavours.

Marienberg Shiraz Cabernet

A blend of the two premium varieties, matured in small new wood, both French and American, this wine has considerable varietal flavour, together with very good oak handling. It seems that these wines should develop very well with a few years in the bottle. Certainly they have good balance, are very vinous, have excellent fruit characters and are extremely well made.

Mildara Wines Ltd

Mildara Cabernet Shiraz Reserve Bin

This famous line was introduced in the early fifties by Ron Haselgrove, Esq., O.B.E., who had been running Mildara Wines, one of the more famous of the medium-sized wine companies of Australia, which is located at Merbein, just outside Mildura, on the River Murray. Mildara have long been famous for their brandies and sherries. In the late forties, Ron Haselgrove was intent upon making a dry red wine. Mildara did not have the material in their own area, so he sought to find it elsewhere, to put it together and mature it to make a firm, clean, dry red, perhaps based on the Bordeaux style of wine. I know that he used to get shipments of Bordeaux wines from France so that he could taste them from time to time and examine them to see how he could balance his own wines to approximate that style.

The first commercial wine that came out was Bin 21 of 1951. This was mostly made from material grown south of Adelaide and many, many years later I had the pleasure of tasting it, having found some in the cellar of the Renmark Hotel at Renmark. The wine was quite remarkable with a tremendously well developed bouquet and flavour, a beautiful balance of soft, clean, lingering finish, surely a top Australian red.

There was no wine sold of the 1952 vintage, but from the 1953 vintage he made Bin 22 and thus started having numbers, one year after the vintage year. This has carried on to this day. The Bin 22 was a rich wine, very full with quite remarkable development; a very rich flavour which lasted and lasted and it had a particularly long, savouring aftertaste. The Bin 23 of 1954 was a very famous wine, a Gold First Prize winner in the days when there were only three prizes in each class—First, Second and Third. This was a mature, elegant wine with very rich nose and flavour, well-balanced and of quite considerable staying power.

The Bin 24 of 1955 seemed to have good flavour but was somewhat lighter and a little thinner on the palate, with perhaps a harder, more acid finish.

There was no wine made in 1956 as far as I know. In 1957 they had the Bin 25, a fairly straight-forward wine of good flavour that did not have the complexity of some of the other wines and appeared to be rather hard.

The Bin 26 was made in the same year. This was a wine in which Mr Haselgrove experimented with various blending materials and found that he didn't quite get the desired result. I think that this was the only time the wine included some malbec, a practice later discontinued.

The Bin 27 was a 1958 wine and this was another wine of strong cabernet character. By this time the blends had evolved into material from the Southern Vales district south of Adelaide, both cabernet sauvignon and shiraz being used, together with Coonawarra material. Mr Haselgrove was very impressed with the quality of Redman's wines and he bought these wines for his blending purposes.

When he first approached Mr Bill Redman to buy some wine from him, he refused to buy at the price quoted per gallon and in fact wanted to pay more. He wanted to encourage Bill Redman to maintain the supply of very good quality wine, and believed he should be rewarded for his efforts.

In 1958 Ron Haselgrove also put together an extraordinary wine which was one of the most remarkable

Australian dry reds ever made. This was the famous Mildara Hunter Coonawarra of 1958. In 1957 they had put together a wine which was predominantly Hunter (over 60 percent) together with Coonawarra shiraz. There was no cabernet in this wine at all, though the label did state Cabernet Shiraz, being the general label used for this line. In fact the wine was a straight shiraz from the two districts. The 1957 wine was rather interesting, fine flavoured, and elegant, with considerable finesse—a rather austere wine with a fairly hard finish. The reason for this is that traditionally Coonawarra wines have a fairly firm finish and the 1957 vintage in the Hunter Valley district was much finer than usual.

But in 1958 they really hit the jackpot when they reduced the Hunter proportion so that the wine was half Hunter, half Coonawarra. (The Hunter material coming from Doug Elliott of 'Oakvale'.) The wine also had some oak maturation. Consequently it was a flavour blend of Coonawarra region, Hunter region, shiraz fruit and oak and the whole thing came together magnificently. I have enjoyed many bottles of this wine over the years. There is considerable bottle variation—one bottle will be picked as a Hunter because there is tremendous Hunter flavour; the next bottle is full of Coonawarra character. Often the wine has been picked as French. It has an extraordinary volume of bouquet reminiscent of some Bordeaux wines. As long ago as 1963 I saw the wine tasted blind by Les Ekert, who worked for the company, and he thought it was a French wine. It still drinks tremendously well, still has quite gorgeous flavour and is unquestionably one of the top wines of Australia.

In 1959 the Bin 28, a slightly bigger wine, contained a measure of Hunter material and this approximate proportion has been in the blend since then. The blend has now settled down into being a regional and varietal blend as follows: approximately ten percent or so from the Hunter Valley— all shiraz; from the Southern Vales forty to fifty percent of the remainder—it varies with the year depending entirely on what is produced, made up of roughly half cabernet sauvignon and half shiraz; from Coonawarra, the forty to fifty percent remaining with a dominance of shiraz.

Bin 28 was a fuller wine—for 1959 was a fairly big year in South Australia—with lots of flavour and style and a very pronounced bouquet. I thought it was a very good wine, though it was too big for some people.

The Bin 29 of 1960 was a more fragrant, lighter and elegant wine, which had an intense full nose, very strong cabernet character, and lovely flavour and balance. It was a most complete wine. The Bin 30 of 1961 was another excellent wine; fuller and softer this time with very good flavour. It was soft and round with a very clean, elegant finish and a beautiful nose. The Bin 31 of 1962 perhaps had a little less Hunter in it, and had quite marked

Coonawarra character. This was evident on the finish of the wine which was rather austere, firm with clean tannin.

The Bin 32 of 1963 was (and still is) absolutely first class—and unquestionably it will live for many years. It seemed to have very strong shiraz character on the tongue, with a rather forward cabernet flavour on the front of the palate and on the bouquet itself. There was also oak showing. This wine was beautifully balanced, the mid-palate filled out with delicious, elegant soft fruit.

The 1964 blend was Bin 33, another top wine that contained a fair proportion of Coonawarra cabernet and shiraz. By this time Mildara had established vineyards of their own in Coonawarra which produced the famous 1963 Cabernet Sauvignon. But the 1964 vintage at Coonawarra was affected by frost and hence there was no straight bottling of cabernet sauvignon. They blended cabernet and shiraz together to make a very good single wine from Coonawarra which had excellent balance and character, but there was a fair amount of material left over to go into the general cabernet shiraz blend. This wine therefore contained Coonawarra, Southern Vales cabernet and shiraz and Hunter shiraz. It had excellent fruit, superb middle palate flavour balance, and again, at the price it was sold for in those days, was a real bargain for those who were establishing a cellar at the time.

The Bin 34 of 1965 did not seem to have the same elegance. It was again a poor year in Coonawarra. The wines were not very good and although this wine contained plenty of Coonawarra material, if you have a poor year there's not much you can do about it. The wine seemed to have less middle palate fruit and certainly the nose never built up as well as the other wines.

1966 was a better year throughout Australia and it is reflected in the Bin 35 which is a full-flavoured wine, still maturing well and which will still need more time to reach its peak. The proportions of this wine varied slightly from normal. The Bin 35 of 1966 contained Coonawarra cabernet and shiraz, approximately half the wine being from this district; plus forty percent Southern Vales shiraz and ten percent Hunter Valley hermitage (shiraz). The blend was matured in new French small oak, so there was a multiplicity of flavours in the wine; the varietal flavours of cabernet and shiraz, the regional flavours and characteristics of Coonawarra, the Southern Vales and the Hunter and the oak extraction from the new casks. At the time I said these flavours would take some time to come together, and indeed this is what happened; but now the Bin 35 of 1966 is starting to drink extremely well and will go forward for some considerable time yet.

The 1967 Bin 36 was a bigger fruit wine. There was oak evident but the oak wasn't as strong as that of the Bin 35 of 1966. The Bin 36 has extremely good discernible cabernet and Coonawarra flavours which greatly added to the elegance of the wine. In fact, they probably gave more finesse to the wine because the chief characteristic of the Bin 36 was a great big, sort of Southern Vales character; we've used various words over the years to try and describe the flavour—some people call it 'chocolatey', others 'burnt toffee', others 'smoky' and even one friend of mine—of great wine repute—said it has the flavour of 'crushed ants'. Certainly it was a very big, voluminous sort of nose and flavour and it combined very well with the more austere flavours that cut it back a bit. The palate of this wine was very round, soft and supple and there was a slight oak astringency on the finish. I suppose one could add that this wine perhaps didn't have the elegance and finesse of some of the previous wines, but certainly had a lot going for it and at the time it was sold it was very cheap and represented a great buy for cellaring purposes.

Both the wines of the latter vintage of the 1960s seem to be disappointing, the Bin 37 of 1968 and the Bin 38 of 1969. The 1968 wine had pleasant fruit, was well put together, and was touched up nicely with small oak, but it didn't seem to have that depth and flavour of character of previous years. The 1969 wine, Bin 38, reflected the generally poor year in South Australia. At the 1969 vintage the grapes were picked at Coonawarra after the rains fell and I think this is reflected in the light, rather colourless wines that came from the area from that company. A lot of the wine went into the Bin 38 of 1969 and it shows. It is a nice, lighter style of wine, well put together, quite elegant and having quite good flavour—but without that lovely, generous, rich completeness and perfect balance of wines like the Bin 31 and Bin 32. These wines have a very special place in my wine tasting memory. I always regarded this line as being extremely important as far as Australia was concerned. It was a great development. A blend that completely slaughtered those people who said that you couldn't have good wines if there were blends, and it showed how one company could chase integrity to produce a complete style and line. Doug Seabrook, Melbourne wine merchant and well-known judge, wrote about 'the absolute integrity and devotion to standards of the Mildara bottlings'; and George Fairbrother, chairman of judges at Sydney, Brisbane and Adelaide, said of Ron Haselgrove, 'He's chased quality all his life.' I think that this is reflected in this very famous line of Cabernet-Shiraz dry red wine and I believe that over the years these wines have provided some of the very best value for money in this country.

Mildara Chestnut Teal Sherry
This is a very good semi-sweet style of sherry which was first produced in 1950 from palomino grapes and blended from various types of wine. The sweet portion of the blend requires extensive small oak maturation, and the remainder is composed of Flor sherries grown and matured in those famous Flor sherry houses at Mildura and then put into oak for further maturation.

The great flavours, wood character and the Flor characters are evident on the palate. Though sweet, it is a very good style, towards an Oloroso style, which has always remained extremely good drinking and good value for money.

Mildara Coonawarra Cabernet Sauvignon
This is made from straight cabernet sauvignon grown on the Mildara's vineyards at Coonawarra, on the red and black soils that cover the limestone subsoil. The grapes ripen to optimum maturity before picking. Then they are gently handled and crushed through the Amos Mill. All the wines are then treated in new small oak. and this is reflected in the final flavour. There is no question in my mind that Cabernet Sauvignon, especially Coonawarra Cabernet Sauvignon, and small oak are made for each other.

Of the wines that have so far appeared under this label the 1963 was the first and by far the most outstanding. This wine had an incredibly intense flavour, fantastic fruit, beautiful oak and it was so outstanding that it simply walked away with all the honours when it was first shown in Sydney. I think it finished up 'best wine of the Show'. It certainly was 'best red of the Show', which for a young wine is not a bad accomplishment. This wine had great richness of character, and its flavour is difficult to describe. Someone once said it had almost a 'blackberry-mint character' and one could understand exactly what he was trying to say.

There was no wine in 1964 under the label, nor in 1965 and then there were three consecutive vintages, the 1966, 1967 and 1968.

The 1966 wine had tremendous colour, a great deal of depth, a lovely fruit nose, very good oak—all the factors adding up to make it a very good wine indeed. My only criticism of this wine was that it appeared to be rather dumb. It showed this character quite early and the dumbness is still there. Indeed I think it will take quite a lot of time for the 1966 to fully mature. There was also a bit of that dusty, chalky sort of nose which I think comes from the limestone subsoils—something evident sometimes in wines from Coonawarra.

So, although I considered the 1966 Mildara Coonawarra Cabernet Sauvignon an extremely good wine, at a tasting of all the wines produced so far under that label, it was the least developed. It didn't have the estery fruit, the intensity of flavour that the other wines did, *although* it is an extremely good wine of considerable character which will mature well into the future.

The 1967 was a better wine. This had less of the limestoney nose of the 1966 and a great deal more of the cabernet fruit. The colour, a very dark purple red that still stays with it; the aromatic fruit nose was backed up with plenty of fresh new oak and there was almost aggressive cabernet flavour on the palate—the finish showing a lot of good, clean acid and firm tannin. This is a wine which obviously needs to go a great deal further. Indeed, talking to Ron Haselgrove's son years ago, he said he expected the wines could take at least ten years in bottle age and probably a great deal more.

The 1968 edition of the wine had more complexity still. (Though one mustn't get the idea that the wines of 1966 and to some extent 1967 are now being denigrated by the enthusiasm for the 1968.) This wine had all the usual characteristics of the line; a very deep, dark, dense colour, purple-hued; extremely strong varietal fruits, strong cabernet berry showing through; very strong regional character—Coonawarra is always there and always evident; very good strong new oak. It is almost as if the wine has too much of the flavour goodies. When these are integrated together they should provide a wine of wonderful power and flavour. The point about the 1968 was the balance. It has a lovely harmony of characters, and even though the flavours have not yet come together, you can still see the potential of the wine. The finish is very clean, soft and firm. A wine which one could put away with enthusiasm and anticipation.

So speaking broadly it appears that the masterly 1963 is the wine that is still going forward and still has tons of character going for it. It will live and mature and build up flavour and bouquet for years and years. The 1968 is somewhat behind it. It did not have the exquisite flavour of the 1963, but a magnificent wine none the less. It is followed by the 1967 and 1966: the 1966 still perhaps the 'dumbest' of them all, one which shows less estery and varietal character, but still an extremely good wine. In fact there has never been anything even remotely approaching a poor wine in the lot, because if, as in the years 1964 and 1965, the wine doesn't approach the required standard, they simply use the material elsewhere.

Mildara Coonawarra Cabernet Shiraz

We are not likely to see this wine again since plantings of malbec which had been made by the company in Coonawarra came into bearing in the mid-1960s, and it now appears that this will always be blended with the shiraz to make another unique style of Mildara Coonawarra wines. However, two bottlings were made and are worthy of mention.

The 1963 Cabernet Shiraz never received the accolades of its celebrated big brother, the 1963 Cabernet Sauvignon, but this wine was still extremely good. I saw it in a Brisbane show some years ago when I thought it should have walked away with the top red honours of the day. It was a wine which always had an extremely good fruit (the shiraz fruit being quite evident on the palate) and the oak certainly was extremely well-balanced. A wine which drank well quite early but which is still

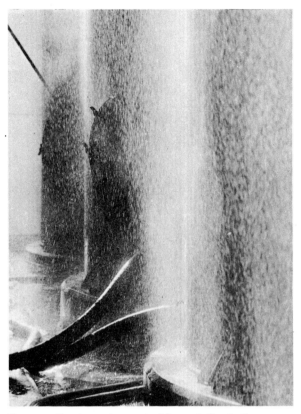

Water cooling is used to control fermentation in these oubide stainless steel tanks at Mildara, Vic.

drinking well today and will certainly go on for a few years yet.

The 1964 edition was the only wine made. In 1964 the wine wasn't considered good enough to be bottled as a straight Cabernet Sauvignon and the two varieties were put together. The wine had less oak than the 1963 and probably a slighter fruit, but it was a well-balanced, harmonious wine, with a very nice soft middle palate and a rather pleasant, soft tannin finish.

Since 1964 there has been no repetition of this label—the Coonawarra Cabernet Shiraz—and it appears unlikely that we shall see it again.

Mildara Coonawarra Cabernet Shiraz Malbec

Though I have long been a supporter for elimination of the use of overseas names in Australia, this title does show how unwieldy some of ours can become.

This is a blend of the three varieties that Mildara grow at Coonawarra and was first brought onto the market in 1966. It replaces the former cabernet shiraz blend that appeared for two vintages. This is a very soft, round wine with considerable suppleness and smoothness on the middle palate. The oak character tends to dominate on the nose. There is still plenty of fruit, however, and it is interesting to see that the proportion in this wine was fifty percent cabernet, thirty percent shiraz and twenty percent malbec, and yet the latter variety tends to show through. Mr Ron Haselgrove wrote to me about this many years ago and said that it was quite remarkable to him how assertive the malbec variety was. The wine was always much more forward than the Cabernet Sauvignon, being a much rounder, softer, smoother wine that would appear to mature early. In fact some judges made the comment that they did not think that it would last very long. I feel that the wine had so much going for it, fruit, plus oak, plus pure body, that it would need time to mature, fully ripen, enrich and soften.

The 1967 wine was even slightly better. The proportions in the wine were much the same. It had an extremely deep colour with just a trace of development on the outer meniscus of the wine. The nose was powerful, very rich and voluminous, showing plenty of fruit as well as the strong oak. Again the palate was extremely supple, with a very rich, mouth-filling quality, and plenty of fruit and body. The whole wine is certainly so well-balanced that you could drink it quite young, even though you could see the extraordinary future development that lay in store for it. The cabernet character was quite strong among these complexities, and yet there wasn't the dip on the back of the palate that is so often associated with the variety. On the contrary, the rich roundness of the wine on the tongue was one of its most interesting features. I suspect that the Malbec, which is used in Bordeaux for much the same purpose (to fill out the middle palate) was in fact doing the trick with this wine. This roundness and softness carried straight through onto the back of the palate and through to the finish which was quite soft, even when the wine was young.

So, overall, I liked the balance and completeness and fruit of the wine and look forward to seeing it develop, even though it was very soft.

The 1968 wine didn't impress quite so much. It had a sort of lighter style to it and there appeared to be that lack of volume of fruit and flavour that I had come to associate with the wine style. The 1969 also seemed to be lacking and this could be put down to the slighter years. I understand the material in the early 1970s was quite extraordinary and I am looking forward to seeing these wines when they are ready to be shown.

Mildara Coonawarra Rhine Riesling

This style was first introduced in 1967 and is produced from 100 percent rhine riesling grown at Coonawarra. The wine does show that the famous Coonawarra red soil belt, the terra rossa, may have the ability to produce extremely good quality white wines.

The 1967 was an extremely attractive wine of the fuller style. It didn't have the light estery, sort of 'head and shoulders' quality of the Watervale and the Eden Valley rhine rieslings, but it had a quieter nose, although what was there was still of good varietal character. On the palate the wine was rich and round. It achieved this quite quickly in the bottle and so although you could see the rhine riesling quality there it didn't have that sharp intensity of flavour which is associated with other bottlings. It is a very soft, pleasant wine.

The 1968 wasn't quite so good, for I think they had some trouble with the fermentation in that year. It appeared to me that there was a certain amount of residual sugar in the wine which also lacked enough aromatic fruit quality to really carry it as a sort of moselle—it was too broad.

The 1969 was a good interesting wine; and the 1970 I liked very much. It had an estery pungent sort of nose, full of rhine riesling fruit. The flavour was quite strong and again this middle palate was filling out at a comparatively early bottle age. The finish was clean and fresh, in spite of the volume of the flavour on the palate. It was therefore a fairly big wine—none of your wispy, delicate styles—very mouth filling and satisfying; altogether, an interesting style.

Mildara George Dry Sherry

This famous sherry is made from pedro ximenez, palomino and doradillo grapes. The material comes from vineyards at Irymple in the Mildura District along the River Murray, from the Southern Vales south of Adelaide and from Coonawarra. It is a carefully selected blend of oak matured Flor sherries of between three and ten years age. The wine is completely sugar-free and it really has a dry, almost flinty, acerbic sort of palate. It was rumoured that this was produced originally for a man who loved sherry, but who was a diabetic. Consequently it is highly recommended for those people who have sugar problems. It is completely bone dry. Therefore the wine does not attract a lot of people unless they understand this completely fine, delicate dryness, which is a combination of good grapes, good fruit material from different areas, matured in oak for some considerable time and this marvellous Flor character.

Mildara Golden Bower Riesling

A blend of Hunter River riesling (semillon) and Coonawarra semillon. Up until the 1969 vintage this wine was an adaption of a straight Elliot wine from the Hunter Valley. Doug Elliot makes wines at his 'Oakvale' winery from material from Belford, Fordwich and Oakvale and Mildara used to buy some which they then put into this bottling. Wines I remember with affection are the Bin 16 of 1967 and the Bin 18 of 1969. Possibly the addition of the Coonawarra semillon will now slightly take away some of that full, rich 'honey' character which is not necessarily anything to do with sweetness, but rather a characteristic of the flavour.

The first wine we have seen of this blend is well put together, pleasant and soft, with good flavour, good balance and soft fruit, and with none of that aromatic esteriness which is characteristic of most South Australian wines. If one has to describe it in structure form, it is rather more of the white burgundy style than any other. It develops with bottle maturation, acquiring an additional full, rich character. The flavour deepens and the nose builds up bouquet. It is very good drinking indeed, especially with strong flavoured white meats or mild cheeses—quite a unique style of white wine.

Mildara Golden Oriole Champagne
This is produced from clare riesling grapes, grown in the Mildura area and made into a base wine. From this base wine a sparkling wine is made, using the traditional Methode Champenoise.

Mildara Hermitage Claret
A pleasant, light dry red made from shiraz with some grenache. It is matured in oak for from one to two years and then bottled. Long bottle ageing is not recommended.

Mildara Merebin Estate Hermitage
A pleasant red made from shiraz together with a small proportion of grenache and a blend of various vineyards at Mildura, Southern Vales and Coonawarra. This fairly firm dry red is matured in oak for from one to two years prior to bottling and with some bottle age provides pleasant everyday drinking.

Mildara Merebin Estate Moselle
This is a slightly sweet, white table wine with balanced acidity made from riesling material grown at Coonawarra and Irymple. The riesling material includes rhine riesling, clare riesling and semillon.

Mildara Merebin Estate Sauterne
Produced from semillon and clare riesling grapes grown at Coonawarra and Irymple. Shows considerable improvement after two or three years in the bottle, having pleasant sweetness on the middle palate and good balance.

Mildara Merebin Estate Riesling
A light, crisp, dry white made from rhine riesling and clare riesling grapes, grown at Coonawarra and Irymple. Pleasant, undistinguished; good value.

Mildara Monopole Claret
This is produced from shiraz grapes grown in the Mildura area. Fermented in stainless steel, it is bottled as a quaffing wine and is not intended for bottle maturation. However, it always provides very good, pleasant, well rounded, soft drinking.

Mildara Monopole Riesling
Produced from riesling material grown in the Mildura area. A wine with pleasant varietal character, some considerable flavour on the middle palate and a pleasant, crisp finish.

Mildara Reserve Bin Port
Made from grenache and shiraz grown in the Southern Vales district of South Australia. This wine is fortified with Mildara Pot Still Brandy and matured in oak hogsheads and quarter casks for some considerable time. The various vintages are then blended together to make a very soft, pleasant, developed Tawny Port; a very high quality dessert wine.

Mildara Rosé
An interesting light, pleasant dry wine made from grenache grapes.

Mildara Rio Vista Cream Sherry
This wine has a Flor sherry base which has been blended into a soft, mellow, rather grapy dessert wine.

Mildara Rio Vista Flor Dry Sherry
Made from doradillo and palomino grown in the Mildura area. Mildara are famed for their Flor sherries and this is a typical one, in which the Flor sherry material is blended into a softer, more fulsome flavoured wine, more towards the Amontillado style.

Mildara Rio Vista Medium Dry Sherry
A semi-sweet, soft, Flor sherry, made from palomino grapes grown in the Mildura area.

Mildara Rio Vista Muscat
A rich, fruity muscat made from gordo blanco grapes grown in the Mildura area; fortified with brandy, which has been distilled from muscat gordo blanco which adds an interesting dimension to the flavour of this wine.

Mildara Rio Vista Old Port
Made from brandy-fortified shiraz grown in the Mildura area.

Mildara Rio Vista Sweet Sherry
A soft, pleasant, sweet, fortified wine made on a Flor sherry base.

Mildara Supreme Dry Sherry
Made from pedro ximenez, palomino and doradillo grapes, grown at Mildura, Coonawarra and in the Southern Vales district of South Australia. This is an extremely popular, pale, dry, delicate wine, which has long been one of the most highly regarded Flor sherries in the country. It is quite delicate and has a nice middle palate nuttiness, which is a combination of fruit, oak and Flor and there is just a trace of some

slight residual sugar on the middle palate, which prevents it being one of those very bone dry sherries; always consistent and always good value.

Miranda

This company in the Riverina district of New South Wales at Griffith, sells fortified and table wines in flagons and bottles. There is a large range of different sherries, muscats, ports, vermouths and marsalas. Mr Jim Miranda, the winemaker, also makes some dry reds and whites of which he is especially proud. Wines worthy of special mention include the following.

Miranda Bin Burgundy
An interesting wine of considerable fruity character and a rather assertive flavour reminiscent of the Italian Barbera wines. It is made from shiraz grapes, crushed at 12 Baumé and fermented by the Duscillier method.

Miranda Bin 52 Dry White Clare Riesling
A light, crisp, white wine with full-flavoured body and pleasant acid balance, made entirely from clare riesling grapes grown in the Wyangan district. The grapes were late picked at 12 Baumé; the juices immediately run off the skins after crushing, with fermentation being conducted at 14.4 degrees C.

Miranda Bin 66 Dry White Trebbiano
This is a light wine with a soft flavour and dry finish, made entirely from the trebbiano (white shiraz) white variety. The flavour is rather straightforward and the wine is best enjoyed when fairly young.

Miranda Bin 76 White Burgundy
Made from trebbiano (white shiraz). The wine has a light golden colour, a round fruity flavour, a soft smooth finish, and is pleasant straightforward drinking.

Miranda Cabernet Shiraz
A good quality red made from cabernet sauvignon and shiraz, fermented by the Duscillier method; then aged in oak barrels for twelve months prior to bottling, and further bottle matured before release. A soft, round, pleasant wine with an interesting berry character.

Miranda Claret
Produced from sixty percent grenache and forty percent shiraz. A pleasant, well-made everyday drinking wine.

Miranda Golden Crown Liqueur Frontignac
Made entirely from frontignac. A mellow, red, sweet wine which is aged in small oak barrels for six years. The wine has a pleasant combination of fruit and oak and finishes clean, with an excellent spirit quality.

Miranda Golden Crown Liqueur Tokay
Made entirely from tokay and aged in small oak for five years and more. A mellow, fortified, sweet wine of quite distinctive 'honey' flavour and with a smooth, soft, clean spirit finish.

Miranda Golden Crown Mature Port
Made from shiraz and grenache and aged for many years in small oak vessels. It is a rich, sweet red wine having a full, round, fruity flavour with some wood showing.

Miranda Rosé
Made entirely from grenache grown locally. A clean, fresh wine of no particular distinction, but ideal for everyday consumption.

Morris Wines Pty Ltd

Morris Blue Imperial Dry Red
Made from blue imperial (cinsaut) grown at the 'Mia Mia' vineyards in north-east Victoria. Matured in 350 gallon oak casks for 16 months and then in oak puncheons for a further two months prior to bottling. The wine is light in style, but heavier in body than are most wines made from this variety. It has a very good straightforward flavour, with plenty to it, and finishes agreeably crisp and firm.

Morris Brown Muscat
A blend of Rutherglen brown muscat (frontignac), muscat gordo blanco and grenache grapes; matured in wood for approximately three years. It has about 5.5 degrees Baumé and is a pleasant wine with a strong muscat bouquet and flavour.

Morris Cabernet Shiraz Dry Red
Made from cabernet and shiraz grapes in equal proportions and grown at 'Mia Mia', picked at 13 degrees Baumé and fermented together on the skins for three days. The wine is matured for eighteen months in 350 gallon old oak casks and has a further two months in new American oak puncheons. The wine has won numerous medals in wine shows, mostly as a Burgundy, because of its softness on the middle palate. It has a full, earthy bouquet with cabernet character showing quite strongly. The wine is big and fruity on the palate, with a nice soft roundness to it; but it still shows a touch of astringency on the finish. It has a very good violet colour, and holds this colour for quite a while. It will mature for a considerable period.

Morris Claret (Flagon)
Made from shiraz and grenache grapes fermented separately, the wines are blended together later. They

Sherry in the storage cellars at McWilliams Wines, Hanwood, N.S.W., where a winery was built in 1917.

are usually matured for about eighteen months; nine months of this time is spent in concrete and then nine months in wood. This is a pleasant wine with some nice fruity bigness of the shiraz on the middle palate, which is combined with the softness of the grenache.

Morris Club Sherry
An amontillado style sherry of fortified white, mostly coming from pedro ximenez material. Aged in wood for three years, blended with approximately fifteen percent Flor sherry and slightly sweetened. This is a well-matured, full-bodied, rather full-flavoured dry sherry.

Morris Cream Sherry
A blend of white hermitage, tokay and muscat gordo blanco grapes, matured in large oak casks for three years prior to bottling. The wine is approximately 6 degrees Baumé and is much fuller, softer and darker in colour than the majority of cream sherries on the market. Therefore it is nearer the Spanish type of sherry which is sold as a Cream in Britain. It has proved to be a very popular wine.

Morris Shiraz Dry Red
Made from shiraz grapes, which are picked at 12½ to 13 degrees Baumé and fermented on skins for three days. Matured in oak casks for approximately sixteen months before bottling. There is a trace of wood on the bouquet and palate, but this does not dominate because the flavour of the variety is so strong. The wine is fairly dark in colour, has an earthy, north-east Victorian character and flavour. It is a bigger wine than most of the commercial wines available today.

Morris Dry Vermouth
Made from a neutral sherry-base wine, which has had imported vermouth herbs steeped in it until the right amount of herbal flavouring has been infused.

Morris Durif Dry Red
This unusual grape variety was first introduced by Francois de Castella from France about 1908, when replanting was being carried out in the Rutherglen district after phylloxera had devastated the area. The grapes are picked at 13 degrees Baume, fermented on skins for three days and then matured in 350 gallon old oak casks for 16 months; after which time they are transferred to new oak casks for about two months prior to bottling.

This wine has taken numerous prizes in Australian wine shows, mainly in the Burgundy class. It is a big wine with a very dark colour which has a pronounced purple tinge to it as a young wine; it holds this purple for some considerable time. There's a distinct varietal nose, very fruity, a big palate with a good balance of acidity and rather astringent tannin on the finish. The wine will mature for a long time.

Champagne at McWilliams, Yenda, in the Riverina, N.S.W.

It is a very good, straightforward, rather robust flavoured dry red.

Morris Hock
Made from white hermitage and riesling grapes and bottled after six months in old big wood. A rather fulsome, broad white wine with a pleasant, soft, acid finish which balances it.

Morris Marsala
The base wine is a sweet red wine made from grenache grapes, matured in large oak casks and to which marsala essence has been added. This is made specifically to meet the continued demand for these wines from a section of the market.

Morris Medium Dry Sherry
An 'each-way' wine, it is a blend of dry and sweet sherries, that has general appeal.

Morris Miafino Flor Sherry
The base wine is made from palomino, pedro ximenez and white hermitage grapes. It is fortified to 27° proof and left on Flor culture in oak hogsheads for two years and then fortified to 31° proof and left for a further 12 months to mature. The wine has a distinctive Flor bouquet and palate, is fairly well balanced, soft and smooth and has a rather nice, soft, lingering, nutty sort of finish.

Morris Moselle
Made from white hermitage and riesling and sweetened with grape concentrate. It is a rather full, nondescript white wine with some sweetness, which is bottled about six months after vintage.

Morris Muscat
This Muscat is of the liqueur type and is labelled as such. One of the most interesting and finest wines in Australia, it is made from Rutherglen brown muscat (frontignac) which are picked at about 17½ degrees Baumé, fermented slightly, pressed and fortified. The resultant wine is usually 9-11 degrees Baumé. The wine is then matured for a considerable time in casks of various sizes. The bottled wines are usually a blend of different vintages, rather than being of one particular vintage. It is the job of the winemaker to sort out the characters of the wines that he has on hand, to put them together into a blend which will finally have total character.

These bottled wines from Morris' always show a strong, clean-scented muscat bouquet of the highest character, combined with extremely good use of oak. The muscat flavour on the palate is compared to a dry raisin character, which combines excellently with the oak. Although showing a great deal of luscious sweetness, the wine has plenty of style and character to prevent it from being sickly sweet, and the finish is always clean, nutty and rather astringent. The wine has won numerous Gold Medals in wine shows and the Show Muscat, the one that is there to be tasted and sometimes to be bought, has an incredible richness of character. It is said that some parts of this wine go back into the nineteenth century.

There is no doubt that the Brown Muscat wines of the north-east Victorian districts have tremendous significance. They are wines which cannot be made overseas and they lay claim to being the truly indigenous wines of this country. It is a great shame that they have not had the recognition they deserve. They are ideal at the end of the meal with a plate of muscatels and nuts. A glass of old muscat is a deeply satisfying, sensuous and tactile experience.

Morris Riesling
Made from riesling grapes, grown at Morris' 'Balldale' vineyards in New South Wales. The grapes are picked at 11° Baumé and control fermented. The wine is bottled after six months' maturation. It is a fairly full-flavoured white of no great finesse, but pleasant drinking.

Morris Rosé
Made from grenache grapes, it is a light wine with a slight fruitiness.

Morris's Royal Reserve Port
Made from grenache and shiraz grapes and matured in wood for two to three years before bottling. It is of the lighter, ruby style and is fairly sweet, having about 5½ degrees Baumé.

Morris Sauterne
Made from white hermitage and riesling grapes and sweetened with grape concentrate. A rather fulsome, sweet wine.

Morris Sparkling Moselle
A straight commercial offering, this fairly sweet, sparkling wine is made by the Charmat method.

Morris Sweet Sherry
A sweet wine of the minimum price bracket, made from pedro ximenez and muscat gordo blanco grapes and matured in wood for two years.

Morris Sweet Vermouth
A fairly sweet wine of about 6 degrees Baumé with darker, richer colour than the majority of sweet vermouths. Made by steeping imported herbs in light, wood-matured port base wine until correct herbal balance is achieved.

Morris Tawny Port
A port made from grenache and shiraz, aged in wood for a number of years before bottling. The wine is fruitier than most aged tawny ports, being about 6 degrees Baumé. It is quite dark in colour, and is probably too sweet and a little too dark to be called a true tawny port style. The wine has great popularity.

Morris Tokay
This is one of the famous grape types of the district which makes a magnificent dessert wine. According to Francois de Castella it is the Hungarian grape harslevelu, one of the most highly esteemed grapes of the Tokay district in Hungary, but which is totally distinct and different from the furmint variety, which is the dominant grape of the Tokay district, which helps to make all those famous concentrated wines of Hungary. The grapes are picked at about 15-16 degrees Baumé and after fermentation the wine finishes out at about 8½ to 10 degrees Baumé. It is then matured in wood for several years.

The resultant wine has a most delightful, clean-scented aroma, which is somewhat earthy and fragrant, and has a big, luscious soft palate, fairly low on acidity. These wines have deservedly taken countless prizes in the main Australian shows in the sweet wine classes. They do not have the rich, raisiny grapiness of the muscat varieties, although they have much the same structure. Whatever, they are formidably good dessert wines of the highest quality.

Morris Vintage Port
Mick Morris, the winemaker at 'Mia Mia', is a student of port styles. He says that this wine is called vintage wine for want of a better name. It is made from shiraz and durif grapes and has about 5 degrees Baumé of sweetness. The wine has a very deep colour and a pleasant, sort of liquorice-style nose. The palate is full and fruity and although the finish is slightly dry, it is by no means as dry as the best of the real vintage ports from Portugal. Mick says this may be because they use a low strength spirit for fortification, whereas we use very high strength clean spirit for fortification.

This wine has taken many prizes at Australian shows in the one and two-year-old, full-bodied sweet red wine classes (a class which the public rarely sees). The wine is usually bottled after about eighteen months in wood. If anything it is probably nearer the L.B.V. (late bottled vintage) style of Portugal. Although vintage ports in Portugal are bottled after about eighteen months in wood, this wine certainly is fruitier, fuller, far less dry and has less tannin than those extremely elegant great wines from Portugal. Still, it is a very good sweet red of the highest quality and has tremendous fruit and character.

Morris White Burgundy
Made from white hermitage and palomino grapes, the palomino giving some softness and the white hermitage fullness and acidity. It is bottled after six months' maturation in old oak casks. With all these

factors—the climate, the grape varieties used and the oak—the wine, not surprisingly, is rather a robust style which lacks finesse.

Morris White Port
Made from muscat gordo blanco and pedro ximenez grapes, matured for two years in wood. A pleasant sweet wine of a rather full style.

Mudgee Wines

Mudgee Wines Cabernet Sauvignon
Interesting wines of powerful fruit and very strong colour. These wines have quite strong, marked flavour and a considerable future. In 1970 a quantity of cabernet sauvignon was set aside and matured in separate kinds of French and American oak. The American oak wine had a rather straightforward non-complex flavour, but was very mouth-filling in style. The finish was soft, smooth and clean; definitely a wine for those who like big, straightforward character.

Mudgee Wines Chardonnay
A rather full-flavoured white wine of good balance, softness and smoothness with a nice clean finish; very mouth-filling flavour. There is a big future for this variety in this district.

Mudgee Wines Hermitage
Made from shiraz grapes. A wine of considerable flavour and character, having good colour, a pleasant fruit, a rather robust vigorous palate, and a quite clean and pleasant finish.

Mudgee Wines Muscat
A light, clean, fortified wine of some wood maturation.

Mudgee Wines Muscat Liqueur
A rich style of wine which has had more time in wood and which shows considerable muscat flavour and character.

Mudgee Wines Pinot Noir
A most interesting wine made entirely from new pinot noir plantings. These plantings have just started to yield and they have produced a wine in the early 1970s which gives much scope for conjecture. The wine has that intense pinot colour, which shows none of the density of the cabernet sauvignon, but which has a lovely typical hue. The resemblance between the colour of the Mudgee wine and the colour of the top wines of the Burgundy districts of France is extremely marked. At this stage the material has obviously come from young vines and this is quite marked in the flavour, but there is extremely good fruit on the palate as well and it shows considerable finesse for this district. The pinot noir grape is difficult to grow and in the

Hunter Valley, further south, there is a problem in extracting sufficient colour. Certainly this is no problem in the Mudgee district and one looks forward with great interest to see if this variety will prosper in the future.

Mudgee Wines Port
Made from shiraz grapes grown in the district. A dessert wine, matured in wood for some years.

Mudgee Wines Semillon
Made from straight semillon grapes grown in the district. A straightforward, rather broad-flavoured, soft white wine of pleasant flavour and good for early drinking.

Mudgee Wines White Shiraz
Made entirely from the white hermitage variety grown in the district, having a rather negative flavour, but a clean, acid balance to the finish of the wine.

Norman, A, and Sons, Pty Ltd

Norman's Angle Vale Burgundy
This is processed from shiraz and grenache grapes grown in the 'Angle Vale' vineyards of the company twenty-five miles to the north of Adelaide and five miles to the west of Gawler.

This style of red wine has extremely pleasant fruit and good oak character. The 1967 won the Montgomery Trophy for the best young Burgundy of the Adelaide Show and the 1969 has already won Silver Medals in open classes at Melbourne.

Norman's Angle Vale Claret
Made from shiraz and chardonnay grapes and matured in new oak puncheons for two years. The 1967 Claret was a celebrated wine. It won the Sheppard Trophy for the best dry, young red in the Adelaide Wine Show. The 1969 has won Silver Medals in Brisbane and Perth and Bronzes in Adelaide and Melbourne in open classes. This shows that the judges agree that the style has developed extremely well over the last two years. There is an extremely good balance of fruit, especially cabernet fruit, and oak. These are undoubtedly high quality, South Australian reds that are becoming more and more celebrated.

Norman's Angle Vale Rhine Riesling
Made from straight rhine riesling grown on the company's vineyards, having very good fragrant aromatic nose and a pleasant varietal character on the palate. The wines have a good, crisp, clean finish.

Norman's Angle Vale White Burgundy
Made from rhine riesling and pedro ximenez grapes and fermented under controlled refrigeration. These wines are very well flavoured. They have a rather

delicate, full nose, plenty of flavour with a very soft, generous fruit on the middle palate and a crisp, clean finish. The 1971 White Burgundy won Gold Medals in Adelaide and Melbourne.

Norman's Angle Vale White Frontignac
Made from white frontignac grapes, fermented under controlled conditions. The 1970 Angle Vale was a very aromatic, rather pungent-flavoured wine with a considerable grapy nose and full flavour. The wine won a Gold Medal in the Melbourne Show and two Bronze Medals in Brisbane.

Norman's Claret
Other than the famous Angle Vale reds there are various other claret style wines made from cabernet, grenache and shiraz which range from light to medium-bodied.

Norman's Muscats
Norman's produce dessert wines, such as the Liqueur Muscatel and the Special Muscatel, which are made from the muscat gordo blanco variety, and the Liqueur Frontignac. This is a wine of considerable flavour and wood character.

Norman's Ports
The selection of ports available include the Special Aged Reserve, the Invalid Reserve, the Old Reserve and a Pedro White Port. Of these the port which enjoys the most popularity is the Special Aged Reserve Port, a blend of shiraz, grenache and pedro ximenez grapes, matured in oak puncheons. This port is fifteen years old.

Norman's Sherries
The company makes a large range of sherries which include Cream Sherry, Special Reserve Dry Sherry, Sweet Sherry, Dry Sherry and Medium Dry Sherry. The Special Vintage Sweet Sherry is one of the most popular. It is processed from pedro ximenez and palomino grapes and matured in old oak hogsheads for three years.

Norman's Whites
Other than the Rhine Riesling, White Frontignac and White Burgundy, Norman's make a range of white wines for local trade purposes. These include Hock, Moselle, Riesling Hock, Riesling Moselle and Sauterne.

Olive Farm

Olive Farm Burgundy
A full-bodied, dry red wine, made from straight shiraz. The grapes used are from the Bindoon district of Western Australia, noted for its high quality dry red wines which are very fruity, full-flavoured, soft and rather aromatic.

Olive Farm Chablis
A full-flavoured, rather big-bodied dry white, made from chenin blanc under controlled fermentation.

Olive Farm Claret
This is a full-bodied dry red made from shiraz and under controlled fermentation. The grapes come from the Bindoon district. The wine has a good, soft tannin and a rather distinctive berry flavour character.

Olive Farm Cream Sherry
A light, sweet fortified wine made from a blend of muscat gordo blanco and sultana with no wood maturation.

Olive Farm Dry Sherry
A dry fortified wine, made from a blend of pedro ximenez and semillon and matured in wood for some time.

Olive Farm Frontignac
A sweet, fortified wine made from the brown frontignac variety and matured in wood.

Olive Farm Hock
A blend of semillon and sultana, made under controlled fermentation; the fermentation taking place at about 12.7 degrees C.

Olive Farm Liqueur Muscat
A concentrated raisin-flavoured wine made from muscat gordo blanco and matured in wood for approximately ten years. This wine has a high Baumé and a highly concentrated muscat character.

Olive Farm Medium Dry Sherry
Made from a blend of pedro ximenez and semillon and matured in wood for some years.

Olive Farm Moselle
A slightly sweet, white table wine made from riesling under controlled fermentation.

Olive Farm Muscat of Alexandria
A dry, white table wine made from the muscat of Alexandria (gordo blanco) grapes grown in the irrigated area of the Swan Valley.

Olive Farm Rosé
A soft, pleasant, dry rosé made from shiraz grapes grown under irrigation. There is also a lighter rosé made from grenache, also grown under irrigation.

Olive Farm Sauternes
A sweet, white table wine, rather light in character and lacking lusciousness, which is bottled at an early age for the local market.

Olive Farm Sweet Muscat

A sweet fortified wine made from brown muscat grapes (probably frontignac), grown at Bindoon.

Olive Farm Sweet Sherry

A blend of pedro ximenez and sultana and matured in wood for some years.

Olive Farm Tawny Port

A blend of tokay and shiraz grapes, matured in wood for fourteen years. It has considerable depth of character and flavour.

Olive Farm Vintage Port

Made from the shiraz or hermitage grape, crushed at 16 Baumé and stored in wood for twelve months prior to bottling. A wine of considerable depth of colour, some sweetness on the middle palate and a good firm, rich, clean finish.

Olive Farm White Burgundy

A blend of tokay and semillon grapes made under controlled fermentation conditions at 15.5 degrees C. It has a considerably flowery bouquet and quite a delicate palate for the varieties.

Olive Farm White Port

Free run juice from the grenache grape taken off the skins and matured in wood for three years.

Orlando

Orlando Auslese Riesling

I think there were only two of these wines made—in 1964 and 1972. Every year they have been trying to make the wine, but the conditions are usually not quite right. In this wine the grapes are left on until long after the rest of the vintage—12-14 weeks later—and then are picked when extremely luscious. The 1964 Auslese was a beautiful wine of tremendous fruit and flavour, which developed into a sweet wine of concentrated vinosity and depth of character; a really outstanding Australian sweet wine.

Orlando Barossa Cabernet

Made from forty percent cabernet sauvignon and sixty percent shiraz grapes grown almost entirely in the Orlando vineyards at Rowland Flat. The wine is stored in small American or French Nevers oak for twelve to eighteen months, depending on the body of the wine. Of recent vintages the 1965 and 1966 wines are outstanding, having an excellent combination of small wood and fruit flavours, the cabernet fruit being by far the dominant varietal character. It appears that Gramps have now settled on this style.

The wines of the 1950s, when this style first came out, were rather big, porty wonders, having a great deal of excessive—almost over-ripe—fruit

quality to them. It wasn't until the early 1960s that the wine style started to lighten. The wines of the early 1960s did not have the oak character of the latter wines, but still had a great deal of good cabernet fruit, and were more elegant. They were lighter and cleaner and by now had lost this trace of coarseness.

The 1963 and 1964 vintages, both of which were very good wines, saw the application of more small wood maturation, and this combination of flavours was best in the 1965 and 1966 wines. The 1967 is also an extremely good wine, again having very good oak and cabernet flavours; but the 1968, I thought, was a lighter wine, probably the result of the year. Later vintages returned to this fine combination of oak, cabernet and shiraz fruit flavours and were well-balanced wines with a fairly firm finish. One of the outstanding commercial wines available in Australia today.

Orlando Barossa Fino Sherry

A pale, delicate, Flor fino sherry made from well-ripened pedro, palomino and white hermitage grapes and matured in wood for some years. Pale to gold in colour, this sherry has some extremely good nose combinations of fruit, oak and Flor character. The flavour shows well on the palate and the wine has a very pleasant dry, nutty, slightly astringent finish. The only fault with it is that there is perhaps a trace too much sugar on the middle palate; otherwise this wine is an excellent, fine Australian sherry.

Orlando Barossa Hermitage

Made from selected shiraz grapes grown on different soils (from gravelly to sandy loam) in the Rowland Flat vineyards of the company; matured in French oak for eighteen months, the oak used probably being second-hand (that is, new oak which has previously been used for a vintage or two for another wine style, in this case probably the Orlando Barossa Cabernet).

Early vintages of this wine were rather dumb, ordinary wines without any great complexity or flavour. They were straightforward reds, enjoyable to drink, but with no great finesse or particular distinguishing character. Later vintages, however, have shown more style and have a greater complexity. The 1967 was perhaps the beginning of this, for it had excellent fruit with just a discreet touch of oak. The finish was rather clean, although there was a bit of that soft, furry tannin quality that we identify with a Barossa. It was very good value at the price and drank very well as soon as it was released. It also took a bit of bottle ageing and became a very nice, soft, smooth, flavoursome wine.

The 1968 was perhaps a trifle lighter, probably because of the vintage, but subsequent vintages show very good balance. They handle their wines very well, showing good red winemaking techniques. The result—good fruit, good oak, good combination of flavours and very easy drinking.

Orlando Barossa Pearl

A much denigrated wine which unquestionably deserves a place in the Australian hall of wine fame. Made from a variety of material, probably mostly Thompson's seedless (sultana). In 1956, Gramp's, using a completely new technique, produced this style of wine in Australia—a wine of natural effervescence, with some delicacy, a crisp finish and a rather pleasant, sort of softly-sweet middle palate. The secret, of course, was in the production technique, for it was made on the Charmat pattern.

Its unique qualities, combined with the merchandising ability of the company, the shape of the bottle, a lot of advertising, and many other reasons, resulted in it being widely accepted by all sorts of palates; especially young, uneducated palates and people who had normally loaded their tables with bottles of beer. Orlando Barossa Pearl rapidly rose to leadership of the table wine field, and more of it was sold than any other table wine. It also enjoyed considerable popularity overseas, being marketed throughout the world. I believe the significant thing about the wine was that it launched thousands of people into drinking wine. Perhaps they don't continue to drink Barossa Pearls, perhaps they do. But the fact is that they began to see the benefit there was in wine and in the enjoyment of wine. There is no question that Barossa Pearl was the great educator. The wine industry should be immensely thankful for it.

Orlando Barossa Pink Pearl

A delicate, slightly sweet, rosé table wine made from grenache, grown in the Barossa Valley. Its natural effervescence and pearl effect give the wine a refreshing character. Really it is nothing more than a slightly differently flavoured sparkling wine of a rosé colour, very much on the Barossa Pearl line; perhaps with a little more flavour character.

Orlando Barossa Rhine Riesling Moselle

Made from specially selected rhine riesling grapes which have been allowed to get a little riper on the vines. It is vintaged according to the same process as used for the Barossa Rhine Rieslings and, in fact, is much the same style of wine, except with a slightly richer flavour with greater depth and a little sugar on the middle palate. This, of course, appeals to a number of palates who don't like to have their wines bone dry.

This is a good wine which, although a trade wine, consistently wins Gold and Silver Medals at shows. A quite personal thing, but I feel that the Barossa Rhine Riesling Moselle does not have the fame it should have, simply because of its atrocious label which must be one of the worst wine labels in this country.

Orlando Barossa Riesling

A famous dry white wine, vintaged entirely from rhine riesling grapes which are grown in the vineyards around the winery at Rowland Flat. The grapes are control fermented under a process that Orlando started in 1953. The wines are temperature and pressure controlled during fermentation, which means that the fermentation rate is slowed down. The carbon dioxide gas is not allowed to escape, and as the pressure builds up so it slows the fermentation down. The control of temperature also has the same effect. The resultant wine has a crisp delicacy, because all the flavour characters are retained.

In 1953, when Gramp's made their first Barossa Rhine Riesling, they revolutionized the white table wine industry of Australia, and particularly that of South Australia. South Australia always had the material to make good Rhine Rieslings, but until 1953 the wines had been mostly rather big, often verging on coarseness, and they lost a great deal of their varietal character—their true essence character—the distilled intensity of flavour which is the hallmark of the great German wines. Gramp's won prize after prize with their 1953s and other earlier Barossa Rhine Rieslings. Indeed, they deserved them, because they brought a new character altogether to these wines—of freshness, cleanness and intensity of flavour—all of which greatly lifted the standard of the Rhine Rieslings. Of course, other companies have since followed suit and the competition is now quite tough in that field, but Gramp's continue to make outstanding wines of this character. The Barossa Riesling is still an outstanding wine, especially as a trade wine at its price. Gramp's now make finer wines which are more expensive, being from more selected rhine riesling material; but the Orlando Barossa Rieslings remain outstanding value year in and year out.

Recent vintages like the 1968, 1969 and the 1970 prove this beyond any doubt. The wine is always crisp, fresh and has a very powerful aromatic nose and a beautifully fresh, refreshing, varietal rhine riesling character on the palate. The finish is always crisp, clean, delicate and quite delicious. Incidentally, the wine is always available in green and amber bottles—Gramp's state that the green bottle Barossa Riesling caters for those who like their rhine riesling youthful, spritzig, fresh and young. Limited quantities of each vintage are set aside in amber bottles, because the light is not allowed to affect the wine so much as in a green bottle and therefore the delicate character of the rhine riesling grape is retained. It is an interesting argument. Some of the older amber bottled matured Gramp's I've seen have picked up this quite definite, so-called kerosene flavour, the rather rich flavour of the developed rhine riesling, but others have retained outstanding freshness and delicacy with increased richness. These wines are outstanding examples of Australian white wine styles.

Orlando Blue Ribbon Barossa
The base wine is made from clare riesling and semillon. This undergoes a secondary fermentation under the Charmat process and then the resultant sparkling wine is liqueured with selected frontignan to give it a rather pleasant, raisiny type of quality.

Orlando Brown Muscat
A two-year-old sweet wine with some muscat character, mainly derived from the percentage of high quality muscat variety frontignac.

Orlando Champagne
A pleasant, light sparkling wine, made from selected varieties. It is made as a commercial wine, since it is not too dry and not too sweet and is reasonably delicate and well balanced.

Orlando Conto Port
This is a popular sweet wine; fruity, rather light and nondescript.

Orlando Coolabah Claret
I've always been impressed with this wine which remains amongst the best of the flagon reds available in Australia. Made from a blend of grenache, mataro and shiraz grown in the Barossa Valley, with grenache from Ramco on the Murray River, and control fermented on skins, headed down in open tanks. The wine is then aged in wood for twelve months, some of which is American oak puncheon storage. It is then available for bottling and marketing. It has a light to medium colour, is very fresh and fruity on the nose with the grenache aromatic fruit dominant. There is a touch of shiraz coming through on the tongue and the finish is pleasant, soft and smooth; very good drinking always at the price and without the coarseness which is associated with some flagon lines.

Orlando Coolabah Dry White
A light refreshing dry, white wine, made from clare riesling from Ramco and pedro ximenez from the Barossa Valley. I've been fond of this wine for

some time and always find it extremely good value for money as a flagon wine. The wine has a rather fresh, appealing apple sort of nose, a clean, soft palate and a crisp, clean finish. It has always had this quality of freshness and fruit on the middle palate which is not always the same for a flagon white wine. The freshness is the result of temperature control fermentation. The company gives these flagon wines a great deal of attention and skill which is why they are so sound. The Coolabah Dry White is excellent value for money and year after year is one of the outstanding dry white flagon wines available. It is an interesting reflection, but when you consider the quality of this wine against the quality of some of the vins blancs *ordinaires* of France it does show what sort of market we could have in the future, in some countries.

Orlando Coolabah Moselle
Another light, refreshing white wine, much the same style as the Coolabah dry white, except there is a measure of sugar retention, which gives a slightly more fruity taste. The wine has pleasant softness and a touch of sweetness on the middle palate. It appeals to those people who don't like their wines quite so dry as others.

Orlando Coolabah Rosé
A pleasant pink-coloured wine made from grenache and clare riesling. The nose is a bit flat and is fairly uninteresting, it could do with a lift I feel, since they're not using extremely aromatic fruit. The palate is very fresh and quite reasonable. I quite like the fruit on the middle palate and there is a pleasant fresh acidity on the back of the tongue. It is quite dry and very much recommended as a rosé flagon wine. The grenache material in the wine comes from the Barossa Valley and Ramco on the River Murray. The juice is separated from the skins through M.A.C. gravity separators, and control fermented in 10,000 gallon tanks under its own CO_2. It is a good indication of Gramp's tremendous winemaking techniques.

Orlando Dry Sherry
A straightforward, moderately priced trade dry, fortified wine.

Orlando Dry Vermouth
A white wine made from selected varieties and then infused with imported alpine herbs and afterwards fortified with pure grape spirit to 32° proof. This is a light, quite delicate, aromatic wine with an astringent finish.

Orlando Estate Burgundy
This is the carafe line put out by Gramp's which contains a litre of wine and sells at a most reasonable price. The wine, generally speaking, is of fairly high quality. The Burgundy is produced from shiraz and

grenache grapes grown in the Barossa Valley, blended and matured in large American oak casks for eighteen months prior to bottling.

Orlando Estate Claret

Made from shiraz, grenache, mataro and carignane, grown throughout the Barossa Valley on the Orlando vineyards, and then matured for eighteen months in large American wood (500s). A pleasant wine with some body, good straightforward flavour, a fair degree of tannin, and clean acid. I prefer the Burdundy, but this is a personal thing. As far as I am concerned, if the wine is to have clean tannin and a firm finish it must have compensating rich development of fruit.

Orlando Estate Moselle

The various vintages are made from blends of selected white varieties, such as clare riesling, rhine riesling, semillon, frontignac and tokay, all grown in the Barossa Valley at Moorooroo, Jacobs Creek, Miamba, Lyndoch and Kluge vineyards.

The Estate Moselle is a good fruity wine with a touch of quite marked essency fruit on the middle palate. The finish is crisp and clean. This is a good wine for those who like a touch of sugar and, as stated, the presence of this quite marked varietal character is appealing.

Orlando Estate Riesling

A blend of selected riesling grape varieties grown on the company's Ramco vineyards on the River Murray and their Barossa Valley vineyards. By riesling I suppose they mean rhine riesling, certainly clare riesling, and semillon which sometimes is given the riesling title. This is a fresh, fragrant, flowery wine, with pleasant palate and crisp finish—it has the Gramp's mark of quality upon it and is very good value for the money.

Orlando Estate Rosé

Produced from grenache grapes grown in the Lyndoch Valley, Kluge and Ramco. It has a good, clean quality, a pleasant fruit nose, a touch of sweetness on the palate, it is fresh at the finish, well balanced and good drinking.

Orlando Estate White Burgundy

Made from the clare riesling variety grown at Ramco and matured in large American oak. Well made, a soft, pleasant, clean wine, smooth on the palate with a soft finish. It has no great depth of flavour or character, but is a very pleasant quaffing wine.

Orlando Gold Medal Liqueur Muscat

A very sweet, fruity, dessert wine produced from fully ripened muscat gordo blanco (muscatel) grapes. The wine has spent many years in wood and has a rich, smooth character.

Orlando Gold Medal Port

This wine has done very well in European wine shows, such as Montpellier in France and Ljubljana in Yugoslavia. It is a tawny port made from selected shiraz, carignane and mataro grapes which are allowed to get quite ripe. After picking they are made into wine which is then fortified. It is aged in casks for about eight years and picks up a tawny port character, rather sweet on the middle palate with a faintly amber tinge to the edge of the wine. This port is quite fruity, the oak is evident, and it has a pleasant nutty flavour and character.

Gramp's Gold Medal Tokay

This is a pleasant, luscious, sweet-flavoured dessert wine made from tokay grapes, with the familiar earthy bouquet of that variety and a quite concentrated flavour.

Orlando Grec Rosé

This is one of their top rosé wines made from the variety which they call grec rosé, grown in the Barossa Valley and also at Ramco. The style of this wine is most interesting, because it has been evolved over the years and is a quite dry style as against the sparkling, slightly sweet style. The wine is very well balanced and has a quite marked interesting flavour; it is not a pink dry white, nor is it a light, dry red. It is an *individual* wine. I like the grape flavour and I am very pleased to see that Gramp's decided to concentrate on this dry style, as I believe that this is eventually the required classic rosé style of Australia.

Orlando Mature Dry Sherry

A blend of palomino and pedro ximenez varieties matured in oak for five years, producing a well matured dry sherry of good colour, pleasant flavour and distinctive oak character.

Orlando Mature Medium Sherry

Made from a base material of palomino and pedro ximenez with the addition of some verdelho and tokay material which gives a slightly richer character and flavour to the wine, and, of course, more sweetness on the middle palate.

Orlando Medium Semi-Sweet Sherry

An 'each-way' bet, suit anyone who likes an occasional glass of sherry. It has no great character.

Orlando Mature Sweet Sherry

Made from pedro ximenez, tokay and verdelho and matured in wood for several years; a sweet sherry of quite pleasant smoothness and fruitiness.

Orlando Miamba Vintage Chablis

A very good dry wine made from clare riesling and semillon grapes grown on the Orlando 'Miamba' vineyards. I've always liked this style because I thought it such good value. The 1967 vintage Chablis was very pleasant and well-balanced with a good flinty finish. The 1968 was perhaps slightly more delicate, it didn't have such a pronounced character and had a softer finish. These are very good wines at the price.

Orlando Miamba Vintage Hermitage Cabernet
Again a wine with considerable appeal at a most reasonable price, made dominantly from shiraz grapes (sometimes called hermitage in the Barossa Valley) plus some cabernet sauvignon. It has a pleasing bouquet and fruity palate, is quite light in style and there is always a measure of oak with the wine.

Orlando Miamba Vintage Moselle
Very pleasant white wine produced from the blending of tokay, clare riesling and semillon varieties, grown in the Barossa Valley; it has quite a fruity bouquet, a depth of sweet grapiness on the middle palate and a crisp finish.

Orlando Miamba Vintage Riesling
Made from rhine riesling, semillon and tokay grown in the 'Miamba' vineyard at Lyndoch in the Lower Barossa Valley. It has quite a good, fruity nose and a soft, fresh, flavoursome palate with a good, crisp finish. There is just a touch of sweetness on the middle palate which appeals to many people. This wine is good value for money.

Orlando No. 1 Invalid Port
Having never been a No. 1 invalid, I don't quite know how to classify this wine. It is a fruity, full-bodied dessert wine with plenty of sweetness, balanced by a certain amount of astringency. This is a popular line which has been going for some years, probably being a relic of other drinking standards (which is not to denigrate it, for I don't think that Gramp's could make a bad wine if they tried).

Orlando Pink Starwine
A pink version of the sparkling Starwine which has been so successful throughout the country.

Orlando Satin Cream Sherry
This is a light, sweet sherry which is blended with natural grape juice, giving the wine a creamy fruitiness for which it was named. I remember when this wine came out with a huge advertising campaign. Unfortunately, it came out at a time when table wines were really taking on and somehow it never made the impact that I think the company wanted it to make.

Orlando Spaetlese Frontignan
This is an interesting wine style developed by the Gramp's in the 1960s, vintaged from a selected late picking of frontignan (frontignac) grapes grown in the Barossa Valley. The actual time of gathering varies

according to the climatic conditions. However, on all occasions the picking of the grapes takes place several weeks after most of the white table grapes are picked in the Valley. The frontignan grapes at this stage are thoroughly ripe and the quality notable for passing the average of the vintage. The fermentation is cold and pressure controlled, thus enabling the full, delicate and aromatic quality of the grape to be retained. The residual sugar is retained in the wine by arresting the fermentation.

It is a very fruity, sweet wine with quite considerable density of flavour. I've never liked the wine as much as the rhine riesling spaetlese styles, but it is a matter of individual choice. This wine has an aromatic quality on the nose and a marked flavour. But to me the wine has always been slightly coarser, compared with the elegance of the other; consequently, I always compare it with the other and have always judged it the lesser wine. However, there is no question that there is a lot in the wine and that it does appeal to a considerable number of people.

Orlando Spaetlese Riesling
This is a remarkable wine in that it contains a tremendous density of fruit, enormous flavour, extreme grapiness of character and matures extremely well. Of course, it is a late-picked wine, the grapes being left on the vine considerably longer than at other times—often up to four and six weeks later. The company takes a considerable risk with this and on a number of occasions they have lost the wines through rain. The grapes at this stage are thoroughly ripened, have high Baumés and have started to shrivel. This wine gets its character from the high natural sugar content plus the fruit of the variety which is retained by the fermentation process. There are not many grapes available for this style, and therefore there is not much of it made, but what is made is of exceptional quality. The Gramp's Spaetlese (late pickings) are usually much fuller and richer in character. They are something beyond

Over: Sunset over the vineyard.

a spaetlese, in my opinion. They have a richness and character to them which is not commensurate with the other spaetlese styles. However, they make extremely luscious wines and with maturity they arrive at a stage which is quite magnificent. I have enjoyed several of the older ones and I think this is one of the finest sweet wine styles in Australia, if not *the* finest, year after year.

An interesting point in this flavour and viscosity is that since it is always stronger than other sweet wines it is almost of the composition of a Sauternes. It can't be a Sauternes, because it is not of the right variety, nor from the right country, yet it does seem to have more of a Sauternes composition and character. The reason may be that the rhine riesling grapes grown for the wine are mostly grown on the Jacobs Creek Estate. This is a mixture of soils, alluvial type, sand to gravelly, black loam. The grapes, as I have said, are left until much later than usual—this can be as much as twelve weeks after completion of the rest of the vintage—and consequently, they are extremely ripe and full; quite luscious. Because the grapes are grown on the Valley floor and not at high altitudes, a delicate acidity/sugar ratio cannot be achieved, as in the Eden Valley, Watervale District and so on. Hence this fuller, richer style. I like it for its flavour. I like it for its character; and I like it very much with chilled fruit.

Orlando Sparkling Carte Blanche
An attractive white, sparkling, hock style of wine which has a measure of sugar on the middle palate. It is a sound commercial sparkling white.

Orlando Sparkling Printz
This is a sparkling rosé type of wine which has a distinct fruitiness, plenty of sweetness on the middle palate and is promoted by an interesting advertising campaign.

Orlando Sparkling Spar Rouge
This is really a light, sparkling burgundy, but not as deep and full-coloured as some sparkling burgundies are. It is made on the Charmat method.

Orlando Sparkling Starwine
Again this is a commercial pearl-type wine, made as a successor to the Barossa Pearl and which has since become extremely popular.

Orlando Special Muscat
An aged, fruity dessert wine made from ripe muscat gordo blanco (muscatel) grapes.

Orlando Steingarten
The improvements with rhine riesling wines which have occurred in the last ten years have been largely the result of improved techniques. Now it appears that if we want to make the ultimate in rhine riesling styles in Australia we also have to improve our vines.

It seems that most of the best rhine riesling wines which are made in Australia come from altitude plantings, from which the balance of sugar and acid may be retained sufficiently long to develop the full flavour in the grapes. To obtain crisp freshness with this concentration of intense flavour (which is necessary to make a great rhine riesling wine) it is important that the grapes are picked when they still contain a fairly high natural acidity, which is retained while the grapes fully ripen. The over-abundance of sun in Australia makes this fairly difficult since to obtain the natural acidity in the resultant wine many grapes have to be picked before they are fully mature. This most vital and important flavour component in rhine riesling is only brought about by this perfect acid/sugar balance. Orlando accepted this challenge in their experiment at Steingarten.

In 1962 they planted two acres of the rhine riesling vines on the eastern face of the Barossa Range, situated up a very steep winding track behind their winery and cellars at Rowland Flat. This vineyard is approximately 800 feet higher than the original rhine riesling plantings at Rowland Flat and therefore is a total of about 1600 feet above sea level. The soil is scarcely that, since after about an inch of topsoil there is almost pure rock—soft rock known as schist. It was deep-ripped and then broken up, first mechanically and then by hand with an old-fashioned stone hammer. The pebbles up there now are two to three inches in diameter. The soil was so tough in places that they actually had to dig holes first to get the stakes in. The usual trellis was discarded and the vines were individually basket-pruned around each stake. These stakes were planted only four feet apart—four foot rows, four foot apart. Consequently, there are 2,760 vines per acre, as against the normal 700-800 or so—and because the bunches are extremely tight and small they are very difficult to pick. It was amusing talking to the vineyard workers. On one particular vintage they didn't think much of the experiment at all. The grapes ripen slowly, and are rather susceptible to climatic conditions on the top of that high and windy hill. The vineyard is picked, therefore, about four to six weeks later, compared with the rhine riesling picked on the Rowland Flat vineyards. So far, one wonders if the experiment has been worth it. They collected a few bunches in 1965, but in 1966 the crop was damaged by hail; in 1967 the conditions were poor; the 1968 was quite a good wine; in 1969 again, the conditions weren't good. The wines that have come off this vineyard have shown a strong, marked depth of flavour on the middle palate, yet with steely elegance and finesse, which is the hallmark of the great German wines. I feel this is a most worthy experiment and one looks forward to future Steingarten wines with tremendous interest.

Orlando Sweet Vermouth

A full-flavoured, full-bodied table wine base is used here and then infused with astringent alpine herbs. After the period of infusion the vermouth is sweetened and again fortified with pure grape spirit and its colour darkened with caramel. It has quite a full, aromatic character and a sweet, rich palate with an astringent, rather firm acid finish.

Orlando Trockenbeerenauslese

One wine only was made of this style; yet it remains a wine of considerable significance and curiosity value. One of the winemaking staff noticed that the stalks coming out of the destemmer contained some small, tight little berries which were extremely rich and ripe. They were so shrivelled on the vine that they could not be removed by the fingers on the machine that knocks all the grapes off. Consequently he had these picked off by hand and they made a couple of buckets of wine. It has great richness and vinosity of flavour and now sells at auctions for an incredible amount of money.

Orlando Vintage Tawny Port

An exceptional dessert wine made from a selection of material from shiraz, carignane and mataro grapes. These grapes are allowed to reach full maturity and then are picked and made into the wine which is then fortified. The wine, stored in wood for many years—anything up to twenty—in special casks becomes very rich in flavour and vinosity. One amusing thing, of course, is that the wine is called a Vintage Tawny Port because it is made from one particular year, although it is a tawny port, and tawny ports are usually blends of various years. Orlando concentrate on one year because they like to have a wine of one particular vintage so they know exactly whence it cometh, how old it is and the pattern of maturation.

These dessert wines are very rich, have a lot of character and are outstanding after-dinner drinks.

Orlando White Burgundy

Made from chenin blanc grown in the Barossa Valley. This is a fairly pungent variety which gives this soft, fruity, white wine with quite a marked flavour on the middle palate. This is blended with the variety they call madeira, but which is almost certainly semillon.

Orlando White Port

This is a fruity, sweet dessert wine, aged in wood for some time. It is made from selected white grape varieties grown in the Valley and matured in wood for a few years. It is soft, pleasant and fruity.

Orlando Yellow Label Sweet Sherry

A very popular trade sherry which is sold at a fairly low price.

Parri Wines

Parri Dessert Wines

A limited range of dessert wines is made by Ken Mallett from grapes grown in the Neerabup district of Western Australia. The range includes a Muscat, a Ruby Port which is made from the grenache variety; a Marsala, called Rosita—which contains various herbs and spices, and some cocktail Marsalas, including cherry and almond.

Parri Dry Reds

A range of full-flavoured, rather full-bodied dry reds, is made from various varieties. The wines include: a house Burgundy, made from shiraz, malbec and grenache; a house Claret, made from shiraz and grenache; a Dry Red Bin 39, made from shiraz, grenache and pinot noir; a Burgundy Bin 28, made from shiraz and malbec grapes; and a Cabernet, which is a blend of cabernet and shiraz.

Parri Dry Whites

Two white wines are made from blends of semillon and pedro ximenez: a house Moselle and a White Burgundy.

Parri Sherries

A range of sherries is made for local consumption— Dry, Medium and Sweet.

Parri Sparkling Wines

The company makes a range of sparkling wines by the Charmat method, which includes: Sparkling Apollo, a white party wine; Sparkling Carina Rosé, a rosé party wine; Spumante Tipo Asti, a sweet sparkling wine from the muscat variety; Sparkling Burgundy, which is made from shiraz and malbec; Demi-Sec Champagne, from semillon; and Sparkling Champette, a non-intoxicating sparkling white made from apples and grapes.

Penfold Wines Ltd

Penfold's Bin Red—Cabernet Sauvignon Bin 707

In the past few years this famous dry red line has slipped a little from its very high pedestal. There is no question in my mind that during the mid-sixties it was one of the top dry red wines of Australia.

The wine is made entirely from cabernet sauvignon grown in the 'Kalimna' vineyards in the Barossa Valley and is matured in 'second-hand' wood.

The 1964 Bin 707 was, and is, a magnificent dry red; full of complexity and tremendous fruit with an almost minty character which one associates with other regions, such as Coonawarra; this came from the extremely high quality fruit used to make this wine. Touched up with some small oak, this wine had beautiful balance and superb style. It will live for many years.

The 1965 was almost as good a wine, again showing delightful balance of oak and fruit; a wine which was extremely well priced at the time it was sold.

The 1966 was also a good wine. It seemed to me that it didn't have quite the intensity of flavour and character that the other two wines had; perhaps the wine was becoming more popular; perhaps there was a little more made of it; or perhaps the material used would have been better for other things. However, it was still an extremely good wine and again remarkably low-priced. Penfold's have always adopted this policy of selling many of their very good red wines (apart from their two most expensive ones— Grange and St Henri) at most reasonable prices.

Both the 1967 and the 1968 vintages appeared to me to be lighter. They were still very good wines, well worth the price; but they were not the tremendous bargains that the previous wines were. Perhaps they didn't have the overall depth of flavour and character that the other wines had; though I felt that with some bottle age they would mature well.

The 1969 was quite disappointing, maybe it was the particular bottles that I tried. It seemed to contain a trace of H_2S (Hydrogen Sulphide) and this, of course, is not pleasant.

However, at its best Bin 707 is a magnificent Australian dry red wine. A wine of considerable complexity of fruit; full-bodied with a lot to it; a high tannin finish which is very much in balance with the whole wine; an outstanding firm dry red.

Penfold's Bin Red—Cabernet Shiraz Bin 389

'Poor man's Grange' is the tag often given to this wine and it is actually a compliment. The wine appeared in the early 1960s after some experiments had been made with various cabernet sauvignon and shiraz blends from Magill in the Adelaide foothills, from the Barossa Valley and from various other sources.

The 1965 wine was excellent, with extremely good fruit—a very pleasant combination of cabernet, shiraz and in addition some small oak character, which is so much a part of Penfold's winemaking. The wine always appeared to be of the Grange style, though lighter. Hence the tag.

At one time these wines were sold for a price somewhere in between their standard private bin range and their top two wines, Grange and St Henri, but lately the price has been kept to a lower level. This must make it one of the great bargains in Australian wine, because it matures extremely well and within five or six years of its bottling into a wine of tremendous flavour and character; one which can be enjoyed at all times.

Succeeding vintages seem to bear out this thought. The 1966 is a very full-flavoured, rich wine which is maturing extremely well. The 1967 was a top wine. It was a blend of cabernet sauvignon and shiraz from Magill and also from 'Kalimna', in the Barossa Valley. There is at least thirty percent of cabernet in the wine.

The fruit was first-class, with a strong mint varietal overtone which is said to be typical of Coonawarra, but which I think in fact is closer to some styles of Australian regional cabernet. On top of this the oak was quite strong: certainly probably the strongest seen (until that occasion) in the Bin 389 line. The oak was American and the wine took some considerable time to come together but it was one which would live and improve for years. The flavour and the bouquet would build up to create a wine of complete distinction. I think it sold at about $1.50 a bottle, which indicates the kind of bargain (if it were available) this was amongst the top Australian wines.

I've said many times that 1968 and 1969 were disappointing vintages in South Australia—the 1969 in particular—but again the 389 showed well on both occasions. The 1969 stood out in the range as having by far the best flavour, character and overall composition.

At blind tastings some of the older 389's often covered themselves with glory. Invariably they are not spotted. Invariably there is a lot of discussion on them and almost equally invariably there is never a bad comment. The wines are hard to spot because, while they are so obviously of the Penfold's style, of oak and fruit, they mature into something which is generally considered to be better than they are supposed to be. Thus we often see the wines picked as a St Henri, as a Grange or as a 707. Certainly as far as I am concerned it remains one of the wines of best value amongst all the dry reds that are available.

Penfold's Bin Red—Coonawarra Claret Bin 128

Another repetitive Bin number. Penfold's use the same number year after year. This is made entirely from shiraz grown on Penfold's vineyard at Coonawarra in South Australia. They are a most interesting line of wine in that the wine varies enormously.

Going back over some of the years, the 1969 was a wine which was quite light, reflecting the rain which fell half-way through vintage at Coonawarra. I don't believe Penfold's had picked at the time and consequently their wine was much lighter than the wines which were picked before the rain fell. The wine is very clean, pleasant, quite austere, but without the fruit normally associated with the style of wine, and it will mature well as one of those lighter rather high acid Coonawarra wines.

A magnificent wine was produced in 1968, with rich fruit, and very much the regional character of Coonawarra; a character very much beyond shiraz fruit normally. One could easily pick this as having cabernet in it and all touched with the delightful small oak handling which is associated with Penfold's and which Max Schubert, their chief winemaker (and now Director of the company) handles so well. The 1968 was a beautiful rich wine, tremendously appealing when young even, because it was so beautifully put together, superbly balanced and with so much complexity of fruit; a wine that would live for many years.

The 1967 didn't have quite the same oak character and not so much fruit. Most of the 1967 Coonawarra wines appear to be quite light and this wine was clean flavoured, though it would grow bigger in the bottle. It was bigger than the 1969, but was somehow reminiscent of some of the previous Rouge Homme wines of lighter years.

On the other hand the 1966 was of the 1968 scale; again plenty of fruit, body, and oak, with much going for it. It appears that if Penfold's have the black fruit, the heavy fruit, then they are more inclined to use the oak. When they have a lighter wine they are much more sparing with the oak because they know the oak will dominate and the wine will be nothing else except an oaky special. The 1966 was and is a very good wine indeed. A top Australian wine that will live and improve for years. And when one considers that it was available when it was released in 1969 and 1970 for $1.40 a bottle, it shows what value there was.

The 1965 was a rare wine for little was made. It was not considered a top wine although a bottle I saw was very good indeed when it had some age upon it. The 1964 was a bigger, fuller wine with a lot of character, though of course at this stage it didn't have the same beautiful oak handling. The 1963 and 1962 were both good wines, slightly on the lighter side, but wines of good fruit which matured very well in the bottle.

Incidentally, of the 1968, I wrote some years ago, 'the oak/fruit/regional character on the nose is tremendous; very estery and assertive; yet there is no hint of coarseness. The wine has plenty of colour, high, bright and handsome and is quite dense. The palate is medium-bodied, clean fruity, flavoursome, austere, complex and the tannin acid finish clean and delicately abrupt. That's not a bad description of a good wine.' Well that's *not* a bad description of a good wine and I am very pleased that I was able to recommend an outstanding example of an outstanding line.

The 128s are interesting wines of good flavour and style and always good value. Once more, they are readily available in restaurants and wine shops. The 1966 and 1968 remain outstanding vintages.

Penfold's Bin Red—Hunter Valley/South Australian Blend Bin 333

Another interesting repetitive Bin which comes out year after year and which does vary. I've always felt that the Hunter Valley and South Australian blends can make extremely good wines and certainly other winemakers have proved this from time to time.

This line started in the early 1960s. The 1962, available for some time, was a very pleasant wine which drank very well up to ten years after being made. The 1963 was also a good wine with a lot to it.

Of later years, the 1966 impressed tremendously. This was a blend of shiraz grapes from various areas, being fifty percent hermitage from the new 'Dalwood Estate' at Wybong in the upper Hunter districts and forty percent Coonawarra shiraz from their own vineyards and ten percent Southern Vales shiraz. The wine reflected the very good year of 1966. Subsequent vintages have not had the same style and character, but they have been good, pleasant wines which grow after two or three years in the bottle and which provide good easy drinking with nice, pleasant, well-balanced flavour.

Penfold's Bin Red—Kalimna Dry Red Bin 28

Made entirely from shiraz at 'Kalimna' in the Barossa Valley. This has always been a good standard dry red line of Penfold's, not of the most distinguished kind, but of good quality and very good value for money. Of the 1969 Bin 28 I wrote, 'nice Barossa shiraz nose; pleasant, well put together wine, showing no great character, but good value. No defects, soft, slightly furry tannin finish; nice clean fruit; good touch of oak; pleasantly astringent. Very much a good quality Barossa wine without any jamminess.'

The 1968 wine was another pleasant wine. However, I think the 1967 wine was the pick of the line. It had good fruit and was without that kind of furry quality which I usually associate with the area, and it was also touched up with very good oak. A very nice fruity, oaky wine which matured well.

The 1966 was also quite a good wine and one which will improve for quite a time. The 1965 was rather coarse and seemed to pick up a slightly edgy, corky quality in many of the bottles.

The 1964 was a pleasant, soft Barossa Valley wine which didn't have much distinction of character. The Penfold's hallmark wasn't upon it, but it was a pleasant wine that matured fairly well and drank quite nicely.

All these wines of the early 1960s seem to be pleasant wines, of good fruit character; but I think the line has developed and improved now but I would still regard the 1967 as the best wine to date.

Of the 1970s there is very good material around. It has been extremely well handled, and is now maturing in all sorts of different oak. I have no doubt that in the next decade we shall see some very good examples of this line.

Penfold's Bin Red—Shiraz Mataro Bin 2

Made from mataro grown in the Adelaide foothills and shiraz from the Barossa Valley—the blend being about fifty-fifty. This is another repetitive bin line that has come out for the last ten years or so. I believe the first wine was made in 1959. I tasted the experimental wine at that time and thought it had nice appealing fruit, quite soft, pleasant. It was put together in order to create a line which did not need the maturing time of the shiraz by itself.

I liked the 1960 Shiraz Mataro Bin 2. It won a lot of prizes and could be enjoyed for many years after it was released (I drank the last bottle of that wine in the early 1970s and it was in splendid condition). Then for some years I didn't bother with this line too much for it was a wine that was always there. If on a restaurant list there was little offering, it was a wine that was always dependable, of good quality, and a seasonable drinking wine that never excited one. However, I thought the 1969 was the best wine of the number since the 1960. Though the familiar mataro fruit shows through (and I'm still not very fond of that) the wine had plenty of other things going for it. The shiraz part of the fruit was clean, soft, very pleasant and there was just a touch of wood to the wine. Again there was the famous Penfold's wood handling which was most agreeable. Interestingly, the company must have thought that they had something a bit special for they entered the 1969 in one show and this was the first time they had done this to the line since the 1960. The Bin 2 won a Silver Medal, which is not bad for a trade line. It is good drinking now and a wine which definitely builds up character in the bottle.

Penfold's Bin Red—Shiraz Oulliade Bin 426
An unusual combination of shiraz grapes from the Clare district of South Australia and oulliade from the 'Kalimna' vineyards in the Barossa Valley has produced a light, easy drinking wine, of very soft style. I like the wine because it has never pretended to be anything it isn't, and always seemed to be the most honest of the commercially expedient wines (i.e., those wines which are made to be drunk and enjoyed young). So often the winemakers seem to resort to 'false' stretching—too much white in red or too much irrigated material in a supposed dry area wine. Penfold's at least make no bones about this wine. The oulliade, which is not a great variety in any circumstances, is used to soften the more flavoursome shiraz and since the latter from Clare is often quite soft—and in this case is soft, though quite full-bodied—the result is a very round, appealing sort of drinkable red, very pleasant when young. A light touch of oak is blended in very well with the fruit and this adds dimension to the wine. It is not wine to be kept for a long time, but it is a very good, soft drink. I think it better to drink this kind of wine when it is available, than a bigger wine with more to it but which needs a lot more age.

Penfold's Blanquette Bin 700
Another repetitive line, this time a dry white wine which comes entirely from the Hunter Valley in New South Wales. The company has two sources of material in that area—the H.V.D. Vineyard, Pokolbin, and also the Wybong new 'Dalwood Estate' near Muswellbrook.

The variety produces a most distinctive bouquet and flavour, rather big in volume, with a full flavour and of distinctive character. I have always felt that there was not much complexity to it, that it starts and goes straight through with the same rather vigorous, almost pungent, character; but distinguished judge Rudy Komon likes the variety very much and has always stood by it.

The Bin 330 of 1959 was an outstanding wine which I feel has swayed Rudy into always following the line so well. Whatever, the wine has plenty to it, plenty of character and plenty of flavour. It has an interesting, quite individual nose; fresh, fruity *and* quite appealing. The flavour character is evident on the nose and naturally carries straight through onto the tongue. The wine always has a good, clean acid finish which is most refreshing. But as I have said there is straightforward flavour, with not much complexity, but always plenty to the wine.

Incidentally, students of grape varieties really should get cracking with this wine. The Hunter blanquette is quite different from the South Australian blanquette, though they do bear the same name. The South Australian variety is thought to be very similar to doradillo. The Hunter one was thought to be mauzac, blanquette and mauzac being the same thing in France. But now it appears that it might be neither of those varieties at all, but the clairette blanche!

Penfold's Champagne (Demi-Sec)
A light, refreshing sparkling wine containing considerable sweetness and made from white shiraz grapes at the Minchinbury Cellars at Rooty Hill in New South Wales.

Penfold's Claret Bin 747
Made entirely from shiraz grown in the Clare and Barossa Valley districts of South Australia. This is a soft, quite pleasant, well-flavoured wine, which takes some bottle maturation, but which does provide easy drinking quite early in its life.

Penfold's Club Port
Made from selected shiraz grapes grown at Nuriootpa in the Barossa Valley, South Australia and fortified with a brandy spirit. This is matured for many years in small oak casks and is a true tawny port style. Penfold's have a large volume of fortified wines which are maturing in a huge open store in the Barossa Valley. This is a roof store with wire sides, called 'the bird-cage' and there is a tremendous amount of very good fortified wine maturing there, the idea being, of course, that the roof provides shelter, aids evaporation and there is plenty of air circulating through it the whole time to carry away fumes.

This port has perhaps a little too much sweetness on the palate; but for the price remains one of the best of the ports consistently available throughout Australia year after year and which provides very good drinking.

The pot still room at Penfold's 'Grange' at Magill, S.A. At this winery money has not been spared in installing the latest machinery, equipment and scientific apparatus.

Champagne shaking tables at Romalo. Australian Wines Pty. Ltd. produce large quantities of sparkling wine each year.

Penfold's Cream Sherry
Made from the muscat gordo blanco variety grown in South Australia. A typical soft, round, fruity, muscaty, sweet fortified wine.

Penfold's Dalwood Burgundy
This is made from both shiraz and mataro grape varieties from a variety of sources. It is a very pleasant, soft, round wine which is very good drinking quite early in its life. As a trade line I like it because of its straightforward honesty of purpose; it is there to be drunk young and enjoyed young. It has no characteristic which offends and is a very pleasant, soft, easy drinking wine at all times. In the 1966 Dalwood Burgundy over half the wine was south Australian shiraz. A fifth is Griffith shiraz and another fifth, 'Dalwood Estate' (Wybong) hermitage.

Penfold's Dalwood Chablis
This wine is very good value for its price, it has always been made up of a lot of Hunter Valley material. The 1966 was a straight lower Hunter Valley wine from their H.V.D. vineyards in the Pokolbin district and was a mixture of semillon and white hermitage.

The 1968 I know wasn't, for it was a blend of twenty-five percent Griffith semillon with seventy-five percent semillon from the H.V.D. vineyard.

Both of those wines were very good. Generally Dalwood Chablis is the most consistent line of good flavour. I think Penfold's now have returned to the straight Hunters, because they blend Wybong material with the H.V.D. material. Certainly the wine is full of flavour, has good Hunter character, with that flinty, rather dry, acerbic finish which is often associated with Hunter Valley wines; and it remains extremely good value for the money. This wine matures well in the bottle and will hold up for many years, but it can be drunk young as a good fresh wine.

Penfold's Dalwood Claret
I tasted both the 1966 and the 1967. The former was the bigger wine and reflected the year. It had good fruit flavour, some detectable oak on the nose and palate and quite a firm tannin finish. The wine has a much darker colour than the Burgundy and the middle palate is much firmer. It was very good drinking many years later.

The 1967 Dalwood Claret was lighter in colour and body and showed a slight stalkiness. Both were very clean wines, of good balance and character.

Penfold's Dalwood Hermitage Claret
This is a well-known and very popular line, made predominantly from shiraz grapes obtained from various sources. There is some Hunter in it plus some Griffith material but the majority of the material comes from South Australia.

Penfold's Dalwood Hock
A medium-bodied, quite clean and refreshing white wine made from rhine riesling and semillon grapes; suitable for drinking as a relatively young wine.

I tasted the 1968 which seemed good value. It had freshness and soft fruitiness, with some aromatics showing. There was some rhine riesling in the wine which was a blend of Barossa and Modbury rhine riesling, nearly forty percent, Hunter Valley semillon, again forty percent, and the balance of twenty percent being semillon, from the Griffith district of New South Wales.

Penfold's Dalwood Riesling
Made from semillon and rhine riesling grapes. This is a clean, light, refreshing wine which is quite consistent in quality.

The 1968 was the vintage tasted. It had a pleasant, rather negative nose, was light on aromatics, with a soft, fruity palate and a clean, fresh acid finish of about 6.2 grammes per litre. This wine is made up of ten percent Minchinbury semillon, fifteen percent Griffith semillon and seventy-five percent semillon from the H.V.D. vineyards of Pokolbin and the Wybong and the Upper Hunter.

Penfold's Dalwood White Burgundy
A very pleasant, well-made, rather full-bodied dry white wine, made from white shiraz and semillon grown in the Hunter Valley. The wine is fermented in temperature controlled stainless steel tanks for a period of 14 days. After a short resting period it is bottled and matured for eighteen months in the bottle at the Tempe Cellars.

It is very round and soft, and has a really good, full, satisfying flavour. This is one of the better trade white burgundies on the market. The 1960 vintage was considered good enough to win a Gold Medal in the 1967 Adelaide Wine Show, for example. I understand there was no 1966 of the line.

The 1967 was another good wine. It was made up of fifty percent blanquette and twenty-five percent white hermitage from the Hunter Valley and twenty-five percent semillon from South Australia. The blanquette aroma was quite apparent on the nose and this fruity quality went right through. However, again the wine was very soft, very round, very flavoursome and improved with further ageing.

The wine, of course, varies from year to year. I don't think any winemaker should be compelled to stick to a blend. It is up to him to put together what he considers best with the year's material from the available sources. Dalwood White Burgundy has always been a consistent wine of good flavour and style, which matures well in the bottle.

Penfold's Dry Red Claret
A very light, dry, inexpensive table wine made from shiraz and grenache grapes and suitable only for early drinking.

Penfold's Dry Red Flagon

Made from shiraz and grenache—mostly from the Griffith area in New South Wales. A wine of good composition ready for early drinking.

Penfold's Dry White Flagons

Very light, dry table wine, made from semillon and white shiraz. It is always well put together—having quite nice, clean fruit and flavour; a very good drinking for the price.

Penfold's Dry White Riesling Hock

A light, dry table wine of a most inexpensive bottle line, made from semillon and white shiraz grapes, grown mostly in the Griffith district of New South Wales.

Penfold's Eden Valley Moselle

A light and refreshing, slightly sweet white wine, made from rhine riesling, clare riesling and semillon grapes grown in the Barossa Valley and the Eden Valley districts of South Australia. It is a wine which has pleasant fruit, some middle palate sweetness and a nice clean finish.

Penfold's Extra Dry Sherry

A high quality sherry made from pedro ximenez and grenache grapes grown in the Barossa Valley. This is made at the Nuriootpa Cellars of the company. The sherry has been produced by the Flor process and matured in small casks to give the wine full character. A very good dry wine.

Penfold's Grange Hermitage

This famous line was established in the early 1950s by Max Schubert and Jeff Penfold-Hyland. They had both been to Bordeaux, in France, where they had seen the effect of small wood maturation upon red wines; particularly upon the cabernet sauvignon grape. The cabernet sauvignon variety, one of great fruit and flavour, particularly lent itself to combining with the flavour derived from a small oak barrel. The smaller the size of the barrel and the newer the oak, the greater the flavour of oak concentration to go into the wine. Therefore, both Schubert and Penfold-Hyland surmised that this style could be introduced into Australia, particularly when combined not only with the cabernet sauvignon variety, but also with a particularly strong wine made from the shiraz variety, which was so prolific in South Australia, the home of Penfold's wines.

They started their experiments in the early 1950s and indeed, in some cases, used cabernet sauvignon as well as shiraz. The Australian synonym for shiraz, in some cases, is hermitage. This name comes from the Hermitage district of the Rhone, in the south of France. They brought in particularly full-flavoured hermitage wines and matured them in small oaks of various kinds for a period of twelve to eighteen months. They used Troncaise, Limousin and also American oak; no oak from Australia, or, indeed, other wood from Australia, was suitable.

In 1952 they made a wine which has matured into something of superb elegance and style. In 1953 they used a greater proportion of cabernet in the wine; and this wine is remembered until this day. It has matured now, and indeed will mature further, into a wine of unsurpassable flavour and quality—one which has superb balance, tremendous nose and body; indeed, one of the greatest wines Australia has ever made.

The 1954 Grange Hermitage was not its equal, but it drank enormously well for a long time before it became rather tired; or at least, in the writer's knowledge, until certain bottles of it became rather tired.

The 1955 Grange was another of the greatest wines ever made in Australia. This wine was being shown sixteen and seventeen years after vintage and was still winning Gold Medals. It would be difficult to quote the number of Gold Medals this wine has won and, indeed, I doubt that Penfold's themselves know the total number. This wine has shown variously. Most of the time it has had tremendous bouquet, very rich, full flavour on the middle palate and a soft, lingering finish. Indeed, this finish became so soft that one wondered if it should have been shown in Burgundy classes. To drink this wine is a great privilege and I have never seen a single bottle of it open badly, although some have been softer and more advanced than others.

The various Granges, 1956 to 1959 were a disappointment. Indeed, I can remember rejecting the 1956 Grange some years ago and refusing to stock it at the hotel for which I was the wine buyer. The 1957 wine was not a bad wine, but it lacked the usual great 'sweet' oak of previous wines. The 1958 and 1959 were both disappointing, though some experimental bottlings of great quality were made. Perhaps the reason for the lack of so-called Grange character was that the makers at the time were not allowed to purchase a great deal of new oak. There had been enormous criticism from various sections of the wine industry and, indeed, there were very few people who supported the introduction of this new style. The wines were rather plain with big, rather dumb fruit. This dumb fruit not being lifted by the amount of small oak formerly used, the wines did not have the quality, nor the character, of the previous wines of the early 1950s.

Luckily, all this changed in the 1960s. There was a change in the attitude of the company, since the Grange was being accepted by more and more people, so they decided to go ahead with a full production programme. The 1960 Grange is one of the better wines of the range and has all the typical qualities of a true Grange Hermitage; lovely combination of fruit and new oak, very good balance and a soft, lingering finish with this immense concentration of flavour character on the middle palate.

In 1961 I thought the wine was excessively hard. Whether this was the fault of the grapes themselves when they were picked and made into a wine, or whether there is an excess of oak, I do not know. However, the wine has always been rather hard and still remains so, in spite of an extremely good oak flavour and general character.

The 1962 rivals, and may pass one day, the famous 1955. The 1962 wine had an enormous flavour and, surprisingly, was drinkable very early. Again, I liked the combination of oak and fruit flavours, the superb middle palate flavour—such density of flavour—and the soft, lingering finish. It won a large number of medals.

The 1963 wine was rather like the 1960 and somewhat behind the 1962 in the final line-up. This wine also won many Gold Medals. Bottles that are available are still drinking extremely well.

The 1964 was a surprising wine in that it did not have as much Grange character as others. Although not a wine like those of the late 1950s (in that it was dumb and lacked the new oak character of the typical Grange) it still lacked that final 'sweeter' character which we have come to regard as the definition of the true style. I liked it quite a lot as a red wine, but it seemed to have an extra austerity and a lack of roundness and generosity which characterized other Granges.

The 1965 Grange was an extremely good wine with heavy black colour, strong flavour and heavy tannin. Perhaps it lacked sufficient oak for the fruit. The 1965 was a very big, generous wine, with many, many years in front of it before it could be fully enjoyed.

The 1966 Grange was a return to the standard of the 1962 and the 1955; a deep purple, almost black, colour denoted a wine of great strength of alcohol and body. The 1966 year was an extremely big one, almost throughout the whole of Australia. This wine was also matured in small American oak and had extremely 'sweet' flavour character. Some of the characteristics of the wine were close to those of the 1955 and I believe that this wine will eventually mature into the same character, plenty of fruit and oak, very good balance, extreme fullness and flavour on the middle palate and a soft, lingering finish. Indeed, of all the Granges, after the experimental wines of the early 1950s—including the magnificent 1953—I would say that the 1955, 1962 and the 1966 have been the outstanding wines to date.

In 1962, when trying to define wine flavours—a job which I still find extremely difficult—I described the Grange Hermitage as having the mixed flavours of raspberries, strawberries, violets, truffles and old boots. Today I still think that was a good description of the wine.

Penfold's are to be congratulated on the fame of Grange Hermitage, because they have established this style within the last twenty years and because, in the first ten years the style wasn't really at all well accepted except by one or two very discerning judges. Grange Hermitage has won medals mostly during the last ten years when it has swept the board, winning far more Gold Medals than any other single dry red style in Australia—and probably any other style of wine. Indeed, the style is quite unique. I have seen judges looking at it, almost automatically place the wine right to the front of the judging table. They didn't exactly say 'this is the Grange and therefore it must get a gold', but you can see that the depth of interest in the wine and the fame of it, over a period of time, has more or less established in their minds that the style itself, not each individual bottle, deserves a Gold Medal. Indeed, one year I spoke to Max Schubert and told him that I hadn't thought the wine in the show had been particularly good. I was surprised to find that he agreed with me, for he thought that that particular vintage was fading a bit, but since it was still getting the Golds—well, 'good luck to it!'

We must be grateful for their having established such a different flavour of wine. Certainly, in this relatively short space of time the Grange Hermitage has come now to hold a distinct place in the affections of Australian winelovers. In fact, in some people, it has formed a unique disease called 'Grangeomania', which is the obsession to own Granges at almost any price and to sometimes even drink it. It doesn't always happen. I know one young gentleman who has a cellar of Grange wine and he is obsessed with the thought of increasing it all the time. Yet, he told me, he very rarely drinks it and he just likes to gloat over it. This manifests itself in auctions, in which up to $20, and even more, has been paid per bottle for wines of the 1960s. Even some of the poorer Granges —the vintages I have already mentioned—have achieved prices of $10, $12 and $15 per bottle. The 1962 Grange, even as a comparatively young wine, was reaching $10 and more a bottle. I remember recommending it in only 1968 and complaining that the price was $2.40! Had I taken my own advice and bought and stored what I could I would certainly have a considerable liquid asset today.

But these prices show that the Grange Hermitage has a very special place now amongst the most distinctive wines of Australia and that Penfold's really have created something extraordinary which, I hope, will be with us for many years to come.

Penfold's Hunter Valley Pinot Riesling Bin 365

This repetitive Bin number is a descendant of the famous Bin 302 Pinot Riesling of 1959, which came from the H.V.D. vineyards of the company, which are in the Pokolbin district of the Hunter Valley. That wine had tremendous flavour and style. It matured in the bottle for some considerable time and was a magnificent dry white of concentrated flavour and unique complexity.

The 365 was then established in the early 1960s and since then they have kept the number year after year. Incidentally, this keeping the same number happened because so many customers complained that when a particular Bin number (which does, after all, only represent a limited 'bin') was no longer in supply they stopped buying the next wine. It took too much effort for them to keep up with the bins. Now the blend of chardonnay (which is actually what pinot is) and semillon (Hunter Valley riesling) comes from either of the company's sources in the Hunter Valley, the Pokolbin district or from Wybong, in the Upper Hunter.

The grapes are picked and crushed together, then fermented together. The proportion is not exact—it varies from year to year—but, generally speaking, it would be about one part chardonnay to three parts semillon. It appears to me that the semillon provides the structure for the wine, being soft and round with good after-palate and smoothness, and that the chardonnay provides a hint of distinction, a touch of fine flavour. I like this wine very much indeed. It matures very well with some age in the bottle and drinks extremely well.

The famous Gold Medal winning 1962, a 365 Pinot Riesling, which kept going for many years, contained riesling material from South Australia. It was a wine of exceptionally high acid and this probably had something to do with its long life; but it had great flavour and did extremely well at shows. Whatever, the Bin 365 is a line which is always quite good drinking when young and does build up a certain amount of character in the bottle. It is always most dependable and extremely good value for money.

Penfold's Hunter Valley Riesling Bin 568
Made entirely from the semillon variety, grown in the Hunter Valley of New South Wales, this is another dependable wine. Penfold's tend to make it on the slightly bigger side, so that in actual fact, they are producing a rather soft, round, so-called white burgundy style. It always has plenty of maturation to it when it is sold. Full of flavour, soft, and very well-balanced, it is a good example of almost the older style of Hunter Valley semillon. This one has been a consistent medal winner in wine shows throughout Australia.

Penfold's Mantillo Flor Sherry Dry
Made from pedro ximenez and palomino grapes, on the Flor process, specially selected and matured in small wood casks. The wine is made in Penfold's Magill cellars. After the wine has picked up enough Flor character it is kept in small wood for some considerable time and finishes with a delightful bouquet and fairly rich, full flavour.

Penfold's Medium Dry Sherry
A very popular line which is a fairly round, soft, fruity wine, with considerable flavour.

Penfold's Minchinbury Champagne—Brut
Made from a blend of semillon and chasselas grapes at Penfold's Minchinbury Cellars at Rooty Hill in New South Wales.

Lately, this wine has changed style. It used to be a fairly rich, full-flavoured, rather hard style, with plenty of flavour, perhaps lacking delicacy and rather hard on the back of the palate. The wine is now considerably more delicate, with a finer flavour and a softer finish. Penfold's make this wine by the traditional Methode Champenoise. The extreme care which they take with this wine is reflected in the cracked yeast character which shows in the flavour. I prefer the latter, which is the style now being sold, because the wine has more distinction and character.

Penfold's Minchinbury Champagne—White Seal
Made from various grape varieties which can vary from year to year, but a typical blend could contain something like this: fifteen percent Hunter semillon from Penfold's Hunter Valley vineyards; some tokay; sixty percent semillon from South Australia; and perhaps ten percent chardonnay from the Hunter Valley.

The wine also is made by the traditional Methode Champenoise and the maturation on yeast lees is allowed to take place over two years. It is then disgorged, cleaned up, relabelled and rested for a further period prior to marketing. Again the style has changed; again, this wine was always slightly hard, perhaps a slightly bigger, firmer style, and now is lighter and more delicate. An extremely popular Champagne, it is made in South Australia and in New South Wales.

Penfold's Minchinbury Sparkling Burgundy
A red sparkling wine made from shiraz grapes by the traditional Methode Champenoise; slightly sweet in flavour, with a good, clean acid finish.

Penfold's Minchinbury Sparkling Moselle
A white sparkling wine made by the traditional French process. The wine is fruity and sweeter than the Champagne style the company makes.

Penfold's Muscat
Somewhat sweeter than the Special Muscat, but with the same characteristics of flavour and bouquet. Very rich and fruity, made from the muscat gordo blanco.

Penfold's Pale Dry Fino Sherry
A dry and delicate sherry, with an abundance of bouquet and flavour. It is matured on the Spanish Solero System and the quality is quite high. It is a pleasant wine with just a trace of sugar on the middle palate.

Penfold's Rosé—Flagon
This is entirely made from the grenache grapes, most of which come from the Griffith district in

New South Wales. A clean, pleasant, well put together wine.

Penfold's Royal Reserve Port
Made from selected shiraz grapes grown in South Australia; matured in small wood casks: a quite reasonable example of a good quality tawny port.

In spite of the old-fashioned label and all the connotations it possesses, it is actually quite a sound and well-flavoured wine. Penfold's have a magnificent store of port and they use it well. This wine is very good value, having had considerable years in the wood.

Penfold's Royal Reserve Sweet Sherry
Made from pedro ximenez and white hermitage grapes grown in the Barossa Valley this wine maintains the traditional sweet sherry style with plenty of flavour and character.

Penfold's Royal Sauternes
An old-fashioned line, this sweet table wine is made from semillon grapes.

Penfold's St Henri Claret
This is one of the two top Penfold's wines and certainly one of the most celebrated wines in Australia. This wine was started as a hobby by John Davoren, the winemaker at 'Auldana'. Penfold's were looking for some wines to make up as Dalwood Hermitage. (It is no secret that many of the big companies buy various wines and their skill lies in putting these wines together with their own material to produce a commercial wine.) Some material was found at Paracombe, just through Paradise, an outer suburb of Adelaide. Jeff Penfold-Hyland saw it and thought it so good that it should be marketed as a special. But what to call it? In an old loft of the famous 'Auldana' winery they found a batch of labels which dated from 1870, among them was one that, with some adaptation, became the St Henri Claret label today.

The first actual vintage was made in the early 1950s during the time of the experiments and it was crushed by foot. In fact, the whole wine was foot-crushed until the 1960 vintage and they also used to keep the fermentation going on stalks. In this case they didn't remove the stalks when the grapes were crushed, but left them on the vine. This, of course, promotes a much greater activation in the fermenting must; but there is that slight stalky character that St Henri has to this day. By the mid-fifties they had settled the style and there was a 1956, although I think 1957 was the first commercial wine made.

A recent tasting of all the St Henri's ever made promoted the thought that the line showed again—as most Australian wine styles do when they are seen together—that there are considerable discrepancies between the various vintages of any line. The St Henri showed once again that indeed there are variances,

although they all had very elegant fruit, rather pleasant perfume and there was always a slight trace of stalky character which goes through the wine.

The 1956 wine was very good drinking; a dark, heavy, very perfumed wine with a great deal of character. I don't know that this wine was ever sold for release.

The 1957 was a well-balanced wine; it had plenty of fruit and character, with quite a lot of vinosity and a very firm and clean finish. The 1958 had a slightly porty nose. This was a very good wine, but rather a big wine with the porty nose, a very full palate, a strong alcoholic wine and finishing rather hard. The 1959 was also a big wine. I don't think it was quite as big nor had quite so much character as the 1958. Certainly the wine seemed to be dumber with a flatter palate and also a slightly hard finish.

The 1960 wine was lighter, a very palatable wine with good fruit going for it. I think there were one or two different bottlings of this, probably the company was still trying to find its true style. One of the bottlings certainly was light, quite clean, very palatable; was drinkable early; whereas there was another one marked 'Para' which had a big fruity nose, was also slightly porty with a very big flavour, a slightly stalky character on the middle palate and an austere finish. But I think that the trade St Henri of the day, 1960, was a fairly light wine and a very good, clean one of tremendous charm.

The 1961 wine, with a lot more finesse, was a very good, well-balanced wine of excellent fruit and fine character; everything came together well in the wine and it had a very clean, pleasant finish.

The 1962 was also very good, although there were several versions of it. I believe there was an Adelaide and a Sydney bottling, and also a St Henri marked 410. But just talking of the top bottlings, they had very full flavour and, again, a slightly stalky character was always there. There was tremendous integration of the different fruits and compositions of the wine: a lovely balance, a very lingering, soft after-palate with, again, this slight stalky character evident, and a smooth, soft finish.

The 1963 was also a good wine that drank very well when it was about four or five years old. It was slightly austere on the back of the palate; by this I mean a rather firm, persistent tannin with a slight trace of hard wood—but a wine of good fruit.

The 1964 had very good flavour; was well-balanced and less porty, certainly, than some of the others and perhaps with less stalkiness than the usual style. A good type of wine, well made, well put together and again with a very nice soft, clean finish.

The 1965 St Henri was an excellent wine with very good style. This wine had an abundance of fruit—a lot of style, a lot of flavour; but all in balance with a very nice, clean finish.

The 1966 I think, typical of the year, was a slightly bigger wine with big flavour and very big fruit indeed; a rather more voluminous wine altogether. Again, there is some stalkiness showing, perhaps even a trace of portiness, but full of style·and a very nice generous wine altogether, with a big finish. A lot of people would like this wine.

The 1967 was another good wine. A big wine; very characteristic again, with plenty of style, shiraz fruit and character; and a rather firm finish. This wine should go forward for many years and mature well.

The 1968, perhaps, was disappointing. It was much lighter and rather dumb, the stalkiness had gone and, perhaps, some of the fruit had gone, also. Certainly, it was not a true member of the St Henri family. I think this also applied to the 1969 wine which was well put together, you could see the quality winemakers' touch with the wine, but did not have that final depth of fruit and character that encourages one to lay the wine down. Consequently, one tended to dismiss it at the price—because the price *is* important. At this time St Henri Claret (together with the Grange Hermitage) was the most expensive single release in Australia. Now, since it sells for the same price as Grange Hermitage, the buyer has to decide on his preference. I certainly would go more for the Grange style, although I have liked many of the St Henri's, but they are a lighter, perhaps more elegant, style and they need understanding. They certainly are very popular and there is never enough of this wine in Australia.

Penfold's Sauternes—Flagon
A sweet, white table wine made from semillon grapes.

Penfold's Show Sauternes Bin 414 1962
Although this wine is no longer available it deserves a mention, being probably the best sweet table wine of the so-called Sauternes style ever made in South Australia. It was a wine of enormous richness and sweetness which won many Gold Medals during its show history and was outstanding value for money. It was released finally in the late 1960s and early 1970s and was snapped up immediately; but occasionally the wine is still to be found. A rich, delicious wine, of great character, made from the semillon variety.

Penfold's Sibon Dry and Sweet
These are new wine-based mixed drinks which can be served over ice or as mixers.

Penfold's S.A. Burgundy
A soft, easy drinking red made from shiraz and grenache grapes grown in the various wine areas in South Australia.

Penfold's S.A. Burgundy—Flagon
A soft, easy-drinking red, also made from shiraz and grenache grapes from various areas in South Australia.

Penfold's S.A. Rhine Riesling Bin 231
Made entirely from rhine riesling from the Eden Valley area, north of Adelaide, an area in which the grapes ripen more slowly with greater acid retention. They make a wine of greater fragrance, flowery varietal character and style with a crisp, acid finish.

Penfold's Sparkling Mardi Gras
A popular sparkling wine, light pink in colour and made from a blending of riesling and shiraz grapes grown in the Barossa Valley.

Penfold's Sparkling Tiffany
A natural sparkling white wine, made on the Charmat process which is very popular with the younger market.

Penfold's Special Cream Sherry
A delicate, sweet sherry, possessing a pleasant bouquet and rather fruity palate.

Penfold's Special Golden Sherry
This dry sherry, a mixture of Flor and non-Flor sherries, is made from pedro ximenez and palomino grapes grown in the Barossa Valley and elsewhere.

Penfold's Special Muscat
This is made from the muscatel (muscat gordo blanco) grape grown in the Barossa Valley. It has plenty of fruitiness and generous flavour.

Penfold's Special Sweet Sherry
A smooth, easy-drinking wine made for the commercial market.

Penfold's Traminer Riesling Bin 202
This is made from traminer, together with rhine riesling, although the material source does vary from year to year. Now, it seems, the wine comes from traminer, grown at Wybong, in the Upper Hunter, traminer from the 'South Ridge' vineyard at Minchinbury, and rhine riesling from Modbury, in South Australia. There may also be some rhine riesling from Wybong.

The line started in 1961 when Penfold's, faced with the fame of their tremendous Trameah, which was hardly ever released for sale (made entirely from plantings at Minchinbury), knew that they couldn't reach the market with the small amount of wine that they had; so they decided to use the very big, aromatic fruit of the traminer, combined with rhine riesling, to produce a wine which would have general commercial acceptance. The year was 1961 and the bin number was 177 and it was a very good, popular wine.

In 1962 they made the Bin 202 and the number has remained ever since, simply because customers could not keep up with the change in numbers. There have been many good wines since then. I particularly liked the 1968 and the 1970 wine. These

This small shack of gum tree slabs built by Edward Tyrrell in 1858 still stands adjacent to the present winery at 'Ashmans'.

wines have won 31 Gold, 29 Silver and 29 Bronze medals—including four special trophies at State wine shows. This is a tremendous feat for a wine of this nature and I believe that the character of both the show-winning wines and the commercial wine is carried through into this wine which is often available on the market.

The Traminer Riesling, I think, is best enjoyed when quite young. I do not see why the incredibly full aromatic fruit should be kept for longer than just a short period, for it is best enjoyed in the first year or so. When the wine is kept in the bottle the flavour broadens, the gorgeous so-called essence character is lost and the wine just seems to get a bit fatter and not to have the final grape lift and character it has when quite young. Certainly, the Bin 202 is an extremely good wine on all occasions. It has delicious character and fruit, and a lovely true aromatic style. A very good wine, indeed.

Penfold's Vermouth Dry

A dry, straw-coloured aperitif made from a selected dry white base and infused with herbs.

Penfold's Vermouth Sweet

A sweet amber aperitif, made from a selected sweet wine base and infused with herbs imported from Italy.

Penfold's Vintage Sauternes

A white, sweet table wine of light golden colour, made from fully ripe semillon grapes, grown in South Australia.

Penfold's V.O. Invalid Port

As indicated by its colour, this wine tends towards the ruby style. It is a popular, nourishing, wood-matured dessert wine.

319

Penfold's Wybong Park Blanquette Bin 32
Made entirely from blanquette grown at the 'Dalwood Estate' in the upper Hunter Valley. The Bin 32 has the soft, round characteristic flavour of the blanquette grapes, with a slightly softer finish than is usual with the variety in the lower Hunter. This wine is made under controlled fermentation, is quite delicate, soft and round; it has an agreeable flavour and is a most pleasant drinking wine.

Penfold's Wybong Park Semillon Bin 29
A full-bodied white burgundy style made from semillon grapes from the young vines grown on the 'Dalwood Estate'. The wine is fermented under controlled temperatures, bottled fairly young and then kept in the bottle for some eighteen months before being marketed. It is a high quality wine with a very soft, smooth palate and a fragrant, fruity, extremely pleasant nose, and a soft, clean acid finish. This wine will go on for many years, developing bouquet and flavour. The acid is quite clean and pleasant and will hold the wine together for some time.

Penfold's Sacramental Wines
Light, sweet red wines suitable for use during certain solemn ceremonies.

Peters Wines

Peter Talijancich of Millendon, in Western Australia, is another of the highly enthusiastic band of smaller winemakers who produce quality wines from their own vineyards, mostly for local consumption. Peters produce a full range of fortified wines: Cream Sherry, Dry Sherry, Medium Dry Sherry, Marsala, Port, Sweet Muscat and Sweet Vermouth. They specialize, however, in dry reds and these are the biggest sellers of the company. They are made nearly entirely from the shiraz variety. In the Perth Royal Show of 1971— a show which has always done much to support the local winemakers by having separate classes for them—Peters' red wine won a Bronze Medal. They also gained Bronze Medals for a Sweet Muscat, Port and Cream Sherry; and Silver Medals for Cream Sherry and Port.

Pokolbin Winemakers

Pokolbin Winemakers Flor Fino Sherry
As most people know, the Hunter is not a sherry-producing area. So South Australian Flor fino sherry was selected for re-sale in the Hunter Valley. This was made from pedro ximenez and palomino, developed under the Flor culture and matured in small oak.

Pokolbin Winemakers Hermitage
This style of wine is featured for sale for the local and visiting trade in the Hunter Valley. It is made from red hermitage (shiraz) from their own vineyards, together with high quality McLaren Vale shiraz wines, and was matured in small oak before bottling.

Pokolbin Winemakers Pokolbin White Burgundy
A big, full-bodied style of white wine from semillon and blanquette grapes grown in Pokolbin and blended with material from McLaren Vale.

Pokolbin Winemakers Private Bin 114 Hermitage
In 1970 a rather firm style of red was made of seventy percent local material (mostly hermitage, but with some cabernet sauvignon from new vines), which was blended with thirty percent of high quality McLaren Vale shiraz. This wine has plenty of colour, strong flavour and a firm finish.

Pokolbin Winemakers Private Bin Hermitage Mataro
This very soft, round and rather aromatic wine is a blend of red hermitage (shiraz) and mataro grapes, matured in French oak for eighteen months. This company is one of the few which has plantings of mataro in the Hunter.

Pokolbin Winemakers Semillon
Made from semillon, the main white grape variety of the Hunter Valley district, grown in their own vineyards in the district. A full-flavoured, aromatic and rather pungent wine with a soft finish.

Pokolbin Winemakers Semillon Blanquette
A rich, full-flavoured Hunter dry white, made from semillon and blanquette from the vineyards of the company. It has a rather full palate with some coarseness, and a soft finish.

Quelltaler

Quelltaler Brut Champagne
This Champagne is made entirely from the ugni blanc or white hermitage variety, planted at the 'Chateau Remy' vineyards at Avoca, Victoria. These vineyards were originally planted to make brandy and this is still the main purpose of their being; but John Robb, the manager of the venture, being an inquisitive man, played with all sorts of different materials and styles and noticed that the white wine made to be distilled into spirit was extremely delicate, had a very nice clean, fresh acid and would be quite suitable for making Champagne. After several experiments he decided to make the first wine in 1968. At the time of picking, the grapes had a Baumé of 10.5 degrees and a total acidity of 10.8 grammes per litre which was quite high. After fermentation the final strength was 18 degrees proof spirit and the acidity had adjusted to some-

thing over 9 grammes per litre. The wine was exclusively made by the Methode Champenoise and all the bottles were hand disgorged (which is not so common these days).

It is a good wine showing very clean well-balanced flavours with an interesting delicate nose. I like the nose and palate which show no coarseness or hardness. The whole wine is very well balanced as long as you can accept the rather clean, crisp acid on the back of the palate. I like this wine. To me it is the sort of wine that the Pol Roger people produce in France, though of course this Australian wine has not got the final chardonnay flavour which makes those wines so great. Whatever, this is a very good clean wine with a nice composition and character, and available at a reasonable price.

Quelltaler Chablis
This wine is a blend of pedro ximenez and semillon grapes all grown at the company's vineyards at Watervale, where various wines are selected to make a rather full, fruity style of wine with a clean, dry finish.

Quelltaler Champagne
This wine is very much like the Brut Champagne previously described, with the exception that the Expedition liqueuring is increased and the wine has a rather full, soft, fruity palate and a clean, dry finish.

Quelltaler Granfiesta Sherry
This is one of Australia's outstanding dry sherries. It is made from pedro ximenez and rhine riesling grapes grown on the company's 'Springvale' vineyards at Watervale. These vineyards are situated about 1,200 feet above sea level and the soil is light clay over a limestone base.

Wood-matured dry whites are put under Flor for about two years and then fortified to approximately 34.5 degrees proof spirit. They are then blended on the Spanish Solera system, preparation time to sale being about seven years. Over the years they have developed their own strain of Flor yeast culture and this gives the sherry a distinctive character. Though delicate, the wine is not as light as other Flor styles and has a delightful combination of Flor and oak flavours. The oak character is marked on the finish of the wine, which has that delightful clean astringency so typical of any top Jerez finos.

I like this wine very much for it is most reliable, has extremely good flavour, is well put together and there's plenty to it. It is very much like one of the bigger Spanish finos. A very good wine indeed. And incidentally, other judges must think so because the wine has gained numerous awards, including many Gold Medals over the years.

Quelltaler Graves
A medium sweet wine, made from pedro ximenez and semillon grapes grown at Watervale. Maturation is carried out in imported oak casks.

Quelltaler Hock Bin 65
This is probably the most popular of all the Quelltaler dry whites and it is interesting to see that they use the Hock name, simply because it has been so popular for so many years. It is one of the longest established table wines in Australia.

Blended from a variety of grapes grown at Watervale, which includes rhine riesling and semillon, it is then matured in selected oak casks and allowed to acquire bottle age prior to being marketed. The wine has won numerous show awards over the years. It has pleasant flavour and one can detect the wood in the wine. It is a rather full-flavoured wine, but still clean and rather austere, with a dry, crisp, acid finish.

Quelltaler Moselle Bin 66
Made from pedro ximenez and semillon grapes grown at Watervale. The pedro ximenez variety when grown on Watervale soil provides a high quality, rather pungent wine. This wine is not fermented out to complete dryness and although slightly sweet is still balanced by good acidity. This is a somewhat fuller style of wine, with some residual sugar for those who like the style.

Quelltaler Old Bin Port
As the name implies this is an old port which is blended from selected tawny ports made from shiraz grapes grown at Watervale. The wine is matured for fifteen years in selected oak casks prior to bottling. It has a very good brandy spirit finish and is lighter in character than some of the bigger liqueur ports of the Barossa Valley and other districts.

Quelltaler Oloroso Sherry

This is an old semi-dry sherry, made from pedro ximenez grown at Watervale. It is matured for several years in oak casks. The wine is then blended with matured sweeter wine to impart a slight fruitiness.

Quelltaler Pastilla Cream Sherry

These are carefully blended sherries of various kinds (sweet, cream, medium, dry). They possess the expected characteristics for commercial purposes being rather smooth and well put together. The large stock reserves of the wine enable high standards to be maintained and all the wines have plenty of wood since they are kept in casks for some considerable time in the cool cellars of the company at Watervale.

Quelltaler San Carlo Claret

Rather fruity dry red, blended from shiraz and grenache grapes grown at McLaren Vale, south of Adelaide. The wine is matured in small wood which shows up on the nose with a pleasant oak flavour. The tannin is evident, giving a slight astringency which balances the fruit. A standard dry red of no great distinction, but of quite pleasant character.

Quelltaler Sauternes

A luscious, golden wine made entirely from pedro ximenez grapes grown at Watervale. It has a pleasant bouquet, is distinctly sweet in flavour and has some oak character.

Quelltaler Tawny Port

A blended, wood-matured dessert wine, made from shiraz and grenache grapes grown· at Watervale. This wine is developed in selected smaller casks for at least eight years before bottling. It has a fairly pleasant flavour, slightly lighter in character than some of the other tawny ports that we have seen.

Quelltaler Vermouths

The company makes· both Italian and French style vermouths, which are produced from selected base wines and then infused with imported herbs.

Quelltaler Vintage Port

Occasionally the company produces a rather full-flavoured, full-bodied port which is neither vintage nor tawny. These wines are kept in the wood for some time. They have big blackberry character, plenty of flavour and body; and, if they were bottled young and had more tannin they could make quite a good vintage port style. As it is, they are nearer the L.B.V. (late bottled vintage) style of Portugal. There is obvious wood to them, but they are not allowed to develop in the wood and do not have any of the ruby or tawny character of wines

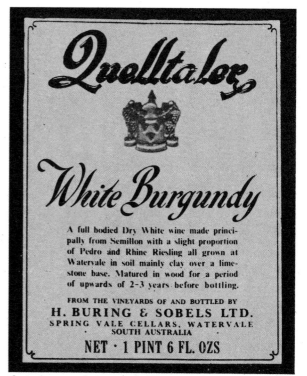

that are wood matured. They are interesting wines which can be drunk much sooner than vintage ports and have a lot of flavour going for them; very popular with wine drinkers who enjoy robust wines, and particularly in winter.

Quelltaler Vintage Riesling

This is a true varietal wine produced solely from rhine riesling grapes grown at Watervale. It is matured in selected oak casks and given a period of maturation in the bottle before being marketed. Consequently it has a different character from some of the wines being made today which are fermented in stainless steel under enclosed fermentation methods and which are bottled extremely young to retain the fruit ester. This wine has a bigger body and character. Perhaps it has less volume of ester, but it certainly has a lot of varietal character, has a very soft full palate, and a clean acid finish; a most interesting wine of the old style.

Quelltaler White Burgundy

A full-bodied wine which is vintaged from semillon grapes grown at Watervale where the soil is mainly red-brown over a limestone base. It is matured in imported oak casks and there is a very pleasant combination of oak and fruit flavours. The wine has a fairly soft, clean, slightly pungent nose; a broad full palate, with the oak showing through, and a very clean, soft, satisfying finish. It is a very good class White Burgundy which has won several Gold Medals in open shows.

Owen Redman's new Redbank Winery, Coonawarra, S.A.

Redman, O. & L.

Redman's Coonawarra Claret

From 1966 to 1969 this wine was made exclusively. from shiraz grapes grown on the red soil at Coonawarra. In 1965, after Redman's had sold Rouge Homme Wines to Lindeman's, Owen Redman bought 40 acres from Arthur Hoffmann, a descendant of one of the original colonists. Since 1965 he has bought a further 10 acres of red soil and has increased his plantings of cabernet sauvignon. The grapes therefore used for the 1966 to 1969 wines came from his first purchase. In that time he made some very fine wines, indeed.

The 1966 was an extremely rich, full-flavoured wine of great fruit character. Oak influence was not strong; the wine had beautiful fruit, tremendous regional character and is one which will live for years. The 1967 was a much more austere wine. It very much had the character of the Rouge Homme wines made by Bill and Owen Redman years before; there was little oak influence and very good fruit, and, as stated, it had great elegance and finesse. The 1968 wine was a softer, more subtle wine, having very good fruit with nice regional character, but being a more rounded and quicker maturing

wine than either the 1966 or the 1967. The 1969 wine was very famous, for it was the first wine made at Redman's new 'Redbank' winery—located not far from the original plantings of Rouge Homme— a very good unit, devoted entirely to producing one wine, the Redman Claret. The 1969 wine, made entirely from shiraz grapes, was matured in various kinds of French and American oaks. I prefer the American wood for that extra dimension of 'sweetness', a very delicate character being added to the extremely high quality fruit of the 1969 material. This wine will live and develop for years. The 1970 wine also had great character. It was probably lighter than the 1969 and the 1966, but had extremely good style, a ton of fruit on the middle palate, an aromatic fruit nose which would obviously build to a great bouquet.

By this time Owen Redman's handling of small new wood became very subtle and he was evolving what in fact seems to me to be the third Redman style; after the rather full wines of twenty years ago, and more, the lighter wines of the early 1960s, we now find a wine of different style to both, with great regional character, tremendous fruit and delicious handling of oak.

The 1971 vintage produced wines of outstanding quality. There is little doubt that these wines will impress everybody who sees them in the future. For as they build up bottle character upon their wood development there is no question that they will produce wine of extraordinary complexity of bouquet and intensity of flavour. Owen Redman's great knowledge of the district, his ability to pick his grapes at the right time plus his new-found skill in handling the wines so well in different kinds of small new oak, are all skills which can add this extra dimension. There is no question now that Owen Redman aims to make one of the most outstanding red wines in Australia. To quote his own words to me at one time, 'in specializing we aim to have the reputation that every vintage under this label will be recognized not only as straight Coonawarra Claret, but one of the best Coonawarra's and one of Australia's best.' I believe that Owen Redman, after only a limited number of years in his new winery, is going to fulfil exactly this and produce one of the outstanding wines of Australia. It is most interesting, too, to note that this is probably the first time that any one major company in Australia has produced just simply one wine. The cabernet plantings of 1966 and 1967, which are now coming into bearing, are having an influence upon the wine. They are already among the 1970 and 1971 wines and at present it seems that Owen Redman will include the variety altogether with the shiraz to make just one wine, it being representative of his vineyard and of his project. I wish him every success in the single-mindedness of his aims and ideals and I think that we shall all benefit in the future from his efforts of today.

Renmano

Renmano Brown Muscat
A very sweet dessert wine made from muscat gordo blanco grown by the River Murray in the Renmark district of South Australia.

Renmano Champagne
Made from the trebbiano (white hermitage) variety grown in the district, of Demi-Sec style with fairly full character.

Renmano Claret
Made from shiraz and mataro grown in the district, matured in oak casks; having good balance and a soft after-palate.

Renmano Cream Sherry
Made from muscat gordo blanco. A very sweet dessert sherry, quite light in colour, having plenty of flavour and fruitiness.

Renmano Dry Sherry
Made from palomino and pedro ximenez grown in the district. A full-bodied wine, matured in oak; very fruity, yet has a dry finish.

Renmano Frontignac
A dessert wine made entirely from the brown frontignac variety, it has plenty of fruitiness.

Renmano Hock
Made from clare riesling grown in the Renmark district of South Australia. A neutral, bland sort of wine usually showing some developed bottle age.

Renmano Madeira
Made from the madeira or semillon variant; rich and full with a dry after-palate.

Renmano Marsala All'uovo
An extremely sweet wine, popular with the Italian trade. Herbs and a quantity of eggs have added with other ingredients to give it a quite distinctive character.

Renmano Medium Sherry
An each-way dessert wine, matured in oak casks, being neither too sweet nor too dry.

Renmano Montessa Cabernet
Made from cabernet sauvignon grown in South Australia. This wine has had French oak maturation and is round on the middle palate, with a pleasant grapy middle palate and a fairly astringent wood tannin finish. A fairly full-flavoured, full-bodied wine, perhaps lacking in complexity and finesse, but certainly with plenty of flavour.

Renmano Montessa Cabernet Malbec
A blend of cabernet sauvignon and malbec grown in South Australia. It is a soft, rich wine which has a rather full palate and is showing some oak on the back of the tongue, with a clean tannin finish.

Renmano Montessa Chablis
Made from clare riesling and pedro ximenez grapes. It shows a rather clean, crisp, acid style with fairly full-flavoured fruit on the middle palate. This, however, is balanced by the rather clean, sharp, somewhat steely finish.

Renmano Montessa Late Picked Riesling
Made entirely from clare riesling ripened to full maturity before being harvested. Fermentation is carried out under refrigeration and then further chilled to leave a residual, natural, pleasant sweetness. A rather full-flavoured, slightly coarse wine, but one which would appeal to many people.

Renmano Montessa Late Picking Individual Vineyard
Made from rhine riesling grown on the company's own vineyards. The grapes ripen to full maturity and are then fermented under refrigeration. The wine has a high residual natural grape sugar giving it a great deal of full-flavoured style, plenty of essence character, some sweetness and plenty of body to the middle palate.

Renmano Montessa Moselle
A rather spicy, fruity, slightly sweet wine with a clean, acid finish.

Renmano Montessa Pettilant Rosé
Pettilant is a French term referring to the amount of effervescence in a wine. This wine is made from grenache and they induce this effervescence (residual gas, CO_2) to give the wine a bit of life, flavour and character.

Renmano Montessa White Burgundy
A full-flavoured, round, soft wine with a smooth finish.

Renmano Moselle
Made from semillon and pedro ximenez grown in the Renmark district. A fruity, full-flavoured style, with considerable sweetness on the middle palate.

Renmano Rich Port
A fruity wine made from shiraz and grenache, and matured in wood for up to three years. It has a pleasant spirit finish.

Renmano Riesling
Made from clare riesling, this fresh, dry, reasonably delicate wine, is fairly light-bodied with a clean finish and quite pleasant flavour.

Renmano Rosé

Made from the grenache grape. This wine has had considerable success in shows, including one Gold Medal. It has quite full flavour, good balance, a pleasant light pink, slightly orange colour, a little sweetness on the middle palate, and yet the finish is quite delicate and light.

Renmano Sauternes

A rather full-flavoured sweet wine, made entirely from semillon grown in the Renmark district.

Renmano Sparkling Burgundy

This wine, made from shiraz for the trade, has considerable sweetness and a lot of gas.

Renmano Sparkling Moselle

Made from semillon and pedro ximenez, this wine contains much residual sugar and has plenty of full flavour.

Renmano Spumante

Made from the muscat gordo blanco and pedro ximenez varieties, this wine is similar to the sparkling moselle style, except that it is much more 'raisiny' and fruitier, with a great deal of muscat character.

Renmano Sweet Sherry

Made from pedro ximenez and palomino grapes, this wine is quite dark in colour due to plenty of wood maturation. It has a pleasant fruity flavour with a smooth, soft finish.

Renmano Tawny Port

Made from shiraz and grenache grapes grown in the local district and picked at a much later stage of maturity to get as high a Baumé as possible. Matured in wood for some years, the wine has considerable density of flavour and a pleasant, clean, spirit finish.

Renmano Telsta

A sparkling, sweet, white wine, made from muscat gordo blanco and semillon.

Renmano Vermouth

Renmano makes several vermouth style wines— French, Italian and Bianco. The wines are made on a sweet white wine base and are infused with various herbs in relation to their style.

Renmark Montessa Rhine Riesling

A typical wine of the area and made from high quality rhine riesling, it has a fairly full palate and a clean, acid finish.

Renmark Montessa Sparkling Montessa

A sparkling, sweet wine made from local material.

Walter Reynell & Sons Pty Ltd

Reynella Alicante Flor Sherry

A pale delicate dry sherry made from palomino and pedro ximenez grapes grown at Reynella, McLaren Vale and Bow Hill in the southern districts of South Australia.

The juice is drained from skins immediately after the grapes are crushed. Only the free run juice is used for sherries and this is fermented at low temperature. It is clarified immediately after vintage and inoculated with the Flor yeast. Then it is allowed to ferment on Flor until spring when it is fortified with neutral grape spirit to kill the Flor yeast and, finally, stored in small oak casks. A certain amount of doradillo grape juice, concentrated by boiling down, is fortified with neutral spirit and also stored in small wood each year.

Every year a blend is made of a proportion of the Flor wine production of the last twelve years, plus a small proportion of old, matured, boiled and fortified grape juice. This careful blending maintains a high and unvarying standard of quality.

There is no question that the Reynella Alicante Flor Sherry is one of the top dry sherries of Australia, with its tremendous 'sherry' flavour and bouquet, an extremely delicate, delicious palate and a lovely, almost nutty, astringency on the back of the palate. It is a wine I have always enjoyed, and a fine example of the winemaker's art; one of the most consistent and reasonably priced sherries on the market.

Reynella Bone Dry Flor Sherry

This very fine wine is made in only small quantities. It is made by the same methods as the famous Reynella Alicante, except that it apparently does not have the same amount of concentrated doradillo grape juice in it. This is a finer, more delicate wine, possibly a more elegant wine. Very much for those who like the Manzanilla style (although this is possibly a bit older than the general run of Manzanillas in Spain). Whatever, Bone Dry is an excellent sherry; older and drier than the Alicante.

Reynella Cabernet Sauvignon

One of the finest red table wines made at Reynella, although there isn't much of it made and it is not made every year. I have been very impressed with these wines over the years, although I have not tasted them when they have reached their full maturity. It has always seemed to me that the wine still had such a long way to go.

At one tasting, some years ago, we tried the 1965, the 1963, the 1962, the 1957 and the 1954; all were outstanding and all had extremely good character. I remember in particular the 1957 which had tremendous character, fruit and elegance, plus the austerity which is always part of the Reynella Cabernets—I think it is something to do with the soil which is a variable red clay loam over marl and limestone subsoils. The limestone accounts for the austerity and the rather firm, clean finish that the wines have.

Of the Cabernet Sauvignons, I thought the 1963 quite outstanding; the cabernet fruit had been balanced and complemented by the very good use of the oak. It seemed to me that the winemakers had achieved the right degree of oak to match the very good fruit of the wine. This was a wine that was going to live for years and years. Since then I have liked the 1967 quite a lot. Generally I am impressed with these Cabernet Sauvignon straight wines, although I am not very fond of straight cabernet sauvignon, except with some makers. I feel that they sometimes lack fruit on the middle palate and that they get a bit thin on the back of the palate. This wine certainly has plenty of bouquet, plenty of flavour and I think my only disappointment is that I can't say that I have ever seen one fully matured and at its top.

Reynella Champagne

A straightforward, very clean, pleasant wine made by another company in Adelaide for Reynella.

Reynella Del Pedro Amontillado Sherry

A fuller and rounder style of wine with Flor character evident. It is not quite so concentrated as in the Alicante sherry and appeals to those who find the Fino wines a trifle too austere.

Reynella Dry Moselle

This is a blend of rhine riesling, clare riesling, semillon and the rare variety gouais; the material comes from Reynella, Happy Valley and the Bow Hill districts south of Adelaide.

The wine has pleasant flavour, a rather full palate and—as its name suggests—is quite dry. Perhaps there is a trace of coarseness on the back of the palate. Certainly there are many wines in South Australia which are more delicate, but, for those who like plenty of flavour in the mouth, this wine can provide pleasant drinking.

Reynella Dry Red Bin 2

Made from shiraz, cabernet sauvignon and grenache grapes from the Reynella vineyards and other vineyards in the Southern Districts. It is put into small new oak storage as soon as it is clarified after vintage, and bottled at about fifteen months old. Within two or three years it is drinkable and will improve for some years after that. It is a lighter style than the famous Vintage Reserve of the company and has pronounced wood character. The wine is always reasonably priced and provides very good early drinking; although the longer you leave it in the bottle, the more the oak and flavour come together —in spite of the fact that the flavour is rather light.

The 1969 Bin 2 was a particularly good example. It had a nice, soft, subtle middle palate; there was very good oak showing, and it was nicely backed up by fruit. The finish was clean and had a good, firm astringency. This wine will benefit from further bottle age. So Bin 2 remains a good 'each-way' bet; pleasant drinking young and one which takes three or four years' age very nicely indeed.

Reynella Hunting Sweet Oloroso Sherry

A blend of old Flor sherry with old matured, concentrated and fortified grape juice added. It is somewhat sweet but with a dry finish imparted by the Flor yeast.

Reynella Marsala All'uovo

This is made from an infusion of traditional herbs and egg extract with a rich old brown wood-matured sweet wine. In this case the blending expertise of the company is shown to full advantage.

Reynella Port Royal

An old wood-matured tawny port made from two-thirds grenache and one-third shiraz, grown at the company's 'Wylpena' vineyard in McLaren Flat. It is fermented on skins, fortified with pot still brandy, then matured in small oak casks stacked in a hot part of the wine store for ten to twelve years. There is no need for cellaring, of course, as the wine is quite mature when bottled and ready for sale.

Reynella Rich Reserve Wines

Available both in flagons and bottles, the Rich Reserve range comprises Frontignac, Madeira, Muscat, Sweet Sherry and Port. They probably get more wood age than most commercial wine, and illustrate the skill of the blenders and makers in the company. These wines are excellent examples of standard commercial lines. They are good value for money for those people who are looking for a reasonably priced, fortified wine.

Reynella Riesling

A blend of rhine riesling and clare riesling varieties grown at Reynella, Happy Valley and Bow Hill; fermented and stabilized at low temperature and bottled in the years of vintage. Again a bigger style of Rhine Riesling—much bigger than what we are used to today from other companies—a wine of full flavour and style.

Reynella Royal Duke Port

A well-matured, tawny port of medium price and made from grenache and shiraz grapes, fortified with pot still brandy spirit.

Reynella Sparkling Burgundy

Another purchase from a wine company in Adelaide which specializes in turning out high quality sparkling wines.

Reynella Special Flagon Wines

This range of flagon wines consisting of Special Claret, Burgundy, Rosé, Hock, Riesling, Moselle and Sauternes, are not the cheapest flagons available on the market, but they provide extremely good, reliable wines for everyday drinking. I am particularly impressed with the reds of the range which are made from local material and which have plenty of body and flavour. Often the Reynella Claret is by far the best flagon buy because it has more to it than some of the more insipid varieties available, although its flavour and astringency are too much for some.

Reynella S.V.O. Medium Dry Sherry

A fortified wine, mid-way between the dry amontillado and the sweet oloroso styles.

Reynella Vermouth

The company produces a very good range of vermouths including Rossi (red) and Bianco (white) in the sweet Italian style, and a light dry vermouth, which could be compared with French wines of the same style.

The sweet vermouths have a luscious muscatel base wine and the dry vermouth is based on a pale dry sherry. The secret of the production of quality vermouth lies firstly in the selection of the wine base; and secondly in the choice and blending of the herbs with which the wine is infused. These wines are very well handled; they are matured in wood for some years and have very good style.

Reynella Vintage Port

Made from one part grenache and two parts shiraz from grapes grown at the 'Wylpena' vineyard at McLaren Flat; fermented on skins and hydraulic pressings blended back with free run juice. The wine is then fortified with pot still brandy to finish at 5 degrees Baumé and 20 percent alcohol by volume. It is stored in wood for two years and then bottled.

Only special vintages are bottled. The wine usually crusts heavily in the bottle after years and must be decanted carefully. It is drinkable from about five to seven years on, but preferably you should wait until at least twenty years to take full advantage of these wines. I have tasted some of the special Vintage Ports from Reynella. They are rather stalky and aggressive in the first ten years, but then they soften quite marvellously and have extremely good style. Sometimes I think perhaps there is a trace of too much sugar on the middle palate. I would like to see them probably a couple of degrees Baumé lower; but they have good style and are very well made, fruity wines of considerable character.

Reynella Vintage Reserve Burgundy

Made from shiraz material grown locally; fermented dry on skins. The free run juice only is used and

is matured in 500 to 1,000 gallon oak vats for eighteen to twenty-four months before bottling. This wine is drinkable at about four to five years old but it is said to be best around ten years.

As the Burgundies don't have the same character as the Clarets, they can be enjoyed younger. Of recent vintages I particularly liked the 1968 and the 1969. This is a consistent line of full-flavoured wines.

Reynella Vintage Reserve Claret

Made from cabernet sauvignon and shiraz grapes with the composition varying. At present the blend is probably round about one part cabernet sauvignon to two parts shiraz; whereas in the middle sixties the proportions were roughly equal. All the grapes are grown at Reynella then fermented dry on the skins. The free run juice and hydraulic pressings are blended together and then the wine is matured in large vats for six months or a little more. Then it is further matured in small French oak for a year before bottling.

This is another wine that needs considerable time. I don't think it is very drinkable when it is young for it shows much better from five to six years on; and is at its best at ten years or more.

Of recent vintages I particularly like the 1968, which I thought was a very well-balanced wine with plenty of grip and fruit, but it needed a lot more time. The chocolate character is again evident; there is plenty of character to the wine, and it has a very firm tannin finish which means that this wine should keep for many, many years. I quite liked the 1967 edition of the wine which had good fruit flavour and was well balanced. The 1966 seemed to be lighter. It was a pleasant wine but lacked the finesse and final quality of some of the others in the line.

The 1965 was a magnificent wine with terrific character. Words mentioned before for the style can describe its general composition: lightness, austerity, firmness, abundant fruit; again a chocolatey character and a wine with quite pleasant oak. Certainly I felt that this wine would live a long time and show very well. I have seen it recently and was impressed with my original favourable writings. The 1964 was quite a pleasant, fresh, light wine, well put together, but one which didn't have as full a character as the others. The 1963 was rather soft and round and lacked the usual firmness of the style. The 1962 was a very good wine which had a lot of Cabernet varietal character and very full bouquet. A well-balanced wine, with a clean finish. I didn't like the 1961 which has been talked of here and there, but I have never seen a particularly good bottle of it. The wine always had a sort of funny, sacky sort of flavour which didn't appeal.

The wines go back and back. The 1959 wine was outstanding. The 1958 was a rounder, softer wine;

Liqueuring champagne at Romalo, a subsidiary of Wynns, at Magill, east of Adelaide.

Cleaning the stainless steel storage tanks at Seppeltsfield, S.A.

perhaps without the full fruit of the 1959, but a wine which would live a long time with this rounder, softer palate. The 1955 and 1957 both contained some gas—evidence of continued malo-lactic change, with a milk-powder sort of lactic acid nose showing quite clearly on the 1955. The 1954 was a good wine. I found some of this wine in the Renmark Hotel many years ago, then kept it for some years in my own cellar. It had good fruit and was a well-balanced wine that still showed plenty of life and undoubtedly would live further. The 1953 seemed slightly unbalanced with 'a hard finish. This hard finish, like so many of some of our heavy summer wines, was not compensated for by the fruit on the middle palate.

There are even older wines in this line. I remember buying a bottle of 1943 Reynella Claret in a restaurant in Adelaide in about 1965. At the time I paid the big price of 32/6d for it. This wine was beautiful with a magnificent nose; a delightful, delicate perfume; terrific balance and flavour and a lovely soft finish; it really was in top condition. I also saw a 1940 which had much the same type of flavour, though the wine was rather soft and more delicate and apparently a little more aged on the nose. The balance was outstanding throughout and the finish lingering and soft. And then at a tasting we saw a 1928—an incredible wine showing considerable wood age and a huge developed bottle age; a most complex estery sort of nose, delightful flavour on the palate and a soft, clean finish that was still fresh. Ray Shipton (the celebrated wine man from the Hunter Valley now working for McWilliam's) donated this particular bottle, and described the character as 'crushed ants'. Don't laugh at his description, for he always picks the wines quite easily at blind tastings by seeing this quality. Whatever, the wine—when tasted—was forty years old and in absolutely superb condition. I think this shows what can happen to material from the area and I have no doubt that Reynella produced some Vintage Clarets in the sixties and will produce some more wines in the seventies which will have the same kind of longevity.

Reynella Wylpena Range

These are bottled wines that are basically the flagon wines with a little more maturity and some more wood age on them. They are then bottled and given some bottle age to bring out the bouquet. They are available in Claret, Hock, Riesling, Moselle and Rosé. The Moselle is sweeter than the Chateau Reynella Dry Moselle.

The white wines have full flavour and style and the red wines have some surprising depth of colour and abundance of fruit.

Riverside Vineyard

Riverside Vineyard Burgundy

This wine is made entirely from shiraz grapes grown in the Swan Valley district of Western Australia by Mr L. Nicoletto. He is one of the legion of winemakers of different nationalities who have settled in Western Australia and who have contributed much to the lore of that state. These winemakers have been helped considerably by the W.A. Department of Agriculture and particularly by gentlemen such as Bill Jamieson and Durham Mann. It is interesting to visit the area, to talk to them about what they are doing and what they are providing for the local market.

This is a typical Western Australian full-flavoured, rich wine full of all sorts of grapiness and fruitiness. It has been awarded prizes in shows both locally and interstate.

Riverside Vineyard Claret

Basically a flagon wine of which the main grape variety used is grenache. This wine is made to be drunk when young and to be enjoyed as an everyday drinking wine.

Riverside Vineyard Dry Muscat

A very fruity, full-flavoured, dry white wine made from muscat gordo blanco grapes. These people serve it well chilled and enjoy it very much for its fruitiness and abundance of flavour.

Riverside Vineyard Dry Sherry

A blend of sultana and pedro ximenez, which is then aged in the wood for two years.

Riverside Vineyard Hermitage

A full-bodied wine with a round, soft palate, made entirely from shiraz grapes grown in the Swan Valley.

This wine is not matured in wood and is bottled in the year of making to encourage immediate drinking. Many of the customers of these small vineyards demand that their wine be available for ready consumption. I can remember a Shiraz which I quite liked one year when I judged in Western Australia and I asked the age of it and I was told that it was one year old. 'It's no good', the winemaker said. 'It's too old for many of my customers, they like their wine young.' Indeed, it seemed to me that several of them liked their wine straight out of the vat. Anyway, this is the style of wine that is made for them. It has plenty of fruit and a ton of life. Sometimes the wines have a slight bit of residual gas but they have pleasant acid.

Riverside Vineyard Medium Sherry

A blend of sultana and pedro ximenez which sees very little time in maturation. It is a pleasant, soft, round, sweet fortified wine.

Riverside Vineyard Port
Produced from grenache grapes and matured in wood for some time—more of the ruby style.

Riverside Vineyard Sweet Muscat
A pleasant, fruity, fortified wine made from muscat gordo blanco grapes.

Riverside Vineyard Sweet Sherry
This round, soft, sweet wine for the local trade is made from pedro ximenez grapes and aged in wood for two years.

Rossetto

Rossetto's Arancito Vermouth
A smooth, mellow, light, sweet white vermouth. Normal vermouth base wines and herbs are used and there is a special infusion of orange oils to give orange undertones. This is a line that sells extremely well locally.

Rossetto's Beelgara Dry Red
The introduction of this wine commenced in 1969 when the winemaker decided the time was right to produce a typical 'geographic' wine from the Murrumbidgee Valley. Hence, this regional wine was named Beelgara as a direct product of the vineyards of that name.

The grapes used are shiraz picked at an average of 12 degrees Baumé. Wood maturation varies from year to year as does the handling of the wine in an effort to maintain constant style. This is a big dry red—garnet red in colour—with a pronounced varietal and regional nose, and which can be termed earthy. It has a medium palate and potential of quite a long life. This is a good all-round hearty red.

Rossetto's Beelgara Dry White
An effort to produce a white counterpart to the Beelgara Red, pressed from the white hermitage grapes. Plenty of wood maturation showing; very deep gold in colour; and there is a ton of flavour. Perhaps there is an excess of wood evident, but it is 'a wine of unusual style and which is quite definitely from the maker. I know that he is proud of it because of its regional character.

Rossetto's Bianco Marsala
A White Marsala produced as a counterpart to the large range of Amber Marsalas. It has distinct herbal overtones of considerable delicacy to match the over-soft palate. There is good wood maturation showing and the whole wine is well balanced.

Rossetto's Burgundy Bin 5F
In an effort to produce a full-bodied dry, soft style of red from one hundred percent shiraz, the juice

was drained from the skins very early. There is some excess tannin evident, but this is compensated by a large full flavour. This wine has good ageing potential.

Rossetto's Cabernet Sauvignon
The company has taken full advantage of this famous variety to make an aggressive, yet versatile and potentially outstanding, dry red. The line was introduced in 1970. It is made entirely of cabernet sauvignon, picked at 12 degrees Baumé, and fermented for three weeks under controlled temperature conditions at 15.5 degrees C. The wines were left on the skins for long duration and then put into oak for two years. It has a strong, gripping palate, with excess acid for the time being, plus tons of cabernet fruit character as one would expect. This is an item of great interest which could result in a quite new style after many years of bottle age. It has been a constant medal winner at various Australian wine shows.

Rossetto's Chardonnay
The wine has a very soft, mellow flavour and a very pleasant grapy bouquet. The variety is not as assertive and yet it is quite different from any other variety in the district. This wine has won Silver Medals and other awards at various shows throughout Australia.

Rossetto's Clarets—Bins 3H, 6H and 9H

Three medium-dry reds of varying flavour and intensity. Shiraz, mataro and grenache grapes are used to aid the balance of flavour and body. These are well-made, average reds, with no great faults and perhaps greater potential than at present indicated. The wines have twelve months' wood maturation.

Rossetto's Mount Bingar Port

A medium-bodied, sweet, fortified red wine with plenty of colour—as all fortified sweet wines produced by the company have. Once again the regional character is of an 'earthy musty sweet odour'. The winemaker feels this is typical of the area and adds to the spectrum of interest in the wine. This line was introduced in 1967 and is doing extremely well. It is a cross between a light vintage port and a tawny style. The grapes used are shiraz and mataro.

Rossetto's Pinot Chardonnay

Made entirely from the famous grape—which has been available to the area for a few years now. The chardonnay is picked at 11½ degrees Baumé. Fermentation is rapid in stainless steel. Then the wine has a slight wood maturation and is binned. It is a soft, fruity wine—not typical of the area—but extremely pleasant, well made and well put together. I remember seeing these with Alan Rossetto some years ago when he first made them and was impressed with their flavour. The line was introduced in 1969 and it will be interesting to see how the wine turns out in the future.

Rossetto's Vinette Hermitage

A delicate dry red, pressed from low Baumé shiraz and back blended with a little dry white made from the palomino grape. It is wood matured for eighteen months and then put into round, squat Portuguese style bottles.

This is a rather clean, light wine, with a nice soft acid finish. It is extremely popular locally.

Rossetto's Vinette Trebbiano

A slighter dry white, full of tiny bubbles which are the result of some secondary clean fermentation. The trebbiano (white hermitage) grapes are picked at the end of April every year, which results in the gold colour of the wine. It has been likened to a cross between a Vinho Verde wine from Portugal and a medium quality Rhine White Wine. This is a very interesting style. It is refreshing on a hot day and is a great local favourite.

Rothbury Estate

See The Rothbury Estate.

Rovalley Wines

Rovalley Cabernet Shiraz

Produced at Rowland Flat in the Barossa Valley by B. Liebich and Sons, a company which did not make table wines until the latter part of the sixties. The first Cabernet Sauvignon was made in 1971 and this was blended with the 1971 Shiraz. It won a Bronze Medal at the Adelaide Wine Show. It is a very full-flavoured and rather big wine that will need considerable bottle ageing to soften and develop the style.

Rovalley Frontignac

A rich dessert wine made entirely from the frontignac variety and one which has spent considerable time in wood. The resulting wine is rich, highly-flavoured and shows a pleasant balance of developed fruit and oak.

Rovalley Moselle

Made entirely from clare riesling grapes this is a very full, round, rather fruity wine with a broad palate and soft finish.

Rovalley Reserve Port

Made from shiraz and grenache and matured in wood for some time, it shows good tawny port style.

Rovalley Rhine Riesling

Made entirely from rhine riesling grown on a vineyard a mile from the cellars in the foothills of Rowland Flat. The 1970, which had a very good aromatic flavour and plenty of depth of varietal character to the palate, won a Gold Medal at the 1970 Adelaide Show.

Rovalley Shiraz Claret

These are very heavy and long lasting red wines. The material used comes from Rowland Flat and the Lyndoch area of the Barossa Valley.

Many other wines are produced under the Rovalley label by the company but they sell chiefly as cheaper lines to much of the hotel trade in Adelaide. Their only sparkling wine is 'Charmane', which is sold in champagne bottles and is the Liebich's fastest seller.

Roxton Estate

Roxton Estate Brookhill Claret

Made from shiraz grown on the sloping 'Brookhill' vineyards of the company in McLaren Vale, it is a soft, clean, dry red wine of some considerable fruit.

Roxton Estate High Crest Burgundy

Made from shiraz and cabernet sauvignon grapes grown at 'Brookhill' Looking towards Clarendon at the rear of these vineyards is a crest of land—thus the name 'Highcrest'. The addition of the cabernet in the Burgundy gives a round, soft style with a very pleasant fruit character and a soft, clean finish.

Roxton Estate Magnum Burgundy

Made only from esparte (mataro) and shiraz to give a very fruity character to this round, soft style. The wine is matured in the wood for eighteen months and is then bottled in big bottles—Magnums—to provide a most interesting and quite arresting pack.

The first release of this wine was the 1968 vintage which was first sold when the wine had only had three weeks in the bottle. Consequently it was rather unsettled and aggressive; and it was difficult to really classify. Now the wine has had more bottle age it is showing a different and softer character.

Roxton Estate Magnum Claret

Again the first release of this wine was the 1968 vintage. It is made from shiraz, mataro and grenache grapes grown in the McLaren Vale. Both pressings and free run juice are combined in the blend. Shiraz and mataro are the main varieties. The addition of the shiraz pressings gives a bit of depth to the wine and sufficient balance for long keeping. Before bottling the wine is kept in large wood for over eighteen months.

Roxton Estate Private Label Burgundy

Made from shiraz grapes only grown in the vineyards of the company at McLaren Vale, it is stored in 500 gallon casks, transferred into small wood and then back into large wood before bottling. This wine is also interestingly packed and sold with a cane basket as the basket-packed Burgundy.

'Roxton Estate' was the name of the original vineyard in this area. It became the Valle D'Oro Company until recently, when Dalgety's took it over as the first of their aquisitions, and reverted to the original name. It will be interesting to see what they intend to do in the future with the wines and the style of wine and I have no doubt there will be considerable upgrading.

Ryecroft

Ryecroft Cabernet Sauvignon

This wine is made entirely from cabernet sauvignon grapes planted some seventy years ago on Ryecroft's original acres at McLaren Flat just east of the town of McLaren Vale where Ryecroft is situated. There is a small percentage, about an eighth, of shiraz grapes planted across the block. This has been the amount thought to enhance the cabernet when made into dry red. In the past the wine has been aged in small wood for about twelve months and bottled within two years of vintage. White of egg fining has always been used.

Outstanding years have been 1957, 1958 and 1964. If the standard is not high enough this wine is not released. After some years in bottle the wine softens considerably and the character builds up. This wine develops an outstandingly big, rather floral voluminous bouquet, and a very rich, soft, broad palate with a clean tannin finish.

Ryecroft Shiraz

Made from grapes grown at Ryecroft, mainly from blocks known as 'Fern Hill' and 'Pruning Match Hill'—both on sand over gravel. These two blocks produce the well-known fruity, dry red style of the McLaren Vale area, with rich colour and full tannin finish. The wines are aged in bottle rather than having a long spell in wood. The 1971 and 1972 vintages are very good, rich, full-flavoured wines that will live for many years.

St Clare Wines

St Clare Dry Red Cabernet Malbec and Shiraz

Made from a blend of cabernet, malbec and shiraz from the 'Benbournie' vineyards, together with some grenache from the 'Burton Cottage' vineyards of St Clare. The 1969 vintage, which won a Silver Medal in the vintage claret class at Adelaide, shows good colour and distinctive fruit. It is quite difficult to ascertain which of the several different varietal fruits are dominating at this time. The wine was matured in American oak for two years, and is a good combination of fruit and oak.

St Clare Dry Red Cabernet Sauvignon

Made entirely from the famous variety grown in the 'Armagh' and 'Benbournie' vineyards of the company at Clare. This wine has an immensely rich, deep colour; a full fruit flavour, a ton of power and body and will live for many years.

St Clare Dry Red Cabernet Shiraz

A wine of quite distincitve flavour showing good cabernet fruit, still having plenty of colour, though slightly lighter than the straight Cabernet Sauvignon. The varietal fruit flavours have married well, and are nicely touched with oak. The 1968 vintage wine won a Silver Medal in Brisbane in 1971 and showed very well as a wine which would take considerable bottle age.

St Clare Dry Red Malbec Shiraz

A soft red wine of deep colour and pleasant flavour from malbec and shiraz grapes grown in the 'Benbournie' vineyards of St Clare, crushed and fermented together and then stored in American oak puncheons for two years before bottling.

St Clare Rhine Riesling
A delicate wine made entirely from rhine riesling grapes grown on the 'Watervale' vineyards of St Clare and having very good aromatic fruit, a very pleasant fruity middle palate, quite light and delicate, and a soft, clean and crisp finish.

St Clare Three Sisters Riesling
This wine is blended from the three so-called riesling varieties, two of course are complete misnomers—the varieties are rhine riesling (the true riesling), clare riesling and semillon—which has also been called 'shepherd's riesling' and is called 'Hunter Valley riesling' in New South Wales. The varieties are grown in the high hills of the Clare Valley. This wine has considerable fruit, a rather broader middle palate than the Rhine Riesling and a pleasant, soft acid finish. It is a consistent Bronze Medal winner in shows.

St Hallett's Wines

St Hallett's Anniversary Port 1944
Made from shiraz grapes grown in the Hallett's Valley area of the Barossa Valley. This wine was left to mature in hogsheads into a very rich, full-bodied liqueur port.

St Hallett's Burgundy
Made from shiraz and grenache grapes and aged for eighteen months in oak casks. It is a dry red of lighter style.

St Hallett's Carl Special Dry Red
Made from shiraz and grenache grapes, then aged in French oak quarter casks for twelve months. A pleasant, soft, full-flavoured wine.

St Hallett's Claret
Made from shiraz and grenache grapes and aged for twelve months in oak casks. A wine of lighter dry red style.

St Hallett's Dry Red (Vintage)
Made from premium quality shiraz and grenache grapes grown in the Barossa Valley and then aged in French oak hogsheads. This is a full-flavoured, rich dry red with plenty of character and style and with a soft, rather pleasant tannin finish.

St Hallett's Dry Sherry
Made from pedro ximenez grapes grown in the Hallett's Valley and Vinevale areas of the Barossa Valley. It is allowed to ferment on skins for approximately two days, then run off and fermented out. The wine is then fortified and matured for a period of approximately three years in small casks. It is a well-balanced, fairly full-flavoured, dry sherry.

St Hallett's Fine Old Port
Made from grenache grapes grown in the Barossa Valley on dark, loamy soil. It matures in wood for approximately four years to attain a well-balanced port more of the ruby style.

St Hallett's Frontignac
Made entirely from frontignac grown in the Barossa Valley. The wine matures in hogsheads for a period of about five years, in which time it achieves a smooth, soft dessert wine style, of considerable raisin flavour.

St Hallett's Hock
Made from tokay, doradillo and madeira (semillon) grapes, grown on dark loamy soil types in the Hallett's Valley area of the Barossa Valley. This wine has matured into a very full-flavoured wine with a lot of varietal character showing, and a clean, crisp finish.

St Hallett's Liqueur Muscat
Made from muscatel (muscat gordo blanco) grapes grown in the Hallett's Valley area. It is matured for a period of six years in wood, during which time it has plenty of time to acquire some wood character. This wine has considerable sweetness.

St Hallett's Liqueur Shiraz Port
Made only from shiraz grapes grown in the Barossa Valley from selected vineyards to attain a well-balanced, fruity flavoured finish; matured in small oak casks. This is a wine of pleasant varietal character with a smooth, clean middle palate, and a soft finish.

St Hallett's Marsala
Made from the well-matured port wine which has been kept in hogsheads and then infused with herbs and spices; allowed to marry for a period of three months. It is then filtered and bottled.

St Hallett's Medium Dry Sherry
Made from pedro ximenez, grown in the Hallett's Valley and Vinevale areas of the Barossa Valley; allowed to ferment on skins for approximately two days and then run off. The fermentation is arrested by spirit when the right degree of sweetness has been achieved. It is matured in small casks for approximately three years and then bottled.

St Hallett's Moselle
Made from madeira (semillon) and clare riesling grapes grown on the sandy loam soils from the Vinevale area of the Barossa Valley. Again, a full-flavoured, bigger style of semi-sweet wine with a very fruity taste and clean acid finish.

St Hallett's Muscat

Made entirely from muscatel (muscat gordo blanco) grapes grown in the Hallett's Valley area in the Barossa Valley and matured for five years to obtain a fairly rich, muscat dessert wine.

St Hallett's Pearl

A typical light sparkling wine of considerable sweetness.

St Hallett's Pedro Ximenez 1959

A rather sweet, sherry-style of wine which matured in French oak quarter casks for a period of eight years. It is very rich, with a distinctive nutty flavour and a nice clean finish.

St Hallett's Rhine Riesling

Made entirely from rhine riesling grown on sandy loam soils in the Vinevale area. Control fermented, the wine has a pleasant, flowery bouquet and plenty of varietal character.

St Hallett's Riesling

Made from clare riesling grapes grown on the sandy loam soils of the Vinevale area. Again, rather full-flavoured, plenty of substance to the wine and a crisp, acid finish.

St Hallett's Rosé

Made from grenache grapes grown on dark loamy soil in the Hallett's Valley area. The wine has matured into a light, crisp, fruity type with rather strong after-taste.

St Hallett's Sparkling Wines

The company makes a variety of sparkling wines—Champagne, Sparkling Moselle, Pink Champagne and Sparkling Burgundy—by traditional methods.

St Hallett's Special Old Port

Made from grenache and mataro grapes grown in the Barossa Valley on dark loamy soil. It matures for four years in large wood and is then put into hogsheads for an extra year to achieve a well-balanced, full-bodied, full-flavoured port.

St Hallett's Special Old Sherry

Made from pedro ximenez grapes grown in the Barossa Valley. Allowed to mature in wood for a period of approximately six years. This is a well-balanced, full-bodied old wine.

St Hallett's Sweet Sherry

Made from pedro ximenez grapes, it matures in wood for a period of approximately four years. A wine of considerable sweetness.

St Hallett's Vermouth

The company makes a dry vermouth from a well-matured and balanced dry white wine and a sweet vermouth from a well-matured, older sweet sherry. In both cases herbs and spices are added to the wine and mixed every day for three weeks. The flavours are then allowed to marry and the wine is bottled.

St Hallett's Vintage Port 1954

Made from shiraz and grenache grapes grown in the Barossa Valley. The wine was matured in hogsheads and achieved some considerable wood development. It is more of the tawny style, but of one particular year; hence the rather misleading name.

Saltram— Salter, W., & Son Pty. Ltd.

Saltram's Alameda Cream Sherry

A more distinguished type of soft sweet sherry, matured for many years in small oak casks; made principally from albillo grapes.

Saltram's Alameda Fino Extra Dry Sherry

Made from palomino and pedro ximenez grown in the foothills just south of Adelaide. Again the Flor is developed over two or three years and then the wines are racked off, fined and filtered ready for bottling. The Flor character is quite pronounced. It is a very dry sherry and the oak is less assertive than usual in the style.

Saltram's Alameda Fino Sherry

A pleasant, dry Flor sherry made from the pedro ximenez and palomino grapes which have been grown on the Adelaide Plains. It spends two to three years on Flor and then the middle palate is broadened slightly with an old Mistelle (sweet white wine). After further fortification this wine is then stored in oak for some time further to produce a good fino style that is not bone dry.

Saltram's Alameda Liqueur Muscat

Made from muscatel (muscat gordo blanco) and frontignac grapes grown in the Barossa Valley and matured in oak for some considerable time. This wine has a good combination of fruit and oak flavours.

Saltram's Alameda Port

A pleasant, light style of tawny made from grenache and shiraz grapes, grown in the Barossa Valley and areas south of Adelaide. This wine has been matured for approximately seven years in small oak, thus giving it a tawny appearance and a very pleasant character. It is slightly lighter than some of the heavy, old liqueur tawny ports of the Barossa Valley.

Saltram's Alameda Special Show Tawny Port

Made from shiraz, tokay and semillon and matured in small wood for some considerable time. A very well-balanced, high-quality wine of considerable depth of character.

Saltram's Birnenwein

Described by Bryce Rankine as evidence of the work of an oenological humourist—Peter Lehmann; simply because this wine comes from Duchess pears which are grown near Angaston. It is a very pleasant drink.

Saltram's Brut Champagne

A pleasant Champagne made entirely from the tokay variety and by the traditional bottle fermentation method—the Methode Champenoise. During this process two years are spent on the yeast lees in the bottle, which allows the wine to pick up a good cracked yeast flavour. It is then sold with very little or no liqueuring.

Saltram's Chablis

Made from clare riesling, tokay and semillon grapes grown locally near Angaston and also in the Eden Valley. A pleasant, clean-flavoured wine, not aromatic, with pleasant fruit on the middle palate and a very crisp acid finish.

Saltram's Dry Champagne

A crisp, pleasant wine made by the same methods as the Brut wine; but containing some liqueuring.

Saltram's Dry Sherry

A good young sherry with some wood age, made from the doradillo grape.

Saltram's Flagon Burgundy

A soft, pleasant dry red, made from the various varieties available, but this may change from year to year. This Burgundy has pleasant middle palate softness and a rather soft, easy finish.

The company also makes a range of bulk wine which is available in barrels or casks for bulk bottlers. These, like the flagon wines, are usually blends of shiraz, mataro and grenache.

Saltram's Flagon Claret

Again a pleasant, dry drinking wine with a little more flavour on the middle palate and a rather firmer finish than the Burgundy.

Saltram's Frontignac Blanc

Made from white frontignac from grapes grown in the Barossa Valley and River Murray district; picked early and with immediate separation from the skins to retain the full flavour of the variety. The nose is extremely aromatic, very fragrant and flowery. This follows through to the palate which remains fresh and pleasant. Too many of these frontignac styles coarsen too much at this point and one tends to look out for this. There is some fleshiness apparent with this wine, but it remains fresh, quite light and very acceptable. It has a trace of sugar and the acid is on the lowish side at the end of the wine. I quite like this wine and gave Peter Lehmann a chance to deliver one of his favourite lines. I asked him what he would serve with the wine and he replied a 'highly perfumed Persian lady'.

Saltram's Hock

A pleasant, rather negative wine made from clare riesling, semillon and tokay and bottled early to retain freshness and crispness of flavour.

Saltram's Mamre Brook Cabernet

A top dry red of which the predominant part is cabernet sauvignon. The 1967, for example, was seventy-two percent cabernet sauvignon and twenty-eight percent shiraz. The cabernet comes from their own vineyards; one, the 1964 plantings behind the winery at Angaston; and two, the 1958 plantings on Hatch's Flat on the left-hand side of the road before you come to the winery (that is coming from Nuriootpa to Angaston). The soil of the 1964 plantings is a clay and limestone mix and Hatch's Flat is rich river silt. The shiraz also comes from Hatch's Flat where the vines are probably over sixty years old.

This is a very good line of wine and I don't think we have seen the best of it yet. Of the wines that have been released thus far, the 1967 is a very good wine indeed: big, full, grapy character, a trace of the liquorice character which I associate with the highest quality reds from the area. It has a very full, rich palate and is a firm wine the whole way through, with a slightly austere finish. The 1967 has won numerous Gold, Silver and Bronze Medals in both Claret and Burgundy Classes, amusingly—which shows that the judges aren't quite sure what style it is. It is a noble red that will go on for many years. The winemaker believes that it needs at least four more years in the bottle and I say six or more. One reason there may be some argument over the style of wine is that although the finish is firm the middle palate is surprisingly soft, very round and smooth with tremendous depth of volume of flavour.

The 1966 wine wasn't quite so generous and round but was very high quality cabernet fruit, with deep fruit varietal character. It was also a more austere wine—a rather firmer wine, slightly harder style on the finish, but an extremely good wine. It needs many more years and will develop very well over those years.

The 1965 again had a very ripe style: big fruit, the big, voluminous, almost liquorice, style of fruit; yet the wine still has considerable finesse. I imagine that the grapes were very ripe at the time. It is a round, soft wine; big volume of flavour in the mouth; soft and smooth on the middle palate and finishing with less austerity than the younger wine.

The 1964 has a huge voluminous nose—I would call it 'smokey', perhaps due to a combination of smoke and fruit. I saw the wine picked at a masked tasting by an eminent judge as a Chateau Haut Brion, one of the top of the Great Growths of Bordeaux. The 1964 does have a definite combination of oak and fruit flavours so I could understand the

mistake: it has a very rich flavour with a soft, pleasant finish—with a hint of firmness at the back of the palate.

The 1963, which was the first of the line, is of the same style, although perhaps it is just a fraction lacking, in relation to the other wines. The undoubted quality of the line is revealed when one understands that this wine, although it is probably not the best of the line, still won Gold Medals in Melbourne and Adelaide. It just seems to me to be a bit thinner than some of the other wines which have so much going for them.

Altogether the Mamre Brook style, within a matter of years, has impressed and Peter Lehmann has established it as one of the major wine styles of Australia.

Saltram's Moselle
Made from clare riesling and tokay grapes grown in the Angaston and Wilton districts of the Barossa Valley. Fermentation is very carefully controlled and the wine is bottled early to retain freshness and crispness. It has a trace of sugar on the middle palate.

Saltram's Muscat
A pleasant, soft, fruity wine made from muscatel (muscat gordo blanco) grown in the Barossa Valley.

Saltram's Port
A well-priced, young, wood-matured port of good character, made from grenache and shiraz grapes grown in the Barossa Valley, and made to be enjoyed fairly young.

Saltram's Rhine Riesling
A straight Rhine Riesling from grapes grown on the upper slopes of the company's own vineyards behind the winery at Salter's together with material from the Eden Valley in Wilton. The local vineyards are comprised of clayey loam over limestone, the latter being quite near the surface. Heavy ripping has brought much of it to the top and this steely, delicate sort of character that these wines have is due in part to it. The wines have a very big, voluminous nose. Fermentation takes two weeks at 10 degrees Centigrade and very good sugar/acid ratios have always been used with the grapes. The palate has plenty of flavour and the finish is very good, clean and crisp. A top quality Rhine Riesling. It is most interesting to see Peter Lehmann, who is a celebrated red winemaker, doing so well with his white wines over the last few years.

Saltram's Rosé
Made from grenache and oeillade grapes grown in the Barossa Valley. A traditional Portuguese style rosé, delicate with a touch of residual sugar and slight 'spritzig'. The wine generally has some age on it and has a nice depth of flavour on the middle palate for those people who like rosés with some

sugar. Incidentally the order form of the company is most amusing in that it states that orders for consigning interstate are requested in even dozens as the rosé bottle is not of the conventional shape—not a bad selling gimmick!

Saltram's Sauternes
A sweet wine of no remarkable character made from various varieties grown in the Barossa Valley. Fermentation is controlled and a relatively high percentage of grape sugar is retained. The wine does not have much oak maturation.

Saltram's Selected Vintage Burgundy
This is a very good line of wine which is always pleasant drinking. The grapes are usually predominantly shiraz, although there have been wines which have had some of the white variety, tokay, added and also the dolcetto, which is grown in the district. The result is a very soft, full-flavoured wine, which has a lot of fruit, just a touch of this so-called liquorice character, which one associates with the district; a pleasant, round, varietal flavour, some oak showing; and a nice soft, smooth finish.

These wines are very good drinking when they are young, but they mature nicely after three or four years in the bottle to provide very good quality dry reds. They are always very well priced.

Saltram's Selected Vintage Claret
One of the more famous of the lines of the company as some remarkably good well-priced wines have been made within this style.

The wine is usually a blend of cabernet sauvignon from Saltram's Angaston vineyards, shiraz from their vineyards and also purchased from Eden Valley growers, in the proportion of about forty percent to sixty percent. They also use some tokay, the white variety, mostly purchased from growers in the Light Pass district. The shiraz is picked at 13 degrees Baumé, the cabernet at 12½ degrees Baumé and the tokay at 14 degrees Baumé. It is usual practice to attempt to crush the tokay with the other grapes so that maximum colour pick-up is obtained. Blend proportion is usually about 20-30 percent cabernet, 15-20 percent tokay and the rest is shiraz. Fermentation takes a fairly long time to complete in open concrete tanks under heading boards, and maturation lasts about eighteen months in large old 1500 gallon oak casks. Consequently there is not a great deal of wood showing on the palate. But there is very good flavour, quite a high volume of varietal fruit showing on the nose, a pleasant firm palate and a good clean, quite firm finish.

The wines always show up well. They are not big heavy wines and have an immediate impression of drinkability. There is no question that they last and develop for many years. Of the various wines I liked Bin 53 of 1969, which was a very good wine in spite of 1969 being a very poor year. It had good

Small wood storage at McWilliam's Wines, Hanwood, N.S.W.

character, good balance and is a wine that undoubtedly will improve.

The 1970 Bin 55 was a bigger wine than the Bin 53. It was a wine of considerable substance and one that would need at least ten years in the bottle before showing its best. I quite liked the Bin 47 of 1967 which is showing very well now. I always thought there was a scrap too much tokay in that wine and it was a little lighter on the middle palate than the others.

Other wines to mention are the Bin 39 of 1964, which matured well and is still drinking extremely well; and the celebrated Bin 33 of 1962. The Bin 33 contained no tokay, although there was some dolcetto in it.

In the mid sixties I liked this wine very much and recommended it on the basis that it would improve over the years: the bouquet will build up and the flavour enrichen. Well, in the seventies I can do the same thing. I see the wine quite often and like it very much indeed. It is drinking better all the time and I think it is one of Peter Lehmann's top reds.

In Saltram's museum there were earlier wines with a tremendous amount of character which other winemakers had made. The 1958 was a wine of quite considerable distinction. The 1956 Shiraz was a lovely soft wine of enormous character and style. The wines of the selected vintage claret line are always well priced. The 1970 wine, for example, was on sale at the winery at $1.11 a bottle, which I believe is remarkable value. The wines throughout the years have always been extremely good value in relation to the general range of wine prices.

Saltram's Sweet Sherry
A generous, full-flavoured dessert wine.

Saltram's Tawny Port
Made from grenache and shiraz grapes grown in the Barossa Valley and also in the foothills, just south of Adelaide. This wine has been matured for some considerable time in small oak casks which gives it a tawny appearance and character and a very good combination of fruit and oak.

Saltram's Vintage Port
Made from shiraz and cabernet sauvignon grapes grown in the Langhorne Creek and Barossa Valley districts: matured in large wood to retain some of the ruby characteristics and bottled as required. So although this is not a traditional vintage port and it is bottled young in its entirety, it is of a particular vintage year.

The accepted style of vintage ports is for the wines to be wood matured for two years and then bottled for further maturation. This wine would best be described as a very late bottled vintage port, tending more towards the tawny style, although the colour is quite dense and there is a tremendous volume of non-wood-matured fruit with the wine. The wines available are usually from ten to fifteen years old.

Saltram's White Burgundy
Another very soft, round, pleasant wine from the local districts of the Eden Valley, Wilton and Angaston. The blend is usually about forty percent semillon from Eden Valley and Angaston; thirty percent clare riesling from the company's own vineyards at Angaston and thirty percent tokay from Wilton. The fruit is picked at about 11 degrees Baumé and the wine contains pressings material which accounts for its bigger, fuller style. The wine is also allowed to remain in contact with the skins for a short time and this gives this extra depth of flavour on the middle palate.

The 1968 was a very generous flavoured wine which won a Gold Medal at Perth and several Silver and Bronze Medals at other shows. It was a wine that broadened out on the middle palate after some bottle age and drank very well for a considerable time. The 1969 reflected the vintage. There was less sunshine during the year and the grapes were picked at higher acid than usual, although they were quite ripe and had much flavour. Consequently, the 1969 was firmer and crisper than the 1968 and it seemed that it would take bottle age for longer. This was a wine of very good balance and considerable subtlety of flavour. Again I was impressed by the strides being made within this style by South Australian winemakers.

Both the 1970 and 1971 White Burgundies were very well-balanced wines; again with this middle palate flavour which probably is the result of the skins being in contact with the fermenting must for a short time.

These wines also are always economically priced and extremely good value.

Savage Wines
The Savage Brothers of Griffith specialize in bulk wines. They sell fortified wines, Claret and Riesling in 45 gallon, plastic lined drums to the trade, and in addition supply bulk wines in returnable ten gallon, stainless steel containers for home bottling purposes.

Seaview
Seaview Amontillado Sherry
Matured in oak hogsheads, this wine is made from palomino grapes grown at the 'Seaview' vineyards in McLaren Vale, south of Adelaide. The wine is blended on the Solera system.

Seaview Cabernet Sauvignon
Some extremely good wines have been made under this label. The cabernet used in the wine is grown

at 'Seaview', where plantings have been increased year by year since Ben Chaffey established the Cabernet Vineyard in 1952. The vineyards are within sight of the sea and this has the effect of the sea breezes helping cool down the grapes during vintage. I think this is one of the reasons (the aspect reason) that Seaview wines have been so good at different times. The ripening is slower, the acid is retained while flavour builds up. The soil of the Cabernet Vineyard is also good, being of an ironstone gravel mixed with loam.

Some splendid wines were made in the fifties. I have tasted superb 1957 and 1959 Cabernet Sauvignon from the company and the wines of 1960, 1961 and 1962 all had considerable delicacy in spite of their very flavoursome fruit and character. These wines were among the most elegant dry reds I have seen from the district and I attributed this to the effect of the aspect of the hillside in relation to these sea breezes, and to the winemaking abilities of Ben Chaffey.

The line seemed to suffer towards the mid-sixties. The wines seemed to get lighter, and there are one or two which suffered from volatile acid. This seemed to me to be a great pity, because Ben Chaffey had unquestionably established the Seaview Cabernet Sauvignon as one of the great red wines of Australia; and at their best some superb top class wines have been produced.

Seaview Cabernet Shiraz
Made from cabernet shiraz grapes, grown on the 'Seaview' vineyards at McLaren Vale. A pleasant wine of medium body, soft fruit and clean, acid finish.

Seaview Flor Sherry
Mainly using palomino grapes, this Flor sherry was made over three to four years in the cool centre cellar at 'Seaview' and is blended before bottling with older wine on a Solera system.

Seaview Moselle
A crisp, slightly sweet, moselle style, using pedro ximenez, semillon and sauvignon blanc grapes grown at 'Seaview'.

The white wines at 'Seaview' are made from material planted on a rather light, sandy loam. The sauvignon blanc is a most interesting variety. Ben Chaffey obtained the cuttings of the vines from Thomas Hardy and Sons, at McLaren Vale in 1954, who had long had the variety and used it for making a dessert wine. Ben Chaffey thought that he could use it for making other varieties and, indeed, he has been most successful with it. In the Moselle category he has made one or two splendid wines with a great deal of sauvignon blanc in them.

I remember one particularly well which contained fifty-five percent sauvignon blanc and forty-five percent rhine riesling. This wine was served, masked, to John Avery, the son of the famous British wine merchant, on television. He said, 'This is a top quality German wine which would sell for about 25/- to 30/- sterling in England and which has all the character and style that we expect from the Mosel area.' André Simon, who didn't talk much about our wines when he came out here, also praised this wine as having very good flavour and acid. There is no question to me that the sauvignon blanc adds an extra dimension to wines and, if properly handled, can make some very fine wines, indeed. The variety is also used in other wines.

Seaview Rhine Riesling
Made entirely from rhine riesling, grown on the higher slopes surrounding 'Seaview', Willunga and McLaren Vales. There have been some quite celebrated wines of this particular line. At one time some of the most interesting Rhine Rieslings in Australia were being made from this winery—wines that saw a bit of wood and were bottled when fairly young to retain fresh acidity and plenty of flavour. I think it is likely now that the progress of other companies with their rhine riesling variety has overshadowed the present wines of 'Seaview'; but certainly some very interesting, full-flavoured wines were made. These wines had considerable character and balance, and showed good varietal fruit.

Seaview Sauvignon Blanc
Made entirely from sauvignon blanc grapes, grown in the 'Seaview' vineyards. The most interesting wine of a style which is quite unusual in this country. There is a little sulphur apparent on the nose which doesn't take long to go. Then the perfume of the wine comes through. It has a very pleasant character. This aromatic character is nothing like any of the fruity, aromatic grape varieties as we know them— rhine riesling, traminer and so on. It is an individual aromatic character of high quality. The palate is very good; full, round, fruity, of good flavour, and there is some sweetness evident on the palate; the finish is clean and pleasant and the wine is very well-balanced.

I would prefer to see more lusciousness, and encourage the winemakers to leave the grapes longer on the vine to make a wine which is sweeter, more luscious and of greater complexity. Still, this wine is an interesting wine of good style.

Seaview Tawny Port
Made entirely from shiraz grapes, grown at 'Seaview', this wine originates in a blend of 1955 wines blended on a Solera system. It is a wine of good colour and flavour, with pleasant balance of sugar and acidity.

Seaview Vermouth
A prize-winning dry vermouth made in the usual way in which a base wine is used and infused with imported herbs.

Seaview Vintage Port

Made only when the shiraz grapes are formidably ripe enough to make this kind of extremely full-flavoured, heavy, high tannin wine that is bottled young and keeps for so many years.

Seaview White Burgundy

Semillon and sauvignon blanc grapes, grown at 'Seaview', make this very soft, round, pleasant, dry white style. The grapes are picked a little earlier than for other wines and bottling takes place in October, following the vintage. This wine has enjoyed considerable success. I wouldn't classify it as a white burgundy, because it strikes me as not being quite full, rich or deep enough. It is a round, soft wine, well-balanced, and with an assertive grape character. There is a very distinctive flavour and a nice, clean finish.

Seppelt, B., & Sons

Seppelt's Arrawatta Riesling

This well-known dry white is named after a vineyard, south-east of Seppelt's Great Western winery, in Victoria. Rhine riesling and clare riesling grapes are grown at Great Western to help produce this wine, although the material may not necessarily all come from Great Western. The 1970, for example, was made up of rhine riesling, clare riesling and tokay— the fruit coming from the Barossa Valley and Clare, in South Australia, as well as from Great Western.

Arrawatta Riesling is bottled within six months of vintage and is further matured in the bottle before being labelled and sent on its way. Generally, the wine has a light colour and a definite clare riesling character. The nose is fresh, soft and clean, the palate light and fruity, and the finish crisp and pleasant. This is a good quality, standard commercial wine.

Seppelt's Chalambar Burgundy

This vintage dry red is produced from malbec and hermitage grapes. It derives its name from Mount Chalambar, in the Great Western area, where the wine is made. The wine is matured in oak hogsheads for two years and is a blend of selected wines from the Great Western, Barossa Valley and Rutherglen areas.

The first Chalambar wines came out in the early 1950s. They were wines of immense power and flavour, and examples of the 1952 vintage, recently enjoyed, showed tremendous flavour, tremendous depth of intense aged character, with the wine still in perfect condition and still beautifully blended. a wine which had an enormously good nose. In fact, many people at masked tastings tend to think this wine is a very good old French Burgundy.

Most of the material of those days came from Great Western. It was put together with great care and attention by Colin Preece, the famous winemaker, who did so much to establish the great sparkling wines of the district. I believe that during the 1950s, the early fifties especially, some of the greatest red wines ever made in Australia were produced at Great Western, the Chalambar Burgundy of 1952 among them. Since then, of course, both the demand for red wines and the fact that the line has become extremely popular, has led to the wine becoming lighter. It is a very round, soft, clean wine now. The Chalambar Burgundy, today, is a blend of the different districts and has good balance, good flavour and fruit, but it lacks the sustaining power and depth of body and fruit that the wines had so many years ago.

Recently, I enjoyed a 1962 Chalambar Burgundy, with the old label, which I thought had a great deal of character and style—it certainly was an extremely good Australian red wine.

Seppelt's Extra Dry Solero Sherry

This is made from grapes grown in the Barossa Valley and River Murray areas. The varieties used are palomino, pedro ximenez, white hermitage and sherry (probably the albillo). It is a blended wine of different vintages. It is also a blend of cask-matured non-Flor sherry and sherry which has been made on the Flor process. This system of blending was developed at Seppeltsfield many years ago and is individual to Solero.

Seppelt's Frontignac

A blended wine made from the frontignac grape grown in the Barossa Valley and matured in sub-heated buildings at Seppeltsfield. This variety

Maintenance work on the diatomaceous earth filter at 'Chateau Leonay', Barossa Valley, S.A.

produces a wine with a distinct fruity character, to which is added extremely good wood flavour.

Seppelt's Great Western Imperial Reserve Champagne

This is perhaps the most famous of all Australian Champagnes and is celebrated for its fine bubble and excellent flavour. It has a nice, clean, crisp finish and fine varietal character. The variety is one of the most interesting things about the wine. When Great Western Champagne came entirely from that district they said it was based on the pinot blanc or chardonnay variety. Then ampelographers suggested that it wasn't a pinot variant at all, but a variety called folle blanche. Immediately the company renamed the variety Irvine's white, after the famous Hans Irvine, who did so much to raise the standard of the wines in the early twentieth century.

The ever-growing thirst of the Australian public and the ever-growing demands for Great Western Champagne have resulted in, perhaps, a lower standard than the very fine wine that was achieved when it could be made in relatively small quantities. There is no doubt that Colin Preece, who retired in 1963, did a great deal for establishing this line. As he did not have the huge quantities to handle, he was able to devote more of the Irvine's white to the wine than is perhaps now done; and these wines benefited from it. They won medal after medal in show after show, and have always been regarded as the top Australian Champagne.

Since then they have lightened in style. The wine flavour has become, perhaps, more negative and more material has been used from other districts. They have also had to forgo certain operations, such as the old hand disgorging methods after second fermentation. Now the wines are cleaned up and filtered by the Star Transfer method. All of which means that Great Western Champagne is still one of the top sparkling wines of Australia, but that it is not so likely, with the standard Imperial Reserve, to have the exquisite flavours of ten or more years ago.

Seppelt's Great Western Sparkling Burgundy

This is undoubtedly the best of the sparkling burgundies of Australia, and is a consistent medal winner at shows. A wine of very good fruit, indeed, it is made from specially selected hermitage grapes and matured in oak storage before undergoing bottle fermentation. It is then kept in the underground tunnel, just as the Champagne is, for about three years before shaking and disgorging and final preparation for market.

The red wines used in this wine are especially selected for their quality, their balance and flavour. The final liqueur which goes into it makes it slightly sweeter than is the case for Champagne.

There have been some extremely good wines made within this line. They are always consistently high value for a sparkling red with just a trace of sweetness. The 1943 sparkling Burgundy, still being shown in shows, is an outstanding wine which has shown this wonderful quality for years and years; which shows that if a 1943 wine can do it, there is no question that these wines of today can be enjoyed for many years. They are wines of tremendous flavour and character within the style.

Seppelt's Great Western Vintage Brut Champagne

A vintage-dated, selected Champagne, made from the famous Irvine's white or folle blanche variety, grown at Great Western, in Victoria. The Brut is made up of selected wine from a particular vintage. After initial fermentation the wine is kept in oak storage casks for one year before secondary fermentation is undertaken in the bottle. It is then bottle-aged for three years before shaking down and final preparation for the market, which still includes the famous hand-disgorging method. The Star Transfer process is not used here. The final Expedition liqueur is not as heavy as with the ordinary Imperial Reserves, and consequently this wine is a very delicate, delicious wine of good flavour.

Brut Champagne is always of high quality, with a fine, delicate flavour, and extremely good balance. It is a wine which matures in the bottle for many years, developing depth of character and tremendous style. There have been many, many famous wines in this line and very rarely a disappointment. To me, Great Western Brut Champagne has remained the outstanding sparkling wine of Australia. Indeed, I believe it to be among the high quality sparkling wines of the world. I just wish they would drop the name Champagne and call it Great Western Brut.

Seppelt's Greenock Sauterne

A blended wine made from semillon, grown in the Barossa Valley, matured in oak casks for one year before bottling and then for a further year in the bottle. A pleasant, round, sweet white wine.

Seppelt's Medium Dry Solero

A blend of wine grown in the Barossa Valley and River Murray areas and matured at Seppeltsfield. It is a compromise between a dry sherry and a fuller-bodied sweet sherry; but it is a soft wine of great acceptability. This is probably the most popular of the medium dry wines.

Seppelt's Melita Moselle

A wine made at 'Chateau Tanunda', in the Barossa Valley, from tokay and clare riesling grapes. The wine is bottled within six months of vintage and is then bottle-aged for a period before marketing. It is a soft, pleasant, semi-dry wine with some residual sugar on the palate and a soft, clean finish.

Seppelt's Mount Rufus Port

This old tawny port is made from shiraz, mataro and

grenache grapes grown in the Barossa Valley. It is matured in oak casks at Seppeltsfield. This wine has an average age of about eleven years. The Port Store at Seppeltsfield is a sight to behold and it really does contain a tremendous amount of ageing, wood-matured ports of character. The Seppelt's people are very good at blending these wines to make extremely good, acceptable wines of great depth of character.

The Mount Rufus Port, named after a hill near Seppeltsfield, has a very soft tawny colour; plenty of flavour and character; a nice, clean spirit finish. It is a most acceptable medium-bodied port.

Seppelt's Moyston Claret

The name was derived from a small village in the Great Western district. The grape varieties used are cabernet sauvignon and hermitage and the wine comes from Great Western, Rutherglen and the Barossa Valley. It is brought together at Great Western and stored in oak hogsheads for an average of two years and then, after bottling, is matured in the bottle for six months or so before release onto the market.

The Moyston Clarets of the fifties were superb wines and the 1952 will long live in my memory as one of the fine wines of Great Western. I can remember the 1956 which matured magnificently; the 1958 which was an outstanding wine; the 1960, which had enormous depth of flavour; the 1962 which appeared to me to be the last of the wines that had the great character of the Great Western fruit.

Since then the style has become lighter. This cannot be avoided. There are only two things that can happen: One is that the price goes up as the material becomes scarcer and the costs rise (the individual vineyards of Great Western are not very heavy

bearing, in fact, they are rather shy bearing, and they are rather costly vineyards to operate); or, the wine can be stretched under the famous name so that more becomes available and the price stays down. You can't have it both ways; otherwise the wine would become extremely rare and virtually a private bin, only enjoyed by a select few.

Seppelt's Muscat

A sweet dessert wine made from several of the many varieties of muscat, including muscat gordo blanco and members of the frontignac family, grown in the River Murray area of South Australia. It is a soft, sweet wine with a powerful scented raisin character.

Seppelt's Muscatel

A sweet, fruity wine made from the muscatel (muscat (gordo blanco) grape; matured and blended at Seppeltsfield.

Seppelt's Para Liqueur Port

An aged tawny port made at Seppeltsfield and matured in oak casks, during which time it becomes greatly concentrated, due to tremendous evaporation through the wood of the cask.

This vintage wine is the oldest marketed in Australia and one of the oldest of its style in the world. It is made from shiraz, mataro and grenache grape varieties. Seppelt's bring this wine out habitually and it is always of a specific year. The wines of the past few years have been 1927, 1930, 1937 and now the 1940s. The wines have enormous flavour and character; although I believe now they are getting a little dry in style. Previous liqueured ports were really just that: immensely strong, viscous wines of enormous flavour and concentrated character; even too much for some, being too sweet and having too much wood style.

The 1944 example, at present on the market, is a lighter wine, though it still has an extremely concentrated character. It has a touch more austerity to it, and is, perhaps, a finer wine. The nose is very good and the port and wood flavours are extremely well married together. This wine has an excellent spirit finish.

There is a great store of these old wines at Seppeltsfield and some wines go back to 1875; of course, that particular vintage is now so concentrated it could be spread on bread. I was honoured some years ago, when working in the hotel business, to be presented with a birthday present of a Seppelt's Para Liqueur Port. The vintage label was not on the wine—instead, my birthday had been painted on and the wine, I was told, was an authentic wine of that year. Seppelt's have a huge range of these wines of all different years and they even gave André Simon a bottle of a wine made in the year of *his* birth, which was in the 1870s.

Para Liqueur is a fine wine. I liked the lighter style and I believe that this is one of the most important ports for sale in Australia. It is certainly one of the priciest!

Seppelt's Para Port
A light, tawny port matured in oak casks in sun-warmed buildings at Seppeltsfield. Again, a blend of wines made from the shiraz, mataro and grenache grapes. It has an average age of about four years.

Seppelt's Rhymney Chablis
A vintage-dated dry white made mainly from Irvine's white and semillon grapes, grown in the Great Western area. It is matured in large wood before bottling and further matured in the bottle before sale. Its name is derived from the small settlement in the Great Western area, known as the Rhymney Reef.

This is a full-flavoured wine which has good varietal character, plus certain evidence of wood maturation. It is a broader style of wine and today, when lighter and more estery wines are becoming fashionable, it remains a very nice old anomaly. It is a wine of the older style with full, broad flavour and a good clean, rather firm, finish. It matures for some considerable time in the bottle. Old examples of Rhymney Chablis have shown great power and flavour. They pick up extraordinary bottle character and live for years.

Seppelt's Sedna
This wine is produced from selected matured port in which certain aromatic herbs and kola nuts have been added. Therefore, it is a tonic wine.

Seppelt's Seppelt B.V. Burgundy
This blended wine is produced from hermitage and esparte grapes, grown in the Barossa Valley. It is matured in 500 gallon oak casks for one year and then bottle-aged before release; a soft, round, pleasant wine.

Seppelt's Seppelt B.V. Claret
Made from the hermitage and mataro grapes, grown in the Barossa Valley; also matured in 500 gallon oak casks for one year before further bottle ageing. A firmer wine which is quite drinkable when young and one which represents very good value for money.

Seppelt's Seppelt B.V. Hock
This is a blended wine made from the pedro ximenez and tokay grapes, grown in the Barossa Valley; bottled while young and fresh and then bottle-aged for a period before release. It is a pleasant, round, soft wine of some grapiness and is good value.

Seppelt's Seppelt B.V. Moselle
A blend of pedro ximenez and tokay grapes of good fruitiness with some sweetness on the middle palate and a crisp, acid finish. Made and bottled at 'Chateau Tanunda'.

Seppelt's Seppelt B.V. Riesling
Also made at 'Chateau Tanunda' from especially selected clare riesling and semillon grapes from the Barossa Valley. It is bottled while still young and has quite good fruit with a clean, acid finish.

Seppelt's Seppelt B.V. Sauterne
This blended wine is made from semillon, grown in the Barossa Valley. It has considerable sweetness on the middle palate, though it is not a cloyingly sweet wine. Before release to the market, it is matured in oak casks for one year.

Seppelt's Seppelt B.V. White Burgundy
A blended wine made from semillon and tokay grapes grown in the Barossa Valley and made and matured at 'Chateau Tanunda'. It is also matured in wooden casks for a period of one year. This is a round, soft, mouth-filling wine with a smooth, soft finish.

Seppelts' Serita Sweet Sherry
A fruity, sweet sherry made from muscatel (muscat gordo blanco) from the Barossa Valley and muscat gordo blanco from the Murray River. It has a very 'raisiny' character and plenty of sugar.

Seppelt's Solero Sherry—Pale Dry
A selected dry sherry which has undergone the traditional Spanish Flor Process. It is made from palomino grapes, grown in the Barossa Valley, and is matured for some considerable time in oak at Seppeltsfield. A wine of some delicacy with reasonable oak and Flor character showing through and just a touch of sugar on the middle palate.

Seppelt's Spritzig Rosé
This wine has been developed by joining two varieties, grenache and miguel d'arco. The latter comes from the Rutherglen winery, in Victoria, and

'Seppeltsfield' winery near Tanunda in the Barossa Valley was founded by German settler, Joseph Seppelt, in 1852.

Salter's, a division of H. M. Martin & Son, market their product under the name of 'Saltram', from their vineyard near Angaston. Barossa Valley.

*In the bottling department at S. Smith & Sons 'Yalumba'
cellars at Angaston, S.A.*

gives the wine its particular bouquet and palate, which distinguishes it from other rosés on the market. The spritzig style obviously follows the Portuguese rosé style, as does the bottle shape and the label. But, whatever, this is an extremely popular well-made, well put together wine, containing some sweetness, and of good flavour and pleasant gas.

Seppelt's Sweet Solero Sherry
A soft wine with a slight fruitiness, made from pedro ximenez, sherry (albillo) and sercial grapes, grown in the Barossa Valley and matured in oak casks at Seppeltsfield.

Seppelt's White Port
A dessert wine, vintaged from grenache, pedro ximenez and sultana grapes, and matured at Seppeltsfield.

Sevenhill Cellars

Sevenhill Dry Red Table Wine
Made from cabernet sauvignon and shiraz in proportions that vary; generally, cabernet sauvignon comprises from thirty-three to forty percent, and shiraz makes up the rest. It is matured for two years in big wood and then bottled. The wines are extremely big and fruity, with a great deal of colour, tremendous depth, and power. They need plenty of time before they start to show their best. They are saved from portiness by the considerable austerity of the finish. Although the wines have full, rich flavour, they finish very clean and actually have quite an elegant character, even though they are as big as they are.

Most of the wines have been made by Brother John Hanlon, a great friend of many in the trade. Brother Hanlon was a man of tremendous charm, tremendous spirit and tremendous generosity of character. It is unfortunate that he will no longer be tasting wines with us, since he died in early 1972.

He was proud of this line which, he was always careful to point out, was a by-line. It was nothing more than something he did on the side and was sold mainly to visitors at the cellar door. He was very fond of making this line and fond of drinking it.

Sevenhill Cellars Dry Sacramental Wine
A dry wine of the Hock style, made from pedro ximenez.

Sevenhill Cellars Dry White
Made from clare riesling, which originated in this vineyard, being brought from Germany in 1869. It is bottled at about six months and drunk young.

The bulk of this wine is sold in bulk to be made into Champagne. It makes extremely good Champagne

material, being delicate, yet having full flavour and a very clean, acid finish. These wines have a lot of appeal. They do not have the estery nose and rather thin palate of so many wines of the area, but have, perhaps, slightly less nose, making up for this with considerable vinosity and depth of flavour on the middle palate and an almost steely finish.

Sevenhill Cellars Fortified Wines
There were some old fortified wines in the cellar when Brother Hanlon took it over. He continued to make them and keep them in wood. They were produced mainly for local trade. Among them were a Tawny Port, a Frontignan, a Tokay and a Verdelho.

All these sweet wines were fortified to about 34 percent and had a sweetness of about four degrees Baumé, none of them being less than five years old and most of them containing bits and pieces of considerably older material. All the wines were developed under a modified Solera system, by which new wine was added to the older wine in casks and the equivalent amount taken out as required.

Sevenhill Cellars Sweet Sacramental Wine
The main product of the vineyards and cellars, being a blend of shiraz, grenache, pedro ximenez, frontignan, tokay and verdelho; its strength is about 33 proof spirit and sweetness about 3.5 degrees Baumé.

Production of sacramental wine was the purpose of the Sevenhill Cellars and Brother Hanlon was always careful to point out that that was what he was there for. The other wines on which his fame as a winemaker rested were only sidelines that earned a little bit of money at the cellar door.

The Sacramental Wine, however, was sold all over Australia, New Zealand, the Pacific Isles, to Japan and Korea, India, Indonesia, Malaysia, Singapore and Zambia; and Brother Hanlon once told me that in places where it couldn't be sold, because there was, no money to buy it, it was given away.

Sevenhill Cellars Vintage Port
Occasionally, Brother Hanlon made a very robust, extremely full-flavoured vintage port from both the cabernet sauvignon and shiraz pressings; a wine of tremendous body, strength and huge tannin. One that would live in the bottle for many, many years before softening and settling down. I remember tasting one such port which had some age upon it and it was a marvellously exciting drink of extraordinary flavour.

The famous 1925 Sevenhill Cellars Port, made by Brother Hanlon's predecessor, Brother Downey, was tasted in Melbourne and this wine was almost of the same character, in that it had not yet developed to show what it could do. It still had fantastic flavour and a superb balance; but at the same time had a long life in front of it. This wine was made from straight cabernet sauvignon.

Stainless steel fermenter and storage tanks at the 'Rothbury' vineyards at Rothbury, near Pokolbin, Hunter Valley, N.S.W.

South Coast Wine Company

South Coast Wine Company Shiraz

Made by Keith Genders in his small winery in the heart of the McLaren Vale district of South Australia. Keith Genders has long been a grape grower in the district and has lately turned to making his own wines.

The Shiraz wine has distinctive, full-flavoured characteristics, with a rather flowery nose, plenty of full fruit and a very strong, full tannin finish. Although he has only made a few examples during the last three or four years, recognition has already come in the form of a couple of medals from major shows and also from the increasing number of people who visit him, wishing to buy this wine. The reds are enclosed fermented on skins and allowed to settle for six months in stainless steel tanks before being transferred to small American oak casks for further maturation. They have plenty of style, plenty of fruit and plenty of character.

South Coast Wine Company White Burgundy

A most interesting style of wine made in enclosed stainless steel fermenters under temperature control. Keith Genders has been experimenting with wood maturation, using German oak, and he has great hopes in this direction. There is no doubt that an extra dimension of flavour is picked up by the use of oak and this could match the rather full-flavoured, full-bodied, almost coarse white that the area tends to produce. These wines have a great deal of robust character and it is my belief that small wood could aid their style considerably.

Southern Vales Co-operative Winery Ltd

Southern Vales Cabernet Bin 27

A fine, full-flavoured blend of cabernet sauvignon and shiraz, grown in the McLaren Vale district. A very big berry nose, a full, round flavour and firm tannin finish. This wine needs considerable bottle maturation.

Southern Vales McLaren Vale Hermitage Bin 8

Made by the Southern Vales Co-operative Winery Limited in the heart of the town of McLaren Vale, in South Australia. This wine is made entirely from grapes grown on the red loam slopes of the McLaren Vale district and follows the trend towards a lighter style, with a touch of oak. It is pleasantly flavoured, soft and round, with a smooth, soft finish.

Stanley Wine Company

Stanley Clare Special Claret

Blended from shiraz and grenache, this wine is soft and round with plenty of flavour and a pleasant tannin finish. It is a wine that may be enjoyed young and represents very good value for money.

Stanley Clare Vintage Riesling

A blend of rhine riesling and pedro ximenez with a delightful fruity nose and loads of flavour—well-balanced and containing pleasant 'spritzig' (natural effervescence). Again, a good-value wine.

Stanley Leasingham Bin 43 Burgundy

Named after the vineyard of the company in the Watervale district. This wine is a blend of cabernet sauvignon and grenache grapes, grown at Leasingham and Clare and bottled after maturation in small oak casks and larger wood. The grenache is taken off the skins and fermented on cabernet skins. It is a very pleasant red, having good medium density, lively colour, soft floral cabernet nose; round, soft palate and a smooth finish with some typical varietal tannin evident.

Light, but good drinking now of a slightly more substantial kind than is usually available. Not recommended as a long-term cellaring proposition, although it will improve for two or three years in the bottle. It has good fruity flavour and character.

Stanley Leasingham Bin 49 Cabernet

Of the 1966 vintage a Cabernet Bin 14 was released which was of extremely rich, full character, tremendous cabernet fruit and style. There were very small quantities of it, but it was a wine that would undoubtedly last for twenty years and improve for most of that time.

The Bin 49 was of the 1967 vintage and created a great deal of interest when it came onto the market. It was actually a blend containing eighty percent cabernet sauvignon and twenty percent malbec from grapes grown at Leasingham and at Clare. The colour is a good, deep, thorough red. The wine shows lots of cabernet character on the nose and this follows through onto the palate with an astringent and mouth-puckering finish. The malbec helps to fill the hole that sometimes appears on the back of the palate of a straight cabernet.

Clare reds are noted for their longevity and Bin 49 is no exception. It needs years and years for the cabernet and wood to soften out and its quality, when the wine has lots of age, should be well worth waiting for.

In 1970 another Cabernet Malbec was produced—again in the proportions eighty percent to twenty percent. This was blended to make this good claret style, the malbec adding interest to the big cabernet character. The wine spent nine months in new, small wood and was a wine which should lay down very well, thus representing a very good cellaring proposition.

Stanley Leasingham Bin 6 Mosel

A light, fresh, flowery rhine riesling, with a touch of the spicy sauvignon blanc character on the middle palate. This wine drinks well now, but it will develop with some cellaring. It has a slight sweetness, crisp acidity and plenty of gas evident. Again from the Leasingham vineyards at Watervale. It is a clean wine with a pleasant, soft finish, and has won some medals in shows. I prefer the 1970 to the 1971 version.

Stanley Leasingham Bin 5 Rhine Riesling

A straight Rhine Riesling, made from grapes grown at the Leasingham vineyards where the soils are basically red over limestone. Altitude is 1,300 feet above sea level—roughly comparable to the Eden Valley (Pewsey Vale, incidentally, is at 1,800 feet).

The grapes are crushed with a Coq Mill, which features rubber rollers to eliminate stem damage. The juice is fermented in enclosed stainless steel containers at a temperature of 12.7 degrees C, fermentation taking about a fortnight. The wine is then cleaned up straight after vintage and bottled in late May to retain freshness and a trace of gas.

It looks quite brilliant with a lovely greeny-gold colour. The nose is tremendous—big, full-powered, flowery varietal smell, with the barest trace of sulphur. The flowery smell carries through to the palate which is soft and balanced. With age, the wine fills out on the palate; it is rather thin to start with, but with age it fills out into something quite substantial; very mouth-filling and fine.

That description, basically, was for the 1968 Bin 5, which went on to win three Gold, two Silver, two

Bronze Medals and a Haywood Trophy for the best Hock of 1968 in Adelaide. At the time the wine was being sold for less than a dollar a bottle.

In 1971 another Bin 5 was made. This was blended from wines made from grapes picked at the end of the season and were thus riper and lower in acid. It gave Bin 5 a fuller, softer palate and a somewhat lower acidity than the more austere Bin 7 of the same year. I liked this wine very much, indeed. It does not really have a soft, full palate, but had marvellous flavour and quite intense fruit (essencey almost) which I enjoyed very much. The nose was very full and flowery, the finish clean and fresh. This wine is a top Rhine Riesling, although the price had gone up considerably.

Stanley Leasingham Bin 7 Rhine Riesling

There have been several Bin 7s of different years, all made by the brilliant winemaker, Tim Knappstein. The Bin 7 is a blend of early wines made from mid and late season grapes grown in the Leasingham vineyards of the company and is very delicate, with a fairly high, crisp acidity. The finish is firmer, as well as being more acid. Delicate, but lacking in full flavour; perhaps slightly dumb. Mick Knappstein, the gentleman who has done so much to make the Stanley Wine Company the success that it is, believes the wine will pick up more flavour with a year or so in bottle and this is certainly a strong probability.

The Bin 7 of 1970 was the wonder wine of the industry for the 1970 vintage. It won six or seven Gold medals, gained from almost every show in which the wine was entered, plus a couple of special trophies as Best Wine of Show. Again the wine is a blend of local rhine rieslings, picked at different times. Thus the Baumé and acid levels vary for each selection in relation to the time picked. The Knappsteins firmly believe that this helps the final wine in that the first pickings have very crisp, clean acid and the latter pickings the full ester, flavour and build-up. The different Baumés in this case were 10 degrees, 11 degrees and 12 degrees—fermentation took twelve to fourteen days at the controlled temperature of 12.7 degrees C. The soil is red soil over limestone.

This wine is extremely well made, with tremendous volume of flavour and character; beautiful varietal aromatic nose—very fresh and abundant; high ester quality which hits the front of the mouth quickly. It stays in the mouth right through, although I would always like to see more depth and intensity of flavour on the middle palate. The finish is crisp and clean.

The Bin 7 of 1969 also did well in shows. A wine of considerable aromatic fruit, delicious flavour—although, again, light on the palate—and a clean acid finish.

Both the Bin 7 and Bin 5 may now be celebrated as among the top Rhine Rieslings in the country. They are prizewinning wines which are being brought out year after year, and always good value for money.

Stanley Leasingham Bin 9 Spatlese Riesling

This is a very good wine, indeed, especially if you like elegant, sweetish wines. I certainly do, but I don't like sweet wines if the material is not of the highest quality. There are not many great Australian sweet wines, although we are seeing more of them lately.

This wine has all the hallmarks of the Leasingham-Rhine Riesling quality: massive forward fragrance of fruit, balance, acid freshness, and remarkable cleanness and finesse, all qualities recognized now as being typical of the line. Add the obvious sugar—the result of late picking, add the late-picking flavour that is nothing to do with sugar, but seems to be an actual flavour constituent, and you get a delicious depth of flavour on the middle palate.

The one criticism I had of these Rhine Rieslings in the past has been this lightness, lack of depth on the middle of the tongue, but this has been overcome in this wine. It certainly has something to do with the touch of sweetness, but it is also an extra flavour dimension. I like it very much and remember enjoying it with a couple of chilled peaches from Mudgee, a really superb experience. The wine has already won Gold and Silver Medals and I believe it will improve considerably with extra age in the bottle as the flavour deepens and the bouquet builds.

Stanley Leasingham Bin 3 White Burgundy

Another quality white wine from this company, remarkable in that it is not of their usual flowery, aromatic style. It is made from semillon, tokay, clare riesling and sauvignon blanc grapes grown at Leasingham and at Clare.

When I first saw this soft, full, round wine, my tasting notes read: 'Soft, pleasant nose. Good, soft round palate, good fruit flavour, pleasant soft finish...' which sums it up quite well.

It is a very good style of soft, fruity white; good drinking now and one which will develop further. The 1970 won several Silver Medals and although, perhaps, the wine lacked the final essential complexity of flavour on the middle palate that some other district wines have, it still remains very good value for money and good drinking at all times.

Stanley Leasingham Cabernet Sauvignon

Made entirely from cabernet sauvignon. Tim Knappstein has been making a range of superb, full-bodied cabernets in the late sixties and early seventies which are of excellent varietal composition. These wines have tremendous berry fruit, a full, rich palate, and a firm tannin acid finish. The 1969, which was matured for some months in small wood, won several show awards, amongst them a Gold Medal in Brisbane in 1970. Vintages of the 1970 show even more complexity of character and they are being very well balanced against the flavours that can be derived from small, new wood. This is a line of which a great deal more will be heard in the future and we look forward with enormous interest to seeing and tasting them when they have some degree of age upon them.

Stanley Riesling

A blend of clare and rhine rieslings, this wine is somewhat softer and rounder than a true Rhine Riesling. It has excellent flavour and slightly lower acidity. A very good all-round drinking wine, suitable for most occasions.

Stanley Rosé

A most interesting wine made from straight grenache. I liked it very much because of its dry style, as I am not enthusiastic about the sparkling, slightly sweet rosé style, and prefer the drier, more flavoursome style.

The 1971 Rosé was an excellent wine of young, fresh fruit, considerable complexity of flavour; all-round body and very clean acid finish.

The 1970 was a magnificent wine which won numerous prizes. It was made from grenache grapes, grown at Watervale, and specially culled for various reasons. Stanley aimed for fairly light-coloured grapes, low in sugar, not too high in acidity, and I believe there are vineyards in the district that meet these requirements. After crushing, the juice is left on the skins overnight and then run off in the morning. From that time the rose is treated as a white wine and finishes its fermentation in closed, stainless steel tanks at 12.7 degrees C to give a fragrant, delicate wine. It is cleaned up and bottled as soon as possible. The development in the 1970 was most appealing. Its freshness flattened slightly, but this gave way to a most distinctive flavour, with a strong bouquet—a

very definite getting away from the wishy-washy rosés which are nothing more than slightly tinted whites.

Both the 1968 and 1969 Rosés also won many Gold Medals and both of them won the Sheppard Trophy for the best Rosé in the Adelaide Show.

So the company has contributed a most worthy and authentic rosé style to the market; one which is appealing when it is young, because of its fruitiness and pleasant flavour; but one which, after a year or so in the bottle, develops a most distinctive and worthy character.

Stanley Shiraz

Made from straight shiraz, grown in the Clare district, these wines represent good value for money. The 1969 was a very good wine—a trifle lighter than usual, but quite fruity—and a wine which was very good drinking when young and also one that would take some age. The fruit was good, typically Clare; the colour was quite vigorous; and the palate had plenty of body that needed some time in the bottles to settle down. The 1968 wine was tremendous and was offered at a very cheap price at the time: A vigorous, young unpretentious wine, good solid drinking and a wine that will cellar well into a softer, but still full-flavoured dry red.

Stonyfell

Stonyfell All'uovo Marsala

A very sweet dessert wine, made from a port wine base and grape juice concentrate, and delicately flavoured to provide the traditional style.

Stonyfell Amontillado Flor

Made from palomino and pedro ximenez grapes, grown in the Adelaide foothills and in the Langhorne Creek area. After fermentation, which is allowed to go

out completely dry, the wine is slightly topped with spirit to approximately 26 degree proof spirit, after which it is put into small oak, filling only to two-thirds, and the Flor yeast is seeded on the surface of the wine. This is allowed to go on for two or three years while the Flor film imparts the characteristics required, after which the wine is racked off, further topped with spirit to approximately 32 degree proof and blended with a wood-aged, slightly sweet sherry to give a delicate combination of Flor character and wood. A very pleasant, soft, well-made wine which has been extremely well put together and is very good value for money.

Stonyfell Amorita Sherry

A soft, oloroso style, matured in small oak for many years in warm conditions to reach a nice, soft pleasant flavour and full, deep colour.

Stonyfell Austral Cream Sherry

A soft, mellow cream sherry; matured for many years in small oak casks; made principally from the albillo grape.

Stonyfell Crema Marsala

A velvety, cream, liqueur-style wine with a high degree of sweetness, but not as highly flavoured as the Marsala All'uovo.

Stonyfell Fino Extra Dry Sherry

Made from palomino and pedro ximenez grapes, grown at Stonyfell. After two to three years in oak casks, when the Flor character is developed, these wines are racked off, fined and filtered ready for bottling. The Flor character is pronounced and it is absolutely dry sherry.

Stonyfell Ilfracombe Table Red

A light, fragrant, dry red made from selected pickings of grenache and shiraz from the Langhorne Creek, Barossa and Burnside areas. This is packed in a most individual bottle, rather like a Paris Pot. The size is 20 oz which they consider to be an ideal 'table-for-two' size. This wine has a nice pleasant, grapy character; the slightly stalky character of the grenache is always evident. It can be served chilled in summer and is a very pleasant, light, unpretentious quaffing red.

Stonyfell Ilfracombe White

Again packed in the distinctive 20 oz 'bottle-for-two' size. This is a light, white wine made from tokay and clare riesling varieties, grown in the Barossa Valley. It is a pleasant, fresh, round, soft wine with a clean, crisp finish.

Stonyfell Metala Claret

One of the most distinguished of the company's red wines and one of the most interesting reds of

Australia. This has been called Stonyfell Claret Private Bin, but is now generally called Metala Cabernet Shiraz. The labels are numbered and are packed full of information.

The material for the wine comes from Langhorne Creek where there is a fair amount of cabernet sauvignon and shiraz grown. Stonyfell have been making the grapes from their vineyard sources in the area since quite early in the twentieth century. Since 1955 the whole storage and winemaking have been removed to Stonyfell, in the foothills of Adelaide, only 5 miles east of the G.P.O.

The wine matures in 500 gallon oak casks in approximate proportions of forty percent cabernet to sixty percent shiraz, although this can vary. A small quantity is also kept in French oak and these wines are then balanced and blended and put together. The style is rather a formidable one, big and rich, with much depth of flavour. Perhaps the wine sometimes lacks finesse, but the finish is quite firm. Plenty of bottle age is needed and I don't think we have seen the best of the wines fully mature as yet. Some of these wines need ten to fifteen years bottle age to get the most out of the fruit and flavours that are there. The wines have a very big, rich volume of varietal nose, to start with. There is some oak evident; and I have no doubt that with age this fruit and oak will build up into a very fine, rich, perfumed bouquet.

These wines are quite hard to obtain. They appear to be on quota most of the time and only a limited quantity is made, although they are distributed throughout Australia.

Stonyfell Montagne de Pierre Brut Champagne
A very good quality, rather soft-flavoured Champagne, made entirely from the tokay variety and processed by the Methode Champenoise. The wine spends from two to three years on its yeast lees before being disgorged, cleaned up and re-bottled. It is a fairly dry wine, and I doubt that there is much liqueuring in it at all.

Stonyfell Montagne de Pierre Champagne
A pleasant, soft, sparkling wine, again made by the Methode Champenoise and from the same material as the Brut, but in this case the wine is slightly liqueured at the Expedition liqueur stage.

Stonyfell Moselle
A delicate wine with a small percentage of the natural grape sugar retained in it by chilling the wine down before the fermentation is complete. It is made from clare riesling and tokay grapes, grown in the Barossa Valley and bottled early to retain freshness. The 1970 wine did particularly well in open classes, winning several Silver and Bronze Medals in Perth, Brisbane, Melbourne and Adelaide.

Stonyfell Mountain Mist Sauterne
A pleasant, sweet, delicate white table wine of no great distinction of character and no great lusciousness or depth of flavour.

Stonyfell Old Liqueur Muscat
A fairly luscious, full-flavoured dessert wine of considerable age and character, made from muscatel (muscat gordo blanco) combined with frontignac. It has good depth of 'raisiny' character with considerable rancio flavour from the wood.

Stonyfell Old Lodge Port
An old tawny port made under an old system of blending. Each year about one-third of the wine is drawn off for bottling and the 500 gallon casks are refilled with wine which has already spent ten to twelve years in small oak, so that the standard remains practically constant. It is made from grenache grapes, grown on the slopes of the Stonyfell Vineyards, above Burnside in the suburbs of Adelaide.

Stonyfell Pale Tawny Port
Made from grenache and shiraz, grown in the Barossa Valley and Stonyfell areas. This wine has been matured for approximately seven years in small oak casks, giving it considerable character and flavour.

Stonyfell Pepita Sherry
A delicate dry Flor, made from pedro ximenez and palomino varieties, grown on the Adelaide plains. After two to three years on Flor it is sweetened slightly with some concentrated old sweet wine. After blending and fortification this wine is held in 500 gallon oak casks to minimize further maturation.

Stonyfell Private Bin Burgundy
A full-flavoured soft wine made from shiraz and tokay, grown in the Angaston and Eden Valley districts; matured in 500 gallon oak casks prior to bottling. This wine is very good drinking when young, because it has a very full, rich, soft, pleasant character; but two or three years bottle age softens it further and builds up the depth of flavour and the bouquet. Always very good value for money.

Stonyfell Private Bin Claret
Made from cabernet sauvignon and shiraz grapes grown in the higher, cooler regions of Angaston, Eden Valley and Light Pass. It shows a good balance of varietal character and tannin and is a wine which will improve with further bottle age. It is matured in Nevers oak puncheons prior to bottling.

Stonyfell Rhine Riesling
A very delicate and completely dry table white wine made from rhine riesling, grown in the cooler ranges of the Eden Valley and Springton area of the Barossa Valley. The grapes are picked at approximately 10

degrees Baumé and undergo prolonged fermentation at quite low temperatures (approximately 3 weeks at 10-12 degrees C). This wine is bottled in July, when it is about three months old.

It has very pleasant, fragrant fruit; a good aromatic nose; a soft, pleasant bouquet with good varietal character and a very clean, crisp, rather acid, finish. Recently, the wine has been a medal winner. In 1970, for example, it won Gold, Silver and Bronze Medals at various shows around Australia.

Stonyfell Rich Port
A reasonably priced, young, ruby port of pleasant character; made to be enjoyed when quite young.

Stonyfell Rosé
Of the so-called Portuguese style, made from grenache and oeillade grapes grown in the Barossa Valley and Langhorne Creek districts. It is slightly sweet with a suggestion of gas and has a crisp, clean finish.

Stonyfell Royal Cream Sherry
A modestly priced, soft, sweet sherry.

Stonyfell Royal Reserve Dry Sherry
A wood-aged, medium priced dry sherry, of considerable fruitiness.

Stonyfell Royal Reserve Muscat
A mellow dessert wine showing the full fruity, 'raisiny', character of the muscatel (muscat gordo blanco) variety.

Stonyfell Royal Reserve Port
A medium-priced tawny port showing a little age and pleasant fruit.

Stonyfell Royal Reserve Sweet Sherry
A typical medium-priced, full-flavoured, sweet dessert wine.

Stonyfell Sparkling Wines
The company sells a range of these traditional wines that have some sweetness: Sparkling Burgundy, Sparkling Hock, Sparkling Moselle.

Sparkling Burgundy has considerable residual sugar. The Sparkling Hock is slightly sweeter than the standard Champagne; and again, the Moselle is sweeter than the Hock.

Stonyfell Spatlese Riesling
Made from rhine riesling grapes which have been left on the vine until early May, thus increasing the depth of flavour and character of the wine, whilst the acid is retained. The wine has good aromatic nose; plenty of flavour; and some residual grape sugar on the middle palate with a clean, crisp finish. This wine will develop further in the bottle.

Stonyfell Special Dry Sherry
A finely-priced young sherry with a little wood age, made from doradillo.

Stonyfell Special Muscat
A modestly-priced dessert wine showing plenty of muscatel (muscat gordo blanco) character.

Stonyfell Special Sweet Sherry
A very popular trade line.

Stonyfell Vermouths
The company makes a range of vermouths, using good base material which is infused with herbs, especially imported from Turin in Italy. The range includes a Dry Vermouth, a Sweet Red Vermouth and a Sweet White Vermouth.

Stonyfell Vintage Burgundy
A soft, round style made from shiraz grapes, grown in various areas. It is a pleasant wine which drinks well when quite young.

Stonyfell Vintage Claret
A blend of shiraz and mataro grape varieties, grown in the Langhorne Creek and Barossa Valley areas. There is slightly higher tannin content in this wine than the Burgundy; although, after wood ageing and further maturation, this is soft and pleasant. A wine that is extremely reasonably priced; it can be drunk when young, but does benefit from a couple of years in the bottle.

Stonyfell Vintage Hock
A light, dry white made from semillon, grown in the Barossa Valley. Controlled fermentation and early bottling ensure a natural freshness and some crisp acidity. A pleasantly flavoured wine.

Stonyfell Vintage Moselle
A delicate dry white made from straight semillon, fermentation being arrested just prior to completion, thus retaining a certain amount of fruitiness, with a trace of residual sugar.

Stonyfell Vintage Port
This wine is now made from shiraz, grown at Langhorne Creek. The style of wine is normally bottled quite early—vintage ports should always be in the bottle fairly young. This one, however, is a late bottled variety, having spent some considerable time in large oak casks kept in a cool cellar. This raises an interesting point. If the wine is kept in small oak in a warm cellar the evaporation is high and the tawny character is hastened. In this case they like to have the big, rather 'blackberry' style of wine, although it is still wood matured. Consequently, it has a much stronger, deeper colour which is much more purple-hued than the wines matured in the traditional

way in wood. It is an interesting style, containing considerable sweetness, and it drinks very well.

Stonyfell White Burgundy
Made from semillon, clare riesling and tokay grapes, grown in the Angaston, Eden Valley and Wilton districts. A very good, full-flavoured wine which remained in contact with the skins for a short time in order to develop more character. It has a soft and smooth middle palate; good flavour; and is a wine that will improve with bottle maturation.

Stonyfell White Frontignac
A dry wine, made entirely from frontignac grapes, grown in the Barossa Valley and River Murray districts. It is separated from the skins immediately after crushing and made under controlled fermentation conditions. The result is an extremely full-flavoured wine with a very aromatic, muscaty nose; extremely big volume of fruit; and yet there is a certain delicacy to the palate for the variety with a clean, crisp finish. This wine is best drunk and enjoyed when quite young.

The Rothbury Estate

This is a rather difficult area for me to discuss. Firstly, Murray Tyrrell and I put this company together, and in only a few years it has developed into something big, from virtually nothing. Secondly, there are no wine names.

The Rothbury Estate is an attempt to make highest quality wines from a single, famous district. Proven varieties have been planted to form the 'bulk' of the wines to be made, although several other famous varieties are also flourishing. These will be used to improve the quality of the final wine if they are good enough. Thus hermitage (shiraz) and semillon are the basic varieties. These have made many great wines in the Hunter Valley, and indications are that the Rothbury Estate vineyards will produce classic material from these types. However, there are also substantial plantings of cabernet sauvignon and chardonnay, and experimental vineyards of sylvaner, gewurztraminer, clare riesling, blanquette, merlot and pinot noir that have been established.

The intention is to make a white and a red wine. Should a particular cask of wine show exceptional quality, a quality that would be lost in a final cuvee, then it may be bottled separately. Otherwise, one red and one white each year. As simple as that. Perhaps strangely to some, these will sell under the same label, one which simply gives the name of the company and the area. It is assumed that people will make up their own minds about the style, and names such as 'burgundy', 'chablis', and 'white burgundy' have been rigidly eschewed. A back label gives details of the particular grape percentages used in each vintage, although this may vary from year to year.

The job of the selection committee (Rudy Komon, Murray Tyrrell, Len Evans, together with the wine-maker, Gerry Sissingh) will be to choose, from all the wines made, those which will best make up the final wine.

Thus, in 1971, although over twenty thousand gallons of wine were made, only two thousand gallons of white wine were considered good enough to bottle under the austere label of the company. No red was selected from the same vintage. Some of the balance of the white and red, pleasant wines of good flavour, were bottled under a 'First Crop' label which will be discontinued when all vines are in full bearing. The rest of the wine was sold in bulk.

The 1971 white of The Rothbury Estate is a delicate, fine-flavoured wine that will take some years of bottle maturation. The nose is fruity and building all the time, the palate clean and beautifully balanced. It is reminiscent of some of the fine Lindeman's Hunter white wines, which is not surprising, since the winemaker, Gerry Sissingh, worked for that company for over ten years.

In 1972 over sixty thousand gallons were produced, including some great whites and good quality reds. The whites included a thousand gallons of a magnificent chardonnay/semillon blend, the grapes being picked and fermented together. This wine was variously matured, in stainless steel, bottle and new oak, in an attempt to determine the best maturation method for a wine of such quality. In addition, a remarkable white, from straight semillon, was made, but this will need some time in the bottle to show its best. It has a full, rich flavour, perfect balance, and a soft, smooth finish. Less than half the white made will be sold under the Estate label.

The reds of 1972 are still maturing, and among them are some high quality casks of Hermitage and some very good Cabernet Sauvignon. About a third of the material may appear to be of sufficient quality to be sold under the Estate label.

Only time will tell how good these wines will be. Sufficient to say that *every* attempt is being made to make great wine, and that the selection committee and Board of The Rothbury Estate will only present those wines under their label that are considered completely worthy of the concept. It is a wonderfully exciting time.

Tolley, Douglas A., Pty Ltd
Tolley's Hope Valley Bianco Dry White Vermouth
Made by the firm at Hope Valley, South Australia, from pedro ximenez grapes, grown in the local vineyards. This wine is infused with imported herbs, and shows good herbal character.

The impressive winery at The Rothbury Estate, Hunter Valley, won the prestigious Blacket Award for architecture in 1970.

Tolley's Hope Valley Bianco Sweet White Vermouth
This wine is golden in colour, and has good balance with a strong herbal character. It is produced from palomino grapes grown at Qualco on the River Murray.

Tolley's Hope Valley Cream Sherry
This sherry is golden to amber in colour with fresh, fruity flavour, made predominantly from muscat gordo blanco, grown at Qualco, and aged in large wooden casks.

Tolley's Hope Valley Dry Sherry
Matured in oak for two years the base material coming from pedro ximenez and palomino, it shows a slightly sweet edge.

Tolley's Hope Valley Frontignac
Full-bodied, soft and round; showing good wood age. Produced from frontignac grapes grown in the Barossa Valley.

Tolley's Hope Valley Medium Dry Sherry
Matured in oak for two years. The base material comes from pedro ximenez and palomino grapes, grown in the Barossa and elsewhere. The sweetness is quite apparent.

Tolley's Hope Valley Moselle
A light, delicate wine with a fresh, flowery flavour, made from riesling grapes grown in the Barossa Valley. Some sweetness is apparent on the middle palate.

Tolley's Hope Valley Muscat
A pleasant dessert wine showing strong varietal character; produced from muscat gordo blanco, grown at Qualco. It is sweet, with a soft, fruity finish.

Tolley's Hope Valley Port
Medium-red to amber in colour; full and fruity, and matured in wood for two years. Made from grenache

grapes, grown at Modbury, just outside Adelaide, in South Australia.

Tolley's Hope Valley Rosso Sweet Red Vermouth
Made from grenache grapes which have been matured in wood for some time, this wine has strong herbal character and a dark red colour.

Tolley's Hope Valley Sauternes
A distinctly sweet, light golden table wine, made from pedro ximenez and riesling grapes, grown at Modbury, in South Australia.

Tolley's Hope Valley Sweet Sherry
Blended from pedro ximenez, grenache and muscat gordo blanco grapes. A sweet dessert wine with a good fruity and aromatic bouquet; gold to amber in colour.

Tolley's Hope Valley White Port
Made from free-run grenache juice, from Modbury in South Australia. It is gold to amber in colour and shows good wood age.

Tolley's Marsala All'uovo
A blend of old aromatic sweet wines, further enhanced in body and style by the addition of specially selected flavourings.

Tolley's Pedare Cabernet Sauvignon
Made from cabernet sauvignon material from the company's Medlands Estate in the Barossa Valley. After delivery to the Hope Valley cellars, nine miles north-east of Adelaide, the grapes are vintaged in a manner ensuring maximum extraction of flavour and character from the skins. After a traditional maturing in old 500 and 1,000 gallon French oak casks for at least two years, the wine is then bottled for further development.

This is a limited edition bottling and is usually in short supply. On the palate it seems to me that the wine also sees a shade of new oak, because this flavour was evident in, for example, the 1968 wine. I like the mint character of the fruit, a typical intense sort of cabernet influence, and I also liked the trace of spiciness that I find on many wines of this company. The wine is well balanced and finishes soft and clean. It drinks quite well now, though it will benefit considerably from further bottle age.

Tolley's Pedare Cabernet Shiraz
A full-bodied dry red showing strong varietal character. Vintaged at the Hope Valley Cellars, it is a blend of twenty percent cabernet sauvignon from the Medlands Estate at Dorrien, and eighty percent shiraz from the company's Tea Tree Gully Estate in the Adelaide foothills. After two years' maturation in 1,000 gallon French oak casks, the wine is bottled and given further ageing prior to marketing.

This is a very pleasant, well-flavoured wine and the cabernet always shows quite well. It has an appealing softness and again a familiar hint of spiciness on the middle palate.

Tolley's Pedare Champagne—Brut
Made from clare riesling grapes grown predominantly in the Clare district of South Australia and bottle fermented under the authentic Methode Champenoise. It is light in colour with a crisp, dry flavour. Bottle ageing on yeast lees is quite evident on the palate.

Tolley's Pedare Champagne—Dry Imperial
Made from clare riesling grapes, predominantly from the Clare district and bottle fermented again under the Methode Champenoise. Light in colour with a fresh, fruity bouquet, it has much the same style as the Brut, but with a trace more liqueuring.

Tolley's Pedare Champagne—Pink
A delicate pink wine made by the Methode Champenoise.

Tolley's Pedare Claret
Selected shiraz grapes from the company's Tea Tree Gully vineyards are used to produce this well-balanced dry red which is matured in old 100 gallon oak casks for two years and then given some more bottle age prior to marketing. This is a lighter style, with a rather firm, clean finish.

Tolley's Pedare Flor Dry Sherry
Light golden in colour with strong Flor character; produced from pedro ximenez grapes from the Hope Valley, and palomino from the Barossa Valley. Matured in small oak, the wine is full on the palate with an exceptionally dry, astringent finish which shows some oak character.

Tolley's Pedare Old Black Label Port
Made from shiraz grapes grown at Medlands Estate at Dorrien and at Tea Tree Gully. A ten-year-old port matured in small wood, including quarter casks, hogsheads and puncheons. There is a good medium to dark red colour, with a deep amber tinge showing through. It is full in flavour with a soft middle palate flavour, and finishes dry.

Tolley's Pedare Old White Label Port
A five-year-old wine made from shiraz grapes grown at Modbury, South Australia, it is matured in small wood.

Tolley's Pedare Pearl
A slightly sweet sparkling wine made in the Barossa Valley.

Tolley's Pedare Red Hermitage

Shiraz (hermitage) grapes from the company's Tea Tree Gully Estate were used to produce this special red. Its distinctive oak flavour is from French Nevers oak puncheons (110 gallon casks) in which it is matured for twelve months, prior to further wood ageing in larger casks. A well-balanced wine showing a good grape tannin flavour with a firm astringent finish.

There is not much of this wine around and it is always at a most reasonable price. Its interesting feature is that the oak is so strong when the wine is young that it really does overcome the varietal character; although the varietal character is quite deep, there is a spiciness which I always see in their big fruit wines, but the oak is unquestionably the dominant flavour factor. I believe that the wine will soften and mature over the years and it will be most interesting to see the style after the wine has at least ten years bottle ageing.

Tolley's Pedare Rhine Riesling

Made from selected rhine riesling grapes from the Modbury district. It has a nice flowery bouquet with a rather full style of flavour, more of the traditional old Australian white style, rather than the elegant flowery kind. A nice soft round wine with a good soft acid finish.

Tolley's Pedare Sparkling Burgundy

Showing some bottle age, light ruby in colour with a pleasant dry finish.

Tolley's Pedare Sparkling Moselle

A slightly sweet wine with a fresh fruity bouquet showing bottle age.

Tolley's Pedare White Burgundy

A blend of rhine riesling and semillon grapes from the 'Austral Estate' at Qualco on the River Murray. The fruit matures a little longer on the vine and is subjected to a warmer ripening period, so the wine produced is full-bodied with a pleasant acid finish, but still retains a fresh bouquet. After maturing in a large 1,000 gallon oak cask for twelve months, the wine is bottled and laid down for a further ageing period.

I feel that this wine has not quite the delicacy one would like to see in this style. Even though the style is basically broad and soft, it still must have finesse. However, this wine is a very big, rich, full-flavoured, full-bodied style that does have a lot of appeal.

Tolley, Scott & Tolley

Traditionally this firm have been top quality brandy makers, but they have undertaken an extensive programme of vineyard production and winemaking.

All manner of new wine equipment has been installed under the ebullient direction of their technical manager, Mr Wolfgang Blass. I have no doubt that in the mid-seventies we shall see some extraordinarily good wines from them.

As yet no wines have been marketed, except to the trade; but I understand it is their intention to set up branches and to distribute their own range of wines throughout the major States. This range will include: Commercial Red, Rhine Riesling, Moselle, Hock, White Burgundy, Sparkling White, Dry, Medium and Sweet Sherry, Port, Champagne, and a limited number of Special Bin Reds.

I look forward, especially, to the latter. I know that Wolfgang Blass makes some very fine Rhine Riesling wines, but he basically specializes in reds. At present, they are building up stocks of red wines which have been made since 1969. The 1969 Cabernet Shiraz, which I have inspected several times—both in wood and bottle—won the Champion Claret in Sydney and Brisbane in 1972. An extraordinarily good wine of magnificent balance of flavour, thoroughly deserving its high award. I have no doubt that some of the wines that have been made in the seventies will do as well. Wolfgang Blass handles both the material and the wood maturation extremely well and he is being backed in every way by the company.

I look forward with great interest to the future when we shall see these red wines on the market.

Toorak Wines

Toorak Brown Muscat

Made from eighty percent black muscatel and twenty percent frontignac grown in the Leeton district of the Murrumbidgee Irrigation Area in New South Wales. The grapes are not crushed until they reach required maturity of 13 degrees Baumé or over, in order to retain the fruity muscat flavour and character.

Toorak Cabernet Sauvignon

Produced entirely from cabernet sauvignon grapes grown in the vineyards of the company at Leeton, it is matured in American oak. This is a wine of full flavour, well-balanced with a firm, clean finish.

Toorak Cabernet Shiraz

A bin dry red vintaged from fifty percent cabernet sauvignon and fifty percent shiraz, selected grapes grown in the company's vineyards at Leeton. It is matured in American oak puncheons to give the wine full character, flavour and style.

Toorak Dry Reds

Made from sixty percent shiraz and forty percent grenache and classified as a light, quaffing wine.

Toorak Sweet Sherry

Made from white hermitage grapes grown in the Leeton district and matured for two years prior to bottling.

The company also makes a full range of other fortified wines, produced from local material.

Tulloch, J. Y., & Sons

Tulloch Glen Elgin Bin 22 Dry White

A vintage wine which comes from various grape varieties, but predominantly a Hunter River riesling (semillon), together with white hermitage. A wine of the broadest style, being round and soft on the middle palate, with a very smooth, soft, pleasant finish.

Tulloch Pokolbin Dry Red

A well-known line developed by Hector Tulloch, a man who did a great deal to promote the Hunter Valley and to promote table wine drinking in general. He avoided using the Burgundy and Claret names on his wines and indeed was always amused by the success of the famous 1954 Private Bin wine, which he produced and which won Gold Medals in both Burgundy and Claret classes in various shows. It is said that from 1957 the Tulloch Pokolbin Dry Red contained some imported material brought in from other districts. I was told that this was done because it would improve the all-round quality of the wine for it was felt that certain of the Hunter characteristics were extremely beneficial to classic wine styles, although the wines lacked in other departments; to 'freshen them up a bit' I was once told. Certainly, the wines, after some years in the bottle, matured to achieve a very nice standard in which the Hunter flavour appears to dominate. I remember drinking the 1954 standard line against the famous Private Bin Pokolbin Dry Red of the same year, with Hector Tulloch many years ago; and Hector said he preferred the lighter wine for everyday drinking. His statement was that the Private Bin Wine was just too big to enjoy all the time.

In years such as 1965 and 1966 the standard line of this wine is very good indeed; the Hunter flavour showing strongly throughout the wine, which has an extremely pleasant varietal and regional nose and flavour, with a smooth, soft finish.

Tulloch Pokolbin Dry Red Private Bin

A famous vintage dry red and a celebrated wine in Australia; made for many, many years by a sturdy, independent family, the Tulloch family, in Pokolbin; members of which, Hector, Keith, Mrs Tulloch (Eileen), did so much to promote wine in Australia and in the Hunter Valley region in particular. The company has now been taken over by Reed Consolidated Industries.

The wine varies from year to year depending on the vintage, but has provided some of the classic soft, fulsome, full-flavoured dry reds of this country. The 1969, for example, a wine of great potential, has a very strong deep colour, an almost minty nose of very fresh aromatic fruit, big Hunter shiraz, then broadens onto the palate into a big, full, rich, mouth filling, flavoursome red. There is much complexity of flavour present and the wine seemed a natural for future development. It has a very soft, pleasant finish.

The 1968 and 1967 wines were somewhat lighter—the 1968 in particular was lighter. There were two 1967 straight bottlings, one from Fordwich and one from Glen Elgin, which took Gold Medals in Young Burgundy Classes. They were sold as straight Pokolbin Private Bin Dry Reds. The 1966 was a great keeper—a wine of full volume, full character, and one that will live for many years and will be classic drinking. The 1965 was a very good wine also; a big wine without, perhaps, complete finesse, but a wine that had very strong Hunter flavour and character and which was very well balanced.

The 1964 I remember as being about the best wine of that vintage. I reviewed the wines one year at the Vintage Banquet in the Hunter District and this wine was among the 1964 Reds on view. It was definitely the outstanding wine of the dinner.

The 1963 was light, again reflecting the year, but with pronounced Hunter Valley character. I don't think it would last for many years but was a wine that was to be enjoyed in the late part of the sixties and early seventies. The 1960, 1961 and 1962 wines weren't great, for the wet years were reflected in the wines. They are not bad wines in the sense that they were undrinkable, but they lacked complexity and character, being thin, and rather uninteresting.

The 1959 was an extremely good wine; round and soft with plenty of flavour, a clean, smooth, soft, lingering finish and after-taste. The 1958 at one time seemed to be fading a bit, the fruit was not big enough and yet, one tastes certain bottles and changes one's mind. Quite recently I tasted a bottle which had a great deal of character, a beautiful finish and a delightful 'smoky' bouquet that augmented the familiar so-called 'sweaty saddle' character of Pokolbin Hunter River Reds.

In 1957 it was hot and all the wines show a degree of tannin. They have good flavour and strong bouquet, but always a very firm finish. The 1956 was a rather unbalanced and hard wine, but the 1955 was most interesting. It wasn't considered a good year, yet the wine was surprisingly pleasant, well-balanced and soft, with a slight touch of the earthy character which is stronger in the fuller wines of bigger years.

The 1954 is one of the most famous Australian wines ever made—a fantastic old red; big and firm, tremendous flavour and nose; sturdy, strong; firm, clean finish; a magnificent wine and one that will still be drinking well in the eighties.

Of the the older vintages, the 1952 was a nice delicate wine, which developed considerable finesse on the middle palate; the 1947 and the 1945 were both big wines that reflected the years. Once I attended a tasting that actually featured some of Tulloch's very old wines—the 1932 was a magnificent wine with a superb bouquet. One that had delicious flavour, there was every small oak character in the wine— although there is no record of what was used. It was a delicious wine and one that still had fine power; I would always pick it as French.

The 1931 I have seen several times. This wine was stored by Thomas Hardy and Sons in their Mile End Cellars in Adelaide in the famous 'Black Hole', a very tiny inner cellar inside the cellar complex. These wines had been bought by Roger Warren, the famous Hardy winemaker and blender many years before and he had kept them in the cellar. So I was privileged to taste the wine on three or four occasions; including the head-wetting of my son Toby, the day after he was born, a day we tasted many of these fabulous Tulloch's range.

Bob Scott opening a cask at 'Glen Elgin' now owned by Reed Consolidated Industries (Photo: A. F. D'Ombrain).

The 1931 was a straightforward, gracious old Hunter. I wrote about it some years ago and said, 'It tasted bloody marvellous—as a magnificent old Hunter in top condition should and that was all there was to it—which is quite enough for me.'

At that tasting we went back to a 1929 Tulloch bottled by Caldwell's which had an incredible flavour of Hunter and Beaune. This wine would undoubtedly fool a host of experts—it was light and yet had intense character and a complex series of taste sensations. It was still living and one could see no reason for it not living for some time yet. All of which proves that the Tulloch Pokolbin Private Bin Dry Red is an outstanding wine and a wine which, at its best, develops for years.

Tulloch Pokolbin Riesling

Made from the Hunter River riesling (semillon) at the 'Glen Elgin' winery of the company in Pokolbin. A wine of pleasant varietal fruit with some softness on the middle palate and a clean, sometimes rather hard finish.

Tulloch Pokolbin Riesling Private Bin

Made predominantly from Hunter River riesling (semillon) and also occasionally containing some chardonnay and verdelho, depending on the year. Sometimes it contains both these varieties backing up the predominant semillon variety used. A well-balanced wine of interesting complexity of flavour and style, with good fruit, again sometimes a rather hard finish.

This wine is highly acceptable as a young wine after bottling but develops with the years into a more full-flavoured style. On my very first visit to the Hunter in 1959 I drank this wine with Hector Tulloch on a very hot day and we had tumblers of the Private Bin Riesling with large blocks of ice in it. The sun beat down on the valley, the wine tasted good and was deliciously cold—the world was a splendid place.

Tyrrell's Vineyards Pty Ltd

Tyrrell's Hunter Valley Blanquette Shiraz

This is Murray Tyrrell's second line of white wine which, being a somewhat unusual style from the Ashman's vineyards in the Hunter Valley, has a great following amongst certain people. The grapes are carefully blended in equal proportions to give a wine that has plenty of flavour and also considerable freshness. This wine takes a certain amount of bottle age with the flavour of the blanquette grapes developing; the freshness being preserved by the white shiraz.

The best of these wines produced are, generally, Vat 3, Vat 20 and Vat 50—Murray Tyrrell having great regard for different vats which have different characters and which usually follow some sort of consecutive pattern in that the wines from the same vineyard are put in much the same cask, year after year. He considers the Vat 50 of 1968 an outstanding wine. I don't enter into the argument because, although Murray is a great friend of mine, I don't like Blanquette very much; indeed, the best Blanquette I saw was one made in the 1972 vintage. To me the flavour of the wine is always rather common; it has plenty of flavour, but it hasn't any great finesse or delicacy to it at all. But many people like this rather forward, fruity style of wine. They like the nose and the straight through flavour of the blanquette, which carries on from the nose and is balanced by the acidity of the shiraz.

Tyrrell's Hunter Valley Dry Reds

In the Hunter Valley this company has long pursued a policy of keeping separate many of the different red wines from different vineyards. Generally they are put in the same vats year after year from the same particular vineyard patches. This is an attempt to produce a continuity of style with the different vats. Of course, this is somewhat offset by the variations in the year.

In 1965 Murray Tyrrell started the system of selecting a number of wines from these vats, which is his Winemaker's Selection. The demand has gone up so much these days and there are so many followers, not only of his wines, but also certain Vat numbers, that he finds it difficult to allocate his Winemaker's Selections. If the wines are not good enough he will blend them with other wines for more commercial purposes, or sell them as other Vats under a simple label.

The reds, which are in great demand (there's never enough of them), are sold while they are actually in the barrel. They are sent to the people who have asked for particular wines as soon as they are bottled. These reds are made from the hermitage or shiraz variety and the body varies from year to year. The flavour ranges from light to full; there's always plenty of it even in light wines; there is a softness on the middle palate; the tannin varies; there is a delicacy and finesse about the wines at all times, and they drink at their best generally after about five or six years bottle ageing. Of course, if they are big years like 1965 and 1966, they will take much longer to mature than that.

For many years in the mid-sixties Vat numbers 12, 11, 5, 9 and 8 were outstanding wines; but it seems that during the last few years the Vats 84 and 85 became dominant. It may be no coincidence that these vats have had some oak staves replaced in their ends. The oak used was new Californian oak which gives a lift to these wines. I believe that unless Hunter wine is made from cabernet sauvignon it does not take too much oak too kindly. Oak is a dominant flavour characteristic which overcomes the Hunter flavour in no mean terms. But a touch of new oak can be a great help and, certainly, the Vats 84 and 85 of the last few years have been extraordinarily good wines. Vat 84 of 1970, Vat 85 of 1968 and Vats 84 and 85 of 1967 are remarkably good wines. The 1969 wines are also good.

A quick look at the years: 1970 was an agreeable year which produced some very good red wines; 1969 a fairly big year; 1968 a very light year; 1967 a medium year; 1966 a huge year—some of the wines have extraordinary character—Vat 9 was the pick of both Murray and myself for many years. Unfortunately it was perhaps bottled too late and consequently picked up a strange character in the bottle which still hasn't gone. In fact, Murray was so disappointed with it that he took it out of the bottle and rebottled it with great success. The wine is now quite outstanding. The Vat 9 came from the same patch of vineyard as the historic 1954, which is celebrated as one of the best Hunter wines ever made.

Other 1966 wines that were outstanding were Vats 67, 10 and 8; but all the wines of that year could take a great deal of age for they were wines that would show great flavour in years to come. Another big year was 1965. The wines perhaps had more austerity in that year—Vats 14, 12 and 70 were brilliant wines. They had a brilliant ruby colour that lasted and lasted and didn't turn at all to the usual brick of the Hunter within the four or five years. Of that year the Vats 5, 7 and 11 were slightly lighter, but the wines turned out very well. I tasted Vat 7 quite recently and it was getting a most generous flavour on the middle palate, of great character. The 1964 was a sort of medium-bodied year. Vat 11 was probably one of the better wines of that year. It drank very well in the late sixties and early into the seventies. I think that if the wine is of a light or medium year there is no point in keeping it for years. It is best to be drunk within five or six years in the bottle.

The early sixties were not very successful. 1963 was a light year, but some very pleasant wines were made. I remember buying Vats 5, 7 and 9 for the Chevron—it seems ages ago now—and those wines were highly drinkable at the end of the sixties. Again Vat 11, which was light with a very pleasant character, was probably the best wine. 1962 was not a good year in the Hunter, yet the Vat 5 won a couple of Gold Medals in shows. It was a light wine but had good flavour and soft tannin, and that definite Hunter earthy quality was there. It was a very well-balanced wine and both nose and flavour developed considerably in the glass. This came from grapes grown on the old vines of the new vineyard, which was planted when Murray was born, nearly fifty years ago. It epitomizes what is supposed to be the Tyrrell style; although personally I find that the Tyrrell style changes from year to year, and very much depends on what the year does.

For wine students here is a brief resume of the tasting we did years ago in which we collected many old Tyrrell wines. These wines were made by both Murray Tyrrell and his uncle, Dan, who died in 1959 at the age of ninety.

1961: Light and inconsequential. 1960: Hard and green, suffering very much from the hail. 1959: Dumb and a little volatile. One great wine. 1958: Big and slightly sweet and of very full flavour. A wine that possibly had a future. 1957: Firm, with a very good flavour, but considerable, rather hard, tannin. The wine would obviously live for years, but would the fruit last? 1956: A light and agreeable wine, typical of the year which was very light. 1955: Also a very wet year and the wine was hard and thin. 1954: Absolutely magnificent, famous wine, famous reputation. rich and full-flavoured, with

wonderful nose, considerable finesse; a wine that I showed overseas visitors again and again; and a wine that they, without exception, thought superb. These people included some of the greatest palates in the world of wine. The question when they came from England was always 'why don't we see these wines back in the U.K.?' The French were equally astonished and you could see them, after the initial shock and making the inevitable comparisons against Bordeaux and Burgundy, just enjoying it. Such was the great charm that it had. 1953: Light and pleasant and very drinkable. 1950: Seemed full of pressings; a very big, dumb wine. 1949: This wine had a slight volatility, but it had a magnificent generous flavour; beautiful balance, very soft in the mouth, and a delightful intensity of character which I enjoyed. And enjoy still, for fortunately a few bottles were saved and occasionally we can try one of these wines. 1948: Very big and full, with tremendous balance and style; another wine of the historic forties, those great hot years that produced wines that will live and live for ever.

I have no doubt the 1965s and 1966s will do much the same thing in the future and maybe some of the 1969s.

In conclusion, I suppose I have drunk as many Tyrrell wines as anyone, with the exception of the winemaker himself and I have done so with considerable pleasure over the years. I find that it is not necessary to keep them for ages and ages, especially the medium years; and even if they are slightly bigger years (short of the biggest years) they do have that gorgeous quality of being able to be enjoyed within two or three years in the bottle. Probably in the future one shall regret drinking them, but the fact is they provide very good drinking at all times.

Tyrrell's Hunter Valley Pinot Chardonnay
A relatively new development, being one hundred percent chardonnay from the carefully matured five acres over the road from Ashman's in front of Murray Tyrrell's house. 1971 was the first time there had been a straight bottling of the variety. Before that, Murray had blended the material available with suitable semillon. The grapes are picked at 10½ degrees Baumé and 7.9 grammes per litre total acid. There was a very heavy precipitation of Potassium Bitritrate and at bottling the acid was down to 6.3 grammes per litre. Fermentation was fairly warm, 21.1 degrees C most of the time; though it did take ten days to ferment right out. Murray Tyrrell feels that because of this fairly warm fermentation the wine settled very quickly by itself and required little final attention.

The chardonnay is difficult to grow in the Hunter for it is extremely susceptible to downy mildew. On the other hand, and to compensate, it matures early—about three weeks before the semillon. The top yield is two tons. It is therefore too costly to produce, unless a top wine is made from it. Missing a lot of the rain that fell in 1971, it was brought in at the stated sugar/acid ratio, which appears to be about the mark for the variety. The flavour is delicious: a delicate, fine, clean flavour that subtly fills the mouth, without any hint of coarseness or roughness. The aroma of the variety is also delicate. One doesn't expect big volumes of fruit from it at this stage. The wine had great flavour when young and did develop some flatness on the middle palate with some bottle age; yet it was a great joy in the mouth—a different sensation altogether, and a quite new sensation in Australia, because the flavour of the chardonnay is most marked. It has, of course, the gorgeous delicacy that professional wine people enjoy so much.

In 1972 the Chardonnay was of enormous quality. It had a bigger, richer flavour; again a very delicate wine of considerable finesse. I would like to see some of this wine put into a sparkling wine because I am quite sure it would provide magnificent drinking after two years on yeast lees. Certainly now, I have little doubt that a new wine style has been evolved that is of great interest and that we shall see some wonderful wines in the future from this variety in the Hunter Valley. The 1972, at the first show in which it was entered, won a Gold Medal (Brisbane, 1972).

Tyrrell's Hunter Valley Pinot Riesling
Until 1971, when he first made a straight bottling of chardonnay, Murray Tyrrell used the chardonnay obtained from the developing vineyard to blend with riesling to make very agreeable wines. The same thing was done in 1972. This was such a good year for white wines all round that the Pinot Riesling blend of that year (which of course is actually a Chardonnay Semillon blend), was a truly outstanding wine that would mature tremendously over the years and pick up wonderful character and balance.

It appears that the winemaker now intends to produce this blend of varieties as well as the single Chardonnay every year. The 1971 Pinot Riesling also won a Gold at Brisbane in 1972.

Tyrrell's Hunter Valley Riesling
These wines are made from semillon which has been called the Hunter River riesling for the last 140 years. There is no point in changing the name now. The Riesling line has shown many changes over the years. Fifteen-twenty years ago the wines were very big, rich, robust Hunters of the so-called old traditional style: lots of flavour, and very golden coloured. I've seen many of them and have always enjoyed them, slightly coarse wines perhaps, but wines of immense flavour and character.

In the early sixties Murray Tyrrell attempted to lighten this style considerably. He picked the grapes much earlier to make very fresh wines and in some cases he made wines that seemed too acid to many of us. Now he seems to have settled on a style which produces wines of great freshness and delicacy with quite abundant flavour; very well made wines of considerable finesse. They drink very well when they are young and also have this 'each-way' character; they mature very well in the bottle and provide splendid drinking with some years age upon them. I think I would go so far as to say that I haven't seen a really poor Tyrrell white wine for several years. If they are not good enough the wines are not bottled and are blended with other material. This means that the wines have a dependability and a consistency which is very good for the wine consumer.

Of the white wines I suppose I prefer Vats 1 and 18. Vat 1 generally wins the top wine of the year award, though I have a sneaking regard for Vat 18, which often appears more delicate to me. Vat 1 of 1972 is superb and (also a Gold Medal in the 1972 Brisbane Show) the 1971 wine was a good wine; the 1970 wine was fairly big; and the 1969 was also a big wine. Many of these wines did very well in shows. They all have an intense flavour that was developing even further in the bottle.

Vat 18 is also very good. I particularly liked the 1969 and 1970 Vat 18s, which were delicious wines of considerable character and style. Incidentally, the Vat 18 comes from the Long Flat Vineyard which is mostly composed of semillon vines planted in 1880 by Murray's grandfather. The vines are five feet apart in rows eight feet wide. The soil is composed of a light loam sandy topsoil that goes straight into podzolic clay. This is very little to do with the Long Flat Dry Red, which is one of the company's

The vintage comes in at Hungerford Hill in the Hunter Valley.

'Chateau Tahbilk' winery, Vic. The vineyard was established in 1860 and is now owned by the Purbrick family. The winery and cellars have been classified by the National Trust of Australia as buildings of historical and architectural interest.

commercial wines, being a blend of wines from other districts.

For the technically minded, these wines are generally picked at 10-11 degrees Baumé, the total acid is something over 7, perhaps nearly 8, grammes per litre; and after fermentation total acid comes down to about 6 grammes per litre. Obviously then the wines are light, delicate, rather soft and with all the care and attention that goes into them they finish very fresh and delicate; yet with very deep flavour in them.

Valencia Wines

Valencia Cellar Claret
A flagon red; dry, full-flavoured, with some tannin on the finish which is made to be sold and enjoyed young and fresh.

Valencia Chef's Choice Cookin' and Sippin' Claret
This is the same style as the Cellar Claret. It is claimed it is ideal at barbecues for discerning cooks. Certainly the title must be one of the most extraordinary throughout Australia.

Valencia Cream Sherry
A blended wine, based on muscat gordo blanco grapes; smooth and sweet with pleasant 'raisiny' flavour.

Valencia Crema Marsala All'uova
This full-flavoured dessert wine is aged in wood, and infused with the delicate extracts of egg, coffee, cinnamon, cocoa and vanilla. It is very popular as an after dinner liqueur.

Valencia Dry Sherry
Made from pedro ximenez grapes; a rich, full flavoured sherry with generous flavour and a touch of residual sugar.

Valencia Dry Vermouth (French)
This pale amber coloured wine is spiced with herbs to give a true vermouth flavour.

Valencia Light Port
A pale wood-matured port; blended to suit local palates; aged in wood for three years; made from predominantly hermitage (shiraz) grapes.

Valencia Malbec Rosé
A fresh, fragrant table wine with an appealing pink colour, a round and smooth palate. It has a nice clean acid finish and quite a pleasant varietal taste, and is made entirely from malbec grapes.

Valencia Manzilla Flor Sherry
Produced from pedro ximenez and palomino grapes, this sherry is made on the Flor process and matured in small casks.

Valencia Medium Sherry
An 'each-way' wine of some sweetness, made from palomino and pedro ximenez grapes.

Valencia Muscat
Produced from non-irrigated muscat gordo blanco grapes grown in deep loam, it is a wine of considerable varietal character.

Valencia Perry Lakes Burgundy
A full-bodied dry red with an appealing fruity bouquet and rather full, rich flavour that has a soft finish. It is produced entirely from hermitage (shiraz) grapes.

Valencia Perry Lakes Chablis
A straw-coloured, dry white table wine; rather full bodied, with a very pleasant, fresh, fruity flavour. The acidity is medium. This can be a very good drink, well chilled on a hot day, and it has a more pungent flavour than a lot of the more delicate wines of South Australia. It is very well made and the rather full character is pleasant and mouth filling.

Valencia Perry Lakes Claret
A dry red table wine with well balanced acidity and body and a firm tannin finish. It is produced from hermitage (shiraz) grapes.

Valencia Perry Lakes Moselle
A nice soft, fruity style, produced from semillon grapes grown in the Swan Valley. It is a pleasant, full-flavoured wine, with a soft acid finish and having some slight residual sugar on the middle palate.

Valencia Perry Lakes Riesling
A full-flavoured dry white table wine, made from rhine riesling grapes grown in the Valencia vineyard in the Swan Valley. A fuller style of rhine riesling; with a round, rich middle palate and plenty of varietal fruit.

Valencia Reserve Port
A wood-matured port produced from hermitage (shiraz) grapes, grown in rich loam in the Swan Valley and matured for five years in small casks before bottling.

Valencia Rich Port
A wood-matured port produced from hermitage (shiraz) and grenache grapes.

Valencia S.V. 170
A light dry red; youthful, with good flavour and balance. Produced from hermitage (shiraz) grapes grown on loam over red clay in the Swan Valley. This wine shows development of bouquet and has a soft tannin finish. It is matured in oak casks for twelve months before bottling.

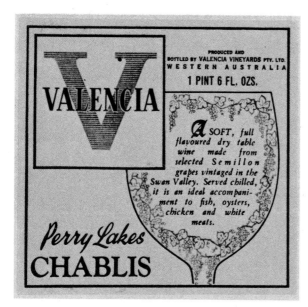

PRODUCED AND
BOTTLED BY VALENCIA VINEYARDS PTY. LTD.
WESTERN AUSTRALIA

1 PINT 6 FL. OZS.

A SOFT, full flavoured dry table wine made from selected Semillon grapes vintaged in the Swan Valley. Served chilled, it is an ideal accompaniment to fish, oysters, chicken and white meats.

VALENCIA

Perry Lakes
CHABLIS

Valencia Sauternes
A rich, generous, sweet wine, with considerable depth of bouquet and a rather full flavour, made from a blend of semillon, muscat gordo blanco and grenache grapes.

Valencia Sweet Sherry
A blend of pedro ximenez and muscat gordo blanco grapes. It is aged in wood for two years; a smooth and sweet sherry.

Valencia Sweet Vermouth (Italian)
An Italian-type sweet vermouth, pale amber in colour; considerably sweet, with a smooth, appealing taste.

Valencia White Port
Produced from pedro ximenez and semillon grapes, this port is smooth, rich and fruity.

Waikerie Co-operative

Waikerie Co-operative Rhine Riesling
This is a good wine made by Vince Berlingieri, the energetic Production Manager of the company, who has only been with them since 1970, but who has already made a considerable impact. Traditionally the Waikerie Co-operative supplied all sorts of standard wines to the trade. In the last few years bottling under the firm's name has begun and a bottle trade has been established.

The Rhine Riesling is typical of the advances made by this company. The 1972 wine was of very good fruit and character with a pleasant fruity nose, clean palate and crisp finish. It was produced from grapes picked at the estate of Mr F. G. H. Solente.

Waikerie Co-operative Ruby Port
A blend of two medal winning ports—a 1970 Shiraz Port, which won a Bronze Medal in Victoria and another at the Royal Perth Show; with the 1971 Shiraz Port, which won a Silver Medal at the Royal Perth Show.

This is a well-balanced wine of pleasant fruitiness and a clean spirit finish.

Waikerie Co-operative Vintage Port
A rich full-flavoured wine, made from shiraz grapes which are harvested at full maturity.

Waldeck Wines

Waldeck Bi-Centenary Claret
A full-bodied, dry red, especially selected to mark the historic celebration 1770-1970. The well-rounded qualities of this full-flavoured wine have been balanced by new French oak in the first year. The grapes used were shiraz grown in the Swan Valley of Western Australia.

Waldeck Bin A.45 Shiraz
A fine light dry red of the claret style showing prominent acid and persistent tannin which is characteristic of the Swan Valley. These qualities have been balanced by oak used in the first year.

Waldeck Bindoon Burgundy
Produced from grapes grown exclusively at the Bindoon vineyard of the company. A lighter style of wine; round, soft and smooth.

Waldeck Bindoon Shiraz
A full-bodied dry red, made from shiraz grapes grown on the Bindoon vineyard where the soil is loam, ironstone over a clay subsoil.

This wine has a most distinctive regional character which is entirely different from the famous Swan Valley dry red style. Bindoon Shiraz 1971 won Gold Medals at Brisbane and Melbourne and Silver Medals at Adelaide and Perth Royal Shows that year. It was a wine of considerable fruit; well-balanced, with a very clean, well-made style that has a most agreeable flavour. A wine of obvious maturing potential.

Waldeck Cabernet Hermitage Claret
Produced from cabernet sauvignon and shiraz varieties and aged in oak, including a little ageing in new French oak. This wine has a most distinctive character; well-balanced and with a soft but firm tannin finish. The 1968 was a celebrated red that won the award for the best Western Australian table wine of that year.

Waldeck Chablis
Produced from semillon mainly, with a little chasselas added; the result is a light, crisp, rather pleasant wine with a flinty finish.

Waldeck Claret
A light, crisp red wine made from shiraz and grenache, and sold only in flagons.

Waldeck Cream Sherry
Made from pedro ximenez and sultanas, with a little muscat gordo blanco added to give a fruity lift to the wine.

Waldeck Dry Sherry
A soft, clean, pleasant wine made from semillon and pedro ximenez.

Waldeck Dry White—Hock/Riesling Style
This style is made from semillon, blended with sultanas, and is sold only in flagons.

Waldeck French Vermouth
To make this wine, dry sherry is used as a base, plus various herbs and flavours.

Waldeck Hermitage Claret
A fruity light red made entirely from shiraz, and sold only in flagons.

Waldeck Italian Vermouth
In this vermouth sweet sherry is used as a base, plus various imported herbs.

Waldeck Liqueur Muscat
Made from extremely ripe muscat gordo blanco grapes picked at 23 degrees ·Baumé and stored in old English oak for fifteen years.

Waldeck Marie Rosé
Made from grenache grapes grown in the ·Swan Valley. It is a light and fruity wine. Named after the wife of the present winemaker.

Waldeck Marsala All'uovo
A very sweet Mistelle made from pedro ximenez plus imported Italian essences to give a rich, full flavour, which is very popular.

Waldeck Moselle
Made from semillon, the fermentation being arrested at· 1/2 degrees Baumé to produce a smooth, slightly sweet table wine.

Waldeck Port
A ruby port made from shiraz and grenache grapes grown in the Swan Valley.

Waldeck Rhine Riesling
Made entirely from rhine riesling grown at Waldeck's 'Caversham' vineyard on gravelly loam over a clay subsoil. This has produced a soft, full-flavoured white table wine.

Waldeck Romany Claret
Named after the property 'Romany' at Bindoon. A light-bodied Claret made from sixty percent shiraz and forty percent grenache. This wine has something of the subtle bouquet of the grenache, combined with the firm but soft tannin of the shiraz. The property 'Romany' was named after a ticket-of-leave man of that name who, when given his freedom in the middle of the nineteenth century, settled in the area.

Waldeck Sauternes
Made from semillon grapes that have ripened very well; the fermentation being arrested to leave some residual sugar on the palate.

Waldeck Sweet Muscat
Made from muscat gordo blanco, a large proportion of which comes from Bindoon.

Waldeck Vin Rose Sec
Grenache grapes are used entirely in this wine which is well-balanced and has a crisp and acid finish.

Waldeck White Burgundy
Made from semillon and white tokay grapes grown in the Swan Valley. This district is renowned for its soft white burgundy styles and this wine is extremely well made with a full, round flavour and soft, pleasant finish. It has considerable nose. The 1970 vintage won several awards at shows, including a Gold Medal at Melbourne Royal Show.

Waldeck White Frontignac
Made from the frontignac variety, which has a most distinctive grape character. When young, the wine has a very strong aromatic varietal bouquet and a light fresh palate. With age the flavour and bouquet build up considerably and the wine becomes much broader and the finish softer.

Wilsford Wines

Wilsford Burgundy
A full-bodied dry red made from shiraz grapes, lightened with a small proportion of carignane. These grapes are grown on the non-irrigated, red hillside soils of the Lyndoch Valley in South Australia and are picked when quite ripe. The wine is matured for two years in oak before bottling and then has further bottle age before being released for sale.

Wilsford Claret
A fresh, light to medium-bodied dry red wine made from shiraz, carignane and mataro grapes, picked early enough to ensure the fresh character that the

winemakers are looking for. It is bottled earlier than the Burgundy.

Wilsford Frontignac

A liqueur dessert wine of the brown muscat style, made entirely from the quality frontignac grape. The aromatic flavour is preserved by the addition of grape spirit before fermentation proceeds too far. The wine aged in oak, becomes very mellow, and has a very nice, soft, agreeable wood-acid-spirit finish.

Wilsford Hock

A light, fresh white wine—completely dry; made from semillon and palomino grapes.

Wilsford Lyndoch Rosé

A light, delicate dry red made from grenache and mataro grapes.

Wilsford Lyndoch Sauterne

A light, sweet table wine made from semillon and tokay grapes that have reached a high maturity at picking time. This shows in the golden colour of the wine and the smooth taste and finish.

Wilsford Marsala

A rich velvety liqueur wine, highly aromatic, with imported ingredients added to mature red wine.

Wilsford Moselle

Made from semillon grapes from the company's own vineyards with a little of the palomino variety added. It has some residual sugar on the palate and is bottled fairly early to maintain freshness.

Wilsford Muscat

A dessert wine made from muscat gordo blanco grown in the River Murray district. The aromatic flavour is balanced with a sufficient degree of natural sweetness and the wine is aged for three years before being bottled.

Wilsford Riesling

A rather light crisp wine, quite dry; made from clare riesling and semillon grapes grown in the Lyndoch Valley and carefully made in small lots to achieve as much delicacy as possible. It is stored in cool underground tanks for eighteen months so the wine gains bottle age before being marketed.

Wilsford Sherries

Made from pedro ximenez and palomino grapes grown on sandy loams at Lyndoch and Williamstown. After maturing in oak hogsheads, the base sherries are blended for uniformity and type.

The Cream Sherry is finished off with a very old liqueur wine. The whole range, in degrees of sweetness, will satisfy most palates. The wines range from Dry Sherry, through Medium Sherry to Sweet Sherry and, finally Golden Cream Sherry.

Wilsford Tawny Port

Well-ripened grenache and shiraz grapes give richly-coloured and flavoured juice which after partial fermentation has grape spirit added to it to maintain most of the natural sweetness and fruity character of the varieties. This wine is wood matured. The company also markets an Old Port, which has a much longer time in oak casks.

Wilsford Vermouth

For this vermouth a sweet base wine is used, infused with imported Italian herbs.

Woodley Wines

Woodley's Amber Medium Dry Sherry

An amontillado-style dry sherry, made from pedro ximenez, it exhibits some sweetness on the palate.

Woodley's Burgundy

A vintage wine made predominantly from shiraz, with some blending of mataro and grenache grapes. It has a full, soft, round palate and follows the traditional Australian burgundy style. For part of its life before bottling, maturation is carried out in small casks and it is normally bottled about two years after vintage. It is a full-flavoured wine, but soft and agreeable on the palate. While it may be enjoyed young, it undoubtedly will improve with further bottle ageing.

Woodley's Cabinet Sherry

A full-bodied, dry sherry, this is a blended wine containing some amount of Flor. It is made principally from pedro ximenez grapes.

Woodley's Chablis

A dry white wine made from semillon, exhibiting the clean, slightly acid character of the traditional style. Of somewhat less bouquet than is found in a Riesling, but showing pleasant character on the palate with a clean acid finish.

Woodley's Cream Sherry

A sherry of medium sweetness, golden in colour, and made from palomino grapes.

Woodley's Dry Fino Flor Sherry

A high quality, very dry sherry, made by the Flor process. It is almost bone dry.

Woodley's Est

Est is a very old label from Woodley Wines, and for a long period this was Woodley's best seller; and indeed it was one of the most popular wines in Australia. Est's descriptive label recalls the story of Baron Fugger, who set out from Rome—sending before him his servant to sample the wines of the country. The servant was to indicate his choice by chalking on the gates of the hostel 'Est'. At the Monastery of Montefiascone he found a wine of such excellence that he enthusiastically chalked 'Est! Est! Est!'. The Baron, upon his arrival, heartily agreed and settled at Montefiascone, willing upon his death his fortune to the makers of this Est—on the condition that each year one barrel of the wine should be emptied over his grave. (Est is from the Latin, meaning 'It is'.)

Woodley's Est is in the traditional style—a light sweet wine made from the muscat gordo blanco grape.

Woodley's Fino Bianco Vermouth

A traditional Bianco Vermouth, golden in colour and of quite high Baumé. The herbs used are not as strong as those used in the making of the heavier Sweet Vermouth. The grape used to produce the basic wine is palomino.

Woodley's Fino Dry Vermouth

A light dry vermouth, not of great age, retaining the freshness of the herbs. The basic wine is comparatively neutral with very little sweetness and some acidity. Its outstanding feature is its comparative delicacy in both its basic wine character and the background of selected herbs. The grape variety used is the doradillo.

Woodley's Fino Sweet Vermouth

A vermouth of several years age. The grape variety of the basic wine is pedro ximenez. It is of quite high Baumé and with the years spent maturing in wood, attains a full-bodied character and flavour. The character of the herbs is strongly evident, but well-married with the wine.

Woodley's Gold Label Champagne

Made by the traditional Methode Champenoise; the base wine being of clare riesling and tokay grapes. There is some slight sweetness on the palate.

Woodley's Golden Muscat

A full-bodied wine of medium sweetness; soft and light in colour. It is aged in wood for some years.

Woodley's Hock

A clean dry white wine with some acid apparent; it is slightly astringent but well-balanced. This wine is made from the semillon variety.

Woodley's Liqueur Muscat

This muscat is slightly less aged than the Golden Muscat, but is matured in wood and a little lighter in colour.

Woodley's Moselle Bin L

A reasonably delicate wine, quite full of flavour on the middle palate and somewhat sweet.

Woodley's Old Chimney Claret

The Old Chimney label commemorates the stone chimney standing on the hill near Glen Osmond. The chimney was used in the mid-1800s in the smelting of the ore taken from the silver-lead mines then operating about the Glen Osmond foothills, south of Adelaide. The chimney has been proclaimed by the National Trust as being of historical interest. It can be seen as the traveller leaves the Adelaide suburbs on the road to Melbourne, just above the tollgate near Glen Osmond. It lies approximately half a mile south of the cellars of Woodley Wines. The Old Chimney label has been adopted for two good quality table wines.

The Claret is predominantly of the shiraz variety with sometimes a touch of mataro added. It has good flavour and a clean, dry, firm finish.

Woodley's Old Chimney Riesling/Hock

This is the other wine which bears the Old Chimney label. It is a blend of riesling and semillon grapes, and has a fresh character and a clean acid finish.

Woodley's Old Woodley Port

A high quality tawny port marketed at fifteen years of age. Maturation is carried out in small casks. This wine has limited availability.

Woodley's Osma Glen Green Ginger Wine

A very old label of the company and a very old recipe. Three flavours are blended into the neutral basic wine which is normally made from either pedro ximenez or palomino.

Woodley's Queen Adelaide Claret

The Queen Adelaide label is reserved for some of the high quality wines of the company. It is named after Queen Adelaide, wife of Henry IV, whence the City of Adelaide got its name. The wine is principally made from shiraz grapes grown in the Clare and McLaren districts and in the Barossa Valley. Most vintages are blended with some small amount of mataro and part of the life of the wine before bottling is spent in French or American oak casks. However, the oak character of the wine is carefully controlled and is not overstrong. Bottling is usually about two years from vintage.

The first Queen Adelaide Claret was from the 1953 vintage and most vintages since have been represented. The wine is usually full fruited, rather full-bodied, with a clean, crisp, astringent finish; and greatly benefits from some bottle age.

Woodley's Queen Adelaide Riesling

A high quality dry white which is a blend of rhine riesling and clare riesling grapes, both grown in the Barossa Valley. The wine is made under controlled temperatures under pressure fermentation conditions and bottled shortly after making. Whilst very drinkable at an early age, the makers prefer to see it acquire some bottle maturation.

This wine first appeared with the 1961 vintage and the makers claim that the wine is still very sound and enjoyable after eight or nine years bottle age. Some vintages exhibit a spritzig characteristic.

Woodley's Red Label Frontignac
A dessert wine of fairly high sweetness, it is very smooth and has a rich golden colour. It is made principally from the frontignac variety grown in the Upper Murray area of South Australia. This wine is full-bodied with excellent flavour.

Woodley's Reserve Port
A quality tawny port aged in small wood, the blend contains ports aged from eight to ten years. A heavy, full-bodied wine with some amount of spirit noticeable on the palate.

Woodley's Riesling
A clean, slightly acid wine, but exhibiting a full riesling character both on the palate and in the bouquet. It is made from specially selected clare riesling grapes grown in the upper Murray areas of South Australia.

Woodley's St Adele Claret
A very old label of the company, St Adele Claret has been marketed for well in excess of twenty years. It is vintage wine, principally made from grenache grapes grown in the McLaren Vale area of South Australia. Grenache from this area is a high quality grape, yielding quite good colour and flavour. Each vintage contains some amount of shiraz, also grown in the McLaren Vale area. The wine is matured in wood for two years.

Woodley's Silver Sherry
The silver label is a very old one used by the company for several years on both the dry and sweet sherry. Both sherries are aged in wood.

Woodley's Sparkling Wines
The company sells two sparkling wines, both of which are fermented in the traditional way in the bottle. The Sparkling Burgundy is made from high quality shiraz grapes and is almost dry. The Sparkling Hock is made from a blend of clare riesling and semillon and has some sweetness.

Woodley's Tawny Port
A full-bodied dessert wine made from a blend of shiraz and grenache grapes and normally aged for four to five years in wood.

Woodley's Three Roses Sherry
A quality sherry of high Baumé with some years ageing in wood. This wine is made from a blend of three grape varieties: frontignac, muscatel (muscat gordo blanco) and shiraz. It is a very full-flavoured wine, full-bodied and quite smooth on the palate. Some part of its life is spent maturing in small wooden casks. It is marketed as a speciality line, above the usual price range of sweet sherries.

Woodley's Top Royal Port
A very old label of the company and a good standard port made from a blending of shiraz and grenache.

Woodley's V.O. Dessert Wines
The company makes three wines in this range: an Invalid Port, which is a light dessert wine four to five years old and matured in wood; Dry Sherry, which is a good standard dry sherry of the amontillado style, aged in wood four to five years; and Sweet Sherry, made from the palomino grape.

Wybong Estate Wines
Dr Bob Smith, in the Upper Hunter district of New South Wales, has yet to achieve his winemaking destiny or to arrive at a definite style. His winery is constructed from an old jail which he bought, pulled down and rebuilt on the site.

In 1971 he produced a white which has a most definitive character, but the 1972 wines were much better. He made two whites; one, a free run semillon which was cold fermented, and the second a combined free run and pressing wine. The free run was a very good, clean, flavoursome wine. The red wine of 1972 is predominantly shiraz with a small amount of cabernet and mataro. The wine was subjected to various oak treatments to help the ebullient Bob Smith achieve his winemaking destiny.

Wynn, S., & Co.

Wynn's Boronia Marsala All'uova
A liqueur wine blended from aged wines, Italian herbs and egg, to a secret formula.

Wynn's Boronia White
A white Marsala, flavoured with fruit and herbs.

Wynn's Coonawarra Estate Cabernet Hermitage
Due to the peculiarities of the weather during the 1969 vintage—this was the year in which the rains came half-way through vintage—the company gathered in the cabernet sauvignon at the same time as the hermitage and vintaged them together. For the first time (and it may never occur again) they have produced a Cabernet Sauvignon/Hermitage.

It is a balanced wine of very interesting character and with a deep rich colour. The twenty percent cabernet sauvignon in the blend comes through quite clearly, giving an added dimension of finesse and elegance to the whole wine; and the hermitage part is not as full-flavoured as usual, which heightens the cabernet. The wine was matured in big wood—500s—for something over twelve months, and then bottled. In spite of this lack of time the big wood character is quite evident.

Over all, the wine is very elegant—austere if you prefer. It has considerable finesse; a dry clean firmness on the back of the tongue and, although light, it will undoubtedly benefit from bottle age.

Wynn's Coonawarra Estate Cabernet Sauvignon

This is by far the most famous of the Wynn's wines. There is no doubt that David Wynn in particular, did a great deal to establish the fame of Coonawarra, fame which Bill Redman (the grand old patriarch of the Redman family) had long before established in the minds of a select few. His wines were unquestioned for their quality. But David Wynn was the man who really (commercially) put Coonawarra on the map.

This wine is made from a straight cabernet sauvignon grown in the area by the company and provides interesting variation for the grapes are grown on red and black soils. Indeed, it would be most interesting to see if within the company the wines varied before blending. One wonders also how long the wines will live. The company has been making Cabernet Sauvignon since the early fifties and yet in some cases wines which have been brought to the table from those early vintages still appear immature.

The 1968 has all the marks of a top Cabernet from the company. It has extremely good varietal fruit, a deep colour, a strong berry nose and sturdy flavour, yet the wine still has finesse and considerable elegance; and a smooth, but firm, finish. No doubt this wine will take considerable bottle age—how long one wouldn't know—and in that time the nose will build up into a definite fragrance; the character will richen on the palate; and the typical cedar-like finish will appear.

The 1967 was a lighter wine; a softer, rounder wine on the middle palate; and a wine that would appear to be maturing earlier. The 1966 was a very good wine: full-flavoured, well balanced, and again a wine that needed at least ten years in the bottle before you start to decide when you are going to drink it.

The 1965 seemed to me to be rather unbalanced. I have seen several bottles of this at different times and they seem to have changed. Again I wonder if this is the method of maturation of certain places. Certainly it had a great robust character and style, but it seemed to want to come together and it hasn't done this yet. Maybe in the future this will be a wine to watch. Certainly it needs a long time to settle down properly, to throw a crust and then to develop its own character.

WYNNS
COONAWARRA ESTATE
CLARET
CABERNET SAUVIGNON—HERMITAGE
VINTAGE 1969

AUSTRALIAN WINE 26 FL OZ

The 1964 was a pleasant soft, light wine which was very well put together. It had a smooth, lingering finish, a rounded style and one would sense this wine coming forward quickly, say like the 1967. There was no wine in 1963.

The 1962 was a big wine with strong flavour, but rather heavy and slightly unbalanced; it still had a long way to go. I feel this wine has a great future.

The 1959 was another big wine, having great depth of flavour, a lot of extra fullness to it and beautiful balance; a wine of considerable finesse. I like this wine very much and look forward to its future.

The 1958 was a rounder, softer style, with a more floral nose; a smooth palate; and a clean, dry finish —without that aggressive tannin that the wine sometimes has. Certainly the 1957 had it. It remained hard for years; but eventually softened into austerity —and into a softer, delicate style of great flavour and complexity, which retained considerable firmness on the back of the palate.

I loved the 1954 wine; it had great flavour, and was beautifully put together. Over the years it developed enormous fragrance, and is a wine that, unquestionably, will live for years.

This line is a most interesting one—a line that I still cannot finally make up my mind about. Undoubtedly there are wines of great character in it; undoubtedly they are wines that will live for years. I don't think that we have had time yet to decide on the complete destiny of the line.

Wynn's Coonawarra Estate Hermitage

Made from hermitage grapes, grown at the Estate and matured in medium-sized oak casks for approximately two years before bottling. After some time in bottle, the young wine attains a nose of some complexity; a deep, rather full, rich palate and a firm tannin finish. Although the makers claim that it can be drunk when quite young, I think this is taking a bit of commercial liberty, for undoubtedly it needs a great deal of age. Fortunately, the wines don't suffer from the volatility that was evident in some of the earlier bottlings. This acetic acid volatility was caused by the fact that the casks were ullaged slightly to allow the malolactic organism to get to work, so they ran a risk at the same time of being affected by the acetic acid bacteria. Now this organism, to induce the malolactic, can actually be seeded into the wine and so there is no longer need for the ullage; hence, no volatility.

The Hermitage line has been variously labelled Hermitage and Claret. Recently, I enjoyed a 1958 Claret which had a tremendous volume of flavour; very good style; was well put together; elegant and had considerable finesse; and with a lovely soft, full palate—a wine of tremendous distinction. On the other hand there were wines like the hard wine of 1962 and the volatile wine of 1963—which really did no justice to the name.

At their best, these wines have tremendous character—at their worst, they can be pedestrian. The 1966 Hermitage had considerable flavour and style and still has a future before it. I liked the wine when young and I think it is going to develop very well. The 1967 was a light wine and a wine which, although of good flavour, did not appear to have the cellaring future ahead of it.

Wynn's Coonawarra Estate Rhine Riesling
This was first made in 1968 and there was quite an interesting story behind the making of that vintage. The grapes were picked on March 27th, when the sugar/acidity ratio was correct. Picking began very early in the morning and the grapes were crushed as soon as they came in. The must went into an open fermenting tank that had been fitted with stainless steel draining slats and the drained juice was pumped into a wine tanker that was standing by. By the end of the day the tanker was full. It travelled overnight to Melbourne, where the juice was transferred through refrigeration to lower the temperature and to closed stainless steel storage. It was seeded with yeast culture and held at 10 degrees C for the whole of the thirty-one days it took to ferment out. Then it was racked, chilled and fined; racked again off its heavy tartar deposit, then allowed to return to normal temperature and immediately bottled. The whole thing took eight weeks from grape to bottle.

It is a very pleasant wine with a delicate, fragrant perfumed nose and a clean, fresh palate. I like the acid on the finish, which was clean and slightly firm. In fact the whole wine reminded me of the true Mosel style—not the sugary, lolly wonders—but the real, austere Mosel wines.

The 1969 was a good wine, as was the 1970 which was a fresh, elegant, delicate, clean, fragrant wine, showing extremely good fruit and character. It will be interesting to see how the style develops in the future. There is no question among professional wine people that Coonawarra will be able to produce classic Rhine Riesling wines and recent plantings of the variety tend to confirm that companies are most interested in growing the variety in the district.

Wynn's Estate Aged Port
Made from a blend based on the touriga grape variety, grown at the Wynn's Yenda Estate in the Riverina district of New South Wales. This wine has considerable age and therefore is beautifully mellow with a true, clean spirit finish.

Wynn's Estate Claret
Shiraz grapes grown at 'Modbury Estate' have been selected for this wine which has been matured for two years in small oak casks to complement the distinctive characteristics of the grape variety. A pleasant, soft wine which makes for very reasonable easy drinking.

Wynn's Estate Cinsaut Rosé
Grown at the 'Modbury Estate' in the Adelaide foothills, the cinsaut grapes are picked early for fresh acidity. The free run juice is separated from the skins for light colour and tannin and fermented under controlled conditions to give plenty of delicacy and freshness. It is a wine without great depth of character, but it is very well made and put together and drinks very easily.

Wynn's Estate Dry Flor Sherry
A distinctive Flor Sherry made from palomino grapes grown at the 'Modbury Estate'. The wine is kept under Flor at Wynn's Romalo Cellars in small oak casks and the traditional Spanish Solera system is used.

Wynn's Estate Medium Sherry
Doradillo from the 'Modbury Estate' is the grape variety used for this wine. The wine is matured in small oak casks for some considerable time and then slightly liqueured, resulting in a true amontillado style.

Wynn's Estate Sweet Sherry
A luscious wine made from pedro ximenez grapes, ripened to their full sweetness, at the 'Modbury Estate'. After many years of oak maturation, this sherry has achieved typical oloroso characteristics.

Wynn's Modbury Estate Moselle
Produced from a blend of semillon and riesling, picked early in the vintage to achieve light freshness. This delicate wine has the best characteristics of the style and is clean, with some residual sugar.

AUSTRALIAN WINE 26 FL OZ

WYNNS
MODBURY ESTATE
MOSELLE

WYNN WINEGROWERS LTD

E2003

Wynn's Modbury Estate Riesling

Made from rhine riesling grapes, picked young for lively acidity and fermented under controlled temperature conditions. The resulting wine is crisp and has retained the typical flowery character of the grape variety, with the traditional clean, crisp finish.

Wynn's Modbury Estate Semillon (Sauternes).

Made from a selection of late-picked semillon grapes left on the vines to develop their full sweetness. The controlled temperature fermentation technique is used to produce this luscious, honeyed wine which, although it has considerable sweetness, still finishes clean and dry.

Wynn's Modbury Estate White Burgundy

A unique full-bodied wine made from semillon. The 'Modbury Estate' is located on the lower western slopes of the Mount Lofty Range, its vineyards are gently undulating and protected from the cold of the high levels of the range and from the hot summer conditions of the nearby plains. They comprise 561 acres of contour planted vines in the Adelaide foothills, only 13 miles from the G.P.O., at an elevation of 550 to 700 feet above sea level. The soils vary between red loam over limestone topsoils, to chocolate loam over quartzite and ironstone and rubble which makes it possible to cultivate a wide range of grape varieties suitable for producing high quality wines.

I like the White Burgundy because it has plenty of broad, clean flavour; almost a nuttiness in its

flavour and a very smooth, soft finish. It is a wine which develops very well in the bottle and is sold at most reasonable price.

Wynn's One Gallon Wine Casks

The company is blending a special range of wine for this very interesting package called Wine Casks which are very fairly priced. The grapes have been grown on the estates of the company at Modbury in South Australia and Yenda in the Riverina.

The Claret is a very pleasant type of wine with a shiraz/grenache blend nose: reasonably fruity; well-balanced, with a clean, soft finish; with some tannin and acid apparent and a hint of firmness on the back of the palate.

The Burgundy is a mellow, soft red wine, blended from shiraz grapes; a wine of soft, fruity style that appealed to me very much as a quaffing wine.

The Moselle is quite an impressive wine, made from semillon grapes with a pleasant touch of crisp, natural sweetness. I like the style—pleasant, light, ordinary, clean—it is good value.

The Riesling I thought was a little overdone and I liked it least of all. Obviously it is popular, but it did not appeal to me because it was rather fat and coarse. There was a little too much of a muscat character about it, which tended to dominate the semillon content. On the other hand, if you like plenty of aromatic fruit in a fairly unsubtle way, you will enjoy this wine.

The Rosé I found to be a light, crisp wine, made from grenache. It was a pleasant wine without fault, although of no great character; clean, fruity, pleasant, with a soft clean acid finish.

The fortified wines include Dry Sherry, which is a quite well made wine from pedro ximenez and palomino grapes; Medium Sherry, which is an amontillado, fairly sweetish style produced from doradillo grapes; a Sweet Sherry, which is a mature blend of pedro ximenez and muscat gordo blanco (obviously having considerable fruit); and an Old Tawny Port, which is a mellow wine of considerable age, produced from grenache and shiraz, with perhaps a touch of touriga grapes.

The Sauternes in the One Gallon Wine Cask involved me in an argument. This is a blend based on semillon grapes which have developed their full flavour and characteristics. I quite liked the wine and wrote in my tasting notes that it was a 'sweet wine with no great character and without fault'. My staff thought this a condemnation, but it was not so. I couldn't see any fault in the wine although it lacked character. Any resemblance between it and a true French Sauternes would be quite coincidental; yet it certainly was a pleasant enough wine for those people who like sweet softness, and certainly a lot of people do.

In conclusion I must repeat that I thought the package an outstanding one, designed to cater for people who want a glass at a time. I tested several packs of the wine for some weeks and found there was no deterioration at all and that there was very little container flavour pick-up.

Wynn's Ovens Valley Shiraz (Burgundy)
Made from shiraz grapes grown in north-eastern Victoria and oak matured for two years before bottling. The vineyards of the Ovens Valley are within sight of the Great Dividing Range and they receive copious winter rains. The hot summer sun ripens the shiraz to quite a degree, producing a wine which is soft, yet full in flavour.

There have been some most interesting wines produced under this label. I suspect that in recent years some of the material has been blended—the original Booth's material with other sources. The Ovens Valley burgundies of the late fifties were remarkable wines of considerable strength of character, with a vaguely irony, ironstone quality in them. They crusted very well and had great flavour and staying power. In the mid-sixties the wine seems to have softened down, and has become lighter, rounder and smoother: although, of latter vintages, I noticed a greater depth of flavour on the palate. Certainly they are wines that are very drinkable at all times. Certain vintages took a great deal of bottle age to mature into something which is quite remarkably interesting and of great distinction and flavour.

Wynn's Romalo Pink Champagne
A bottle fermented Champagne made from shiraz and oeillade, grown at the 'Modbury Estate'. The juice is separated immediately from the skins to give some pink colour. A very crisp, clean, refreshing wine with some sweetness.

Wynn's Romalo Sparkling Burgundy
Bottle fermented and made from a blend of shiraz and mataro grapes grown in the Clare district. It is aged in wood—500's—for two years prior to bottling and then spends a further two years in the bottle before marketing. A full-bodied, soft wine showing some sweetness.

Wynn's Romalo Sparkling Moselle
A bottle fermented sparkling wine, made mainly from clare riesling grapes from the Clare area. It is slightly fruity on the nose, fairly sweet, with a crisp acid finish.

Wynn's Romalo Vintage Champagnes
These wines are made exclusively by the authentic Methode Champenoise at the Romalo Champagne Cellars at Magill in Adelaide. Each bottle bears the label 'Fermented in this bottle'. The company supplies a number of other wine companies with their champagnes, which are labelled under their labels, and also certain merchants.

Wynn's Romalo Vintage Champagne Brut
Bottle fermented Champagne made from selected clare riesling and tokay grapes grown in the Clare district. The wine was bottled when approximately twelve months old and allowed to mature on yeast for three years before disgorging. A further short ageing period is allowed before sale.

It is a very dry, delicate style of sparkling wine, showing a fair amount of character from its maturation in the bottle on yeast lees.

Wynn's Romalo Vintage Champagne Brut De Brut
Made from clare riesling grapes vintaged in 1965, this wine is the oldest and driest in the range, and it has tremendous austerity and very fine flavour. It has spent considerable time on its yeast lees after secondary fermentation and has obviously picked up a great deal of character from this. A bone dry, sparkling wine of considerable elegance and austerity; very much an ideal aperitif wine for those people accustomed to using sparkling wines for this purpose.

Wynn's Romalo Vintage Champagne Cuvee Reserve
This wine, without being too sweet, is not as dry as the others in the range and appeals to popular taste. It is made in the same way as the Brut, except that the final liqueuring is heavier and the wine has two years maturation instead of three.

Wynn's Romalo Vermouths
The company makes both a dry and sweet vermouth from a base of fortified dry white wine, sweetened with Mistelle and blended with an infusion of imported herbs.

Wynvale Flagons
Wynvale flagons are a range of eight table wines, fourteen fortified wines and two apple wines. The wines are produced and matured at the Yenda Estate of the company in the Riverina from grapes grown at vineyards associated with the estate. *Grape varieties:* Shiraz and cabernet for red table wines; semillon, rhine riesling and white hermitage for white table wines; palomino and pedro ximenez for sherries; touriga and shiraz for ports.

The Vermouth and the Marsala are made from a blend of fortified dry white, infused with imported herbs to a secret formula.

Maturation: Red table wines, in large wood; sherries and ports, in wood ranging from hogsheads and puncheons to 500 gallon vats; Flor sherry produced by Flor method in small wood; Apple Wine, modern winemaking techniques are used to produce a double strength, natural, still cider; carefully controlled fermentation methods fully retain the crisp, clean taste and aroma of fresh apples. I like this very much, especially on a hot summer's day. The dry one is particularly good.

Yalumba

Yalumba Autumn Brown Sherry
A luscious, fruity, sweet sherry, which has a deep golden-brown colour, full flavour and a clean spirit finish. They fortify with brandy spirit to approximately 33 degree proof spirit. It is made from selected varieties of sweet grapes and is very good value in the middle of the commercial price range.

Yalumba Barossa Cream Sweet Sherry
A smooth sweet sherry, made from muscat gordo blanco and other varieties. It is quite sweet and has a rich texture and full flavour. A very popular wine of the minimum price range.

Yalumba Barossa Dry Sherry
Made from palomino, pedro ximenez and other varieties and wood-matured. A fairly young wine which is excellent value as a medium sherry in the minimum price range.

Yalumba Barossa Frontignac
A wine, light in texture, made mainly from frontignac grapes. It is on the fruity side and has been matured for at least two years.

Yalumba Barossa White Port
A smooth, sweet white wine made from muscatel (muscat gordo blanco) and other varieties grown in the Barossa Valley.

Yalumba Brandivino
A very popular liqueur type of sweet white wine with a distinctive brandy flavour, which has popular appeal. Made from mainly madeira (semillon) grapes, grown in the Barossa Valley and elsewhere, and fortified with brandy. This wine is also used as a 'mixer' with dry ginger, etc. The name and the process of making are exclusive to Yalumba and registered under Patent and Trademark Acts.

Yalumba Carramar Chablis
Made from semillon and madeira grapes grown around Penrice at the high end of the Barossa Valley, approximately half a mile from Angaston. There is no such grape as the madeira. On Madeira itself, the magnificent fortified wines of the Island come from sercial, verdelho, boal and malmsey (or malvasia). The South Australian madeira is none of these. No one knows exactly what it is, except that it looks like the local semillon and makes a wine which tastes much the same. The grapes are picked quite early. Consequently considerable acid is retained and the fruit flavour is delicate. The wine is then held in large wood for about twelve months. This oak is noticeable in the flavour and adds to the complexity of character.

On the flavour there is just a hint of the spiciness of the semillon from the Barossa. It is a nice flavour, very clean and rather austere on the back of the palate. This is a good under-rated wine which always provides excellent value for money.

Yalumba Carte D'Or Riesling
A delicate white table wine of considerable fame, made mostly or entirely from rhine riesling which is grown in the cool ranges around the Eden Valley. The wine is made under temperature controlled conditions and bottled early so as to get full flavour of the grape, crispness, freshness and slight spritzig.

This is a line which has been sold for many years. I think it was first started in the thirties and there are many great stories about the power and body of the wines of those days. Certainly I have tasted one or two of the thirties, including the 1937, which had tremendous flavour and was still full of character.

The 1941 and other wines of the forties were in splendid condition up to thirty years after they were made.

There have been average years of this wine, but a recent vintage, the 1969, was outstanding. It provided very good value for money selling at something not much more than a dollar a bottle, having all the hallmarks of a true, authentic, high-quality Rhine Riesling. It was a wine of delightful freshness and fruit, very well balanced, clean, fragrant, flowers —all the rest of it—a ton of flavour on the palate; well balanced with a clean finish. I liked the wine very much.

Subsequent Carte D'Or's have shown the same character. It now seems that the style has returned to its former position, and its rightful position, of considerable reputation.

Yalumba Champagne

Made from selected clare riesling grapes grown in the Eden Valley district, picked and vintaged at Yalumba. The wine is then made in the traditional manner by the Methode Champenoise and after fermentation is completed the wine has twelve months' maturity on its yeast lees. It is a very well-balanced drink of good flavour and character, with pleasant soft, acid finish.

They also make a Pink Champagne as above.

Yalumba Chiquita

A pale, delicate, very dry, Flor sherry, made from palomino and temperano grapes. The sherry is placed into casks and seeded by placing a small portion of Spanish Flor yeast on top of the wine. It rapidly grows, covering the surface of the wine—completely sealing it off from any contact with the air. This process takes from three to four years before the full Flor character is developed. As is usual in the method, the wine is then racked off the Flor and fortified to 32 degree proof spirit. It is then matured again, in oak, for some considerable time and when the balance of flavour between Flor, fruit and oak is complete it is fine-filtered and ready for sale.

Chiquita is very dry and clean and there is a slight nuttiness on the back of the palate. It is extremely good quality for money.

Yalumba Directors Special

A tawny port, lighter in colour and texture than the famous Galway Pipe of the company. This port is closely akin to some high quality Portuguese tawny ports, in that it has a lightness and balance about it and gets away from the over-sweet style. It is made from specially selected ripe shiraz and tokay grapes of a high Baumé which are then made into wine, fortified and put in wood for at least ten years. This is an excellent wood-matured port of the lighter style.

Yalumba Dry Frontignac

Made solely from white frontignac grapes from selected vineyards in the cool Eden Valley and Springton districts; carefully fermented under modified cold pressure to produce a light wine, crisp and delicate on the palate with a fragrant and aromatic nose. It is most suitable for drinking not long after bottling.

Yalumba Dry Vermouth

A dry sherry-type wine infused with imported herbs. This is one of the better dry vermouths on the Australian market. It is excellent for mixing and is a very good drink by itself.

Yalumba Fino Championship Show Sherry

This is a light bone dry sherry which has won numerous show championships throughout Aus-

tralia. It is made from palomino and pedro ximenez grapes grown in Yalumba's Barossa Valley vineyards. After being on Flor for several years it receives further maturation in fine oak casks. The nose is superb, with good nutty, matured Flor character—beautifully combined with oak. It has a fine fino style on the palate: very delicate and quite astringent with further evidence of its years in wood showing. The flavour is quite outstanding. This is one of the best of the wines in this category in this country.

Yalumba Four Crown Burgundy

A soft medium-bodied wine, made from shiraz, and occasionally from other varieties such as cabernet sauvignon, carignane and grenache. The cabernet sauvignon comes from Yalumba plantings at Oxford Landing on the River Murray. The grenache and the shiraz come from the Barossa Valley. It is matured in a mixture of French Nevers oak and some large old wood for a period of at least twelve months. The wine is very good value, being soft, round, fruity, easy to drink when young and a wine which takes a couple of years bottle age very gracefully.

Yalumba Four Crown Claret

A non-vintage blend of selected, slightly firmer but light-bodied wines basically made from shiraz grapes with some cabernet sauvignon added. The wine also has some age in the bottle before release. It is a light style of wine, with nice fruit and a good clean firm finish. Very good value for money.

Yalumba Four Crown Liqueur Muscat

A luscious, sweet, fruity wine, made from very ripe muscatel (muscat gordo blanco) grapes. It contains ten percent grape sugar and has been matured in oak casks for five years. There is good flavour of ripe muscat, plus oak, and is extremely good value for money in the medium price range.

Yalumba Four Crown Port

This wine is outstanding value. It is a very full-flavoured wine, made mainly from shiraz grapes matured in wood for about seven years. It is soft and smooth on the palate. In South Australia this port is by far the most popular of all brands in its price range. The fruit flavour, plus the oak maturation, plus the low to medium price indicate the depth of excellent port material the company has. Yalumba have been famous for their appetizer and dessert wines for many years under the control of a top winemaker, Rudi Kronberger, and his band of dedicated winemakers.

Yalumba Four Crown Sherry

A rather full-bodied amontillado style of sherry. After they have spent some time on the Flor process, some of the 'bigger' Flors—those wines which have picked up more Flor character than is required perhaps for the more delicate fino styles—are blended with matured sherries to make this style. This is then matured in wood for an average time of five years. It has some residual sugar on the middle palate, is very well-balanced and has a very clean spirit finish.

Yalumba Galway Fino Sherry
This delicate Flor sherry is made under the Flor process from palomino and temperano grapes grown in the Barossa Valley. It is a pleasant, round wine, slightly sweeter than most fino styles to cater for popular demand. It is fairly low in acid. The sherry remains on the Flor for a minimum of three years and its total age is usually five to six years. The wood character is pleasantly nutty. This is a wine for those who don't like the bone dry style.

Yalumba Galway Oloroso Sweet Sherry
A full-bodied, smooth, sweeter style made from tokay and madeira (semillon) grapes, grown in the Barossa Valley. The grapes are picked over-ripe and fermented to a high alcoholic strength, then fortified. It is aged in imported oak casks for eight to ten years and remains a very high quality sweet style.

Yalumba Galway Pipe Port
Perhaps the most famous single wine of the Yalumba range. It is an old, wood-matured, tawny made from the choicest shiraz, dolcetto and tokay grapes and then fortified with brandy spirit. It is a very carefully blended wine, matured in selected oak and casks. I have been in the port loft of Yalumba on numerous occasions and have tasted various wines that are being wood matured before they are selected for final blending. This is an extremely responsible job and it is most interesting to watch them at work.

The average age of the wine is approximately twelve years. The wine took its name from a former Governor of South Australia, Governor Galway, who during his frequent visists to Yalumba always selected it as his favourite type of port; hence the wine was eventually named Galway Pipe. The wine has won innumerable championships and many, many Gold Medals. It is a very soft wine but has a marvellous concentration of flavour and remarkable finesse; a beautifully balanced, beautifully clean, old dessert wine. There was a special batch of it from the mid-fifties which was quite the best tawny port I have ever seen in Australia.

Yalumba Galway Vintage Burgundy
This is a soft and rather full-bodied dry red made from fifty percent Yalumba River Estate cabernet sauvignon from Oxford Landing on the River Murray; twenty-seven percent Eden Valley and Springton shiraz and twenty-three percent Barossa

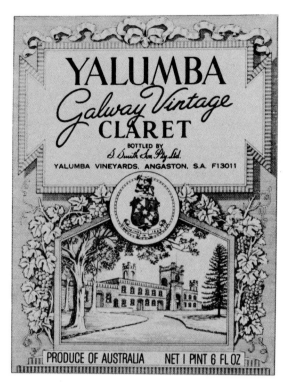

Valley carignane. The wine is matured for approximately eighteen months in French Nevers oak puncheons and in 800 gallon oak vats, then bottled and binned for further age. It is always sold under the vintage year. This is a very good, soft, round wine of considerable fruit and charm. I believe the breed has improved over the years since the first wine was released—I think in 1965—and now represents extremely good value for money.

Yalumba Galway Vintage Claret
This is a celebrated line which goes back some years. The composition of the wine varies from year to year, but a typical blend could be something of this nature: one-third cabernet sauvignon from the Yalumba River Estate vineyards at Oxford Landing, plus some material from the Barossa Valley; one-third shiraz from the Eden Valley and Springton areas, together with a touch from the Barossa Valley; one-third carignane and cabernet gros, from the Barossa Valley. The wine is matured in big Nevers puncheons. It always has a pleasant nose, shows good fruit with that trace of sweatiness that can be sometimes associated with River material. The cabernet fruit shows through well. The palate is medium-bodied; clean and balanced, and the finish quite firm and pleasant. This wine can be drunk when it is quite young, but it does take some years of bottle age quite kindly. It is sold at a very competitive price, and is consistently good within its range.

A recent tasting of these wines showed that whilst they didn't represent the highest quality of dry red wines of Australia, they certainly had always been good value for money. The 1967 was a pleasant wine of nice fruity nose, round palate, slightly firm, with perhaps too much hardness on the back of the palate; but a good wine of good fruit. The 1966 was a pleasant wine with a lighter nose; a fairly furry finish on the back of the palate, but again the wine was very well-balanced. The 1965 was a nice wine, showing good development, a well-balanced palate, very clean and very good drinking after about four years in the bottle. The 1964 was a fuller-flavoured wine and had quite something to it. The 1963, a well-balanced, pleasant wine, was slightly thin on the palate, with just an unfortunate touch of volatility.

The 1961 was a very pleasant light wine, which was extremely good value for money when it was brought out; sixty cents a bottle or something. This is a very good, well-balanced wine with a light to medium body, but overall a good composition of character.

The 1960 was a rather volatile, slightly thin, almost watered down wine—balanced and light, but not particularly likeable. It seemed to start the lighter style of the line. Before then the wines were much firmer bodied and had much more to them: a very good 1959; a rather over-the-hill 1958; an outstanding 1957; two wines, the 1954 and 1956 which had seen better days; and a very porty, rather vigorous, big-flavoured 1955.

It was certainly a very interesting tasting. Today the wines are pleasant, well-balanced, have good character and, as stated previously, represent good value for money.

Yalumba Galway Vintage Claret (Special Bottlings)

From time to time the company has released special bottlings of high quality cabernet and shiraz wines which have no definite consistency of character, but which from year to year show interesting styles. These include such examples as the 1966 Alf Wark Red, made from cabernet and shiraz, named after a celebrated character who worked for many years for the company. It was a very big, highly perfumed wine, slightly stalky on the middle palate and rather hard. It needs a long time to mature. 1966 saw the Harold Yates wine—a softer, rounder wine, with very good flavour, very good fruit showing good development; a wine made up of eighty percent cabernet sauvignon from the Barossa and twenty percent of the same variety from Waikerie, from the Yalumba River Estate. This wine also had some oak on the middle palate and again is one (although, because of its big soft fruit it was very pleasant to drink) that will take further bottle age.

In 1964 there was a wine called Percy's Blend; a slightly volatile wine of very good flavour and fruit with a slightly hard finish. Sidney's Blend of 1963 was a lighter wine of nice development with rather a matty sort of nose and a slightly furry finish on the back of the palate, but overall a wine of pleasant flavour and style and one which was starting to show some nice development after about six years in the bottle.

In 1962 there was a wine called Samuel's Blend; a slightly hard wine which needed a lot more time, for it hadn't quite come together. One could see there was much room for development still even though it was eight years in the bottle.

In 1961 there was a famous wine called the Menzies Claret—so-called because Sir Robert Menzies (then Prime Minister) said it was the best Australian Claret he had ever tasted. This is a very nice wine; very good nose and flavour; a well-balanced wine; in my opinion not quite the wine that Sir Robert thought it was—but a wine of good character. I always preferred the 1960 Special which had a lot of fruit, very good nose and flavour and was building up lovely character. It had a slightly hard finish and after ten years in the bottle still needed further time. Both the 1960 and the 1961 came from the McLaren Vale area, combined with cabernet grown in the Angaston district.

I have also had the pleasure of sipping the 1958, which was mostly from the McLaren district and put together at Yalumba. This is an excellent wine of delicious character; very rich, with great depth of flavour; and well-balanced. I am delighted to say that we generally see a bottle, when I visit the district, on the table of Mark and Margy Hill Smith at Yalumba.

Yalumba Golden Ridge Riesling (Late Picking)

Made from rhine riesling grapes grown in the Eden Valley and Springton districts. Only the most carefully selected, top quality grapes are used. These stay on the vine long after most grapes are harvested. This late picking produces a sweeter Riesling than normal, full of flavour, crisp and clean. It is a wine which also takes some considerable bottle age. I prefer to see these sweeter wines with bottle age upon them, because in this time it seems that the lusciousness and depth of character and flavour on the middle palate develops and they build up a greater volume of bouquet. All this added richness adds to the character of the wine, which is most suitable for having at the end of a meal with chilled fruit.

Yalumba Hermitage Claret

A light, dry red made from eighty percent shiraz and twenty percent cabernet sauvignon grapes from McLaren Vale and vineyards of the company in the Barossa Valley and on the River Estate. After blending, it is matured in oak, bottled and binned for further age and then sold under a vintage label.

It is a round, light, clean style, which is good value for money.

Yalumba Hock
Another dry white table wine made entirely from rhine riesling grapes, slightly fuller than the more celebrated Carte D'Or Riesling style.

Yalumba Koorianda White Burgundy
Made from clare riesling and trebbiano (white hermitage) grown in the Lyndoch area of the Barossa Valley. It is a smooth, soft, round wine, fairly full-bodied, but not of great depth of flavour; a fairly ample, broad style with a nice clean acid finish.

Yalumba Medallion Rosé
A light, soft, pink wine with a suspicion of sweetness and a fair degree of spritzig. It is made mostly from grenache from the Barossa Valley vineyards of the company.

Yalumba Mexican Vale Estate Burgundy
A medium-bodied red wine; soft and smooth, made from shiraz grapes from the Barossa and Eden Valley areas. It is matured in French oak, mostly 'second-hand' puncheons of Nevers oak; a soft, pleasant drinking wine, which is good value for money.

Yalumba Mexican Vale Estate Claret
A red of good colour and soft character made from shiraz, carignane and malbec grapes. An easy drinking wine which has developed a pleasant finish after spending some time in French casks. A fair quantity of River material is used in this wine which makes it drinkable quite early. The whole of the Mexican Vale Estate range, which is a low priced line, provides some extremely good drinking at a low price.

Yalumba Mexican Vale Estate Moselle
Made from semillon and clare riesling grapes grown in the higher areas of the Barossa. A clean, fresh wine, showing attractive fruit character, it is bottled young to retain freshness on the palate.

Yalumba Mexican Vale Estate Riesling
Made from rhine riesling and clare riesling grapes grown on the higher areas of the south-eastern Barossa Valley. A clean, crisp wine bottled early, retaining the true fragrant character of the riesling grapes. This is one of the best wines of the range and represents very good value for money. It has all the characteristics of the fine handling of this type of material that the Yalumba winemakers are capable of.

Yalumba Mexican Vale Estate Rosé
A very light, slightly sweet spritzig Rosé.

Yalumba Mexican Vale Estate Sauternes
A full-bodied sweet white wine made from fully ripe Barossa semillon grapes and sauvignon blanc grapes grown on the River Estate vineyards of the company. It has a certain amount of lusciousness but lacks complexity. Good value for money.

Yalumba Mexican Vale Estate White Burgundy
A fuller, softer, rounder style of white made from semillon and tokay grapes grown near the winery.
All these wines get their names from the Mexican Vale Estate, which is next door to Yalumba. Local legend tells of a Mexican who lived in a slab hut close to the Yalumba boundary. James Trescowthic, a miner from Cornwall, found a fortune in the Victorian goldfields and in 1854 he bought the property and named it Mexican Vale. He set up in winemaking and for many years grew good quality grapes, many of which were vintaged by Yalumba. Yalumba's records show that at the 1896 vintage he delivered 12 tons 2 cwt. 2 quarters of shiraz grapes at £4.10.0d a ton.

Yalumba Moselle
Another wine made from rhine riesling grapes grown in the ranges along the eastern side of the Barossa Valley. It has considerable fruit, some sweetness on the middle palate and a clean acid finish.

Yalumba Muscat and Barossa Muscat
A very popular sweet white made from muscatel (muscat gordo blanco) from the local district. It is smooth and pleasing to the taste and a popular line in the minimum price group.

Yalumba Pearlette
A light, slightly sweet, gassy white table wine made from rhine riesling and semillon grapes, on the Charmat process.

Yalumba Pewsey Vale Hock
Some nice wines are being produced from the semillon variety from this joint venture of Yalumba and Mr Geoffrey Parsons of 'Pewsey Vale', on the site of the old vineyards established by Mr Gilbert, the Government Surveyor, in the early 1850s. His winery ruins are still there and worth a visit if you are in the area.
'Pewsey Vale' is noted for its plantings of rhine riesling which have done extremely well recently in shows. The plantings weren't made until the early sixties and some semillon was also planted there. I'm not generally impressed with the semillon quality in South Australia, but the Pewsey Vale variety seems to perform much better.
The 1971 has a fine nose, and is clean, fruity and pleasant. I would pick it as a clare riesling or even a rhine riesling blend at a masked tasting. The wine has good colour; it is very fresh and aromatic; there

is a developing fullness on the middle palate, and I think the wine would round off and acquire a greater depth of flavour on the palate with some bottle age. However, it is a very good wine to drink now and is selling at a reasonable price.

The 1969 was also a good wine that developed in the bottle. It was fairly low in alcohol, being about 18 degree proof and the total acidity averages about 6.5 grammes per litre. It had a freshness of character and style, a hint of spiciness on the palate, and a fresh, aromatic esteriness which I liked very much indeed.

Although the line does not have the final complexity of its sister plantings, it is still an extremely interesting wine of good character.

Yalumba Pewsey Vale Rhine Riesling

This wine is made exclusively from the true rhine riesling grapes grown on the high slopes of the 'Pewsey Vale' operation. 'Pewsey Vale' is probably the highest altitude commercial vineyard in Australia. Because of the cool climate and high rainfall, the ripening period is longer and more even than any lower altitude vineyards, which of course allows the grapes to be picked at a perfect acid/sugar ratio; the acid being retained while the sugar develops slowly and the flavour therefore develops more slowly.

The wines produced have tremendous delicacy and concentrated rhine riesling character. Of the wines released so far the 1969 is probably the most celebrated and, writing about it some years ago, I said, 'It is a mighty wine that is as fresh as a daisy, light and clean, with wonderful aromatic fruit of the most elegant kind. This is a classic Hock. The nose and flavour, intense flowery fragrance sustained; are balanced by a fresh, clean acid... compensated by the tremendous fruit flavour.' This wine went on to win several Gold Medals (after my review) and it unquestionably established that the Pewsey Vale Rhine Rieslings are outstanding Australian wines.

The 1970 was slightly lighter but it was still extremely good. The 1971 wine had considerable flavour again—almost back to the 1969 standard. The 1972 wine was another outstanding wine that I am sure we will be hearing a great deal more of in the future. Intensity of flavour on the middle palate—that's the thing we're after; certainly these wines have it.

Yalumba Prince's Reserve Port

Made from shiraz and grenache grapes, this wine is younger than some of the others sold, normally being matured for about four years. The addition of grenache hastens the maturation, which permits the wine to be sold at a lower price. It still has plenty of character.

Yalumba Royal Reserve Port

Made from shiraz and grenache grown in the Barossa Valley, it is smooth to the taste and fairly light in style.

Yalumba Sauterne

A sweet, round, full, white table wine made from semillon grapes which are picked when quite ripe. It has a pleasant golden colour and a clean finish.

Yalumba Selesto Sherry

A straight wood sherry, being slightly fuller than the Four Crown style and tasting sweeter. It is matured in selected oak and casks to make a medium-dry, balanced wine in the middle price field.

Yalumba Sparkling Burgundy

Made from a base wine of shiraz, and then processed by the Methode Champenoise.

Yalumba Sparkling Moselle

Also made by the authentic champagne method; the variety being used is clare riesling and the wine is usually more highly liqueured than Champagne.

Yalumba Sweet Sherry

A sweet wine, lighter in colour than the more celebrated Autumn Brown and younger. This wine commands big sales in the price group. It is not a muscat, but is made according to accepted sherry techniques.

Yalumba Sweet Vermouth

Made from sweet, neutral wine, infused with an extraction of the best Italian vermouth herbs from Turin.

Yalumba V.O. Invalid Port

Made from grenache and shiraz grapes, it is a medium-bodied port, aged in wood for two years (which would appear to deny the V.O. label). However, it remains good value for a wine in the minimum price group.

Sunlight sparkles on the vineyards during vintage time in the Barossa Valley, S.A.

FROM VINEYARD TO TABLE

Anders Ousback

Wine is for everyone, to be looked at, to be smelt, to be tasted, to be enjoyed.

12 From Vineyard to Cellar

Many people incorrectly consider that any collection of bottles is a cellar, but this is merely a collection or store of wine. The experienced storeman or collector has a wine for every occasion: a fresh crisp white, and something more developed; the youthful red and a more mature one; a bottle of champagne for a christening, and a sweet sherry for a favourite Aunt. Once you become interested in mature reds and developed whites and discerning in your choice and price of wines it is time to start a cellar.

A wine cellar should really be below ground level and contain 'bins' of maturing wine and incorporate the wine store. However, if the 'bins' are above ground level the expression of cellar is still accepted.

Determining your cellar requirements

Let us assume that in a week you drink three bottles of white and four of red wine. One bottle of red and white is inexpensive, pleasant and ideal for quaffing; purchased in dozen lots when quantity is at a minimum. The second white is a crisp young aromatic such as a rhine riesling or traminer; this can be picked up from time to time in half-dozen lots. The final white is a developed wine such as a Hunter or Great Western white burgundy or chablis style and requiring perhaps four years (cellar) maturation. To enjoy the luxury of drinking one four-year-old white per week you will need to have on hand eighteen dozen wine of this type—ranging between one and four years old.

The second and third bottles of red can vary from five to seven years in age. Before purchase these wines have spent two years in wood and bottle before being released by the various wine firms. To drink two a week, you will need just on thirty-seven dozen red of this group with new wines constantly replacing the mature wines as they are consumed.

The final red may be a wine of, say, eight years cellar age; made up of the ends of bins you used to drink with five to seven years age on them; and a few special wines purchased and put aside until they reach maturity. Add to your list another four and a half dozen bottles.

So finally you have a stock of just on sixty-two dozen drinking and maturing wines that has taken you a total of eight years to attain, and on the basis of purchasing the wines when first available, you have waited three years before you get your first glass of developed wine.

Obviously one just doesn't start a cellar by going out one day, purchasing sixty-two dozen bottles of wine and sitting back waiting for the wine to reach maturity. The cellar develops from the store. Every now and then you drink a youthful red that you enjoy. Suitably impressed, you buy a dozen. Perhaps a small winemaker, whose wines you enjoy, makes a good vintage available, and knowing the demand for his wine you purchase a dozen while you can—and so the cellar begins.

Storing wine

Obviously my suggested cellar of sixty-two dozen is based on one bottle of wine being drunk each night; and that a certain percentage of the wine is youthful and the balance mature. This will vary greatly from person to person but everyone must make reasonable allowance for the storing of both youthful and maturing wine.

Modern homes have little provision for a suitable storage area for the maturation of wine. Not all wines need be contained within the one area for everyday drinking wines are often more easily stored in the kitchen or sideboard for easy access. Despite insufficient space for his maturing wines rarely does the true wine lover stop purchasing wine because of lack of space! Somehow there is always room for one more bottle.

The storage area (cellar) must be cool with a constant temperature: 10° Centigrade to 13° Centigrade (about 50°-55° Fahrenheit) is ideal. Wine can tolerate temperatures up to 24°C (75°F) but this, and temperature fluctuation, causes rapid maturation. This must be avoided for the slower a wine can mature, the greater will be the complexity and subtlety of the developed flavours. Avoid light also as this can cause wine colour to fade.

Some humidity is desirable but excess humidity can damage labels and the general appearance of the bottle. Too dry an atmosphere may enable cork weevils to breed which could damage the wine. Good ventilation prevents mould or stale air and removes any strong odours near the cellar. These odours could eventually permeate the cork and taint the wine.

The cellar should be free from vibrations and movements which, over a long period of time, can adversely affect the quality of the wine.

With the exception of tawny port, sherry, madeira and muscat, wine to be stored for any length of time must be kept on its side so that the cork remains moist. This stops excessive amounts of air entering the wine, causing it to become 'oxidized'.

Wine purchased in any quantity should be stored in a 'bin' or container, in which bottles of the same wine are kept. This gives easy access to the wine and enables one to know at a glance how much of that wine remains.

Whatever their construction, be it wood, metal, agricultural pipes, plastic foam, etc., the bins should be of uniform shape to facilitate easy stacking; strong enough, so that they can be built onto (should space permit it), and large enough to hold 6, 12, 24 bottles, i.e. the multiples in which you purchase your wine. Cost should also be considered. The initial cost for a few bins may not be high, but multiply this by the number of bins you intend to have and you will soon find that it equals the price of another couple of dozen bottles. In a large cellar the bins are numbered, corresponding to those kept in the Cellar Book which is described later in this section.

What to cellar

When buying for cellar maturation, buy wine that will become better with age (i.e., build up flavours that we recognize as being synonymous with quality in an old wine). What is the point in cellaring a wine, be it white or red, unless it can improve? A wine may have fresh grapiness, but there is no point in keeping it a few years just to soften the acid and tannin if the fruit becomes stale.

To be able to determine if a wine when young is suitable for cellaring is probably the hardest thing to do in the 'wine game'. It requires years of experience in constant tasting; examination and retasting. A young wine, particularly a red, is often firm, hard, dumb, and showing excess of tannin and acid. But is there the right amount of acid and tannin? Will the wine lose that hardness? Will the fruit develop? All questions that only an expert can answer, and even then, he can make mistakes.

Never presume that just because you like a wine, that it is suitable for cellaring. Wine merchants (not the local bottle shop), food and wine magazines, articles, experienced friends and your own knowledge and understanding will all help.

Ageing and maturation

Ageing and maturation are perhaps the most mystical and misunderstood aspects of wine. Quite a few opinions are available, the majority backed by extensive scientific research and experimentation, but for each opinion there is an exception that prohibits any rules being made.

Chemically, ageing is a continuous state of decomposition which occurs very rapidly during the initial stages of winemaking, through de-stalking, crushing, pressing, alcoholic fermentation and possible malolactic fermentation. From this point onwards the rate of decomposition slows down, though the speed varies within the individual wine styles.

Total acidity decreases and alcohol, sugar, acids and other components are transformed into innumerable complex compounds such as esters, aldehydes and acetals. The precipitation of salts is also important. All wine ages up until the point when it is drunk. Maturation is more positive, and is the ageing of the wine to increase its quality, consequently not all wine can be said to mature.

Generally speaking, white and rosé wines lack the tannins and pigments (maturation constituents) of red wines and, as a result, have somewhat less capacity to mature after bottling. These constituents as well as acid, sugar and alcohol, although themselves changing their structure and producing flavours with age, tend to act as preservatives enabling grape flavours to 'develop' resulting in those that we recognize as being synonymous in a mature wine.

Wine can mature in two ways:
1. in cask
2. in bottle

In the first group are the styles such as tawny port, sherry, madeira and fortified wines in general, whose excellence comes from a process of oxidation resulting in the formation of aldehydes (notably acetaldehyde) and other compounds as well as those derived from the cask, giving the wine an aged character. Once bottled these wines have no capacity to mature.

In the second group, quality is related to specific odourants and flavours supplied by the grape variety, the absence of air, and good reducing conditions. The length of time required to produce a maximum of desirable flavours varies considerably within the table wine styles. A few months in the case of some white wines, to fifty or sixty years in that of a vintage port.

Cask ageing/maturation is the time wines of the second group spend in wood prior to bottling and is important in hastening the clarification and stability and also imparting wood flavour to the wine. Wine in cask is also susceptible to air (oxygen) entering via the pores in the wood and between the staves. This initial contact with air is strongly related to quality of the bottled wine, particularly red wines, where the casks themselves vary in the amount of air they allow to come in contact with the wine resulting in 'cask characters' quite unrelated to the wood flavours picked up.

In Bordeaux, volatility is a positive quality factor in a great claret. In the Hunter Valley, initial exposure to air, while the wine is in cask, highlights wine flavours by oxidation. Tyrrell, for example, retains his best wines for maturation in cask numbers such as 9, 11 and 84, and even if the same wine went into all three casks, each for the same length of time, three different wines would emerge for bottling. When a wine is bottled, sulphur is used as a sterilizing agent to prohibit oxidation $(S + O_2 = SO_2)$. Although bottle ageing is not completely understood, it has been determined that the finest wine flavours will be formed in the absence of air. This statement is supported by the fact that wine ages as well in hermetically sealed tubes as it does in corked bottles. The importance of air entering the wine via the cork is much over-rated as long as the cork is sound and prohibits wine weeping from the bottle, in which case, air will take the place of the displaced wine. What is generally overlooked is that 8-10 millilitres of air are present in the average bottle of wine which can play a role in the changes that occur. Care is always taken at time of bottling so that oxidative changes are at a minimum and reducing conditions can be set up.

'O'er the hill and far away'

Any wine, regardless of its style, should be drunk at its best, that is, when there is a maximum of desirable flavours. As mentioned in the preceding section, the length of time varies considerably depending upon the style of the wine. With age the acid riesling loses its freshness, the fruit becomes stale and the finish coarse. The red wine from a good vintage, however, may require many years to reach the quality level, during which time it will soften, the basic elements of wood and fruit will marry and flavours will be built up. The complication (fascination) that arises with maturing wine is when to pull the cork, which can be largely open to debate in regard to a specific wine. The French prefer the freshness associated with youth and drink their wines considerably younger than the English, the latter favouring the complexities and nuances derived from extensive bottle ageing. The French are quick to call the Englishman's delight Vieillarde, passé (old, past its best). The English can only go so far and beyond a certain stage a wine goes 'over the hill'. It's very much a matter of 'One man's meat ...'.

The understanding of old wines (those past their best) is complicated by their scarcity and the consequent lack of exposure one gets to them.

Within this old wine syndrome, whites possibly suffer the most. Much the best part of old sauternes are the flavours produced by oxidation even though the sugar content decreases with age. Madeirization rears its flavoursome head in many types, and old dry white champagne styles can, and often are, drunk as delicate old white wines when they have lost their sparkle.

When one is fortunate enough to taste these very old wines, don't denigrate them simply for being old and not drinking at their best, for age itself is not a fault. Judge a 30 year-old Hunter as a 30 year-old Hunter and a 15 year-old Eden Valley Riesling as a 15 year-old Eden Valley Riesling. Considering the class and keeping an open mind are the essentials.

On crusts and deposits

During the process of maturation (viz. decomposition) it is not uncommon for wines to form a deposit in the bottle. This deposit can range from fine crystals in a white wine, to large sheet formations adhering to the sides of a vintage port bottle.

The fine deposits present in some white wines are a crystallization of the excessive amounts of tartaric acid (the predominant acid in wine) that precipitates to form tartaric crystals (notably calcium tartrate and potassium bi-tartrate).

Normally this excess is removed before the wine is bottled by chilling it to a near freezing point, and holding the wine at this temperature for five to seven days. This process is known as stabilization. Occasionally one can see this deposit in white wines made before the availability of suitable refrigeration equipment. At any rate, their presence is neither harmful to the consumer, nor derogatory to the quality of the wine.

The crust in a red wine is not only natural, but is desirable. It is a process by which a wine gets rid of its excesses. The crust in a mature vintage port is greater than that of a mature red because of the larger amounts of tannin and colouring (organic) matter present in the former, and also the fact that fortified wines cannot tolerate, in solution, as much iron and copper as can red wines.

The actual state of the crust—i.e., fine, coarse, granular, sheet, etc., depends not only upon the style of the wine, as previously mentioned, but also the way in which the wine has been cellared. Movement and too high temperature will inhibit crust formation thus limiting the precipitation of any excesses a wine may have.

Where to buy your wine

Having reached a stage where you have space to mature some wine, and a desire to fill those empty bins, where are you going to get your wine? The answer to this is not as simple as it may first appear. As soon as one becomes a little discriminating, you will find that not every wine and spirit shop stocks the particular wine you want. So get in touch with the particular company who will be able to tell you of a local outlet for their wines.

If 'only available from the vineyard—no local agency' answers your query then find out the address of the vineyard (it's always on the bottle) and write to them. As a rule these small makers are most helpful. Ask to be put on a mailing list and you will receive regular information about their wines.

There is an increasing number of wine lovers making annual pilgrimages to various vineyards and winemaking areas in order to purchase new vintages. Much can be learned from these trips, both in seeing the vineyards, and tasting the wines available for purchase. Often the vigneron himself is available, and only too pleased to answer questions and advise on the purchase of his wines. Direct vineyard buying has the advantage of obtaining wine at prices considerably less than in urban centres.

Don't be deterred by some reactions to your request for a particular wine.

'On quota.' Most of the time a problem of scarcity creating its own demand. To get some, you have either to pay above the suggested retail price, or purchase a quantity of lesser wines.

'The wine has been unavailable for a couple of months.' In this case arm yourself with a wallet and go on a wine hunt, stalking your vinous prey from bottle shop to bottle shop. These hunts can be rewarding in that you may stumble across something a little older or even a previously wanted wine. No good huntsman ever returns to the table empty-handed.

'Never heard of it.' A common cry, so try elsewhere. If the cry becomes too common make sure that you're asking for the correct wine.

Wine auctions

Merchants in Sydney, Melbourne and Adelaide are conducting wine auctions with some regularity. These are serious auctions in the sense that they are free from the hysteria of charity auctions and their 'tax-deductible' high prices. A great feature of the Barossa Valley Vintage and Rutherglen Festivals are the auctions that are attached to them. These auctions bring to light a great number of rare and old wines that, apart from the satisfaction that it gives the wine lover just to know of their existence, also enables him to fill a number of gaps he may have in his cellar. The tasting held prior to some of these auctions represents a rare opportunity to taste many famed but rarely seen wines. Even if you don't purchase anything, there is always the satisfaction of being with other lovers of wine, and seeing the prices that the market is bearing for older wines. It is unusual for a collector to walk away disheartened with prices realized for wines that he may have in his own cellar.

Wine labels

Unlike the large wine producing countries of Europe with their heavily policed 'Appellation Controlée' system, Australia has no direct regulations governing its wines; which, although to the advantage of certain vignerons, is a great disadvantage to the consumer. Be aware that there is no assurance, by regulation, that the wine named on the label should be that which is in the bottle. One has only the integrity and reliability of the winemaker or merchant to rely upon.

How to buy wine

With the exception of the 'wine hunt' and auctions, where one may come across an old bottle, nearly all the wines purchased will be young—generally one to three years. The older a wine is the greater the risk of it being faulty. That, however, does not mean that all young wine is sound.

The following notes may be useful when purchasing and unsure of condition. Rules such as never buying wine that has been stored standing upright, or has been exposed to extremes of temperature, should go without saying.

The cork should always be flush with the top of the bottle. If the cork is protruding from the neck it indicates either that the wine has been exposed to high temperatures—causing the wine to expand and thus forcing the cork out; or that the cork has been put in incorrectly in the first place (often the case with small vineyards still using hand corking machines). Ensure in both young and old wines that there are no signs of the cork 'weeping'. In an old wine 'weeping', or wine slowly seeping from the cork, can indicate that the cork has lost its elasticity and has started to contract. If this is the case check the ullage, or the air space in the bottle. If excessive, the two almost guarantee an unsound wine. In the case of some young wines, however, it is not uncommon to find that excessive moisture has built up under the capsule. This is due to capsuling taking place immediately after corking, without giving the cork time to rest. When a cork is put into the bottle the solution in which it has been soaked to sterilize it and make it sufficiently elastic to fit into the bottle is displaced with some of the wine in the bottle. The solution then seeps out of the cork and accumulates under the capsule. This natural displacement, however, is not to be confused with 'weeping'.

Heavy ullage also is quite natural in the case of very old wines, and is not really a problem so long as the cork is firm. These wines, however, must be treated with caution.

Colour should always be considered. Golden or brown shades in a white wine are strong indications of over-ageing. No matter what their age, reds should always have a red colour about them. Shades of brown are acceptable; indeed, in old reds they are expected; but it is rare for a red wine to have lost its colour and still be drinkable.

'Chateau Tahbilk's' large wood and bottle cellars under the winery at Nagambie, Vic.

13 From Cellar to Table

Decanting

Since the crust in a mature wine is an 'excess', it is logical that to best appreciate a wine and to take advantage of this natural process of 'excess elimination', it is necessary to remove the crust from the wine before drinking. This is done by carefully pouring the wine from the bottle into another vessel, so that one is left with the pure wine, free from the crust. This is known as decanting.

As age is no rule to the amount of crust a wine has or should have, decanting for the removal of the crust may not be necessary for wines ten, even fifteen years old; but, when it is necessary, care should be taken.

The wine to be decanted can either be stood upright for some twelve hours, depending on the size and structure of the crust, before opening, so that the deposit in course suspension may slide down the side of the bottle and accumulate on the base; or, the bottle to be opened can be removed directly from the bin. In the case of this latter method it is advisable to decant as close as possible to the bin where the wine is kept, as moving the bottle from cellar to dining room could disturb the crust. For the same reason it is necessary to have a wine basket or cradle to keep the wine free from movement when drawing the cork.

With a sharp knife, or similar instrument, cut the capsule around the neck of the bottle. Move the blade around the neck—not the neck over the blade. Lift off the top of the capsule and, with a clean cloth, wipe any deposit that may have accumulated on top of the cork. Carefully insert the corkscrew and draw the cork. Rewipe the neck of the bottle.

Many people prefer to rinse the decanter with a small amount of the wine before the actual process of decanting begins. This will remove any foreign odours or deposits that may be present in the decanter. To rinse a decanter from a bottle that has been standing upright is not advisable, unless the bottle, once moved from the vertical, can be kept in that position while rinsing.

If using a basket it will now be necessary to remove the bottle, ensuring that it remains as close to the horizontal as possible.

Over a light (a candle is most suitable), pour the wine, slowly at first until sufficient air has made its way into the bottle to stop the gurgling sound that will cause a current, into the rinsed decanter. The light, best under the shoulders of the bottle, will allow you to see when the crust is approaching the neck. At this point stop pouring to reveal the clear wine in the decanter.

When purchasing a decanter make sure that the decanter will hold the contents of a wine bottle. Many decanters, particularly those that form part of a suite, are made to be artistically pleasing first, and practical second. It is not uncommon to find decanters holding no more than 20 fluid oz, which in the case of the average 26 fluid oz bottle has obvious consequences. Nothing is more embarrassing for the gracious host than, with gaze fixed intently upon sediment creeping slowly towards the neck of the bottle, the wine is running out of the decanter and onto the table.

Decanting funnels

To aid the passage of the wine from bottle to decanter, a 'decanting funnel' is most useful, particularly for those new to this skill. These funnels are hard to come by, but a great asset if you own one. They vary from the traditional conical shaped funnel, in that the narrow end turns at an angle directing the course of the wine to the side of the decanter, instead of splashing onto the wine below. This more gentle handling of the wine causes less aeration, or breathing.

Apart from the bend at the narrow end, the true decanting funnel has a sieve in the form of a piece of fine metal mesh, normally attached to the base of a cup that fits snugly into the top of the funnel. This sieve is particularly useful in the case of old vintage ports as it stops any large flakes that may have become liberated from the body of the crust from entering the decanter.

Do not limit the use of the decanter for crusted wines only. Why serve wine at the table in the bottle from the cellar? Remember, a decanter is a practical ornament, a bottle is only a temporary home for the wine.

The Cellar Book

No matter how large or small your collection of wines may be, a 'Cellar Book' is a practical necessity. One can gain much pleasure from owning a cellar, by recording the when and where of a wine's origin, its price and so on.

The provision of a space in the Cellar Book for one's tasting notes, such as in the example below, will enable you not only to follow the development of various wines, but more particularly the changes in tastes and the palate of the author.

NAME: LINDEMANS WHITE BURGUNDY BIN 3870. VINTAGE: 1970.

DESCRIPTION: SEMILLON FROM BEN EAN VINEYARDS.

ORIGIN: PURCHASED FROM SYDNEY CELLARS ON 3/8/71 PRICE $2.20.

DATE	QTY	BAL	OCCASION	TASTING NOTES
3/8/71		12		
9/8/71	1	11	FIRST TASTING	GOOD HUNTER FLAVOUR, CLEAN ACID
				FINISH. NEEDS MORE TIME.
21/9/71	2	9	DINNER PARTY WITH	AS ABOVE – SEEMS TO HAVE
			SMITHS AND JONESES	FILLED OUT A BIT. ALL THOUGHT
			GRILLED WHITING-TOO	IT BEST WINE OF THE EVENING
			OILY FOR THIS WINE!	

Although not essential, a section for 'Occasion' provides space for useful commentaries that may be related to the drinking of the wine, necessary in avoiding repetition of serving the same wine or food to your guests. Also, by making a note of the food, you will have a record of which wines go well with what foods. With time the Cellar Book develops into a fascinating record of the wines that have passed through your cellar, and, therefore, over your palate.

As a subsidiary to the Cellar Book, the enthusiast will have a tasting book for recording his own impressions and the opinions of others on wines outside his own cellar. Constant thought in describing a wine's flavour will enable you to become, firstly, more exacting in your appraisal of a wine; and, secondly, more fluent in relating your tasting experiences to others.

Very often you will hear or read of a wine that takes your interest, or of the success of a particular vintage. If unavailable either for tasting or cellaring, keep a list of these wines (for convenience in the back of either the Cellar or Tasting Books), so that at a later date you will not forget about the wine.

Within either of these volumes it is a good idea to make a list of the various times of the year that the large and small wine companies make their wines available for purchase. As a result of the continual demand for, and scarcity of, fine wines, far too often one only gets to hear about them when they are no longer available.

If you cannot be bothered with a Tasting Book, a popular practice is to fasten the labels from the wines consumed into a book; relevant notes being recorded on that page. I have even heard of people who keep the corks from the wines they drink, writing on them the date the wine was drunk and their opinions—brevity and a clear hand being vital requirements.

Home Bottling

Home bottling is becoming increasingly popular, particularly amongst people with whom wine has a strong acceptance. The bottling (as well, no doubt, as the use to which the balance of the wine is used) is as good an excuse for a party as any. Half a dozen friends, some empty bottles, wine, corks, and a length of plastic hose are really all that's necessary to produce one's own 'Private Bin'.

Many wine firms sell their produce to the public in either wood, stainless steel, plastic or enamel lined drums for bottling. One should never expect to get a great vintage wine from these companies, since a 'great' wine is too valuable to appear under any label save that of the company that produces it. Also

there is the possibility that the wine may not be bottled correctly and with time, 'goes off'. The first cry from the owner will be that he has been sold poor wine—not that he could be at fault for not bottling correctly. What one can expect, at best, is a very good drinking wine, sometimes capable of undergoing maturation in bottle, and most important of all, it will be at a reasonable price.

If the wine for bottling is in cask allow it to rest for at least a week so that any matter in suspension will settle. Apart from the necessity to bottle with greater care, the only other disadvantage of sediment is that a few bottles towards the end of the cask will have to be discarded.

Bottles

If the wine is of quality and has the constituents for maturation, one is advised to buy new bottles, in case any off-flavours develop, possibly years after bottling, due to unclean bottles. There is very little against using second-hand bottles, so long as they are known to have contained nothing else but wine—if in doubt discard. The mistake that many make is in supposing that a quick rinse is all that is necessary. Thorough washing is essential to remove any harmful germs or bacteria that may contaminate the wine, and also to remove any chemicals that may result in chemical spoilage.

Firstly the bottles should be thoroughly washed by scrubbing with a bottle brush or a powerful hose. The bottles should then be soaked in a complex detergent, providing that it is odourless, or for best results, use 1 or 2 g. of Sodium Metabisulphate (available from any chemist). The solution is then heated to a temperature of 50°C. The bottles must again be rinsed free of all washing products, and stood base up to allow them to drain properly.

Bottling

Rarely will any home bottler come in contact with any bottling machine more sophisticated than a length of plastic hose pipe for siphoning the wine from cask to bottle.

If the wine is in wood open the cask by banging with a hammer around the 'bung'. In this way the bung will slowly rise because of the vibrations set up by the hammer. Never drill a hole into the cask—you will forfeit the deposit paid on the cask as well as expend a lot of effort in repairing the 'stave'.

Attach the end of the hose that comes into contact with the wine to a length of wood (a broom handle is most suitable) with a few bands of wire, ensuring that the end is about an inch and a half from the end of the piece of wood. In this way the hose will be kept close to the bottom of the cask, yet sufficiently above it so that no sediment will be drawn off. A tap can be fixed to the other end of the hose to minimize waste.

The cork

Unlike the bottles, it is essential that the corks are new. Prepare them by first rinsing in cold water to remove any dust. The corks must then be heated to give them the elasticity required to fit into the bottle. This can be done by soaking in warm or boiling water, though this may dissolve some of the elements responsible for a cork's elasticity. More preferable is to steam the corks in a colander over boiling water for 5 to 10 minutes.

Before the wine is bottled it is advisable, as a final precaution, to rinse the bottle with a little of the wine to follow. Pass the rinse from bottle to bottle, changing it every couple of dozen of so.

Corkers

For the backyard bottling set up, nothing more elaborate than a manual hammer or beer action corker is required.

Capsules

Though unnecessary, the addition of a capsule is a final touch that removes the wine from a backyard effect. Aluminium capsules are available in a variety of colours and only require a crimping ring to mould the capsule in place. Plastic caps are fixed by heat (a little hot water) whereby they shrink into place providing an easy effective seal. It is preferable, though not always practical, to capsule a few weeks after bottling. The resting time will allow the cork to displace any wine and adjust to the bottle.

Labels

It only remains for the bottle to be labelled. Again, though not essential, it is a finishing touch. Inevitably a friend with some artistic ability will produce a label suitable for the wine and the occasion. The variations on 'Fred's Rough Red' are endless. No special glue is required to keep the label in place but a labelling stand, simply constructed from a few pieces of wood, is advisable to keep the bottle in place to ensure the label is put on straight.

On opening the bottle

Unlike many popular beverages, opening a bottle of wine isn't just a matter of lifting a crown seal. Before you can get to the cork it is necessary to cut the capsule, the neater the better, in aiding presentation.

Capsules

The composition of the capsule varies, plastic, aluminium foil, sealing wax and lead being the most popular materials employed. Nowadays the capsule is mainly used to aid the presentation of the bottle, although it can be effective in stopping cork weevils from burrowing into the cork and spoiling the wine. Sealing wax is perhaps the most effective in reducing the displacement of wine with air. Lead, by far the most desirable, is considered a possible source of lead poisoning. For this reason, a plastic disc or cap is inserted above the cork, under the capsule to avoid possible lead contamination by contact with the wine.

Corks

Air is kept from any quality wine by a cork, of which there are four groups:

1. *The flange cork:* This type appears on the majority of fortified wines and consists of a length of cork between 1"-1¼" in length, on top of which is a plastic top or flange preventing the cork falling into the bottle. Since fortified wines, unlike table wines, are not drunk at one sitting, the flange cork is convenient for resealing the bottle until it is empty.

2. *The standard cylindrical wine cork,* used for table wines and the odd fortified. These vary in length from 1 to 2, or more inches. (During the war years the scarcity of corks necessitated their being cut in half. Consequently, many wines from this period have corks only ½" in length. This is a rare exception and is nowadays never practised commercially.) These corks should be of one piece, although cheaper and lesser quality corks can often be found comprising two longitudinal pieces.

3. *The layer cork,* used almost exclusively for sparkling wines. Here discs of cork of various thicknesses and qualities are cemented together, the highest quality cork being at the end which comes in contact with the wine. The advantage of using this type for sparkling wine is that the hardest cork, generally that which is the lowest quality, will be at the opening of the bottle. Should too porous or soft a cork be used, it will be ineffective in keeping the gas in the bottle.

4. *The composite cork*—again used almost exclusively for sparkling wines. The cork is 'composed' of many small pieces of cork, mainly remnants that are cemented together and moulded to the required shape. Although appearing quite frequently in French Champagne, the layer cork is still retained for the finest wines of this style.

Still wines

Having cut the capsule on a still wine, any deposits that may have accumulated due to age should be wiped from the top of the cork lest they fall into the wine when the cork is drawn. Insert the corkscrew, preferably at an angle, with even and constant pressure, and draw out the cork in the manner dictated by the type of screw being used. Opinions vary as to the best type of corkscrew. The single shank corkscrew with its steel spiral I find the best, since it burrows into the cork whereas the actual 'screw' type cuts the cork, often causing it to break. Whatever the type of screw being used, the tip should be sharp otherwise the cork will crumble.

Often in both young and old wines, the cork breaks. This is due to the screw not being inserted correctly (as mentioned previously), the age of the cork or mainly because of the vacuum created when the cork is drawn from the bottle. Particularly in old corks it is advisable to turn the corkscrew till its end protrudes from the base of the cork in the bottle. This will allow air to enter the wine prohibiting a vacuum forming.

Regrettably, with some wine bottles, the sides of the neck are not parallel and flare out to the shoulder, making the cork easier to push into the bottle. The cork is also more difficult to remove since it is conical in shape and acts like a wedge when being removed. Extra care is needed with this type of bottle.

Sparkling wines

Peel the foil, and remove the wire cage securing the cork from the top of the bottle. Take a cloth or similar to get a good grip on the cork. If necessary, a special pair of nippers can be used. Slowly turn the cork one way and the bottle in the opposite direction, gently pulling on the cork till it rises from the bottle. There should never be a 'pop' only ever a 'sigh'. To avoid losing any froth, hold the bottle slightly inclined thus giving the wine a larger surface area when the wine is opened for the excess gas to escape. Return the bottle to the vertical and wipe the top of any dirt or deposits common on sparkling wines which have undergone a second fermentation in the bottle.

Glass temperature

The temperature of the glass receiving the wines is of importance mainly when serving sparkling wines. The warmer the glass the faster a wine will lose its sparkle. Apart from over-chilling the wine to compensate for this, pour a little of the sparkling wine into one of the glasses, rotate it in the glass, and pass it on like-wise to the other glasses. This will lower the temperature of the glass and also remove any impurities that may be present from which the bubbles stream. On no account should ice cubes be placed in a glass to chill it for inevitably moisture will be left in the glass and this can affect the flavour of the wine to follow.

Breathing

Breathing refers to drawing the cork on a bottle of wine some time prior to it being drunk. This removes certain scents and odours and allows other flavour components to develop.

The correct breathing of wine is one of the most neglected facets of wine appreciation, and isn't just a matter of drawing the cork of a young red or decanting a vintage port some time prior to drinking.

What happens is that a current of air passing over the wine allows off-flavours that may have been collected during vinification, or have built up as a result of maturation, to evaporate. Many of these off-flavours are more volatile (i.e., evaporate quicker) than the actual flavour components of the grape produced by fermentation. Breathing, therefore, not only improves the drinking qualities of a wine by the removal of off-flavours, but also by allowing the more complex and subtle grape flavours to appear.

Breathing times

The higher the molecular weight of a wine, the longer the breathing time required. Young red wines and vintage ports with their high levels of tannins, acids and sugars, require more breathing than old red, rosé and white wines (lower in molecular weight). Vintage port is the only exception to fortified wine styles requiring breathing to develop flavours, although sherry, madeira, and so on, may have off-flavours due to bottling in which case a certain amount of breathing is necessary.

Temperature is important as the higher the temperature, the greater will be the speed at which odiferous substances leave the wine. This does not mean that one should warm wine to hasten its breathing, since these volatiles leave a wine at different stages, depending on their rate of volatility. An increase in temperature will cause evaporation of some aldehydes and esters (flavour components) and alcohol that would normally remain.

Just as one should never heat a wine with the intention of hastening its breathing, so too, should one never re-decant or shake a wine in order to aerate it further. If, when the wine is poured, it is found to require further breathing, allow it to develop ('bloom') in the glass. It is always better to under breathe a wine and have to wait for it, than it is to over breathe and be unable to bring the wine back.

Off-flavours in wine

During vinification the grape juice comes in contact with a variety of containers and substances capable of passing on flavours to the wine. Some of these flavours are desirable, others, though undesirable, necessary, and the balance totally undesirable. Some of these may leave a wine on breathing; others, due to their low concentration and nature, will be taken over by stronger characters as the wine develops/matures. The balance, however, will become an integral part of the wine removing it from any claims to greatness.

Recognizing off-flavours requires skill and continuous exposure. Unless these flavours are pointed out by someone familiar to their characters, the taster may, although recognizing their presence, confuse them as a positive quality factor in wine.

As mentioned, any receptacle with which wine comes in contact is capable of tainting it. Those in the list below appear with some regularity. Although the majority are self-explanatory, their causes and characters appear in the glossary.

Cork
Filter Pads
Chemical (sterilization agents and insecticides)
Yeast
Rubber hose pipe
Earthy (soil contamination)
Concrete
Metallic (metal contamination)
Dirty wood
Mould
Sulphur
Burnt sugar

Serving temperatures

Temperature plays a very important role in our appreciation of wine. Too cold a red and it appears dumb and ageless; too warm a white, and it tastes flat and flabby. The reasons for this variation are quite simple. White wines have a lower molecular weight than do red wines, and as such require a lower temperature to allow the volatile flavours to vaporize. The importance of volatiles in relation to taste has already been discussed. Temperature governs the amount of volatiles a wine makes available for olfaction.

There are no cast iron rules as to the temperature at which wines should be served, for just as in the selection of wine, the kind that is most pleasant to him that drinks it, is the best. Personally, I prefer my Hunters slightly warmer than my Coonawarras. The views as to the exact temperature of sparkling wines vary considerably, and no doubt each opinion has validity.

The context in which the wine is being served is very important. A rich Hunter White Burgundy served at the beginning of a meal needs to be considerably cooler than the same wine drunk with a soft cheese at the end of a light luncheon.

Good quality red wines should be served at room temperature, approximately 18.3°C. What lesser quality wines lack in their flavour they compensate for by being refreshing, consequently their temperature should be cooler, say 15.5°C. One could scarcely call the ancient red around which a dinner party has been planned, refreshing!

To bring a red wine up to room temperature, stand it in the room in which it is to be drunk a few hours before serving. This procedure is termed *chambre* and

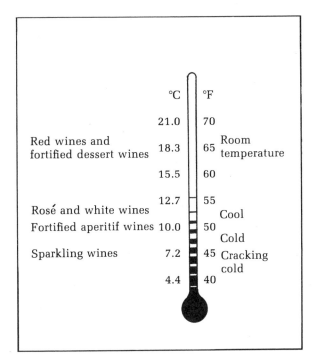

°C	°F	
21.0	70	
Red wines and fortified dessert wines 18.3	65	Room temperature
15.5	60	
Rosé and white wines 12.7	55	Cool
Fortified aperitif wines 10.0	50	Cold
Sparkling wines 7.2	45	Cracking cold
4.4	40	

relies, of course, upon the fact that the cellar is cooler than the dining room, and hopefully that the latter is at 18.3°C. Above this temperature the alcohol in red wines, any wines for that matter, begins to evaporate adding its own smell to that of the wine. Don't expect much from the room temperature red if it is 43.3°C in the shade, and heaven stop the zealous host standing his reds in front of a radiator to increase the temperature. If a red is too cold, hold the bowl of the glass in the palm of the hands. No artificial way is sufficiently gentle.

Generally, white wines and rosés should be served between 4.4-10°C, sparkling wines more specifically at 7.2°C, although I have never seen a thermometer thrust into a glass and a wine being declared too hot or too cold.

A small amount of trial and error influenced by personal preference is the best advice one can give.

As for ice buckets versus refrigerators in the chilling of whites, I know of no reason, nor have tasted any difference, between wines chilled either way, although each has its own advantages. The ice bucket fails to chill the neck of the bottle, quite important in the case of sparkling wines where the difference in temperature causes considerable loss of gas. On the other hand, I know of no refrigerator as portable as an ice bucket.

With the exception of the driest sherry styles that are often chilled to advantage when served as an aperitif, all other fortified wines such as madeira, port and muscat, remain at room temperature.

From Table to Palate

Wine tasting

The term 'wine tasting' is somewhat of an antithesis, for after all, it is rare that one is incapable of detecting flavour when drinking wine. The term, though, is more specific in meaning and refers to the conscious examination of all facets of a wine for the assessment of quality. By all means drink wine to make the meal merry, to quench the thirst and raise the spirits —for that is the purpose of most wine. When, however, you are presented with a wine of quality, treat it with the respect it deserves and allow yourself to extract the maximum pleasure, by tasting.

How to taste

Apart from the practice of 'listening' to the crackle of champagne and 'feeling' the viscosity of certain fortified wines, when tasting one brings into play three senses—sight, smell and taste (their approximate importance being in the ratio of 3:7:10 respectively, according to judging systems).

SIGHT. The first step in tasting a wine is to examine the colour and condition; far too often this first step is neglected, or not given the necessary consideration.

It should be remembered that there are two constituents comprising colour: hue and density of hue. 'Hue' is the actual shade—be it red, yellow, brown, etc.—whereas 'density' is the concentration in which that hue manifests itself.

In order to appreciate the nuances of colour, tilt the glass (to achieve a range of depths) over a source of light; or preferably a negative background, such as a piece of white paper. Examine closely that area just past the meniscus and into the wine, for it is here that the final subtleties of colour are best detected.

Characteristics of a wine detectable by sight:

STYLE: Whether the wine is still or sparkling; red, white or rosé. Strength can be related to density of hue (body).

CONDITION: Cloudiness can indicate an undesirable presence of protein or bacteria with the result that the wine is unsound or decomposed. Sediment can indicate age or method of winemaking (i.e., degree of fining, stabilization). Shades of brown in both red and white styles can indicate a wine past its peak, madeirized or oxidized.

AGE: Some red wines change from purple/garnet in colour to orange/red, brick red or brown-red; whites from pale green/yellow to golden-yellow.

GRAPE VARIETY: The purple of cabernet sauvignon, the red of shiraz, the green of rhine riesling, the yellow of semillon, etc.

REGION: The dense red/purple of Clare; the brick/red of the Hunter, and so on..

ALCOHOL (and Glycerine) CONTENT: Determined by the 'tears' a wine forms on the inside of the glass (Legs).

OXIDATION: Indicated by the presence of brownness.

VISCOSITY: The more viscous a wine, the slower it will move in the glass.

NOSE. Nosing a wine refers to the detecting of flavours by smell. To best appreciate this facet of a wine, rotate the glass, allowing the wine to rise up the sides and release its smell. The wine is easier to smell by employing this practice, for it follows that volatile flavour components are leaving the wine. Do not, therefore, swill the wine for too long a time—a few turns are sufficient.

The first smell will tell you the most. Re-smelling will enable the taster to detect further nuances. Nosing a wine before introducing it to the palate can get to the stage where no new flavours can be perceived; and the level of perception is diminishing, since the olfactory sense has become familiar with those flavours given off by the wine. Don't dwell any longer than is necessary. If further examination is required, the sense of smell can be momentarily refreshed by exhaling in short blasts via the nose.

Characteristics detectable by smelling:

AGE: The freshness of the aroma or the extent to which the bouquet has developed.

GRAPE VARIETY: The 'blackberry' scent of cabernet sauvignon, the 'sweet' smell of grenache, etc.

AREA: The higher the quality of the wine the stronger will be the regional character. The famed 'mint' of Coonawarra; the 'cow sheds' of McLaren Vale; the 'fruit salad' of Northern Victoria, and so on.

VOLUMINOUS: Related to volatility. The bigness of a wine's 'nose'.

QUALITY: The absence of faults and the presence of desirable scents; their number and degree of complexity.

SOUND: A wine without fault is said to be sound. This does not, however, imply that the wine is of quality.

FAULTS: A variety of faults are readily detectable on the nose:

Firstly: Those collected during vinification:
- chemicals and insecticides used for sterilization and inhibiting bacterial growths;
- substances with which a wine has come in contact that have imparted their own flavour, e.g., rubber hose pipes, concrete fermenting tanks;
- flavours resulting from poor winemaking; excesses of oak, acid, sugar, tannins, greenness (malic acid) resulting poorly balanced wines.

Jim Ingoldby noses a young dry red at 'Ryecroft', McLaren Flat, S.A.

Secondly: Flavours that have developed due to bottle ageing:
- primarily aldehydes produced by the oxidation of alcohol;
- oxidation of delicate flavoured components.

PALATE. Though a misnomer, palate refers to the detection of flavour whilst the wine is in the mouth.

Taste results from chemicals in solution stimulating nerve endings (taste buds) on the lips, palate, and primarily the tongue. Sweetness is detected at the tip of the tongue; sourness (acid) at the sides; salt behind the tip and bitterness at the back.

It is important to remember that with the exception of the four primaries, most tastes are in actual fact smelled. What happens is that volatiles are detected in the upper nasal cavity, while the wine is in the mouth.

When tasting a wine's palate, take a good quantity of wine into the mouth, to ensure that all areas of the tongue come in contact with the wine. The polite sip allows saliva to reduce the effectiveness of a wine. Drawing air through pursed lips will enable more volatile flavours to penetrate the upper nasal cavity.

When tasting a large number of wines, particularly fortified wines, don't swallow—spit. This practice is never considered undignified—it is expected.

Characteristics detected by the palate:
PRIMARIES: Sweet, salt, sour, bitter. Often these tend to act against one another. For example, certain sugars reduce the taste of malic and tartaric acid, the more bitter a wine, the less sugar will be apparent and so on. Degrees of perception vary between individuals—one man's sweet can be another man's sour.

GRAPE VARIETY: Determined by structure as well as flavour. Cabernet sauvignon has a firm finish; Australian rhine rieslings tend to lack flavour on the middle of the tongue ('head and shoulders').

STYLE: Burgundy style falls off at the back of the tongue, whereas the claret style does not. The Hock style has a delicate acid finish; the White Burgundy style is softer and richer.

CONDITION: Whether the wine is sound and free from fault.

AREA: Relative degrees of flavours, acids, tannins, peculiar to certain winemaking areas.

AGE: Amounts of acid and tannin; the degree of development.

FAULTS: *See* 'Nose'. The majority of faults appear on both the nose and palate; excesses of primaries, lack of balance.

BODY: The apparent viscosity.

QUALITY: Related to the absence of fault. Balance, finish, suppleness, etc.

ALCOHOL (Content): Spirit detectable at the back of the palate.

Order of tasting

The best order of tasting is firstly to examine the colour, then nose and finally palate. It is strongly advised that this order be adhered to since it is a regular sequence of appreciation that will allow the taster to examine the widest range of wine characters, and therefore derive the greatest satisfaction from the wine he drinks. Unaided by the nose and palate a taster can form a series of opinions on colour alone, which can be later confirmed or rejected by further tasting. To drink a wine before smelling it familiarizes the olfactory sense with the majority of flavours normally derived from nosing, and will consequently lessen the perception to the balance of scents and odours.

Comparative tasting

Just as one should taste in an order that will allow a wine to show a maximum of characters, so too should a group of wines be tasted without allowing one wine to dominate another.

Few people are able to completely remove themselves from the atmosphere that surrounds them when tasting. How often the wine drunk amongst friends at the end of an enjoyable meal appears lacking when tasted in sobriety. Similarly many of the nuances of a great wine drunk singularly are lost. It is perfectly possible to judge a fine wine on its own but its real qualities will be thrown into perspective if tasted alongside another wine, even if it is dissimilar in style.

Order of serving

Whereas a dry wine stimulates the palate, a sweet wine satisfies it. An acid wine will taste excessively sour if tasted after a sweet wine. The same thing occurs when a light wine is drunk after a full bodied wine, the former will appear thin and lacking in character. So too, with a delicate wine and a fully flavoured wine. As a general rule for tasting, serve dry before sweet, light before full, young before old.

Apart from tasting in an order that allows flavours to appear in their true perspective, our level of appreciation is also affected by comparative quality. Taste a great wine before a lesser one and the latter will show poorly, whereas if tasted with wines of its own class, it will not appear as inferior. Both style and class must always be considered when tasting.

Note Taking and Judging Systems

Unless you possess a god-gifted memory capable of recalling the characters and names of all the wines you drink, you should take notes when tasting. With time, you can build up a vinous vocabulary allowing you to become more exacting when describing wine flavours. The vocabulary also enables you to converse more fluently (no pun) with fellow tasters.

Although not for the beginner, judging wines by awarding points is excellent for evaluating the merits of individual wines tasted en group. The following example is based on the French Brunet System and is employed in Australian Show Judging.

Vat No. or Identification	Gallons	Colour and Cond.	Nose	Palate	Total Points	Ranking		Remarks and Recommended Treatment
		3	7	10	20	Personal	Group	
......								
......								
......								
......								
......								
......								
......								

ORIGIN .... TASTED AT .... DATE ....

TASTER .... CLASS ....

Wine Judging

Some Judging Systems:

1. Out of 200 Points:

colour	10
limpidity	10
bouquet	40
alcohol	10
suppleness	20
body	30
finesse	20
flavour persist.	10
general balance	50

2. Out of 30 Points:

Sight	colour	1-5
	limpidity	1-5
Smell	bouquet	1-5
	persistence	1-5
Taste	body	1-4
	suppleness	1-3
	mouth aroma	1-3

3. System using a series of numbers:

colour
bouquet
equilibrium   all out of ten
freshness   & optimum score = 10
finesse
body
character   all 1 to 10
acidity   opt. 5-6
hardness   excess 6-10
state of devel.   lack 5-1

e.g., a good young wine 67778 67564

Wine preferences

I'll never forget the comment made by a friend when I presented him with a glass of my great Australian Sauternes. He considered the colour, examined the bouquet, pondered over the palate, and spat out the wine, declaring: 'Brilliant! I could imagine no better Sauternes. Such flavour, so complex and so perfectly balanced.'

'Then why did you spit it out?' I enquired.

'Oh, I hate sweet whites,' he replied.

The experienced taster judges a wine without being affected by personal likes and dislikes. Far too often a wine is denigrated because of the taster's dislike for the style, mostly a case of lack of understanding and familiarity. Remember: Just because you like it doesn't mean it's good. By all means have preferences and specialize in these, but keep an open mind, and approach all wines trying not to be swayed by the comments of fellow tasters, and your own lack of experience.

Successful tastings

A successful tasting depends not only upon the quality of the wine served, but is strongly related to the amount of appreciation that can be gained by the tasters. The following points should be considered by those organizing a tasting to ensure this appreciation.

One of the greatest failings of many tastings is the presence of odours or smells in the room where the tasting is to be held. Strong cheeses, floral decoration, a poorly aired room, all contribute to reducing the performance of the taster.

Smoking when tasting is not only considered ill-mannered, but lessens the perception of the smoker as well as that of his fellow tasters. Colognes, strong perfumes and make-up (particularly lipstick) should never be worn for the same reasons as smoking is undesirable.

Ensure that a sufficient number of clean tasting glasses are available. Often when serving a large range of wines, or there are quite a few tasters, one may not have the quantity of glasses required. This can be remedied in two ways: Firstly, the 'community' glass method where one or two glasses are placed in front of each wine available for tasting, and are shared by all those attending. Apart from being somewhat unhygienic, the glasses will readily pick up many scents (particularly perfumes and colognes) from the previous taster. Secondly, and more desirable, every taster is given a glass for each group of wines served—i.e., one glass for reds, one for whites, and so on. Before starting on a new wine a small amount of it is put into the glass and 'rinsed' to remove any previous wine. The main disadvantage of insufficient glasses is that it prohibits comparative tasting.

There must be sufficient light and a white background to best appreciate the colour of the wine.

Make sure that the wines available for tasting are at the correct temperature.

The importance of serving wines in their correct sequence has been mentioned previously. To make sure the taster will have no difficulty in following the order, mark the wines numerically either on the labels or on tags to avoid confusion.

With any tasting involving a large number of wines, palate cleansers should be provided for the tasters. Each taster will no doubt have a cleanser that appeals to him more than others, so a variety may be needed. The most common are mild cheese, dry biscuits, and olives. Cheese has a tendency to coat the palate thus reducing the effectiveness of the taster. Olives, though popular, are really too strongly flavoured. Dry biscuits (water crackers and the like) should be salt free and not served with butter. By far the best palate cleanser is cold soda water. It is neutral in flavour, refreshing and revives the palate.

Almost as an afterthought, though not to be neglected, is the presence of note paper, tasting sheets and writing implements. Although fundamental they are absent from many tastings or forgotten by many tasters.

When organizing a serious tasting, bring together interested people. It is so off-putting to the enthusiast to be surrounded by hard drinkers scarcely thinking about what they are drinking. Try to have one experienced person or professional at the tasting. Apart from being the best way for a newcomer to learn, the presence of an expert will eliminate many differences of opinion that arise through the uncertainty of the inexperienced.

Don't embarrass your guests by exposing them to too large a number of wines, or to a style with which they are not familiar. Although the latter may be interesting, unless the taster has some background knowledge, the range will appear little more than confusing.

Just as various wines should be drunk in certain classes, so too should various tasters only drink certain wines. How it hurts to see one's last bottle of a great wine slide down the gullets of the disinterested or the uninitiated.

Masked bottles at twenty paces

'Blind tastings', or tasting a wine not knowing under what label it appears, is perhaps the most honest way to evaluate quality, for what an impressionable lot we are. No matter how knowledgeable or experienced the taster may be, his opinion of the wine can only be affected by his awareness of the label.

Through blind tastings the palate of many an expert has crumbled and often that of the amateur has risen to illustrious heights. But just how valid is blind tasting?

An 'expert' can be wrong. The reason for his inaccuracy can simply be that he isn't the expert he or others make him out to be. On the other hand he could have been given a glass from a poor bottle; the wine may not have been authentic to label. Perhaps through his expertise he may have been confused by many subtleties unrecognizable to one not so experienced. It must be remembered that we taste wines to assess their quality—not to pick them as being such and such, nor to praise one palate and denigrate another.

When and how to taste blind

Nothing is more agitating than being expected to perform the blind tasting sleight of hand when you are either incapable or not in the mood. Before the exercise begins, ensure that everyone wants to taste blind. Don't produce a 'masked bottle' at the end of a long tasting, when the palate is tired and beyond its best, and allow sufficient time for the tasters to give their answers.

Try not to give the tasters any idea of what the wine is. For this reason decanting is the best solution. A glimpse at the bottle shape, the colour of the capsule, even seeing the cork, will limit the options a taster may allow himself, and the majority of times he'll come up with the wrong answer.

It is advisable to ask a series of questions, or options, as opposed to the one 'What is it?' For example: 'What is the dominant grape variety of this wine? From which winemaking area does the wine come? What is the vintage, is it pre or post '67?' In this way an initial mistake can be corrected, allowing the taster to progress with less uncertainty. Try not to drag out the questions and ask only those which can be related to the actual flavours of the wine.

Bottle variations

It is significant to mention at this point the important role bottle variation plays in tasting. The saying, 'there are no great wines, only great bottles', although coined when winemaking lacked its present sophistications, is still valid. Bottle variation isn't really that surprising when one considers the different conditions to which a wine can be exposed.

At any wine tasting, particularly at Shows, two or more bottles of every entry or sample are always on hand. One for tasting and the second to be called for should the first have an outstanding fault or off-flavour. Except for the trained eye that can distinguish the subtleties in the variation of colour, the only positive way to determine any differences is by tasting.

The biggest single factor contributing to variation is the cellar. Since no two cellars can experience the same temperature, light, movement and such, so it follows that bottles drawn from such cellars will vary according to the cellar differences. A wine

Several growers in the Riverina, N.S.W., make their own wine. Among these are Rossetto's wines at Beelbangera, five miles from Griffith. Rossetto's market a full range of wines and liqueurs.

that was purchased young, and kept in the one cellar all its life, will be better than the same wine that has changed hands many times and will have therefore had more exposure.

The cask from which the wine was drawn is relevant. Large wine companies with their scientific bottling and blending facilities are more capable of producing variation free wines than small makers. Though this is not to say that they do. The first bottle drawn from the cask can differ from that bottled last, particularly when filtering is done on the bottling line. A new set of filter pads can strongly taint the initial wines passed through them, giving the wine a strong asbestos flavour.

After bottling, differences often exist in the levels or ullage of the wine. As a result, one bottle will have more air (viz. oxygen) to act upon it. Corks differ in their lengths, condition and porosity. One cork will allow more wine to seep from the bottle than a second. Another may contain bacteria, which through inadequate sterilization will manifest itself giving the wine a 'corked' character.

The more full bodied and higher in alcohol a wine is, the less susceptible to variation it will be through its resistance to bacteria and odours. Fortified wines have nowhere near the variation of table wines. A fresh acid riesling has less resistance than a Sauternes, and so on.

In this highly mechanized world, wine, the manmade product of the vine, continually defies standardization. Perhaps this is the true mystique. Having realized the differences to which a wine can be exposed, don't now cry out 'bottle variation' whenever disappointed by a wine.

Travelling wines

Often when you visit a wine growing region, you can come across a particular wine that takes your fancy. Suitably impressed you buy a quantity of the wine and take it with you, or have it delivered. A few weeks later, the wine arrives at your home, you pull the cork and taste it to find that it is nothing like the wine tasted at the vineyard. The first reason for this difference can be the wine isn't the same, either by a confusion in the ordering of the wine, or through the lack of integrity of the winemaker. The second possibility is, at the winery, amongst the casks, the grapes, and after quite a few glasses of wine, with the senses mellowed and the heart light, one was apt to become over enthusiastic about the wine, with the result that when it is received in sobriety, it only has a measure of its previous character.

Another reason is that the wine was tasted in cask, possibly before clarification and fining. Bentonite, a fining agent, can account for considerable loss of flavour in a new wine, though with age the wine will have its former flavour restored. Filtering, bottling

and sterilization agents all take their toll of a young wine, resulting in it being termed 'bruised' or 'knocked'. Some winemakers consider the pumping of a wine so harmful as to have their wineries designed employing gravity in the movement of the wine, considering this to be the most gentle method of handling.

The last hypothesis, travel, is perhaps the soundest reason for the variation in the wine, particularly if it has not been given sufficient time to rest, and is not just peculiar to newly bottled or young wines. Indeed, the effects of movement over a considerable length of time and fluctuations in temperature, will have a greater consequence in an old wine than in a young wine. The effect of transport, movement and temperature fluctuation, is such that in the past the rolling motion of ship transport was used on wines in cask as a means of ageing.

Wine in the bottle

The ullage in a bottle of wine is responsible for much of the loss of quality resulting from travel, for here the air space tends to percolate through the wine as well as causing currents in the bottle. Certain elements of wine—the colour, and tannins in particular, are not really dissolved but are in a state of colloidal suspension. Nothing is more fragile, chemically speaking, than these suspensions. They can be broken by fluctuations in temperature, by oxidation, movement, even prolonged high and low frequency sound waves. Ullage is important, and any wine for long transport should have as small an air space as possible. The fragility and changeability of the bouquet is notorious, breathing being a good example of just how instable it is. It is not surprising that transport can change its chemical balance and modify this even more.

Most owners of private cellars allow their wines to rest after transport before attempting to taste them, but usually they are not left long enough. Several weeks to several months are necessary for a wine to recover its full bouquet and taste.

Not all wines will suffer from travelling. I know of many examples of wines that contradict any rules on travel. Max Lake has written extensively on the 'travelability' of Hunter wines (Hunter Winemakers Ch. 13 pp 118-125).

To minimize the effects of movement and temperature fluctuation wine should be transported upright so that the air space, as mentioned, will not percolate through the wine. If the wine is old, with considerable ullage and sediment, it is advisable to decant it into a smaller bottle such as a German riesling bottle which only holds 24 fl. oz. In this way the wine can be decanted free of sediment and, when the cork is replaced, will be free of ullage. This is only advisable if the wine is going to be drunk no more than a few days after decanting, since the quality of the rebottling cannot be guaranteed.

Bottling and packing at S. Smith & Son's 'Yalumba' Winery in the hills just out of Angaston, S.A.

Ullaged bottles

Every wine deteriorates once the cork has been drawn, though the rate of deterioration depends on the style of wine. It is essential to drink sparkling wines as close as possible to being opened, for once flat they have lost their most appealing character.

Often a bottle of table wine is not drunk in the one sitting, and is held over till the next day when it is finished. Re-corking the wine immediately after pouring helps minimize the amount of volatiles that will evaporate, otherwise by the second day it will appear flat and lifeless. White wines will carry over better, and should be stored in the refrigerator. Much the same practice applies to flagon wines, but particularly in the case of reds, it is advisable to decant the flagon into three bottles, recorking each. Depending upon the care that is taken when bottling, the wine is capable of lasting a few weeks.

Fortified wines, because of their higher amounts of alcohol, can be opened considerably longer than table wines before there is a marked change in their character. But after a few weeks, or particularly towards the end of the bottle, they will lose flavour and become stale. As a general rule the more full bodied the fortified, the longer it can be opened— e.g. Fino sherry should be finished before an old liqueur port.

Glassware

The varieties and patterns of glassware are innumerable. The great vineyards of Australia, unlike their European counterparts, have not influenced a design to equal their magnificence, so there is no unique Australian glassware, such as the Romer of Germany, or the classic Claret and Burgundy glasses.

The best glassware for drinking wine is made from the purest lead crystal, which, because of its brilliance, enables the colour to be best appreciated. Coloured glassware (unless one possesses an extraordinary understanding of colour blending), is for the crystal cabinet and not for the table. Decorated, engraved or cut glass is tolerable up to a certain point. Other drinking vessels are available crafted in silvery pewter, wood and a variety of other materials. Although they may reflect the great skill of the silversmith or pewter craftsmen, they do not allow a wine to show its colour, have no advantage over crystal (save durability) and are little more than affectations.

The shape is most important and in any style the lip should be narrower than the bowl enabling the wine to be swilled in the glass so as to condense the bouquet for olfaction. The most suitable glass for still wine styles is that with a total capacity of 6-8 oz. of wine. A stem to elevate the bowl from the base is essential particularly in the case of white wines where the temperature of the wine will be affected by that of the hand. One glass of five ounce capacity, two-fifths full, is perfect for the enjoyment of fortified wines, brandies and liqueurs. As for the bird-bath in which champagne and sparkling wines so often appear, I appeal to manufacturers to cease their production and governments to ban their use, for there is no surer way to rid a wine of its finest quality, its sparkle, which is often the product of years of work.

Decanters

Decanters are either used for receiving a wine after it has been poured free of its sediment, or as a decoration in the case of spirits and fortifieds. There are four groups of crystal decanters:

1. For spirits, traditionally rectangular in shape and short neck with a large stopper and generally heavily patterned cut.
2. Decanters for fortified wines such as sherry and madeira either round or rectangular in shape, with a long neck and decorated in the lower half of the decanter.
3. Port decanters. Because of the popularity of vintage port in England, a type of decanter was designed expressly for this style of fortified. It is similar in shape to that used generally for fortified wines, but is cut with a simple angular design over the whole of its surface.
4. The wine decanter. Simplest in design, round and with a tall neck. Two sizes are found capable of holding one or two bottles respectively.
    The larger size was most popular in Victorian times and is rarely seen nowadays.

Care of glassware and decanters

All the work in decanting a fine wine will be wasted if the decanter and glasses are not free of smells which result from incorrect cleaning and storing. Glass and crystal, although appearing so, are not smooth substances but have microscopic pores capable of being filled with cleaning fluids or housing substances that can communicate a foreign taste to the wine.

To clean either decanter or glassware, avoid using perfumed detergents. Pure soap flakes and a little warm water is all that is necessary. After washing they should then be rinsed thoroughly in cold water and a final time in warm water so that they will dry without streaks. Glassware should be inverted on a tea cloth and left to drain. This is not as easy with a decanter because of the weight of their base and small top. Before putting either wine receptacle away, polish them with a lint-free tea cloth, good linen being the best.

If the decanter is encrusted with the colouring matter of red wines, a little chlorine bleach will

Recommended wine glasses: l to r—all-purpose wine glass serves any type of wine in style; a tulip Champagne glass; sherry glass; another all-purpose glass; port or dessert wine glass; a long-stemmed Rhine wine glass for white wines; traditional hollow-stemmed glass for Champagne (Photo: Wine Institute, California).

remove it. Use vinegar to remove a lime deposit that may be caused by hard water. Take care to thoroughly rinse the decanter, lest traces of these agents remain.

Store crystal in as negative an atmosphere as possible. Many new building materials, plastic, and the like, can transmit very strong smells to the air which will be absorbed by the glass. Wooden cupboards, due to their lack of airing, readily build up an unfavourable musty smell. Generally glasses are stored upside down to prevent dust from getting in, although by doing this the air inside the glass has no chance to circulate and will readily give a foreign smell to the glass (the so-called cupboard stink). Decanters should never be stored with their stopper in for no air is able to circulate within them. Whenever taking glasses from their storage place, smell them first, to ensure their neutrality. It may be necessary to rewash them.

Wine and food

Within the natural affinity between wine and food lies one of the purest and most natural pleasures available to modern man. Many consider the importance of combining wine and food flavours overrated, or its pleasure exaggerated. These unfortunates have obviously never been exposed to the true marriage of wine and food.

Within this realm one will stumble across such thoughts as the 'drink what you like with what you like', 'white wines with white meat, red wines with red meat', and an endless stream of this dish with that wine, or this wine with that dish. Yet another appears at the end of this section. Although having some validity, these generalizations are rarely taken to heart by those of even the most meagre interest. What is required is an understanding of the compatibility of flavours and textures—an understanding that is only gained through extensive personal experience. No food ever did such justice to the '57 Hardy's Golden Nectar Sauternes than the cold Mango Soufflé I made when the fruit was at the height of its season. Conversely, no longer having this Sauterne in my cellar, I have yet to find a sweet wine capable of enhancing the soufflé as well.

Although balance of flavours is essential, a certain amount of contrast is desirable. Serve an acid white with avocado vinaigrette and the flavours will fight till the end of the dish. On the other hand, what chance does the delicate flavour of mudcrabs have against a Great Western Red?

Apart from their flavour harmonizing ability, wine and food allow one to highlight the other. Red wine cleanses the palate of fats. Fresh acid white wines remove the coating egg and cream sauces leave on the palate. Food, correspondingly, excites areas of the palate not brought into use when drinking wine, as well as reversing those areas already employed.

A happy combination of New Zealand wines and cheeses for a party (Photo: N.Z. Woman's Weekly).

The fundamental rules of dry before sweet, light before full, young before old, are equally applicable to drinking wines with food, as they are when tasting. Just as one aims at a balance of colours, flavours and textures within the menu, the wines served should be treated similarly. There is little point in serving one developed white burgundy after another, no matter how well they complement the food. Serving a fresh riesling style before the white burgundy will both enhance the second wine as well as offer variety to the palate.

Champagne and high quality champagne styles have a reputation of being able to be served throughout any meal. If only one wine is being served, champagne will combine better with a variety of dishes than any other wine style. Rarely though, is it the one wine served, the progression being from Brut, through to sec and demi-sec styles, which in themselves offer considerable variety.

The more delicate or subtle a wine, the more delicate the food that should go with it. For this reason you will often find a great old red being drunk with nothing more than a soft cheese and unsalted cracker biscuits. A fine tawny port lends itself perfectly to freshly cracked nuts, though this instance is more a result of menu compilation than the requirements of the wines.

Whatever the wine, whatever the meal, remember the ability that one has of enhancing the other. Have fun experimenting, creating dishes for particular wines and being selective in the wines you serve with different foods.

Yet another wine and food compatibility chart

Young S.A. Rhine Rieslings and Riesling/Hock styles	Simple seafoods, salads.
Youthful Hunter and Great Western Whites Developed S.A. Riesling styles	Melon, oysters and seafood in general. Poached fish.
Mature Hunter and Great Western Whites	Cold chicken, ham. Special seafood dishes.
Moselle, Spatlese and Sauternes styles	Light pastry, sweet soufflés, Fresh and poached fruit
Rosé styles	Cold poultry, ham, Seafood Provéncale.

Youthful, light reds, any area	Paté, terrines, roast chicken, pork.
Young reds, notably Eden Valley, Clare, Tahbilk, Coonawarra, etc.	Farinacious foods, such as pasta. Roast beef, lamb, cheeses.
Mature reds	Roast beef, lamb, cheeses.
Very old red wines	Soft cheeses, dry biscuits.
Vintage Port	Alone. Dry biscuits, nuts, cheeses.
Tawny Port	Dry biscuits, nuts, cheeses.
Liqueur Port	Fruits glacé.
Dry Madeira	Alone. Consommé.
Sweet Madeira	Alone. Unsalted nuts.
Muscat	Raisins, dry biscuits.
Old Muscat (North Victorian)	Dry biscuits, walnuts.
Dry sherries— Flor, Flor Fino	Hors d'oeuvres, lightly salted nuts.
Amontillado Sherry	Cream soups and bisques.
Oloroso Sherry	Fruit glacé, nuts, etc.
High quality cream sherries	Fruit glacé, nuts, etc.
Brut Champagne and dry sparkling wine styles	Paté, smoked salmon, any simple seafoods.
Demi-Sec and Sec Champagne and sweeter sparkling wines of high quality	Sweet soufflés. Fresh fruit, nuts, etc.

Cooking with wine

Wine is a wonderful medium with which to cook since it can take the place of any liquid when cooking a dish, as well as lending an extra dimension to the dish because of the flavour it adds. Regrettably, low quality wine is far too often used when cooking, 'the anything handy will do' attitude. No matter how competent the cook, his culinary results will be disappointing unless he uses the best ingredients. The point is best illustrated by the food and wine lover who went into his wine merchant and after ordering a few wines for his cellar, added, almost as an afterthought, 'Oh, you'd better send me a case of the Beaune-Marconnets '67—I need something to cook my Coq-au-Vin.' Often faulty wine (e.g., corked) is used when cooking—a valid practice up to a point. An oxidized red can enhance the flavour of a stew but can also give it an off-flavour. Any wine found to be so affected should be brought to the boil first and allowed to cool. In this way, the presence of the off-flavour is less noticeable. (During the cooking of wine the alcohol evaporates and is therefore quite suitable for children.)

Uses of wine when cooking

The main reason for adding wine to food is the flavour it lends to the completed dish. Splash some red in a stew, or add 1 tbsp. sherry or madeira to a soup. Red wine, apart from the flavour it adds, tends to colour the dish, making it more appealing to the eye.

Tough meat will tenderize and acquire extra flavour if soaked overnight in red wine. Red, white and occasionally fortified wines can be used for a marinade.

The Court-Bouillon used when poaching fish, poultry or meat is usually wine based, with herbs, vegetables and spices added. Try poaching fish in a Court-Bouillon with a red wine base. After cooking reduce the wine, thicken with a little beurre manié and finish the sauce with butter (red wine with white meat!!).

Basting beef with red wine and chicken with white will moisten the meat and flavour it.

Some of the greatest sauces of French Haute Cuisine are those involving wine, sauces bordelaise, bourguignonne, and madere (involving claret, burgundy and Madeira wine, respectively) being perhaps the most famous. Vary your everyday white sauce, by using half white wine and half milk. A good pan gravy cries out for a 'slurp' of red.

Use an acid white wine instead of vinegar in your next salad dressing. Try half red wine, half oil, seasonings and a little sugar for tomatoes.

How often those previous juices from meat fried or grilled, are wasted. Deglaze the pan by splashing in some red wine, returning the pan to heat, and reduce until the required quantity of sauce is produced. Finish with butter.

A refreshing sweet dish for summer, is to place ripe fruit, peaches for example (peeled, de-stoned and cut into pieces), into a tall glass and chill. Just before serving fill the glasses with cold champagne.

The uses of wine when cooking are numerous, but experience is necessary to know how big the 'splash' and how long the 'slurp'. Use wine sparingly at first and taste frequently. In any dish wine should be *a* flavour, not *the* flavour.

THE CHANGING SCENE

Ross Turkington, B.Sc.Agr., R.D.Oen., is a graduate from Sydney University with a Diploma in Oenology from Roseworthy Agricultural College in South Australia. He has been with the N.S.W. Department of Agriculture since 1959 and holds the position of Principal Fruit Officer (Viticulture). Before this present appointment he undertook extensive viticultural studies at the Department's research station at Griffith.

Michael Baume, B.A., a former finance journalist, is now a Sydney stockbroker and panelist with Len Evans in the ABC television program 'Would You Believe'. He is married, has three sons, and lives at Woolwich, N.S.W.

Mr Harry F. M. Palmer joined the Australian Wine Board as chief executive officer in 1955 and resigned his position as General Manager in May 1972. He has made seventeen trips around the world promoting Australian wines and is recognized as a marketing expert. At present Mr Palmer is Export Marketing Manager of the Barossa Co-operative Winery Limited, makers of Kaiser Stuhl wines.

Keith Dunstan has been the daily columnist on the **Sun News Pictorial**, Melbourne, for the past fourteen years. He has written four books—**The Paddock That Grew, Supporting a Column, Wowsers and Knockers.** He has always shown a devoted interest to wine.

Mildara's new stainless steel storage area at Merbein, five miles west of Mildura, Vic.

15 New Plantings of Grapes

It's happening everywhere—grape vines are springing up all over the place. Land prices in areas suitable for viticulture have soared to record heights, and all as a result of the wine boom. The big companies have spent huge amounts of money and manpower, and increased their plantings all over the place. Many wine lovers, from dilettante to the truly dedicated, have rushed to get in on the act. A vineyard of one's own has become a much-envied status symbol regardless of the quality of the wine made.

There has been some conflict of opinion over whether all this activity will lead to another big grape bust. One rotund Cassandra has predicted all kinds of doom, while other writers, would you believe, are confident that the new grapes will not even begin to fill the increasing demand for premium quality wine. That argument will not concern us here.

What does concern us is some knowledge of the new plantings; that is, who is planting what—and where. After all, there have been and will continue to be numerous new labels appearing on the shelves of your local bottle shop—Avoca, Drumborg, Keppoch, Naracoorte, and so on, and so on, and it helps to know something about them.

One problem in a chapter such as this is when a new planting stops being a new planting. It takes many years to establish a vineyard. Some developments which were begun even eight to ten years ago are not yet fully established; and only time will tell what the future holds for some of the more recent enterprises, large and small. Thus, here we have concentrated on very recent developments and on general trends of new plantings. Further information on the happenings of the sixties is given in the descriptions of the vineyards of the various states.

What follows is a brief outline of the new developments. And the picture is far from complete. Despite lots of letters and enquiries it was impossible to get complete details on the many new developments taking place. However, we have all done our best.

Grateful thanks are due to Ross Turkington (B.Sc. Agr., R.D.Oen.) of the New South Wales Department of Agriculture; R. S. Harper, Chief of the Division of Horticulture of the Victorian Department of Agriculture; his counterpart, J. P. Eckersley, in Western Australia, and also Dorham Mann; W. F. Walker, Chief Horticulturist in Tasmania; R. C. Cannon, Director of Horticulture for Queensland; E. W. Boehm; and splendid stalwart in times of stress, Jack Ludbrook.

Len Evans
Jaki Ilbery

Ross Turkington

Wine grape planting trends in New South Wales

In response to the rapid increase in Australian wine consumption since 1965, heavy plantings of wine grape varieties have been made in New South Wales during the last seven years. In 1965 there were 8,202 acres of vines intended for wine grape production, but by 1971 the area planted for wine grapes had more than doubled to 18,530 acres.

The total vineyard area in New South Wales in 1971 was 31,040 acres and this represents 19 percent of the total area planted to grapes in Australia.

There is a strong upward trend in the area of wine grape plantings in New South Wales *(figure 1)*. It is apparent that most of the new plantings have been made since 1967 and that the imposition of an excise on wine in 1970 caused no reduction in the rate of increase in plantings. The main bulk of the new plantings comprise the table wine varieties shiraz, semillon and cabernet sauvignon, while the distillation variety doradillo has actually declined in area *(figure 2)*.

Full details of New South Wales grape plantings as at 31 December, 1965 and 31 December, 1971 are compared in *Table 1*. Plantings of varieties intended for the production of table and drying grapes are also included because these varieties are often processed by wineries. Unlike wine varieties the area of drying grapes has increased only slightly while the area planted to table grapes has declined.

Because of the need to replant vineyards after about forty years, the non-bearing area should comprise at least 5 percent of the total planting if present area of vines is to be maintained. A non-bearing area of less than 5 percent indicates that the area planted to a particular variety is declining and this is certainly the case with doradillo which has a non-bearing area of 1 percent. On the other hand, a non-bearing area of greater than 5 percent indicates the area planted is increasing. The overall non-bearing area of 32 percent for wine grapes contrasts with the now declining acreage of drying varieties (2 percent non-bearing) and the stable acreage of table grapes (5 percent non-bearing). This implies that 32 percent of the wine grapes planted in New South Wales have yet to produce.

Grape plantings in New South Wales are situated in three major districts and three minor districts with other small isolated plantings scattered throughout the state.

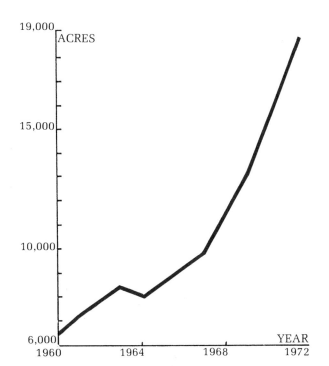

Figure 1: Total area of wine grapes planted in New South Wales.

Major Districts

1. Murrumbidgee Irrigation Areas (M.I.A.)

The M.I.A. is by far the most important wine producing district in New South Wales. At present it has 9,344 acres of vines, of which 8,555 acres produce wine grapes.

The M.I.A. is located 300 air miles west of Sydney and its main towns are Griffith and Leeton. Most of the vineyards are located at the western end of the M.I.A. around Griffith and its satellite villages of Hanwood, Yoogali, Bilbul, Beelbangera and Yenda. Twenty miles to the south of Griffith is the Coleambally Irrigation Area (C.I.A.). The vineyard area of the C.I.A. is relatively small and it is included in the M.I.A. for statistical purposes.

With an annual average rainfall of 16 inches, it is essential that M.I.A. vineyards are irrigated regularly and in consequence yields are high (8 tons per acre).

Orchard fruits such as citrus, canning peaches, apricots, prunes, apples and pears are also grown in the M.I.A. and most of the individual orchards grow a 'fruit salad' mixture of these fruits and vines.

The holdings are generally small with an average area of 43.14 acres* with 21.24 acres devoted to vineyard including 17.70 acres of wine grape varieties. The majority of orchards and vineyards are owned and operated by Italian migrants and their descendants. There are only a few farms specializing in grape production but their number is increasing because of the greater production efficiency possible with large specialist vineyards.

The maximum size of orchards and vineyards that can be held by any one person (home maintenance area) in the M.I.A. and other irrigation areas has been limited in the past to fifty acres by the Water Conservation and Irrigation Commission (W.C. & I.C.). The W.C. & I.C. supply and control the delivery of irrigation water to the individual farms and have imposed area limitations to prevent exploitation of the land by large monopoly interests. However, because of increasing economic pressures on farmers to improve their operating efficiency by increasing the area of land farmed, the maximum permissible area of orchard and vineyard was increased to 100 acres in 1970. As yet there is only a handful of individually owned vineyards exceeding fifty acres in area.

The planting of wine grapes in the M.I.A., apart from maximum acreage restrictions, is controlled on a voluntary basis through the M.I.A. Wine Grapes Planting Advisory Committee. The Committee meets annually prior to the planting season and comprises delegates from the N.S.W. Wine Grapes Marketing Board, the M.I.A. Winemakers Association, the N.S.W. Department of Agriculture and CSIRO. Planting and production trends are reviewed and winemakers' requirements are discussed. A general recommendation is then issued to growers who, in consultation with their individual winemakers, make their final planting decisions. In this way the planting of wine grapes is well regulated and the danger of shortages and surpluses of particular varieties minimized.

The total area of plantings has increased substantially since 1960 with a particularly rapid increase from 1967 on. The increased plantings have not only been a direct result of the boom conditions in the wine industry but also a result of replacement of peach trees that died during the wet winters of 1968 and 1969. The heavy plantings made in 1963 were associated with the record crop and yields produced in 1962 and the allied increased profitability of wine grape growing.

M.I.A. winemakers, in relation to those in other irrigated districts, can be considered most fortunate because of the excellent choice of varieties they have at their disposal. The distribution of varieties is:

Shiraz: 24.0 percent
Semillon: 20.5 percent
Trebbiano: 13.8 percent
Grenache: 7.5 percent
Muscat Gordo Blanco: 6.0 percent
Palomino: 6.0 percent
Doradillo: 5.5 percent
Cabernet Sauvignon: 4.6 percent
Pedro Ximenez: 3.4 percent
Others: 9.6 percent

*Economic Survey of the Wine Grape Industry, Quart. Rev. Agric. Ecos., *XXIII*, 3 July, 1970.

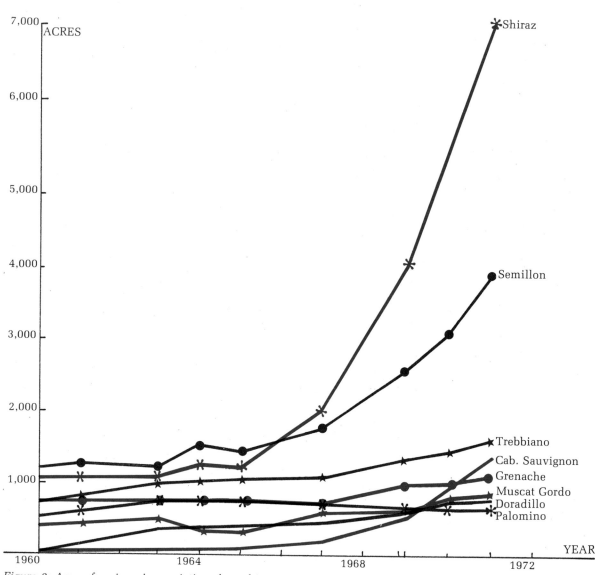

Figure 2: Area of major wine varieties planted in New South Wales.

The acreage of wine grapes in the M.I.A. increased from 5,687 in 1965 to 8,555 in 1971. The strong upward trend in plantings of wine grapes is continuing in contrast to the fall off in table grape acreage and despite the 1971 recommendation of M.I.A. Wine Grapes Planting Advisory Committee that a 'severe brake should be placed on the further expansion of M.I.A. wine grape plantings'. However, it is expected the rate of planting will slow down in the near future as the full effects of the present difficult wine grape marketing situation are felt. The most rapidly expanding varieties are, in order, shiraz, cabernet sauvignon, semillon and trebbiano, all of which can be used for the production of table wine.

A substantial area of suitable land for wine grapes is still available in the M.I.A. and could be planted to vineyard should a demand for increased wine grape production arise.

Lower Murray

The Lower Murray district in New South Wales forms part of the Sunraysia area which has its centre at the town of Mildura, Victoria, and is more widely known for its importance in dried fruit production rather than wine grape production. With an annual rainfall of 10 inches, the climate is eminently suited for the production of dried vine fruit. Naturally irrigation is essential and the

Wine	Dec. 31, 1965			Dec. 31, 1971			No. of Growers
	Bearing	Total	% N.B.	Bearing	Total	% N.B.	
Blanquette	41.00	42.75	4	66.99	110.56	40	15
Cabernet sauvignon	11.69	95.72	88	424.00	1252.61	66	154
Chardonnay+				36.98	67.93	46	16
Clare riesling+				23.08	30.58	25	5
Doradillo	819.21	832.70	2	640.34	644.72	1	215
Frontignan	143.50	159.80	10	128.91	153.37	16	47
Grenache	786.73	797.70	1	961.33	1091.68	12	310
Malbec+				5.46	13.46	59	6
Marsanne+				4.50	4.50		*
Mataro+				55.71	117.43	53	36
Muscat gordo blanco	249.91	308.17	19	687.04	739.92	7	218
Muscat Hamburgh	88.03	116.38	24	150.81	152.81	1	101
Oeillade	48.15	48.15	0	48.27	48.27	0	22
Palomino	217.88	400.18	46	641.18	666.26	4	183
Pedro Ximenez	421.70	438.55	4	341.82	343.40	1	107
Pinot noir+				41.14	42.14	2	8
Rhine riesling+				67.91	228.86	70	42
Semillon	1102.96	1503.09	27	2606.20	3758.68	31	446
Shiraz	1270.17	1670.96	24	3831.86	6806.41	44	590
Tokay+				2.30	10.36	78	*
Touriga+				7.72	13.72	44	*
Traminer	36.50	48.50	25	85.80	110.84	23	19
Trebbiano	1019.20	1181.93	14	1317.64	1468.55	10	352
Verdelho	34.00	34.00	0	43.21	45.21	4	*
Others	573.01	639.90	10	404.96	607.28	33	168+
Total wine	6863.64	8318.48	17	12624.86	18529.51	32	880
Total drying	8626.25	8797.00	2	9597.53	9751.10	2	637
Total table	2433.48	2741.27	12	2599.07	2720.13	4	804
Ungrafted stocks					39.58	100	23
Total—all varieties	17923.87	19856.75	9	24803.46	31090.32	20	1634

Table 1: *Acreages of vineyard in New South Wales in 1965 and 1971. (New South Wales Department of Agriculture Fruit Planting Census.)*

* Less than five growers.   + Included under others.   N.B. Non-bearing.

vines are watered by pumping from the Murray River.

The principal town in the New South Wales Lower Murray River district is Dareton. Most farms were established as soldier settler blocks after World War II. At present there are less than a thousand acres of true wine varieties, but because of a diversion of the drying varieties, sultana and muscat gordo blanco, into the Mildura winery and the more recent winery of International Cellars at Buronga, the Lower Murray is the second largest production centre of grapes used for wine in New South Wales.

Vineyard orchard holdings are similar to those of the M.I.A., averaging 44.34 acres of horticulture (vines and citrus), with 25.83 acres devoted to vineyards, but only 8.48 acres of wine grape varieties. There are virtually no specialist wine grape producers, but a small number of growers specialize in grape growing.

As in the M.I.A., the W.C. & I.C. limit the maximum area of orchard and vineyard that may be held by any one person to 100 acres, but there are virtually no holdings at this stage exceeding fifty acres.

Bearing in mind that drying varieties can be used for the production of wine, the area planted to true wine varieties represents only 9 percent of the total vineyard area. The distribution of wine varieties is:

Grenache: 30.9 percent
Shiraz: 26.1 percent
Doradillo: 19.0 percent
Palomino: 9.3 percent
Cabernet Sauvignon: 5.5 percent
Others: 9.2 percent

The large proportion of grenache reflects the demand for this variety in the Melbourne 'case trade' in which grapes are shipped to Melbourne in cases for sale to home winemakers.

Plantings of wine grape varieties in the Lower Murray district have increased almost ten-fold since 1962.

The strong upward trend in plantings of wine grape varieties since 1967 is associated with the opening of the new winery of International Cellars at Buronga and associated contracts agreed on by certain growers to supply grapes. However, it appears that the requirements of this winery are now being fulfilled and the expansion in wine grape plantings is halted. Table grape varieties increased three-fold from 1965 to 1971, plantings extending from 100 to 351 acres in the period. There is a large area of sultana in relation to the small area of grapes for winemaking which shows that there is ample scope for diversion of this variety into the wine industry should the need arise.

It is unlikely that further expansion in the area of wine grapes will take place, at least until it is clear that markets can be found for the production from extensive newly planted vineyards, many of which have yet to come into full bearing.

Hunter Valley

Prior to 1960 Hunter Valley vineyards were confined to a small area around Pokolbin near Cessnock, 130 miles north of Sydney, and Broke, some 30 miles west of Pokolbin on the Wollombi Brook. These vineyards were owned and operated almost entirely by established proprietary and family wine-making companies.

In 1967 private investors, syndicates and public companies began to stake their claim in the Hunter Valley wine industry and sparked off an unprecedented heavy planting programme. Some of these newcomers will be growing grapes for established wineries, while some plan to, and others have already, constructed their own.

Because of the unavailability of large areas of suitable soil in the traditional area around Pokolbin, many of the new vineyards have been established further up the Hunter Valley around the towns of Muswellbrook, Denman and Scone. To supplement the lower rainfall of these new areas most of these vineyards have installed trickle irrigation systems, using water either from Wybong Creek, the Goulburn or Hunter Rivers.

Vineyard size ranges from twenty to the 1,600 acres planned for a new vineyard in the Upper Hunter. When planting is completed it will be the largest vineyard in Australia.

Since 1960 the area planted to wine grapes in the Hunter Valley has increased by a factor of nearly seven. In the period from 1965 to 1971 the area under wine grape varieties increased—from 1,323 to 7,135 acres. The dominant varieties are shiraz (53.3 percent), semillon (26.7 percent) and cabernet sauvignon (9.4 percent).

The 56 percent non-bearing area of Hunter Valley wine grape varieties is much higher than that of the M.I.A. and indicates that substantial increases in the production of Hunter Valley wine can be expected during the next few years. While there is ample suitable land available in the Upper Hunter Valley area, future expansion will be dictated by the size of the market for the different Hunter Valley wines. However, indications are that planting of established vineyards will continue for at least another two years and it is expected that the area planted to wine grapes will exceed 10,000 acres by 1973.

Because table grape varieties are not used in the Hunter Valley wine industry, it is not proposed to present data on them here.

Minor districts

Smaller but significant plantings of wine grapes also exist in the Mid-Murray, Corowa-Barooga, Forbes (where plantings are relatively static at 40 acres) and Mudgee districts.

Mid-Murray

Located near the towns Goodnight and Koraleigh, the Mid-Murray district produces mainly drying varieties, little of which are diverted to wineries. However, plantings of wine varieties have increased slightly and it is likely that this trend will continue in view of the establishment of a co-operative winery at Woorinen, Victoria.

Corowa-Barooga

Plantings have been very static in this district and no further expansion is expected except possibly further north in the Berrigan Irrigation District. Corowa-Barooga plantings are owned wholly by wineries.

Mudgee

Wine grape plantings are expanding rapidly at Mudgee. In 1965 there were 147 acres of wine grapes. This figure had increased to 648 acres by the end of 1971. The vineyards are being developed mainly by city based investors for table wine production and are not irrigated. Further plantings are expected but their extent will depend on the development of outlets for Mudgee wine.

New wine grape districts

Plantings of wine grapes have been made during recent years in the previously untried districts of

Bob Hazelgrove at work in the laboratory at Hungerford Hill's Buronga winery, N.S.W.

Wee Waa, Young and Inverell. A major problem facing the proprietors of these vineyards is the lack of a nearby winery to process the grapes.

Wee Waa

An area of wine grapes (shiraz) is being grown under irrigation from bores by a private developer. Future expansion will depend largely on the outcome of this venture.

Young

Small plantings have been made at Young and Cowra by private landholders. Further expansion is expected to take place with the establishment of a large vineyard at Cowra this year.

Inverell

A small area has been planted on a trial basis. No immediate further expansion is expected.

Future trends in New South Wales

It is clear that, despite the continued rapid expansion of New South Wales wine grape vineyard area during 1971, unless the availability of markets for Australian wine improves overnight there will be a rapid decline in the rate of planting in New South Wales during the next three years. By 1975 it is expected that plantings will be sufficient to only maintain the existing area of vineyard.

Victoria

Along with the rest of Australia, plantings of vines in Victoria increased dramatically with the boom of the sixties. The acreage of established areas was increased, and vines were planted in areas previously not used for viticulture, such as at Drumborg. Further, some revivals were begun in areas long dead, such as at the former famous wine grape area of Yering near Lilydale.

North-east Victoria

This area has had a very up and down history of winemaking. At the beginning of 1970 there were 1,428 acres under vine, of which sixty acres were non-bearing. New plantings in this area have not been extensive since that time, and would amount to approximately 100 acres. The position is, however, a healthy one compared to the decline which the north-east had suffered for so many years.

Goulburn Valley

This area includes the main irrigated district between Kyabram and Shepparton, the biggest vineyards being owned by Messrs Darveniza, Conte and Gravina. In 1970 there were 500 acres of vines in bearing, with a further 200 acres of non-bearing vines. Only small extensions of plantings have been made in this district. In the Seymour-Nagambie area small increases have been made by 'Chateau Tahbilk' and Fitzpatrick Bros.

Bendigo

This area extends from the Goulburn River westward and includes several small plantings from five to fifteen acres. At the beginning of this decade there was a total of 205 acres under wine grapes. However, only seventy-five acres of these were bearing. The most significant area is that established by Mr Ross Shelmerdine with over 100 acres at Mitchells Town, near 'Chateau Tahbilk'.

Western Victoria

This area includes the plantings at Great Western and Avoca. The largest plantings are controlled by Seppelts and Bests (Thomson Bros) and 'Chateau Remy' in conjunction with Messrs Nathan and Wyeth Pty Ltd. Other plantings which could become significant in the area are those of J. Barry, Avoca, and Wal Henning, who is establishing a 400 acre vineyard of premium varieties, at Moonambel. In addition, Des McRae and his two sons are establishing a vineyard on their property at Ararat, and the Dalkin family have planted twenty acres only a few miles from Great Western.

Mildura

It is assumed that approximately 200 acres of additional wine grape plantings would have been made in this district since 1970. Before this time there were 1,137 acres under vine for wine, of which 619 acres were not bearing. The main plantings have occurred in the Nangiloc area and in areas south and west of Mildura where additional water has become available. Several of the larger plantings of 100 acres-plus, in the Mildura district, are being established under local management by syndicates and business people. Quite a number of smaller individual plantings have been made by growers who have decided to diversify from their normal production of dried fruits, citrus and vegetables. In almost all of these instances the growers or syndicates have an arrangement with either the Mildara winery, Merbein or the Hungerford Hill winery at Buronga to take their grapes.

Robinvale

In 1970 there were 154 acres of wine grapes planted, of which only thirty-one acres were bearing. Very little change has occurred since this time, but there has been an expansion in the McWilliams installation, and it is understood that this winery absorbed large quantities of local grapes, including gordos and sultanas.

Swan Hill

Of the 382 acres planted in 1970, 215 acres were in full bearing. Approximately fifty acres of additional wine grape plantings would have been made in this area since then. Three local wineries, including the long established installations of Bullers and Bests take considerable quantities of local grapes and the new installation which has been established under the general guidance of Hungerford Hill by the Woorinen Fruitgrowers Co-operative was processing grapes this season.

Portland

The major vineyard in this area is that of Seppelts at Drumborg. There has not been a large increase in plantings and in 1970 there were 160 acres under vine, only a quarter of which were bearing grapes.

Metropolitan

This district includes an area mainly east of Melbourne and comprises quite a number of small vineyards, none of which would be greater in area than thirty acres. Recently there would have been approximately an additional thirty acres planted in this area.

Tieing up plantings at Hungerford Hill's new vineyard at Coonawarra, S.A.

South Australia

At the end of March, 1971 the area planted to vines was a record 68,332 acres, representing an increase of 3,495 acres on the record area of vines twelve months earlier. Three years earlier, in March, 1968, there were ten thousand fewer acres of vines (58,129 acres). Ten thousand acres in three years is not to be sneezed at!

The largest areas of young vines, i.e., those planted in the past two or three years, are found in the varieties grenache, used to produce 'general purpose' wine; cabernet sauvignon and shiraz, for red wines; and rhine riesling and clare riesling for whites. It is a pleasing prospect for those who enjoy fine wine that the new plantings have been of these quality varieties.

It is of interest here to examine briefly the varieties crushed at the 1971 vintage. It is rather 'bringing-down-to-earth' to examine the following figures in view of all the talk of planting of the exotics, such as gewurtztraminer and pinot noir. The following Bureau of Census and Statistics figures bring home strongly the present position, where the highly prized and much-talked-about exotics hardly figure at all in terms of quantity.

The principal variety crushed for the State as a whole was gordo, with 33,047 tons. Second was sultana, 30,788 tons, followed closely by grenache, 30,215 tons, in third position.

Other prominent varieties in the State total were doradillo, 23,019 tons; pedro ximenez, 18,293 to and shiraz, 17,806 tons, while down the list were palomino, 9,877 tons; semillon, 5,404 tons; mataro, 4,679 tons; clare riesling, 4,447 tons; rhine riesling,

3,263 tons; trebbiano (ugni blanc or white hermitage), 2,787 tons.

The Riverland, as would be expected, accounted for almost the whole tonnage of the gordos crushed, 32,379 tons, and the whole of the sultanas, 30,788 tons.

Of the other varieties, the Riverland totals were: grenache, 14,725 tons; doradillo, 18,438 tons; pedro ximenez, 7,878 tons; shiraz, 5,590 tons; palomino, 6,214 tons; semillon, 2,962 tons; mataro, 1,743 tons; clare riesling, 1,865 tons; rhine riesling, 575 tons; trebbiano, 1,466 tons; common palomino, 1,866 tons.

Leading variety crushed in the Barossa Valley was grenache, 5,809 tons, closely followed by shiraz, 5,616 tons, and pedro ximenez, 5,079 tons. Other Barossa totals included clare riesling, 2,434 tons; semillon, 2,260 tons; doradillo, 2,165 tons; rhine riesling, 1,934 tons; palomino, 1,343 tons; trebbiano, 1,260 tons.

In the Adelaide and southern grape growing areas the main crushings were of grenache, 8,184 tons, followed by shiraz, 5,052 tons; pedro ximenez, 2,979 tons; doradillo, 2,416 tons; palomino, 2,320 tons.*

It is interesting that a mere 2,235 tons of cabernet sauvignon were crushed in the whole of South Australia in 1971. No comment!

Some new grape varieties are currently being developed in the State, though no commercial wine has been made as yet from these. Eight varieties have been tested: sylvaner, chenin blanc, white riesling, ruby red hybrid, pinot noir, gewurtztraminer, zinfandel and pinot blanc. Of these, gewurtztraminer has been the most successful, with chenin blanc next.

In March, 1972 the South Australian Government approved the importation of six new grape varieties into the State. These are the French colombard, a high yielding white variety; chardonnay, a high quality, moderately yielding grape, famous for white burgundy; a French clone of malbec, to substitute for the virus infected South Australian material; pinot gris, a white variety; pinot meunier, a black grape from the Champagne region of France; and cardinal, an early red table grape from California.

There has been some agitation within the industry for the more rapid introduction of new varieties and clones. The Government, however, is concerned to keep South Australia as virus free as possible and has a policy of the utmost caution with regard to the importation of new vines.

Here follows an outline of new developments in some of the winemaking companies. G. Gramp and Sons (Orlando) have carried out new plantings, mostly at their Eden Valley Estate. Their total acreage there is eighty, of which twenty-five to thirty acres were planted in 1971 and about twenty acres are planned for this year. The main variety is rhine riesling (seventy acres), with five acres of gewurtztraminer and some experimental cabernet sauvignon and shiraz. Large scale new plantings are not planned at this stage.

*Commonwealth Bureau of Census and Statistics, quoted in *The Murray Pioneer*, 21 October, 1971.

Thomas Hardy and Sons have 330 acres at Keppoch, of which 100 acres were planted last year. It is expected that about sixty acres will go in this year. Shiraz is the main variety grown (210 acres) with sixty acres of cabernet, forty of malbec and twenty acres of rhine riesling.

Penfolds have in the past decade maintained a steady replanting programme of the high quality varieties. This has been their major area of activity, rather than new planting. Of the 560 acres at Kalimna, thirty acres were replanted in 1971. At their recently acquired Truro vineyard, the total acreage of which will be eighty acres, Penfolds plan to plant twenty-five acres this year. At Kalimna the varieties are mainly shiraz, mataro, oeillade and clare riesling, with some experimental plantings of traminer and pinot noir. At the Truro vineyard they have extended these two experimental varieties, and will put in more as they become available. At Coonawarra, Penfold's total acreage is 240 acres. In 1971 they planted ten acres with rhine riesling, and plan to put in another ten to fifteen acres of rhine riesling this year.

The company has established a new eighty acre experimental vineyard at Dimchurch in the Barossa Valley, five miles east of Kalimna. Drip irrigation on the Dapkos System, developed by Keith Yore, and used in the Upper Hunter Valley, will be used at Dimchurch. The vineyard will be planted with new wine varieties that have become available, including traminer, sylvaner, pinot noir, chardonnay and white pinot. The plantings will be on a scale sufficient to enable 1,000 gallons of wine to be made from each of the varieties. It is estimated that the overall outlay involved in the planting of the vineyard will be at a minimum rate of $1,700 an acre.

Quelltaler Wines at Watervale have a total acreage of 840; 571 of these under vines. This is made up of pedro ximenez, 140 acres; rhine riesling, 220 acres; semillon, 74; shiraz, 48; grenache, 69; doradillo, 14, and six acres of mixed varieties. In 1971 they planted fifteen acres of rhine riesling and plan to put in thirty acres this year; about fifteen each of shiraz and rhine riesling. Over the past four years Quelltaler has put in mostly rhine riesling. The company is concerned with replanting and increasing their acreage.

St Clare Wines have 108 acres at Ben Burnie, Burton Cottage Vineyards at Clare and St Clare Vineyards at Watervale. There were no plantings in 1971, or this year, as they concentrated on their Auburn development. The 'Chateau Clare' vineyards at Auburn cover 440 acres under vines. They were planted in two sections of 120 acres, in 1969; the balance in 1970. The first planting was mostly shiraz and cabernet sauvignon; with all cabernet sauvignon in the second planting. A site for the winery is currently being excavated and the building will be ready for the 1973 vintage.

Grape pickers at work at Hungerford Hill, N.S.W.

The Seaview-Glenloth Company is expanding in several new areas. The 'Glenloth' vineyards in the Keppoch area cover 400 acres, of which 300 acres are already planted with cabernet sauvignon, shiraz and rhine riesling; and they expect to plant the other 100 acres this year. At Willunga, seventy-five new 'Seaview' acres were planted in 1970. The majority is cabernet sauvignon, plus twelve acres of malbec. Planting at this vineyard is now complete. 'Seaview' have acquired 120 acres at Bethany, between McLaren Vale and Willunga. 100 acres were planted last year with rhine riesling, cabernet sauvignon and shiraz; the majority being cabernet sauvignon. The other twenty acres will be planted this year to rhine riesling. At Chapel Hill, up behind 'Seaview' Winery, there are eighteen acres of which twelve acres are under cabernet sauvignon, and the balance will be planted to shiraz this year. Another vineyard, opposite the winery, 'Blencowe', has ninety acres. Half will be planted this year to shiraz, rhine riesling and sauvignon blanc (the main varieties, with just a few smaller lots of other varieties), the other half will be completed next year.

Seppelts have their traditional headquarters in the Barossa Valley, but these are maintained more for historical than practical reasons. The country in the Barossa is too marginal in rainfall to be expanded for viticulture. The company's policy is to encourage private growers to deliver grapes to them in this region. Qualco on the River Murray was primarily purchased for sherry and spirit production, but has been converted to table wine production. The project will conclude at 500 acres within the decade. Seppelts have made an enormous investment in the Keppoch Valley since they moved in in 1964. To date they have planted cabernet sauvignon, malbec, shiraz, frontignac, tokay and some small acreages of rhine riesling, sylvaner and pinot noir. Development at Keppoch is expected to be completed within the decade. Seppelts believe that there is need to place more emphasis on the growing of better wine grapes, and at the same time improving efficiency to reduce their cost of production.

The Stanley Wine Company has a total of 780 acres, with another 400 acres to plant. In 1971 they put in sixty acres, and another sixty to seventy acres are projected for this year. Emphasis has been on rhine riesling and shiraz, with some cabernet sauvignon and clare riesling. Stanley are still developing their experimental vineyard which was begun in 1968 with two cuttings of each new variety. No quantity of grapes have been picked yet, and no wine made. Varieties are gamay beaujolais, pinot noir, sylvaner and gewurtztraminer.

Douglas A. Tolley has seventy acres planted in the Barossa Valley. No plantings are planned for this year. Last year one and a half acres each of gewurtztraminer, sylvaner, pinot noir and gamay were planted in the Barossa. At Qualco, near Waikerie, D. A. Tolley has 141 acres under vine.

Three acres each of cabernet sauvignon and rhine riesling were replanted last year and seven new acres of shiraz put in. There will probably be no more this year. At Hope Valley, Modbury and Teatree Gully the company has 275 acres. The last planting was in 1970 (two and a half acres each of rhine riesling and shiraz) and small replantings are carried out each year. Six acres of grenache will be replaced this year.

Tolley, Scott and Tolley have 1,254 acres in all at Waikerie. Of these 1,000 acres are fully planted—of which 800 are in production; the balance will commence production next vintage. The main varieties are grenache, 323 acres; trebbiano, 144 acres; cabernet sauvignon, 150 acres; doradillo, 140 acres and shiraz, 100 acres.

Early in 1970 Tolley, Scott and Tolley purchased 450 acres of land in the Barossa Ranges, three miles west of the Eden Valley township. 100 acres have been planted—last year sixty acres of rhine riesling and forty of shiraz. This year another 150 acres are going in: thirty acres of cabernet sauvignon; sixty of rhine riesling and fifty to sixty acres of shiraz. The whole property is being planted on contour because of the soil structure there. The rate of planting depends largely on the weather, last year being a perfect season for planting young vines. A small nursery is being established at Eden Valley for the propagation of recently released varieties, such as gewurtztraminer, chenin blanc and pinot chardonnay. This vineyard will be called the Woodbury Estate Vineyard. Tolley, Scott and Tolley are also doing some experimental work with the rubired variety.

Yalumba (S. Smith) has a total acreage in the Barossa Valley of 461. Within the last two to three years more black varieties than white have been planted. The company has concentrated on cabernet sauvignon and shiraz, plus rhine riesling, and suggest these varieties to growers. When completed the total acreage at Mexican Vale will be about thirty acres under drip irrigation. Last year twenty acres were planted, and this year nine to ten acres will go in. Of that figure, about half will be cabernet sauvignon and the rest shiraz.

Last year about twenty acres of experimental vines and shiraz were planted by Yalumba at Waikerie; about ten acres of new varieties; the balance being the old faithful, shiraz. Another twenty acres are being planted at Waikerie this year; the varieties will depend on what rooted vine stocks are available.

Coonawarra and Keppoch

With regard to regions, Coonawarra and Keppoch have probably enjoyed the most attention in recent years. The increase in plantings at Coonawarra has been nothing short of dramatic. In 1959 there were only 250 acres under vine there. By 1968 this figure had grown to 1,480. Although final figures have not yet been confirmed, it is believed that after the 1971

At Buronga, N.S.W., Hungerford Hill have established an open-air winery. It will have the capacity for handling 2½ million gallons of wine.

plantings there were 2,485 acres under vine at Coonawarra.* Of these, shiraz was the main variety, 1,243 acres; with 732 acres of cabernet sauvignon, 367 acres of rhine riesling and whites, and 143 acres of other varieties. E. W. Boehm has estimated that in 1971, 478 acres of cabernet sauvignon, 170 acres of shiraz, 75 acres of rhine riesling and other whites, and three acres of other varieties were planted. The bald figures do not really convey the amazing increase—the area under vine at Coonawarra increased almost ten-fold in the twelve years from 1959 to 1971.

Another dramatic development has taken place in the nearby Keppoch area. Bear in mind there were *no* wine grapes in the area in 1959. By 1968 there were 120 acres. After the 1971 plantings it has been estimated that there were 1,451 acres of vines. Of this total, about 593 acres were planted in 1971. This means that 40 percent of a not inconsiderable area was planted only last year. At Keppoch the main variety is shiraz, 638 acres; with 343 acres of rhine riesling and whites; 276 acres of other varieties and 194 acres of cabernet sauvignon.

Adelaide Hills

The Adelaide Hills is emerging as a 'new wine region', despite high land prices. The wineries there have been described as 'boutique cellars' as thousands of Adelaide motorists tour the Hills every weekend. Grape acreage expansion in the Hills is limited by high land prices and all the wineries there buy grapes from southern areas.

One of the biggest wineries in the area, 'St Francis', has impressive plans for development. It is situated close to the main South Road at Reynella, and was established by winemaker, Karl Lambert, who previously spent sixteen years with Penfolds. The winery specializes in reds and buys grapes from contract growers in the McLaren Vale area. 'St Francis' has made rapid strides since its first vintage two years ago. The company plans to develop picnic areas and build a banqueting hall, as well as to establish a 'wine museum' in the 102 year old cellars.

In the nearby Happy Valley, the Torresan family is making a name for itself. Gino Torresan started six years ago with ten tons of grapes, and now buys more to make up his yearly 200-ton vintage, although he has about fifty acres under grapes. Only thirty acres of grapes will be retained, as the land has been re-zoned as residential, and in the next five to ten years the majority of the family's grapes will come from land bought at McLaren Vale. The Happy Valley Winery offers the usual wide range of wines, concentrating mainly on reds.

Practically next door is the 'Marienberg' Winery, run by winemaker, Ursula Pridham. Mrs Pridham has had considerable success in shows. Her vintage is now about 120 tons, and Mrs Pridham plans to concentrate on quality rather than on increasing size. 'Marienberg' had its first small vintage in 1968—at which time winemaking was only a hobby for Ursula Pridham.

Light Wines have, near Clarendon, a brand new winery on the brow of a hill which undoubtedly impresses many Sunday drivers. They have now had three vintages ranging from 400 to 800 tons.

Don and Barbara Paul of the 'Trennert' winery at Clarendon boast that their enterprise must be the smallest in South Australia, because they make only just over the ten ton commercial minimum. They have only had a licence since the beginning of 1972, winemaking being only a hobby before this. The Pauls are proud to have already had show success.

The Murray River districts

From the smallest winery in the State, we move to the largest region—the River districts. It is expected that wine grape production from these areas will increase by fifty percent in the next three years, resulting in a total production of 210,000 tons. This was revealed by the State's first comprehensive survey of horticultural plantings along the River Murray. The figures showed a downward trend in production for drying vine varieties; namely, sultanas, currants and gordos, due to old age.

The River areas have been hardest hit by the slump following the Government-imposed excise tax on wine. In addition, when the new plantings of premium varieties come into full bearing in the next few years, it can be expected that the irrigated areas will be further affected, unless demand takes a sudden (and unexpected) upswing.

Western Australia

The Swan Valley and adjacent areas

It must be appreciated that suitable viticultural soils in the Swan Valley area are fully planted and that expansion of vine growing in this region is limited. The position is complicated owing to the region's close proximity to Perth and subsequently inflated land prices. Acreage in the area has been steadily declining owing to old Currant vineyards going out of production.

The wine grape position is rather brighter than the overall area figures indicate. Most replanting is being carried out to wine grape varieties, particularly better quality varieties. Thus the wine grape acreage is being maintained and there is a desirable trend towards a higher proportion of high class varieties. Wineries, both small and larger, have been generally active in this regard with their own plantings. The wine industry in the Swan Valley represents a picture of consolidation and improvement with several of the small winemakers beginning to produce some fine table wines of the local styles. This is being achieved through better grape varieties and improving technology.

New areas

Of particular interest are the developments in new districts outside the Swan Valley.

Valencia have initiated large new plantings at their 'Moondah' property in the Gingin area some fifty miles north of Perth. This is a warm region (over 4,000 day degrees heat summation for the growing season) and should produce table wines of generally similar style to those from the Swan Valley. It is assumed that the firm's basic objective in going to Gingin is to produce table wines to supplement the established Houghton styles, particularly White Burgundy. They have about 300 acres planted to varieties including Swan Valley semillon (chenin blanc), verdelho, tokay, shiraz, cabernet and malbec.

There has been a lot of interest in developments in two regions in the cooler south west of this State; the Mount Barker/Frankland region and the Margaret River/Busselton area. These regions have climates possibly better suited to the production of traditional table wine styles than any areas in Australia. Heat summations are 2,600 (Mt Barker) and 2,200 (Margaret River) day degrees, winter rainfall is generous, there is freedom from spring frost and little potential for summer rain problems.

In the Mt Barker/Frankland region, there are several new plantings. The Western Australian Department of Agriculture has an experimental vineyard at Mt Barker (5 acres—half cabernet and half rhine riesling) from which the first grapes have just been processed. There are several individuals with small new plantings. The only varieties in the area are cabernet, malbec, shiraz and rhine riesling. The Frankland River Grazing Co has a large new planting under way which is unquestionably a significant commercial venture. We are looking forward to the young wines from this region and can anticipate fine table wines with trends towards traditional European styles.

There are also several individuals active in the Margaret River/Busselton area. This area has a unique climate with a very long, but very cool growing season. It enjoys freedom from summer rain to almost the same extent as Perth, so will be a very consistent and safe region for wine grape production. The pioneer in the area is Dr T. Cullity and he has a small planting of the better varieties with a small processing plant. He has just completed his second vintage and his young wines show excellent promise. There are others with small plantings and plans

for development in the region. Large scale development is anticipated in this area in the near future.

As for the future of these new areas, much will depend upon the quality of wines produced in the next few years and subsequent larger scale developments. The costs involved can be appreciated. The Department of Agriculture is confident that the regions have the capacity to produce table wines of exceptional quality. However, the areas have yet to be actually proven.

If Western Australia is to expand its wine industry, it has an opportunity in the high quality table wine field. The Eastern States have a firm grip on the flagon and standard quality wine trade. They are looking towards high quality varietal table wines made from non-irrigated grapes and having distinctive regional characteristics.

Queensland

While there has been considerable interest in wine production in Queensland, to the knowledge of its Department of Agriculture there have been no recent plantings of any commercial extent.

The total production of wine in the state is less than 100,000 gallons. The bulk of this comes from near Stanthorpe, in the high land Granite Belt, and is made not from wine grapes but from the tail end of the table grape crop. Only one winery, that of Bassetts of Roma, is based on wine grape varieties, and there have been no substantial recent plantings.

In response to widespread interest, the Queensland Department of Agriculture is initiating pilot trials in several districts to determine the potential for wine production in the State. To do this, it has first been necessary to introduce most of the wine grape varieties from the southern States, as very few of these are to be found in Queensland.

Tasmania

In recent years there has been a revival of interest in the growing of wine grapes in Tasmania, many years after the unsuccessful early attempts. These developments are however quite small in scale and very much in the initial, experimental stages.

In the last decade, Claude Alcorso planted vines at his 'Moorilla Estate' at Berridale, near Hobart, with the main planting in 1966. He now has one acre of vines. In 1965 'Windemere' vineyards was planted on the West Tamar, near Robigana, which also consists of one acre. 'Chateau Legana', situated near the town of that name, was started in 1969, and now has four acres of vines. There are several other plantings from which wine is made in small quantities, mainly for home consumption.

Further details of these developments are given in the section on Tasmania.

Small wood storage, McWilliam's Wines, Hanwood, N.S.W.

16 Takeovers in the wine business

Michael Baume

Sixty million dollars worth of takeovers in the space of three years, or many millions of dollars more than the total of all the mergers and acquisitions that had taken place during the previous 130 years or so history, of the Australian wine industry. That, in a nutshell, is the measure of the remarkable changes that have come so quickly to what was basically, a family business. Wine has become one of the greatest centres of takeover activity in Australia. And the biggest, most significant takeovers are all by companies owned by, or closely associated with, overseas interests. As a result five of the top ten Australian wine groups have suddenly become foreign owned or controlled. And the five remaining locally owned companies in the big league have been consistently wooed by rich suitors keen to buy their way into one of the fastest growing businesses in Australia.

Not that it has been a massively profitable one; the huge purchase prices for many of the wine groups that have been sold reflect expectations of future high profits rather than what has been achieved so far. For example, it would take more than thirty years for the buyers of Lindemans to get their money back if the company's profits were to remain at last year's level. There is nothing surer than that the buyers mean to make a lot more money out of the wine business than the previous owners; so it looks as if there are going to be a lot of very significant changes in the structure (and marketing policies in particular) of the major members of the Australian wine industry. Not much has happened yet, but there is no doubt it will. And this could mean some big changes too for the companies that have elected to stand independently against the flood of foreign takeover.

This is not to say that the industry in the past had not been achieving remarkable growth in local consumption of its product. The marketing triumphs of such leaders as Lindemans in quality wines and Wynns in making flagon wines respectable, had been reflected in the huge increases in consumption per head in Australia in the last five years or so. But the newcomers think that a lot more can be done, and already Orlando under its new control from the British dominated Reckitt and Colman group has shown what can be achieved with a good marketing gimmick like the one litre carafe.

But for most of these big companies, clearly one of the most interesting sales prospects is in exports, where so far only Seppelts, and to a lesser extent Kaiser Stuhl, have really been trying terribly hard (excepting, of course, the British-owned Emu Wine Co, which still produces its medicinal Australian burgundy that is guaranteed to cure most of the ills suffered by Midlands housewives in Britain while keeping its good quality wines for local sophisticates under the Houghton label).

Many of the major companies acquiring wine businesses in Australia are involved in the wine trade in other countries. Allied Vintners Pty Ltd, which now owns Wynns, Seaview, and Glenloth, is itself jointly owned by Allied Breweries of the U.K. with Tooheys Ltd, the Sydney brewery, and there seems every prospect of the Australian product getting reasonable distribution through Allied Breweries' British outlets. Reckitt and Colman, which now owns Orlando and Morris wines, is a major bottler of Rhine wines through its U.K. parent and it has an American associated company which has interests in one of New York's major wine companies.

But for all the speculation about what these big newcomers are going to do in a marketing and managerial sense to their winemaking acquisitions in Australia, it seems certain that they are not going to muck about with the wine itself. It is striking that so far the companies doing the taking-over have gone to great pains to retain the winemaking skills that came with their acquisitions.

Some companies have even promoted the oenologists to high managerial positions—and all have endeavoured to keep the old family connections in their businesses. As a result, there are still Gramps at Orlando, still a Morris at Morris', still a Chaffey at Seaview, and a Tulloch at Tulloch's, and Egerton Dennis of the Ryecroft-McLaren Vale operation is chairman of the whole of the Reed Consolidated wine interests. And, of course, Philip Morris have pretty much left the successful Lindeman people to run their own show. The agreement with Rothmans and Hungerford Hill leaves Hungerford Hill in charge of wine production and Rothmans controlling marketing. What the big companies say is lacking—and what they are providing—is skill in management and marketing. They say that the industry was, in simple terms, badly managed and that good management will bring markedly improved profits. But it is not only because of the great marketing and management potential that so many millions of dollars have been poured into takeovers in this business in the last three years. There is a lot more to it than that.

In the first place, there are taxation benefits involved for a big profitable company in moving into primary production. And clearly the fastest growing and potentially most profitable primary area is wine.

There are special depreciation allowances that make it relatively cheap for companies to expand. These taxation benefits available to primary producers have, ironically, encouraged the big newcomers to the industry to make things more difficult for the genuine primary producers who have been growing grapes for years.

With tax concessions making it so cheap to do so, the big companies have been increasing plantings, particularly of higher quality wine grapes, so reducing the dependence on grapes produced by independent grape growers, particularly in South Australia. This trend was already in evidence before the bout of big takeovers began, but it has certainly increased; the proportion of grape acreage in South Australia owned by the wineries had grown from 11 percent a few years ago to 25 percent by early 1972 according to the Minister for Primary Industry, Mr Sinclair. This has not been the result of acquisition so much as of increased planting and the development of new groupings. As a special Commonwealth Government report on the wine industry recently done by Professor Grant points out, there could be a surplus of wine grapes emerging as a result of plantings in the late 1960s and 'if such conditions occur, proprietary wineries will use their own grapes and cut down on their purchases of grapes from growers and on their purchases of bulk wines from the co-operatives and small producers who do not market their own products. The trend towards vertical integration in the industry, that is, for winemakers to grow more of their own grapes, has and will amplify the effect of the burden of sales and production variations in the industry falling on the residual suppliers.' There has already been plenty of evidence of this as the big merged companies appeared to suffer far less during the latest year's downturn in per capita wine consumption (brought on by the 1970 wine excise) than did the small grape growers of South Australia, many of whom experienced serious financial difficulties.

Probably the most important taxation advantage to big companies in this industry lies in their ability to hide profits in their wine stocks. This applies particularly to the higher quality end of the business, where stocks of wine are held for some years at very low valuations, so providing hidden assets and deferring the emergence of taxable income. An added advantage, of course, is that the stock situation is sufficiently flexible because of the quality differences and blending involved, to allow considerable scope for hiding profits in good times and pulling them out when needed in bad times.

But why did the takeovers in the wine industry begin with such a burst only three years ago? One reason, of course, is that the remarkable developments of the previous few years had by then become clearly apparent. Certainly, the stock market had recognized the great potential in the listed companies, Lindemans (which had a succession of bonus issues during its listed life) and Penfolds, by pushing their shares up to record heights. If that sort of growth could be maintained, then clearly the buying companies would be on a good thing.

But it takes two to consummate a takeover and the very growth that was bringing such increased fortunes to Australian companies in the wine industry provided a large amount of the motivation for them to sell out. Growth costs money; many of the big local companies, particularly the family controlled ones, simply did not have the resources to keep up the pace being set by the market leaders. As Mr Henry Martin, the Deputy Chairman of H. M. Martin and Sons (Stonyfell and Saltram Wines) and who has remained a director of the company after its acquisition by Dalgety (the British dominated pastoral group) said recently: 'Operating as a family company our resources were stretched too far; we could not expand and that is what a company has to do. At least now we have the capital backing to do anything we think feasible.'

This reason for selling out can be spread right through the industry. And as the number of take-overs increased, it became increasingly evident to those companies that were left that they would either have to find a big brother too, or make some suitable alternative arrangements. Penfolds and Kaiser Stuhl are two of the wine producers that have chosen to go their own way and are spending large amounts of money on winery development and grape planting. There is no doubt that this problem is going to become increasingly serious. As a spokesman for McWilliams Wines said recently, 'The greater financial resources of large organizations like Philip Morris and Rothmans give them an advantage over the smaller independents in marketing situations where a lot of cash is needed at short notice to carry the retail trade.' Not that this was worrying the McWilliams man; he was confident that companies with a good name and prestige could meet the marketing competition of these newcomers.

Another reason for the widespread sell out by Australian wine companies was the extent to which the families themselves were keen to sell for family reasons. As Professor Grant pointed out in his study, some winemakers had accepted takeovers because for years profits had been ploughed back into the business and family members were locked in financially and found it hard to get any cash out of the enterprise. For instance, the Tulloch family which had owned the original 'Glen Elgin' property at which Tulloch wines had been made in the Hunter Valley for over 100 years, had twenty-two members of the family financially interested in the business at the time of the Reed takeover. It is natural that as families become more fragmented with succeeding generations, the ties that bind them to a wine business that returns them· very little, but which has a great capital worth, become weaker and weaker. As Professor Grant noted, an additional inducement to sell was that profits which had been ploughed back over the years could be at least recovered free of tax as a capital profit—and, at best, a great deal more could be gained tax free. This even applied to the listed companies where the families in control had not only gained the capital benefit involved in selling their wine businesses to the public company they floated in the first place, but also got the tax free capital gain when they were acquired by their new foreign masters.

The big question for the Australian consumer is whether or not these new foreign dominated groups are going to change the quality and style of the wines that have now become so popular on Australian dinner tables. It seems that the answer will be no, although there is a prospect of some improvements in quality as the result of newer and better equipment being now within the reach of many companies that could have been pretty stretched for cash. As Reckitt and Colman, for instance, have stated, their strong intention is to retain the quality and distincfive regional characteristics of both their Orlando South Australian wine and their Morris wine from Victoria. There is no intention to make one label the 'quality' label and the other the cheap mass label. This is in line with Lindemans' approach when they acquired Leo Burings; they put out flagon wines exclusively under the Buring name for some time before they allowed the Lindeman name to appear on flagons, but they nevertheless produced some very high quality show-winning wines under the Buring label. So while companies like Reckitt and Colman and Allied Vintners, who will be co-ordinating their various wine acquisitions under one managerial structure, the present .plans are for the wines to remain distinctively different.

Has the combination of factors that brought this burst of takeovers now ended? Probably not, even though there are clear signs that some of the ventures have been none too successful. Not much more than a year after spending close to a million dollars in buying the W. J. Seabrook wine business, Kiwi International has opted out and sold the business back to the Seabrooks. And there appear to have been some financial problems facing the local listed public company, Pokolbin Winemakers Ltd, which floated late in 1970 to take over the Drayton family's 'Happy Valley' vineyard at Pokolbin in the Hunter Valley.

But not even the recent downturn in per capita consumption of Australian wine during the 1971 financial year has dampened enthusiasm by many potential buyers of Australian wine businesses. There are still plenty of foreign-based accountants doing their sums on the sorts of profits they could get out of a jazzed-up Australian winemaker; there are still plenty of managing directors and chairmen of large international groups taking their dusty trips through the dirt roads of the Barossa and Hunter Valleys 'just to have a look'.

But there are not many companies left, and all of the big ones have been rejecting suitors for some time. There are the two listed public companies, Penfolds and Seppelts, which the share markets value at a total of more than $25 million. And then there are the big privately owned companies like McWilliams, Smiths (Yalumba) and Hardys. But it seems inevitable that there will be more takeovers, not only from those companies that have so far missed out in the rush into the Australian wine industry, but also from those already in it in a modest way who clearly have greater aspirations. For instance, it seems unlikely that the great H. J. Heinz organization will be content simply to own the fairly modest sized Stanley Wine Company.

No matter what the speculation is about the future, there can be no disputing the facts about the recent rush of takeovers. Before September, 1969, there had been very little takeover activity apart from such relatively modest moves as the Lindemans acquisition of the struggling Leo Buring business and of the smallish Rouge Homme operation. But then the British controlled packaging company, Reed Consolidated Industries Ltd (the Australian subsidiary of the giant Reed-IPC group that dominates the U.K. paper and newspaper industries) bought out the old-established Hunter Valley wine business of J. Y. Tulloch and Sons for $2 million or so. (Coincidentally, the company secretary of Reed who signed the letter announcing the acquisition, was named Tulloch.) Before twelve months were up, Reed made its second venture into wine, this time in South Australia, buying Ryecroft Vineyards Pty Ltd and its marketing company, McLaren Vale Wines Pty Ltd, which marketed Ryecroft, Ingoldby, and McLaren Vale Estate labels. Reeds are clearly aiming at the top quality end of the wine business.

The next move was Hungerford Hill Ltd, which had only been formed in 1969, with the petroleum and shipping company H. C. Sleigh taking up a major shareholding. Hungerford Hill (whose major assets also included a cotton farm at Wee Waa) paid $1.3 million in February, 1970, for the long-established southern vales producer, Walter Reynell and Sons Pty Ltd, whose Reynella wines had a sound reputation and whose winery is one of the most picturesque in Australia. But since then Hungerford Hill itself has sold out its wine operations to International Cellars Australia Pty Ltd, a company it owns jointly with the major cigarette maker, Rothmans of Pall Mall (Australia) Ltd, a subsidiary of the British Rothmans group. Hungerford received $2.8 million for its wine business, and then reinvested $2.3 million of this to acquire 50 percent of International Cellars with Rothmans subscribing another $2.3 million.

The next takeover was in October, 1970, only a month after Reeds acquired McLaren Vale when the small 'Glen View' winery was bought up by Melbourne interests. The following month, the modest 'Arrawarra' Winery and its adjacent 'Paradale' Winery at Tanunda in South Australia were acquired by BernKastel Wines Pty Ltd which was backed by Investment and Merchant Finance Corporation.

Then in December, 1970 came the first of the really big takeovers, with Reckitt and Colman buying G. Gramp and Sons (the Orlando group), having already acquired the Rutherglen winemaker, Morris Wines Pty Ltd, in August for an undisclosed amount of shares and cash. The Morris family interests included two producing vineyards of over 200 acres under vines, the 'Mia Mia' vineyard at Rutherglen, and another nearby at Balldale in New South Wales, also two wineries, one at Rutherglen and the 'Chateau Charles' at Griffith.

Like the Morris family, the Gramps had been in the business for more than 100 years, but the Gramps were a much bigger bite, having over 1,000 acres in full bearing in the Barossa and near Ramco on the Murray River, and also buying several thousand tons of grapes each year from independent growers. The Gramps had achieved considerable respect with some of their high quality Orlando wines and considerable profit with their sweet effervescent wine, Barossa Pearl, which stimulated a whole new market for wine. These two acquisitions made Reckitt and Colman one of the top five wine producing and marketing organizations in Australia. With the evident trend towards wine sales out of grocery shops and supermarkets, which Reckitt and Colman already serviced with their food, household products and toiletries, the company clearly has some interesting marketing opportunities available.

Another joint British-Australian company that moved into the wine business was Allied Vintners Pty Ltd, jointly owned by Britain's Allied Breweries and Sydney's Tooheys Ltd to buy the Seaview Winery at McLaren Vale for about $2 million in October, 1970. Five months later Allied Vintners also bought control of Glenloth Wines at O'Halloran Hill, south of Adelaide. And to bring the cost of its investment in the Australian industry up to the eight figure mark, Allied Vintners bought out Wynn Winegrowers Ltd for $7½ million, or more than thirty times Wynns' latest profit. This gives Allied Vintners a range from top quality wines right through to the bulk flagon trade.

In the midst of all these acquisitions, small Australian listed public companies were floated to participate in the wine boom. Pokolbin Winemakers Ltd was floated late in 1971 after taking over the Drayton family's 'Happy Valley' vineyard at Pokolbin in the Hunter with results that so far do not appear to have been particularly happy. And Alan Pond's Pokolbin vineyard property became the basis for formation of Hermitage Wines Ltd which raised $465,000 in its public float in 1971.

But the biggest bid of all came in April, 1971, when Philip Morris Australia Ltd paid $22.5 million for Lindeman Holdings Ltd, Australia's biggest and most successful wine company that had gone public in 1959. In one go, Philip Morris became one of the 'Big Three' in Australian wine, but paid thirty-one times their earnings to do so.

Shortly after this, H. J. Heinz bought out the Stanley Wine Company (whose wines are marketed under the Stanley and Leasingham labels) which is a fairly modest operation with 600 acres under vines at Clare, forty miles north-east of the Barossa Valley, and buying in grapes from many local vineyards in the area. It seems a fairly modest beginning in the wine trade for a large company like Heinz. But once again this takeover demonstrated the classic need of a small company having to get a big brother in order to do the things it wanted to do; its modest bottling capacity had hampered the growth of its brand names, forcing the company to sell much of its production to other vintners.

The next big company to move into the business was Dalgety Australia Ltd, the local subsidiary of the large British-based pastoral group. For many years, Dalgety had been a wholesaler of wines and spirits and owned a one-third interest in a company specializing in the bulk cartage of wines from South Australia. In July, 1971 it bought an 80 percent interest in Valle d'Oro Pty Ltd which has a winery at McLaren Vale in South Australia producing wine from its own vineyard and from independent grape growers. For Dalgety this was natural vertical integration, as the company had been Valle d'Oro's distributor in the Eastern states for several years. Dalgety followed this up by buying the Augustine Barossa Valley Estates Pty Ltd and in January, 1972 the Glenview Winery. But its biggest move in the wine business has been its latest one; in March, 1972 it acquired H. M. Martin and Son Pty Ltd, proprietors of the Stonyfell Winery just out of Adelaide and the Saltram Winery in the Barossa Valley. Once again, this was a natural vertical integration move, as Dalgety had been Martin's distributor.

There are plenty of much smaller takeover moves in the industry, too. One of the founders of X.L. Petroleum Ltd, which gave the major petroleum companies a run for their money with discount petrol, Mr Brian Fitzpatrick, has a winery, restaurant and cellars and a bottling house at Seymour, sixty miles north of Melbourne on the Hume Highway. His company, Fitzpatrick Bros Vineyards, bought out the renowned but small Clare winemaker, A. P. Birks, in November, 1971. In December, 1971, a group of Adelaide businessmen bought O. Basedow Wines Pty Ltd of Tanunda. And Industrial Equity Ltd acquired the Woodley Wines section of Crooks National Holdings when it was taken over in 1971.

There have also been many forays into the wine industry by large companies aimed at developing new vineyards, often with the objective of supplying grapes to associated wineries. For example,

W. R. Carpenter Ltd, the large island trader and investor, bought a two-thirds interest in Arrowfield Vineyards Pty Ltd and announced it would put $2 million into its development over five years. This property, of 2,800 acres, is on the Hunter and also runs cattle. It is associated with Penfolds Wines. In the same way, Adelaide Steamship Co has joined with South Australia's oldest winemaker and vigneron, Hamiltons, to plant the Mt Dangar vineyards in the Upper Hunter at Sandy Hollow. By June, 1971, the partners had spent about $700,000 in planting 450 acres to establish a winery late in 1972.

There seems no doubt at all that these major changes in the ownership and control of so much of the Australian wine industry must bring significant changes also in the way that industry, formerly a family dominated one, goes about its business.

Just how substantial those changes will be is still an open question; all the big companies doing the taking over swear that they will do nothing to reduce the quality of the wine made. And the taxation concessions available mean that success in financial terms of these takeovers will not necessarily be reflected in their profit and loss accounts. But it is not just the companies that have been taken over that are in for a change; the prepared defences of those outside the new order are rapidly going up. It may have been hastened by the impact of the 1970 wine excise on the fortunes of the smaller independent growers, or it may be simply a recognition of the threat they face in the future, but seven co-operative wine producers at Renmark, Berri, Loxton, Waikerie, Barossa, Southern Vales and Clarevale, all with a string of brand names going from high quality red and white table wines down to pretty rough fortified wine, have banded together to form Universal Wine Cellars Ltd. There are reports that a big U.S. controlled food and drink corporation was keen to gain a large stake in the new company, but nothing along these lines has happened yet. Universal plans to market under its own label in Sydney, Melbourne, Adelaide and Perth by the end of 1972, and is gearing up for an export drive to the United States. One of the independent members of Universal is Kaiser Stuhl which has already placed its wines on the shelves of the Safeway supermarket group which has 3000 stores across the United States. But for the small wine grower, there appears little prospect of making any meaningful defences apart from on a political level.

The big changes in this industry may mean progress to the consumer in supplying him with more good wines; to the Australian balance of payments, by increasing exports, and to the big companies involved by lifting their profits. But to many of the small grape growers this may mean disaster. Growing grapes and making wine in Australia is becoming less and less a way of life, and more and more an industry.

Champagne storage, McWilliam's Wines, Yenda, N.S.W.

17 Wine Exports *H. F. M. Palmer*

It was not the prospect of profit that provoked Australia's early vignerons to test their products in overseas markets. They knew there was a vast quantity of wine available for export from the Continent of Europe and they also knew the high regard the world markets had for the top quality wines produced on the Continent. However, they were adventurous souls and they were very proud of their wines.

Many of the nineteenth century Australian winemakers were born in Europe and had been brought up on Continental wines. Some had learned the winemakers' art in Europe. They were aware of the type of competition to expect but they were confident they could sell their wines on quality and they were successful.

The first shipment of commercial wine from Australia was made to Britain in 1854 when 1,389 gallons of Australian wine were imported by British merchants. Trade grew steadily and reached half a million gallons by 1893. This is about the same quantity as was shipped to Britain from Australia in 1972.

The early settlers recognized that with a temperate climate and good soil, Australia's coastal areas were ideal for the cultivation of the vine and even before settlement began it was predicted by first explorers that Australia would become the vineyard of Great Britain. This prediction has not been fulfilled, but during the 1930s Australia was exporting nearly four million gallons a year to that country.

The early export trade was confined mainly to the British market but by the 1970s Australia was exporting wine to more than eighty countries throughout the world; however, the quantity was only half that shipped to Britain alone in the 1930s.

Trade up to the First World War was mainly in table wines and full bodied burgundies comprised a very large part of the shipments. These wines were most popular in Britain at that time and competed very successfully against similar wines from the Continent.

The burgundy trade continued to dominate Australian exports until the mid-1920s when a new field opened up. By this time soldier settlement areas were coming into production in irrigated areas in Australia and, at the same time, there was a growing demand in Britain for sweet fortified wines, particularly in Port style. The Australian Government introduced an export bounty to assist the marketing of sweet wines and this was the beginning of a new era for Australian wines in the British market. The market for sweet wines soon became a most attractive proposition for Australian exporters and many winemakers turned to this field. As a result of the bounty the export trade boomed until the late 1930s but there was a severe set-back during World War II owing to lack of shipping space.

The sweet wine trade was great business from a point of view of quantity, but during the build-up of this trade Australia's reputation for quality suffered considerably. Much of the wine was good, sound wine but it was catering for a market suffering from the economic depression of the 1930s. Price was the vital factor and there was strong competition from Europe and other wine producing countries.

Wine connoisseurs and wine writers are usually not lovers of bulk sweet fortified wines and, although the wines were sound and palatable, Australia's quality reputation was damaged mainly by comparison with the finer wines consumed by the connoisseur.

In most English speaking countries there is a large market for sweet wines but mainly in the lower price field. The merchants interested in selling Australian wines in Britain in the boom years should have been complimented on their marketing expertise but they were condemned frequently for their complete disregard for our higher quality wines. However, they were in business to make a profit and our growers were keen to dispose of their crops. Looking back it may seem short-sighted but the trade was essential for the livelihood of Australia's winegrowers and without it the industry might have died instead of expanding to the thriving business it is in the early 1970s. Unfortunately there are still occasions when some of the old die-hards rubbish Australian wines because of the links with the old sweet wine trade.

Our early vignerons were very pleased with the quality of their wines but they could not have envisaged the vast improvement in both the quality and range of wines exported to so many countries today. The sweet wine trade still plays a big part in the export scene but there is now a wide variety of excellent table wines exported alongside them. There is a place in export markets for our sweet wines, and a place for our table wines, and in the relative price fields our competitors find it very difficult to match us.

Referring to statistics we find that our overseas trade is only half what it was in the 1930s. There are many reasons for this—elimination of the export bounty, diminishing the value of import duty preferences, relatively high costs of production, the long distance from traditional markets and so on. Perhaps the most important factor has been the attraction of the home market to winemakers. Consumption of wine in Australia more than doubled between 1960 and 1970 when sales exceeded 24 million gallons for the year. The big increase was in table wines and most winemakers were devoting their energy to improving quality and matching the strong competition for the new business. Exports continued, and similar to the pattern in Australia, there was a greater swing to table wines in most markets. However, the total quantity of wine shipped from Australia remained around two million gallons a year despite an upward swing in consumption in many of Australia's traditional overseas markets. The winemaker's job is to make wine, and he must sell it at a profit. He was able to do this in Australia but many export markets were becoming less profitable.

In the early 1970s, the indication is that plantings of vines in Australia are more than adequate to meet demand for wine in the home market and this is one reason why winemakers are beginning to take a new look at export markets. The scene is set for Australian winemakers to build their export business and there is no doubt they can do this on the score of quality alone. With rising costs in many other wine producing countries our export prices are competitive and this has been proven in markets as far apart as East Africa and Canada, and also in the nearer markets such as South-East Asia and New Zealand.

Export marketing policies

Many views have been expressed on export marketing policies. Some have promoted the idea of marketing one brand of Australian wines in overseas countries, others have pushed the idea of a national symbol. Many of the proposals put forward have had some merit but the main deterrent has been the desire of the winemakers themselves to retain a free hand with individual marketing methods.

At one stage in the early 1950s a proposal to establish a company to export wines under one national brand came close to adoption by the industry but in the end the scheme was dropped because of the lack of interest in nationalizing any aspect of the wine business. The decision to abandon the idea was probably a wise one. Wine is a sophisticated product and no consumer wishes to have his choice restricted to a national brand. One brand marketing would be more simple and less costly, but from a wine consumer's point of view there is more appeal in having a multiplicity of brands from which to choose.

The use of a symbol for Australian wine has many supporters—however, the idea also has many critics. The main objection seems to be that a symbol becomes a common denominator, irrespective of quality and price. Consequently it can be expected that if a symbol were used it would be found on the highest quality wines exported from Australia and also on the much lower quality wine shipped to satisfy a particular demand in certain export markets. The exporter of fine wines is not keen to risk the identification of his product with lesser quality wines bearing the same symbol.

A quick reflection on export statistics serves as a reminder that Australia has traded heavily in countries such as Britain, Canada and New Zealand, where preferential import duties have been available. These preferences have diminished in value over the years owing to changes in currencies and variations in rates, and are therefore not as valuable as they were. This, along with the thought that preferences will be lost in Britain as a result of the European Economic Community, and perhaps in other markets due to preferences to developing countries, is leading Australian wine exporters to explore new avenues of business in export fields.

Of the eighty-five countries to which Australian wines were shipped in 1971 only fifty-five took 100 gallons or more. Almost half the total wine shipped went to two countries, namely Canada and the United Kingdom. However, the fact that so many countries were interested in importing Australian wines, even in small quantities, indicates there must be prospects for expansion in those markets. Most wine consuming countries have been importing wines from Europe throughout their history. This has led to what might be described as the traditional acceptance of European labels. In many overseas markets Australian wines are comparatively unknown. It is therefore much harder to sell Australian wine in competition with wines from the continent. Our wines have to be sold whereas a European label sells itself. It is fairly well known that, in some markets, all that is needed is an impressive bottle and an impressive name. Quality is of little importance. Australian wines cannot be sold with those features alone. We have had to rely on quality in post-war years and our reputation is being built on quality.

Nomenclature

There has been a certain amount of criticism of Australian wine names in overseas markets. Names such as burgundy, claret, champagne, sherry, port, sauternes, have become generic through more than a century of use. However, some of these names have a geographic origin and, in more recent years, there have been moves to prevent the use of the names except by countries which claim origin of the word. Some of the international trade in wine has been built up on the use of generic wine names, not only by Australia, but by many other wine exporting countries. Now, owing to trade agreements, litigation and other factors, some countries have either dropped or been forced to stop using generic wine names.

To the layman it is a simple matter to think of the type of wine he wishes to buy before choosing the brand. This is why the generic name is such a convenient one. However, because of the strong opposition from European producers there is a tendency in overseas markets to regard a wine with a generic name as being a copy rather than a high quality wine in its own right. This fact alone has influenced many Australian wine exporters to use district and varietal names in their export business.

It is difficult to change labels where trade had been built up on the use of generic names but the new move is a very sound one in the face of the public relations work being done by European interests who are endeavouring to prevent the use of the names. With Australian wines there has been no attempt to mislead consumers into believing they are purchasing continental wines and, in fact, the word 'Australia' is very prominently and proudly shown on the labels of Australian wines sold in overseas markets. Some winemakers adopt the attitude 'why should we change'. People have been eating brussels sprouts and french beans for generations and they have also been drinking burgundy and sauternes. However, the test comes when the wine is to be sold and if the customer believes he is buying an imitation product when he sees a generic name, then the course of our exporters is clear.

Travelling wines

Nomenclature is one problem Australian exporters have had to face, another is the propaganda fed to consumers and the trade, by wine countries more closely located to export markets, that wines won't travel. The fact is, of course, that most wines improve with travel and the remainder are not affected in any way provided simple precautions are taken. Australia has probably had more experience than any other country in shipping wines over long distances and we pay more attention to the simple precautions

Preparing for racking at Campbell's 'Bobbie Burns' winery, Rutherglen, Vic.

than some countries which are located closer to their markets.

Sweet fortified wines, sherries and red table wines all show improvement through the continual movement in transit and even more so if the wines are shipped in wooden casks. The delicate white table wines are seldom shipped in wood but, if they are, the casks are heavily paraffined to avoid any oxidation. The usual practice in recent years has been to ship these wines in steel containers to eliminate the possibility of oxidation. The movement of the wine on the voyage will only help round off the wine and will certainly not cause any deterioration in quality.

Future exports

The demand for quality wine throughout the world is increasing each year and with the greater appreciation of wines by consumers the more discriminating are prepared to pay higher prices for the required quality. Australian wines for export are priced realistically and are very good value in most export markets. We are not attempting to compete against the *vin ordinaire* of which Europe can produce such large quantities. The present policy of our exporters is to compete in the quality wine fields and this is where, on a quality-price basis, Australian wines are hard to beat.

Australian visitors overseas frequently complain that Australian wines are not available in many countries. Americans visiting Australia probably make similar complaints about Bourbon, Canadians probably complain about the lack of Rye Whisky, the Germans possibly complain about the scarcity of their beer. It would be a truly remarkable feat by wine exporters if they could place Australian wine in all of the countries visited by Australian tourists to the extent that our wines were freely available in most licensed outlets. This. is an ideal which Australian wine producers would hope to achieve—however, we must be realistic.

Producers seldom find an easy course when they wish to market their products in a field where there is intense competition and this is the case with wine marketing in most overseas countries. However, Australian winemakers can look with confidence to the future of their export trade. They have excellent products and with continual rising costs in many of the European wine producing countries, Australia is able to compete favourably. The growing demand for wine throughout the world, especially among large affluent nations, means that Australia must be able to place its wine abroad, provided it sticks to quality and works hard to establish market openings. Japan and the U.S.A. are already making representations to Australia and looking at the wine supply situation for their countries. There is little doubt that quality wine could become a major export earner in the next ten years.

Garrulous wine labels *Keith Dunstan*

You must have noticed that Australian wine labels are terribly in. Our local lighting shop is featuring wine label lamp shades. You can have your room lit with the warm glow of Dalwood Hermitage, the marvellous shine of Chateau Gay and the noble strength of Moyston Claret.

The big store in the city has a show of wine label wallpaper. You can now surround yourself utterly with the warmth of the vineyards from Purple Para Port to Minchinbury Champagne.

It has all happened since the year 1965. Perhaps we could call '65 the year of eloquence. Pre-'65 most Australian wine labels merely contained the dull information: year, name of vineyard, wine type and quantity.

Now they are covered in information. Some companies put labels on front and back of the bottle, so that you practically get a potted version of the Decline and Fall of the Roman Empire.

I first noticed the remarkable influence of this thing in a lunch up at Carlton. It was the meeting of our regular wine team. We had oysters, minestrone, chicken livers venezia, yet by the time we reached our third course we were still on our first bottle and obviously lunch was going to take until four o'clock.

The reason? It was those damned wine labels. They contained so much reading matter we weren't getting time to do our serious tasting.

Actually it became so interesting from now on we will hold regular masked wine label lunches. It will work this way: the labelmaster of the day will cut off from the labels the proprietary brands. Then to the assembled gathering he will read excerpts.

After reading several paragraphs he will say: 'Standish, I wonder if you will give us your comments on the label?'

'Certainly, Mr Labelmaster. Here we have an example of a beautifully balanced prose style. His adjectives I think tend to be a little over-fruity. And if I had to make a criticism I would say they lacked rather in freshness. By his use of "generous full-body" and his enthusiasm for phrases like "grown in the rich, glorious chocolate cake soil of Western New South Wales and fanned by the soft breezes blowing direct off the smooth flowing waters of the Murrumbidgee" I would suggest that this was a McWindeman's wine. Indeed, I would go further. I would say the copy was written by a junior of around 25 years and that he came from George Patterson Advertising. The style of material hasn't a long life. I wouldn't give it more than two years. Yet on the day I found it a fairly satisfying label.'

Oh, you think I am exaggerating. The truth is that we have developed the most eloquent, the most garrulous wine labels in the world. You want examples. Certainly. One of the wines we had at this lunch was a McWilliams, Mt Pleasant Philip Hermitage 1965. This was on the label:

As far as can be determined the Hermitage grape originally came from Persia and it is now one of the main red grape varieties grown in the Rhone Valley in France where it is known as 'Petite Syrah'. It is also grown extensively throughout Australia where it is renowned for the high quality of the wine which it produces in the Pokolbin district of the Hunter Valley. The wine produced from the Hermitage grape on heavy volcanic loam on the slopes of Mount Pleasant is a full-bodied, robust, dry red which should continue to age and improve.

Yes, it was a beautiful wine, and we all enjoyed that little lecture on the history of the shiraz grape, but I nearly died of thirst waiting for our host to take the cork out of the bottle. Another good bottle we had was the Lindeman's Bin 50, vintage 1967. Hearken at this:

This wine was produced from Red Hermitage grapes grown in the Hunter Valley, Eden and Clare Valley and at McLaren Vale, Corowa and Langhorne Creek. It was matured in small oak casks prior to bottling and is a diWtinctive Lindeman's 'cellar style' wine. Bin 50 is a soft, round, generous wine with an attractive flavour and great delicacy. It may be enjoyed now or safely binned away for years to come.

Ah yes, this is wine obviously made for masked tastings. It calls for a brilliant subtlety of palate. Can't you see the master expounding: 'An extraordinarily interesting wine, but when you examine the nose, when you look into the fascinating complexity of fruit flavours it all becomes too obvious. I am happy to say, without fear of contradiction, that this wine comes from the Hunter River, Eden and Clare Valley, McLaren Vale, Corowa and Langhorne Creek districts.'

To the assembled cheers of the audience he sits down.

The Houghton's White Burgundy label is nice:

A full-bodied white wine which is only produced in Western Australia and developed as a distinctive white burgundy style from semillon and tokay grapes. The Indian Ocean plays an important part in the production of this wine. The long dry summer and cool ocean breezes at night combine to eliminate the acidity found in grapes grown in colder climates. The wine gives a pleasant softness on the palate and is usually served chilled.

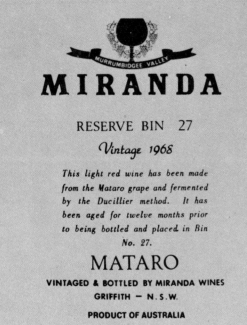

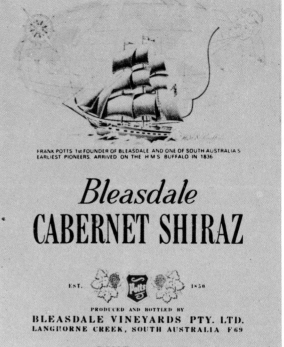

I love that part about the long dry summer, the breezes off the Indian Ocean. Throw in a sunset and it would be better than a Brian Fitzpatrick travelogue.

Then there was the Leo Buring DWY 13. Aren't you intrigued by that numbering? It sounds like a marvellous new rocket fuel. The blurb said:

Produced from Rhine Riesling grapes grown in the Barossa Valley and Leo Buring vineyards at Watervale. Medium in colour with a shade of green it has a clean, fresh, flowery Rhine nose, excellent balance and is soft with full wine character.

This is a great help. When a wine is described as precisely as this it is a convenience to wine lovers. The job is done, so there is no need to taste the wine at all.

Then there are those people who number their bottles as if they were rare folios produced by monks in a lonely Alsatian castle. Some winemakers like Orlando have printed labels but they have a typewriter script. Immediately you get the feeling that this was a terribly small binning. The winemaker really only made thirty or forty bottles of this rare wine, just for use by his own family, so he typed out the label on the battered, old vineyard typewriter.

Over yonder in our cellar there are some prized bottles of Metala and the label has this to say:

A distinctive claret vintaged at Stonyfell from cabernet sauvignon and shiraz grapes grown in the vineyards at Metala Langhorne Creek. After three years' maturing in 500 gallon oak casks it was filled into 30,672 pint bottles and binned. This is bottle 14,921 and we recommend it as a truly fine claret which will continue to live and improve for years to come.

Immediately the thought comes to mind what was bottle 14,922 like, or how about 14,923? Or perhaps the labels are even more valuable than the wine? What say, one collected all the labels from that vintage, would they in time be as valuable as a full collection of old BDV cricketer cigarette cards? But Stonyfell didn't stop there. Their reading matter goes right round the bottle. On the back there was a map with the message:

The clay topsoil and limestone subsoil has been enriched with alluvial soil brought down from time to time by the flooding of the river Bremer. In this beautiful countryside bordering the River Bremer where the shiraz and cabernet grapes flourish, the yield is seldom more than two tons per acre ensuring a wine of remarkable character.

Hungerford Hill for a brand new winemaker is showing remarkable promise. Recently I hurried home with the first bottles from their first vintage.

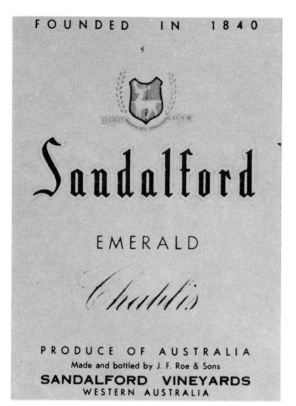

FOUNDED IN 1840

Sandalford

EMERALD

Chablis

PRODUCE OF AUSTRALIA
Made and bottled by J. F. Roe & Sons
SANDALFORD VINEYARDS
WESTERN AUSTRALIA

SEPPELT

MELITA.
MOSELLE

A light, delicate style Moselle best served chilled. The wine was cold fermented to retain the characteristics of the Tokay grapes grown in the cooler regions of the Barossa Valley. The grapes were picked early during the vintage. A small portion of Barossa Valley Semillon was used in the final blend.   F. 13017

BOTTLED BY B. SEPPELT & SONS LIMITED, SEPPELTSFIELD, S.A.
PRODUCE OF AUSTRALIA · 1PT 6FL OZ CONTENTS

The label began 'Hungerford Hill Collection'; I liked the use of 'Collection'. It smacked of a rare gathering of Louis Quinze furniture or early English water colours. Here is some of the very precise information on the label:

Pokolbin Vintage.
Semillon 1971.
The first white wine from the Hungerford Hill
Pokolbin Vineyards. The semillon grapes were
vintaged under controlled fermentation
and bottled in June, 1971.
Picking date February 8, 1971.
Vintage No. 7c/302.
Gallons vintaged 3500.
Bottled June 9, 1971.

I have been so over-awed by this label I have been too timid to open any of my bottles.

Rothbury on the Hunter is another new vineyard. Their first label is classically correct. It doesn't tell you anything. It doesn't even say that there you are getting white wine. They leave it to your powers of observation to note that. The label in its entirety says:

THE ROTHBURY ESTATE
HUNTER VALLEY
Produce of Australia.
25 Fl. Oz.

But wait, the label is by Fred Williams, Australia's top landscape artist. You get an intriguing, almost mysterious Williams interpretation of a vineyard and up at the top there is a free form chunk of black, no doubt depicting a chunk of vine. When you consider that a Fred Williams landscape can bring maybe $8,000, once again you are over-awed. Yes, I'm keeping my Fred Williams labels to see how they increase in value. But how will the other vineyards compete? Will they fight back with Blackmans, Nolans, Drysdales or will they go for Percevals, Pughs and Boyds?

One can even foresee the day when a traditionalist wine drinker might send back a bottle at the restaurant with the announcement: 'I never drink a red by a non-figurative artist.'

There are other ways, of course, of producing a graphic label. Glenloth have a Coromandel Riesling. It depicts the old sailing ship Coromandel and it tells us that this ship arrived at Port Adelaide on 12 January, 1837 and that this 'crisp, clean white wine was made from riesling grapes grown at Langhorne Creek and on properties overlooking Happy Valley Reservoir in the historic Coromandel district south of Adelaide.'

The tie up is just a trifle tenuous, but then perhaps the use of the Coromandel might be symbolic of oak or teak character in the wine.

'Chateau Tahbilk' labels are quite beautiful. They feature the historic Chateau tower of the

winery at Tahbilk and it looks rather more French than anything that ever came out of France. The back of the bottle looks like something created by Angostura Bitters. You can only read it if your eyes are in remarkably good shape and you haven't been drinking.

There is a map of the district and a complete history of the surrounds starting in 1836 when Major Mitchell crossed the Goulburn right on to Tahbilk country to 1964 when they extended the vineyards.

Then you get the companies which try to get a wash-off from France by labelling their bottles claret or burgundy. I remember asking one very distinguished Australian wine judge: 'What is the difference between Australian claret and burgundy?' He replied, 'I haven't the slightest idea.'

He went on to explain that claret in the Bordeaux tended to be more acid and usually was made from cabernet sauvignon grapes. The burgundies of Burgundy were made from pinot noir, were softer, rounder, had great finesse and flavor, yet were often lighter in colour.

Douglas Crittenden, a famous wine man of Melbourne, tells the classic story of the lady who came into his store and said: 'I'd like to buy some of your burgundy but it has too much shiraz in it.'

For once Mr Crittenden did not know what to say. Was it correct to argue with a customer? He was about to tell her the hermitage grapes of New South Wales and the shiraz grapes of Victoria

were both exactly the same variety, but he thought better of it.

It is hard to pin down the grapes in South Australia. Leasinghams have a wine under a burgundy label which, ah me, contains cabernet sauvignon and grenache. Another big company has switched its entire 'burgundy' line into claret shape bottles because they find wine sells better in claret bottles.

But it is not the curious use of moselle, chablis, champagne and such that really worries me. It is the stepping up of the printed matter on the labels that is the problem. I fear this will expand. Competing vineyards may soon bring out paperback books with every bottle and winemaking will become a major publishing venture.

Why are Australians so garrulous? At one shop recently I came across a single bottle. The price was $58.30. The label read:

> CHATEAU MARGAUX
> Grand Vin
> Premier Grand Cru classé
> 1928

That's all. A bottle nearby for $17.20 had even less:

> Grand Vin de Latour
> 1964

No wonder they weren't selling. I mean, at those prices you should have received at least 2,000 words.

A hydraulic wine press in operation at G. Gramp and Sons 'Orlando' winery at Rowland Flat, S.A.

*Refrigeration system to control fermentation at Penfold's
'Grange', Magill, S.A.*

On a steeply sloping site and stony ground in the hills
above Rowland Flat, in the Barossa Valley, G. Gramp
and Sons planted experimental rhine riesling grapes in
1962. Here, Mr Colin Gramp, a fourth-generation Gramp,
tends the grapes on high German trellising at the
appropriately named Steingarten (garden of stones).

WINEMAKING

John Stanford, R.D.Oen., M.A.S.E., is a graduate winemaker from Roseworthy Oenology School in South Australia and a Member of the American Society of Enologists. He operates his own wine technology and marketing consultancy. For three years he was Federal Manager of the Australian Wine Bureau. He has acted as a Senior Judge in wine shows for the past fifteen years.

Dr Don Francois settled permanently in Australia in 1962 after obtaining a Ph.D. in fisheries from Cornell University, U.S.A. He became N.S.W. Director of Fisheries in 1966, a position he still holds. Dr Francois' keen interest in winemaking led him recently to acquire a small property at Pokolbin which he is developing as a vineyard.

White wine grape fermentation at an advanced stage at McWilliams, Hanwood, in the Murrumbidgee Irrigation Area, in southern New South Wales.

John Stanford

Wine is made from grape juice and over eighty strains of grapes are used, about half red and half white. Their juices are mostly white or greenish-gold, but some are pink, and a few are purple-red. The flavours of the juice are sweetness, with fruit and acid after-tastes. The skins contain colour and additional flavours, which become dissolved in the juice during winemaking processes. Fermentation transforms the juice into a complex, inspired beverage with remarkable qualities of keeping, and also of developing new accents on the original flavours as it matures.

Behind this simple definition is a vast, world-wide structure of capital, specialized technology, engineering and marketing. There is an involvement of consumers ranging from casual appraisal, to cultist fervour.

The art of the winemaker, whether on a large or small scale, is in a precise understanding of the nature of grapes and wine. On this depends his capacity to recognize, and where necessary, influence, the many changes which take place during fermentation and ageing to create the characters of his wine.

Most fruits will make a type of wine, but grapes are the usual and most natural source. They are more juicy, have more complex flavours, and when ripe, contain enough sugar to produce a level of alcohol which preserves the wine.

Commercial winemaking has developed from an ancient art, practised as a cottage industry, into an exact, imaginative science. It employs sophisticated, often large-scale handling and control equipment.

Its object is to protect the juice from the time it leaves the grape-skin until it is safely in the bottle, and guide the processes of fermentation and clarification.

The two main factors affecting quality are still, and probably always will be, the quality of the fruit and the individual skill and judgement of the winemaker. A third factor, the quality and capacity of winery equipment, has become more significant in recent years.

Today's winemaker is much closer than any of his predecessors to producing, at will, a great wine, with near-perfect balances of flavours, given perfect fruit to work with.

However not all the wine of any crop can make the ultimate standard. In most cases, the first, free-run juice from the skins is superior to that extracted by pressing the skins. There will always be bad seasons, damaged grapes, missed opportunities in the vineyard and winery, and the demand for plainer wines at a cost which does not allow for the individual care and treatment required by these rarer wines.

There are four basic steps in the winemaking process:
1. Selection, growing and harvesting of the grapes.
2. Crushing and separation of the juice.
3. Fermentation, clarification and stabilization of the young wine.
4. Maturation and blending, and the protection of the wine against spoilage and loss of flavour.

19 In the vineyard

Selection of grape type

Of over eighty different strains of the European *Vitis vinifera* type, some have distinctive, intensive fruit characters, e.g., cabernet sauvignon, malbec, pinot noir, etc., for red wines; rhine riesling, traminer, white sauvignon, aucerot riesling, frontignac and other muscats for white wine.

Others have less intensive fruit character, but develop additional flavours after ageing, e.g., shiraz, merlot, grenache for red wine, and semillon, trebbiano, chardonnay and chenin blanc for whites. Some have neutral flavours, e.g., palomino, sultana.

Almost all grapes make their best wine when picked near the peak of optimum ripeness. Some set fruit and mature fast enough to reach this peak of ripeness in cold districts. Others mature slowly and are better suited to warm areas. Fluctuations in seasonal conditions vary the degree of ripeness possible. They may eliminate a variety from the field of quality winemaking in one district, and make it ideal for another, or limit it to making one type of wine in one place and a different type in another.

In the oldest winemaking areas, the best way of using each grape variety planted there has become established and all other ways of using such grapes have been discarded. Along with this process of elimination, other varieties unsuitable for making the wine style on which the district bases its reputation have also been largely discarded. For this reason the colder Rhine and Mosel Valleys in Germany specialize in making light, white table wines, and the riesling grape is their most important planting. They buy their red wines from France, Italy and Spain because their own red grapes will not ripen adequately.

Younger wine-producing countries are still working through this process of elimination, and establishing their optimum wine styles. It is a slow process and it may take a winemaker fifteen to twenty years to exhaust his ingenuity and prove that a variety is unsuitable for his district and should be replaced with another. In Australia this process has indicated that riesling grapes produce high quality fruit in the Clare, Eden Valley and several upper Barossa districts, but because of the temperate climate, high quality red wines are also grown.

This effect is paralleled in the Coonawarra and Central Victorian districts. The Hunter Valley's warmer climate places the emphasis on red wines, but has established a bigger, more richly flavoured white wine, from semillon grapes, and more recently, from new plantings of more definite flavour types.

Degree of ripeness

Varietal flavour and colour are determined when the vineyard is planted, by the climate of a district and the type of grape. Sugar and acid balances influence most of the remaining flavours of a wine and relate to the degree of ripeness at which they are harvested. These are varied by seasonal weather conditions on one hand and controlled by the precise timing of the day they are picked on the other.

As the berry ripens, the hard, starchy texture softens, colours, and is converted to grape sugars. At the same time the high level of green malic acid decreases and gives way to softer tartaric acid. By late summer, the balance between the rising sugar level and falling acid level reaches a point suitable for making each alternative type of wine.

Grapes picked before optimum ripeness make wines with sharp acidity. After optimum ripeness, the sugar and colour levels continue to rise, but the acid levels fall away very quickly. In cold climates, this transition may take a week or more (and in fact winter may close in before the grapes ripen). In hot areas the peak may be passed in a day.

Dry table wines made from over-ripe grapes tend to lack freshness and crispness created by the presence of acid. Sweet wines usually benefit from the additional richness of flavour of over-ripeness.

Harvesting

The colouring and flavouring substances which give each grape its character are highly complex materials which remain stable and protected as long as the skin of the grape is not broken. They will begin to oxidize, or lose their delicate flavours and aromas by chemical reaction as soon as they are exposed to the oxygen in the air, in the same way, and as rapidly, as a sliced apple or a pear will turn brown as you watch.

Those picked by hand are carried to the winery in loads ranging from one to fifteen tons. Where the vineyard and winery are at the same place, small loads can be run to the winery in shallow trailers which do not damage the fruit. Carried in heavy loads, or by long journeys on rough roads, the grapes may suffer loss of quality before they reach the winemaker.

The Renmark Growers' Distillery was the first co-operative winery in Australia. The wines are sold under the Renmano label.

Hot weather will speed up this process, and hail or insect damage to the skins may allow mould growth to develop before the grapes are picked.

Mechanical harvesting machines now being developed may provide one means of overcoming some of the losses incurred in large loads over long distances. The winemaker is able to counter these effects by controlled additions of sulphur dioxide added to the loads of grapes as they are harvested, or as soon as they arrive at the winery.

In the field, if they are mechanically harvested, or hand-picked, crushed and de-stemmed, they can be pumped into sealed tankers, treated with sulphur-dioxide, and blanketed from air contact with an inert gas such as carbon dioxide or nitrogen. Sulphur dioxide acts as a deterrent to air-borne moulds and bacteria, and the inert gases displace the air in storage containers and reduce the risk of oxidation without otherwise affecting the juice.

Summary of stages of winemaking

All winemakers are individual thinkers, and tend to plan their own solutions to the physical problems of winemaking. They favour different approaches to the same problem, or specialize in different types of wine, requiring some variations of handling methods. For this reason few wineries appear identical, but the schematic diagram (Fig. 1) indicates the normal flow of processes which happen in each.

2O Inside the winery

There are six stages inside the winery (if crushing is not done in the field).

Crushing
Separation of the juice
Fermentation
Clarification
Storage and maturation
Bottling

The first four stages happen quickly—in three to six weeks in the majority of wine districts. The final clarification, maturation and bottling can be effected in another few weeks, in the case of very delicate white wines, but usually take from one to three years for table wines, and even longer for ports and sherries which need extensive wood maturation.

In spite of this, a breakdown of the winemaker's control in any one stage can result in a spoiled wine, or one lacking some of the quality and flavour potential that the grapes were capable of producing. For this reason, the first frantic weeks of the vintage can make or break a wine, and the quality of a winemaker and his equipment are of major importance.

Winemaking processes
Crushing

The object is to gently crush and de-stem the bunch without cracking the seeds or stripping any of the flesh from the stems. Both would add undesirable bitter flavours to the juice which would persist in the finished wines.

Of the many types currently available the Amos type (German) and the Coq (French) represent one approach, and the Whitehill a simpler and less flexible process (*See* Fig. 2).

The first two use rollers to gently burst the berries (the Amos type after de-stemming, and the Coq before). The stems are then picked out and discarded by fibreglass or metal fingers set on a slowly rotating shaft in a perforated cylinder. Both can optionally by-pass the de-stemming phase and include stems with the skins and juice to allow quick draining of white wines.

The Whitehill type thrashes the berries from the stems through a perforated cylinder and throws the

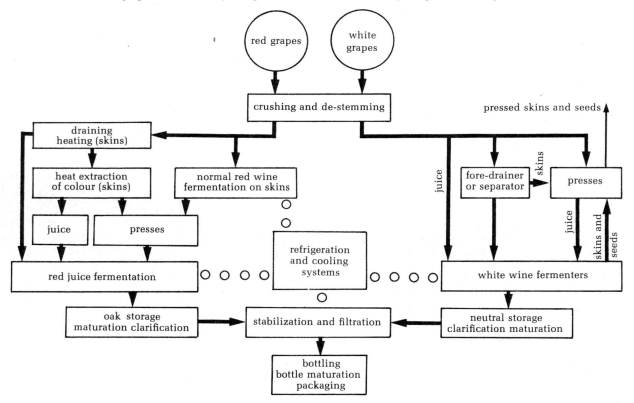

Figure 1: Schematic winemaking outline

stems out along the central shaft in one operation.

There is another design which pulverizes and disintegrates the whole mass, where extraction of sugar is the objective, and bitter flavours are not important, as with crushing of grapes for distillation of spirit or brandy. The crushed, de-stemmed mixture of skins, seeds and juice is called 'must'.

Separation of the juice

Juice is separated from stems, skins and seeds after varying periods of contact, ranging from an hour to a week, according to the type of wine being made. When light, delicate wines are needed, e.g. light dry white, sparkling wine, fino sherry and dry vermouth, the juice is drawn immediately after crushing.

This is the case also where white wines are to be made from red-skinned grapes (as in France for champagne-making) or if hail or insects have damaged the grapes and secondary moulds or bunch rots have appeared. If stalks are left in during crushing, they act as a filter bed and speed the rate of separation, but they are seldom left in during fermentation because they import green, bitter flavours. The must may be fed directly into one of a range of fore-drainers and de-juicers (*See* Fig. 3), or directly in one of several types of press (*See* Fig. 4).

Where limited skin contact is required, as with more robust dry whites such as white burgundy, or sherry or sweet white from muscat or pedro grapes, the grapes are de-stemmed and put into a closed fermenter tank with a seeding of fermenting juice.

After several hours or several days, the gas bubbles having floated the skins to the surface, the juice is drained clear, and the drained skins are transferred to a press (*See* Fig. 4) and squeezed dry. This wine from pressings has more intense skin flavours and is usually made separately and blended back, as required, after vintage.

The separated wine is still sweet and fermenting and is transferred to another tank to complete the process, or, if for a sweet fortified wine, is stopped

from fermenting by the addition of neutral grape spirit or brandy.

Where red wines are to be made, the fermentation is allowed to consume sixty to eighty percent of the sugar before separation and the skins are pressed in the same way.

Although yeast spores occur naturally on grape skins, most wineries now use cultured strains of selected wine yeasts to start the fermentation, because, in many vineyards, the grape skins also carry inefficient yeasts and spoilage bacteria.

Fermentation

The oldest wineries may still use open fermenter tanks made of concrete or wood. There is a greater risk of flavour and colour loss by exposure to oxygen in the air of the top layer of skins. Fermentation in closed stainless steel or enamelled tanks is now generally accepted as the best way to protect the wine during this critical stage of making.

The rapid multiplication of yeast cells and the energy created by them in converting sugar to alcohol increases the temperature in the juice. If this temperature rise is unchecked, the yeast action becomes inefficient and the fermentation may produce undesirable flavour by-products in the same way as people become less efficient and effective in prolonged heat waves over 40°C. In extreme cases, the temperature may rise high enough to stop the yeast action completely, resulting in a 'stuck' fermentation which leaves the wine prone to bacterial spoilage.

These factors surrounding the separation and fermentation are key processes in good winemaking. It is here that judgement and experience allows the good winemaker to sense changes, and correct them before drastic action is necessary.

The tools he uses, apart from instinct and know-ledge of his wines, are regular instrument checks on the rate of conversion of sugar, and change of temperature. His principal aids are cooling, and clean, effective equipment. Most wineries have refrigeration plant and heat exchangers.

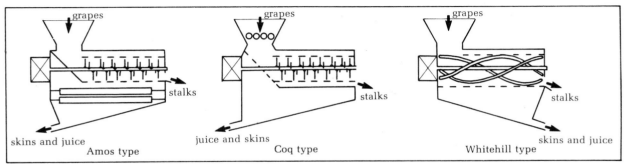

Figure 2: Crusher—de-stemmers

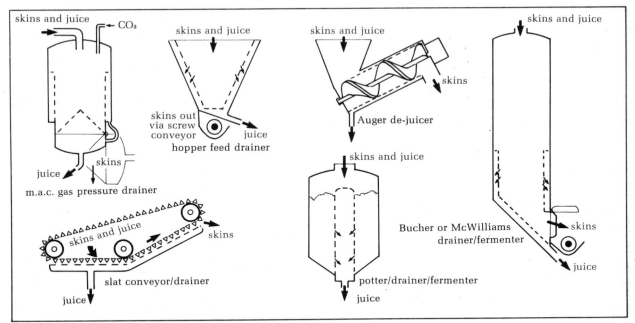

Figure 3: Fore-drainers and de-juicers

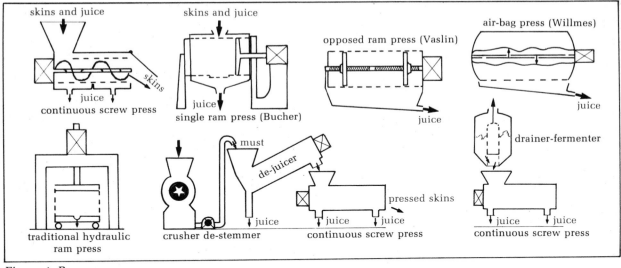

Figure 4: Presses

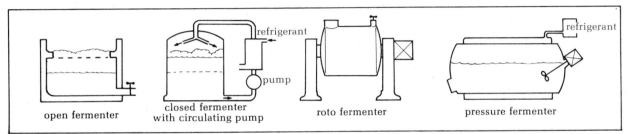

Figure 5: Fermenters

White wines are held to a range between 16°C and 21°C. Red wines ferment and extract colours best at higher temperatures—24°C to 29°C. The danger point is only 2-3°C above this range and strict control is exercised on red wine fermentations.

Clarification

Finely divided particles of grape pulp, small shreds of skins, broken-down yeast cells, and other organic matter are present in freshly drained wine and can add undesirable flavours if they disintegrate and dissolve. In some wines, suspended solids tend to settle out quickly at the end of vintage, forming a deposit on the bottom of the tank called 'lees'. In others, the finest particles may remain in suspension for several months if allowed to do so, and may need some urging or mechanical assistance before they will settle.

This assistance is given in several forms. Chilling a wine will increase the rate of settling. Adding neutral materials which collect fine particles into bigger ones, heavy enough to settle out, is the process of 'fining'. Wyoming bentonite, a neutral powdered earth, and several forms of gelatine, or powdered casein, are the usual forms now used.

Other protein substances such as egg-white or skim milk are sometimes still used, because they coagulate in the presence of alcohol or tannin. One which, happily, has fallen out of favour, but which was used as late as this century, was blood of animals, slaughtered over a vat.

High-speed centrifuges are used in many countries for separation of very cloudy juices and wine.

The final clarification is one or another method of filtration, either instead of, but usually in addition to, fining or centrifuging. The process of draining the clear wine from the settled deposit is called 'racking'.

In hotter winemaking districts both in Australia and other winemaking countries, significant improvements in quality have been achieved by chilling, settling and filtering the juice freshly separated from white grapes, before fermentation as well as after.

Filters used employ asbestos or cotton pulp mats, or a slurry of diatomaceous earth—finely divided coral-like skeletal powders—which are mixed with the wine and then filtered out on fine screens, carrying the layers of slimy or sticky yeast deposits which would otherwise clog up a filter.

Storage and maturation

The usual means of storage for many centuries, apart from stone jars, was wood. This was the easiest material to shape into the various sizes needed for small winemaking units of tribes or families. It was replaced about a hundred years ago by lined concrete vessels, and we have now graduated to vats of enamelled steel or stainless

New concrete storage under construction at Brown Brothers', Taminick, Vic.

steel. During this evolutionary process, it was found that certain types of wood, such as oak, lent distinctive flavours to wine. The most readily available cask timber in Greek winemaking areas was pine, which created another flavour fashion in the 'retsina' wines.

These flavour fashions are apart from the basic purpose, which was to contain the finished wine away from the air and to allow its fruit, acid and tannin flavours to mellow and settle down together without the wine spoiling.

Neutral containers are now used for most wines during the early stages of winemaking. Stainless steel is the easiest to keep clean without re-treating the surfaces from year to year to prevent bacteria, lurking in porous surfaces, from emerging to spoil the clean fresh flavours. Concrete tanks, lined with special neutral surfacing materials, such as waxes, or enamels, are widely used because they cost less than stainless steel.

Oak casks of the American White Oak (*Quercus Alba*) and the French and German oaks (*Q. Robur* and *Q. Pedunculata*) are generally used in Australia and other winemaking countries for simultaneously maturing the wines—mainly dry red, port, sweet white and sherry—and imparting their distinctive flavour, which has become part of the traditional

Evaluation of last year's dry red before bottling at Campbell's winery, Rutherglen, Vic.

flavour pattern of these wine types. English oaks, chestnut and other timbers similar to these white oaks are unsuitable for wine or brandy storage because of their individual flavours and pigments, which react with wine to form bitterness and black colours.

Bottling of wines

The selection of the precise time for bottling a wine is part of the winemaker's art.

Wines stored in oak casks, for instance, are matured at a much faster rate than those stored in sealed, neutral containers without contact with air, possibly because the porous surface of the wood carries more air to dissolve in a wine than the smooth surface of a polished steel or concrete vessel, or a glass bottle.

When a wine is first made, there is a phase of early, rapid integration of a number of differing flavour and colour substances. The winemaker controls the speed and extent of this settling-in stage by the temperature at which the wine is stored and the amount of oxygen it is allowed to absorb.

White wines with delicate, perishable fruit flavours need very little of this, and are, therefore, usually bottled early.

Red wines need more because they have more of the stable, rough tannin flavours to soften down before they are geared back to the much slower rate of ageing which results from sealing them into the bottle.

Ports and sherry have freshly added grape spirit and brandy to integrate with, as well as their normal range of acids, sugars and tannins, and are usually bottled later again.

The selection of the right time for bottling each wine determines if it will retain its best characters and develop them all together, when the cork comes out, or if some of them have already been lost before the wine is bottled. It becomes a matter between the winemaker, with his imagination and experience of similar wines, and each individual wine he bottles.

The effect can be varied by his skill as a blender— in knowing which vats to put together to achieve a balance at some time in the future and by his observation of the rate of progress shown by each wine through the early making and maturing process. When very young, a number of vats of similar wines, made from the same vineyard, may appear almost identical to a casual observer. To the winemaker who made them they have distinct characters which will age and develop in different ways.

450

Winemaking programmes

21

All wines separate into two basic groups—those consumed at the strength at which they ferment (dry reds, dry whites) and those which have been increased in strength by blending back grape spirit or brandy distilled from similar grapes.

Within these two groups, are wines which have developed from secondary winemaking processes using one or another of these as a base, e.g., Champagne or sparkling burgundy from re-starting the fermentation in dry white and dry red.

Sauternes and other light sweet wines made by stopping the fermentation or blending back similar wines or juices of high sugar content.

Or in the fortified group: Sherry is made from dry white, fortified, and then impregnated with a special yeast growth. Vermouth is made from dry sherry or sweet muscat base by infusing a carefully balanced mixture of herbs. Other flavoured aperitif or dessert wines use sherry, port or madeira or muscat with different herbs or flavouring added.

In all these cases, the traditional flavour patterns have been tested and accepted over many years, in some cases, centuries, and processes have been developed by winemakers which recognize and avoid spoilage, or exaggeration of the desired sophistication of the natural base wine.

The principal group of established wine types falls into one of the following categories:
a. Wines of natural strength
White table wines
Red table wines
Sparkling wines
b. Fortified wines (for aperitif or dessert use)
Sherries
Ports, madeiras, muscats, etc.
Flavoured wines (vermouths, marsala, etc.)

White table wines

The three main groups are:
Light, delicate dry (riesling or hock styles)
Full-bodied dry (white burgundy, chablis, etc.)
Sweet (ranging from late-picked styles at 1-2 percent sugar to rich sauternes at 7-10 percent sugar).

The first objective of the programme for all such wines is to reduce exposure to air at all times, because the relatively low concentration of skin tannins makes the juices prone to browning or oxidation. If this becomes apparent to the eye, many of the volatile fruit flavours which give these wines their character will have already been oxidized and lost to the consumer.

The grapes used for this type include riesling, (rhine riesling, white riesling, rizling, etc.), semillon (Hunter River riesling), muller-thurgau (sylvaner x riesling hybrid), sylvaner, clare riesling, and more highly aromatic types such as aucerot riesling, traminer, frontignac, etc.

a. Crushing

The grapes or the juice are dosed with sulphur dioxide immediately to protect against oxidation and spoilage bacteria.

In many modern installations in Germany, as well as Australia, the crushers are enclosed with sealed covers connected to cylinders of inert gas which exclude all air and the must enters an atmosphere of carbon dioxide or pure nitrogen as soon as the skins are broken.

b. Separation

Pumps at the crusher transfer the must immediately to one of a number of drainers (*See* Fig. 3), or to de-juicers, or draining tanks. The free run juice is usually kept separate from pressings. The juice may then be chilled and filtered, or chilled and settled (before yeast is added), or simply seeded as it is drained with a vigorously fermenting juice containing the selected yeast culture. In hot districts, pre-fermentation cooling and clearing is essential to production of better quality wines without loss of flavour.

c. Fermentation

The fermenting wine is usually held in a closed tank or vat with refrigerated cooling systems attached, to constantly control the temperature level. In colder climates, partial fermentation on the skins can give more intense fruit flavours without risk of browning or excessive skin bitterness. In hot districts the risk of excessive flavour and colour pick-up is too great and juice is separated quickly.

Sulphur dioxide is used in all winemaking countries to protect against both colour loss and bacterial spoilage. The precise dosing is of great importance, because it evaporates as the wine warms up and ferments.

High residual levels of sulphur dioxide, e.g., the levels used in most non-alcoholic aerated waters and cordials, are considered excessive in wine and detrimental to the more delicate and complex flavours. The winemaker maintains a constant check on the levels and adjusts frequently by small additions.

Fermentation of a white wine may take one to five days longer than that of a red wine because temperatures are kept lower, reducing the activity of the yeast culture.

d. Clarification

In most districts, the wine is allowed to settle for a week or two after the sugar is fermented. In the hottest areas the wine is clarified by filtration or centrifuging immediately the gassing stops. In colder areas, after settling, the clear wine is pumped from the deposit ('lees') in a process referred to as the 'first racking'. The sulphur dioxide, acid, alcohol and sugar levels are checked and if necessary, adjusted.

The young white wine is then filled and topped up in a vat for a further settling-out period—usually for the next two or three months of winter. The vats are kept filled to exclude all air and checked regularly for sulphur dioxide, clarity and soundness.

When they have settled out again, they are pumped off the deposit ('second racking') and are ready for pre-bottle maturation, or in many cases, immediate filtration and bottling.

e. Storage, maturation and bottling

Fresh, delicate young white wines, especially those from hot districts (e.g. the Murray Valley area of South Australia, or similar districts in Spain, France, Italy, California or South Africa) have a lower resistance to the levels of oxygen from the air usually picked-up during handling and maturation in vats or casks. Such wines are filtered and bottled as soon as they clear, often at the age of three to eight weeks.

White wines of similar type which are made in the more robust, white burgundy style, usually by partially fermenting on the skins, need more time to settle and mature before they are bottled.

Light, delicate rieslings of cold areas, with higher levels of grape acid resulting from slower, colder ripening conditions for the grapes may need handling for up to a year before they have softened and developed the balance of characters which the winemaker recognizes from experience as the right time to bottle.

Full bodied semillon wines from the Hunter Valley, or robust dry or semi-sweet white wines of the Great Western or Barossa districts, or the French Burgundy, may need up to two years maturation, with some storage in oak casks before they have achieved this balance of flavours.

The effect of bottling white wines is to slow down the comparatively rapid pace of maturation achieved in casks by sealing them in glass against any further oxygen intake. As their maturation proceeds at a slower pace, it is possible to more accurately gauge the best time to uncork and drink them.

The ultimate stage of maturation is the end-point of the winemaker's objective in selecting and crushing the grapes, and deserves as much care and attention as the preceding stages of winemaking.

Bottle maturity ranges between the point at which the raw young characters of the grape have mellowed, and that at which the fruit and acid flavouring substances begin to break down and fall apart. In the lightest, thinnest white wines from hot districts, this point of maturity may be six to twelve months of age, and over-maturity may be three to four years. More stable rieslings, pinots or semillons from colder Australian, French or German districts may need two years to show mature balance, and may hold and develop these balances over ten to thirty years.

Red table wines

The main groups are:
Full-bodied, crisp dry red
Soft, aromatic dry red
Fresh, delicate rose wines

The basic differences in approach in making red and white table wines are in the fermentation methods. These produce more intense flavours, extract more of the bitter and aromatic skin characters, including colour, and thus create the need for greater pre-bottle softening and maturation. The exception is the light, delicate rosé wine group which is intended for earlier consumption, and is treated more in the style of a white wine.

The first group, full-bodied red wines, is usually based on the use of flavour-intensive varieties such as cabernet sauvignon and malbec, with shiraz or merlot as a less highly flavoured background blending wine. The French Bordeaux or Australian Claret types are examples.

The softer, more aromatic dry reds relate to the French Burgundy style. In France this type is based on the pinot noir grape, although other varieties are used, such as gamay, grenache or shiraz.

In Australia, shiraz and grenache are currently used, but increasing volumes of pinot noir are becoming available and will be more generally used in the future.

a. Crushing

At crushing, because the tannin substances in the skins act as a protection against oxidation of colour and flavour less sulphur dioxide can be used. The same protection against excessive aeration of the juice during processing is needed, but the penalties are less severe.

b. Separation

The grapes are de-stemmed and primary separation is only practised where rosé wines are to be made, or if heat treatment to extract colour from a proportion of the skins is needed. In all other cases, skins, seeds and juice are pumped together into the fermenter. Heat treatment is a recently developed technique of winemaking in France, Italy, California and Australia.

The separated skins and seeds are heated to temperatures ranging from 45-70°C., the colour cells which are contained in the grape skins break down, the cold juice is returned, extracts the colour and is re-separated, in a continuous process. This allows immediate colour extraction instead of gradual breaking-down of skin cells over 3-4 days of fermentation.

The advantages are in being able to dispose of skins earlier in the winemaking process, and in the easier, more controllable fermentation of a clear juice instead of a mixture of skins and juice. It is not yet proved that an improved quality of wine results in good districts, but greatly improved colour and flavour is obtained in those areas where sufficient colour extraction has been a winemaking problem.

c. Fermentation

Normal red wine fermentations are conducted at higher temperatures than white (26-29°C.).

The yeasts are allowed to consume from half to over three-quarters of the sugar, according to the amount of colour and flavour needed, before the juice is run off the skins. The alcohol level rises in proportion. As the bitter tannins are more soluble in alcohol than in water, the rate of their extraction increases towards the end of fermentation.

The winemaker must decide the best stage to draw off the juice, basing his judgement on the amount of colour he needs, balanced against the amount of tannin the wine will carry. Each grape variety in each season varies in its requirement. Cabernet sauvignon and shiraz usually give higher colour results than malbec, or grenache, but these grapes have compensating flavour values and are usually blended back for this purpose.

Ripe grapes need less time on skins than under-ripe.

The average period of fermentation is 3-4 days, after fermentation starts. In cold seasons, when cellar temperatures are below 15°C., a week or more may be needed to obtain enough colour and flavour.

Ripe grapes with high sugar contents produce high alcohol levels towards the end of fermentation. Combined with high extracted tannin content, this can inhibit the growth of the yeast culture causing a stopped, or 'stuck', fermentation, in which a small amount of unfermented sugar is left in the wine. Apart from its flavour effect, this sugar can provide food for spoilage bacteria, which are often present on grape skins, but which would not normally have the opportunity to develop. When the temperature

of a fermentation is allowed to rise to 35°C. or higher, the yeast culture can be incapacitated with the same attendant dangers.

After the required amount of contact with skins, red wines are drained off and the clear wine is allowed to finish its fermentation in a closed tank until all the sugar is exhausted.

The skins are pressed in either one or two stages, i.e., a light, then a heavy pressing. The amount of tannin and colour which is extracted with the remaining juice varies with the pressure applied. For this reason, most winemakers keep pressings wine separate until after vintage and blend it back into the free-run portion as required.

d. Clarification

Red wines are normally easier to clarify, and because they contain more stable and protective substances, such as tannins, they can be given more time to settle naturally, without the same risks of oxidation and flavour loss as with white wines.

The first and second 'rackings' of clear wine off lees are usually one month and then three to four months after vintage. Wines of delicate flavour balance, or unstable wines, will be clarified in three to four weeks.

Fining with bentonite, or protein-type finings, follows, and at about six months of age, most red wines are filtered and, if they warrant it, stored in oak casks for extended maturation leading to bottling.

e. Storage, maturation and bottling

As a general rule, the biggest and most robust red wines require the longest maturation before they balance their flavours sufficiently to be bottled.

Light red wines, and rosé wines, are bottled young for the same reason as white wines—to preserve their more delicate and fragile characters which could be lost during prolonged wood storage.

The additional flavour drawn from the French or American oak casks must be limited to each wine's capacity to carry it in balance with its own fruit and acid characters.

There is an affinity, and a close chemical similarity, between some oak flavours and those produced by varieties such as cabernet sauvignon. They complement each other when they are present in a wine in the right proportions. It is the assessment of these factors which decides when a wine is ready to bottle.

Most red wines take longer to mature in bottle than white wines, and contain a greater variety of flavours. For this reason, young wines when bottled may have more acid, and rougher tannin flavours, and be less palatable for immediate consumption, unless they have been deliberately over-matured before bottling. The lightest red wines may show some maturity in a year, and pass their peak after four to five years.

The biggest Australian wines, and many high quality European red wines, may be raw and youthful until they are ten years old, but still fresh and alive at forty years.

Sparkling wines

There are five types of sparkling wine in general use:
Bottled fermented (Champagne or Sparkling burgundy style)
Vat fermented (Charmat, caarstens, etc., bulk tank style)
Pearl (bulk fermented as above but at lower pressures)
Spritzig or Petillant (still table wine styles with slight gassing)

All these wines are based on light, delicate dry wines, which have been re-fermented to a greater or lesser degree, or have been chilled and gassed with varying pressures of added carbon dioxide gas. The gas tends to disperse some taste flavours such as acid, but magnifies aroma, due to the fine mist of evaporating wine over the surface of the wine in the glass from bursting bubbles.

In these circumstances, a full-flavoured aromatic still wine becomes strong and over-powering if made into a champagne style. A medium-bodied dry red Carbonated (still wine impregnated with carbon dioxide to varying pressures) becomes heavily scented and too frothy to pour if made into a sparkling burgundy style.

For these reasons, the base materials for sparkling wine production are lighter and thinner than they appear to be when the process has been completed and requires special knowledge in making and selection.

Bottle fermented sparkling wine

The principal style is the champagne type made from a light, acid base wine, with fresh but very delicate flavour balance and ten to twelve percent of alcohol by volume.

Base wines are usually selected for delicacy, fruit character and acidity, and blended together because it is unusual to find one wine with all the required characters. The French word 'cuvée' is the term for this blend.

The cuvée is then fined, cold stabilized (by chilling and filtering cold) and the clear wine transferred to a vat which can be mixed or stirred. A measured sugar solution, a measured volume of yeast culture and a small amount of fining material are then added and mixed in. The amount of sugar is carefully calculated to ferment dry when the maximum pressure of 75-90 lb per square inch has been reached in each bottle. Too much sugar,

and the bottles will burst, or sugar will remain. Too little sugar and insufficient pressure will develop.

The wine is then bottled, and laid down in stacks for periods ranging from six months to three years. The yeast cells, after completing the fermentation, settle out on the side of the bottle, and then begin to decompose, giving up essential oils and conferring 'cracked yeast' flavour on the wine, an essential quality factor in champagne. The longer they remain in the stack, the more of this flavour is conferred.

The bottles are then unstacked and set in 'riddling' tables, where the layer of deposited yeast and finings is shaken down to the cork.

Bottles are then 'disgorged' by blowing the cork with the plug of sediment out of the bottle.

The bottles are then topped up from each other on a pressure filling device, re-corked and wired with the sale or 'expedition' cork, and are ready to label, foil and pack. If a semi-sweet champagne is required, the liqueuring is added at this stage.

Bulk fermentation

The term Charmat is used in Australia to describe this process (after the French winemaker who developed the technique).

The same process is applied to a similar base wine as was used in the pre-bottling stage for champagne types. In this case, the secondary fermentation is carried out in a large pressure tank. Such vessels range from 500 gallons to 15,000 gallons in capacity. When the required pressure is reached the tank is chilled to nearly freezing point. This reduces the working pressure by about half, and the wine is filtered under counter-pressure to a holding tank, where it warms up to bottling temperature, and is filled at pressure—usually into champagne bottles.

Pearl wine

This is a light, lower strength material, which is usually bottled to 40-50 lb per square inch. It is bulk fermented in the same way and is generally aimed at a lower-price market. This is one reason that a lower pressure is used, enabling cheaper, lower pressure bottles to be used.

It is made in white and rosé styles which are sweeter and less delicately balanced than champagne or charmat styles of sparkling wine, and may also be flavoured with fruit essences or cordials.

Carbonated wines

The principle which enables pressured wines to be controlled is based on the increased solubility of carbon dioxide at very low temperatures, with a corresponding lowering of pressure. By this means, the charmat wines, when chilled, can be reduced to half their normal pressure and more easily handled.

Still base wines similar to those used for charmat or pearl wines can be reduced almost to icing point, and mixed with carbon dioxide at high pressure. Under these conditions they will dissolve a high level of gas. The same principle is used in making aerated waters.

The wine is then transferred to bottles under a counter-pressure filling system. As the bottle returns to cellar temperature after filling and corking the gas pressure increases.

Such wines can be made with final pressures of 70-80 p.s.i., but the carbon dioxide, not being naturally fermented, exists in larger undissolved bubbles which leave the wine more quickly in the glass.

Carbonated wines of low pressure (spritzig, petillant, etc.) can be made in the same way. In this case the normal level of gassing is less than 1 p.s.i. They should not be confused with the spritzig or petillant wines resulting from early bottlings of riesling, and similar high quality table wines, which are bottled cold with some of the natural fermentation gases still dissolved in them.

Spritzig wines do not froth or taste of gas, but give a beading of small bubbles on the warm glass after they are poured and a faint prickle of gas on the tongue.

Fortified wines

The addition of neutral grape spirit or brandy to a wine has traditionally been regulated to raise the alcohol strength to between 18 percent and 20 percent by volume (30-35° proof spirit).

A natural grape juice of 20-25 percent sugar will ferment dry to between 11 percent and 13 percent alcohol by volume. At this level the yeast conducting the fermentation is approaching the limit of its tolerance of alcohol.

Specially trained, cultured wine yeasts can ferment at up to 15 percent alcohol. Most wines are safe from re-fermentation of sugar over this level, and fortification to 18 percent is intended to prevent it.

Sherries

The two principal grape varieties used are palomino for the light, delicate base wine and pedro ximenez for the full-flavoured or rich, sweet base wine.

The basis of sherry-making lies in the blending together of a range of elements from light, delicate, crisp dry 'flor' wines, to rich, sweet full-bodied oak flavoured wines. Neutral flavour is required in the juice, and the classical sherry characters of flor yeast·flavours and oak flavour are super-imposed on this neutral base.

Other neutral base wines from varieties such as sultana, albillo, madeleine, etc. are also used. Higher-flavoured sweet wines from muscat, verdelho, madeira, tokay, etc., are used in small amounts in blending sweet sherry styles.

Flor sherry

A light base wine of neutral hock style is fermented, clarified and stabilized. Clean, neutral grape spirit is added to raise the alcohol strength to 16 percent by volume. A selected strain of the fermentation yeast (*Saccharomyces cerevisiae* sp. *ellipsoideus*) which can adapt to growing in a dry film on the surface of the wine is introduced, usually by spatula, and allowed to develop a complete cover over the surface of the wine in each of a series of casks or vats.

Over a period ranging from several months to a year, this film of yeast absorbs oxygen from the air-space above the wine and from the wine itself, and converts the part of the alcohol to an aldehyde, conferring the nutty, or yeasty 'flor' flavour on the wine.

This process is mostly conducted in oak casks, resulting in an additional flavour, of oak, being added to the base wine.

The wine is drawn off, fortified with more spirit to raise it to 18 percent alcohol, and stored in oak casks to mature and develop.

Sweet blending sherries

In Spain some of the pedro ximenez grapes are ripened fully, sun-dried on mats, and then pressed to make a rich, very sweet amber wine. Aged in wood for many years, this 'PX' blending wine is used in small quantities to add richness and flavour to sherry blends. Australian sherry makers carry large stocks of similar wine reserved for blending.

The Spanish term 'rancio' is used to describe the combined age, fruit, oak and alcohol character which distinguishes old wines of this type. In simplified terms, 1-5 percent of such wines with a dry fino sherry makes an Amontillado. Seven to fifteen percent would create the Oloroso style.

Higher proportions would over-power the delicate flor character, and in amoroso and cream sherries, a base wine, wood-aged without flor character is used.

Ports

The style originated in the Douro Valley of Portugal, where wines of the 8-900 vineyards along the steep sides of the river valley are grown.

In Australia, portmaking began with the first vineyards and the Australian styles stand second to Portuguese in world quality standards. The main varieties of grape used here are shiraz, cabernet sauvignon, grenache and mataro.

The warmer climate makes grapes ripen enough to high sugar and deep colour, both of which are necessary for good port production. The three traditional styles are:

Vintage Port
Ruby Port
Tawny Port

Vintage port

This port is made from ripe grapes of shiraz, cabernet sauvignon and mataro style. They are crushed, de-stemmed, and fermented until they have consumed about half the original sugar content. They are then run off skins and a measured addition of alcohol is made to raise the strength to 18 percent by volume. The skins are pressed and the pressings usually returned to the same vat as the free-run wine.

The port is then mixed, fined, filtered and transferred to oak casks to mellow, and integrate the tannins and alcohol and develop fruit characters. This material is bottled within two to three years and left to complete its maturation slowly in glass over twenty to fifty years.

The final fortification is usually with a high-flavoured brandy spirit which adds to the complex grape and oak flavours.

Ruby port

This style is based on the vintage port, and is usually lighter, softer and less intensely coloured. In Portugal vintage ports are only made in those years classified by the port.

It is made in the same way, using grapes of lighter colour and body. When ready for bottling, which is much sooner, e.g., one or two years, ruby port has a soft, fruity flavour. It may also be fortified with brandy. It will develop much more quickly in bottle and may be mature in five to six years, with a bottle life of ten to twelve years.

Tawny port

This wine is fortified in the same way, but may be lower in sugar content, i.e. fortified at a later stage of fermentation.

It uses grape varieties of aromatic flavour which produce wines similar to those for ruby port, but the treatment requires wood ageing instead of bottle age. After some years in oak casks, the red colour cracks and becomes a rich (tawny) brown-red.

Like sherries, the flavours of tawny ports depend on skilful blending of a variety of base wines.

Vermouth

A wide range of flavourings have been added to establish types of dry and sweet fortified wines and traditional styles have been created which have achieved classical flavour patterns for more than a century.

The most significant group is the vermouths, which use a wide variety of extracted herb flavours infused in a dry or sweet wine base.

The basic additive to all vermouth wines is the bitter herb wormwood. To this is added almost every aromatic herb in the culinary lists. The common name vermouth probably derives from the German word 'wermut' for wormwood.

Dry vermouth

A light, dry white, of the style of a dry sherry base wine, fortified to full strength, is infused with a carefully balanced herb mixture.

The objective of vermouth making is to have a wide variety of herb flavours in balance with each other and the base wine, without one of the group dominating the flavour effect.

Sweet vermouth

The base wines for the two styles of sweet vermouth are muscats. The red or brown vermouth uses a brown muscat with a firm tannin flavour, the white or bianco style uses a light soft white muscat gordo.

The sweet vermouths use richer, more aromatic herbs with the wormwood base, as they must conform with the sweet aromatic muscat base wine.

Herbs for vermouth

Some come from Asia, some from Italy, others from France and Belgium. The more important herbs and spices used in vermouths are classified into three groups: bitter, bitter-aromatic and aromatic.

In the bitter group are aloe, angelica, blessed thistle, cinchona, century, germander, lungwort, lungmoss, quassia and rhubarb. Bitter-aromatics include allspice, elder, elecampane, gentian, juniper, bitter orange, sweet orange, saffron, sage, sweet flag, speedwell, wormwood (common, gentile and pontico varieties) and yarrow.

Aromatics are anise, bitter almond, cardamon, cinnamon, clove, nutmeg, coriander, dittany of Crete, galingale, marjoram, Roman camomile, rosemary, savory, thyme, tonka bean and vanilla.

Other flavoured wines

Apart from wines flavoured with fruit essences, and 'Pop' wine mixtures, the other established styles are produced by companies such as Dubonnet (ruby port base with cinchona and other herbs) and Byrrh, Boual, Amer Picon, Cap Corse, which are also based on ruby port.

Observations on home winemaking

22

Dr Don Francois

Home winemaking, amateur winemaking, small quantity winemaking, whatever name you wish to call it, encompasses a wide range of alcoholic beverage manufacturing activities from little old Miss Pennyfeather brewing up a drop of dandelion wine to Gino Vitaliano making his full 400 gallons excise free quota in his backyard winery at Leichhardt.

Recipes are given in most home winemaking guides for wine made from virtually every conceivable plant material. They include the conventional fruits and berries, vegetables such as marrows, artichokes and broad beans, flowers such as marigolds and roses and many exotics such as oak leaf wine. Australians have not been immune to making wine from odd ingredients and Gerry Sissingh of the Rothbury Estate tells the story of awarding a gold medal to a kikuyu grass hock at a Newcastle Amateur Wine Show.

Possibly because of the influence of the vast amounts of literature on home winemaking, which until recently did not include Australian home winemaking, we have not taken full advantage of the excellent supplies of fresh grapes available in this cou try. Aside from proper wine grapes, which are now obtainable, table grapes and dual purpose grapes such as sultanas can be purchased when supplies are heavy for as little as 75 cents for a 24 lb. case.

Essentially, a sound, ripe grape is a small package containing all the ingredients necessary to make wine, such as sugar, acid, tannins, vitamins, nutrients, etc. Because of this, making wine from fresh grapes is in my opinion the easiest home made wine to undertake successfully. By comparison most other recipes call for many ingredients to be added and most of the quantities are average requirements and do not take into account the particular characteristics of the batch of fruit used, such as the sugar and acid contents, etc.

In view of the excellent books available for the home winemaker I do not propose to give step by step procedures, but rather to comment on aspects on which I think my remarks or observations will be interesting or helpful. If the reader wishes to make wine, it is recommended that a *good* general instruction book be purchased. With the exception of *Home Winemaking* by B. A. Chatterton (Rigby Ltd), books that I have seen pay little attention to making grape wines. This is generally left to the more complicated professionally orientated texts.

The best beginners text is *The Winemaker's Companion*, by B. C. A. Turner and C. J. J. Berry (Mills and Boon Ltd, London). Other excellent books as a follow on are *AB-Z of Winemaking* by B. C. A.

Turner and E. A. Roycroft, and *Improve your Winemaking* by B. C. A. Turner, both published by Pelham Books, London. Good criteria for the adequacy of a text is whether the book provides tuition on the use of a hydrometer including tables and the use of sulphur as an antiseptic and antioxidant.

Winemaking from fruits and berries, etc., is good fun and some first rate wines can be made from the most unusual ingredients. However, I am confining this chapter to the home making of wine from grapes.

Grapes

In Australia grapes of good quality are readily available to the home winemaker. Table grapes and multi-purpose grapes, which can be used for eating, drying, distillation and winemaking, can be obtained from your local greengrocer. The most satisfactory method to obtain grapes, however, is to visit the markets, inspect the fruit and shop for the best price.

In the table grape/multi-purpose grape field, I recommend black muscat, gordo blanco and sultanas (Thompson seedless in U.S.A.) for the home winemaker. Other grapes such as purple cornichon, isabella and waltham cross may be used but I find they produce wines of indifferent quality. Black muscat is a spicy grape which produces a pungent typically muscat flavoured wine. If care is taken to select very dark fruit, a very richly coloured red wine can be made. One disadvantage with this variety is that it continually deposits a flocculent crust and considerable care must be taken to decant an aged bottle so as not to end up with a glass of sediment. I decant these wines through a kleenex tissue in a funnel. With age, black muscat wine loses some of its aggressive muscat character and improves considerably. As is the case with all grapes which carry their pigment in the skins, a white wine can be made from the juice. Pressing freshly crushed grapes, however, is always difficult and without a reasonable means of pressing the grapes, it should not be attempted by the home winemaker. Because of this, the beginner should start making red wines and graduate to white wines as skill and equipment are acquired.

Gordo blanco is a multi-purpose white grape which can give good results for the home winemaker. Although it detracts from quality, it may be desirable to ferment gordos and sultanas on the skins for twenty-four hours to break down the pulp and make them easier to press.

Sultanas are possibly the cheapest grape available and as mentioned earlier can sometimes be purchased for as little as 75 cents per 24 lb. case. This is roughly 3 cents per lb. and on this cost structure the raw materials for a bottle of sultana wine could run as low as 10 cents per bottle. On low yields of 120 gallons per ton, it takes approximately 3½ lb. of grapes per bottle of wine or 20 lb. per gallon.

Whilst the grapes mentioned above will make an acceptable wine it is preferable to obtain proper wine grapes. Wine grapes have been available at the Melbourne markets for some years now but it is only in the last four or five years that they have come to Sydney in quantity. Wine grape merchants in Sydney purchase grapes from the irrigation areas of Victoria, South Australia and New South Wales. The grapes sell for three to four dollars a case and are available during March and April. Wine grapes are more fragile than other grapes and do not travel well over long distances. Because of this they frequently arrive in the markets in very poor condition so great care must be taken to select sound fruit.

Shiraz, grenache and mataro are the main grapes available but other varieties including the noble cabernet sauvignon are sometimes shipped. Possibly because they are tougher, mataro seem to arrive in better shape and I have had the best results using this variety.

Sulphur dioxide

Because these fragile wine grapes are picked several days prior to arriving at the market and a good proportion of even a sound case damaged, it is essential to sulphur (sulphur dioxide) the crushed grapes to kill undesirable moulds, bacteria and yeast. Sulphuring also aids in later clarification of the wine and acts as an anti-oxidant. Sulphur dioxide is most easily used by the home winemaker in the form of potassium metabisulphite, obtainable in powdered form from any chemical supply house. Depending upon the condition of the grapes from 75 ppm. (for clean, sound, cool, under-ripe grapes) to 250 ppm. (for mouldy, bruised, hot, over-ripe, low in acid grapes) should be used. As a guide, 1 oz. of potassium metabisulphite per 30 gallons of crushed grapes equals approximately 100 ppm.

The easiest way for the home winemaker to use potassium metabisulphite is to start with a stock solution sufficient to treat 30 gallons of wine at the rate of 100 ppm. This is made by measuring 300 ml. of water with a 100 ml. graduated cylinder into bottle and adding 1 oz. of potassium metabisulphite. Ten ml. of this solution would then be added for each 1 gallon of crushed grapes. This should be added as the grapes are crushed or as soon as possible after, and well mixed. By adding more or less of this basic solution you can vary the dosage of sulphur dioxide to suit the condition of the grapes.

I would not like to hazard a guess as to how much potentially drinkable wine has been spoiled for the want of the proper use of sulphur in wine-making by the Italian community in Sydney. A friend of mine recently made about $500 worth of vinegar through dirty casks and lack of sulphur. Therefore I cannot over-emphasize its importance to the home winemaker.

Because sulphur dioxide inhibits the multiplication of desirable wine yeasts, and it is most desirable for the ferment to start as quickly as possible after the grapes are crushed, cultured wine yeast should be added to the crushed grapes either as powdered or granulated yeast or in the form of a starter culture prepared several days previously. A good text on home winemaking will explain fully how to do this.

Hydrometers

Hydrometers measure the specific gravity of liquids. This measurement can be expressed as a standard specific gravity, or it can be expressed in special scales such as Baumé which gives directly from the crushed grapes the potential alcohol content of the wine, or Balling or Brix, which gives the percentage of sugar content of the crushed grapes. A standard specific gravity of 1.090 equals 12.0 degrees Baumé or 21.5 Balling, Brix or Hunter Sugar. A hydrometer is therefore essential to the home winemaker so that he knows where he starts and where he is going. It tells him if his grapes have enough sugar to make sound wine and when his ferment has come to a satisfactory conclusion.

Containers and Maturation

Because wine is so easily made in quantity from grapes and many people do make large quantities, the traditional wooden barrel is commonly used by Australian amateur winemakers. Most barrels used are not new but are second-hand whisky or brandy barrels. Sometimes barrels have been used for less desirable liquids. Storing wine in wooden barrels imparts a pleasant flavour and matures the wine in a gentle manner which cannot be done otherwise. Maintaining wooden containers, however, is a skilled job and many things can go wrong. Much of the vinegar made by home winemakers and many of the off-flavours in home-made wines can be traced back to unsound barrels. I seldom use barrels in my own winemaking and for large quantities I use 44 gallon drums with special inert plastic inserts. They are impervious and easily cleaned and have threaded openings which

Hydraulic presses at Glenloth, S.A.

can be sealed tightly or fitted with a fermentation lock. These same containers are used extensively in the wine industry to ship wine interstate and overseas.

For the home winemaker I consider glass to be the ideal container, but because of size limitations, it cannot always be used. Glass is impervious and easily cleaned but it also has the terrific additional advantage in that it is transparent and the home winemaker can see precisely what is happening. We can see how gas bubbles in fermenting juice behave and how sediment accumulates and how crust particles are sucked into a siphon. We can see the wine clear from the top down and how the cream of tartar crystals form.

By using containers other than wood, however, we miss out on the very positive quality factor of oak flavour. This can be imparted by the use of oak chips, but because of their irregular shapes, they do not lend themselves to a calculation of surface area exposed to wine. In an attempt to overcome this problem I obtained battens of American oak each measuring 12" x 1⅛" x ⅛". Each of these has a surface area of 30.3 square inches. I then calculated the surface area of a 50 gallon oak cask and commenced experiments submerging the battens in wine using various ratios of wine to surface area. These experiments have been encouraging and are continuing. The great advantage in this method is of course that I have a reasonable degree of control and can repeat favourable results.

Most home winemakers will not be making these large quantities of wine, but as grapes are cheap and easy to make wine from, they will probably make wine in larger quantities than the 1 gallon lots suggested in most home winemaking books. In this regard, I consider 1 gallon too small a quantity of grape wine to achieve good results. Oxidation becomes a critical factor with such small quantities and after all the work you end up with six bottles, or two flagons! I have good results with 3½ gallon carboys and larger, and consider a five gallon bottle ideal for the following reasons:

1. It is large enough in my opinion to avoid excessive oxidation through surface contacts, etc.

2. It is small enough to lift thereby facilitating racking by gravity—no pumps to churn the wine.

3. It makes 2½ dozen bottles which is a reasonable quantity of wine to end up with of a particular type.

I have larger carboys, up to 14 gallons, and they are excellent for my purposes but I cannot shift them easily.

Although the home winemaker may work under some disadvantage such as greater risk of oxidation and lack of good equipment, because he makes wine in small quantities and in small containers he also has some decided advantages over the larger commercial operators.

1. Fruit can be carefully picked and culled.

2. Gravity can be used more to shift wine—less pumping—less damage to wine—less oxidation.

3. Small fermentation containers have a greater surface area to volume of wine and therefore a greater heat loss—they are easier to cool. As mentioned, small containers can be picked up and moved to a cooler place. During the heat of the 1972 summer I was able to keep a fermenting white wine below 68° F by simply wrapping the 8 gallon carboy in wet hessian and keeping an electric fan directed at it.

4. Small glass containers facilitate visual inspection of processes.

Most home winemakers bottle their wine too soon and drink it too quickly to get the benefit that bottle age can impart. Except for some white wines which are best bottled as soon as possible and are quite good drunk young and fresh, most wines, particularly dry reds, benefit from several years in a bottle. I would recommend as a general rule that your wine should not be bottled for at least 10 months. With grape wines, this affords plenty of time for a malo-lactic fermentation and also allows for natural clearing of the wine without the use of clearing (fining) agents.

Bottles

Most home wine books give elaborate procedures for cleaning bottles, probably because many people who make wine at home will accept from friends and other sources empty bottles which are not clean. I suggest that you accept no bottles which have been empty more than 24 hours and preferably much less. These are extremely easy to clean with water and antiseptics are not required. Ideally, a bottle should be filled with water as soon as it is emptied. After soaking off the labels it can be rinsed once and drained and dried for storage. Bottles not filled with water immediately after emptying should have water left in them for 24 hours prior to rinsing and draining dry. I store clean bottles in used wine cartons or else I wrap them in a sheet of newspaper to keep the dust out.

The law

The Commonwealth of Australia, in line with most countries, does not unduly hinder the home wine-maker. Home-made wine cannot be sold without the appropriate Commonwealth licence and there is an annual excise free production limit of 400 gallons (1,800 litres), but aside from these liberal restrictions you can do what you wish. As might be expected, however, the home beer brewer is more restricted, and would-be brewers are advised to clarify the legal position.

Storage/fermenter tanks at Tolley, Scott and Tolley, Barossa Valley.

SOILS
AND CLIMATE

Norman Hanckel is Director and Group General Manager of International Cellars Australia Pty. Ltd. —and subsidiary companies which include Walter Reynell & Sons Wines Pty. Ltd. and Hungerford Hill Vineyards Pty. Ltd. He previously held the position of Production Manager for S. Smith & Sons Pty. Ltd., Yalumba Wines.

Pickers at Hungerford Hill vineyard in the Hunter Valley, N.S.W.

Norman Hanckel

Wine quality in Australia has benefited greatly through the use of modern equipment and with the development of new techniques including improved processes in maturation of wine. The major factors in determining the quality of wine, however, are the grape variety used and the environment in which these grapes are grown. An understanding of the importance of environment related to grape quality, based on recognition of the influence of both climate and soil, is essential before an accurate classification of the Australian wines according to district and specific locality within a district can be made.

Considerable research has gone into studying the culture of grapes in Australia and a great amount of information has been compiled on both climatic and soil data to the extent today that it is possible to select a vineyard site capable of producing economic grape crops. There is a serious lack of information, however, which adequately explains the influence of climate and soil on grape composition and the final quality of grapes, particularly those used for the production of table wines.

Any attempt to analyse the influence of soil and climate on Australian wines must therefore be to a large degree subjective in viewpoint and it will be necessary to continue to use wines from the quality districts of Australia together with wine from the vineyards of France and Germany as a standard by which to judge the quality of wines from new vineyard areas.

In Australia there is a continuing collection of information on the suitability of different grape varieties for particular localities gained from experience of grape growers and winemakers. The information is usually confined to finding that a specific grape variety grew extremely well or did not succeed to grow well on one type of soil or in a particular locality, without finding the reasons why the specific grape variety was not suitable. The fact that the specific grape variety grew well has been sufficient reason in most cases and little work has been done to determine the real quality of the wines from this particular locality. With the growing awareness of wine drinkers in Australia towards quality regional wines, we find winemakers are now prepared to pay premium prices for grapes grown on specific vineyards within a small regional area, e.g., the price paid per ton for shiraz grapes grown in the Pokolbin area of the Hunter Valley in 1970 and 1971 has been three times higher than the price for quality shiraz grapes grown in the best areas of the Barossa Valley. This development of awareness of wine quality resulting from grapes grown on specific vineyards is the first step towards the development of locality wines showing details of classifications of area of origin of the grapes.

In the famous vineyard areas of France and Germany the vineyards are usually planted to only a few varieties of grapes, which have been chosen because of their suitability to the soils and climate of the district. The choice of these varieties has resulted from the long experience gained over centuries in the development of quality wine, whereas in Australia we are still in the early development stages where most vineyard areas grow almost the complete range of grape varieties available.

The development of the Pokolbin area of the Lower Hunter in New South Wales and Coonawarra in the south-east of South Australia has followed the pattern of European vineyards more closely than any other areas in Australia. At Pokolbin the majority of quality wines are being produced from one red grape variety, shiraz, and one white grape variety, semillon (Hunter River riesling), while at Coonawarra the plantings are mainly cabernet sauvignon, shiraz and rhine riesling.

There are many subtle differences in composition of wine caused by the influence of soil and climate, and it will be extremely difficult to develop a definition of boundaries for districts and specific vineyard areas within Australia. In preparing a regional classification code it will be difficult to decide whether climatic differences as determined by altitude, temperature, rainfall, topography including mountain ranges, creeks and rivers, soil types or road or parish boundaries should be used as the sole demarcation of one classified vineyard district from the next. It is obvious that a great deal more selective bottlings of area wines, based on these factors, will need to be made to assist in the development of a regional classification code.

Vineyard selection, establishment and management

23

The influence of soil and climate on vine growth and wine quality will be examined by relating the influence of these factors on vineyard selection, establishment and management problems rather than making a detailed analysis of the climate and soils of each district.

New vineyards are being developed over widely differing soil and climatic conditions throughout Australia today. Some of these vineyard plantings are extensions or a rejuvenation of established premium table wine areas such as Pokolbin, Coonawarra and Pewsey Vale; other developments are in areas proven to produce good yields of high quality wines; while other areas are being developed under irrigation to economically produce large tonnages of grapes for use in the growing low to medium price wine market.

A great number of new vineyard development projects have taken place in areas not previously planted to table wine variety vineyards. These new developments are offering a great challenge to both the vineyard owner in the selection and establishment of the property, and to the winemaker in producing the first wine from grapes from these new areas.

Many existing districts are influenced by a micro-climate not apparent in local meteorological records and until accurate weather recording stations are located on individual vineyard properties, the effect of local differences in temperature and rainfall to wine quality will be difficult to correlate.

In districts such as Pokolbin, the vineyards on the slopes receive cooling sea breezes in the late afternoon during the ripening period, whereas vineyards in the valleys closer to Cessnock continue to experience high temperatures.

Therefore, every district in Australia presents different problems in vineyard establishment and management. Vineyards being planted in established areas can be planned using the previous experience of grape growers in the area, relating this to current developments in the wine industry. In establishing a vineyard in a new area, a perceptive analysis is required on all available soil and climatic data to determine whether grapes will grow successfully and whether the wine quality will be acceptable.

Selection of vineyard site

Selection must be based upon the analysis of both soil and climate bearing in mind the practical aspects of vineyard operation as well as assessing the effect of both soil and climate on the quality of the grapes being produced.

It is necessary to initially look at the reasons why the vineyard is to be established, setting out the basic objectives. Production of grapes may be aimed at premium quality wines; medium quality wine; wine from high yielding vineyards under irrigation normally in the warmer areas. Production could be aimed towards table wines, fortified wines, or for the production of brandy and spirit.

Within the objective of producing premium table wines, consideration will also need to be given to the rate of maturity of wines produced from each area as this affects the amount of capital required to hold wine stocks prior to marketing. Thus, the Pokolbin area of the Hunter Valley has traditionally produced both red and white quality wines which mature early with full softness, whereas at the opposite end of the scale, the red table wines from Coonawarra require a lengthy period of bottle age prior to being at their optimum marketable age.

Climate

Rainfall

Wine grape varieties require an average annual rainfall of between 25 and 30 inches per annum to satisfactorily produce economic crops of grapes. The majority of vineyard areas, with the exception of New South Wales coastal vineyards, Coonawarra and Western Australia, receive less than 25 inches of rain and grape yields often reflect this moisture deficiency.

In many areas irrigation is used to supplement rainfall. The majority of grapes produced for wine-making in Australia are now produced in these irri-gated areas using water supplies from the River Murray and its tributaries. Winemakers are yet to make the necessary assessment of the effect of continued or excessive irrigation on the quality of grapes when these grapes are grown in premium quality areas normally relying on natural rainfall. Irrigation schemes, if they are to be installed, must be planned, and should be installed prior to planting as total layout is affected.

In non-irrigated areas the total rainfall shown as annual rainfall is not a sufficient guide to determine whether the rainfall is adequate for vine growth. The pattern of rainfall throughout the year is most important. Soils require a capacity to hold moisture if the climate is a winter rainfall pattern, having soil conditions able to allow penetration of water into the soil at all times and with adequate contouring in undulating or mountainous areas to prevent run off of water. Rainfall statistics can be inadequate even on a monthly basis as a showery weather pattern rather than soaking rains can be misleading in terms of effective rainfall.

The majority of grapes grown in Australia are grown in Mediterranean type climate with dry summers which allow vine growth to be relatively disease-free. The Hunter Valley vineyards and other vineyards on the East Coast of Australia have a pattern of high summer rainfall which changes the pattern of vine growth and also encourages rapid development of diseases, of which downy mildew would be the most severe. The summer rainfall pattern, after discounting the cost of controlling diseases, and allowing for the risk of rain damage to fruit during harvest, gives conditions for vine growth which are far more ideal than under dry summer conditions. Summer rainfall reduces moisture stress during the period of rapid vine growth, has a cooling effect during the hot summer period, and in most cases gives conditions of high humidity throughout the growing period, reducing vine transpiration rates and preventing scorching and drying up of vine leaves. The development of modern spray chemicals, and the use of both fixed wing and helicopter aerial spraying techniques, has reduced risks of the damaging effect of disease in these high summer rainfall areas to a degree where they are no longer a significant threat to the vine crop.

Adequate growing season

Vines require a sufficiently long period of warm summer conditions to allow the vine to flower, set fruit and mature grapes so that the fruit arrives at an adequate balance of sugar and acidity.

Frosts

The green parts of growing vines will be damaged at temperatures below 30 degrees Fahrenheit. This precludes development in vineyards in areas subject to late spring or early autumn frosts. Most of the vineyard areas in Australia, with the exception of the East Coast of New South Wales, are subject to occasional damage from spring frosts, and this particularly applies to the more southern vineyards of Victoria and South Australia.

A great amount of climatic data has been compiled on the likelihood of frosts in various regions of Australia and much of this has been summarized in 'Frost in the Australian Region' Bulletin 32 of the Australian Meteorological Bureau. Within any one locality the likelihood of frost occurrence varies with soil type, height of the vineyard site related to adjoining land, direction of the slope and general air drainage conditions. Soil management techniques and irrigation techniques and vine training patterns can do much to alleviate frost damage even under extremely adverse conditions.

Temperature

Areas experiencing extreme heat during the growing and ripening season should be avoided if possible due to the likelihood of damage to the grape berries. This condition can be aggravated under conditions where application of spray chemicals is required for disease control.

A great amount of research is being carried out to determine the effect of temperature during the growing season on wine grape quality. Regions most suited for producing quality table wine grapes require moderately cool weather during the ripening period, as this allows the fruit optimum development of aroma and flavouring character leading to the development of bouquet in flavour of wines.

It is generally accepted that the cooler the district, within the climatic limits of growing wine grapes, the greater the chance of wine being of high quality. Detailed research was carried out by Professor M. A. Amerine and A. J. Winkler of California in the United States to determine the effect of temperature on grape maturity and quality. They related the total temperature for the growing season for each vineyard area in California and expressed temperature as a heat summation in degree days where temperatures are above 50 F. for the period concerned and the base was set at 50°F. as there is little vine growth below this temperature. This resulted in a division of regions in California—five regions from very cool regions to extremely warm regions and this basis has now been applied throughout the world including Australian vineyards. The only vineyard area within Australia which does not fit the pattern relating degree days directly to the capacity of the district to produce premium quality table wines is the Pokolbin area in the Hunter Valley of New South Wales where available climatic data indicates on a degree day basis the area would be too hot to grow wines other than the fortified wines whereas in actual practice, the district produces premium quality table wines and cannot easily obtain the sugar levels required in the production of fortified types. A comparison shows that very few areas in Australia are as cool as the white wine growing areas of Germany and it is possible that future white wine plantings in Australia will follow much more the pattern of selecting extremely cool regions using this heat summation formula as a guideline.

Region 1, Under 2500

Country	District	Degree days
Germany	Geisenheim	1709
Germany	Trier	1730
Germany	Rheingau	1745
France	Auxerre	1850
France	Chalons-sur-Marne	2060
U.S.A.	Oakville	2300
France	Burgundy	2327
U.S.A.	Sonoma	2360
France	Beaune	2400
France	Champagne	2449

*Region 2, 2501-3000

Portugal	Douro	2765
Australia	Barossa, S.A.	2838
U.S.A.	St. Helena	2900
Italy	Asti	2980

Region 3, 3001-3500

Australia	Seymour, Vic.	3050
Australia	Coonawarra, S.A.	3175
Australia	Clare, S.A.	3231
U.S.A.	Livermore	3260
Australia	Adelaide, S.A.	3458

Region 4, 3501-4000

Australia	Gt. Western Stawell, Vic.	3505
Italy	Florence	3530
U.S.A.	Codi-Stockton	3590
Australia	Rutherglen, Vic.	3654
Australia	Benalla, Vic.	3715
Australia	Berri, S.A.	3840
U.S.A.	Davis	3970

Region 5, Over 4000

Italy	Naples	4010
Australia	Swan Valley, W.A.	4079
Italy	Palermo	4140
Australia	Griffith, N.S.W.	4170
Spain	Jerez de la Frontera	4194
Australia	Pokolbin, N.S.W.	4538
U.S.A.	Fresno	4680
U.S.A.	Bakersfield	5030
Algeria	Algiers	5200

The two sluice gates controlling the irrigation supply to the Potts' 'Bleasdale' winery, Langhorne Creek, S.A.

Average daily temperature records do not necessarily give a complete picture of the effect of district temperature on wine quality. Districts having a low variation of temperature between day and evening temperatures produce more delicate table wines than districts experiencing extremely hot day temperatures and cool evenings. Hours of sunlight and day length also influence vine growth and wine quality. Relation of these factors to Australian wine quality is not understood, but it is argued that reduced hours of sunlight during the ripening period are part of the explanation of why quality table wines can be produced in a warm climatic region such as the Hunter Valley.

Grapes grown in various regions of Australia at identical latitude can have marked differences in quality due to variations in actual temperature patterns. Altitude is the most significant influence on these and this effect is shown by the difference in ripening dates and wine quality of grapes grown in the Eden Valley-Springton area of South Australia when compared with vines in the Barossa Valley proper where there is an average of 800 ft difference in altitude. This effect of altitude on wine quality has been demonstrated by the outstanding quality wines being produced from the vineyards at Pewsey Vale, one of the highest commercial vineyards in Australia. The direction of slope, whether towards or away from the sun, the effect of sea influence and the effect of prevailing winds, all give specific localities within a district temperature variations which, in turn, affect the quality of wine produced.

Freedom from hail

In selecting a vineyard it is important to give consideration to the likelihood of damage from hail storms. The extreme local nature of hail makes it impossible to maintain district records due to the

*1. **Source of Data:** California Section Climatological Data Reports.
   U.S. Weather Bureau and U.S. Trade Consuls.
2. Commonwealth Meteorological Department.

damage from hail storms normally occurring in only a very narrow strip of vineyard during any one storm. The selection of vineyard sites must be based on gaining local knowledge from existing grape growers.

The East Coast of New South Wales suffers hail damage mainly in the mid-summer to harvest period and damage at this time is usually of a severe nature and does not allow recovery of the vine crop. Hail damage in the southern regions of Australia usually occurs in October/November and it is possible for vines to recover and still bear satisfactory crops after being damaged particularly if vine shoot growth is given correct treatment.

Soil

Grapes can grow under a wide range of climatic and soil conditions. In each district throughout Australia there is a developed preference to plant vines on well drained rich red loam soils with deep clay loam subsoils in non-irrigated areas. Vineyards in irrigated areas are usually on sandy loam to loam soils with a preference for no clay subsoils whatsoever to allow for adequate soil drainage of surplus irrigation water. The selection of these broad types of soils has been based upon the ease of working the vineyard and potential yield rather than the quality of the grapes produced. It is only with the growth of interest of premium quality table wines in Australia that winemakers are learning to assess the effect of a specific soil type in a particular vineyard area.

Within Australian premium quality vineyard areas there appears to be a relationship between the presence of calcium carbonate or limestone in the subsoil and the development of full bouquet and flavouring constituents in the grape. Grape vines are able to grow satisfactorily in soils with 50-70 percent calcium carbonate and wines made from grapes from these soils appear to be better balanced. The rich red volcanic soils at Pokolbin, the terra rossa soils at Coonawarra, the sandy loam soils at Reynella and the red-brown earths at Watervale all have limestone subsoils and the wines made from these areas reflect this influence. The heavy rich black alluvial flats and other areas of similarly rich soils are generally unacceptable for the production of quality table wines, but are admirably suited for the production of fortified wines and vintage port. In some cases the extreme vigour of vines grown on these rich soils leads to heavy cropping and unbalanced sugar/acid ratio. As a general rule heavy yielding vineyards result in wines with an unbalanced composition.

In selection of a vineyard it is of utmost importance to locate the best quality soil available for the purpose of producing a specific type of wine required. There is no substitute for good soils over the period of the life of a vineyard and the use of fertilizers including trace elements only maintains vine growth, but seldom overcomes long term soil deficiencies. Most of the experimental work which has been carried out throughout the world and within Australia to date indicates little response to fertilizer application and this in part is due to the very deep rooted systems of most vine varieties.

Widely differing opinions are held on the suitability of individual soil types in any district for each specific grape variety. As a broad guideline, it is usual to plant white wine grapes on sandy to sandy loam types of soils and to plant red wine grape varieties on soils ranging through from sandy loam to clay loam soil types. This results in unusual patterns of vineyard plantings. The rich red soils in the Pokolbin area of the Hunter Valley are found on the tops of the ridges and the lighter sandy soils found in the valleys, whereas in South Australia the reverse applies with the lighter soils being found on the ridges and the richer loam to clay loam soils found in the valleys.

The type of soil, together with topography and rainfall patterns, must be considered in relation to soil conservation in selection of the vineyard site. Heavy soil types and heavy rainfall patterns will require a much more complicated and expensive system of contour planting than on sandy or sandy loam soils where rainfall can be quickly absorbed. A great deal of work is being done on contour planting of vineyards in Australia under a wide variety of soil and climatic conditions and expert help is available in all cases from the individual State Departments of Agriculture. Soil conservation is essential to ensure adequate intake of rainfall, and to prevent soil deterioration and soil erosion over the period of the life of the vineyard.

The development of the use of weedicides in vineyards is giving the grape grower the opportunity to reduce the amount of cultivation necessary. Because of this it is now possible to plant vines on soil types and to plant steep slopes using under vine weedicides to overcome problems of working the vineyards that would otherwise be very difficult.

In the selection of a vineyard, consideration should also be given to the problem of grape harvesting. Planting of heavy yield vineyards for mechanical harvesting of grapes is essential. This is particularly so if the vineyard is located in an area where it is difficult to obtain casual labour for the harvest period. Mechanical harvesting requires relatively level land, and also requires well drained soils to allow heavy machinery to work in the vineyards as soon as possible after rain during the vintage period.

The large investment required to establish a new vineyard in Australia makes it essential to maximize production relative to the quality objectives. This production should be maintained over a period of thirty years and will require preservation of soil structure using cover crops and conservative soil management techniques, aiming also to retain vigour through adequate disease and insect control.

Ground preparation

It is advisable to prepare ground as far ahead as possible prior to planting. Sandy soils and deep sandy loams require little preparation whereas vineyard sites with heavy clay subsoils could require deep ripping which is an expensive operation.

Some types of clay sub-soil are self-cracking and a soil with this capacity does not require ripping to the same extent as ordinary clay soils. Ripping is usually carried out to a minimum depth of 24 inches along the planned planting row to allow early establishment of a deep rooting system. As a rule there seems little purpose in ripping between the rows prior to planting. In soils experiencing winter drainage problems, it is advisable to consider cross ripping down the slope at the point of each row where the vines will ultimately be planted. Ripping, to be effective, must be done when the soil is in a dry condition to allow fracturing of the soil, and under no circumstances should the soil be ripped in extremely wet conditions as the only effect is to restrict future root growth into the narrow rip mark. In very heavy clay soils it is possible to incorporate a percentage of the friable top soils down through the rip mark to assist early establishment of root growth.

Selection of rootstock

Both climate and soils are significant factors in the selection of a vineyard rootstock, and it is possible in any one vineyard area to see remarkable variations in vine growth and vine yield of individual varieties of grapes. For example, in irrigated areas it has been normal practice to plant sultana grapes on the sandier soils, while muscat and doradillo varieties yield best on heavier loamy soils.

Earlier reference has indicated little work has been done on the selection of individual vine varieties on specific soil types in the production of premium quality table wines. Individual winemakers have opinions which are reasonably substantiated relating specific varieties to individual soil types within their vineyard properties. Most of these opinions vary from winemaker to winemaker and do in fact often conflict with each other.

There is the increasing problem of nematode in vineyards to be established on sandy soils throughout Australia. Nematode is widespread in the majority of sandy soils whether or not the area had been previously established to vineyards. Hot water treatment of vine rootstocks to be introduced to these soil types is essential to ensure that rootstocks are nematode free. Vineyard soils can be fumigated, but the most advisable practice on sandier soils is to consider planting out the complete vineyard with nematode resistant rootstocks, and grafting over to the desirable vine variety at the second year.

Planting layout

The pattern of planting layout of the vineyard, once decided, cannot be changed except with extremely costly adaptions. Decisions made on planting layout are normally related to the soil and climatic conditions prevailing in the district and these must be carefully considered before a planting pattern is decided upon.

Vine spacing

The most economical vineyard pattern to develop and operate is a pattern of long straight rows uniformly spaced with adequate turning space at the end. This pattern of planting is the easiest to cultivate. Widely spaced vine rows again are cheaper to cultivate and work and reduce trellising coasts.

Vine spacing varies greatly throughout the different grape growing areas of Australia. Although many areas have continued to space vines through the traditional pattern set up in the early vineyard development of Australia, there is a move in new vineyard plantings toward assessing such factors as temperature, soil fertility, soil structure, moisture supply and direction of prevailing winds.

It appears one of the only points in favour of close planting is the fact that the first few crops are larger and unless wide spacing is carried to the extreme, vineyards can benefit by spacing to allow adequate access for planting and machinery. The most desirable spacing is the widest which can be made without affecting grape yields or upsetting normal vineyard operations.

Under conditions where ample moisture supply is available development of a pattern of planting and trellising to allow foliage to almost completely shade the soil of the vineyard is gaining favour, as this allows vines to absorb and utilize the full effects of sunlight. The development of under vine weedicide has allowed reduction in the amount of working required under the vine row, but does require sufficiently wide rows to allow access of tractors and normal mid-row equipment without disturbing the weedicide-treated under vine mounds. Under conditions of soil and climate where vine growth is extremely vigorous, row width needs to be increased to at least 12 ft. to allow tractor access unless trellis systems are designed to keep foliage off the ground.

In areas of low rainfall it is often necessary to increase distance between the vines, most effectively achieved by increasing row width, in order to allow vines to survive extremely dry seasons. Where there are no specific requirements of row direction through either irrigation or soil conservation, consideration should be given to planting the vine row in a direction which takes into account prevailing winds and the effect of sunburn, e.g., in the hot irrigation areas of South Australia prevailing winds in the early period

The Wyndham Estate is a 300-acre property on the banks of the Hunter River, N.S.W.

of vine growth are south westerly and sun-scorch normally occurs on the northern side of the vine. By planting the vines in an east/west direction the prevailing winds move the majority of the leaf canopy of the vine to the northern side which gives adequate protection throughout the summer months against sunburn.

Experimental work carried out in the United States has indicated little variation in quality wine made from grapes at different vine spacings and it appears the only influence on quality is the capacity of the vine to absorb sufficient sunlight through the training method to allow full colouring of the grapes.

Contouring

Many of the premium quality vineyards in Australia are located on undulating to steeply rising slopes. These include vineyards in the Pokolbin area of the Hunter Valley, Pewsey Vale and Clare-Watervale districts, where the premium quality wine produced can warrant the additional expense of contour planting and vineyard operation. Vineyards on these slopes need to be planned in such a manner to prevent soil erosion, and to prevent any reduction of rainfall intake.

Development of contour systems is at an advanced level in Australian vineyards and varies from district to district and from State to State due to differences in soil types and rainfall patterns. In areas experiencing a winter rainfall pattern the intensity of rainfall in any one period is usually lower than in areas experiencing summer rainfall. In these winter rainfall areas contour banks can be more widely spaced and of longer length and smaller size because they do not need to carry large volumes of water over a short period, but rather act as catchment drains. Vine rows between the banks are usually planted equally spaced each side of a centre line and designed with a fall throughout the length of the contour bay. This means that vine rows are equally spaced at all times and implements can completely cultivate between the rows. Occasionally a design of this nature does create a situation where a vine row occasionally rises instead of having a continuous fall and this can lead to waterlogging and erosion in these areas.

In these winter rainfall patterns the problem of wet conditions during the summer does not arise. Provision does not need to be made for quick access after heavy rains for spraying operations and for harvesting. In areas of heavy summer rainfall it is common to experience downpours of up to three inches in an hour. The design of contours must be made to cope with large volumes of water and to quickly take this excess water away from the vineyard. Row lengths must be short to allow drainage of the water before the volume rises to a level where the individual vine rows can no longer discharge water and the water cuts down across the slope. For example, in vine rows on the steeper slopes of Pokolbin the length should not exceed 400 ft. to allow for adequate discharge of water at the end of the row. This matter is aggravated in heavy soil types and it is essential that design takes both these factors of soil type and rainfall completely into consideration. The most suitable design under these conditions is where the vine row individually follows the contour pattern at a rate of approximately 1 ft. in 30 ft. to allow adequate and rapid drainage of surplus water. Vine rows under this system of contouring vary in width and do create quite significant management problems particularly in relation to cultivation implements. Vineyards in areas such as these require massive contour banks and extremely well planned and well grassed waterways.

Adequate planning should be made in laying out the vineyard to allow for well drained and consolidated access roads at the top of the property and with a further series of well drained roads at the bottom of each slope.

The direction of vine rows in irrigated vineyards is largely dependent on the slope of the land and the rows should follow a grade that will permit suitable flow of water and allow adequate penetration over the length of the vine row. This is influenced to a large degree by the soil type and the rate of water penetration.

Planting techniques

Time of planting is influenced to a large degree by the climatic patterns of a district. In areas experiencing heavy winter rainfall and conditions of soil waterlogging it is desirable to delay planting to early spring when free soil water has disappeared. In circumstances other than this, it is usually desirable to plant as early as possible in the winter period

to allow the vines to become fully settled in the soil prior to the advent of spring growth. Early planting under winter rainfall conditions can require an excessive amount of vineyard cultivation during the winter and spring months of the first year and is often the reason why vineyard plantings are delayed. In the drier irrigation areas and in areas experiencing a summer rainfall pattern, there is no reason why vines cannot be planted out as soon as the dormant period begins.

Planting techniques vary from district to district due to the carry over of previous practices and to the influences of soil type. Under almost all conditions of vineyard planting it is desirable to ensure that the newly planted vine has adequate moisture supply around the root system and this can be achieved through various methods incorporated with the planting technique. Of the varying techniques used to apply water at planting time the use of a high pressure water gun to prepare a hole through water pressure suitable for planting is the most ideal, and this has the added advantage of allowing insecticides to be incorporated around a root zone at the time of planting. Mechanical planters have been designed and are in use in many areas of the world, but any form of mechanical planting requires large areas of relatively flat land of friable sandy to sandy loam soils to work satisfactorily, and also require relatively dry soil conditions during the planting period to allow access and continued use of heavy planting equipment.

Most methods of under planting are unsatisfactory unless water is applied immediately after planting due to inadequate compaction of the soil around the vine roots and in irrigated areas it is essential to apply an irrigation as soon as possible after the vines have been planted.

The use of posthole diggers for preparing vine planting holes is to be discouraged in all but extremely sandy soil types due to the fact that the soil auger of the posthole digger forms an almost watertight hole in the ground through compacting and polishing the clay on the walls of the hole. There have been many examples in heavy clay soils areas where vines planted in postholes remain stunted throughout the growth of the vine. On removal of these vines, it is usual to find that the roots have circled round inside the original posthole similar to the roots of a pot-bound plant.

Training systems

Some of the factors influencing training systems have been reviewed earlier in 'Planting layout'. The major factor influencing training systems is the vigour of the vines relating to both soil fertility, availability of moisture and the temperature in which the vines grow. Extremely vigorous vines growing under hot irrigated conditions require

Pruning the vines at 'Glen Elgin' vineyard, Hunter Valley, N.S.W. (Photo: A. F. D'Ombrain.)

extremely sophisticated trellis systems able to carry yields of grapes in excess of ten tons per acre whereas in the premium quality vineyard areas yields would not be expected to exceed three tons per acre. In order to carry heavy yields the trellis system needs to be both more extensive in design, the end or strainers need to be much more substantial and additional foliage wires are essential to keep vigorous growth away from the ground and allow adequate disease control measures.

In areas experiencing late spring frosts, it is essential that the trellis be a minimum of 2' 6" above the ground and preferably up to 3' 6" above the ground to reduce the risk and effect of frosts on young vine growth, as frost severity reduces significantly with every 6 inches additional height above ground level. It is also an added advantage in areas prone to frosts to aim to train the vines up to the wire in the first year rather than pruning back to ground level at the end of the first year.

Many of the less vigorous non-vineyard areas of low rainfall have persisted in training systems close to the ground in order to reduce the cost of trellising, or alternatively train the vines on a bush-spur system without any trellising.

Under irrigated conditions and in areas of extremely vigorous vine growth it is essential to trellis in the first year to allow adequate training of the vines and prevent damage to young vines through wind or implements.

Mechanical harvesting

The majority of new vineyard areas being developed have given consideration to mechanical harvesting. Mechanical harvesting requires specially modified trellis systems and in most cases these need to be planted at the initial stages of vine trellising rather than modifying existing systems. Unless vine vigour is sufficient to give vine yields in excess of three tons per acre, it is doubtful whether mechanical harvesting could be considered. Mechanical harvesting is best suited for flat, well drained soils allowing long hours of effective operation of the machinery.

Irrigation systems

Soil type and topography influence the type of irrigation system to be installed. On undulating country, sprinkler irrigation systems allow long straight rows to be planted with selection of the most suitable row direction as outlined earlier in discussing 'Planting layout'. A great deal of research has been carried out on furrow irrigation within Australia on vineyard soils particularly in relation to adequate moisture penetration, and the problems related to salt accumulation and the development of water tables. These are all directly related to the variations and changes of soil type within any vineyard property and in each district. (Refer Reports by the Commonwealth Scientific and Industrial Research Organization of Australia).

Irrigation prior to a frost period has the effect of reducing the risk of frost. Sprinkler irrigation systems have been installed and effectively used in many frost-prone areas to reduce the risk of frost through ground consolidation and through the operation of sprinklers at the critical period of low temperature utilizing the effect of warmer water to prevent freezing of young vine shoots.

Experimental work is also being carried out both in Australia and overseas on the cooling effect of sprinkler irrigation to promote quality in varieties grown for table wine production.

Cultivation techniques

Throughout Australia the general vineyard practice has been to maintain weed-free vineyards through the growing period to conserve moisture, and to leave the soil in a condition to utilize any summer rainfall. Very few areas in Australia have a high enough rainfall pattern to allow permanent sod culture, although in New South Wales it is a growing practice to encourage grass growth from January onward with mowing rather than cultivation in order to consolidate soil prior to grape harvest.

Soil fertility

The maintenance of soil fertility through the use of cover crops is practised throughout Australia, but in many cases the inadequate rainfall makes programmes of cover cropping extremely difficult and at times is detrimental to vine growth through reducing available moisture supplies.

Weed growth

In vineyard areas subject to spring frosts it is essential that weed growth be incorporated in the soil prior to the first date when a damaging frost could occur. The soil should be compacted, preferably rolled and irrigated if sprinkler irrigation is available. This practice has been effectively used in the Coonawarra area over the past few years and has significantly reduced frost damage. High weed growth, cover crop growth or loosely worked up soil increases the risk of frost damage in vineyards. Under conditions of summer rainfall it has been found that application of fungicides after the harvest date will allow vines to continue growing, adding to the vigour of the vine and increasing the future yield potential and longevity of the vine.

Harvesting and winemaking

The rate at which grapes mature varies directly with the temperature of the district in which they are growing, although this could be influenced to a degree by the availability of moisture during the growing and ripening period.

In the hot irrigation areas white wine grapes mature showing a very rapid drop in acidity, often falling from 10 grammes per litre total acid to 6 grammes per litre total acid within a period of seven days, whereas in the cool regions of Coonawarra and in the Eden Valley-Springton areas, the grapes may take up to three weeks to drop from 9 grammes per litre to 7 grammes per litre. Understanding that the relationship of each soil type and the influence of temperature related to each district is essential if top quality wines are to be made and a great deal more research is needed in order to reliably be able to predict the outcome.

The high quality red and white table wines now being produced in the hot irrigation areas is an indication that winemakers in Australia are now learning to appreciate these problems of climate and soil in relation to harvest date. Added to this a greater understanding has been gained in controlling the temperature of fermentation of wine and the storage of wine and many modern wineries in the hot areas are now using refrigeration control during fermentation and using temperature control storage of finished wines, creating conditions for maturation of wine similar to, if not improving upon, maturation conditions in the cooler districts.

WINE OF NEW ZEALAND

Frank Thorpy is the author of **Wine in New Zealand,** *a handsome illustrated book which, up till now, is the definitive book on New Zealand wines. Born and educated in New Zealand he spent fourteen years of his adult life in Europe, has travelled extensively and has visited most of the world's vineyard areas from Chile to Mainland China. In a recent trip overseas he paid a second visit to the vineyards of Chile, Argentina and Brazil on which he has published several articles. His next project is* **Wine in the New Worlds,** *a book dealing with wines in all the countries of the southern hemisphere to which the true wine grape* **Vitis vinifera** *has been transported by man.*

A typical New Zealand winemaker with character and charm always ready to extend generous hospitality (Photo: Marti Friedlander).

24 History of Viticulture in New Zealand

Rev. Samuel Marsden

The honour of planting the first grapes in New Zealand has usually been attributed to Samuel Marsden, a dedicated Anglican missionary, chief Chaplain to the Government of New South Wales. Apart from his great influence as a missionary, he was one of the first to bring European methods of agriculture to New Zealand, and was responsible for introducing new varieties of vegetables, fruit trees, and animal stock as well as grape vines. It was, in part, due to his dispatches to the Church Missionary Society, that the British Government decided to assume sovereignty over the country.

Marsden did not reside for any length of time in New Zealand but made seven visits over a period from 1814 to 1837. He greatly admired the Maoris, whom he had met in Sydney and aboard various whalers and merchantmen. He obtained permission from his superiors, the Church Missionary Society in London, to establish a mission in New Zealand, and on his first voyage in 1814, left at Rangihoua in the Bay of Islands, Thomas Kendall and William Hall, the first missionaries ever to settle in the country.

Marsden took back with him sons of Maori chiefs to train in agriculture at his Parramatta, Sydney, headquarters. He was a practical farmer and wrote in 1818 to London, 'The chiefs' sons who are with me, visit our orchards and vineyards and are astonished to see the fruits and anxious to promote the cultivation of them in their own country.'

In a letter to the Secretary of the Church Missionary Society, dated 27th March, 1817 from Sydney, he wrote, 'We have engaged a very respectable young man, Charles Gordon, as superintendent of agriculture.' Gordon, together with William Carlisle, and six Maoris who had been engaged in agriculture at Parramatta for up to eighteen months, proceeded to the Bay of Islands in April, 1817. Later Marsden wrote, 'I have directed Mr Gordon to apply himself solely to agriculture...They have taken over with them fruit trees of various kinds. Settlers have already got peaches in perfection. I think vines would do well from the nature of the soil and climate. I shall, from time to time, send over different plants as they may be useful at some future day.'

Gordon spent almost three years in New Zealand engaged exclusively in agricultural work for the Mission. No mention of what he had planted is extant but in view of Marsden's letters concerning the possibilities of vine growing, there is little doubt that Gordon planted these among other fruits. Marsden, after his second voyage to New Zealand in 1819, was able to report that over forty varieties of farm and orchard produce had been introduced and all were flourishing. Gordon resigned in 1820 and returned to Sydney.

Marsden, on his second journey to New Zealand, decided to make a further settlement at Keri-Keri and on Saturday, 25 September, 1819 recorded in his Journal, 'We had a small spot of land cleared and broken up in which I planted about a hundred grape vines of different kinds brought from Port Jackson. New Zealand promises to be very favourable to the vine as far as I can judge at present of the nature of the soil and climate. Should the vine succeed, it will prove of vast importance in this part of the globe....'

On 12 October, 1819 he returned to Keri-Keri and in his Journal recorded, 'I was much gratified with the progress that had been made. A number of seeds had been sown in the garden which had been brought from England to Port Jackson and were up. The vines were many of them in leaf.'

No mention is made of his planting vines at the two earlier settlements, Rangihoua and Waitangi, but it is reasonable to assume that they had already been planted there by Gordon who had probably taken vines as well as other fruit trees with him to New Zealand in 1817.

Darwin in 1835, when on his journey round the world in H.M.S. *Beagle,* landed at Keri-Keri and noted that the grapes were flourishing at Waimate (north) a few miles inland, and were being tended by the Maoris attached to the Mission.

Soon grapes were growing in many parts of the north.

James Busby

The next man to bring grape cuttings to New Zealand was a man who had already made his mark on the Australian wine scene, James Busby. He was one of the fathers of Australian viticulture and had already planted a vineyard in the Hunter River Valley at 'Kirkton'. Busby did not remain to see the fruits of his labour, for in 1833 he left Australia to become the first Resident British Agent in New Zealand under the New South Wales Government.

Although Busby brought cuttings with him and planted a vineyard at the present site of Waitangi, he became more and more involved in land speculation and litigation arising out of it, with many petitions later on to the government of the day. The *Treaty of Waitangi* was the culmination of Busby's work (on Hobson's instructions, he drafted the actual treaty) and we hear little of his viticultural activities after that, except that in 1845 part of his vineyard was destroyed in the war against Hone Heke and mention is made of his wine being sold to Her Majesty's soldiers in 1846.

After twenty-seven years of agitation, in 1869 he was awarded £38,000 by the Colonial Government in compensation of his land claims. The following

Spraying copper sulphate in a Hawke's Bay vineyard (Photo: N.Z. National Publicity Studios).

Cook's modern winery and part of the newly planted vineyard near Te Kauwhata (Photo: Cook's N.Z. Wine Co.).

The complex electronic control panel at Cook's winery (Photo: Cook's N.Z. Wine Co.).

year he journeyed to England for medical advice, caught a chill and died outside London in 1871.

Busby's was perhaps not the first wine to be made in New Zealand, but it was the first New Zealand wine to be appraised by a Frenchman, Dumont D'Urville, the French Commander of the *Astrolabe,* who revisited the Bay of Islands in 1840. It was a most anxious and embarrassing time for the principal actors in the drama, apart from the most interested parties, the Maoris. Captain Hobson had been appointed the first Governor of New Zealand, supplanting Busby who was the British Resident under the New South Wales Government. France did not recognize Britain's claim to New Zealand and even at that time an expedition of French colonists was about to land at Akaroa. D'Urville wanted to meet Hobson but Hobson declined to see him, pleading illness, and D'Urville called on Busby. Busby was away and a Mr Flatt was in charge of the estate. D'Urville wrote, 'As I was going over Mr Busby's estate, I noticed a trellis on which several flourishing vines were growing. I asked Mr Flatt if the vines produced any grapes in this climate and contrary to what I had been told in Korora Reka [Russell] I heard to my surprise that there had already been attempts to make wine from New Zealand grapes. On reaching his house Mr Flatt offered me a glass of port, I refused it, but with great pleasure I was given a light white wine, very sparkling and delicious to taste which I enjoyed very much. Judging from this sample I have no doubt that vines will be grown extensively all over the sandy hills of these islands and very soon New Zealand wine may be exported to English possessions in India.'

Busby was not the first man to plant grapes in New Zealand as he was not the first man to plant grapes in Australia. His influence in both countries has been immense more so in Australia, where his foresight, his enthusiasm and his systematic approach to selection and planting helped lay a firm foundation for a flourishing industry.

French settlers

A few months after the time D'Urville was appraising his first New Zealand wine, his French compatriots were landing to form a settlement at Akaroa. Naturally, they brought vine cuttings with them. In 1842 Captain Smith, Surveyor-General to the New Zealand Company, said in a report to Colonel Wakefield, 'The French at once started to prepare their gardens and to grow grapes, some of them developing their branch of horticulture to a high degree of efficiency making excellent wine therefrom.'

But the French were bedevilled by lack of capital, misrepresentation by their sponsors, the Nanto-Bordelaise Company, and sheer bad luck, for they had been promised that their land would be under the French flag and Hobson had forestalled them.

Though the British interfered with them little and they were allowed to retain their French customs and even their flag, and indeed, Akaroa is a little corner of France today, they were disillusioned and most of them returned to France.

They made very satisfactory wine; travellers record 'a good red wine' and when Romeo Bragato visited Akaroa in 1895, he saw several vineyards. 'In the early days a French settlement was established here and those settlers sought to establish in their new home the industry in which some of them have doubtless been interested in the land of their birth. At this pioneer French settlement the wine industry prospered so long as those by whom it was started remained at the helm but immediately they began to die off, the vineyards became neglected and in consequence the vines died out. It would seem that the pioneer French settlers of Akaroa failed to communicate to their offspring even a small percentage of that enthusiasm over the cultivation of the vine which they were in such a large measure possessed of, or that it may be their descendants suspended work by reason of the vines becoming attacked with oidium [mildew] thus causing the disappearance of vineyards which had been to their forefathers as a bit of the fatherland.'

In 1838, two years before the landing of the French settlers at Akaroa, there arrived at Hokianga, the forerunner of a different wave of French immigrants who were destined to have a much more permanent influence on winemaking in New Zealand.

Bishop Pompallier of Lyons had been appointed the first Catholic Bishop of the South Pacific. After a journey of thirteen months in which he touched at Valparaiso (Chile already had a flourishing wine industry), Tahiti, the Wallis Islands and Sydney, he landed at Hokianga in January, 1838. Pompallier was an indefatigable organizer and soon vines brought from France, for both sacramental wine and the health of the fathers, were sprouting in many small mission outposts throughout the North Island.

There has been some doubt up till now as to whether the Bishop had brought vines with him, or whether he was first given some by his Protestant brethren at Keri-Keri or Russell, or obtained wild vines from the Maoris, particularly as the journey from France took over twelve months.

But in the course of correspondence with the present Bishop of Wallis Island, Monseigneur Michel Darmancier, the author has established that a vine was planted on Futuna Island (part of the Wallis Island group) by either Fr Peter Chanel or his companion Brother Marie Nizier, who were landed there in 1837 by Bishop Pompallier on his way to New Zealand. St Peter Chanel was to be martyred by the islanders shortly afterwards.

Monseigneur Darmancier writes that the vine, after one hundred and thirty years, is in good health but naturally enough does not produce fruit in that tropic climate.

The planting of this vine on Futuna proves that Bishop Pompallier had vines on board ship; whether they came from France, or were picked up in Valparaiso, is a matter of speculation. One can hardly imagine the Catholic missionaries leaving France without vines.

That some of the Marist vines did come from France is shown by the following extracts from reports in the archives of the Marist Fathers now in Rome.

Brother Elie-Regis wrote from Whangaroa to Father Colin at Lyons on the 7 May, 1842, 'We cultivate the vines, they do very well here, the first which we planted three years ago already commence to bear fruit.' Similarly, Father Petit-Jean in notes on the Mission of the Epiphany at Whangaroa and Maunganui, undated but, from other evidence, mid 1842, wrote: 'From next year we will have plants that will give us wine for Mass at Whangaroa, among the plants are some young ones and others two years old, in all, 2,500. It is a task which gives much hope to our dear Brother Elie-Regis.'

Conclusive proof that plants were sent from France is contained also in APM208 (Archives des Peres Maristes—Z208 Rome).

Father Forest, Bay of Islands, writing to Father Colin, Lyons, on 2 June, 1842 said, '...we hope that in two or three years they will give us wine. I thank the good sisters of Ste Foix (France) who procured them for me and the good gardener who gave them to us.'

The present Mission Vineyard at Greenmeadows in Hawkes Bay, which is the indirect result of Bishop Pompallier's efforts, has had its ups and downs.

In 1850 by the effort of the original missionaries, plus reinforcements from France, Catholicism had taken a firm hold.

Bishop Pompallier, who had the whole of the South Pacific as his parish, decided to divide New Zealand into two bishoprics, himself as a secular priest taking the north, whilst he appointed Bishop Viard S.M. to operate from Wellington with the Marist Missionaries.

The dividing line was roughly between New Plymouth and Napier and in that year, 1850, Father Lampila and Brothers Basil and Florentin set out from Wellington for the northern-most part of their diocese, Hawkes Bay. However, an ill wind took them off course and they landed at Gisborne in Poverty Bay.

Father Lampila had been there before when he had been stationed at Whakatane under Bishop Pompallier. He set about converting some of the Maoris he already knew, so they settled there and planted grape vines. Later on in the year, their superiors discovered the mistake and they were ordered to proceed to Hawkes Bay.

James Busby (1800-1871) who planted a vineyard at Waitangi in 1833 (Photo: Alexander Turnbull Library).

They replanted their vineyard at Pakowhai, eight miles south of Napier, early in 1851 and though they moved twice to different sites in the same district before settling at Greenmeadows, Mission Vineyards is today regarded as the oldest vineyard in New Zealand under the same management, i.e., The Society of Mary.

Meanwhile the planting of grapes spread rapidly through the North Island in the nineteenth century.

Joseph Soler

In 1890 before the Flax and Other Industries Committee of the House, Joseph Soler, a Spaniard of Wanganui, testified that he had been growing vines since 1865 in Wanganui and had been growing vines in Spain before that. He stated that he first went to Victoria and later to New Zealand and when he saw that the climate of New Zealand was more suitable for winemaking than Victoria he returned there, obtained suitable cuttings, planted them and in time made his first wine. He contended that New Zealand had the soil and the climate to make good wines; all the growers needed was government encouragement, not bonuses. He detailed the kinds of grapes he considered the best for wine-making—all European classical varieties.

Soler must have been a formidably strong-minded character for he stated that he kept his wines as long as eight years before he sold. 'I keep the wine to create the alcohol naturally.' He did not use sugar in his wines except for sparkling wines. Proof that his methods paid off was his outstanding collection of overseas awards in Australia and London.

Later his nephew, Anthony Vidal from Spain, joined him and, after his death, moved to Hawkes Bay where, until a few years ago, Vidal's was the largest vineyard in the area.

William Beetham

Also testifying before the Flax and Other Industries Committee in 1890 was William Beetham, a gentleman farmer, from near Masterton who had spent several years in France and had brought back, along with his French wife, the desire to grow his own vines. He must have had good advice for he brought the right grapes and soon was in business. His enthusiasm communicated itself to other landowners and very soon J. N. Williams, Hastings; Bernard Chambers, Te Mata; and Henry Tiffen of Greenmeadows Station were all planting grapes of the classical variety.

Cross examined by the Chairman, William Beetham stated he had been growing vines for seven years, i.e., from 1883 and the success that had attended his efforts had made him believe that over a large area of New Zealand the vine could be cultivated profitably and an excellent wine could be made. He thought that the wine to encourage in New Zealand was table wine, as the country did not have sufficient heat to produce the dessert wine of Spain and Portugal.

The value of the wine industry was that, if established in New Zealand, it would give value to land not adapted to grain growing or pasturage, in fact, to the poorer type of land, particularly the pumice lands. He recommended, as did Soler, the classical type of grapes as used in European winemaking.

A Mr Kingdom of Omata, Taranaki, wrote stating he was a producer of wines but found that the present restrictions prevented him from doing so with profit. He forwarded samples of his Taranaki vat which the Committee analysed, the results being as follows:
'Character: clear colour red, full bodied, pleasant flavoured and sweet. Contains 12.2 percent of alcohol by volume. No noxious matters present. An excellent colonial wine: would keep well if allowed to age.'

Many a present day winemaker would be happy to have such an accolade!

Romeo Bragato

The direct result of the Commission was the establishment of a Department of Agriculture and the indirect result was the request by the Premier, Richard Seddon, to the Premier of Victoria in 1894 for the loan of the services of Romeo Bragato, then viticultural adviser to the Victorian Government. He came with impressive qualifications having spent four years at Italy's famous school of viticulture at Conegliano, where he obtained a Diploma of Oenology.

Signor Bragato arrived at Bluff on 19 February, 1895 and was escorted by government officials from one end of the country to the other. His report, submitted to the Premier on 10 September of the same year, was expert, reasoned, and enthusiastic, and the advice given is as good today as it was then. Had it been followed New Zealand now would be producing table wines as good as the best produced in other countries of the southern hemisphere to which the true wine grape, *Vitis vinifera* had been transplanted from Europe. In his report he said: 'Fear may be felt in some quarters that, if the wine growing industry were established to a large extent in New Zealand, markets may not be found. Misgivings on this point are quickly dispelled. The wine consumption in the large centres of the world is enormous and the demand ever increasing. The climatic conditions of New Zealand not only favour the production but also the consumption of wine, hence the local market will increase with the output.... I firmly believe that growers will year by year find it vastly to their advantage to increase their area under vines.... In order that the industry be pursued after the most scientific methods, I would recommend the establishment of a technical college of viticulture presided over by a gentleman who is thoroughly educated in every feature of the industry and under the strict supervision of the Department of Agriculture. This college would serve as a medium of education to those deserving to embark on the vine growing and fruit industries, and to the rising generation of agriculturists in your colony.'

Bragato urged that associations be formed in the various districts; 'a competent body in each district would determine the most suitable varieties for planting, collect and spread local data and thus in great measure secure the industry against failure. Each district would subsequently gain notoriety for the wine produced as in the famous wine districts of the Continent.'

He had found phylloxera in the Auckland vineyards of Mr Bridgman and Mr Harding of Mt Eden Road, and strongly recommended an inspection of all vineyards. He also recommended the importation by the Department from Europe of cuttings of American resistant vines.

He said that few places in New Zealand were unsuitable for the cultivation of the vine, an observation since borne out by a procession of experts down to the present day, including André Simon.

At the end of his report he appended a short treatise detailing how the planting and subsequent work of a vineyard should be carried out.

'The first condition necessary to ensure good results in the cultivation of the vine is that the climate and the soil shall be·suitable for the perfect maturing of the fruit.

'There are very few plants to the successful growth of which the sun's rays are more necessary than the vine. Therefore, so far as the temperature and the brightness of the sun's rays are concerned, no fear need be entertained but that the greater part of New Zealand will adequately satisfy the demands of the vine. Given a suitable climate the vine displays no epicurean instincts as regards soil but has been found to luxuriate in all classes. It is essential, of course, that the soil should be well drained as cold, wet, and sour soils operate against the vine... . The land in your colony, if properly worked, should yield a very large quantity of grapes per acre from which wine of the finest quality both red and white and champagne could be produced....'

'The question which next presents itself is what are the varieties best adapted to your colony. It is of the first importance that the intending planter should obtain the particular varieties of vine which are most suitable to his land. I would strongly urge persons about to embark on the industry to adhere to two or three varieties and not more as a large number of varieties produce a different wine every year thus rendering it quite impossible for the grower to provide a wine of uniform quality and type, preventing reputations being made and good prices obtained...."

He then went on to detail what were in his opinion the most suitable varieties for this climate—all European classical varieties.

Signor Bragato returned to Australia, leaving behind him a farming population excited by the prospects of wealth from viticulture. But two pests, phylloxera and the oidium mildew, and a lack-lustre policy by the Department of Agriculture dampened the enthusiasm of most except the wealthy gentlemen farmers of Hawkes Bay, the missionaries, and a new breed of wine growers entering the field, the 'Austrians', as they were popularly known.

The 'Austrians'

These were men from Dalmatia on the Adriatic coast, now part of Yugoslavia. They were Austrian citizens as part of the Austro-Hungarian Empire but the Yugoslavs had little in common with their overlords, and those in a position to leave Dalmatia did so. They were hard workers. They needed to be,

for the only work they could get was digging for Kauri gum in Northland. By 1890 more than 500 of them were concentrated in the north and the reserves of gum were being quickly depleted.

Seventy-five percent of the 'Austrians' had been engaged in agriculture in Dalmatia and many of them, though not possessing specific skills as winemakers, had assisted in the cellars and vineyards.

The wines of Yugoslavia are becoming well known in England but the best of them, particularly the white, come from Slovenia. Ljutomer Riesling, Sylvaner, Traminer, etc., are all good clean wines with a perceptible bouquet and find ready acceptance in England at a price level below the Alsatian and Rhine wines to which they are akin.

Dalmatia makes sweet red and white wines which, though pleasant, are usually not exported. The best known is Dingac, a strong, dark, slightly sweet wine, and sampling it one gets a clue to the taste of our local Yugoslav winemakers.

With this tradition of viticulture behind them and having become painfully familiar with the heavy clay soils from which they had wrested an honest living, it was natural enough that the Dalmatians should turn to viticulture and fruit farming. Soon tiny patches of vines were dotted all over the north. The colony at Henderson grew larger as more and more Yugoslavs, including fresh immigrants, congregated near their largest market, Auckland.

Bragato returns

However, we are out-running our story and must return again to Bragato, the man who, in my opinion, stands in relation to New Zealand viticulture as Busby does to the Australian industry.

In 1901 there was another flicker of interest by the New Zealand Government in viticulture and they asked Bragato to come back and report on the phylloxera which by now was exacting a heavy toll in the vineyards of New Zealand, as it had done so earlier in the vineyards of Europe. He had already given New Zealand the answer in his report of 1895—root out the diseased vines and import and plant American resistant vines, root stock, grafted with European varieties.

This time he was offered a permanent position and assumed the newly created post of Viticulturist and Head of the Viticultural Division of the Department of Agriculture in 1902, styling himself 'Superintendent of Viticultural Stations, Viticulturist and Oenologist to the Government of New Zealand.' In spite of indifference from high up and criticism and sometimes overt obstruction from his colleagues in the other Divisions of the Department of Agriculture, he plunged into his work with gusto.

In 1898 the government had set aside a small area at Te Kauwhata as an experimental nursery and planted it with vines and fruit trees. The purpose was to show what could be done with that type of land. Te Kauwhata was never visualised as being the best spot to establish a Viticultural Research Station. However, the growing of grapes proved successful and a winery was erected and the fruit farm eventually discontinued.

Under Bragato's directive, Te Kauwhata became the centre for instruction in winemaking and viticulture; he also established the field day for growers which continues to this day. In 1908 a wine from Te Kauwhata was awarded a gold medal by the Franco-British Exhibition in London for a wine 'approaching the Bordeaux clarets in lightness and delicacy.' No New Zealand wine today, to my knowledge (with a single exception mentioned in Chapter 27) would win a prize under the same conditions.

Bragato imported disease-resistant stocks and in his handbook *Viticulture in New Zealand*, published in 1906 by the Department of Agriculture, showed growers how to graft the European classical varieties which predominated in the country at that time, on to the American root stocks. But many of the smaller growers, learning that the American varieties would produce greater quantities of albeit inferior wines, simply did not bother to graft.

In the same year that Bragato obtained his appointment, two important vineyards were established in the Henderson area.

Assid A. Corban

Assid Abraham Corban came to Auckland from Beirut in 1892. The family had been winemakers for many generations in the Lebanon and in 1902 Corban planted his first vineyard of four acres in the poor heavy clay of the gumfields. Today the flourishing vineyards extend over hundreds of acres and form one of the three most important wineries in New Zealand.

Stephen Yelas

In 1890 a Dalmatian, Stipan Jelich, landed to try his future in the gumfields. After some years up north, he and a partner purchased several acres in the Henderson area for gum digging. The partnership was dissolved and Stipan, who had now changed his name to Stephen Yelas, began market gardening. In 1902 he decided to make wine from the table grapes he used to send to market and from that humble beginning has spread the largest vineyard owned by New Zealanders of Dalmatian extraction, ably managed by his son, Moscow Yelas, and now named the Pleasant Valley Vineyards.

Hawkes Bay development

In Hawkes Bay, the vineyards mentioned earlier increased their production in 1896. The Marist Fathers bought part of the estate of Tiffen's

'Greenmeadows' property (but not the vineyards) and started their own vineyard. In 1897 Brother Steinmetz left the Order to plant his own five acres of grapes. In 1927 Tom McDonald, who worked for him, took over the vineyards and started McDonalds Wines. Today the property still produces some estate-bottled wines of high quality but it is now merged with McWilliam's Wines of which Tom McDonald is now a director and production manager.

Vine and Wine Instructor

In 1906 Bragato stated there were 550 acres under vines; in 1909 there were 668; by 1923 it had dwindled to 179 acres only.

By 1909 the first golden flush of winemaking was over. Apathy in high places and the rise of prohibition had proved too much for the nascent industry.

Bragato was disheartened. He complained of frustration and lack of co-operation, even though he tabled a cheerful confident report in the House in 1908. He resigned early in 1909 and left the country.

He was certainly unlamented by the hierarchy of the Department of Agriculture—the Annual Report tabled in the House the next year merely stated 'one of the changes of staff effected by last year's re-organisation was the retirement of Mr Bragato and the resumption of his duties by this Division (i.e. Horticultural Division).

'In November last Mr S. F. Anderson, a member of my staff was appointed Vine and Wine Instructor.' Thus the Viticulture Division which under Bragato achieved almost independent status was abolished and the Vine and Wine Instructor became a mere appendage under the Orchard, Apiaries and Horticulture Division.

The Prohibitionists

In 1908 the prohibitionists registered their first victory in wine districts when Masterton and Eden (part of which was the Henderson wine district) voted 'no licence'. As a direct result of this, Dick Scott, in *Winemakers of New Zealand*, notes that 7,000 pinot noir vines established at 'Taratua' vineyard near Masterton in 1897 were destroyed in 1909 and the land returned to other agricultural pursuits.

Twentieth Century developments

In 1912 the New Zealand Viticultural Association petitioned the government 'to save this fast decaying industry by initiating such legislation as will restore confidence among those who after long years of waiting have almost lost confidence in the justice of the government. Through harsh laws and withdrawal of government support and encouragement that had been promised, a great industry had been practically ruined.'

During the 1914-1918 War the industry languished. There was not the labour available, the prohibitionist element was strong and more dry districts were established, depriving the winegrowers of their outlets.

By 1923 the area under grapes was only 179 acres. Nevertheless, it gradually crept up to about 655 acres in 1938 of which, according to the Department of Agriculture Journal half were table grapes.

In 1932 there were one hundred licensed winemakers in New Zealand. The number had increased by sixty within the preceding six or seven years.

The advent of the Labour Government in 1935 proved to be of considerable benefit to growers.

In March, 1938 the government, at the request of the winemakers, increased protection of New Zealand wines by raising the duty on still wines imported from Australia and South Africa. This policy resulted in an increased sale of New Zealand wines by enabling New Zealand port and sherry to compete on a price basis with imported varieties.

The Import Control Regulations of 1938 limited imports of wine to fifty percent of what they had been previously.

But the greatest fillip of all to the winemakers was to be the outbreak of war in 1939. Overseas supplies were greatly reduced and the demand greatly increased by the advent of American servicemen who, like their New Zealand brothers overseas, demanded alcohol of any kind. The Henderson wine acreage and wine production increased by over 300 percent from 1940 to 1950. But more than 85 percent of vineyards were under five acres in extent. Such was the demand that many new smallholders entered the industry and grape vines not suitable for winemaking were planted.

The Royal Commission on Licensing 1946

By the end of the war, the lush artificial conditions had so affected some of the wine growers that, in evidence before the Royal Commission on Licensing in 1946, the Department of Agriculture stated that 'more than sixty percent of the wine made by the smaller winemakers is affected with bacterial disorders of one form or the other...' and that 'fifty percent of the product was poor and markedly inferior, that a considerable quantity of wine made in New Zealand would be classified as unfit for human consumption in other wine-producing countries and that this was due to the lack of knowledge on the part of winemakers.'

The report of the Commission stated that from the evidence before it there appeared to be no restrictions on the amount of sugar which could be used and the representatives of a large Australian winemaking company stated that the wine then being made in New Zealand was not really the produce of grapes but to a much larger extent of cane sugar, and that the product should be labelled 'Grape and Sugar Wine'. The reply of the Department of Agriculture was that the industry would come to an end as practically the whole demand in New Zealand was for a fortified sweet wine which, they maintained, could not be made commercially in New Zealand without the use of cane sugar.

It appeared, too, to the Commission that for the previous forty-five years, water, though forbidden under the Sale of Food and Drug Regulations, had been used to reduce acidity and also to allow fermentation despite the addition of so much sugar. It also appeared that for the previous forty years the fortifying spirit used in the making of port and sherry and other dessert wines had been made out of the spirit marc (or lees) and that further sugar had been added to the marc in order to enable the spirit to be produced.

Clearly, all was not well with the wine industry and the Commission in its report (Chapter 108, pages 346 & 347) courageously set out its conclusions and suggested remedies.

'The evidence concerning the wine industry shows that a large proportion of the wine made in New Zealand, perhaps half the quantity, is of poor quality, yet the evidence as to the reason and the lines of remedy are so conflicting that we strongly recommend a survey of the industry by an independent expert from a country where wine is made under climatic conditions somewhat similar to those of New Zealand. An expert from one of the Universities of the North-Eastern States of U.S.A. might be the most suitable. It is important that the expert should not only be competent but be independent of this country.

'The report should be factual and concern for example:

1. An assessment of the conditions of the soil and climate in the various districts.
2. A report on the kinds of grapes suitable for winemaking in the various districts.
3. What kinds of wines the various districts are suitable to produce.
4. The extent to which sugar must be used in the production of wine in these districts.
5. Whether if sugar to the required extent is used, the resultant product should be properly termed "grape wine".
6. What kind of wine could be produced in any district when the use of sugar was limited to the amount that would be approved in a winemaking country with climatic conditions similar to those in that district, and in what quantity could such wine be produced.

Stainless steel holding tanks each with a capacity of 25,000 gallons, Montana winery, Titirangi (Photo: Montana Wines Ltd).

7. Whether satisfactory light wines can be produced in any district and if so whether on a commercial basis.
8. Whether a changeover from the production of strong fortified wines to light wine is desirable and if so, what steps would be needed to effect the changeover during a period of time.'

This was the finest report produced on the wine industry since Bragato had electrified the farmers of New Zealand with his report presented to Richard Seddon in 1895.

But it was not to be implemented. The wine industry was but a minor part of the report and the main part dealing with breweries and hotels recommended that the control of the breweries in effect should pass to a State Corporation. The report was shelved by the government of the day with every evidence of haste.

Winesellers' licences

A Winemaking Industry Committee from the House of Representatives was appointed in 1957 and brought down a report which considerably assisted the wine growers—single bottles could be sold from the vineyard and wine growers were able to establish their own retail outlets by the creation of winesellers' licences. Nearly 300 of these are in existence today, providing a service to the public by the stocking of a wide range of New Zealand wines. Wine licences were given to restaurants and here again another ready outlet was created.

Growth of the wine industry

But the greatest benefit to the industry was to be further severe import restrictions and heavy excise duties on spirits which forced people to turn to New Zealand wines for their alcoholic sustenance. Large Australian companies such as Penfolds and Seppelts bought into existing New Zealand vineyards, bringing expertise and new techniques to the wine industry and Harveys of Bristol lent their name under licence to a sherry and now port, made by a leading Henderson winemaker.

The grape acreage increased from approximately 600 to 1,000 during the Second World War. By 1965 it was 1,252 acres, by 1970 3,628, and now 1972, following an unprecedented boom, reliable estimates put the acreage, not all bearing, around 4,500 from which more than 5,000,000 gallons of wine are being produced.

25 The grapes, climate and soil of New Zealand vineyards

For the making of good wines and particularly good table wines, most experts would agree on the following requirements—the skill of the winemaker, favourable soil, the right climate and quality grapes. How does New Zealand fare in these respects?

This matter has often been discussed with some of the world's leading experts who have visited our vineyard areas. All these experts agree that in parts (and it must be qualified, in parts) we have a suitable soil and climate. This can be tested scientifically but almost without exception they say we are not growing the right grapes in quantity to produce good table wine.

Grape Varieties

The Department of Agriculture conducts a grape survey every five years and the results of the last one conducted in 1970 were published in June, 1971. Naturally, the results are out of date as soon as they are published for the wine growing industry is not a static one and plantings are continuous. For instance, the 1970 Survey showed the total grape bearing area to be 3,628 acres; it is now thought to be over 4,500 acres though not all are bearing. Nevertheless, with some exceptions, the proportions and types of grapes planted would remain about the same today as in 1970.

The most extensively grown varieties in 1970 were as follows:

Variety	Acres	Variety	Acres
Palomino	582.5	Seibel 4643	79.9
Baco 22A	521.5	Pinot chardonnay	76.2
Riesling sylvaner	465.0	Gaillard girerd	67.0
Chasselas	309.4	Baco 2/11	48.5
Seibel 5455	266.2	Pinot noir	45.1
Albany Surprise	194.1	Pedro ximenez	44.1
Seibel 5437	158.1	Baco No. 1	35.9
Pinotage	154.3	Iona	32.0
Cabernet sauvignon	85.7	Niagara	22.6
Gamay gloriod	83.2	Seibel 5409	18.8

As a footnote the Department states that the proportion of *Vitis viniferas* grown (the classical European wine grape) has increased from 32 percent of the total area in 1965 to 57 percent in 1970. This has been hailed as a great achievement and a great improvement in the quality of the vineyards but on a closer examination of the figures one wonders whether it is so, particularly as the vineyards of New Zealand were originally 100 percent vinifera.

The grape varieties that produce the finest wines in other parts of the world are comparatively few. They are loosely known as European or classical varieties all derived from the type *Vitis vinifera*, while American hybrid grapes, which all experts agree produce wine not in the same category, are derived from *Vitis labrusca* or similar types.

For white wines the classical varieties are riesling, traminer, pinot gris, pinot blanc or chardonnay, tokay, semillon and sauvignon blanc. For red wines they are cabernet sauvignon, cabernet franc, pinot noir, pinot meunier, merlot, shiraz, malbec, and one or two others.

Some New Zealand winemakers say what does it matter whether or not we have the grapes that produce the good wines in other countries of the world, we are producing wines to suit our own New Zealand palate.

But there is a little more to it than that. It is a question of breed and style. Just as in improving our great racehorse strains, we import the finest bloodstock, so we must have better stock to make better wine. We do this in every other facet of our great agricultural and pastoral products which are justly world famous but first we had to import the right strains of animals and grasses, seeds, shrubs, etc., and the skill of our farmers and scientists aided by our favourable soil and climate did the rest.

Other countries recognize this. California uprooted a lot of its native stock in the last century and today the leading firms proudly advertise that they grow all the famous European varieties. Chile uprooted all its vines about 1851 and replanted with classical varieties, and now their wines have an international reputation. In Russia, in the Crimea, a reconstruction of the vineyards was made after the war and only European varieties planted. Both South Africa and Australia have planted large areas of these grapes in recent years. In fact, in nearly all countries where wine is made, growers are busy replanting with these varieties in soils and climates which vary considerably. Even in New Zealand, the acreage of these grapes is increasing—but all too slowly.

The sad thing is that originally we had the greater portion of our vineyards planted in these varieties. Early reports from government viticulturists all attest to the excellent quality of the wines made from these grapes and their suitability for New Zealand conditions.

Deterioration in grape quality

Romeo Bragato, in 1909, urged growers to produce wines for which the country was best suited—'pure, light, delicate wines of the claret or hock type'. As mentioned earlier, a red wine made at Waeranga (now Te Kauwhata) from cabernet sauvignon grapes, won a gold medal at the Franco-British Exhibition in London in 1908.

Refrigerated pressurized tanks at Montana winery, Titirangi (Photo: Montana Wines Ltd).

What caused the deterioration in the quality of the grapes planted? The main reasons seem to be:
(a) The detection of the disease phylloxera and the need to replace the existing vines with disease-resistant American hybrid rootstock, on which were to be grafted cuttings of the classical grapes.
(b) The discovery that prolific American hybrid table grapes could be used to make a rough red wine.
(c) More importantly, the American hybrid grapes would resist fungoid diseases and give a *greater yield* than classical varieties, particularly in the very damp conditions of the north.
(d) The constant threat of prohibition hanging over the winemakers' heads forcing them to grow dual-purpose grapes—suited for table or a coarse red wine which they found, when fortified, was readily saleable. There was no incentive to produce better wines.
(e) Apathy covering the wine industry in high government circles, and also in the higher echelons of the Department of Agriculture, which were pre-occupied in improving the quality of our great agricultural and pastoral products. In spite of the efforts of some devoted government viticulturists, others took the line of least resistance and gave the growers what they demanded—grape varieties which would produce in quantity in unsuitable soil and in damp conditions.
(f) Later difficulties in procuring cuttings of the right varieties, due to strict quarantine regulations; however, these difficulties were not insuperable.

The original plantings in New Zealand were of the classical varieties. As late as 1914 in the Department of Agriculture *Bulletin*, mention is made that in three of the principal vineyards in Hawkes Bay, Chambers Te Mata (now T.M.V.), Mission Vineyards and Steinmetz (later Tom McDonald's forerunner of McWilliams), the grapes mainly consisted of cabernet sauvignon, shiraz, pinot meunier, riesling and verdelho.

The first three government viticulturists in New Zealand, Romeo Bragato 1902 to 1909, S. F. Anderson 1909 to 1920, Charles Woodfin 1920 to 1940, all attest to the excellent qualities of the classical grapes grown in New Zealand. In 1902 Bragato, inter alia, said, 'cabernet sauvignon preserves in this country many of the qualities that make it so valuable in France—among these qualities are bouquet and fine delicate flavour.'

Anderson, who had visited Australia, said in his 'Outdoor Culture of the Grapevine in New Zealand'— *Journal of Agriculture* 20 February, 1917, that both cabernet sauvignon and pinot meunier bore heavier crops here than in Australia. He wrote further— 'The vines grown for winemaking are known as *Vitis vinifera*. The specific name vinifera means "wine bearing" and comprises most of the kinds grown in Europe and other places for wine purposes. The varieties are very numerous. Some of the American varieties are also used in winemaking. These are very distinct from the vinifera class and *inferior* for winemaking owing to a peculiar black currant or, as it is generally termed "foxy" flavour that pervades the whole family....

'The American class of vine is moreover *deficient* in the natural saccharine for winemaking. Owing, however, to their hardiness in resisting fungoid diseases, they are grown very largely in the north of New Zealand. They can also be used with some advantage in blending with sweet wines....

'In New Zealand the grape vine will flourish and ripen its fruit from the North Cape to Hawkes Bay and in a few favoured spots as far south as Canterbury, the chief condition required being freedom from frosts at the time of flowering and setting of the fruits, and a dry autumn. The selection of the district should depend largely on the rainfall for the months of January, February, March and April but as a rule vines that do not fully ripen their fruit by the end of March should be rejected....'

Charles (J. C.) Woodfin was to be the unwitting cause of the further deterioration in the plantings of the New Zealand vineyards. That he was enthusiastic about our grape vines is evidenced in his article in the *Journal of Agriculture* in 1930: 'not only are many varieties of vines suitable to our climatic conditions but they come to perfection on our various soils. As a matter of fact, vines are not exacting as regards soil and they produce heavy crops on our poorest lands—gumlands—light volcanic and on almost pure sand.

'What struck me most about the vineyards on my arrival in this country after twenty-five years residence in the vine growing regions of Europe, was the flourishing conditions of the vines and the remarkedly heavy crops they are carrying in comparison with the same varieties in Europe.'

However, growers demanded other varieties and in response to their pleas he imported many hybrid vines regarded as more suited to the damp conditions of Northland (North Auckland). In the *Journal of Agriculture,* 20 February, 1928, he reports: 'Grape Vines for New Zealand conditions...' 'that with a view to extending experiments in suitable grape vines a number of European varieties of vines from France had been imported. These vines had been selected with a view for qualities best suited to New Zealand conditions, particularly from the point of view of early ripening, which is essential to their adaptation for the climatic condition in the cooler parts of the Dominion. Besides some of the best varieties of pure European vines, the collection included a number of American x European hybrids known as direct producers....

'The object of the hybrids is to produce fruit having the finer qualities of the European vines on vines having the disease resistant qualities of the American varieties. Many thousands of the hybrids had been produced in France over the past forty years but *few* had given satisfaction. The quality of the fruit and the wine which had been made from it was the subject of much discussion in the European viticultural world. Taking a mean course through the conflicting opinions expressed, the best of the direct producers are heavy producers of good fruit and wine without attaining to the aristocrats of ampelography, the leaders of which, the Cabernets, the Pinots and the Rieslings, are now *well established* in New Zealand. The direct producers should prove valuable for cultivation in the districts where humid climatic conditions are favourable to the development of fungus diseases and where the cost of spraying is a considerable item in growing the finer varieties.'

Again on 21 October, 1929, Woodfin speaks of continuing the experiment by importing further varieties. The baco 22A and all the seibel varieties that figure prominently in the 1970 Grape Survey list were imported, though a cautionary note was added, 'In view of the conflicting opinion published in Europe on the habits and qualities of direct producers, it is deemed advisable to reserve a more complete description of the above until they have been tried out locally.'

Unfortunately, in spite of the above warning to await results of local experiments, growers, particularly in the north, seized the opportunity of procuring vines which were marketable as table grapes as well as capable of turning out a rough and ready wine which though 'foxy' to the taste was acceptable to many palates. Additional attractions were that these hybrids would bear prolifically, were more resistant to diseases, were able to stand a damp climate and required less attention and work.

Over the past few years, pressure from the public looking for better quality wines plus the success won in competitions by wines made from grapes such as cabernet sauvignon, pinot chardonnay, etc., have induced growers to search for better quality vines to grow. But the problem is not a straightforward one. Tests by the D.S.I.R. Plant Diseases Division and the

Department of Agriculture have shown that many of our vines, both European and American hybrids, are infected with virus diseases, particularly leaf roll and fan leaf. These diseases were not positively identified till 1959 but much research since then indicates that the main effects of these diseases are (a) to decrease yield—it would appear from overseas evidence and local trials that if free of virus the yield of many European varieties could be doubled and in some cases trebled; (b) to decrease sugar content of grapes—the higher sugar content of grapes from virus free vines would not only reduce production costs but would improve quality; (c) to lighten the colour of wine made from dark coloured grapes—New Zealand red wines tend to lack full colour and experiments indicate that virus free vines would double the depth of colour, thus preventing the use of other agents.

The department is aware of the problem and is importing virus free vines mainly from California and also producing heat treated varieties at the Plant Diseases Division. By regulations, all grape vines introduced from other countries must be grown under quarantine and screened for the presence of diseases and pests before they can be released. But facilities are limited and it is really up to the growers to exert more pressure on the government to extend the facilities so as to speed up the production of virus free vines. There is little evidence of that pressure and the obvious satisfaction over the results of the last grape survey does not indicate a great deal of anxiety by the growers in general as to the quality of our vines. As mentioned earlier, a critical examination of that survey would show that all is not as well on the vinifera front as would seem.

Varieties grown

The number one grape in acreage is palomino, a vinifera variety grown mostly in 'hot weather' countries such as Spain and used there for making sherry. New Zealand has not the climate (as will be seen later) to produce fortified wines naturally. Palomino will not mature here with a proper sugar content as the Department of Agriculture admits. When not used for making sherry, it produces a thin acid white wine which requires added cane sugar to make it palatable. Thus the most commonly planted grape is not suited to our climate and will not produce good wine without some 'amelioration'.

Baco 22A, an American-Franco hybrid, noah x folle blanche, is the second most commonly planted grape. Unfortunately, it is late ripening which is a disadvantage in our climate and the dry white wine made from it tends to be excessively acid unless it is blended with a table grape variety such as chasselas or, again, sugar. Growers are hoping that when brandy making commences commercially their stocks of this grape can be utilized. A better brandy would be made by planting the classical variety, the half parent folle blanche, which is one of the main French brandy grapes.

Most growers are basing their hopes on producing a good table white wine on the third grape, riesling sylvaner, which has had a meteoric rise, about 400 acres having been planted between 1965 and 1970, and substantial plantings have been made since. This grape which is known in Europe as the muller thurgau, is a cross between the noble riesling and the more common variety, sylvaner. The resultant hybrid grape produces more grapes per acre than does either of its parents but the product is undistinguished. It is not grown in any of the classic great wine areas of Germany though grown extensively in lesser areas, and in Alsace where it was introduced when under German occupation, it is not now allowed to be given an appelation controlé. A better cross is the scheurebe which bears more fruit and ripens earlier than the riesling and has a greater volume of bouquet. But the riesling sylvaner (the muller thurgau version) has become a 'fashionable' grape producing an acceptable white wine sometimes sold under the name 'Riesling' and undoubtedly the most popular white wine available on the market in New Zealand.

The fourth commonly produced grape is chasselas which is really a table grape but because of its sweetness is greatly prized by winemakers here to blend in with more acid white wine. Several winemakers are now producing a 'Chasselas' wine which is common in Switzerland and Alsace-Lorraine where it is classed as a *vin ordinaire.*

The next five varieties, all red, in order of acreage are: seibel 5,455, Albany surprise, seibel 5,437, pinotage and lastly cabernet sauvignon, and this illustrates for the knowledgeable wine lover why it is so difficult to get a good red wine in New Zealand. The first three are hybrids or American native grapes with no pretensions to quality and the resulting wine does not lose its 'foxy' character. The fourth, pinotage, purports to be a cross between pinot and hermitage from South Africa and, according to André Simon and many others, inherits the virtues of neither. It is grown commercially only in South Africa and New Zealand, an experimental plot on the Rhine having failed completely. Its great asset to the grower in New Zealand is that it is prolific and stands humid conditions and it has become like the riesling sylvaner, aided by some propaganda from the Department of Agriculture, a 'fashionable' grape. It is puzzling that this grape which thrives only in South Africa should have been introduced into New Zealand when good red wines had already been made from shiraz, pinot noir, pinot meunier; grapes which have been tested over the centuries and in different soils and climates in many parts of the world. However, some winemakers are now producing acceptable quaffing wine from this grape.

Cabernet sauvignon, the grape that produces the great wines of Bordeaux, also the premium wines of countries as diverse as Chile, South Africa, California and Australia, ranks only ninth in our list of grapes and increased by only fifty acres between 1965 and 1970, the same amount as the American labrusca, Albany surprise. Under the right conditions and when free from virus, cabernet will produce four to six tons to the acre, a greater tonnage than that produced in most other countries. The wet conditions of the 1972 vintage have proved to some growers that it will stand more rain without splitting than many of the hybrid varieties. In fact, Mel Fry, the progressive winemaker at Montana, says that generally it was the hybrid grapes that were affected most by the rains that fell heavily on all vineyard areas of New Zealand in March, 1972.

It is significant that in California, cabernet sauvignon grapes sell at more than six times the price of the lesser varieties per ton. Cabernet sauvignon, blended perhaps with some other varieties, will in time produce New Zealand's greatest red wines.

Pinot noir, of which there were only forty-five acres planted in 1970 and ranked fifteenth on the list of varieties, is another grape that has done well in New Zealand in the past. It develops its qualities to the full only in temperate zones. New Zealand is the southern hemisphere's farthest south good red wine district and viticulturists from Bragato onwards have attested how well the pinot noir does here. Yet the acreage planted is insignificant.

Climate

The vine is a plant hardy and more adaptable than most, and by its very adaptability has diversified into many thousands of varieties over its long life. Yet there are climatic limits to its successful cultivation.

Temperature

Because it will not stand tropic heat the vine will not flourish and bear reasonable fruit nearer the equator at sea level than, say, 30 degrees. Similarly, it has been found that it is unwise to attempt to grow vines nearer to the polar regions than 51 degrees. So in general grapes can be grown for winemaking anywhere between 30 degrees and 51 degrees. Mainland New Zealand lies between 34 degrees North and 47 degrees South.

In Europe the cultivation of wine grapes extends from Germany to North Africa. The Bordeaux district, the home of the most famous French clarets, lies approximately in the same latitude as Timaru.

It is on the very borders of the northern limits of grape growing that the greatest vineyards are to be found—Bordeaux, Champagne, Burgundy, Alsace, Rheingau, Moselle, Tokay. In these places, subject to frosts and extreme cold at times, the wine presents its greatest delicacy and the greatest range of its charms. As one goes further south to Italy, Spain, Portugal, Greece, the Languedoc in France, the wine becomes heavier, more alcoholic, more commonplace.

So it seems a temperate climate is that which suits the vine best and New Zealand in general is the temperate zone personified. All manner of agricultural experts have testified to this and all manner of men interested in viticulture such as Marsden, Busby, D'Urville, Darwin, Suttor, Bragato, Woodfin, and André Simon have affirmed that the New Zealand climate is exceptionally suitable.

If you were to superimpose New Zealand on a map of Europe you would find that 47 degrees, the approximate latitude of Bluff, is practically the same as Dijon in Burgundy, that Auckland is the same latitude as Gibraltar, that Northland extends into North Africa and that the greater part of New Zealand lies in the same latitudes as most of Spain and/or Italy.

No part of mainland New Zealand extends as far into the cold regions as the main quality wine growing districts of Germany, the Rhine and the Moselle which lie about 50 degrees latitude, the same as our Auckland Islands on the way to the Antarctic. Some experts believe that New Zealand winegrowing areas have a cool climate similar to Germany and Switzerland but climatological figures do not suggest that this is correct.

New Zealand, being an island set in a vast ocean, does not necessarily have the same climate as similar latitudes situated in a continental land mass and our mean summer temperatures can be as much as ten degrees lower than, say, similar latitudes in Italy. There is much more rain here but also much more sunshine than might be expected in a moist oceanic climate.

The very able oenologists at the University of California who have contributed so much original research to viticulture believe that the setting and ripening periods of the vine are predominant factors to take into consideration when selecting suitable places to site a vineyard. Accordingly, they have established a norm called a heat summation factor to compare different regions. The heat summation figure is the sum of the mean daily temperature above 50°F (10°C) for the period concerned (from October to April in the southern hemisphere and April to October in the northern). In effect, it is the total amount of solar heat recorded during the growing period of seven months. Grape vines make practically no growth below 50°F (10°C) but in the spring as soon as the average daily temperature reaches round this figure, the dormant vine begins to grow and put out the shoots which will bear this year's crop.

Professor Winkler, who for forty years has researched and taught in the Department of Viticulture at the University of California, in his book, *General Viticulture,* gives figures for various areas in California and abroad:

	Degree—days above 50 degrees (10°C) during the growing period
Trier, Germany (Moselle area)	1730
Geisenheim, Germany (Rhine area)	1709
Chalons-Sur-Marne, France (Champagne)	2060
Beaune, France (Burgundy)	2400
Bordeaux, France (Claret)	2519
Sonoma, California (fine wine area)	2360
Davis, California (natural sweet wines & dessert wines, white & red)	3970

Mr Frank Berrysmith, the New Zealand Government Viticulture Officer, very ably discusses the whole question in a most interesting article in the July 1968 issue of the *Journal of Agriculture.*

Here are some figures for vineyard areas in New Zealand:

	Degree—days above 50 degrees (10°C) during the growing period
Henderson	2659
Auckland	2797
Thames	2876
Te Kauwhata	2594
Gisborne	2454
Napier	2510
Hastings	2412
Nelson	1722
Blenheim	2040
Christchurch	1740
Alexandra	1615

Thus, comparing Professor Winkler's figures for overseas vineyards and Frank Berrysmith's for New Zealand, it will be seen that this country is well within the climatic range generally considered suitable for growing quality vines, and making quality wines, in other parts of the world.

Incidentally, one of the winemakers in the Coonawarra district where, according to some experts, some of Australia's finest red table wines are being produced, advertises his heat summation figure as 2175.

That we have the sunshine and the temperature as compared with selected fine wine growing areas in France and Germany is shown below.

These figures show that climatologically Napier (the Hawkes Bay area) is very similar to the Bordeaux and Burgundy areas though there is quite a difference in latitude—the land mass of Europe being an important factor in retaining heat in latitudes closer to the North Pole than winegrowing areas here are to the South Pole.

Henderson (Auckland), Te Kauwhata and Gisborne have higher temperatures and more sunshine hours than have the three European areas but unfortunately have much more rainfall.

Rainfall

Grape vines like well drained soil and can stand drought better than most other fruits. They dislike a cold waterlogged soil and if rains occur during the ripening period or just before harvesting, the time the water takes to drain away and for dry conditions to return are critical. Rains during the blooming period can cause poor berries, resulting in a light crop. Rains can delay ripening and produce low quality or losses by splitting the berries causing bunch rot and mildew.

Ideally the grapes need a dry period before harvesting and therefore the less rain that falls during the months of January, February, March, the better the wine.

A run through of the *Tables of Temperature and Precipitation for the World,* published by the Meteorological Office of the British Air Ministry, indicates that no well-known vineyard area of the world has a rainfall as high as Oratia-Henderson 62.1 inches and only one area, Caxias do Sul in Brazil, has a rainfall as high as Whenuapai, 53.8 inches.

Apart from Conegliano in Northern Italy, which Bragato states, has an annual rainfall of 50 inches (which I have been unable to verify), no well-known vineyard area in the world has an annual rainfall in excess of 38 inches, in fact, the majority have a rainfall of around 30 inches or less.

Latitude		Yearly total duration sunshine	Yearly average of temperature (°F)	Yearly rainfall in inches
36°	Henderson (Oratia)	2061 hrs (Whenuapai nearest station)	57.4	62.1
37°	Te Kauwhata	2040 hrs	57.9	46.3
38°	Gisborne	2212 hrs	57.1	39.8
39°	Napier	2281 hrs	57.0	31.2
41°	Blenheim	2433 hrs	54.8	25.8
45°	Alexandra	2081 hrs	50.8	13.2
50°	Geisenheim* (Rheingau)	1643 hrs	48.95	20.85
44°	Bordeaux*	2008 hrs	54.00	35.1
47°	Dijon* (Burgundy)	2044 hrs	50.89	28.82

*(World Meteorological Organisation, Geneva—No. 177.TP52.) (New Zealand figures—Climatological Observations to 1960.)

Vineyards at Havelock North—in the foreground part of Vidals, and in the background T.M.V. Vineyards (Photo: National Publicity Studios, Wellington).

Thus it would seem that to produce fine table wines, growers should concentrate on the proven Hawkes Bay area and look at the so far untried area of Blenheim as well as some other favoured 'micro-climates' in the South Island which, generally speaking, has much less rainfall than the North.

Established areas such as Henderson, Te Kauwhata and Gisborne will always be important wine-wise—there is too much money tied up in vineyards and wineries—but if experience in other countries is a guide, these areas will concentrate on the popular *vin ordinaire* type largely made from hybrid grapes. The better table wines of which New Zealand is capable must come from areas with less rainfall at vintage time.

Gisborne's annual rainfall of nearly forty inches is not as high as the other two districts but unfortunately, it has 154 days in the year when rain occurs. This certainly promotes lush growth but makes more difficult, though not impossible, the production of really fine wines.

Soil

Soils used for growing vines in the many parts of the world range from gravelly sands to heavy clays, from shallow to very deep, and from low to high fertility. Grape vines are adaptable to most types of soil but they particularly like well-drained soils even if relatively infertile. They have very extensive root systems and will dig deep in order to tap the water-table.

In an article in the *Journal of Agriculture* (July 1968) Frank Berrysmith says, 'Viticulture can be successful on a wide range of soil types. Least suitable are heavy clays, shallow soils and poorly drained soils. Good drainage is most essential in regions of heavy rainfall, and rather deep soils to hold moisture are necessary in areas of low rainfall. Soils of moderate fertility which promote medium growth and cropping usually produce higher quality grapes than are produced on deep fertile soils which support large vines with heavy crops.'

The soils of particular vineyard areas will be discussed when the actual vineyards are being visited.

The 'micro-climate'

Both soil and climate influence the success of grape growing and the quality of wine in a given area. Not only the climate of an area is important but also the 'micro-climate' of each vineyard. By establishing vineyards on gentle slopes with maximum exposure to the sun, or in valleys protected from the wind, the grower can help to offset possible climatic problems.

By centuries of observation of success and failure in the older viticultural countries, and more recently by scientific studies in some of the newer countries, the successful vineyard and grapevine complex is developed.

The varieties of grape which should be grown, the types of wine produced, the proper management of vineyards and wineries, is the characteristic of all the famous vineyard areas of the world.

Undoubtedly, here in New Zealand, not sufficient attention has been paid to establishing vineyards in the best 'micro-climate' areas or on gentle slopes. Rather the tendency has been to use flat land that produces grapes in profusion without regard to quality.

Proof of this is evident in the figures which show we produce more tons of grapes and also more gallons of wine per acre than practically any other country in the world. In the Gisborne area ten to fifteen tons per acre of grapes such as baco 22A and palomino have been common.

Auckland: the Henderson and Kumeu areas

Detailed statistics of the vineyard areas are only published at five year intervals by the Department of Agriculture and therefore are out of date almost immediately.

The last survey conducted in 1970 and published in June 1971, shows that at that time there were 39 acres planted in vines in Northland (Whaipopo to Kaiwaka), 1,626 in Auckland (Warkworth to Pukekohe), 461 in Waikato (Thames to Huntly), 686 in Gisborne (Ormond to Manutuke), 807 in Hawkes Bay (Eskdale to Havelock North). There were two acres in Wellington/Manawatu, six acres in Nelson/Blenheim and one acre in Oamaru, with experimental plots in the Central Otago area.

The acreages have increased dramatically since the 1970 survey, as mentioned earlier, the total not all bearing, is thought to be more than 4,500 acres from which over 5,000,000 gallons of wine are being made.

There were at least 320 growers, many of whom sell their grapes under contract to the larger wineries.

In the early days Northland was the main centre. By the end of the century Hawkes Bay, because of the missionaries, and the large farmers, became the most important centre. Much later the Auckland area came into its own and now Gisborne and Waikato, principally due to the activities of large Henderson winemakers, have become prominent wine growing areas.

Close to Auckland city lies the largest wine district —Henderson/Kumeu. The grape survey shows that there are 149 growers in the area. Of the seventy-five or more winemakers, nearly ninety percent are of Yugoslav extraction. However, the largest and the most important vineyards are owned by growers other than of Yugoslav descent.

Though grapes had been grown and wine made since 1902, it was not until the end of World War II that the winemaking industry was firmly established and the district assumed its present character. The main body of predominantly Yugoslav settlers arrived from 1925 onwards.

It was the increased market created by American troops, who demanded alcohol of any kind, that led many of the smallholders, farming mostly fruit and vegetables, to turn what at best had been a sideline or hobby, into a commercial proposition. The vine acreage and wine production at Henderson increased by three hundred percent from 1940 to 1950.

And later as New Zealanders became more sophisticated, so the demand for wines increased—the forti-

fied wines, helped by the high excise duty levied on spirits. Thus Henderson/Kumeu, with New Zealand's largest market, Auckland, on its doorstep, though climatically not the best area for growing grapes on account of the high rainfall, became the largest wine area, now estimated to be around 1,750 acres.

With so many in the area, it seems invidious to name only a few, but among the largest and most important are:

Corbans, Montana, Penfolds, Pleasant Valley, Western Vineyards, Mazurans, Babich's, Gilbey Nobilo, San Marino, Delegat's, Golden Sunset, Lincoln, Panorama, Selak's, Collards, Spence's, Eastern Vineyards and Villa-Maria (Mangere).

Corban Wines Limited

At the end of Lincoln Road on the outskirts of Henderson town, are some of the vineyards and the impressive sprawling winery of Mt Lebanon belonging to Corban Wines Limited, the largest in Henderson and one of the two oldest vineyards in the area, having been established in 1902. The founder Assid Abraham Corban, came from the Lebanon in 1892. In time he established himself in a small shop in Queen Street, near the present Town Hall and then sent for his family. He prospered but living above the shop did not suit the health of his wife and family, so in 1902 he purchased four acres of heavy clay at Henderson covered with natural bush and manuka scrub. Here he grew vegetables and fruit and table grapes for the Auckland market.

The Corbans had a long tradition of viticulture, Assid's father having worked as an inspector of vineyards and a part-time instructor in the Lebanon. So winemaking commenced. Within fifteen years the original four acres had expanded to fifteen, by 1938 forty-five acres were under vines.

In 1940 various properties two miles from the original Mt Lebanon vineyard were purchased and have led to the eighty acres now known as Corbans Valley Road Vineyards.

This large planting, together with the original block of forty-four acres, firmly established Corbans as the largest producers in the Northland area and gave recognition to Henderson as a major grape growing centre.

In 1941 Assid Corban died but vineyard development was vigorously carried on by his sons N. A. Corban, K. A. Corban, A. A. Corban and W. A. Corban, presided over by a remarkable matriarch, Mrs Najibie Corban, wife of the founder, who died in 1958.

In 1959 an area of 44 acres was purchased eight miles from Henderson on the upper reaches of the

Auckland Harbour and called 'Riverlea'. This vineyard produces Riverlea Riesling, a popular white wine made from the riesling sylvaner grape.

Other blocks have been purchased in the Kumeu area.

Recently, Corbans have established a winery at Gisborne.

Today the vineyards are largely planted in riesling sylvaner, malbec, golden queen, black hamburgh, albany surprise, various seibels, palomino, cinsaut, gamay teinteurier, niagra, baco 22A, golden chasselas, cabernet sauvignon, pinotage, muscat, gaillard, baco 9 & 11, pinot meunier and pinot chardonnay. Large areas of riesling sylvaner, cabernet sauvignon and palomino have been planted in the recently acquired areas.

Corbans with their Gisborne holdings and contract growers now control 950 acres of vines—a far cry from the original four acres in 1902.

The sons of Assid are now enjoying the fruits of their hard labour over the years which has resulted in the thriving business of today. Though some wine and spirit merchant shareholders and a large merchandising organisation have been invited into the business, it is still largely owned by the family.

David Corban is Chairman of the holding company, Alex Corban is winery and production manager, Joe Corban is vineyards manager and Assid Corban is Secretary to the Company. Many other members of the numerous Corban families are employed.

The soil of the original vineyard was heavy clay but in pushing out their frontiers, the company have encountered soils ranging from deep peat of low fertility to gumlands, to firm yellow clays underlying a shallow topsoil. Remedial measures, including large scale draining, have been pursued on a basis of trial and error to see which type of vines would suit which soil and location.

'Riverlea' soils, though firm and heavy, are particularly fertile, ranging from warm loam over yellow clay to heavier river silts. Kumeu land consists predominantly of peat and silt deposits with areas of alluvial loam on yellow clays as well as subsoils of white pipe clays.

In the original area round the winery, there have been three or four replantings over the years to ascertain the right varieties, yet vines planted over fifty years ago are still producing a reasonable crop.

Plantings have been made of American and French hybrids but these were balanced by substantial plantings of grafted vinifera types.

As did most of the early winemakers, Corbans concentrated at first on sherry and port and over the years have won a reputation as producers of consistently high quality ports, sherries and muscats. They have won many prizes both locally and overseas and Corban's Cellarman Port is well known throughout New Zealand.

On their sixtieth anniversary in 1962 they introduced the first sparkling wine to be made in commercial quantities. The wine is made in huge steel pressurised tanks under the Charmat process.

Corbans have concluded an agreement with Harvey's of Bristol who now distribute two styles of sherries under the Harvey label made by Corbans. Recently a Harvey's Port has been added to the range.

Two of the white table wines made by Corbans have excited interest overseas, the Riverlea Riesling and the Pinot Chardonnay. But supplies as yet are limited. Spurred on by this success, Alex Corban is contemplating making Traminer and other classical varieties of white wine for which the area is most suited. This year he has put on the market a white wine made from chasselas.

Alex Corban, B.Sc. and a graduate of oenology from Roseworthy College in Australia, is one of the most experienced and capable of the younger vignerons and Corban's future looks assured as the firm increases both its production and its share of the market.

It was a bottle of 1955 Cabernet made by Alex Corban, along with a bottle of Tom McDonald's 1949 Cabernet, that André Simon took with him when he left New Zealand, 'to show my Australian friends what New Zealand can do'.

Western Vineyards

After leaving the hospitable Corbans Winery one turns right under the railway bridge at Valley Road which winds and twists four miles up into the northeastern slopes of the foot-hills of the Waitakere Ranges. At the end of appropriately named Vineyard Road, in its own special 'micro-climate', lies the well-favoured vineyard of Western Vineyards.

'I have never seen a more picturesque vineyard anywhere but in Tuscany where they have been making wines for some 3,000 years. The vineyards of New Zealand are only just beginning—they are the hope of generations to come.' So wrote André Simon in Western Vineyards' visitors book.

Dudley Russell, the proprietor, certainly has an eye for nature and the nine hundred acres of the present holding, of which forty acres are in vines, are well landscaped in trees and rich meadowland which has been painfully wrested from the scrub country of the Waitakere Ranges.

In 1932, when he was nineteen years old, Dudley Russell bought twenty-four acres. From this beginning has spread the most beautifully landscaped vineyard in New Zealand and the largest holding still in the hands of the original owner.

On the present nine hundred acres, 450 steers are fattened annually—Dudley freely admits all this farming has stemmed from the well tended vineyards, which he does not propose to enlarge. No outside capital is employed.

The vineyard is planted with cabernet sauvignon, palomino, riesling sylvaner, gamay gloriod, tintara, baco 22A, baco I, muscadine and albany surprise.

A McWilliam's vineyard—Hawkes Bay. Rows planted wide apart to allow for mechanical cultivation (Photo: McWilliam's Wines (N.Z.) Ltd).

Fifty percent of the wines produced are table wines, anticipating future trends, though already the demand exceeds the supply and a praiseworthy endeavour is being made to name the table wines after the predominant grape—Cabernet Sauvignon, Pinot Chardonnay, Gamay de Beaujolais, Riesling Sylvaner, Palomino, Muscat, etc.

Other wines made, beside the table wines mentioned above, follow the familiar pattern of sherries, ports, sparkling, etc.

Western Vineyards has always been particularly strong on sherries and a Private Bin sherry made from palomino grapes with a natural Flor character, is undoubtedly one of the best dry sherries made in New Zealand. It is fortified with a pure grape spirit.

Dudley has had many attractive offers for his well-favoured vineyard, the fruit of his life's labours, but he will not sell and says his ambition is to make better and better table wines.

Apart from the vineyards and the cattle paddocks, the home area is beautifully set out in flower gardens, swimming pool and Japanese gardens, which form an ideal setting for the many barbecues held there by the Auckland Wine & Food Society, the Chamber of Commerce and other organisations, through the generosity of the proprietor.

Pleasant Valley Wines Limited

Retracing one's steps and a mile further down the road towards Henderson one comes to the very pleasant, well tended Pleasant Valley Wines Limited, the oldest Yugoslav vineyard in Henderson, started in 1902 by the father of the present owner, Moscow Yelas.

Today, Moscow and his family have 115 acres of rolling land, mostly clay, well drained and with its own 'micro-climate' facing north and ideally situated for grapes. The rows of vines run north and south.

On the property is a vine of pinot meunier first planted by Stefan Yelas in 1902. Black hamburghs still survive from that early date but it is interesting to note that the father was advised to plant pinot meunier, when he first turned to making wine, after he had wrested all the Kauri gum from that heavy soil. He had bought the land in 1895.

Sixty-eight acres are planted in vines though all are not bearing at the moment and the vineyard is the third largest in the Auckland neighbourhood, ranking after Corbans and Penfolds.

Twenty-five varieties of grapes are planted in this old vineyard but the greater plantings, approximately five acres each, are of baco 22A, baco No. 1, palomino, riesling sylvaner, pinotage, niagara and seibels 5409. Recently riesling, pinot noir and pinot chardonnay have been planted and varietal wines from the grapes will be made.

Wines made include the usual sherries and ports, vermouths and a Dry Red made from baco No. 1, and a Dry White.

One feature of Pleasant Valley is that all their premium wines bear, on a very well designed label, the inscription 'Chateau Yelas'. The wines have won many Gold Medals at various wine competitions.

The grounds are well landscaped and the house and the winery in first class order showing the pride of the proprietor and the amount of work he has put into his property.

The present owner has extended the area of vines from seven to sixty-eight acres, all without outside capital, and he says he has by no means finished yet—a great tribute to his energy and his foresight.

G. & F. Mazuran

The doyen of the Yugoslav viticulturists, and the man who has done more than anyone else to further their interests, is George Mazuran, proprietor with his wife of G. & F. Mazuran, a holding of twenty-one acres in Lincoln Road, of which part is in orchards, an established tradition among the Dalmatian wine growers.

George Mazuran has been president of the Viticultural Association for more than twenty years and as such has been a vigorous protagonist and lobbyist for the mainly Yugoslav interests he represents. He was recently awarded the O.B.E. for his services to the wine industry.

As the Deputy Leader of the Labour Party, Mr Hugh Watt, M.P., once said at a gathering of the Association, 'There are not eighty members of parliament but really eighty-one. The extra one who comes down to sit in the House does not catch the Speaker's eye but he has almost as much influence as a Member. I refer to the man who conducts public relations of such a high order for you.'

Proof of the success of Mr Mazuran's public relations work is the attendance of many Members of Parliament and Cabinet Ministers at the Annual Field Day of the Association, which features a barbecue and a conducted tour of some of the vineyards—it is always a happy occasion with plenty of generous Yugoslav hospitality.

The Mazurans purchased their holding in 1938 and on the site was an Albany surprise vine which George says was thirty years old when he bought it and is now well over sixty years old and still bearing fruit.

The Mazurans make a Dry Red wine and a Pinot Chardonnay white, but they specialize in medium and sweet sherries and ports for which they have won many Gold Medals.

They were the pioneers in sending wine to be judged at the Ljubljana Fair in Yugoslavia and won their first gold medal there in 1960 for a medium sweet sherry.

The total storage of wines in oak casks at McWilliam's is the largest in New Zealand (Photo: McWilliam's Wines (N.Z.) Ltd).

Penfolds Wines N.Z. Limited

Lincoln Road, where the Mazuran vineyard is situated is dotted with many small vineyards on either side of the road that leads to Henderson township. One of the most important of the larger vineyards in this road is Penfolds, which bought the existing Averill Brothers' vineyard first established in 1922.

Penfolds Wines N.Z. Limited, is a subsidiary company of the well-known Australian Penfolds Wines Pty Ltd, and has a minority shareholding of local wine and spirit merchants.

Under the capable management of Bob Knappstein, a graduate of Roseworthy College, and a member of an Australian family long connected with viticulture, Penfolds have extended the original block to forty acres and have purchased 265 acres of which 230 acres are planted at Waimaukau further north and towards the west coast.

The land of the original block is like most Henderson land after it has been worked for many years—sandy clay loams. The soil in the new block is sandy loam, free draining and has less rainfall than the Henderson block.

The Henderson block is planted with palomino, cinsaut, black and white muscat, various seibels and bacos.

The new block is planted in palomino, pinot chardonnay, riesling sylvaner, cabernet sauvignon, pinotage, various seibels and bacos, and now traminer for which the parent company is famous in Australia.

Penfolds, as one would expect, are turning out very acceptable sherries, particularly an Amontillado sherry, ports, clarets, moselle, rosé, a Barbecue Burgundy and now a bulk fermentation sparkling wine under the name Medallion. They are also experimenting with brandy and with their Australian experience as a guide should turn out a good one in time.

If instead of leaving the northern motorway at Lincoln Road one continues to the end and follows the road to Kumeu, it will be found that many Henderson vignerons have pushed out this way in order to increase their acreage. Corbans and Penfolds both have vineyards in this area but firmly established here are the wineries and vineyards of Gilbey Nobilo Limited, San Marino Vineyards and Mate Selak's.

Gilbey Nobilo Limited

Gilbeys, the well-known English firm, who distribute a New Zealand made gin under their label, as well as importing many other spirits and wines, entered the New Zealand wine scene by joining partnership with Nick Nobilo. The new company under the name of Gilbey Nobilo Limited, has already planted 150 acres in vines. These include riesling sylvaner, pinot chardonnay, traminer and some pinot gris,

along with the usual bacos and palomino. In the reds, cabernet sauvignon, pinotage, pinot noir and some seibels.

At present they market the usual dry whites and dry reds, etc., but these are being phased out as production of the classic grapes increase. They intend to market under a 'Nobilo Private Bin' label estate bottled wines of superior quality. At present they have maturing 1970 Cabernet Sauvignon and 1970 Pinotage. Through Gilbeys' contacts overseas, the firm sent the winemaker, Nick Nobilo junior, on a trip through European vineyards. He returned fully convinced that the future of the company lay in turning out good quality table wines made from varietal grapes and that tendency is already evident.

San Marino Wines Limited

Near the township of Kumeu is the eighteen acre holding of which fifteen acres are in vines, of San Marino Wines Limited, owned by cheerful extrovert, Mate Brakjovich.

Mate bought the vineyard in 1944 and today has probably the only house and small winery which has been architecturally conceived as a whole to form a pleasing entity.

The model winery has been scientifically designed to cater for the needs of a small vineyard and is made of redwood in the same architectural style as the house where lives Mate, his wife and their three children. The grounds of the house and winery have been landscaped by a professional landscape artist.

Mate tends a sixty years old albany surprise vine but has planted pinot chardonnay, pinotage, palomino, baco, riesling sylvaner and now has a further five acres in cabernet sauvignon. He has a further eighty-five acres of vines under contract.

His Kumeu Dry Red made from baco No. 1 has a high reputation—he is also making a Kumeu Pinotage and Pinot Chardonnay as well as sherries and a sparkling wine and now a Riesling Sylvaner. He is convinced of the need to turn out better quality wines, and in time San Marino should be one of the best of the small individually owned wineries in the country.

Babich's Wines Limited

Leaving San Marino vineyards, retracing your path along the Southern Motorway, turning off again at Lincoln Road and following Ranui Road, you come to Babich Road.

Babich's Wines Limited was established first by Joe Babich near Kaitaia in 1916 but moved to the present site in 1919. The fifty acres, of which forty-two are planted, with a further eight acres planned for this year, consist of gently rolling land lying to the sun and well protected from the wind.

Maori pickers at work (Photo: Marti Friedlander).

The main variety planted is palomino plus various seibels, baco 22A, baco No. 1, gaillard, albany surprise, pinotage, cabernet sauvignon and muscat. Six acres of riesling sylvaner and two of the red variety pinotage are being planted.

Wines made at present include Dry White, Dry Red (claret and burgundy types), Moselle, Sauternes, Palomino dry sherry, medium and golden sherry, port and a Vintara Red which is a cross between a table wine and port and has many enthusiastic followers.

Joe is one of the sterling characters of the industry and was a great friend of Government Viticulturist Charles Woodfin who often stayed overnight at the winery. His dry red and dry white have always had a wide popularity. Peter, the elder son, has travelled through European and Californian vineyards and is a dedicated and professional winemaker. His latest effort is a blend of cabernet sauvignon and pinotage which shows every sign, when fully matured, of being in the forefront of Henderson red wines.

Montana Wines Limited

In Titirangi on the Scenic Drive, on a ridge of the Waitakere Ranges lies Montana Winery, the most dynamic and fastest expanding wine business in New Zealand, and owned by Montana Wines Limited.

In 1944 after ten years in New Zealand, Dalmatian born Ivan Yukich started selling wine from a half acre of grapes. Gradually the area of vines increased until today there are fifty acres of vines off the Scenic Drive.

The father is now dead but the two sons, Frank and Mate, enlisting the support of some wealthy and powerful investors, have embarked on the greatest crash expansion scheme ever undertaken in the wine industry in New Zealand.

Already a spectacular winery of pleasing architectural design and with the garden now being landscaped, has been completed on the Scenic Drive.

Up to fifty huge stainless steel tanks of 25,000 gallon capacity are being installed outside to mature dessert wines. These wines need to 'weather' for a period of four years and stainless steel enables the operation to be conducted outside without the expense of having a roof. Total storage is 2¼ million gallons and the winery extends over five acres.

A fully automated bottling and corking machine is now installed and Montana has, perhaps, the most modern and sophisticated plant in Australia and New Zealand and is already a great tourist attraction.

With substantial capital from both private and various Government Development Fund Projects, a $2½ million expansion programme is being developed in stages and the company is now associated with a big brewery complex which ensures outlets for the large quantity of wine it is making.

To support this large modern winery, vineyards have been developed in other areas. Large areas of vines have been planted in the Gisborne and Mangatangi areas and these are discussed in the Chapter on Hawkes Bay, Gisborne and Waikato areas.

Altogether Montana Wines now has 1,500 acres under its control of which 500 are owned by the company. In 1972 1,300,000 gallons of wine were made.

The directors of this progressive company have been quick to realize the potential of classic European grapes and though like all other winemakers they have to make wine from what grapes they have at present, the new planting programme consists of pinot noir, traminer, shiraz (red hermitage), pinot chardonnay, cabernet sauvignon, pinot gris, pinot meunier and gamay beaujolais.

The company has recently bought out the family holdings in Waihirere Wines Limited, the oldest vineyard in Gisborne, and because of its association with the large brewery complex that already held two-thirds of the shares, it had fallen heir to the 100 acre Ormond Block planted some years ago on classical European varieties.

Wines now being merchandised follow the familiar pattern though the company claims to be making a higher percentage of table wines than does any other firm.

Capitalizing on modern trends, it was the first company to produce sparkling Cold Duck which has been enormously popular. It produces a Pearl wine from golden chasselas grapes. In the white, Riesling, (riesling sylvaner), White Hermitage, Gamay Blanc and Lexia are being produced as well as a White Hock and Sauternes. In the reds a Pinotage and a Dry Red. Various sparkling wines are being made. Soon the company hopes to market a Cabernet Sauvignon, Pinot Meunier, Pinot Noir and Hermitage.

The company has always maintained that it will in time develop an export market and at the time of writing, a significant tie-up with a very large overseas wine and spirit organization with world wide ramifications is being negotiated.

Other growers

Unfortunately, space prevents mentioning any more individual winegrowers as there are more than seventy-five winemakers in the area. All are hospitable and, thanks to the tradition of selling wines from the cellar, all welcome the casual visitor. There is no more pleasant way of spending a Saturday afternoon than going from cellar to cellar, sipping the various products and choosing a favourite.

Future development

The acquisition of vineyards and the building of wineries in Gisborne and Te Kauwhata, the pushing out by some large winemakers to Kumeu, Riverhead and Waimuku where the rainfall is lower, have caused many vignerons to wonder what is the future of Henderson as a wine area. Certainly it is a rosy one for the sprawling city of Auckland is encroaching on the area and land values, both housing and commercial, have risen appreciably. Such is the return per acre from wine that urban values have not reached this figure. When it does, one can only envisage more of the smaller winegrowers selling out and retiring.

But large scale capital developments in the wineries by Penfolds, Corbans and Montana and others, indicate that the area will always be important winewise. And it is hard to imagine men like Moscow Yelas, Joe Babich and Dudley Russell who have created particularly well favoured sites by their own efforts, ever wanting to sell. These sites, perhaps the most pleasing in the area, fortunately for wine lovers are not the best sites for either housing or commercial development.

When one considers the annual rainfall of around 60 inches, the Henderson winemaker has done well. There will always be a market for soundly constructed *vin ordinaire* made from hybrid grapes and some of the winemakers have proved that, in spite of the climate, they can make very drinkable wine from the European grapes. For Auckland wine lovers there always will be a Henderson wine area of character, charm and generous hospitality.

Hawkes Bay-Gisborne-Waikato areas
Hawkes Bay

To the east of the main mountain axis of the North Island lies the province of Hawkes Bay. The western part is hilly country which is some of New Zealand's best sheep country. On the coastal plains, taking in Napier from the sea to Hastings and Havelock North, some of New Zealand's best fruit and vegetables are grown and there some of its best wines are made.

The first vineyard in the area was planted by French priests and brothers in 1851. From this small beginning was to stem Mission Vineyards. The actual vineyard was shifted three times before it was finally established at Greenmeadows on the eastern slopes of the hills which form the western flank of the Heretaunga plains, about five miles to the south-west of Napier. It is not the oldest existing vineyard in New Zealand. That honour belongs to Te Mata Wines Limited at Havelock North near Hastings on land that was once part of Bernard Chamber's estate where vines have been cultivated continuously since 1892.

Hawkes Bay owes its prominence as a winemaking centre to a fortunate set of circumstances. One was the decision of Bishop Pompallier to divide New

Zealand into two bishoprics with himself, a secular priest, retaining the north whilst south of a line stretching from Hawkes Bay to New Plymouth, was to be administered by Bishop Viard of the Society of Mary, whose priests had first planted vines in Northland, and being French, quickly realized the climatological advantages of Hawkes Bay for wine-making.

The other main factor was the emergence from about 1870 onwards of a class of wealthy gentlemen farmers who not only had educated tastes but also the leisure and the money with which to indulge those tastes—many of them planted classical grapes and thus the pattern of Hawkes Bay winemaking was formed.

Unlike Henderson, there are comparatively few wineries in Hawkes Bay, the principal ones being McWilliam's (with which is amalgamated McDonald's), Glenvale, Vidals', Mission, Te Mata Wines, McLeods, Brookfields and Lombardi. The total area in vines is thought to be around 1,250 acres.

McWilliam's Wines (NZ) Limited

The most influential firm in Hawkes Bay, and certainly one of the most important in New Zealand both from a quantity and quality point of view, is McWilliam's Industries Limited which controls both McWilliam's Wines (NZ) Limited and McDonald's Wines Limited, owning approximately 600 acres of vines with a further 300 acres under contract growing. Soon the estimated yearly production will be 1,000,000 gallons. Still a private company, it is two-thirds owned by New Zealand shareholders, mostly brewery and wine and spirit interests, and one-third by the parent company in Australia, McWilliam's, which extends technical advice where needed.

This large company stems from a vineyard of 5¼ acres established in 1897 at Taradale on land bought from Tiffens Greenmeadows Estate by a Luxembourg national, B. Steinmetz—a Marist Brother who decided to return to civilian life. In 1927 a young fellow named Tom McDonald, who worked in the vineyard, bought him out. That vineyard has now expanded to 48 acres and today Tom McDonald is Production Director for McWilliam's, which company merged with the wine and spirit interests that Tom McDonald sold out to in 1944.

McWilliam's have two large wineries: one at Greenmeadows (the original McDonald's now much enlarged), the other in Napier itself. Much modern machinery and equipment has been installed and today the capital invested would be around $5,000,000. A third winery is being established.

Wines processed by McWilliam's include most varieties of sweet and dry sherries, port and muscatel, wine liqueurs and cocktails and one of the best sparkling wines made under the bulk fermentation process, Marque Vue.

The commercial table wines, Cresta Doré in the white and Bokano in the red, are almost household words throughout New Zealand. But the wines which are exciting interest among wine lovers are the private bin Cabernet Sauvignon in the red which consistently wins Gold Medals, and the Pinot Chardonnay and Traminer in the white, and now a Riesling Sylvaner (made from the scheurebe grape) which undoubtedly has more bouquet and is more luscious than any other so called riesling produced in New Zealand.

Semillon and pinot noir vines also have recently been planted.

Tom McDonald is one of the outstanding figures in the industry. He learned his winemaking the practical way and now, having successfully built up a large business based on quantity production, is turning his attention and undoubted skill to producing some of the finest private bin wines ever made in New Zealand.

He envisages a gradual increase in the quantity of the wines made from the above varieties and sees a great future for New Zealand wines when, as he says, more of the winemakers decide to concentrate on quality rather than on quantity.

He gave André Simon and myself (in 1964) a 1949 McDonald Cabernet Sauvignon from his own vineyard which he served masked with a Chateau Margaux 1949—'a rare and convincing proof that New Zealand can bring forth table wines of a very high standard of quality' André wrote later in the London *Wine & Food Journal*, No. 124. 'The Margaux had a sweeter finish and a more welcoming bouquet, greater breed but it did not shame its New Zealand cousin of the same vintage; it happened to be on the terrace above, but the terrace below was surely part of the same hill by no means 20,000 miles apart, barely 20 yards apart.'

The total storage of wines in oak casks would certainly be the largest in New Zealand and one of the largest in Australia and New Zealand and Tom McDonald is still buying new oak to mature his yearly vintages of Cabernet Sauvignon.

Mission Vineyards

Next door to McDonald's Winery at Greenmeadows on six hundred acres bought from Tiffens in 1897 (but no part of the vineyard was included) is the Marist Fathers Seminary and in the sheltered sun soaked valley lying gently on the slopes of the Taradale hill is the Mission Vineyards. The oldest established winery in New Zealand though it has shifted—once from Gisborne, then to Pakowhai in 1851, then to Meeanee in 1858 and finally to Green-meadows.

The cellars are the nearest approach we have in New Zealand to authentic European cellars and are full of character and charm. Gleaming brass and ancient oak casks, together with Mission hospitality, make any visit a memorable one.

The wines are made with care and dedication and the winery and vineyards are in charge of two enthusiastic young Marist Brothers—John and Joseph, who have had the benefit of a year's viticultural study in France and have come back imbued with the desire to proceed, as Chile has done, along the lines of French winemaking. Brother Sylvester, who for many years was the cellarmaster and was well known among the wine fraternity in New Zealand, died in 1971.

At present twenty acres are in production comprising cabernet sauvignon, pinot noir, pinot meunier, pinot gris, la folle blanche, pedro ximenez and palomino—all vinifera varieties. A further eight acres, mostly in chasselas, is to be planted by 1973.

Mission Vineyards is the only winery in New Zealand to mature all its table wines for three years before releasing them for sale and they enjoy the honour of producing the lowest gallonage of wine per acre of vines (600 gallons) which is in line with the production of many vineyards in Europe but far below the New Zealand average.

Wines produced include sherry, port, sauternes, hock, a light dry red called Pinot after the grape, and a Cabernet Sauvignon claret.

A sparkling wine called Fontanella is made and it is the only sparkling wine made in New Zealand by the real champagne method, that is, the second fermentation takes place in the bottle. Brother John would be the first to admit that the wine is not as good as real French Champagne but it is certainly the best sparkling wine made in New Zealand. Its condition is clear and brilliant and one can get the whiff of the grape in the aroma. As it is made by hand it is high in price and the quantity is limited. Its appeal has improved considerably since real corks have been used instead of the plastic ones common to the sparkling wine trade in this country.

Some eight miles north from Napier one comes to the Esk river and along its valley both McWilliam's and Glenvale Wines Limited have planted blocks of grapes in sandy silt on river loam.

Glenvale winery

On the coast at Bay View is one of the most picturesquely situated and the most go-ahead winery in Hawkes Bay—'Glenvale'.

Still privately owned and controlled by Robert Bird, it was started by his father in 1933. The original twelve acres have now blossomed into at least 200 acres spread over seven different vineyards and further plantings up to 100 acres are contemplated. The vineyards are planted mostly in various seibels, baco 22A, riesling sylvaner, chasselas, gamay gloriod and eight to ten acres of pinot meunier in flourishing condition. Alas, the juice pressed from these magnificent grapes is mixed with lesser breeds

The wines at Mission Vineyards are made with care and dedication by the Marist Brothers. Brother Sylvester, cellarmaster for many years and well-known among the wine fraternity for his vast knowledge and his jovial attitude, died in 1971 (Photo: Marti Friedlander).

to cope with the high level of demand for Glenvale wines. Wines produced follow the familiar pattern of most New Zealand winemakers—sweet and dry sherry, red wine made from seibel grapes, white wine of various kinds, sparkling wines, red and white, and rosé in some cases named after the grape, i.e., Sparkling Seibel or Sparkling Chasselas. 'Glenvale' is renowned for its special strength sweet sherry (39 degree proof) which was originally produced during the war when spirits were short and now has a devoted following throughout New Zealand.

Robert Bird, who spent a year at Massey University and Te Kauwhata Viticultural Research Station, is a man of great vigour and energy and under his direction the vineyard is possibly the largest in the country in the hands of a private family—the son and daughter of the founder. There is a staff of fifty employed and Glenvale wines are sold through trade outlets in both islands.

Te Mata Wines Limited

Leaving the valley of the Esk and Greenmeadows, through the town of Taradale, passing Hastings, centre of the great fruit and vegetable cannery industries, one comes to Havelock North and the district of Te Mata. Here on the sunny slopes of the Havelock Hills are situated 'Te Mata' Vineyards and part of Vidals' Limited and also Lombardi Wines Limited, all on the original estate of Bernard Chambers who first planted his vineyard in 1892.

Te Mata Wines Limited, which recently changed hands and is now under the direction of Bill Smale, is the oldest vineyard and cellars still situated in the same place in New Zealand. The winery and vineyards have changed hands many times. The original vines need replacing and this is being done by the new owner.

At present 39 acres are planted with cabernet sauvignon, hermitage, pinot meunier, pinot gris, tokay, chasselas both golden and royal. Another 26 acres have been bought at Haumoana and these are gradually being planted with riesling sylvaner, cabernet sauvignon and malbec. Approximately 25 acres of the original 39 acres are now in vines under five years old.

The vineyard has one of the choicest positions in Hawkes Bay and with this background of classical varieties the company intends to increase its range of premium table wines. At present they are marketing a pinot dry white, claret, rosé and sauternes with a hock and a burgundy to come, all under the label of T.M.V. wines. The company also markets the usual dry and sweet sherries, ports, madeira, frontignac, liqueurs, etc. The present specialities are 1954 Port, Amontillado Sherry and Pinot Red.

The ivy clad winery and the cellars of T.M.V. as it is usually called, have the charm of the old wine cellars of France and recently an old stone coach-house, built nearly 100 years ago, has been resurrected

and turned into a tasting room. It was here in 1964 that André Simon tasted a claret born on the premises in 1912. It was the last of a rare vintage and André's verdict was eagerly awaited, 'Remarkable, quite remarkable. One wouldn't have thought it would have kept that long. This is really quite good, there is not the slightest trace of acidity or vinegar. No sign of decay at all. A very mellow wine.'

Warren Toogood, the then owner, told the assembled guests that the vineyard had been producing fine wines for nearly seventy years. The bottle was an old style handblown one and he thought the good condition of the wine was due to the hot wax seal that had been placed over the cork.

Vidals' Wines Limited

Over the road stretches fifty acres belonging to Vidals' Wines Limited. Originally seven acres of the Bernard Chambers' vineyard was purchased and this has been extended to the present fifty acres on light but extremely fertile soil with adequate sunshine and some of the warmest temperatures in New Zealand.

The winery is situated in Hastings and nearer the coast is situated another vineyard at Te Awanga, located on shallow loam on iron farm country making a total of around 100 acres together with 25 acres under contract growing.

The Vidals have had a long and respected history in New Zealand viticulture. They are descendants of Joseph Soler, the Spaniard, who first established a vineyard in Wanganui in 1865, and who later in 1888 was joined by his nephew from Spain, Anthony Vidal. In 1905 Anthony established a vineyard on an acre and a quarter in Hastings growing mostly table grapes. With the help of his three sons of whom two are still active in the business, Leslie and Frank, land was gradually bought at Te Awanga and Havelock North, part of Bernard Chambers' vineyard.

Grape varieties are cabernet sauvignon, merlot, baco Nos. 1 and 22, golden chasselas, palomino and various seibels. Wines made are the usual dry and sweet sherries, ports, madeira, liqueurs, etc., also chablis and sauternes. Vidals' have established a good reputation for their burgundy and claret which contain a certain amount of cabernet sauvignon, are usually consistent from year to year and figure prominently on many hotel lists.

The brothers are well known in the district and respected for their winemaking, which was the oldest continuous family winemaking tradition in New Zealand. In July, 1972 the vineyard was taken over by the Australian firm of Seppelts. Seppelts intend to preserve the family tradition and are, of course, well known and respected in the wine world. It may well be that their expertise and Vidals' well favoured vineyards may produce in time standard blends equally as good as the Moyston Claret and Chalambar Burgundy produced by the same firm in Australia.

The new firm will be known as Seppelt Vidal Ltd.

Hawkes Bay, although not the largest wine district in New Zealand, is certainly the most important in the production of fine wine and this is proved by the number of Gold Medals and Awards winemakers of the district consistently win. It was not the first area to be planted in vines—that honour belongs to Northland but from about the year 1880 it became the most important. Because the vineyards were founded by gentlemen farmers and missionaries who were perhaps not so concerned with an immediate short term gain as were their more struggling colleagues in the North, it got off to a much better start. It maintained the quality of the original plantings of classical varieties much better than any other area—for instance, albany surprise did not find a place in any vineyard in Hawkes Bay until quite recently. It is the only established vineyard area in New Zealand that has a rainfall that can be compared to the well-known vineyard areas in other parts of the world, i.e., under 38 inches in the year; Napier has an annual rainfall (31.2 ins.) less than Bordeaux (35.1 ins.) and a higher average annual temperature and more hours of sunshine. Like Bordeaux, Napier is subject in some years to heavy rainfall at vintage time and also frosts in the setting season can be a danger. Climate-wise, Hawkes Bay is very similar to both Bordeaux and Burgundy, generally agreed to be the two finest red wine areas in the world.

There may be better 'micro climates' in New Zealand—Blenheim could well be one—but until they are tested and proved there can be little doubt that the best red table wines will come from this area which is equally suited for the production of dry white table wines of the Burgundy type.

Gisborne

One hundred and thirty-eight miles further north from Napier lies Gisborne, cut off from the rest of New Zealand by the Raukomona Range and one of the most prolific fruit and vegetable growing areas in New Zealand.

Until a few years ago there was only one wine-maker. Waihirere Wines Limited, founded by a German, Frederick Wohnsiedler from Wurttemberg. At the time of his death in 1956 he had a well established vineyard of ten acres selling mostly ports, madeira, and sherry. At a later date fresh capital was injected from wine and spirit merchants and a 100 acre block planted in cabernet sauvignon, hermitage, pinotage, riesling sylvaner, pinot chardonnay, semillon, pinot meunier, chasselas, etc.

Through various mergers, common to the wine scene in both New Zealand and Australia, two-thirds of the company has been taken over by a large brewery and wine and spirit complex and recently the one-third holding still owned by the descendants of the Wohnsiedler family has been acquired by Montana Wines, who are themselves part of the same complex which already had the major share.

The high yield from the rich alluvial flats averaging ten to fifteen tons per acre from some types of grapes has attracted the attention of two large Auckland growers, Corbans and Montana, and there has been a meteoric rise in the acreage planted, mostly by contract growers. Ten years ago there were 65 acres in grapes, today over 1,000 acres, making Gisborne an important wine centre. Over seventy contract growers are now supplying these companies.

To process these grapes both Corbans and Montana have built modern stainless steel wineries. Both are situated in the downtown industrial area far removed from any vineyard. Corbans was estimated to cost in the vicinity of $750,000 and has a capacity of 600,000 gallons to hold the wine from Corbans' 350 acres which will go to the Henderson winery for final processing and bottling. Corbans have planted six types of vines, riesling sylvaner, chasselas, palomino, baco 22A and two red wine varieties and the hope is expressed in Gisborne quarters that the wine will eventually be bottled there.

Montana, which already had the majority of contract growers under its control, has recently been augmented by the 100 acre Ormond block and the growers contracted formerly to Waihirere Wines. Following a reorganisation it has been decided to close down the Waihirere Winery and all grapes will now be crushed in the Montana Winery at Gisborne, the wine fully processed and transported by tankers to the Auckland Winery for bottling. Montana is estimated to have over a 1,000,000 gallons of storage tanks, more than the entire wine output of New Zealand only a few short years ago.

Waikato

According to the Grape Survey of the Department of Agriculture, this area takes in all vineyards from Thames to Huntly.

The most important vineyards in the region are Totara Vineyards (S.Y.C. Ltd) 12 acres at Thames, Montana Vineyards at Mangatangi (300 acres), Cooks Vineyards at Te Kauwhata (150 acres), the Te Kauwhata Viticultural Research Station (40 to 50 acres of experimental vines) and numerous small vineyards of which the most important is Aspen Ridge (about 10 acres) at Te Kauwhata owned by Alister McKissock, a graduate of the famous wine school at Davis University, California.

Totara vineyards

'Totara' vineyards is probably the only vineyard owned by a citizen of Chinese birth in either New Zealand or Australia. Cheerful, smiling Stanley Chan,

Some of the thirty ports entered at the annual judging competition held by the Department of Industries and Commerce (Photo: Spur Magazine).

a former greengrocer who bought a market garden of 12 acres containing some table grape vines in 1925 and soon started winemaking. The vineyard is particularly noted for its sauternes. Totara Gold Sauternes has won many prizes—other wines made include a riesling sylvaner, the usual sherries and ports and a fruity muscat. Stanley has four sons, three of whom help him in the vineyard, the fourth he sent to Roseworthy College for a course in oenology. He did so well he is now in a responsible position with Lindeman's and is lost to New Zealand winemaking.

Montana Wines

Forty-five miles south from Auckland, just off the Pokeno-Thames highway at Mangatangi, is the largest single vineyard in New Zealand. Its 300 acres were planted in three years by Montana Wines. The heavy clay soil has been broken up, limed, contoured and fourteen miles of drains have been laid. Large shelter belts of trees have been planted— eighteen varieties of grapes are growing and include the varieties common to most vineyards. Impressive, however, is the large nursery housing many varieties of classical vines: cabernet sauvignon, pinot chardonnay, riesling sylvaner, pinot meunier, pinot

gris, sauvignon vert and many others. This nursery is now supplying classical varieties to the new areas either planted by or for Montana.

No wine is made here and the grapes are sent to the Auckland winery for processing. More was said about this dynamic company when the Henderson vineyards and wineries were discussed.

Cook's New Zealand Wine Company

Three miles north of Te Kauwhata on the main North-South highway, a new company, Cook's New Zealand Wine Company Limited, has planted 150 acres to establish what the promoters hope to be a new concept in vineyard and winemaking techniques. The company has done an immense amount of research into winemaking methods as practised in other countries. As the outset Professor Petrucci, Professor of Viticulture at Fresno State College, California, was retained to give advice.

On gently rolling well-drained sand and silt soil with contours lying to the north, riesling sylvaner, pinot gris, chasselas, pinot meunier, cabernet sauvignon, pinotage and palomino vines have been planted. The winery occupies a prominent position on the skyline. Special features of the winery include the gleaming stainless steel silo-like storage tanks in the open which include the new type grape gravity draining system, the tall arched roof and the extensive use of quality control electronic devices including a complex control panel. In fact, the winery is so designed that it can be controlled by two men.

There are many new and novel features in this winery which will come as a surprise to devotees of the use and advantages of wood in winemaking. A system of control over fermentation patented under the name of the Stoutz-Actinator and the first in use in Australia or New Zealand, will excite a lot of interest from other winemakers. It stabilizes by physical means without affecting the composition or the other properties of the wine. It is used extensively in the fermentation of Beaujolais wines and by inhibiting oxidation obviates the use of sulphur dioxide, up till now a fault in most white wines.

Winemaker and manager is Kerry Hitchcock who trained at the nearby Research Station and has spent some time studying winemaking methods in Australia.

Already the first wines have been made, a Riesling-Sylvaner and a Chasselas, on sale in 1972, and a Cabernet Sauvignon which, following the policy of the company will not be released under a maturation period of two years.

All lovers of wine will await the future of this company with great interest. It is claimed to be the only winemaking company planned from the beginning to the end to produce quality wines.

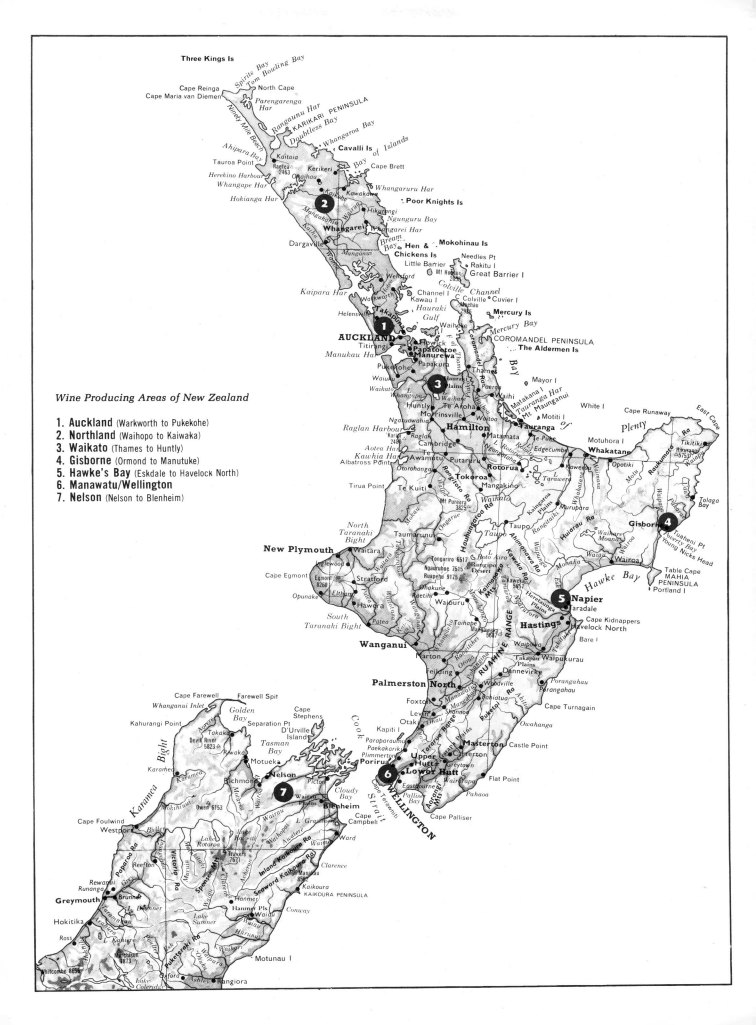

Wine Producing Areas of New Zealand

1. **Auckland** (Warkworth to Pukekohe)
2. **Northland** (Waihopo to Kaiwaka)
3. **Waikato** (Thames to Huntly)
4. **Gisborne** (Ormond to Manutuke)
5. **Hawke's Bay** (Eskdale to Havelock North)
6. **Manawatu/Wellington**
7. **Nelson** (Nelson to Blenheim)

27 Present day New Zealand wines

For too many years, almost from the turn of the century until quite recently, the New Zealand winegrower has been in somewhat of a dilemma.

The demand from the public has been for fortified wines—ports, sherries, madeiras, etc., which as an overseas authority once said, 'are artificially sweet on the palate and kick like a mule in the stomach.'

Experts from the time of the first committee on wines in the House of Representatives in 1890 have testified that the temperate climate of New Zealand cannot produce a sweet fortified wine naturally.

The ports and the sherries of the world are made in countries which enjoy hot climates and little rainfall, thus enabling the grapes to produce natural sugar which in turn forms the alcohol when the grapes ferment.

'Our view is that no area in New Zealand is suited for the production of grapes for the making of sweet fortified wines because the climate is not sufficiently warm to produce grapes of a sufficiently high sugar content,' said the Royal Commission on Licensing 1946. It noted that cane sugar is added to make up the deficiency and that some sweet wines contain as much as thirty percent by weight of added sugar.

Ports and sherries are produced in warmer countries like Spain, Portugal, Cyprus, parts of California, South Africa, Sicily, Australia, etc., but none of these countries can produce the delicate table wines made in more temperate countries such as France, Germany, Austria, Hungary, Chile, Argentine, cooler parts of Australia and now in New Zealand.

And this has been the problem of the New Zealand winegrower; the climate is suited for the production of light table wines, the demand has been for fortified wines.

In the circumstances he has coped very well indeed but with the increased interest taken in wines, a more educated and sophisticated palate all round, he is now able to turn his attention to producing table wines for which the climate and soil, in parts, is most suitable.

As good table wines become available so the demand increases. They are made only from European classical varieties of grapes and not all *Vitis vinifera* varieties will make good wine.

Red wines

The most consistent winner in either red or white wines at Annual Competitions held by the Department of Industries and Commerce and the Auckland Easter Show has been a Cabernet Sauvignon grown in Hawkes Bay. Made by McWilliam's, it is one of the very few New Zealand wines which is accepted overseas as being of an international standard.

The 1965 McWilliam's Cabernet Sauvignon made by the winemaker who made the 1949 McDonald's Cabernet, spoken of so highly by the late André Simon, is well balanced and harmonious and is already developing that indefinable character that makes a great wine.

Wines of later years made in the same style and all, with the typical flowers and fruit bouquet of the cabernet sauvignon grape, are resting peacefully in McWilliam's cellar—1966—1967—1968—1969—1970—1971 (the 1968 has just been released). So, at last, New Zealand is developing a 'classic' wine of the highest quality which is consistent from year to year and of a particular style with one predominant grape flavour.

McWilliam's have only a comparatively small quantity of cabernet sauvignon vines planted but now that the wine has been well received, even at the prices they are charging, they are planting more.

Mission Vineyards have cabernet sauvignon vines and have at times made an acceptable claret but not as yet up to Tom McDonald's standard. Most of their cabernet sauvignon grapes are blended with pinot meunier to form their standard red wine.

Dudley Russell of Western Vineyards has made a Cabernet Sauvignon Private Bin for years with varying success. His 1959 crop was picked green, the 1960 was well rounded and smooth. His later years were not too successful until in 1967 he turned out a very acceptable wine. Small quantities of 1968—1969—1970—1971 wines are now maturing in his cellars.

Corbans of Henderson have had at times an excellent Cabernet—their 1955 was referred to by André Simon as one of the best wines he drank in New Zealand. The wine had the true cabernet flavour and bouquet. It was well rounded and harmonious, heavier than most Cabernets but a wine of quality.

Unfortunately, they have not made a true Cabernet recently but are now blending it with pinot meunier and pinotage to form their standard Claret.

They are busy replanting cabernet sauvignon both in Kumeu and in Gisborne and more will be heard from them about Cabernet Sauvignon wines. The grape is a shy bearer at all times (compared with hybrid grapes) and in the moist conditions of Henderson does not ripen as well as it does in Hawkes Bay.

Vidals' of Hawkes Bay have been bottling for years under the label, Vidals' Burgundy, a sound red wine which has won many prizes. It is a blend of hybrid grapes plus some pinot meunier and cabernet. In some years, and more particularly in the private bin wines made specially for the partners, a whiff of cabernet character can be detected in the bouquet and the wine is always sound and drinkable.

Now that Vidals have amalgamated with Seppelts, and possessing one of the best vineyard sites in New Zealand, climatologically, winelovers may look forward to some interesting wines in the future.

Somewhat belatedly, noting the success of the Cabernet Sauvignon wine at competitions, other growers are busy planting these vines. Montana, Cook's, Waihirere's Ormond Block, Babich's, Gilbey Nobilo, San Marino and Te Mata have planted vines and already Montana, Gilbey Nobilo and Cook's have wines maturing, too young as yet to be evaluated.

Of the more commonly planted grapes for red wine, the only one with any claim to breeding at all is the South African pinotage which has been discussed earlier. The wine made from this grape has been neutral in character. Only one major grower now features 'Pinotage' as a classical red wine. The other large grower who helped to launch the wine on the market has discontinued selling it as such and is making an acceptable 'Claret' by blending cabernet sauvignon, pinot meunier and pinotage together. Babich's have made a good quaffing red by mixing in a little cabernet with pinotage and calling the wine Pinotage-Cabernet. Gilbey Nobilo have produced a 1970 Pinotage, full bodied with a deep red character and pleasant to taste. This wine has not yet been released. Winelovers will be waiting to see if these last two well made wines, when matured, will be sufficient to restore the reputation of the Pinotage to anything like the reputation it enjoys in some circles in South Africa. Juice pressed from the comparatively small acreages of pinot noir, pinot meunier and hermitage (shiraz) grapes is, with minor exceptions, blended in with other wines—however, there is a significant move to more plantings of the above grapes and some wine under the varietal label may soon be on the market.

Western Vineyards for many years have used the Beaujolais grape, gamay de beaujolais, to make a very popular light red wine sold under the varietal label and Montana shortly will be harvesting a significant crop of the same grape.

Growers are planting more pinot noir and hermitage (shiraz) and in time much will be heard of these grapes which produced good wine in New Zealand seventy years ago. Montana have Red Hermitage wine almost ready to be released.

White wines

In the classic white wine field many winemakers are turning out a Pinot Chardonnay wine from the grape which produces the great white burgundies and Chablis. Only two makers, McWilliam's and Corbans, have made good wines—but none as yet have the distinctive crisp, steely clean flavour of the original grape as tasted in Burgundy. Perhaps Nick Nobilo Junr. was right when he was quoted as saying on his return from a trip to the vineyard areas of Europe that our pinot chardonnay vines looked pathetic when compared with the same vines he saw in Europe. He says that virus diseases have taken over and have sapped the quality of the vines. This could apply to the traminer grape which Tom McDonald of McWilliam's says is a very poor bearer here, for it is not so in Europe. Now that experienced winemakers such as Penfolds and many others have planted virus free traminer vines obtained from the Department of Agriculture, some good wines should eventuate in time as the spicy grape seems particularly attuned to climate and soil conditions in New Zealand. In spite of the poor bearing quality of the vine, Baron Philippe de Rothschild declared McWilliam's Traminer to be the most delightful white wine he sampled in New Zealand and said he would be pleased to see it on the wine list of his favourite fish restaurant in Paris, Pruniers. McWilliam's have released the 1968 Roter-Traminer (as they call it) this year.

All the wines mentioned above are available as yet only in limited quantities. The most popular wine available in substantial quantities is a Riesling Sylvaner (or just Riesling) made from the muller thurgau grape. This grape ripens early so it can be cultivated in places where other vines would not ripen, and it produces a wine which is classed everywhere in Europe as a *vin ordinaire*. The wine, which naturally varies according to the winemaker, is generally clean and crisp and is New Zealand's most acceptable and popular white table wine.

Growers are experimenting with the true riesling and in time there may be some very fine wines characteristic of this aristocratic grape. A word of caution—many growers have labelled their Riesling Sylvaner wine 'Riesling' (and there is no law against it) and in order to differentiate, growers here, as in Australia, are labelling their true riesling grape as 'rhine riesling'. This may lead to complications with the Germans who, quite rightly, maintain only a wine grown on the Rhine from a riesling grape may be so labelled.

There will always be a popular demand for the white table wine made from the riesling sylvaner or muller thurgau grape. But it is a great pity that more of the true riesling, sylvaner and traminer had not been planted originally. And if a more prolific bearer is required, the scheurebe, a true cross between riesling and sylvaner and now currently being released from quarantine by the Department of Agriculture, has proved itself in Germany as producing much better wine than does the muller thurgau cross.

Several winemakers are now producing a passable white wine from the chasselas grape which is really a table variety.

Good wine can be made from the American hybrid grapes commonly grown here and these wines will be acceptable always to the average wine drinker but winemakers are deluding themselves if they think that these wines will be acceptable overseas. Only in the Eastern States of the U.S.A., Canada, Brazil and New Zealand are wines made from these grapes accepted with any degree of tolerance. After all, the great wines of France represent less than ten percent of the total quantity produced but it is that ten percent that gives France its reputation as a great wine country. So it will be in New Zealand. The ten percent of wines made from classical grapes, in time, will give New Zealand the reputation of producing the soundest table wines in the Southern Hemisphere. Already the tip of the iceberg is showing.

Fortified wines

Perhaps the most consistent wines produced in New Zealand are the fortified sherries, ports, muscats and madeiras. These are extremely popular, probably more for their alcoholic content than their finesse.

The winemaker contends with all kinds of difficulties in making fortified wine. Dry sherry is increasingly in demand and as the palomino grape does not mature properly in our climate, the winemaker adds sugar to produce sufficient alcohol to make the wine, and then somehow has to give a dry taste to the finished product. On the whole he succeeds very well. In Spain and Portugal, home of the original sherries and ports, the wine is fortified by the addition of grape brandy which is made from the distillation of pure grape wine. Here, a distillation is made from the 'marc', i.e., the lees and the skins and the stalks, etc., left after the original grapes have been pressed. The 'marc' is mixed with more cane sugar producing a lethal alcohol which is used to fortify the wine. This distillation from the marc is not allowed in the sherry and port districts of Spain and Portugal.

Nevertheless, such wine is very much in demand. It provides a pleasant enough drink for unsophisticated palates and because of the high tax on spirits, provides an alcoholic stimulant at a reasonable price. A much better wine could be produced if it were fortified with grape brandy. One winemaker is already experimenting along these lines. The use of grape brandy would have the effect of lowering the alcoholic content, which may not suit all. It would also produce port wines not too sweet and cloying on the palate and with a more satisfactory spirituous farewell.

Sparkling wines

There is a great deal of sparkling wine being made at present. The only sparkling wine produced by the Méthode Champenoise is Sparkling Fontanella from the Mission Vineyards in Hawkes Bay. A dry white is made from folle blanche grapes and a rosé from pinot meunier grapes. The rosé, probably because of the grape, is the better wine; it has a fruity bouquet, is clear and brilliant and has a completely dry taste. Unfortunately, the quantity made is small.

Corbans, McWilliam's, Penfolds and Montana are producing very acceptable wines by the Charmat process in large pressurised and refrigerated steel tanks as first used in Germany. The wine can only be as good as the grapes which go in to the making and though it is usually sound and clean, it has no bouquet. No attempt is made to age these wines and they are bottled and sold almost as soon as they are made.

Many other sparkling wines are made by the Impregnation method. Carbon dioxide is forced into a suitable wine, white or red, which has been cooled under pressure. A wine fairly high in alcohol is used since alcohol dissolves the gas more readily than water does. The sparkle of the wine disappears rapidly in a glass just as the bubble does in bottled beer or soda water. But the wine fills a popular demand for 'bubbly'.

Sparkling Cold Duck, spritzig and pearl wines are also made and find a ready market amongst the affluent younger generation.

Brandy

Experiments have proved that New Zealand can make a brandy at least as good as the ordinary French brandy now bottled here. Some winemakers believe that the distilling of brandy will utilize all their spare production of inferior grapes. It takes approximately eight times the quantity of grapes to produce one gallon of brandy as it does to produce one gallon of wine and the growers are hoping that the large quantities of baco 22A grapes planted here can be utilized for brandy. These grapes will not produce a good brandy but will certainly produce an eau-de-vie with heady qualities.

The production of good brandy as opposed to a fiery eau-de-vie involves many factors. First, the quality of the grapes used, secondly the skill of the distiller, thirdly the type of still and the oak used for maturing

and then the skill of the blender who in older countries blends brandies of varying age to produce a consistent style. A good brandy could contain blends of 30 years old, 20 years old, 10 years old, 5 years old and 3 years old to make a really consistent, pleasant and aromatic beverage.

The grapes used for producing what is regarded as the highest standard of brandy in the world in Cognac, France, are the folle blanche family including St. Emilion, and to a lesser extent, colombard. These same grapes are used to produce the popular South African brandy.

In a masked tasting of five different experimental brandies made by Te Kauwhata, the two brandies made from cinsaut grapes were picked as being outstanding. One was made in 1954 and with years maturing in oak has developed into a brandy bordering on a cognac with a clean dry taste, strong but not unpleasant, light amber in colour and with a pleasant aromatic aroma.

The other experimental brandies were made from palomino and baco 22A but did not have the purity and delicacy of flavour that characterized the brandy made from the cinsaut. Most of the growers who have experimental distillation licences are using baco 22A and palomino grapes simply because those are the grapes that are in abundance.

But perhaps it would be a mistake to give Government support and backing to an industry which as yet has not found the proper raw material.

Baco 22A is a cross between the folle blanche grape and noah, a foxy American grape. It seems wrong to be experimenting with a grape which has had undesirable qualities inbred into it when it was crossed. Cuttings of the original folle blanche which has proved itself in South Africa and California as well as France may be obtained.

There is no reason why growers should not go on experimenting to get the know-how in the actual distilling but it is extremely doubtful whether at present any of them would allow their grapes to be distilled in commercial quantities until they know if the Government will give them an incentive such as the lowering of the excise duty. This should give time for growers who are seriously interested in making brandy to experiment with the right brandy grapes which have been proved in other parts of the world.

It is significant that the Report of the Winemaking Industry Committee of the House, 1957, which examined all aspects of winemaking, quoted the Department of Agriculture as saying that hybrid varieties of grapes grown extensively in New Zealand were unsuitable. Only European or vinifera grapes should be used for brandy distillation. Good brandy could only be made from good grapes and the Department suggested that heavy cropping varieties such as folle blanche (main French brandy grape) and gamay gloriod, would be suitable and economic.

Vintage time (Photo: Marti Friedlander).

The future

As this book is being written there has been some fear in the industry of a glut of wine or grapes. But this is surely a pessimistic outlook. Up-to-date figures are not easy to come by but it is thought that the present consumption of wine in New Zealand is around 1¼ gallons per person. The population now at 2,800,000 will soon reach 3,000,000. On that basis 4,750,000 gallons of wine will be consumed out of the estimated 5,000,000 gallons made. This leaves very little surplus for maturing wines, particularly the ports and sherries, which have traditionally had longer maturation periods than the table wines.

There is now a trend towards maturing some table wines before releasing them and as some leaders of the industry have said, if wine is made only from grapes there should be no glut.

The larger producers, Montana, McWilliam's Corbans and Penfolds, who are responsible for perhaps four-fifths of the total wine production, have slowed down their new planting programme. If new plantings are only of virus free, classical European grapes, and there is every indication that this will be the tendency, then growers of the hybrid grapes commonly planted should have no fears for the future. There will always be a market for a sound quaffing wine made from hybrid grapes, in effect, a New Zealand *vin ordinaire.*

But the wines which will give New Zealand its reputation overseas will come from the classical European grapes which have proved themselves from last century. A stepping up of the policy of importing virus free classical vines is clearly indicated.

Wines currently available

CATEGORY I: Premium wines in short supply, but sometimes available on request at more reputable hotels and restaurants and from some wine and spirit merchants.

Sparkling Wines
Sparkling Fontanella—*Mission Vineyards*

Red Wines
Cabernet Sauvignon—*McWilliam's*
Cabernet Sauvignon—*Mission Vineyards*
Cabernet Sauvignon—*Western Vineyards*

White Wines
Pinot Chardonnay—*Corbans*
Pinot Chardonnay—*McWilliam's*
Traminer—*McWilliam's*
Riesling Sylvaner—*McWilliam's*

CATEGORY II: Good wines which usually are available; these may vary in quality from year to year.

Sparkling Wines
Premiere Cuvée—*Corbans*
Epernay—*Delegat's*
Sparkling Burgundy—*Golden Sunset*
Sparkling White Seibel—*Glenvale*
Sparkling Rosé Chasselas—*Glenvale*
Marque-Vue—*McWilliam's*
Sparkling Grand Cuvée—*Montana*
Sparkling Cold Duck—*Montana*
Medallion—*Penfolds*
Sparkling Cold Duck—*Totara Vineyards*
Sparkling Musca D'Or—*Western Vineyards*
Sparkling Riesling Hock—*Western Vineyards*
Sparkling Burgundy—*Western Vineyards*

Red Wines
Table Red—*Aspen Ridge*
Pinotage Cabernet—*Babich's*

Burgundy—*Babich's*
Claret—*Corbans*
Burgundy—*Corbans*
Riverlea Red—*Corbans*
Pinotage—*Delegat's*
Baieviesta (Rosso)—*Glenvale*
Dry Red—*Golden Sunset*
Dry Red—*Lincoln Vineyards*
Bokano—*McWilliam's*
Mission Pinot—*Mission Vineyards*
Pinotage—*Montana*
Cabernet Sauvignon—*Nobilo's*
Pinotage—*Nobilo's*
Dry Red—*Panorama*
Claret—*Penfolds*
Pinotage Chateau Yelas—*Pleasant Valley*
Pinotage—*San Marino*
Pinotage—*Selak's*
Pinot Red—*T.M.V.*
Claret—*Vidals'*
Burgundy—*Vidals'*
Melesconera—*Villa Maria*
Gamay de Beaujolais—*Western Vineyards*
Rossano—*Western Vineyards*

White Wines
Riesling Sylvaner—*Babich's*
Riesling Sylvaner—*Cooks*
Chasselas—*Cooks*
Riverlea Riesling—*Corbans*
Riverlea White—*Corbans*
Chasselas—*Corbans*
Pearl Wine—*Corbans*
Baieviesta (Bianco)—*Glenvale*
Pinot Chardonnay—*Mazurans*
Cresta Doré—*McWilliam's*
Spritzig Rosé—*McWilliam's*
Mission Hock—*Mission Vineyards*
Riesling—*Montana*
Pearl Wine—*Montana*
White Hermitage—*Montana*
Gamay Blanc—*Montana*
Lexia—*Montana*
Hock—*Nobilo's*
Moselle—*Penfolds*
Chateau Yelas Hock—*Pleasant Valley*
Pinot Chardonnay—*San Marino*
Riesling—*Selak's*
Pinot Chardonnay—*Selak's*
Pinot—*T.M.V.*
Chablis—*Vidals'*
Riesling Sylvaner—*Villa Maria*
Pinot Chardonnay—*Western Vineyards*
Riesling Sylvaner—*Western Vineyards*
Musca D'Or—*Western Vineyards*

Sweet Table Wines
Moselle—*Collards*
Montel Sauternes—*Corbans*
Moselle—*Delegat's*
Sauterne—*Eastern Vineyards*

Sauterne—*Golden Sunset*
Sauterne—*Lincoln*
Te Awanga Sauternes—*McWilliam's*
Sunnyvale Sauterne—*Panorama*
Sauternes—*Penfolds*
Chateau Yelas Moselle—*Pleasant Valley*
Totara Gold—*Totara*
Sauternes—*Western Vineyards*

Dry Sherries
Palomino—*Babich's*
Pale Dry—*Collard's*
Flor Palomino—*Corbans*
Dry Palomino—*Delegat's*
Flor Dry—*Eastern Vineyards*
Dry Sherry—*Lincoln*
Palomino—*McWilliam's*
Dry Sherry—*Montana*
Dry Sherry—*Panorama*
Amontillado—*Penfolds*
Chateau Yelas Fino—*Pleasant Valley*
Amontillado—*T.M.V.*
Extra Dry—*Vidal's*
Reserve Dry Sherry—*Western Vineyards*

Port
Reserve Port—*Babich's*
Cellarman Special—*Corbans*
Rich Port—*Golden Sunset*
Special Port—*Mazurans*
Royal Reserve—*McWilliam's*
Mission Old Port—*Mission Vineyards*
Reserve Port—*Penfolds*
Porto Thames—*Totara*
Port—*T.M.V.*
Reserve Port—*Western Vineyards*

And thus the New Zealand wine scene—a few good wines—many acceptable, drinkable wines—some poor ones. But one thing is certain, if growers concentrate on virus free European classical vines, New Zealand wines will win an international reputation and the prophecies of those two perceptive observers, the French navigator, Dumont D'Urville in 1840 and the Italian oenologist, Romeo Bragato in 1895, will ring true.

The Minister of Agriculture, the Honourable D. J. Carter, opening a national Wine Festival, 'Vintage '72' in Hamilton last August, had this to say: 'New Zealanders today are producing wines which are equal to the run-of-the-mill overseas wines. They have not matched the best wines from overseas but these countries have had centuries in which to perfect their wines.'

In parts, New Zealand has the soil and climate to produce in quantity superb table wines. As the late André Simon observed, the technical efficiency is available—what is needed is more public awareness that good wines can be made only from good grapes and that good wine can never be as cheap as poor wine.

513

GLOSSARY

Acetaldehyde (CH_3CHO): An aldehyde produced by the reduction or oxidation of ethyl alcohol. This compound constitutes much of the flavour of sherry.

Acetic: When a wine has an excess of flavours produced by bacteria having converted ethyl alcohol into acetic acid, it is said to be acetic.

Acetic acid (CH_3COOH): The principal volatile acid, and the acid of vinegar. Tolerated quantities in wine 0.5-1.2 grams per litre.

Acetic bacteria; The organisms in wine which, under suitable conditions, convert ethyl alcohol into acetic acid.

Acid: (i) Notable presence of acid in a wine style, particularly when young. (ii) Unbalanced due to an excess of acid.

Acidity: Usually expressing the total acid content of a wine.

Aggressive: (i) A very young wine, particularly red, high in acid and/or tannin. (ii) An excess of a wine component dominating all others (e.g., aggressive oak). Not pleasant.

Agrafe—agraffe clip: 'U'-shaped clip involved in the making of Champagne and champagne-style wines for securing the Tirage Cork during second fermentation.

Agreeable: A wine without fault, but lacking greatness; nondescript.

Alcohol: Usually indicating the ethyl alcohol resulting from fermentation.

Alcoholic: High in alcohol

Aldehydes: Volatile fluids produced by the oxidation of alcohol. These form a large group of compounds, intermediate between acids and alcohols.

Alkaline: Opposite of acid.

Altar wine: Wine used for sacramental purposes. As such it must be pure and natural without any additives.

Amontillado: Spanish. A wood matured Fino Sherry.

Amoroso: (i) A very old wood matured sweet sherry. older than **Amontillado,** younger than Oloroso. (ii) Sweetened Oloroso Sherry.

Ampelography: The science of classifying vine varieties.

Aperitif: French term for appetiser. Taken before meals to stimulate the palate.

Appellation d'origine: System of guaranteeing the authenticity of a French wine to its region, by the French Government. The strong ruling of the Institut National des Appellations d'Origine are only valid within France itself.

Appellation d'origine controlée: Literally 'controlled place of origin'. A term appearing on French wine labels, not only guaranteeing the authenticity of the place from where the wine came, but also that the wine is indicative of the quality standards of that area.

Armagnac: A brandy made in the Armagnac region in the south-west of France.

Aroma: The scent of a grape variety in a young wine. With age, aroma decreases. (see BOUQUET)

Aromatic: (i) Strong in varietal, odiferous substances. (ii) Characteristic of the variety. (see AROMA)

Arrest fermentation: The addition of spirit to fermenting must to kill yeasts before complete conversion of grape sugar to alcohol has taken place. The resulting wines are sweet.

Asbestos: Fibrous silica used in the manufacture of filter sheets. (see Filter pad)

Ascorbic acid ($C_6H_8O_6$): Vitamin C. Used as a wine anti-oxidant.

Asti: Town in the north of Italy whose vineyards are famous for producing a sweet sparkling wine (Spuemante).

Astringent: (i) Tannins derived from grape pips and wood. (ii) An excess of tannins in a wine; the quality of causing the mouth to pucker.

Attractive: Pleasant to drink.

Auslese: German term referring to the individual selection of bunches of white grapes due to their degree of ripeness. The resulting wines are comparatively sweet.

Austere: Strong in character, though showing no excesses.

Balance: Wine characters and flavours in a complete harmony. No dominance of any one character.

Barriquant: An old French expression for a small wine cask.

These multi-purpose steel drainer-fermenter tanks at McWilliam's Yenda winery near Griffith, N.S.W., have a capacity of 100 tons each.

Barrique: A French cask or hogshead, particularly the Barrique Bordelaise, holding approximately 50 gallons of wine.

Bastardo: Grape variety used in the making of port wines.

Baumé: Measurement of grape sugar. One degree Baumé (1°), is equal to 1.8 per cent of sugar.

Beaujolais: A wine-producing region of Southern Burgundy, France. The majority of red wines produced there are noted for their appealing quality of being suitable to drink when very young— within their first year.

Beerenauslese: German. Referring to the selection of individual over-ripe grapes for the production of very sweet white wines that rank amongst the greatest wines in the world.

Beeswing: A fine sheet crust appearing in an old bottle of port wine.

Bentonite: A colloidal clay used in the fining of red wines for the removal of unstable protein.

Bentonite Slugging: (i) A red wine overfined with Bentonite. (ii) A young red wine recently fined with Bentonite, not showing the amount of grape fruit expected. The wine may appear dumb, flat.

Bianco: Italian term for white wine. Indicates a semi-sweet style of Vermouth.

Bilginess: Off-flavours and odours derived from slime bacteria in water-logged casks.

Bin: A container, space or area in which bottles of the one wine are kept for maturation.

Binning: Cellar term for the storing of wine in bottles for maturation.

Bin—private: Traditionally a personal reserve of wine for the consumption of the winemaker or heads of a wine company; not available to the public. The term has now lost all meaning, save to distinguish one class of wine from another within those produced by one company.

Bin—reserve: (see BIN—PRIVATE)

Bin—special: (see BIN—PRIVATE)

Bitter: Wine fault detectable at the back of the palate. Usually an aftertaste.

Blanc: French term for white wine.

Blended wine: (i) The mixing of two or more wines to maintain a standard or increase quality. (ii) Lack of integrity on the part of many winemakers, accounting for the high output of premium wine-producing areas.

Bodega: (i) Spanish equivalent of the French 'Chateau'. (ii) A large Spanish ground-level cellar.

Body: The degree of bigness or weight of a wine in the mouth.

Bordeaux: One of the most celebrated wine-producing regions of the world. It is situated in the south-west of France, and produces red, white and rosé wines.

Botrytis (*Botrytis Cinerea*): (i) A parasitic fungus or mould that attacks grapes in certain climatic conditions, causing evaporation of moisture and condensation of sugar. When controlled, the fungus is responsible for producing the greatest sweet white wines of the world. (ii) A flavour imparted by the above-mentioned mould.

Bottle sickness: Off-flavours that may be present in a wine after bottling.

Bottle stink: (i) Presence of odours obtained during bottling that leave a wine upon breathing. (ii) Hydrogen Sulphate (H_2S).

Bouquet: Scents produced by maturation.

Brachetto: Italian grape variety.

Breathing: Allowing a wine to come in contact with air by drawing the cork prior to serving. Normally carried out with red wines to allow the development of the bouquet.

Breed: Impeccable flavour of a wine from a great vineyard or area.

Brix degrees: Degrees indicating the approximate sugar content of wine; converts to one degree of proof spirit per degree Brix through fermentation.

Brut: Term originally used to describe entirely unsweetened champagne. It now denotes the driest champagnes and champagne-style wines, which generally contain some degree of liqueuring.

Bung: The stopper in a wine cask.

Burgundy: (i) One of the most famous wine-producing areas in the world, located in eastern France. (ii) Outside France, the name of a style of wine considered similar to that of Burgundy.

Cabernet: (i) The name of grape varieties responsible for many of the finest wines in the world (e.g., Cabernet Sauvignon, Cabernet Franc, Cabernet Gris). (ii) An abbreviation for Cabernet Sauvignon (Australia).

Cabinet wine: German wine term applied to high quality wines. Originally the special reserve of the vineyard owner.

Cahors: Red wine grape (syn. Malbec and Cot).

Cake: Pressed grape skins and pips after removal from the fermenting tank after fermentation.

Carbonated wines: (i) Unfortified wines made sparkling by the direct injection of carbon dioxide gas. (ii) Lowest wine on the theoretical quality list of sparkling wine.

Carbon dioxide (CO_2): The gas released during fermentation, and that present in sparkling wine styles.

Carignan—carignane: A red wine grape.

Cask: A wooden barrel usually bound with iron hoops, used for storing wine. No set volume.

Casse: The presence of clouding or precipitation in a wine, resulting in off-flavours.

Cave: French term for cellar.

Cellar: (i) Area attached to a winery where wine is made, stored and/or bottled. (ii) Area for storing wine (domestic).

Cepage: French term for grape variety (e.g., the 'Cepage' Cabernet).

Chablis: (i) Outstanding white wine-producing area of northern Burgundy in France. (ii) Outside France, the name of a style of wine considered similar to the wines of Chablis.

Chambrer (French—chambré): To place a wine in a room so that the wine takes on the temperature of the room. Usually done with red wines and normally there is an increase in the temperature of the wine.

Champagne: (i) Name of a wine-producing area of north-eastern France, famed principally for its production of finest quality white sparkling wines. (ii) Outside France, the name applied to many sparkling white wines sold domestically.

Chaptalisation: The addition of sugar to the must in order to build up alcohol after fermentation.

Chardonnay: Premium quality white wine grape.

Charmat, Eugene: French scientist responsible for developing an inexpensive process for the making of sparkling wine.

Charmat process: Basically, the making of white wines in bulk in sealed tanks to retain CO_2 gas given off during fermentation. The sparkling wines produced by this method are rated above carbonated wines (see CARBONATED WINES), but much below those produced by the 'Methode Champenoise'.

Chasselas: A white wine grape variety.

Chateau bottling: In France, particularly the Bordeaux region, a guarantee suggesting that the wine is untampered with and authentic, since it has been bottled at the chateau where it was made.

Chenin blanc: A white wine grape variety.

Chianti: Wine-producing region of central Italy.

Cinsault—cinsaut: A red wine grape variety.

Citric acid ($C_6H_8O_7$): Used in winemaking to increase total acidity.

Claret: (i) English term for the wines of Bordeaux. (ii) General term for red wines supposedly bearing a resemblance to the wines of Bordeaux.

Classic: Of the highest quality.

Clean: No outside wine flavours present.

Climat: Term used in Burgundy, France, equivalent to the 'Cru' of Bordeaux. (see CRU)

Cloudy: Matter in suspension, obscuring the colour.

Coarse: Unclean finish; lacking in finesse.

Cognac: Grape-growing region of western France, famed for the high quality brandies it produces.

Collage: Fining process to which wine must be subjected before bottling.

Colour extraction: The gaining of colour by fermenting must with the skins.

Common: Nondescript; ordinary.

Commune: In France, a wine-producing township or parish.

Complete: A wine in which all flavours and components are harmonious and balanced.

Concentrated must: High baumé grape juice racked straight off the skins, boiled down, or concentrated. Useful as a sweetening material.

Concord: An important red grape variety of the American east coast.

Condition: The clarity and soundness of a wine.

Continuous press: A horizontal grape press, somewhat like a conventional meat mincer. The grapes are fed in one end, the liquid is pressed out, and they are ejected as a hard, almost dry core. No wine of any real quality is made in this fashion.

Controlled fermentation: Fermentation so regulated, generally through refrigeration, to slow down or speed up the process as required. Used widely for making clean, crisp white wines in Australia.

Cooper: Craftsman who makes wine casks.

Cooperage: General term for the manufacture or repair of wine casks.

Corked: Wine tainted by an off-flavour derived from a faulty cork.

Cote: French term for a vineyard slope.

Cracked: Odours and flavours produced in a wine by chemical decomposition.

Cream sherry: (i) Very sweet sherry, normally achieved by the addition of concentrate. (ii) A trade name for sweet sherry, often one containing some muscat varietal.

Cru: French term denoting a vineyard of high quality.

Crusher: Machine used for the extraction of juice from grapes prior to fermentation.

Crust: Mostly organic matter precipitated in a young wine.

Cuve: French term for a wine vat.

Cuvée: French term for the contents of a cuve, both in the cask and bottle.

Decant: *Domestic* (i) The pouring of a wine from the bottle to another vessel to aid presentation. (ii) The careful pouring of a wine from the bottle to another vessel for the removal of crust or deposits that may be present.
Cellar (i) The pouring of wines from one bottle to another to hasten maturation by exposure to air. (Oxygen.) (ii) The pouring of wines of the same type into a larger bottle (e.g., to make up rehoboams of champagne).

Delicate: Of good quality. Though light in flavour, without fault. (Normally whites.)

Demijohn: Large wine receptacle holding between one and ten gallons.

Demi-sec: French term for 'half-dry' wines. Normally used for sparkling wines to indicate that the wine is semi-sweet.

Dessert wine: Wine suitable to be drunk with or after dessert (e.g., Sauternes, port, Champagne, madeira).

Developed: Showing maturation.

Distillation: The art of obtaining spirit by vaporization.

Dolcetto: An Italian red wine grape; some grown in the Barossa Valley.

Domaine: French term for a wine estate.

Domestic: Wine term for an everyday drinking wine.

Dosage: French term for sugar solution added to sparkling wines before bottling; the expedition liqueur.

Downy mildew: A vine fungus.

Dry: Showing no sugar: without sweetness.

Dumb: Grape fruit showing no development.

Earthy: (i) Bouquet and flavour reminiscent of certain soil types. (ii) Contamination with soil due to poor winemaking, or by the by-products of soil fungi.

Elbling: (syn. Kleinberger). A white grape of middle Europe.

Elegant: Of high quality, with finesse.

Essence: Strong, complex varietal character.

Estate: Corresponding to the French 'Chateau' (e.g., Wynn's Coonawarra Estate, The Rothbury Estate).

Esters: Organic compounds corresponding to the salts of inorganic chemistry. They have a sweet, fruity smell.

Estery: Strong scents derived from bottle maturation relating to esters.

Ethyl alcohol (C_2H_5OH): The alcohol produced by fermentation.

Expedition cork: This is the cork used for the production of champagne and champagne-style wines after disgorging.

Expedition liqueur: The liqueur added to champagne and champagne-style wine to replace the wine lost from disgorging.

Extra sec: French for extra dry. Normally used on sparkling wines to denote lack of sweetness.

Fading: (i) An old wine past its peak, losing its flavour and character. (ii) A wine left standing in the glass, having lost flavour and bouquet by breathing.

Fat: (i) A big soft wine, normally high in glycerine. (ii) Wine fault; over-developed flavour at the back of the palate.

Fermentation: Usually indicating the change from must to wine; i.e., alcoholic fermentation in which yeast converts sugar into alcohol and by-products.

Fermentation tank: Vessel in which fermentation takes place.

Ferriginous: (i) Tasting of iron. (ii) Iron flavours derived from soil type.

Filter pad: (i) Asbestos sheet used for filtration. (ii) Off-flavour derived from asbestos gained from filtration. (See ASBESTOS.)

Filtration: The removal of solids from a wine before bottling.

Fine: (i) Delicate, distinguished. (ii) Of high quality.

Fine champagne: (syn. grand champagne). The finest cognacs (not the sparkling wine—champagne) blended from the sub-district of Grande and Petite Champagne in Cognac.

Finesse: Term denoting high quality and breed.

Fining: Method of clarifying young wines before bottling.

Finish: (i) The flavour remaining at the back of the palate after a wine has been swallowed. (ii) The end of the wine in the mouth.

Fino: The dryest sherry style.

Firm: Finish at the back of the palate; an aftertaste related to tannin.

Flabby: (i) When a wine finishes (back of the palate) with an over-developed fruit flavour. (ii) A broad soft middle palate with no depth or body.

Flagon: A half-gallon bottle of wine. Outside Australia the expression refers to a vessel for serving wine. It has a narrow neck, a handle and a spout.

Flat: Sparkling wine that has lost its gas. (ii) Loss of freshness, character and/or flavour.

Fleshy: Fresh, youthful, full-bodied varietal flavour.

Flor: A unique yeast which grows on the surface of certain wines; mainly sherry, which imparts its own particular flavour.

Flor fino: (i) A fino sherry upon which the flor yeast has been allowed to grow. (ii) A very delicate form of sherry.

Flowery: The pleasant aromatic quality normally present in white wines.

Folle blanche: (i) The principal white grape from which the brandies of Cognac are distilled. (ii) Probably the variety that makes the most celebrated of the Great Western sparkling wines, previously thought to be Pinot Blanc; now named Irvine's White.

Fortified: Wines to which spirit has been added.

Foxy: Sweetest scent and flavour of wines produced from Vitis Labrusca.

Frappé: French term for serving temperature—'chilled'.

Free run: Wine that runs freely from the grape skins after fermentation. Often it is bottled separately from the 'pressings' that follow.

Fresh: (i) Appealing quality of a young wine showing no off-flavours; high in acid. (ii) An unexpected character that may be present in an old wine.

Frontignac: White grape producing aromatic wines. Also renowned for the unsurpassed quality of the Muscat-style wines it produces in northern Victoria.

Fruity: Fleshy quality of a young wine with strong varietal character.

Fuder: German term for a wine cask holding 1,000 litres (220 imperial gallons).

Full: (i) Wine at optimum maturity. (ii) High degree of body.

Fut: A French term for a particular wine barrel.

Gamay: A red wine grape planted extensively in the Beaujolais region of France.

Gelatine: A fining agent.

Generous: Full of flavour; strong in character.

Gewürztraminer: A particularly aromatic white grape (gewürz-spicy) planted mainly in Alsace (France) and to a lesser extent in Germany.

Glucose ($C_6H_{12}O_6$): Grape sugar.

Glycerol ($CH_2OH.CHOH.CH_2OH$): A by-product of fermentation. Sweet, viscous.

Gout de terroir: French tasting term used in reference to flavours present in some wines (notably red) imparted by the soil.

Grand champagne: (syn. fine champagne). An expression appearing on a Cognac label, denoting the finest district of Cognac and therefore the finest brandies.

Grand cru: French term for an exceptional vineyard or site.

Grand cru classé: A classification of the best wines of the Bordeaux region of France.

Grape: The fruit of the vine.

Grapy: Showing fresh varietal character.

Graves: (i) A sub-region of Bordeaux, France, noted for its red and white wines. (ii) The name applies to white wines considered similar to those of Graves in France. Two general styles can be found, Dry Graves and Sweet Graves.

Green: (i) Presence of malic acid. (ii) Not yet ready for drinking.

Grüner veltliner: The principal white wine grape of lower Austria. There is a possibility that this may be the Australian variety, Clare riesling.

Gunflint: A wine flavour from chalky sub-soils; found in white wines. True French Chablis is often referred to by this term.

Gutedel: A German variant of the White Chasselas grape variety.

Guyot: A method of training vines.

Hard: (i) Strong tannin in a young wine, lacking a soft finish. (ii) Tannin detectable at the back of the palate, derived from poor quality oak.

Harsh: Presence of an undersirable character, attributed to wood tannin.

Head and shoulders: An expression used to describe wines (usually white) that have fine varietal aromatic characters on the nose and beginning of the palate, but which lack body and intensity of flavour on the middle palate.

Hermitage: (i) Important area of the Rhone Valley in France, producing both red and white wines. (ii) Name of a red grape planted extensively in Australian vineyards (syn. Shiraz).

Hock: (i) British name for wines from the Rheingau region of Germany. It is derived from the Rheingau town of Hochheim. (ii) General term for wines of the Rhine type, particularly those made from riesling.

Hogshead: A cask of varying capacity, used for storing wine.

Hybrid: Cross between an American and a European vine variety by cross-pollination as opposed to grafting.

Hydraulic press: A vertical press used for pressing the skins and seeds after fermentation.

Imperial: A large wine bottle of the capacity of eight normal 26 fluid ounce bottles used in the Bordeaux district of France.

Incrustation: The formation of a crust (see CRUST) in wines, specifically vintage port.

Isabella: Red wine grape of the Vitis Labrusca.

Jammy: Off-flavours resulting from heavy pressing of hot-picked fruit. Found mainly in red wines.

Jeres de la frontera: Town in Spain which is the centre of the 'true' sherry trade.

Jeroboam: A large wine bottle. When used in reference to champagne, the capacity is four standard bottles; in Bordeaux, five.

Keg: Small wine cask, usually of less than ten gallons capacity.

Labrusca (*Vitis Labrusca*): A species of grape vine found in northern America.

Lactic acid: Acid resulting from malo-lactic fermentation.

Lambrusco: A red wine grape propagated mainly in Italy.

Late picked: Grapes left on the vine longer than usual to increase sugar level and lower acidity. Process used in the production of sweet white styles and fortified wines.

Lees: Deposits (residue) in cask or bottle.

Legs: The viscosity from alcohol (and a little glycerine) as seen on the inside of a glass of wine.

Liebfraumilich: (i) By German law, a term applied to the wines of Rheinhessen. (ii) General term implying a hock style of wine to which sugar has been added.

Light: Lacking body, pale in colour; but well-balanced.

Limpidity: The state of clarity and cleanness of a wine.

Long: Great wine; staying power of flavours on the palate after the wine has been swallowed.

Maché: French term used to describe a tired wine; i.e. one lacking in flavour due to travelling, 'bottle sickness'.

Madeira: (i) Island off the coast of Spain famous for its fortified dessert wines. (ii) General term for wines resembling those produced on the above-mentioned island.

Maderization: The oxidation of alcohol to acetaldehyde.

Maderized: An oxidized white wine showing the presence of acetaldehyde. The flavour is reminiscent of Madeira wine.

Maitre de chai: French term literally, Master of the Cellar; i.e. the Head Cellarman.

Malbec: (syn. COT). A red wine grape.

Malic acid ($COOH.CH_2CH[ON].COOH$): The acid of fresh grapes, particularly when unripe.

Malo-lactic fermentation: The decomposition of malic acid by bacteria to lactic acid and carbon dioxide.

Marc: (i) The residue of grape skins and seeds after the juice has been extracted. (ii) A brandy spirit made from distilling the marc.

Marsala: (i) Town in north-west Sicily, producing the principal fortified dessert wine of Italy. (ii) General term for wines resembling those produced at the above-mentioned town.

Mellow: Soft, smooth, mature.

Merlot: A red wine grape; a famous Bordeaux variety.

Metallic: (i) Exhibiting a flavour of a metal. (ii) Contamination by metals with which a wine may have come in contact.

Methode champenoise: A French term often used to describe traditional champagne making; i.e. second fermentation taking place in the bottle.

Methuselah, methusalem: Giant bottle with the capacity of eight bottles, used for Champagne and champagne-style wines.

Mildew: An abbreviation for Downy Mildew. (see DOWNY MILDEW)

Mis en bouteille au chateau: French. Literally, 'put into the bottle at the chateau'. (see CHATEAU BOTTLING)

Mis en bouteille au domaine: French. Literally 'put into the bottle at the Domaine'; the Burgundean equivalent of chateau bottled. (see DOMAINE)

Mistelle: The fortification of high baumé grapes to retain natural sugar and grape juice. Used as a sweetening agent for vermouth.

Moelleux: French term for soft, sweet, fruity wines, particularly sauternes.

Mosel: (i) Abbreviation of the famous German River, the Moselle, noted for its premium quality white wines. (ii) Generally (outside Germany), a sweet white wine style. The sweetness can either be gained by late picking or adding sugar after fermentation.

Moselle: An Australian fruity wine style, generally containing some sweetness. (see MOSEL)

Mouldy: Off-flavours, derived from bacterial infection of grapes or cask, which have been retained by a wine.

Mousseux: French sparkling wines made outside the champagne region.

Mouth-filling: Quality of the wine, the flavour of which excites all our olfactory receptors.

Mulled wine: Wine to which sweetening and spices have been added. This wine is served hot.

Muller-thurgau: A white grape produced from crossing Riesling (Rhine) and Sylvaner vine varieties.

Muscat: A sweet grape, usually white, or many varieties.

Must: The mixture of grape juice, skins and seeds before fermentation. During this process it is termed as fermenting must.

Nebuchadnezzar: An oversized champagne bottle holding the equivalent of twenty normal bottles.

Negative: Lacking character, without flavour or scent.

Noble: Of high breed.

Noble rot (syn. *Botrytis Cinerea*) (see BOTRYTIS)

Nomenclature: The way in which a wine is named; e.g. hock, riesling, cabernet, burgundy.

Nondescript: Lacking character, ordinary.

Nose: The scents and odours of a wine.

Nutty: Characteristic pungent flavour of sherry.

Oak chips: Off-cuts of oak used to give a wine an 'oak' flavour and scent. The flavour at the back of the palate will be notably bitter.

Oak essence: Oak extracts used to give a wine an oak flavour and scent.

Oak shavings: As for OAK CHIPS, except the wood takes the form of shavings and oak dust.

Obvious: (i) Strong in character; lacking complexity. (ii) Of highest quality.

Odour: Off-smells present in a wine.

Oenology: The science of wine.

Oidium (*Oidium Tuckeri*): A vine mildew commonly known as powdery mildew.

Oily: Oils derived from grape pips or stalks present in wine. Result of poor winemaking. (see STALKY)

Olfactory: The sense of smell.

Oloroso: An old wood-matured fino sherry.

Oporto: Centre of the Portuguese 'port' trade. Port gets its name from the abbreviation of the name of this town.

Originalabfüllung: German equivalent for chateau bottling. (see CHATEAU BOTTLING)

Ouillade: A red wine grape variety.

Ouillage: The topping up of casks that have become ullaged due to evaporation.

Over the hill: Wine past its best, over-matured.

Overtones: Secondary flavours and scents individually detectable.

Oxidase: Enzyme introducing oxidation.

Oxidation: Chemical decomposition of a wine due to the presence of oxygen.

Oxidized: The dominance of flavours produced by oxidation.

Pasteurization: Sterilization by heat at less than 100° Centigrade.

Pedro ximenes (ximenez): A celebrated grape variety of Spain used for making high quality sherry.

Perfumed: Powerful scents produced by maturation.

Petillant: French for moderately-carbonated wine.

Petite Champagne: (syn. Fine Champagne) A sub-region of the Cognac District of France, noted for its high quality brandies.

Petite-syrah (sirah): The Californian varietal name for Syrah (Shiraz).

Petit verdot: A red wine grape type.

Phylloxera (*Phylloxera vastatrix*): A parasitic disease of the vine.

Pinot: (i) Family of grape vines responsible for some of the greatest wines of the world. (ii) When used in reference to white wines, generally refers to Chardonnay; when to red, to Pinot Noir.

Pinot gris: (syn. Tokay d'Alsace) White wine grape, member of the pinot family.

Pipe: A large cask of tapered ends used primarily for Portuguese port wines. Contents, 115 imperial gallons.

Port: (i) Portuguese fortified wine. There are two main styles (1) Vintage Port (2) Tawny Port. (ii) General style of fortified wines imitating those of Portugal.

Porty: Red wine showing flavours and character similar to port wine.

Pot still: The old and simplest form of still, employed for making the finest brandies.

Pourriture noble: (syn. Noble) (see NOBLE ROT).

Powdery mildew: (syn. Oidium) (see OIDIUM).

Precipitation: White crystals of excessive amounts of calcium tartrate or potassium bi-tartrate that may 'precipitate' in unstabilized white wines and some red wines.

Pressings: Wine gained from pressing the skins and pips after fermentation. It is higher in tannin and acid than the wine fermented from the must, but lacks the flavour and character of the latter. Often the pressings are put back into the wine to build up any deficiencies of tannin and/or acid.

Pricked: Wine smelling of ethyl acetate nearing volatility.

Puncheon: A large wine cask of varying capacity.

Pungent: Very aromatic, often 'earthy'.

Punt: Indentation (for strength) at the base of champagne bottles and various European wine bottles. Originally the punt was formed when bottles were hand-blown, to give them a flat base.

Pupitre: French. A hinged rack for holding sparkling wines by the neck prior to dégorgement.

Quinta: Portuguese term for vineyard.

Race: French quality term describing distinction and breeding in a wine.

Racking: The drawing of clear wine off its lees.

Rancio: (i) An oxidized flavour found in old sweet whites. (ii) The developed wood character of an old dessert wine.

Rehoboam: Large champagne bottle, equivalent to six normal bottles.

Residual sugar: Sugar remaining after fermentation has been completed.

Rhine riesling: The true riesling grape variety.

Riesling: (i) (syn. Rhine riesling). (ii) Crisp, acid white wine style.

Rioja: Most important table wine-producing area of Spain.

Robust: Rich, full; strong in alcohol.

Root stock: The type of vine root on to which the grape vine is grafted. Selection of the root stock is dependent upon its performance in relation to the topography.

Rosado: Spanish term for Rosé.

Rosato: Italian term for Rosé.

Rosé: A very light red wine.

Rouge: A French term for red wine.

Rough: An unpleasant red wine, usually so due to an excess of tannin.

Round: Well-balanced and mature.

Ruby port: Blended port wine, generally speaking a young sweet wine in its early stages; i.e. the colour has not become 'Tawny' through age.

Sauternes: (i) French sub-region of Bordeaux, famed for its unique sweet white wines. (ii) Sweet white wines, imitations of the above-mentioned region. Far too often they are nothing more than sweetened whites.

Sauvignon blanc: A white wine grape.

Sec: French for 'dry'. Normally used in reference to champagne.

Secco: Italian term for dry wine.

Sediment: Deposits appearing in wines (mainly red) due to ageing.

Sekt: Sparkling German white wine.

Semillon: A fine white wine grape variety.

Sercial: (i) Grade of Madeira. (ii) White grape variety.

Sherry: English term for the fortified wines of Jerex in Spain. Australia has had considerable success at imitating the various styles of sherry.

Shiraz: (i) A city in south-west Iran near the Persian Gulf, which gave its name to the best-known Persian wines. (ii) (syn. Hermitage). One of Australia's foremost red wine grapes.

Soft: A term applied normally to red wines with a pleasing finish that is not hard or agressive. Often a product of maturation.

Solera: Method of producing certain fortified wines, particularly sherry, by rotation of casks.

Sound: Without fault.

Sour: Wine spoiled by sourness on back of palate.

Spatlese: German term for the late picking of white grapes to increase their sugar level and therefore reduce water content.

Spirity: The obvious presence of alcohol.

Spritzig: German; presence of carbon dioxide gas.

Spumante: Italian term for sweet sparkling wine.

Stabilization: The chilling of a white wine to near freezing point to precipitate tartaric crystals.

Stalky: Oily character derived from grape stalks. Mainly red wines; indicative of poor winemaking. (see OILY)

Still: (i) Non-sparkling wine styles. (ii) Sparkling wine that has lost its gas.

Stuck fermentation: Natural fermentation not completed because of the killing-off of active yeasts due to an excessive rise in temperature.

Sulphur Dioxide (SO₂): Agent used for sterilization and as an anti-oxidant.

Sulphurous: Wine showing the presence of sulphur.

Sylvaner: White wine grape of Alsace (France) and Germany.

Sweet: The obvious presence of residual sugar in a wine.

Tannin: Natural ingredient of wine derived mainly from grape pips and stalks.

Tart: Possessing agreeable acidity (malic) to a marked degree.

Tartaric acid (COOH[CHOH]₂.COOH): The principal acid of wine.

Tartrates: Potassium and calcium salts of tartaric acid, which often crystallize.

Tastevin: French term for a small silver wine cup used for tasting wine, principally in Burgundy.

Tawny: (i) The colour of an old red wine; (ii) Style of port matured in the cask.

Thin: Unbalanced; fruit too light to match tannin and acid.

Three star: A quality grading of the brandies of Cognac and Armagnac.

Tirage cork: This is the cork used in the making of Champagne and champagne-style wines, when the wine is first bottled.

Tirage liqueur: Sugar solution added to the base wine in the production of Champagne and champagne-style wine. During the second fermentation in the bottle, it will be converted to alcohol and carbon dioxide gas, the latter giving the required pressure after bottle fermentation.

Tokay d'Alsace: (syn. Pinot Gris when grown in Alsace, France).

Tonneau: French. (i) Only large wine barrel. (ii) Standard wine measure in Bordeaux of approximately 200 imperial gallons.

Traminer: Aromatic white wine grape variety.

Trebbiano: (syn. Ugni Blanc, white hermitage). A white wine grape.

Trockenbeerenauslese: German term for the very late picking of white wine grapes. The wines are extremely sweet, rivalled only by Sauternes as the greatest dessert wines.

Ugni blanc: (syn. white hermitage, trebbiano). A white wine grape variety.

Ullage: The air space present in a bottle of wine, between the cork and surface of the wine; also the air space in the top of a cask of wine.

Unbalanced: Not balanced. (see BALANCED)

Unripe: Wine made from grapes picked before they have reached a total sugar/acid balance.

Vanillan: A wine with a richly developed fruit flavour, similar to that of vanilla.

Varietal: Character of wine derived from the grape.

Vat: A container in which wine is fermented.

Velvety: Soft in texture, mellow.

Verdelho: A white wine grape variety of Madeira; spread throughout Australia.

Verdot (petit verdot): A red wine grape variety.

Vermouth: Basic white wine to which many flavour components are added. Not considered a wine style.

Vigneron: French term for winemaker.

Vignoble: French term for vineyard.

Vigorous: (i) Healthy vines. (ii) A youthful wine requiring maturation.

Vin: French term for wine.

Vinicide: A dinner table term for a great wine drunk before its time.

Vinification: The art and science of making wine.

Vinosity: A tasting term related to the alcoholic strength, and particularly to the grape character.

Vinous: Reminiscent of wine.

Vintage: The gathering of the grapes.

Vintage port: The richest and 'fullest' bodied of the port styles. It is bottled traditionally after spending up to two years in oak casks, after which it matures for many years, like a red wine.

Vintage wines: Wines made in a specific year, indicated on the label.

Viscous: Wine showing the presence of glycerol.

Viticulture: The art and science of winemaking.

Vitis vinifera: The species of vine responsible for most of the world's quality wine.

Volatile: Wine spoiled by acetic acid.

Volatile acids: (syn. acetic acid) (see ACETIC ACID).

Volatile acids: Fatty acids of which the main one is acetic acid. Others include carbonic acid, butyric acid (C_3H_7COOH), propionic acid (C_2H_5COOH) and formic acid (H.COOH). (see also ACETIC ACID)

Volatility: The degree of evaporation of esters as detected by the olfactory sense.

VSO: Grade of Cognac; very special, old.

VSOP: Very Superior Old Pale. Used for both Cognac and Armagnac brandies. The term is being used so loosely for brandies not from Cognac, that one critic suggested it means Very Suitable On Puddings.

VVSOP: Grade of Cognac; Very, Very Special Old Pale.

Weep: Wine leaving the bottle due to a cork that has lost its elasticity.

Wein: German term for wine.

Weingut: Wine estate.

Well-made: Without fault.

White port: Popular sherry-style wine; made in Portugal and imitated elsewhere.

Wine: The fermented juice of the grape.

Wine rape: Drinking a great wine long before it has had time to reach its optimum point of maturity; a dinner table term.

Woody: (i) The presence of oak in a young wine. (ii) An offensive excess of oak present in a wine.

Xérès: French for sherry. Originally the name given by the ancient Romans to the sherry city of Jerez.

XO: Grade of Cognac. Generally the oldest available on the general market.

Yeasts: Single cell organisms responsible for the fermentation of sugar into ethyl alcohol.

Young: An immature wine.

Youthful: (i) A young wine. (ii) An unexpected character that may be present in an old wine.

INDEX